WINDOWS NT
Professional
Library

Windows NT
Enterprise Networking

ABOUT THE AUTHORS

Toby J. Velte, Ph.D. is an experienced Windows NT architect
and consultant. He specializes in the design and integration
of heterogeneous networking environments in the enterprise.
He also designs strategies to help organizations effectively
manage the flow of traffic in complex networks. In addition,
Dr. Velte writes articles for *Windows NT Magazine.*

Anthony T. Velte has more than 12 years of technical and
managerial experience in the information systems industry.
He works with Fortune 500 corporations around the world
facilitating the design and deployment of enterprise
networks. He specializes in physical and logical network
design and management, security, and inter-corporate data
exchange.

WINDOWS
NT
Professional
Library

WINDOWS NT

Windows NT
Enterprise Networking

TOBY J. **VELTE** Ph.D.
and
ANTHONY T. **VELTE**

Osborne **McGraw-Hill**

Berkeley   New York   St. Louis   San Francisco
Auckland   Bogotá   Hamburg   London   Madrid
Mexico City   Milan   Montreal   New Delhi   Panama City
Paris   São Paulo   Singapore   Sydney
Tokyo   Toronto

Osborne **McGraw-Hill**
2600 Tenth Street
Berkeley, California 94710
U.S.A.

For information on translations or book distributors outside the U.S.A., or to arrange bulk purchase discounts for sales promotions, premiums, or fund-raisers, please contact Osborne/**McGraw-Hill** at the above address.

Windows NT Enterprise Networking

1234567890 AGM AGM 901987654321098

ISBN 0-07-882495-8

Publisher
   Brandon A. Nordin
Editor-in-Chief
   Scott Rogers
Acquisitions Editor
   Wendy Rinaldi
Project Editor
   Cynthia Douglas
Editorial Assistant
   Ann Sellers
Technical Editor
   Cory Scott
Copy Editor
   Cynthia Sudha Putnam

Proofreader
   Carroll Proffitt
Indexer
   Claire Splan
Computer Designer
   Jani Beckwith
Illustrator
   Brian Wells
Series Design
   Peter F. Hancik
Cover Design
   Regan Honda

To our mother, Joyce: Thank you for life, love, and happiness.
—TJV & ATV

WINDOWS NT

Professional Library

AT A GLANCE

▼ 1   Networking Overview   1
▼ 2   Building Systems   51
▼ 3   Reliability Through Redundancy   89
▼ 4   Network Administration 125
▼ 5   Connecting Client Workstations. 165
▼ 6   Domain Name System 211
▼ 7   WINS and DHCP 243
▼ 8   Internet Services. 287
▼ 9   Routing and Remote Access Service 329
▼ 10   Security. 373
▼ 11   Tuning and Troubleshooting 401
▼ 12   Network Testing and Capacity Planning 439
▼ 13   Planning for NT 5.0 477
▼ A   Year 2000 Problem Identification and
         Resolution 503
▼ B   Enterprise IP Management. 513
▼ C   Windows NT Resources — Where to Get Help 525
▼ D   About the CD 537
▼   Index 549

WINDOWS
NT
Professional
Library

CONTENTS

Acknowledgments   xxi
Introduction   xxiii

▼ 1   Networking Overview.   1
Standards Organizations   2
    The Open Systems Interconnect (OSI) Reference Model. . . .   2
    NT in the OSI Model.   4
The Physical Network   5
    Comparative Topologies   5
    Throughput Expectations   17
Network Protocols   23
    Common Protocols.   23
    Configuring TCP/IP.   30
    NetBIOS over TCP/IP   34
Routing Protocols.   36
    The Routing Information Protocol (RIP).   37
    The Open Shortest Path First (OSPF) Protocol   38
    The Interior Gateway Routing Protocol (IGRP/EIGRP). . . .   40
Routing Tables   41
    MPR and RRAS   42

The NT Routing Table. 43
Networking Hardware. 45
Bridges and Repeaters. 45
Switches. 47
Routers 48

▼ **2   Building Systems**. 51
Choosing Correct Hardware and Software 52
Hardware Compatibility List. 52
The Microsoft Compatibility Tool 54
Advanced Hardware 57
Installing Windows NT—Know Before You Go 58
Installation Overview 58
Workstation, Server, or Server/E?. 61
Standalone Server, PDC Sever, or BDC Server? 61
FAT versus NTFS 61
Queried Information. 63
Unattended Installation 64
Licensing 68
Removing NT. 69
Workgroup and Domain Models. 69
Domain Models 70
Domain Monitor 73
Server Manager. 73
User and Computer Accounts 75
System Policy Editor. 75
Default Users. 78
Adding Users. 78
Users Have Rights and Need Policies 79
User Profiles 82
User Groups 85
Migrating from NetWare 86

▼ **3   Reliability Through Redundancy**. 89
Hardware Failure Probability. 90
Hardware in Series. 90
Hardware in Parallel. 92
Redundant Components. 92
UPS 93
Dual Power Supplies 97
Multihoming 98
Host Adapter Cards 99

Disks   99
   RAID Levels   99
   Mirroring   104
   RAID Level 5   108
   External RAID Arrays   109
Clustering   110
   Types of Clusters.   111
   Microsoft Cluster Service (Wolfpack)   112
   Third-Party Cluster Solutions   113
Backups   114
   Media Choices   115
   Open Files.   117
   NTBackup and Scheduling   118
   Third-Party Backup Applications   119
   Placing a Backup System   119
Directory Replicator Service.   120
   Redundant Databases   120
   Setting Up Import/Export Systems   121

▼ 4   Network Administration.   125
Systems Management Server   126
   Hardware/Software Inventory.   127
   Software Distribution   129
   Remote Diagnostic Tools   132
Third-Party Administration Tools   134
   RoboMon   135
   Enterprise Administrator   139
Microsoft Management Console   142
Zero Administration for Windows   146
   Zero Administration Kit.   147
   ZAW in NT 5.0   148
Networking Commands.   150
   The Net Commands   150
   Scripts   160
   The AT Command   162

▼ 5   Connecting Client Workstations   165
Client Considerations   166
   Thin Clients.   166
NT Connection Services   167
   Client Access Licenses.   168
   Network Browsing Service   170
   NetLogon Service   178

Non-NT Client Connections. 181
    MS-DOS, LAN Manager 2.2c, and OS/2 Clients 181
    Windows 3.11. 184
    Windows 95. 188
Services for Macintosh. 192
    Installing Services for Macintosh. 192
    Logon 192
    Volumes. 196
Gateway Services for Novell Networks 197
    The NWLink Protocol 198
    Gateway Services for NetWare. 199
    Enterprise Considerations in Novell Integration 204
UNIX Connections 204
    File Servers 204
    Applications Servers. 208

▼ 6   Domain Name System 211
Internet Domains. 212
    Top-Level Domains 213
    Second-Level Domains and the InterNIC 215
    Using Whois 216
Digging into DNS 216
    Zones 216
    Domains and Subdomains 217
    Name Servers. 217
    Name Resolution. 218
    Forwarders and Slaves 218
    Database Files and Resource Records 219
DNS, WINS, and RFCs. 222
    DNS and WINS. 222
    Microsoft DNS RFC Support 223
Installing and Configuring Microsoft DNS 224
    Installing Microsoft DNS Server 224
    Configuring DNS Server 224
    Integrating DNS with WINS/DHCP 229
    Special Configuration Items 232
    DNS Client Configuration 233
    Managing DNS. 235
Integrating DNS into a Diverse Network 236
    Domains. 237
    Redundant DNS 237
    Load Balancing. 238
    Caching Name Servers 238

Tracking DNS Evolution.   240
    IPv6 (IPng)   240
    Dynamic DNS   241
    Secure DNS   241
    Incremental Transfer.   241
Future Role in Microsoft Networking   241

▼ 7   WINS and DHCP.   243
Windows Internet Naming Service.   244
    The NetBIOS School of Broadcasting   245
    LMHOSTS   247
    Using DNS to Resolve NetBIOS Names   248
WINS Essentials   250
    Name Registration, Renewal, and Release   250
    Node Types.   251
    Name Query   252
    Replication   254
    WINS Proxy Service   255
Installing and Configuring Microsoft WINS   257
    Installing Microsoft WINS Server   257
    Configuring WINS.   258
    WINS Registry Settings   265
The Impact of WINS on the Network   266
    Local Area Network Implementation   266
    Wide Area Network Implementation   266
Dynamic Host Configuration Protocol.   269
    DHCP Overview   270
    DHCP Address Allocation Process   273
Installing and Configuring DHCP   275
    Installing Microsoft DHCP   276
    Configuring and Managing DHCP   276
    DHCP Registry Settings.   282
    Security Issues   282
DHCP Network Components.   283
An Important Note on DNS, WINS, and DHCP   284

▼ 8   Internet Services   287
Internet Information Server   288
    Planning the Installation   289
    Installing IIS   292
    Configuring IIS 3.0   299
    Additional IIS 3.0 Components.   307
    IIS 4.0 (NT 4.0 Option Pack).   309

Microsoft Proxy Server   311
    SOCKS Proxy Service   312
    WinSock Proxy Service   313
    Web Proxy Service   313
    Installing and Configuring Microsoft Proxy Server   314
    Managing Microsoft Proxy Server   320
Making the Connection   323
    Connecting to the Internet   323
    Throughput Requirements   326
    Bottleneck Avoidance   327
    Management Tools   328

▼ 9   Routing and Remote Access Service   329
RAS in the Enterprise   330
    Clients and Servers   331
    Remote Node and Remote Control   332
    Thin Client Technology for NT   334
    Superthin Client Technology for NT   335
RAS Protocol Primer   335
    Setting RAS Protocols   336
    Network Protocols   337
    Connection Protocols   339
    Transport Methods   340
Configuring RAS Clients   341
    Installing Dial-Up Networking   341
    Installing a Modem   341
    Adding Phonebook Entries   345
    Using Scripts to Automate Connection   347
    Security Settings   349
    Monitoring the Connection   353
Installing the RAS Server   354
    Configuring Network Protocols   355
    Managing RAS   358
Enterprise Considerations   361
    Before You Roll Your Own   361
    Office to Office Connectivity Using RAS   364
    Hardware Scenarios   365
    Vendors   366
    Modem Options   366
    Routing and RAS (RRAS)   369

▼ 10   Security   373
Security Essentials   374

Key Questions 375
Too Little Vs. Too Much. 376
Policies 377
Goals. 378
Expectations 379
Implementing Firewalls 380
Packet Filtering. 381
Proxy Firewalls. 382
Using Firewalls. 383
The Scoop on TCP/IP Ports. 383
Firewall Vendors. 385
NT Security Issues 385
TCP/IP Filtering 388
FTP and WWW Service Security 389
Securing Servers 390
Restricting Anonymous User Access 390
Common Network Vulnerabilities. 391
Passwords. 392
Audit Trails and Logging 393
Backups 394
Remote Access Security 395
C2 Configuration Manager 395
Emerging Technologies 396
IPSec. 397
Virtual Private Networking. 398

▼ 11 Tuning and Troubleshooting 401
Tuning NT Systems 402
The Seven Habits of Highly Effective Tuning 402
Performance Monitor 404
NT Network Tuning 416
Troubleshooting 418
Problem Resolution 419
Diagnostic Tools for NT 420
TCP/IP Troubleshooting 428
Boot Problems 432

▼ 12 Network Testing and Capacity Planning 439
Benefits of Testing 440
Be Proactive Not Reactive. 440
Costs and Benefits 441
Testing Complements Management 442
Capacity Planning 443

Goals of Testing. 443
    Throughput 444
    Reliability 444
    Functionality 444
    Regression 445
    Acceptance 445
Testing Your Network 446
    Network Monitoring Standards 446
    Tools 450
    Laboratory Network 456
    Testing Applications 460
Simulating Your Network 465
    Preparing to Simulate 465
    Simulators. 468
    Lifecycle Management. 475

▼ **13** Planning for NT 5.0. 477
Upgrading Systems 478
    System Requirements 478
    File Systems. 479
    Dual-boot Installations 479
    New Workstation Options 480
    Two Server Types 480
Domain Organization 481
    Active Directory 481
    Distributed File System 488
Migrating to NT 5.0 490
    Enterprise Organization. 491
    Domain Examples 491
    Upgrading Servers. 493
    Creating an NT 5.0 Tree 494
    Making the Move 501

▼ **A** Year 2000 Problem Identification and Resolution 503
What Will Fail? 504
    Mainframes and Midrange Computers 505
    Personal Computers 505
    Network Infrastructure 505
    Embedded Systems 506
Planning a Year 2000 Project to Prevent Disaster 506
    Building the Project Plan 506
    Estimating Costs 507
    Identifying and Selecting Resources 507

Testing and Certification 509
    The Y2K Lab 509
    Vendor Certification 509
    Running Y2K Tests. 510
    Where to Find More Information. 512

▼ **B**   Enterprise IP Management. 513

Why IP Management? 514
    IP Management Challenges. 514
    Cost Vs. Benefit. 515
    Key Features 517
QIP 4.0 518
    NetID 3.0 520
    Meta IP 3.1 523

▼ **C**   Windows NT Resources — Where to Get Help 525

Online Help 526
    Help Books 526
    Command-line Help 526
    Additional Files 528
TechNet 528
Microsoft Online Support 530
Internet Sources. 531
Newsgroups. 532
    Getting Started 532
    Using Newsgroups 533
NT User Groups 533
    NT Resource Kit 534

▼ **D**   About the CD 537

Admin Tools 538
    Enterprise Administrator 538
    Kane Security Monitor. 538
    Kane Security Analyst. 538
    Storage Resource Manager 538
    Pukka Software. 539
    Winquota Manager 539
    RoboMon 539
    Convoy Cluster. 539
    Administrator Assistant Tool Kit. 539
    Fortress-NT 539
    LAN Licenser 539
    Print Manager Plus 540

XLNT 540
Trusted Enterprise Mgr. 540
AutoLogon 540
BlueScreen 540
ERD Commander 540
NTFilemon 540
NTFSDOS 540
NTRegmon 541
NTSID 541
NTSync 541
NTUndelete 541
VolumeID 541
Diagnostic Tools 541
NetScan 542
Net.Medic 542
Nbench 542
BalanceSuite 542
PerfMan 542
LogCaster 542
Contig 542
CPUMon 543
NTHandleEX 543
WinObj 543
NTRecover 543
IP Utilities 543
Meta IP 543
NetID 544
QIP 544
QIP Subnet Calculator 544
IP Calc 544
Big Brother 544
Hostname 544
RAS Utilities 545
RAS Pro 545
Timbuktu 545
Virtual Motion 545
RAS Manager 545
Remotely Possible 545
Miscellaneous Utilities 545
Diskkeeper Light 546
ER Disk 546
Event Admin 546
EZ Clean 546

RAMCharge 546
SuperDisk NT 546
SmartBatch 32 546
Octopus HA+. 546
Media Mirror 547
SuperCache NT. 547
UltraBac 547

▼   Index 549

ACKNOWLEDGMENTS

There are two authors credited for this book on the cover. However, there are a number of very important people who were invaluable to the creation of this book. Foremost, thanks to Wendy Rinaldi for approaching me to do the book and for managing its progress from its inception to its production. There were other notable individuals who were crucial, including Cynthia Douglas for coordinating the copy editing, Cory Scott for his expert input as technical editor, Sudha Putnam for superior copy edits, and Ann Sellers for keeping all things organized. To the staff at Osborne/McGraw-Hill, thank you for your efforts. We also appreciate all the vendors who provided us with product material and software for the CD-ROM.

Personally, I had unstinting support from Sandra, who had to wait several months for me to re-emerge from my office (I told you I'd come back). During an earlier part of my development, Drs. Miller and Masland both took the time to guide me on the arts of clear thinking and intelligible communication. Special thanks go to John Berg for writing Chapter 1 and Appendix A and to Dr. Jon Gottesman for writing Chapter 5. To my brother Anthony, I couldn't have done it without you. To all of you—thank you very much!

—Toby J. Velte

I'd like to thank all of the people at Osborne/McGraw-Hill who helped turn the late nights and long weekends of writing into the finished book you are reading now. I also want to recognize John Berg for his substantial contributions, not only for Chapter 1, but also for his insightful discussions throughout the process. Special thanks to Chris Cox and Bryan Koch for taking the time to review and comment on the DNS and Security chapters respectively. I also want to mention all the bright and talented people I have had the good fortune to have worked with over the years (you know who you are). You have all contributed to this book in one way or another, and I thank you. Finally, I'd like to thank Mom, Dad, and my two brothers: Tully and Toby. Tully for being one of the wisest and most insightful people I know. Toby, for constantly amazing me with his limitless knowledge and for his intense dedication to getting this project completed.

—Anthony T. Velte

INTRODUCTION

▼

There are countless volumes written about how to use Windows NT in the most basic sense: add a user, configure RAS for one person, install a web server, etc. There are even books on rudimentary networking with NT. However, you are on your own to figure out issues such as how to connect thousands of users with RAS, create models of your network for capacity planning, or configure DNS to be fully redundant—until now. This book takes you beyond basic configurations and single-segment network problems to show you how to implement NT in the enterprise.

We use years of enterprise networking experience to show you how to successfully design, optimize, and secure your NT networks. You'll not only learn about what DNS and WINS are, but also see network diagrams that illustrate *where* you should place these servers within a large network for optimal impact and cost-effectiveness. Sure, we'll show you how to install and configure the latest web server, but you'll also read about how to determine the correct server hardware, network connections, and security settings. In addition to learning about how to use the Windows NT services in the enterprise, you'll also get an insider's look at how to plan for the future growth of your network with Windows NT 5.0. If you have ever looked at a Windows NT book and wanted more, this book is for you.

NT AND THE NETWORK

Networks were originally built to share resources. In their humble beginnings, networks were designed to allow for terminal access to shared applications residing on a central host running what are today considered legacy applications. The next generation of networks was built around departmental local area networks whose purpose was to share information among people working within a common department or on the same project. Users typically shared information such as documents and spreadsheets as well as local print and data-storage devices.

Networks today are based on the same simple premise of resource sharing, although the breadth of resources being shared has exploded. Today, users share files, printers, storage devices, modems, fax devices, applications, and traditional host machines. Modern networking is more complex because these shared services are spread among many devices and aren't limited to a single host computer.

To further compound the complexity of networks today, we've now moved into an era where legacy applications are being replaced, or at least supplemented, with applications running on network servers. Many of these servers now work in conjunction with other network servers, legacy systems, and even other workstations to execute applications and process information.

Users have also separated themselves physically from the server. More users are accessing shared resources remotely via modems. In addition, servers and clients are sometimes separated by great distances but maintain connections using dedicated data lines. What has emerged is a requirement for a widely distributed but highly connected workforce. The diverse distribution of users and resources compounds the challenges facing managers of enterprise networks.

Because of the rapid change in network technology, most networks were not initially designed to meet today's needs—they *evolved* to do so. To meet these needs, advanced operating systems and tools for administration had to be developed. Windows NT systems are being deployed at a phenomenal rate to fill this need, and as NT becomes more scalable and powerful, it is taking on roles previously held by UNIX systems. Almost certainly, every enterprise network has, or will shortly have, NT systems. The following chapters describe how to build, optimize, maintain, access, and secure NT systems.

WHO SHOULD READ THIS BOOK

This book is designed for intermediate and advanced NT network architects and administrators. If you are in the position of making decisions about how NT is deployed or how to design NT into your enterprise network, this book is for you. If you are involved with the deployment of NT in the enterprise, you'll find many useful sections in this book because we cover specific installations on many services and products.

We do not cover the fundamental aspects of NT or networking. The first two chapters give an overview of networking and NT; however, these sections should only serve as a recapitulation, and, subsequently, a reference, because they move quickly through their respective topics and expect the reader to be comfortable with these subjects ahead of time.

WHAT THIS BOOK COVERS

Chapter 1: *Networking Overview*—This chapter provides an in-depth look at the network protocols used in today's enterprise network. It also describes some of the basic hardware components typically used in networks. This is an excellent place to start if you want to refresh your networking skills.

Chapter 2: *Building Systems*—The second chapter gives an overview of the more basic NT administrative tasks, such as creating NT systems, adding new users, and organizing them into groups. We quickly move into more advanced coverage when we talk about how to deploy hundreds of systems automatically and about special hardware considerations for the enterprise.

After the first couple of chapters, this book branches out from all previously written books on NT. Only issues that are important to the enterprise are covered. Some of these topics are covered in other books, but not with the same focus on integrating NT into the enterprise we have here.

Chapter 3: *Reliability Through Redundancy*—This chapter begins with a quantitative look at the probability of failure in computer systems. Next we'll show you how to decrease the odds of having a devastating failure by incorporating redundant hardware, such as power supplies and disk drives. Then we'll show you how to keep your systems up and running using technology such as clustering, data backups, and redundant servers.

Chapter 4: *Network Administration*—You have not seen an administration chapter like this before! We dispense with all the common administration tools you are already familiar with and look at some tools that are truly helpful in the enterprise. For example, you'll learn how to administer user accounts when you have thousands of them and how to use the Systems Management Server to automatically install software on remote computers.

Chapter 5: *Connecting Client Workstations*—We first discuss how different Windows systems connect to each other using the Browser and Logon services. Then we delve into specific examples of connectivity, including Win 3.11, Win95, Macintosh, Novell Servers, and UNIX workstations.

Chapter 6: *Domain Name System*—Critical to every large TCP/IP-based network, DNS will play an even larger role in future NT networks. This chapter focuses on Microsoft's implementation of DNS. Not only do we show you how to set up and configure DNS in the enterprise, we show you how to incorporate it into your existing network. We wrap up this chapter with an overview of the future of DNS and NT.

Chapter 7: *WINS and DHCP*—The WINS name service is critical to the functioning of today's larger NT networks. DHCP can provide a new level of efficiency in managing network naming and addressing on workstations, print servers, and other network devices. Here we discuss how you can configure and manage WINS and DHCP on your network.

Chapter 8: *Internet Services*—This chapter deals with the Internet Information Server and Microsoft Proxy Server. We examine the different IIS versions and options, helping you plan, configure, and manage the HTTP, FTP, and Gopher services. We close the chapter with a look at the Microsoft Proxy Server and discuss how to integrate it into your environment with a focus on security, access control, and maximizing web performance.

Chapter 9: *Routing and Remote Access Service*—The ability to provide remote users with reliable dialup connectivity is an important part of the NT network. Here we explain Remote Access (RAS) and discuss how to use the new Routing and Remote Access Service (RRAS). In this chapter we also discuss the special hardware and configurations required to get a large number of users connected. We wrap it up with a look at the protocols used in remote connections and special issues related to RRAS.

Chapter 10: *Security*—Because information is a valuable asset for large and small organizations alike, the subject of network and systems security is always a hot topic. In this chapter we examine important security fundamentals and look closely at network- and NT-specific security. We also cover existing and emerging security technologies in the areas of authentication, encryption, and Virtual Private Networking. These key security technologies help keep private networks and systems secure, as well as allow your network to be extended beyond the traditional boundaries by using public networks such as the Internet.

Chapter 11: *Tuning and Troubleshooting*—This chapter is devoted to tuning and optimizing NT Servers to work in your enterprise. Your problems are different from the administrator who has only a handful of NT systems. Why take the same advice? Here, we present the Seven Habits of Highly Effective Tuning as well as strategies and solutions to the problems that you are likely to face in the enterprise.

Chapter 12: *Network Testing and Capacity Planning*—One key to running a high-availability network is making sure you have the information and procedures to accurately predict future demands on the network. We'll look at what it takes to test the network and the applications that run on it. We will also look at how to use this information to plan for growth.

Chapter 13: *Planning for NT 5.0*—We bring the future of NT computing to you now by showing you how to start planning a migration to NT 5.0. Get a peek at the next generation of NT and see how you are going to get there. We start by showing you how to upgrade different operating systems to NT 5.0. Then we step through a sample NT 4.0 domain conversion. We end the chapter by discussing the issues you must consider before implementing an enterprise-wide migration.

The appendices bring you more pertinent information on such important subjects as IP management, Year 2000 conversions and testing, where to find more help when you are confronted with a difficult NT-related problem, and the contents of our fully packed CD-ROM.

Appendix A: *Year 2000 Problem Identification and Resolution*—Many organizations must deal with legacy systems that may not comply with the date change to the year 2000. Here we lay out a strategy to attack your year 2000 problems.

Appendix B: *Enterprise IP Management*—Enterprises use TCP/IP throughout their networks. Keeping track of your TCP/IP environment can be quite cumbersome. Here we present some third-party applications you can start using now to gain control over your IP addressing and create a managed TCP/IP infrastructure.

Appendix C: *Windows NT Resources —Where to Get Help*—Ever wonder where to look for answers? Because one book cannot contain all the answers, we'll point you in the direction of some great sources for facts, tips, and solutions.

Appendix D: *About the CD*—Browse the contents of the CD-ROM without being at your computer. This is a descriptive listing of all the utilities and tools contained on the CD-ROM that comes with this book. There are more than 50 programs that you can add to your NT toolkit. You'll find just the utilities you need here without having to surf through the fluff.

Resource Kit

The *Microsoft Resource Kit for NT Server* is highly recommended for anyone serious about Windows NT. We make many references to the *Resource Kit* in this book, and it's just a lot more fun when you can join in. So, if you don't have it yet, pick yourself up a copy, install it, and use it.

CD Contents

CD NOTE   We have a CD-ROM included in the back of the book with numerous programs and utilities that run on NT. We have tested them all to make sure they meet our high standards. Throughout the book, we have a special icon to represent CD-ROM contents. This means that you will find software on the CD-ROM pertaining to the topic presently being discussed. However, there is more software on the CD-ROM than we mention in the text, so feel free to explore!

HOW TO READ THIS BOOK

This book was written so you could easily pick it up and browse—every chapter contains specific subject matter that can stand by itself. Provided you have a basic understanding of NT and networking, you can jump right in wherever you find something interesting. If you feel you have a solid background in networking but not necessarily NT, then start with Chapter 2. If you feel you'd like to brush up a bit on your knowledge of networking, start at Chapter 1 and proceed through Chapter 2 onto any other topic in the book. Naturally, you should feel free to just start at Chapter 1 and read on to the end. In addition, there are many tables and figures that you may find useful as a day-to-day to reference. Enjoy!

WINDOWS
NT
Professional
Library

CHAPTER 1

Networking Overview

Windows NT has incorporated networking since its inception. To play an integral part in an enterprise, NT has had to have more than rudimentary networking capabilities. To meet this end, NT has focused on incorporating existing networking standards. With the release of NT 4.0, Microsoft included full support for many networking and routing protocols, as well as the capability for NT Server to act as a router. But before we jump into how NT fits into the enterprise network, we should cover some basic networking principles.

This chapter outlines the basic networking model that most networking devices use. We will discuss how NT fits into this model. We will also explain how to properly design and configure your NT systems to function with other networking devices, because no enterprise network is comprised of only one type of system. Finally, we will cover physical and software application protocols that are used in networking, and we will illustrate how NT is used with these protocols.

STANDARDS ORGANIZATIONS

Standards organizations have been around for a long time, working hard to ensure a fair and compatible networking environment in the face of fierce corporate competition for market shares. Windows NT has had to find its place among the preexisting standards. This section describes how NT fits in the OSI seven-layer model of networking and in the physical configurations of networking hardware.

The Open Systems Interconnect (OSI) Reference Model

With the advent of the networking industry, it became apparent early on that if different devices on a network were going to be able to communicate with one another, some standards would need to be defined to allow a common communication interface. The International Standards Organization (ISO), founded in 1946, published the Open Systems Interconnect (OSI) reference model in 1978. This seven-layer model has become the standard for designing communication methods among network devices. This section covers the basics of the seven layers and the purpose each layer serves.

The OSI reference model has seven functional layers. Each layer defines a function performed when data is transferred between applications across a network, as illustrated in Figure 1-1. This function may be performed by any number of protocols, which are just rules that control how a process or function works. Any given protocol may perform multiple functions. Each protocol communicates with a peer on a remote system. For example, an application layer protocol will communicate through the protocol stack with the application protocol at the other computer. Each protocol layer is concerned only with communication to a peer at the other end of a link and thus creates a virtual link to the other system at the level of the OSI reference model. For example, Simple Mail Transfer Protocol (SMTP) is an application layer protocol that communicates with peer e-mail applications on remote systems. The e-mail applications do not care whether the

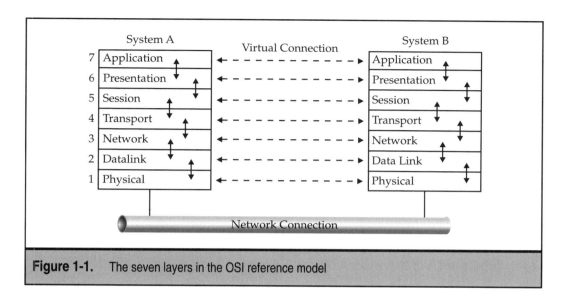

Figure 1-1.   The seven layers in the OSI reference model

physical layer is a serial modem line or a twisted-pair Ethernet connection. It is only concerned with functions within SMTP.

Information is passed down through the layers until it is transmitted across the network, where it is passed back up the stack to the application at the remote end. Although each layer relies on the other layers to perform their functions, the individual layers are not concerned with the workings of the other layers. They only need to know how to pass information up or down from one layer to another.

▼   **Layer one**—The physical layer deals with the actual transport medium that is being used. It defines the electrical and mechanical characteristics of the medium carrying the data signal. Some examples include coaxial cable, fiber optics, twisted-pair cabling, and serial lines. The physical layer also includes physical components like signal characteristics and timing issues. Network devices used at this layer are called *repeaters*.

■   **Layer two**—The data link layer governs access onto the network and the reliable transfer of packets across the network. It controls the synchronization of transmitted packets, as well as the error checking and flow of transmissions. Token passing and Carrier Sense Multiple Access with Collision Detection (CSMA/CD) techniques are included in layer two of the OSI model. Layer two is subdivided into the Medium Access Control (MAC) and Logical Link Control sublayers. Bridges work at this layer.

■   **Layer three**—The network layer is concerned with moving data between different networks or subnetworks. It is responsible for finding the device for which the data is destined. Internet Protocol (IP) and IP routing are functions of layer three.

■ **Layer four**—The transport layer takes care of data transfer, ensuring that the data reaches its destination intact and in the proper order. The Transmission Control Protocol (TCP) and User Datagram Protocol (UDP) operate at this layer.

■ **Layer five**—The session layer establishes and terminates connections and arranges sessions into logical parts. The Lightweight Directory Access Protocol (LDAP) and Remote Procedure Call (RPC) provide some functions at this layer.

■ **Layer six**—This layer is involved in formatting data for the purpose of display or printing. Data encryption and character set translation such as ASCII <--> EBCDIC are also performed by protocols at this layer. Examples of presentation layer protocols are HyperText Transfer Protocol (HTTP) and telnet.

▲ **Layer seven**—The application layer defines the protocols to be used between the application programs. Examples of protocols at this layer are protocols for electronic mail (Simple Mail Transfer Protocol), file transfers (File Transfer Protocol), and remote login.

NT in the OSI Model

Figure 1-2 illustrates how Windows NT implements the OSI seven-layer model. Unlike previous operating systems from Microsoft, NT had built-in networking from its start. Its modular design allows great flexibility and third-party intervention at almost any layer. For example, if a network interface card (NIC) complies with the Network Driver Interface Specifications (NDIS) 3.0 and provides a driver, it can be used with other transport (network) protocols and any application that can run on NT.

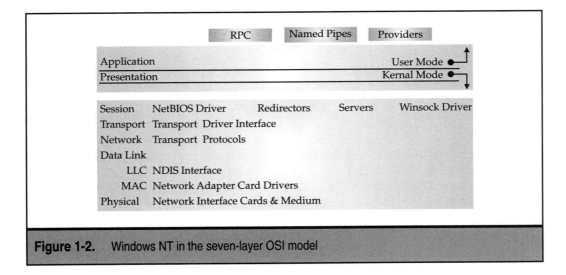

Figure 1-2. Windows NT in the seven-layer OSI model

The NT architecture includes two key components:

▼   **Transport Driver Interface (TDI)**—TDI is a common interface between higher level drivers (such as the redirector or server) and the network protocols. It allows these higher-level drivers to remain independent of any one network protocol.

▲   **Network Driver Interface Specifications (NDIS)**—NDIS also provides connectivity between layers. NDIS is the interface between the upper layer protocols and the network interface card (NIC). NDIS drivers allow multiple protocol stacks to work over the same network interface card. To do this, the NDIS driver requires a protocol manager module that coordinates communication between the card and the different levels of drivers. The protocol manager reads incoming packets, sorts them, and directs them to the correct protocol stacks. NDIS drivers can support as many protocol stacks over a network interface card as the PC memory allows.

Microsoft has incorporated full networking functionality in all NT products. Both NT Servers and Workstations have the capability to be either sources of data (server) or requesters of data (client). For example, let's say a user has an NT Workstation with a 3Com NIC and wishes to use FTP to access another system. Once the user selects the destination and attempts to establish a connection, the FTP application works through the WinSock driver, which works through the TDI (using TCP). The information passes into the network layer using IP, and then passes into the NDIS interface, where it connects with the NIC driver provided by 3Com. Finally, it is placed in the buffer on the NIC for transmission onto the physical medium.

THE PHYSICAL NETWORK

Before any computer can communicate with another, a physical network must be in place. There are three common types of local area network (LAN) topologies in use today: Ethernet, Token Ring, and the Fiber Distributed Data Interface (FDDI). This section is a brief overview and comparison of each of these protocols and their basic throughput characteristics.

Comparative Topologies

Ethernet, Token Ring, and FDDI are three distinctly different LAN interfaces. Each has different advantages and has a different role to play in your networking environment. You will probably have a mix of these different protocols in your enterprise. It is useful to understand the basic functioning of each so you can better choose which one to use in the face of a networking problem.

Ethernet

Ethernet is undoubtedly the most popular LAN topology today. It is a simple and low-cost protocol that was developed in the late 1970s by Xerox, DEC, and Intel Corporations. It saw a series of enhancements and variations in the early 1980s as the Institute of Electrical and Electronics Engineers (IEEE) standards body released the 802.x specifications.

FOUR VERSIONS OF ETHERNET The four primary variations of Ethernet are Ethernet Version 2, IEEE 802.3, IEEE 802.3 Subnetwork Access Protocol (SNAP), and Novell NetWare 802.3 "Raw". The frame format of each type is different. The Ethernet Version 2 and Novell NetWare 802.3 "Raw" frames were developed before the 802.3 standard was released. As a result, they don't use the IEEE 802.2 Logical Link Control (LLC) standard. Ethernet Version 2 identifies the upper-layer protocol in a 2-byte Ethertype field. Novell NetWare 802.3 "Raw" identifies the upper-layer protocols in the data field. The frame format for the Ethernet Version 2 frame format and the Novell NetWare 802.3 "Raw" frame format are illustrated in Figures 1-3 and 1-4.

The IEEE 802.3 and IEEE 802.3 SNAP incorporate a 3 byte LLC portion of the frame to identify the Service Access Point (SAP) for the upper layer. IEEE 802.3 SNAP also has an additional SNAP header to allow vendors without assigned SAPs to become IEEE-compliant. The IEEE 802.3 frame format and the IEEE 802.3 SNAP frame format are illustrated in Figures 1-5 and 1-6.

Some of the most common Ethertypes are listed in Table 1-1.

The most common SAPs are listed in Table 1-2.

ACCESS CONTROL Ethernet uses the Carrier Sense Multiple Access with Collision Detection (CSMA/CD) protocol to control access to the wire and to ensure the integrity of transmission. Before attempting to transmit a message, an endstation determines

8	6	6	2	46-1500	4
Preamble	Destination	Source	Type	Data	FCS

Preamble -- 8 bytes of synchronization
Destination -- 6-byte address of destination node
Source -- 6-byte address of source node
Type -- Specifies upper-layer protocol
Data -- Information received from higher-layer protocols
FCS -- Frame Check Sequence

Figure 1-3. The Ethernet Version 2 frame format

8	6	6	2	46-1500	4
Preamble	Destination	Source	Length	Data	FCS

Preamble -- 8 bytes of synchronization
Destination -- 6-byte address of destination node
Source -- 6-byte address of source node
*Length -- Specifies the number of bytes in the LLC and data fields
Data -- IPX header and higher-layer NetWare protocols
FCS -- Frame Check Sequence

*Novell developed their frame format before the 802.3 specifications were
finished. As a result, they identified the length, but didn't use the LLC
in their frame.

Figure 1-4. The Novell NetWare 802.3 "Raw" frame format

				← LLC 802.2 →				
8	6	6	2	1	1	1 or 2	43-1497	4
Pre-amble	Desti-nation	Source	Length	DSAP	SSAP	Control	Data + Pad	FCS

Preamble -- 8 bytes of synchronization
Destination -- 6-byte address of destination node
Source -- 6-byte address of source node
Length -- 2 bytes; specifies the number of bytes in the LLC and data fields
DSAP -- Destination Service Access Point; receiving process at destination
SSAP -- Source Service Access Point; sending process in source
Control -- Various control information (for connection-oriented LLC,
this is a 2-byte field)
Data -- Information received from higher-layer protocols
Pad -- Pads frame to minimum of 46 bytes of data and LLC
(ensure collisions can be detected)
FCS -- Frame Check Sequence

Figure 1-5. The IEEE 802.3 frame format

8	6	6	2	AA	AA	1 or 2	3	2	43-1497	4
Pre-amble	Desti-nation	Source	Length	DSAP	SSAP	Con-trol	Ven-dor code	Type	Data + Pad	FCS

LLC 802.2 — SNAP header

Preamble -- 8 bytes of synchronization
Destination -- 6-byte address of destination node
Source -- 6-byte address of source node
Length -- Specifies the number of bytes in the LLC and data fields
DSAP -- Destination Service Access Point
SSAP -- Source Service Access Point
Control -- Various control information (for connection-oriented LLC, this is a 2-byte field)
SNAP -- (5 bytes) First 3 bytes identify the vendor; last 2 bytes identify the protocol
Data -- Information received from higher-layer protocols
Pad -- Pads frame to minimum of 46 bytes of data
(ensures collisions can be detected)
FCS -- Frame Check Sequence

Figure 1-6.   The IEEE 802.3 SNAP frame format

Ethertype	Value (HEX)
NetWare	8137
XNS	0600,0807
IP	0800
IP (Vines)	0BAD,80C4
ARP	0806
RARP	8035
LAT	6004
AARP	80F3

Table 1-1.   The Common Ethertypes and Their Values

SAP	Value (HEX)
NetWare	10,E0
XNS	80
IP	06
SNA	04,05,08,0C
NetBIOS	F0
X.25	7E
ISO	20,34,EC,FE,14,54
SNAP	AA

Table 1-2. The Most Common SAPs

whether or not another endstation is transmitting a message on the media. It does this by listening to determine if there is carrier on the wire. If it doesn't hear a carrier for 9.6 microseconds, the endstation will attempt to transmit the message. It must continue to listen while it's transmitting. If two endstations transmit at the same time, a collision occurs. This results in errors called *runt frames*. Both endstations must back off from their transmissions, and then retry their transmissions.

When a node on an Ethernet LAN transmits data, every endstation on the LAN receives the data. Each endstation checks each data unit to see whether the destination address matches its own address. If the addresses match, the endstation accepts and processes the packet. If the addresses do not match, it disregards the packet.

Besides transmitting and receiving data and detecting collisions, endstations are also responsible for detecting *jabbers*. If a device sends more data than is allowed in the largest allowable frame size, the endstation determines that the frame is invalid and the device is jabbering. It then disables the transmission. This prevents a malfunctioning device from causing the Ethernet network to fail.

THE PHYSICAL CONNECTIONS The first Ethernet networks were built using a thick, yellow, semirigid 0.4 inch diameter coaxial cable. With this type of cable, each cable segment can be no more than 500 meters long, with a maximum of 100 stations per segment. These segments can be connected to other segments using a repeater, but workstations can be separated by no more than two repeaters. This limits the distance between any two stations on the Ethernet network to no more than 1,500 meters. This type of Ethernet network is called thicknet, or 10Base5 (10Mb/sec, baseband, 500 meters per segment).

Stations are connected to thicknet using transceivers. These transceivers are typically connected to the thicknet cable by a *vampire tap* , which makes a connection to the outer shielding and the inner conductor without cutting the cable. The stations are then connected to the transceiver with an Attachment Unit Interface (AUI) cable. The maximum length of an AUI cable is 50 meters.

Another method of connectivity was developed to reduce the cost of installation. Thin Ethernet, or *cheapernet* as it's sometimes called, uses a flexible RG58 coaxial cable and moves the transceiver circuitry to the NIC of the attaching workstation. The physical connectivity is still workstation to workstation, but the cabling runs directly to the back of each workstation and connects to the NIC using a British National Connector (BNC) connection. These BNC "T" connectors are installed on the cable by cutting the cable and splicing them in the wire. Thin Ethernet is called 10Base2 (10Mb/sec, baseband, 185 meters per segment). Both 10Base2 and 10Base5 use 50-ohm terminators on each end of the cable so signals do not bounce back and forth along the cable.

Most Ethernet networks built today are using 24-gauge unshielded twisted-pair (UTP) cabling. Ethernet built on twisted-pair cabling is known as 10BaseT (10Mb/sec, Baseband, twisted-pair cabling). 10BaseT uses an RJ-45 phone jack for connections. UTP is typically wired in a star topology. This allows networks to be installed using horizontal cabling plants that terminate in a wiring closet. Workstations connect into a 10BaseT hub in a central location. This makes it much easier to implement moves, additions, and changes. It also allows technology upgrades to be done in a central location without rewiring an entire network, workstation by workstation.

Fast Ethernet

Fast Ethernet, or 100BaseT, has many of the same features as 10BaseT. It uses the same frame formats and frame lengths as 10BaseT. It uses CSMA/CD and runs over Categories 3, 4, and 5 UTP cabling. Interconnections are made using hubs, switches, and repeaters just like 10BaseT.

However, 100BaseT does have some important differences from 10BaseT. Data is transmitted at 10 times the speed of 10BaseT. The amount of time a workstation must detect no carrier on the wire before transmitting is only 0.96 microseconds, as opposed to 9.6 microseconds with 10BaseT. 100BaseT uses a different coding scheme to represent bits on the network. It uses 4B5B and 8B6T instead of the Manchester encoding that is in use with 10BaseT. More information on these encoding techniques can be found in many technical resources devoted to the subject.

Fast Ethernet has been broken into three different physical layer specifications: 100Base-TX, 100Base4, and 100Base-FX. 100Base-TX is fast Ethernet over Category 5 UTP. This uses the same RJ-45 connectors as 10BaseT and requires two pairs of wires for transmission of data. 100Base-TX uses 4B5B encoding.

100Base4 is fast Ethernet over Category 3 or Category 4 UTP cabling. It requires four pairs of wires. Three are used for data transmission, and one handles collision detection. 100Base4 uses 8B6T encoding. It was designed to accommodate large installations of voice-grade UTP.

100Base-FX is fast Ethernet for fiber-optic cabling. Fiber optics allows greatly increased transmission distances. 100Base-FX uses the same MIC, ST, and SC connectors for the fiber optic cabling as FDDI. It also uses both single mode or multimode fiber, just like FDDI. 100Base-FX uses 4B5B encoding.

Token Ring

Token Ring is a LAN standard that uses a token-passing protocol to transmit data. This token-passing protocol eliminates collisions on the network and increases the utilization of the network. Token Ring runs at either 4Mb/sec or 16Mb/sec in a logical ring configuration. A basic Token Ring network consists of ring stations connected into a concentrator. The concentrator may be a Multistation Access Unit (MSAU) or an intelligent hub that emulates an MSAU. Larger networks can be built by connecting multiple MSAUs using special ports called ring in (RI) and ring out (RO), or by connecting multiple token rings with bridges or routers.

TOKEN RING FRAME TYPES   There are three types of frames transmitted on a Token Ring: tokens, media access control (MAC) frames, and Logical Link Control (LLC) frames. The token is a 3-byte frame used to control the transmission of data onto the ring. There is only one token on a ring at a time. Ring stations must claim the free token to transmit. There is an access control bit that determines if the token is free. This means only one station can transmit at any one time, thereby eliminating collisions. Figure 1-7 illustrates the frame format for the access token.

MAC frames are used by the ring stations to communicate with other ring stations. They control the operation of the ring and report errors. Token Ring has a very robust set of built-in controls to ensure proper operation. With the exception of the token, Token Ring uses MAC frames to control the ring. MAC frames are used only on local rings; they never pass through bridges or routers. The MAC frame format is shown in Figure 1-8.

Logical Link Control (LLC) frames carry user data. These frames use protocols like TCP/IP, IPX/SPX, NetBIOS, and SNA.

RING STATIONS   Ring stations, although physically connected to an MSAU or hub, are logically connected to their neighbor on the ring. Each ring station has a separate transmitter and a separate receiver. The transmitter of one ring station is connected to the receiver on the next ring station. The ring station receiving the transmission is referred to

1 byte	1 byte	1 byte
Starting delimiter	Frame control	Ending delimiter

Figure 1-7.   The Token Ring frame format

1	1	1	6	6	Variable	4	1
SD	AC	FC	DA	SA	Data	FCS	ED

SD -- Starting delimiter
AC -- Access Control byte
FC -- Frame Control byte
DA -- Destination Address
SA -- Source Address
Data -- Information received from the higher-level protocols
FCS -- Frame Check Sequence
ED -- Ending Delimiter

Figure 1-8.   The Token Ring MAC frame format

as the *downstream neighbor*. This connectivity is repeated until the last ring station's transmitter is connected to the receiver of the first ring station—completing the ring.

This first ring station is called the *active monitor*. It becomes the active monitor through a process called *contention*. All other ring stations are *standby monitors*. The active monitor ensures the ring is operating properly. It provides master clocking to the ring, removes any frames not claimed by other stations on the ring, compensates for frequency jitter, and ensures there is always only one token on the ring.

If the active monitor doesn't detect a token or a frame on the ring within ten milliseconds, it will create a new token. Before it sends the new token onto the ring, it transmits a *ring purge frame*. The ring purge frame resets the timers on all the ring stations. When the ring purge frame returns to the active monitor, the active monitor transmits a new token onto the ring. If it doesn't receive the ring purge frame within four milliseconds, it will transmit another ring purge. This can continue for up to one second, at which time the ring enters contention and a new active monitor is elected.

There are several other events that can cause the contention process to begin. If any standby monitor doesn't detect an active monitor present frame within a 15 second interval, it will initiate the contention process. If any standby monitor doesn't detect a good frame every 2.6 seconds it will initiate the contention process. Frequency or signal loss errors detected by any standby monitor will also initiate the contention process.

Any standby monitor that detects any of these conditions initiates the contention process by generating a *claim token frame*. A claim token frame can be transmitted without a token. The claim token frame includes the MAC address of the station that transmitted it onto the ring. The downstream neighbor will pull the frame off the ring and compare its MAC address with the address in the claim token frame. If its own MAC address is higher, it appends the claim token frame with its own MAC address. If its own MAC address is lower, it simply repeats the frame back onto the ring with the original MAC address. The ring station with the highest MAC address becomes the new active monitor.

There are a couple of exceptions to this rule. The ring station that was the active monitor prior to beginning the contention process does not participate in the contention process. Ring stations can be configured to simply repeat claim token frames and never become the active monitor. Once the new active monitor is chosen, it sends out a ring purge to reset all the timers, and generates a new token.

The active monitor also initiates the ring poll process. Every seven seconds, the active monitor sends out an active monitor present frame. Because these frames are all addressed as broadcasts, the first ring station to receive one of these frames changes the address recognized (AR) and frame copied (FC) bits to ones. This ring station now knows that the address of the source in the active monitor present frame is its nearest upstream neighbor. The other ring stations will see the AR/FC bits set to one and will ignore the frame. This ring station then sends out a standby monitor present frame. This is also a broadcast frame. The same process takes place as with the active monitor present frame. After every ring station has sent out one of these frames, completing the ring poll, or neighbor notification process, every ring station knows who its nearest upstream neighbor is. This information is used when reporting problems on the ring.

BEACONING   Token Ring also has a method called *beaconing* to identify and attempt to correct hardware errors. This can be a fairly complex process; in essence, a ring station that sees a loss of signal on the ring sends a beacon frame containing its own address and the address of its nearest addressable upstream neighbor (NAUN). If the beacon frame reaches its NAUN, that ring station pulls off the ring and tries to reinsert. The reinsertion process includes a self test that should cause the faulty station to remain off the ring.

In practice, quite often the failing ring station has either a bad cable or bad adapter, and it cannot follow the correct beacon recovery process. This requires human intervention to diagnose the bad ring station and repair it or remove it from the ring.

FDDI

The Fiber Distributed Data Interface (FDDI) is a token-passing interface that uses fiber cabling. It has four key components: the media access control (MAC) layer, the physical (PHY) layer, the physical media dependent (PMD) layer, and the station management (SMT) protocol.

The MAC layer defines addressing, scheduling, and data routing. It also communicates with higher-layer protocols, such as TCP/IP, SNA, and IPX. The FDDI MAC layer accepts data from the upper-layer protocols, adds the MAC header, and then passes packets of up to 4,500 bytes to the PHY layer.

The PHY layer handles the encoding and decoding of data into symbol streams for the wire. It also handles clock synchronization on the FDDI ring. FDDI uses the 4B5B encoding technique.

The PMD layer of FDDI handles the analog baseband transmission between nodes on the physical media. PMD standards include Fiber-PMD for fiber optic cable and TP-PMD for twisted-pair copper wires. TP-PMD is a new ANSI wiring standard that allows 100 Mb/sec transmission over UTP. It replaces the proprietary approaches that have been used to run FDDI over copper.

The SMT protocol handles the management of the FDDI ring. Functions implemented by SMT include neighbor identification, fault detection and reconfiguration, insertion and removal from the ring, and traffic statistics monitoring.

DIFFERENCES FROM TOKEN RING   The MAC processes for FDDI are very similar to the IEEE 802.5 standard used in Token Ring, with several exceptions. One example is when a station waiting to transmit data claims the token, but doesn't convert the token into part of the data frame it wants to transmit. Instead, it pulls the token off the ring completely and then transmits its data frames. Once the station has finished transmitting its data, it puts a new token back onto the ring—even if it hasn't begun to receive the frames it has transmitted. This is similar to early token release in some implementations of 16 Mb/sec Token Ring. Other differences are outlined in the following sections.

SYNCHRONOUS AND ASYNCHRONOUS TRAFFIC   The process of data transmission used by FDDI makes the IEEE 802.5 method of using priority and reservation bits for capacity allocation useless. FDDI uses a scheme to accommodate a mixture of both bursty and sustained throughput traffic. To do this, FDDI defines two types of traffic: synchronous and asynchronous. Each station is allocated a portion of the total available capacity. The data it transmits during this allocated time is called *synchronous* data. Any capacity that isn't allocated, or is allocated but not used, is available for transmission of additional data. This is called *asynchronous* data.

This capacity allocation scheme is defined with the following formula:

$$Dmax + Fmax + Token\ Time + SA_i <= TTRT$$

where:

SA$_i$ = synchronous allocation for station *i*
Dmax   = propagation time for one complete circuit of the ring
Fmax   = time to transmit one 4,500 byte frame
Token Time = time to transmit a token
TTRT   = target token rotation time

The TTRT is determined during the claim token process. Each station stores the same TTRT. The value of SA$_i$ is assigned by the station management protocol. Each station has an initial value for SA$_i$ of zero and must request a change, if desired.

ERROR CORRECTION   If it detects a lost token, any station on the ring can detect the need for initialization of the ring. Each station has a counter it increments if it doesn't see a valid token in the time set for the token rotation timer. If the counter increments to two, the station initiates the claim token process. The claim token process resolves contention of the stations trying to initialize the ring; it also sets the value of TTRT.

Each station trying to claim the token sends a continuous stream of claim token frames. Each claim token frame includes the sending station's bid for the value of TTRT. Each claiming station looks at the information in each claim token frame and determines if it should cease sending its own claim token frames and enter repeat mode, or continue sending its own claim token frames. Its decision is based on three criteria:

▼   The frame with the lowest TTRT has precedence.

■   If the TTRT values are equal, stations with 48-bit addresses have precedence over stations with 16-bit addresses.

▲   If both TTRT and the address lengths are equal, the address with the highest value has precedence.

This process completes when one station receives its own claim token frame. At this point, all other stations should have deferred claiming the token and only this station's claim token frames are circulating the ring. The other stations store the value of TTRT in those frames. All of them now have stored the lowest value of TTRT to be used in the capacity allocation calculation. The station that has won the claim token process sends a token out onto the ring. This token's first circulation on the ring resets each station from an initialization state into an operational state.

BEACONING   The beaconing process is used to isolate faults on the ring. When a station on the ring detects a failure, such as a loss of a token, it enters the claim token process. If there is a failure on the ring, the claim token process cannot complete and the stations time out of it and enter the beacon process.

When a station enters the beacon process, it continuously sends beacon frames onto the ring. Any station that receives a beacon frame from an upstream station defers to that station and stops sending beacon frames. Eventually, only the station immediately downstream from the fault will be sending beacon frames. If the station begins to receive its own beacon frames, it assumes the fault has been restored and initiates the claim token process to initialize the ring.

BUILT-IN REDUNDANCY   The FDDI standard is composed of two parallel rings that connect each station to its neighbors with two links, as shown in Figure 1-9. These rings are called the primary and secondary rings. Each ring transmits in the opposite direction from the other. Under normal operations, the secondary ring sits idle. It is used only if the primary ring fails.

When a failure occurs on the primary ring, the ring isolates the damaged station by connecting to the secondary ring. This results in the two rings becoming a single ring, as shown in Figure 1-9. The same process is used when a link goes down. When this occurs, the ring is no longer fault-tolerant, and measures must be taken to correct the fault.

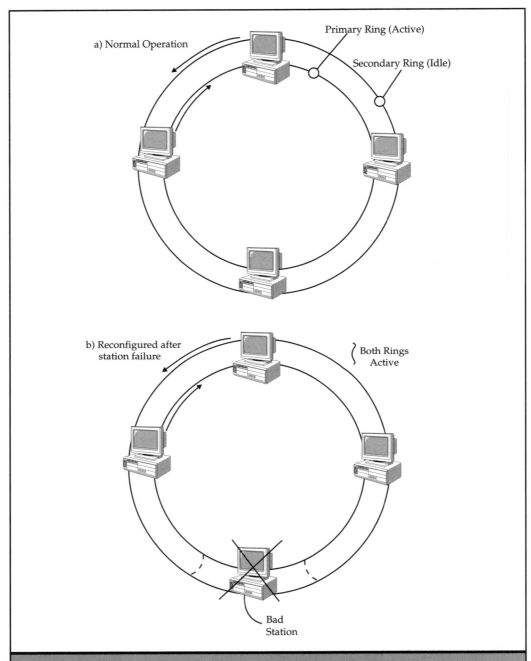

Figure 1-9. A FDDI ring connects all stations with two links for redundancy

Broadcasting

One problem that can plague any type of physical medium is excessive broadcast traffic. Sometimes on a network, a device needs to send data to many, or all, other devices on the network. For example, the NetBEUI protocol broadcasts to all devices on the network when it's looking for a specific NetBIOS name and doesn't know its Data Link Control (DLC) or IP address. TCP/IP may send a broadcast when it's trying to resolve an IP name to an IP address. Some lower-layer protocols broadcast as part of the topology's operation or in an effort to resolve a problem (as with Token Ring). The network devices perform this broadcast function by sending packets onto the network with an address that the other devices understand to be a broadcast, meaning it's meant for everyone.

The problem with broadcasts is that they go to every device on the local network segment. Bridges are used to connect multiple network segments, making them one logical segment; therefore, broadcasts go to every device on the entire bridged network. If too many stations are broadcasting, the network can get bogged down transmitting broadcasts rather than useful data. This is called a *broadcast storm*. The larger the bridged network (broadcast domain), the more broadcasts it must handle. One notable exception is that any MAC layer broadcast, such as a Token Ring poll, will go no farther that its local LAN segment.

One solution to this problem is using routers, which block broadcasts from crossing from one network to another. In essence, they break the broadcast domain into multiple smaller broadcast domains. This was one of the driving forces in the early implementations of routers.

Throughput Expectations

LAN protocols operate at speeds in excess of 100Mb/sec. However, the achievable data rate (*throughput*) is never as high as the protocol's specification. This section outlines some rudimentary methods you can use to gauge the *actual* throughput you can expect for collision and token-based networks. We'll show you how to calculate the maximum throughput that can be obtained under ideal conditions. Because real networks are anything but ideal, these numbers serve only as an approximation of an upper bound on performance. Nonetheless, they give you a place to start. Along the way, you will gain an intuitive sense of how these different protocols work.

Physical Properties

To examine the limitations of networks, we must look at the physical properties of bits on the transmission medium. Here are some useful values for describing the physical characteristics of a network:

▼ R = data rate (for example, 10Mb/sec, 4Mb/sec)

■ d = distance of network in meters (for example, 10m, 100m, 100Km)

■ V = propagation velocity of signal; about 2×10^8 m/sec (for copper wire)

▲ L = length of frame in bits (for example, 1,000 b, 5,000 b)

The number of bits that can be on the wire at any time is defined by:

Rd/V

This is the length of the medium in bits, given a certain data rate and length of the network. For a 10Mb/sec Ethernet segment that is 500m long, the bit length is 25. As the data rate and the length of the wire increase, more bits can fit onto the wire at one time. A useful way to think about the length of the network in bits is to put it in relation to the size of the frame that is being transmitted on the wire. Because only one frame can be transmitted at a time, if another frame is placed on the medium while the first is still being transmitted, it will cause a collision, and both frames must be re-sent. We use the variable a to represent the length of the medium in relation to the frame size.

a = length of wire (in bits)/length of frame (in bits) $=Rd/VL$

If a equals 1, the length of the data path (physical medium) equals the length of the frame. Usually a is much less than 1 for LANs. This means that the frame is much longer than the length of the medium in bits. In our preceding Ethernet example, the length of the wire was 25 bits. Frames are typically much larger than this on LANs (thousands of bits; thus $a = 0.01$ to 0.1). Figure 1-10 illustrates an example of an Ethernet segment that has a value of a that is less than 1 for a given frame size. Because this segment has a value of a that is less than 1, the last station will start to receive the frame before it is finished being transmitted.

Maximum Utilization

The theoretical maximum utilization (percentage of capacity used) of a segment goes down as the value of a goes up. This is because the media must be clear before another frame can be transmitted. If a is large, the stations must wait for the frame to be sent the length of the medium before it is clear. The time when no data is on the wire cuts into the utilization of the medium.

If, for example a equals 1, the maximum utilization of the medium is only 50 percent. As soon as the start of the frame hits the end of the wire, the end of the frame is being transmitted. Then, all stations must wait for the end of the frame to leave the wire. Because the length of the wire in bits is the length of the frame, the same amount of time that was used to transmit the frame is now spent waiting for the frame to propagate all the way down the wire. The wire is used to transmit data only half of the time, so utilization is at only 50 percent This relationship is expressed as:

$$MaxUtilization = \frac{1}{1+a}$$

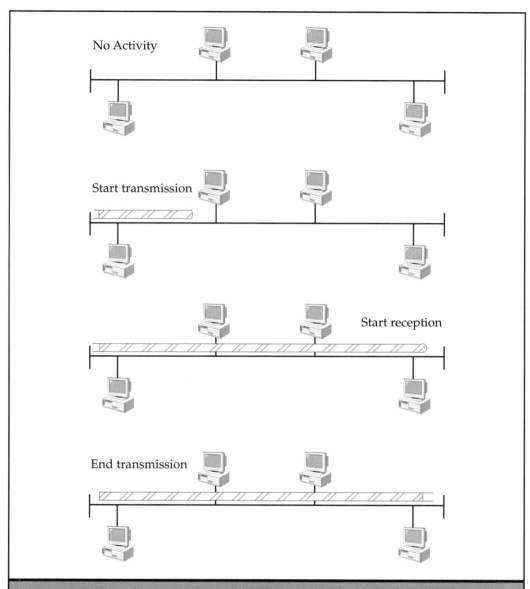

No Activity

Start transmission

Start reception

End transmission

Figure 1-10.   In this Ethernet segment, the length of the medium in bits is less than the length of the frame

This is the best-case scenario; there is no overhead, and there are no collisions, no errors, and no lost data. Table 1-3 illustrates several cases of a 10Mb/sec segment that uses 5,000-bit frames. As the length of the cable increases, a goes up, and the theoretical maximum for utilization starts to go down dramatically. You can see why it is important to keep a as low as possible.

Now we are going to turn our attention to two different LAN protocols: the token-passing and collision-based protocols. The following section discusses a quick method to determine the relative throughput of a given type of LAN. Relative throughput is the ratio of the achieved data rate over the theoretical limit of the throughput. For example, if you measure only 4Mb/sec of data transfer on your 10Mb/sec segment, your relative throughput is 0.4. The equation to calculate the relative throughput for token-based networks is different from the equation for collision-based networks because the two LAN protocols have different methods of carrying data.

Token-Based Protocols

You'll remember that in token-based protocols, a frame is transmitted from the token-holding station to the medium. The frame travels from station to station until the frame comes full circle and is received by the sending station. Then, this station passes the token along to its neighbor so the neighbor can place a frame on the network if it needs to. If this station doesn't have any frames to send, it passes the token along.

For a ring that has little traffic, utilization is not optimal, because the station wishing to send a frame must wait for the token. The time the station waits for the token is time that data is not being sent, so the realized throughput goes down. On a busy segment, token passing works well because the token is passed in sequence so every station has an equal chance to place a frame on the network. Because there is little time spent waiting for

Length (m)	a	Max Utilization
10	0.0001	0.999
100	0.001	0.999
500	0.005	0.995
1000	0.01	0.990
5000	0.05	0.952
10000	0.1	0.909
100000	1	0.500

Table 1-3. Theoretical Maximum Utilization Decreases As Length of Medium Increases

the token (between two stations that have data to send), the realized throughput goes up. The theoretical maximum throughput for token-based protocols is defined as:

$$MaxThroughput = \frac{1}{1+\dfrac{a}{N}}$$

where N is the number of active stations on the ring. Based on the preceding argument, the realized throughput should go up as the number of stations that have data to send goes up.

Collision-Based Protocols

Carrier Sense Multiple Access with Collision Detect (CSMA/CD) LANs function in a entirely different way compared to Token Rings. Instead of passing a token that allows a station to send a frame, collision-based protocols place a frame on the medium when they sense that it is not being used. Obviously, two stations could try to send a frame at the same time. Fortunately, CSMA/CD protocols can detect when a frame has collided with another. Both stations wait a random length of time, and then they try to resend the frame.

If each station has the same probability of successfully capturing the wire for transmission, the probability that a single station has captured the wire is

$$A = (1-\frac{1}{N})^{N-1}$$

And the mean length of the contention interval is

$$\frac{1-A}{A}$$

The maximum throughput for collision-based protocols is the length of a transmission interval divided by the transmission interval plus the interval of contention:

$$MaxThroughput = \frac{1}{1+2a(\dfrac{1-A}{A})}$$

We'd expect that the highest throughput would occur when there are few stations trying to send frames at the same time. This would cut down on contention for the medium and reduce the contention interval. Figure 1-11 illustrates the theoretical maximum throughput for token-passing LANs versus collision-based LANs for two different values of a.

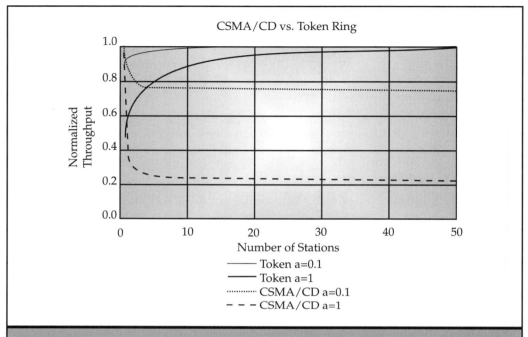

Figure 1-11.   Normalized throughput for collision- and token-based protocols as a function of the number of active stations

As predicted, token-passing protocols have better use of the medium as more active stations are added. They are, nonetheless, still susceptible to the problems associated with an increasing value of *a* as the physical size of the ring grows. Notice that the use of the available capacity is very poor when there are only a couple stations. This is due to waiting for the token to come around, which each must endure until it can transmit again.

Collision-based protocols obviously suffer as more stations try to transmit frames. This is because, statistically, there is a longer delay until a station has the wire all to itself, without the possibility of another station's frame interrupting its transmission and causing a collision. One way to put off contention is to increase the speed of the protocol. For example, moving to 100Mb/sec Ethernet can shorten the amount of time the frame is on the wire and decrease the likelihood of a collision. Another strategy is to reduce the length of the segment. By breaking up large Ethernet segments, you reduce the length of the segment in bits and also reduce the number of active stations.

NETWORK PROTOCOLS

A protocol is a set of rules that governs how a process or function works. Several protocols that work closely with each other often are referred to as a *protocol suite*. This section gives an overview of the primary protocols used in the NT networking environment, paying particular attention to TCP/IP, which is quickly becoming the protocol of choice for enterprise networking.

Common Protocols

In the enterprise, Windows NT has to be able to communicate effectively with all sorts of computer systems. It must be able to communicate with legacy systems, the Internet, and even competitors' products that use proprietary protocols. Much of NT's acceptance into the enterprise will depend on how easily it can be integrated with existing hardware and network protocols.

SNA

In the early days of large mainframe computing, terminals were used for specific applications. If users had to access more than one application, they had to have multiple terminals in their workspace. In 1974, IBM announced the Systems Network Architecture (SNA). SNA defined the framework around which IBM built its data communications functions and protocols. It takes the communication functions out of the applications themselves and provides for shared communication functions among all applications. This simplifies application programming by putting the network definitions into a common networking application with common interfaces that all applications can access. As new communication requirements arise, any changes or additions can be made in one place instead of requiring changes to every application.

SNA SUBAREA NETWORK   SNA is a hierarchical structure consisting of seven layers. Although it is very similar in structure to the OSI model we presented at the beginning of the chapter, the functions that each layer of the SNA stack handles are incompatible with protocols that adhere to the OSI model. This makes SNA a tightly coupled protocol, unlike the modularity of protocols that adhere to the OSI model. IBM has made SNA generally available to network equipment vendors, and there are many companies that have built their businesses on IBM networking, but SNA is still an end-to-end solution and is modular only within the confines of SNA itself.

A hierarchical network is one in which certain nodes control the functions of a lower-level node. In the IBM SNA network, there are four types of nodes. Type 4 nodes and Type 5 nodes are *subarea* nodes. Type 2.0 and Type 2.1 nodes are peripheral nodes. Type 1 nodes were implemented in older SNA systems but are no longer used today. A Type 3 node was never defined.

▼ Type 5 nodes control network resources, transaction program services, network operations, and end-user services. These functions are provided by host processors, sometimes referred to as *host nodes*.

■ Type 4 nodes route and control the flow of data in a subarea network. These are referred to as *communication controller* nodes. Typical Type 4 nodes are IBM's 37xx communications controllers running the Advanced Communications Facility/Network Control Program (ACF/NCP).

▲ Type 2.0 nodes and Type 2.1 nodes are peripheral nodes that connect to either a Type 4 or Type 5 subarea node. These are typically cluster controllers, distributed processors, or workstations. A Type 2.0 node requires the control of a Type 5 node in order to communicate with any other node. A Type 2.1 node has the capability to support a peer-to-peer protocol in addition to the hierarchical subarea network protocol. Reference to Type 2.1 nodes in a hierarchical network assumes they are not using the peer-to-peer functionality.

SNA ROUTING   Routes between different subarea nodes have to be built statically. Only paths to subarea nodes have routes. This means SNA is a routable protocol, but only within the confines of the subarea nodes. Subarea nodes that control the communication between Type 2.0 and 2.1 nodes perform the *boundary* function. The boundary is the delineation point between the routable Type 4 and Type 5 nodes, and the non-routable Type 2.0 and Type 2.1 nodes.

SNA SESSIONS   Certain components within SNA networks can establish sessions with one another. These components are called network addressable units (NAUs). Sessions are temporary logical connections between these NAUs. There are three kinds of NAUs: physical units (PUs), logical units (LUs), and control points (CPs).

▼ **Physical units (PUs)**—These units control the connection between two nodes, such as activation and deactivation of the link. They support sessions with CPs in Type 5 nodes, as well as the CP in its own node.

■ **Logical units (LUs)**—These units manage the exchange of data between two endpoints. End users access SNA networks through LUs. Before the endstations can transfer data, an LU to LU session must be established. LU to LU sessions can only be established between LUs of the same type.

▲ **Control points (CPs)**—These components provide network functions that include managing the resources in their domains and monitoring the status of those resources. In subarea networks, System Services Control Points (SSCPs) control the PUs and LUs in their domain by exchanging control information over SSCP to PU and SSCP to LU sessions. If communication needs to take place between multiple domains, an SSCP to SSCP session between the SSCPs in each domain must be established.

ADVANCED PEER-TO-PEER NETWORKING   SNA subarea networks were designed around large mainframe, processor-centric networks. In 1986, IBM announced an enhancement to its SNA architecture that would lend itself to the evolving distributed environment. Advanced Peer-to-Peer Networking (APPN) took the network intelligence that was centralized in the SNA subarea network, and distributed it across the network. Today, SNA boasts an open networking protocol that allows any-to-any communications between devices on the network.

APPN provides two basic functions. It keeps track of the locations of the devices on the network, and it selects the best path to route data between those network devices. The APPN nodes dynamically exchange information about each other, so creating a massive static routing table, such as that required in an SNA subarea network, is no longer necessary.

NOTE: Microsoft sells an additional product for Windows NT Server called the SNA Server. It acts as an SNA gateway, connecting your NT domain with your legacy SNA machines. You can obtain more information and a free trial at **www.microsoft.com/sna**.

IPX/SPX

The Internetwork Packet Exchange/Sequenced Packet Exchange (IPX/SPX) protocol was developed by Novell for use with its networking product, NetWare. IPX/SPX is a derivative of the Xerox Network Systems (XNS) network protocol developed by the Xerox Corporation.

SPX operates on the transport layer of the OSI model. It ensures the reliability of the end-to-end communication link. SPX guarantees packet delivery and packet sequencing, but it does not play a direct role in routing.

IPX adheres to the OSI standards and operates at the network layer of the OSI model. It handles the addressing of the network devices, keeps track of the routes within the IPX network, and identifies all the services available on the IPX network and the location of those services. IPX is a routable network protocol. It uses one of two routing protocols, Routing Information Protocol (RIP) or NetWare Link Services Protocol (NLSP), to exchange routing information with neighboring routers. The routing protocol keeps track of the locations of all the IPX networks and the best route to pass data between two devices on the network. RIP has been the mainstay routing protocol for IPX networks for years. NLSP is becoming more popular now that it's beginning to mature as a product and the size of IPX networks is getting larger. As we'll discuss later in this chapter, linkstate protocols, such as NLSP, are more efficient in large-scale implementations.

The Service Advertising Protocol (SAP) is similar in concept to RIP. Just as RIP enables routers to exchange routing information, SAP enables networked devices, such as network servers and routers, to exchange information about available services in an IPX network. Services in an IPX network use SAP to advertise their services and network addresses. Workstations use SAP to obtain the network addresses of servers that offer the services they need.

By default, both RIP and SAP broadcast the information they contain onto the network every 60 seconds. This can become a problem as the network—and the information in the RIP and SAP tables—grows.

NOTE: Microsoft NT Workstation comes with the IPX/SPX protocol and services that allow it to act as a client to a Novell server. NT Server has built-in support for the client as well as a gateway service for NetWare. This topic is covered in more detail in Chapter 5.

NetBEUI

NetBIOS was developed by IBM in the mid 1980s as a common application programming interface (API) that application programmers could use to deliver their applications to the network. An API is a set of functions or procedures for a programming language that lets the application access services provided by other software. This functionality relieves programmers from having to know about any of the specific networking technologies their application may use. NetBIOS Extended User Interface, or NetBEUI, was later developed as an extended version of NetBIOS to provide communication within a LAN. It provides a standard frame format for communicating with other devices on the LAN.

NetBEUI locates other devices on the LAN by using NetBIOS machine names. Each device on the LAN is given a NetBIOS name consisting of no more than 15 characters. When a computer has data it needs to send to another device on the LAN, it broadcasts onto the LAN looking for a specific NetBIOS name. Every device on the LAN looks at the broadcast packet to see if its name matches the requested name. The device with the matching name responds to the source device with information about its DLC address. The sending device can then send the data onto the LAN with a specific DLC address. This process is called *NetBIOS name resolution*.

The simplicity of this protocol lends itself to being very quick on a small network. As the size of the network grows and more devices attempt NetBIOS name resolution, this broadcast methodology can quickly utilize more and more of the available bandwidth. This becomes a greater problem when networks are connected over slower wide area network (WAN) links.

NetBEUI, by its nature of resolving names through broadcasting, is not routable. NetBIOS can use other network and transport protocols, such as TCP/IP or IPX, to enable routing in a routed network environment. Windows NT uses NetBIOS over TCP/IP (NBT) to run on a routed TCP/IP network. This will be covered in more detail later in this chapter.

TCP/IP

As the networking industry grew, it became apparent that standards would have to be developed to allow the many different computer vendors to deliver hardware and software that could coexist on the same network. If this didn't happen, developing products that could interoperate while still maintaining unique operating principles would be extremely costly and complex, if not impossible. The OSI reference model is the basis for most networking protocols today.

No single standard accommodates all the interoperability requirements of distributed application processing. Each piece of the process may have different requirements. Every layer of the OSI reference model serves a different purpose. Therefore, the communication requirements to enable these different transactions to operate across a network need to be modular in nature. TCP/IP was developed with these principles in mind by the Defense Advance Research Project Agency (DARPA) and was implemented on the Advance Research Project Agency Network (ARPANET). It consists of a large number of protocols that have been deemed Internet standards by the Internet Activities Board.

The TCP/IP protocol suite operates on the upper five layers of the OSI model. It starts at the network layer, allowing any lower-layer protocols to transport the data. This provides a solution for the entire enterprise, whether you have Ethernet, Token Ring, FDDI, WANs, or all of the above. In the past, most of the protocols in the session layer up through the application layer were developed and used primarily in the UNIX environment. This is becoming less true as vendors realize that TCP/IP is rapidly becoming the protocol of choice for enterprise networking and they adopt it within their product lines as quickly as possible. A few of the many protocols included in the TCP/IP protocol suite are listed here. We'll concentrate on the network and transport layers.

- ▼ **ARP**—Address Resolution Protocol
- ■ **FTP**—File Transfer Protocol
- ■ **HTTP**—HyperText Transfer Protocol
- ■ **ICMP**—Internet Control Message Protocol
- ■ **IP**—Internet Protocol
- ■ **NFS**—Network File System
- ■ **RIP**—Routing Information Protocol
- ■ **RPC**—Remote Procedure Call
- ■ **SMTP**—Simple Mail Transfer Protocol
- ■ **SNMP**—Simple Network Management Protocol
- ■ **TCP**—Transmission Control Protocol
- ■ **Telnet**—Character oriented terminal emulation
- ■ **TFTP**—Trivial File Transfer Protocol
- ■ **UDP**—User Datagram Protocol
- ▲ **XDR**—External Data Representation

IP provides the method to control the transmission of packets from an information source to an information destination. It provides the addressing and segment and reassembly (SAR) functions. It doesn't provide for guaranteed delivery, flow control, or error recovery. Higher layers must provides those functions.

Every connection point on the network is assigned a unique 32-bit address. Each address consists of two parts: a network portion and a node, or host, portion. A network and node designation in an address are required to route packets through a network. We'll cover this in more detail later in this chapter.

SNMP and MIBs

The Simple Network Management Protocol (SNMP) is used to manage TCP/IP-based networks. It runs at the application layer of the OSI model. The intelligence for an SNMP managed network lies in the Network Management Station (NMS). The NMS polls the network devices, or SNMP agents. These agents keep information about themselves in the form of a Management Information Base (MIB). The MIB provides a standard representation about what information is available for the SNMP agent and where it is stored. The NMS keeps a database of all the information extracted from the MIBs from all the SNMP agents it's managing. This method allows low overhead on the SNMP agents themselves, reducing the complexity and, therefore, the cost of implementation.

SNMP MESSAGES   There are five packet types used for SNMP messages:

▼ **Get Request**—Retrieves the values of specific MIB variables from an SNMP agent

■ **Get-Next Request**—Retrieves the next instance of information for a particular variable or device

■ **Set Request**—Alters the value of objects that can be written to the MIB

■ **Get Response**—Contains the values of the requested variables

▲ **Trap**—Contains information about an event that caused an unsolicited message from an SNMP agent

The first three packet types are messages from the NMS to the SNMP agent. The last two are messages from SNMP agents to the NMS.

SNMP was designed to manage TCP/IP networks. As mentioned earlier, it is an application layer protocol within the TCP/IP protocol suite. It uses UDP to pass on datagrams to IP for transport. UDP is a connectionless protocol that does not guarantee delivery. These two features allow SNMP to still function on a network that may be faltering. The NMS must, therefore, be running UDP, IP, and a lower-layer network connection protocol in addition to SNMP. The SNMP agent must also be running UDP, IP, and the same lower-layer network connection protocol as the NMS.

PROXY SNMP AGENTS   In some cases, either devices are incapable of supporting the SNMP-required protocols, or it's undesirable to support them. SNMP proxy agents can be used in these cases to manage these devices. The NMS sends queries concerning the non-SNMP-capable device to its proxy agent. The proxy agent converts the request to the management protocol used by the device and sends it on to the device. When the proxy agent receives the reply from the device, it converts the response back into SMNP format and returns it to the NMS.

POLLING INTERVALS   As the number of SNMP agents being managed in a network increases, the amount of overhead for network management may become excessive. There are several ways to reduce the network management overhead on an SNMP-managed network. One way is to reduce the amount of time that the NMS waits between requests for information from each device on the network. This is called the *polling interval*. This can be reduced even further by using trap-directed polling. Once a baseline and thresholds have been established, the SNMP agents can send information to the NMS only when an unusual event has occurred, such as a link failure, reboot of the SNMP agent, or utilization exceeds a threshold.

SNMP WITH NT   Windows NT has built-in support for an SNMP agent. In this case, the SNMP service accesses the Registry on the local machine and converts this information into a format (MIB) that can be queried by standard SNMP managers.

Windows NT supports multiple MIBs using a separate agent API. Third-party vendors can easily add another MIB for their product or NT itself. Here are some examples of MIBs that you can use

▼ **Internet MIB-II**—Defines objects used for fault analysis as defined in RFC 1213

■ **LAN Manager MIB-II**—Defines objects used for user and logon information

■ **Microsoft DHCP Server MIB**—Contains information about the use of the DHCP server

■ **Microsoft Internet Information Server MIB**—Defines statistics describing the use of the HTTP, Gopher, and FTP servers

▲ **Microsoft WINS Server MIB**—Defines statistics and database information about the use of the WINS Server

The NT 4.0 Server Resource Kit holds the definition files for these MIBs. This CD also contains two applications that you can use to enable a NT system to act as an SNMP manager (NMS): *SNMPutil.exe* and *SNMPmon.exe*.

To use performance monitor counters with a MIB you can use a utility called *Perf2MIB.exe*. This file (found on the resource kit) allows you to create a MIB based on the counters you want to watch, or for which you want to set traps to send information to managers when a threshold has been exceeded.

The Microsoft SNMP service is installed under the Services tab in the network configuration window. Once installed you can use any SNMP manager station to view and configure WINS and Dynamic Host Configuration Protocol (DHCP) servers. You can view performance counters and keep tabs on the general health and status of each machine running the SNMP agent. For example, the NMS could query an NT SNMP agent, as illustrated in Figure 1-12. The agent service looks into its MIB, which was

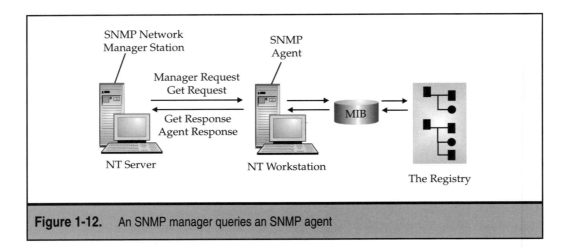

Figure 1-12. An SNMP manager queries an SNMP agent

constructed from examining the Registry, and then returns a response to the SNMP management station.

NOTE: More information about SNMP can be found in the Internet Engineering Task Force (IETF) Request for Comments (RFCs) 1155, 1157, and 1213.

Configuring TCP/IP

The TCP/IP protocol suite is a set of protocols used for transmission on the Internet. Because they are scalable, routable, and reasonably efficient, they have become the protocols of choice within large organizations. Before exploring the suite of protocols, we should take a little time to understand some basic properties of TCP/IP.

IP Numbers and Addresses

IP addresses are 32-bit addresses represented as four eight-bit octets. IP addressing is broken into five classes. The address range of the network portion of the address determines the class. Classes can be identified by the values of the first five bits of the first octet. This is demonstrated in Figure 1-13.

Class A addresses contain a smaller number of bits for networks, and therefore a smaller number of possible networks. But they allow a very large number of possible hosts in each network. These addresses are reserved for very large sites with a huge number of hosts.

Class B addresses have a larger number of network numbers available, with a smaller number of hosts in each network. These addresses are used in networks with a large number of sites that have a large number of hosts at each site.

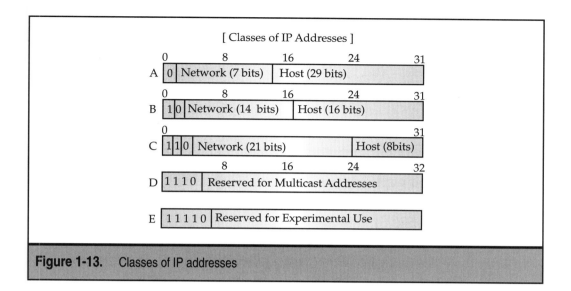

Figure 1-13.   Classes of IP addresses

Class C addresses have a very large number of network numbers available, but fewer hosts in each network. These addresses are used in smaller sites that have fewer hosts on each network.

Class D addresses are used for multicast addresses. For more information on IP multicast addresses, refer to RFC 1112.

Class E addresses are reserved by the InterNIC for experimental use.

Class A, B, and C addresses are described in more detail in Table 1-4.

IP Addressing by the Numbers

The address ranges are represented by the value of the first octet, although the number of networks and hosts are determined by the entire number of bits included in the network and host portion of that address for each particular address class. Class A addresses, for example, use only the first octet for network numbers. Class B addresses include the first two octets as part of the network address. Class C addresses include the first three octets as part of the network address, leaving only the fourth, and last, octet for host addresses.

Subnetting is used to divide the hosts portion of an IP address into separate subnetworks, with a smaller number of hosts assigned to each subnet. This gives the IP address administrator more flexibility in distributing network assignments and host assignments within the IP address assigned to them by the Internetwork Information Center (InterNIC). The InterNIC controls the assignment of all available IP addresses. This ensures that everyone using IP addresses for communicating with other entities using TCP/IP has a unique address. The Internet is a perfect example of this, although corporate communication via alternate pathways is becoming more prevalent.

Address Class	1st Octet	Range of Numbers	Number of Hosts	Number of Networks
A	0xxxxxxx	0 to 127	16,777,214	126
B	10xxxxxx	128 to 191	65,534	16,384
C	110xxxxx	192 to 223	254	2,097,152

Table 1-4.   Number of Hosts and Networks for Different Classes of IP Addresses

IP address subnetting is accomplished through the use of a subnet mask. A subnet mask is a 32-bit binary number that is compared with the IP address using the logical *AND* function to determine which bits of the IP address are part of the IP subnet. The example in Figure 1-14 shows a Class B IP address that uses a subnet mask to increase the number of subnetworks available for use.

Because this is a Class B address, the first two octets represent the actual address as assigned by InterNIC (minus the first two bits, which identify it as a Class B address). The third octet now becomes the subnet because the network administrator has extended the subnet mask to include it as part of the network portion of the address. The dotted decimal representation of this subnet mask would be 255.255.255.0. Now, instead of having a Class B address with one network and 65,534 available hosts, you have 254 subnetworks with 254 hosts available in each subnet. Table 1-5 shows the possible subnet

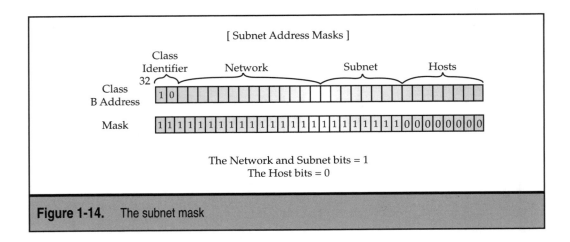

Figure 1-14.   The subnet mask

Subnet Mask (Dotted Decimal)	Binary Representation of 3rd and 4th Octets	Number of Subnets	Number of Hosts
255.255.192.0	11000000.00000000	2	16,382
255.255.224.0	11100000.00000000	6	8,190
255.255.240.0	11110000.00000000	14	4,094
255.255.248.0	11111000.00000000	30	2,046
255.255.252.0	11111100.00000000	62	1,022
255.255.254.0	11111110.00000000	126	510
255.255.255.0	11111111.00000000	254	254
255.255.255.128	11111111.10000000	510	126
255.255.255.192	11111111.11000000	1,022	62
255.255.255.224	11111111.11100000	2,046	30
255.255.255.240	11111111.11110000	4,094	14
255.255.255.248	11111111.11111000	8,190	6
255.255.255.252	11111111.11111100	16,382	2

Table 1-5.   Subnet Masks Increase Number of Available Hosts

masks available for a Class B address and the number of networks and hosts each mask provides.

You'll notice that there are some possible subnet addresses missing in Table 1-5. IP addressing specifications mandate that a minimum of two bits is required for subnet and host addresses. It's also important to note that all 1's in the host portion of an address are a broadcast address for that subnet; therefore they cannot be assigned to a host. Also, all 0's in the host address are used to represent "this subnet"; they cannot be assigned to a host, either.

There are also a number of addresses reserved by InterNIC. RFC 960 identifies the addresses below as reserved by InterNIC.

▼   0.X.X.X

■   127.X.X.X (loopback address)

■   128.0.X.X

■   191.255.X.X

■   192.0.0.X

■   223.255.255.X

▲   224.0.0.0 through 255.255.255.255 (multicast and experimental addresses)

There are certain addresses in each class that are not routed on the Internet, as detailed in RFC 1597. These addresses are commonly used within organizations. They provide a measure of security against outside intruders, and help prevent data from within an organization being placed on the Internet accidentally. These addresses are listed here:

▼   Class A—10.0.0.0 through 10.255.255.255

■   Class B—172.16.0.0 through 172.31.255.255

▲   Class C—192.168.0.0 through 192.168.255.255

The Hosts File

The Hosts file is a good way to simplify the mapping of a network device's TCP/IP name, or alias, to its assigned IP address. Instead of having to remember the four octet dotted-decimal number, the end user simply has to remember the name of the device they want to connect. For example, a server with an IP address of 192.189.225.118 is given a TCP/IP name of Server1.*yourcompany*.com and an alias of Server1. All the end user needs to remember is Server1. When the user issues a command or request using the name Server1, the workstation queries the Hosts file for an entry named Server1. The Hosts file tells the workstation that Server1 is 192.189.225.118, and then sends the request through the network with the required IP address. Except for the initial request, such as "Server1" all this is transparent to the end user.

NOTE: In networks that use DNS, requests will go to the DNS server (or servers) first, and then use the Hosts file as a backup to the DNS servers. DNS will be covered in greater detail in Chapter 6.

The LMHosts functionality is very similar to the Hosts file, except it maps a NetBIOS name to an IP address instead of mapping a TCP/IP name to an IP address. This is a key function in the NT environment, because NT has been developed around NetBIOS, and much of the built-in networking that comes with NT uses many features of NetBIOS. The LMHosts file resides on the NT client, and it is used by the client to resolve NetBIOS names if a broadcast onto the network gets no response.

NOTE: The Hosts and LMHosts files are located in the %*systemroot*%\system32\drivers\etc directory and can be edited with Notepad.

NetBIOS over TCP/IP

The Windows NT NetBIOS implementation for built-in networking is independent of any protocol. NetBIOS is simply an API. NetBIOS alone is not routable, but TCP/IP is completely routable. Because NetBIOS uses names for addressing purposes and IP uses numbers, there needs to be a way to map the two so they are compatible. There must be a layer between the two to map NetBIOS names to IP addresses, and convert IP addresses to NetBIOS names. This layer is known as the NetBIOS over TCP/IP (NBT) service.

Node Types

There are three types of NetBIOS nodes that can be used by NBT in a TCP/IP network. A b-node (broadcast node) uses a broadcast onto the network to resolve a NetBIOS name to an IP address. This is similar to the NetBIOS name resolution process discussed earlier except it resolves the name to an IP address rather than a DLC address.

A p-node (point-to-point node) directs the name resolution request to a specific device that serves as a NetBIOS name server for the other devices on the network to get the IP address for that device. An m-node (mixed node) uses both methods. It first broadcasts onto the network for name resolution. If it gets no response, it sends a request to a specific name server. This combination enables the quick response on the LAN inherent to NetBEUI, yet still enables communication with other devices on a large network without flooding the network with broadcasts.

Name Mapping

There are several ways of mapping NetBIOS names to IP addresses. Windows Internet Naming Service (WINS) associates an IP address with a NetBIOS name. The WINS database is usually populated automatically from a variety of sources. If you are using DHCP, the DHCP server updates the WINS server with its information about IP address to NetBIOS name mappings. Using WINS in conjunction with DHCP greatly reduces the amount of administrative overhead required to manage IP address assignments and IP address to NetBIOS name mapping. DHCP and WINS will be covered in more detail in Chapter 7.

The LMHOSTS database associates a NetBIOS name with an IP address, as we discussed earlier. Using LMHOSTS in an enterprise network can become an over-whelming administrative task. The advent of WINS has rendered the use of LMHOSTS for resolving NetBIOS names in an enterprise network nearly obsolete.

The Domain Name System (DNS) is similar to WINS in functionality except it maps an IP address to an IP name rather than a NetBIOS name. If the network uses the same naming convention for its NetBIOS names as it does for its IP names, DNS can also be used as a method for resolving NetBIOS names to an IP address. DNS, however, is administered manually. DNS will be covered in more detail in Chapter 6.

The NBTStat Command

NBT allows NT to resolve NetBIOS names from IP addresses from WINS server queries, DNS queries, LMHosts files, and Hosts lookups. NT has a useful command line tool for troubleshooting NetBIOS name resolution problems. It is called *NBTstat* and has the following arguments:

V **nbtstat–n**—Displays names that were registered locally by the system using the server or redirector services

■ **nbtstat–c**—Lists the name to IP address mapping that is cached in the system

■ **nbtstat–R**—Causes the system to purge the cache and reload it from the LMHosts file (only entries with the #PRE designator in the LMHosts file are reloaded automatically)

■ **nbtstat–a** *<name>*—Returns the NetBIOS name table for the computer *<name>* as well as the MAC address of its NIC

▲ **nbtstat–S**—Lists the current NetBIOS sessions, their status, and some basic statistics

You can see more information about nbtstat by typing **nbtstat /?** at the command prompt.

ROUTING PROTOCOLS

To accurately maintain the proper information about route paths in a routed network, there had to be a way to make this function dynamic. This was accomplished by developing routing protocols that could keep a current view of the network and all the available routes within that network. The routers running these routing protocols have to be able to keep track of all the other devices in the network, the state of those devices, and the best routes available to pass data from one point in the network to another.

Distance-Vector Routing

The first routing protocols used the distance-vector method. A network using distance-vector routing periodically broadcasts data packets to its immediate neighbors, typically every 60 to 90 seconds. These packets contain all the information they currently have about the network's topology. Distance-vector routing protocols typically use information about link speeds and hop counts to make their routing decisions. The number of hops to the destination is called the *metric* or *cost* to the router.

After receiving this information, the routers consolidate it using their respective distance-vector routing algorithms, and then they pass summarized data along to other routers. Through this periodic checking and broadcasting, which is performed at regular intervals regardless of whether the network has changed, all routers are kept current with the correct network addresses for all devices on the network, as well as with the best route for transferring data between any two devices.

Although routing protocols that use the distance-vector method are simple to configure and deploy, the periodic announcements they use may cause excessive traffic on the network as the network grows. Typically distance-vector protocols are used with networks that have up to 50 routers. Most larger organizations use other routing protocols.

RIP is one of a number of well-known distance-vector routing protocols. Examples of other such protocols include IP RIP, Cisco's Interior Gateway Routing Protocol (IGRP), and the Routing Table Maintenance Protocol (RTMP), part of the AppleTalk protocol suite.

Link-State Routing

Link-state protocols are a relatively recent development and can adapt more quickly to network topology changes than distance-vector protocols. For this reason, they are better than distance-vector protocols for managing large, complex networks.

When a network link changes state (up to down, or vice versa), a notification, called a *link-state advertisement (LSA)*, floods throughout the network. All the routers note the change, and recompute their routes accordingly. This method is more reliable, easier to debug, and less bandwidth-intensive than the distance-vector method. However, it is more complex and more CPU- and memory-intensive. As the size of the network grows, the memory and CPU utilization required to run link-state routing protocols becomes a consideration in network design. Another issue with link-state protocols is the routing problems that can occur if many changes are occurring at a frequent interval, such as a WAN link going up and down, or *flapping*.

Examples of link-state protocols include the Open Shortest Path First (OSPF) protocol (part of the TCP/IP protocol suite), the Intermediate System-to-Intermediate System (IS-IS) protocol (a router-to-router protocol that is part of the OSI suite), and the NetWare Link Services Protocol (NLSP, Novell's link-state protocol for IPX networks).

The Routing Information Protocol (RIP)

The Routing Information Protocol (RIP) is a distance-vector protocol that uses the Bellman-Ford algorithm. RIP routers usually broadcast a routing update message containing known routes every 30 seconds. A timer is started when a route is learned from a routing update message. If subsequent routing update messages do not refresh the route within 180 seconds, the route is assumed to be unusable. Then the route is removed from the routing table.

RIP Limitations

Because RIP cannot detect or correct routing loops, routes learned with RIP that exceed 15 hops are invalid. This means that any given source and destination on your network cannot be separated by more than 15 hops. This hop count limit can make RIP impractical for large networks. RIP routers can also experience inconsistencies in their routing tables. This is due to how long it takes for all of the RIP routing tables to synchronize with each other when a change occurs in the network. The time it takes routing tables across a network to synchronize is called the *convergence time*.

Removing Routing Loops

RIP can use the split-horizon method with poison-reverse for eliminating routing loops and decreasing convergence times. Split-horizon and poison-reverse updating are schemes for controlling the way a router advertises a route to the neighbor from which it learned the route. In split-horizon updating, routes are not sent back to the router that revealed the routes initially. For example, if router A tells router B about routes available to router A, router B does not send this information back to router A in an update. It is never useful to send information about a route back to the router that generated the information in the first place. The split-horizon method eliminates routing loops that occur between two adjacent routers.

The split-horizon with poison-reverse updating method eliminates routing loops that occur when you have many routers. It works by temporarily inactivating routes that have increased in hop count by more than one. An increasing hop count for the same route indicates a routing loop; therefore, temporarily removing or inactivating the route stops the looping. If the route continues to loop, the route is declared invalid and is not used.

RIP Support in NT

The Routing and Remote Access Service (RRAS) formerly code named *Steelhead* includes support for RIP. RRAS is covered in more detail later in this chapter and in Chapter 9. You can pick up a free copy of *RRAS for NT Server* from Microsoft's web site. This implementation of RIP has the following features:

▼ Uses the split-horizon method of updating

■ Allows route filters so you can choose which networks to announce or from which to accept announcements

■ Can filter packets based on IP ports

■ Works with IP and IPX for NetWare

■ Uses a graphical user interface and command-line interface with scripting capabilities

■ Can be managed remotely

▲ Works with Virtual Private Networking (VPN) using the Point to Point Tunneling Protocol

The Open Shortest Path First (OSPF) Protocol

The Open Shortest Path First (OSPF) protocol was developed by the OSPF working group of the Internet Engineering Task Force (IETF). OSPF is a link-state routing protocol based on the Dijkstra link-state algorithm. It was designed expressly for the Internet environment and includes explicit support for IP subnetting, type-of-service (TOS)-based routing, and the tagging of externally-derived routing information. Separate routes can be calculated for each IP TOS. This enables higher-level protocols to identify higher priorities for certain information streams so that the OSPF can give priority routes to those packets.

OSPF also provides for the authentication of routing updates, and utilizes IP multicast when sending and receiving the updates. OSPF routes IP packets based solely on the destination IP address and IP type of service found in the IP packet header.

Autonomous Systems

With OSPF, each router provides information about itself and its immediate neighbors to every reachable router in a routing area or autonomous system (AS). Each router in the AS uses the information gathered from the other routers in the AS, and builds a topological map of all devices in the AS. All routers in the AS have identical topological maps. From these maps the routers use the OSPF algorithm to build a shortest-path tree to all the other routers in the AS. These shortest-path trees are different for each router, because each router builds the tree with itself as the point of origin.

OSPF Areas

OSPF allows sets of networks to be grouped together. Such a grouping is called an *area*. The routers in each area are aware of only the other routers in the area, and they build their topological maps based on those routers. Area border routers (ABR) pass routing information between areas. This reduces the overhead requirements for each router and creates a modular network design that is very scalable. This concept is illustrated in Figure 1-15.

OSPF networks with more than one area require an area numbered as 0, which is called the *backbone*. All areas in the autonomous system must connect to the backbone. The backbone manages all inter-area traffic. In some cases, backbones consist solely of routers belonging to other areas. To free up backbone resources for routing issues, hosts should be located in areas other than the backbone. If the network has only one area, that area is usually designated as area 0.

An advantage of OSPF is that it passes subnet mask information in its routing updates. This allows routers to handle variable-length subnet masks within an IP network. It also enables them to handle IP networks that are noncontiguous. This gives the IP address administrators much greater flexibility and efficiency in the assignment of precious IP addresses.

OSPF Support in NT

Realizing the limitations RIP has in larger networks, Microsoft has implemented OSPF as part of the new RRAS update available free from Microsoft. Incorporating routing as part of NT Server will allow many people access to the traditionally obscure and difficult world of routing. Coupling the router with other services may decrease the total cost of ownership by simplifying management and reducing the cost of hardware. However, it should be noted that Microsoft's router solution does not compete with larger, dedicated hardware routers, which can process many more packets per second compared to a PC running RRAS (40,000 packets per second versus millions). Nonetheless, RRAS and OSPF

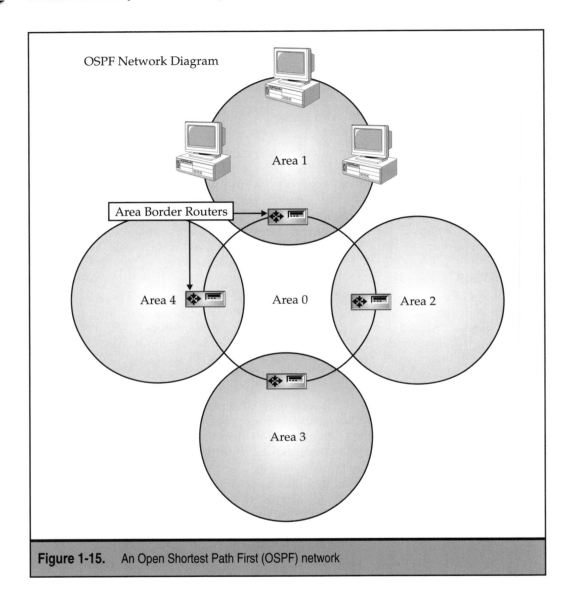

OSPF Network Diagram

Area 1

Area Border Routers

Area 4

Area 0

Area 2

Area 3

Figure 1-15.   An Open Shortest Path First (OSPF) network

may be ideal for smaller- to mid-sized sites and locations where larger routers are not required.

The Interior Gateway Routing Protocol (IGRP/EIGRP)

The Interior Gateway Routing Protocol (IGRP) is a distance-vector routing protocol developed by Cisco Systems to overcome some of the shortcomings of RIP. RIP's hop count limit of 15 and its single metric for basing routing decisions (hop count) doesn't allow much efficiency or scalability. IGRP incorporates several more metrics into the routing decision, including internetwork delay, bandwidth, reliability, and load. Each of these metrics can be adjusted by the network administrator. Another enhancement IGRP made over RIP was the ability to load share traffic over multiple, equal cost links.

Cisco later developed an enhanced version of IGRP that combines the advantages of link-state routing protocols with the advantages of distance-vector routing protocols. Cisco used a new routing algorithm called Diffusing Update Algorithm (DUAL). Enhanced IGRP (EIGRP) is designed to enable quicker routing table convergence. It accomplishes this by propagating only the updates required to advertise topology changes in the network, as opposed to IGRP which, as a distance-vector protocol, broadcasts its entire routing table every 90 seconds. It also has the capability of sending these updated route changes to only the routers that need this information. This feature is known as *bounded updates*.

The two other primary enhancements within EIGRP are support for variable length subnet masks, which was discussed earlier as an advantage of link-state protocols, and added support for other network layer protocols. EIGRP supports IP, as well as AppleTalk's Routing Table Maintenance Protocol (RTMP), Novell RIP, and Novell SAP. It also has the capability to redistribute routes from OSPF, RIP, IS-IS, and the Exterior Gateway Protocol. IGRP and EIGRP work only with Cisco routers, and they do not work with Microsoft's RRAS product. If you have an all Cisco router environment, you are probably using one of these two protocols and may not want to switch over to OSPF just to incorporate NT Servers with your other routers.

ROUTING TABLES

Routing tables are at the heart of a router's capability to transfer packets from one point in the network to the packet's destination in the most efficient manner. Routing tables are where the router looks to find the information to make routing decisions. The routing protocols covered previously in this chapter exist for no other reason than to build these tables.

The information in the routing tables includes all the reachable subnets in the network, the routing cost to reach each subnet, the address of the next router in the destination path, and the interface on the router to forward packets to reach that destination. When a router receives a packet to route, it looks up the destination subnet for that packet in its routing table. Then it passes the packet to the interface with the lowest-cost route to reach the next router in the path. When the next router receives the packet, it repeats the process and forwards the packet on to the next hop. This process repeats until the packet reaches its final destination.

In order for a protocol to be routable, it must contain a network portion and a host portion in its addressing scheme. The routers understand the subnet, or network, portion of the address. The host portion identifies the unique devices on the LAN. In the routing process, the last router in the path is only required to put the packet out onto the subnet where the destination host is sitting. The host is responsible for noticing the packet that is addressed to it and pulling the packet off the LAN.

MPR and RRAS

Microsoft's Multi-Protocol Router (MPR) feature enabled an NT Server to route packets between two LAN segments. Available in Windows NT 3.51 with Service Pack 2, it supported IP and IPX routing using RIP for IP and RIP for IPX as the routing protocols. It also supported Dynamic Host Configuration Protocol (DHCP) using the BOOTP Relay Agent. MPR wasn't really much of a consideration in an enterprise network because the functionality it provided was fairly limited.

Microsoft has recently introduced its new Routing and Remote Access Service (RRAS), which combines MPR and RAS into an integrated product. It delivers a more feature-rich routing service than MPR. It also has improved the administrative functions of the product. The new service provides a graphical user interface for monitoring and configuration, command line-based management for creating scripts, and telnet-based services.

RRAS has also delivered a much more robust set of routing protocols. It now supports RIP versions 1 and 2 for IP, OSPF for IP, IPX RIP, IPX SAP, and DHCP support. It still supports static routes, as well. In addition, RRAS contains APIs to enable third-party vendors to make other routing protocols work with the new service. For example, Border Gateway Protocol (BGP), Interior Gateway Routing Protocol (IGRP), NetWare Link Services Protocol (NLSP), and others can be plugged in. This added functionality moves NT's routing capabilities to a level where they can play a role in the internetwork, but the stability and scalability of RRAS in the enterprise network has yet to be proven.

RRAS brings additional security enhancements to the NT routing arena. RRAS supports Remote Authentication Dial-In User Service (RADIUS). RADIUS is a distributed security solution for use in enterprise and public-carrier networks. This is one of the latest features added to the service. RRAS also has added authentication and encryption support.

Packet filtering is another feature that has been added to RRAS. For IP routing RRAS supports packet filtering based on TCP port, UDP port, IP protocol ID, ICMP type, ICMP code, source address, and destination address. For IPX packet filtering it supports source address, source node, source socket, destination address, destination node, destination socket, and packet type. This greatly enhances the ability of the network administrator to control network traffic—for both security reasons as well as increased network performance.

There are many other enhancements to NT's routing capabilities introduced with RRAS that deal with remote access services. These enhancements are covered in more detail in Chapter 9.

The NT Routing Table

Because even single-homed machines (one network address) need to make routing decisions, all NT systems with at least one NIC have a simple routing table created by default. This table lists the static routes that have been entered manually. Although static routes will work for smaller networks, it would become an organizational nightmare to maintain static routes for a larger network, as you will see. This is why the adoption of routing protocols is so important.

Viewing the Routing Table

All static routing functions are accomplished using the *route.exe* command line utility. For a full list of arguments type:

> **route /?**

at the command prompt. By typing **route print** at the command prompt, you will generate a listing similar to the one in Figure 1-16 for single-homed machines.

The headings can be broken down as follows:

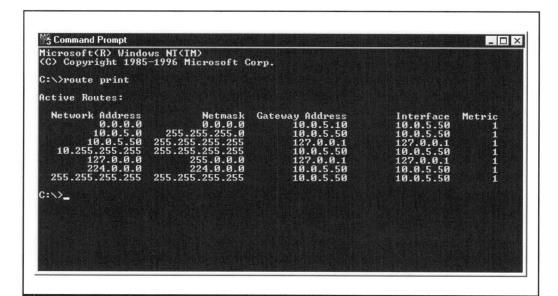

Figure 1-16.   The NT routing table for a single-homed machine

▼ **Network Address**—This is the destination address for routed packets.

■ **Netmask**—This defines the portion of the network address that must match to use that route. A mask of 255 (all 1's) means that the octet in the destination address (that is to be routed) must match exactly that of the network address.

■ **Gateway Address**—This is where the packets need to be sent so they are routed. This is usually the NIC address of the default gateway address.

■ **Interface**—This points to the correct NIC that will be used to get to the gateway. It may be the same as the gateway, a NIC address, or 127.0.0.1, which is the software loopback address.

▲ **Metric**—This is the number of hops to reach the destination address. All local destinations are one hop away.

Static routes solve the basic problem that is illustrated in Figure 1-17. There are four computers and three subnets. The computers in the center (B and C) have two NICs and two IP addresses each, one for each subnet on which they reside. Computers B and C will be able to route packets to either subnet they sit on—provided they have been configured to allow IP forwarding. This is configured under the network properties window for TCP/IP.

The computers are aware only of the subnets that are directly connected to them. If, for example, computer A wants to send something to computer D, it would send it to computer B, because it sends all nonlocal traffic there. Computer B would not know how to reach computer D because it only knows of the subnets where computers A and C reside. Static routes must be added in the routing tables of computers B and C to inform them of the subnets where computers D and A reside.

Adding Routes

Adding routes to the routing table is accomplished using the *route* command with the *add* argument. First you list the destination, and then the netmask (optional). This is followed

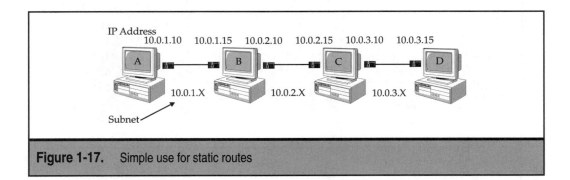

Figure 1-17. Simple use for static routes

by the gateway and the metric (optional). To add a route in computer B's table, we would type the following command at the command prompt on computer B:

route add 10.0.3.0 10.0.2.15

This tells the table to route all traffic destined for the 10.0.3.0 subnetwork to go through computer C.

We also need to add a route in computer C's table so computer D can reach computer A. To do this, we type the following command at the prompt on computer C:

route add 10.01.0 10.0.2.10

Now let's say computer D has some packets for computer A. Computer D will send them to computer C because they are nonlocal and computer D has only one place to put nonlocal traffic. Computer C will examine its routing table and determine that it needs to send the packets to computer B. Computer B receives them and knows about computer A because that subnet is connected directly. Therefore, computer B has no problem sending the packets out its other NIC onto the segment where computer A resides.

You can see from this 'simple' example that static routes can become prohibitively complex in larger networks. You will certainly use dynamic routing protocols there. Nonetheless, static routes are useful for exceptional situations, such as when you have a small site and do not want to dedicate a router or involve the NT Server there with dynamic routing protocols. Sometimes you may need to configure a system to communicate with a network that is located outside of your enterprise and does not participate in your dynamic routing protocol. You can easily set up a static route if your connection isn't going to change often.

NETWORKING HARDWARE

There are many ways, as we've seen, to build networks and send packets from one place in the network to another. The following section describes some of the differences, advantages, and disadvantages of the most common types of technologies in use today.

Bridges and Repeaters

The simplest technology to extend the network beyond the LAN segment is the repeater (it was probably also one of the first technologies to do so). Repeaters take packets off an Ethernet segment and regenerate the packets onto an adjoining Ethernet segment. They operate only at the physical layer, or layer one, of the OSI model, and they make no decisions based on the content of the packet. They simply repeat all packets on the segment.

Repeaters Remove Node Limitations

Repeaters are used to connect two or more Ethernet segments of any media type. As segments exceed their maximum number of nodes or maximum length, signal quality begins to attenuate. Repeaters provide the signal amplification and retiming required to connect segments. A repeater connection takes into account the total node limit on each segment. If, for example, a thin coaxial cable segment is 185 meters in length and has a limit of 30 nodes, it can accommodate 29 nodes, or stations, and one repeater. A thick wire segment that is 500 meters in length and has 98 nodes with two repeaters can accommodate 100 nodes per segment. With the advent of 10BaseT Ethernet technologies, repeaters have almost vanished; signal regeneration has become a role of the 10BaseT hub.

Bridges Are Smarter

Bridges operate at layer two of the OSI model, the data link layer. They make intelligent decisions about packet forwarding based on information in the data link header of the packet. This information could include either the MAC sublayer or the LLC sublayer. MAC layer bridges connect two LAN segments of a similar topology, such as Token Ring or Ethernet. Bridges that use the LLC layer can bridge two LAN segments of different topologies, such as connecting a Token Ring segment to an Ethernet segment. This is sometimes referred to as *translational bridging*.

TRANSLATIONAL BRIDGING   Translational bridging is never an exact science because there isn't always a straightforward conversion from one protocol to another. It's important to keep in mind that although translational bridging is a very useful tool, it's likely some anomalies will occur in the translation.

TRANSPARENT BRIDGING   Transparent bridges (TBs) build a table, mapping host addresses to one of its interfaces. They learn these mappings by analyzing the source addresses of all the packets they see and determining which interface the packet came from. When a packet comes in to the bridge, the bridge compares the destination with its address table and forwards the packet out the appropriate interface. If it has no entry in its table, the bridge broadcasts the packet out all interfaces except the source interface. When the destination host receives the packet and replies, the response packet contains its MAC address as the source. The bridge recognizes the MAC address in the response as the source address and updates its table with the new entry. The next packet destined for that device can then be directed out the proper interface without requiring a broadcast.

SOURCE ROUTE BRIDGING   Source route bridges (SRBs) contain information in the packet header that identifies the specific path through the entire network that the packet will traverse to reach its destination. This information is contained in the Routing Information Field (RIF). It consists primarily of a series of LAN segments and bridges. SRBs were designed to enable bridging on a larger scale, with less overhead than transparent bridging. They require that each LAN segment and each bridge in the network have unique identifiers. In the case of Token Ring, where most SRBs are used, this equates to ring numbers and bridge numbers.

SRBs must first discover the path to find the destination they're trying to reach. To accomplish this, they send out an explorer packet with the destination address in it. Each SRB receiving this explorer packet forwards it out each of its interfaces, adding its routing information. When these explorer packets reach their destination, the receiving host responds to each one using the accumulated routing information on each. When the originating device receives all these packets, it makes a decision on which route is best. Generally it chooses the first packet returned, but it can also use routes with the minimum hop count or the largest allowable frame size.

SOURCE ROUTE TRANSPARENT BRIDGING   IBM developed a bridge that could operate in both TB and SRB modes. It is called Source Route Transparent (SRT) bridging. It is an attempt to deliver a single solution bridge to the entire mixed topology enterprise network. SRT bridges use a field in the header to distinguish between frames using SRB and those using TB. SRT enables intercommunication between SRB and TB endstations, but some of the inherent incompatibilities between the technologies continue to create some problems in these implementations. Incompatible bit ordering and different MTU sizes between Token Ring and Ethernet are issues to consider when designing an SRT installation.

Switches

Switches operate on the same basic principles as bridges, with several notable enhancements. Switches typically are faster than traditional bridges and offer a higher number of ports. In many instances these ports can be made up of different topologies. We now see switches with combinations of Token Ring, Ethernet (10Mb/sec and 100Mb/sec), FDDI, and Asynchronous Transfer Mode (ATM), although very few switches incorporate all these topologies in the same switch.

Advantages of Switches

Switches are beginning to offer some of the functionality of layer three devices. They offer the capability of logically grouping different switch ports to form virtual LANs (VLANs). This gives network administrators some flexibility in creating workgroups or managing broadcast domains.

Each port on a switch can be used to connect either a dedicated device or a shared media LAN. Dedicated devices can often run in full-duplex mode because there is no other traffic on the link with which to contend. This effectively doubles the throughput of the topology. For example, a 10Mb/sec Ethernet port can run at 20Mb/sec if it's running in full-duplex mode.

Network Management

One of the difficulties with using switching has been network management. If dedicated connections are being used, there are no access points on the LAN segment to put any kind of network management devices. Managers are at the mercy of the switch manufacturers to build adequate network management and monitoring capabilities into their products. Although there capabilities were lacking in the first generation switches, great strides have been made to enhance the products being delivered today. Enhanced network management reporting and monitoring ports built into the switches have greatly increased the visibility into the network.

Routers

Routers are the networking components that work at layer three of the OSI model. As covered earlier in this chapter, they implement routing techniques to determine the best path between a source and destination, and to forward packets between them. The latter function is a fairly simple process. Routers simply use the information in the routing tables, and then switch packets through the network until the packets reach their destination. Building routing tables is a complex task. Routers can use a variety of routing protocols to build these tables, or the network administrator can create static routes, which can become complicated as the size of the network grows and changes.

Implementing Routers

Routers were originally developed to increase the scale of networks by interconnecting LANs. They were the first devices that worked together to keep track of the topology of the entire network and make intelligent decisions about the forwarding of packets based on the network layer information in the packet. By adding this intelligence to the network, users were able to transmit information among nodes on the network, but still keep the broadcast traffic inherent to bridges and repeaters within smaller subdivisions of the network.

There are differences in the way manufacturers implement routing. Some manufacturers develop hardware solutions using technologies such as Application Specific Integrated Circuits (ASICs), while others implement software solutions. Some routers use the main CPU to process all the functions of the router, while others offload some processing onto interface cards or daughter boards.

Added Functionality

Routers also incorporate many other added features to enhance the stability and security of the enterprise network. Redundant power supplies can be installed in mission-critical routers. Management modules can be used to track errors, utilization, and environmentals. Access lists can be implemented to control the data that is put onto or taken off of the network.

These features distinguish one vendor's product from another. Each product has its pros and cons. This is why it's critical to understand your networking requirements as well as the routing vendor's capabilities before making a purchase decision. It's a decision you'll live with for a long time.

Multiprotocol Routers

Some routers handle only a single network protocol, but most routers today are *multiprotocol,* meaning they handle several different protocols simultaneously. They do not, however, pass information between different protocols. Each protocol being run by a router is handled as a completely separate process within the router. The process by which multiprotocols run side-by-side, yet are kept completely separate from each other, is called *Ships in the Night* routing.

CHAPTER 2

Building Systems

Building Windows NT systems is much more involved than just putting the product CD-ROM in the drive and typing a few commands. To build systems that work as intended, you must be aware of the environment in which the systems will reside, the standards used within the organization, and the role the computer will play. Too many installations are rushed to put out a fire. Fortunately most system administrators get the chance to actually plan an installation of a new server—at least once in a career. Whether or not you are rushed, it is beneficial to know how to correctly answer the installation questions before you are confronted with the prompt. This chapter describes elements in the installation process you should pay special attention to before you set out to build a new system. To give you a better understanding of the networking environment, we present the differences between the domain models and the workgroup model. Because no network is complete without users, this chapter explains user creation and administration.

CHOOSING CORRECT HARDWARE AND SOFTWARE

Often when you build a new system, you have a specific role in mind for the computer. Typically, the software it will be running dictates the choice for hardware. This is a normal and appropriate way to select hardware. However, the application software you use must reside on top of an operating system, in this case Windows NT. Your selection of hardware must certainly meet the needs of your application software, but it also must meet NT's minimum requirements, whether you choose NT Workstation or NT Server.

Microsoft has defined the bare minimum requirements to run each of the software versions of NT. Table 2-1 compares the requirements for NT Workstation 4.0 and NT Server 4.0 for Intel- based systems. The minimum hardware recommended by Microsoft (shown in the *required* column) will allow you to install NT. However, the system will be all but crippled by its weak hardware. Table 2-1 lists our recommended minimums (shown in the *recommended* cloumn) that provide you with a functioning system. Bear in mind that these values represent a starting point from which to build your system. You will probably need a more competent machine.

Hardware Compatibility List

To help you choose hardware that is known to work with NT, Microsoft has compiled the Hardware Compatibility List (HCL). Initially, the HCL was no more than a few pages in a booklet that shipped with earlier versions of NT. Now the HCL is so extensive that it occupies many web pages on Microsoft's site **(www.microsoft.com/hwtest/hcl/).** Because the HCL is published on the Internet, you can search for specific devices and vendors. Figure 2-1 illustrates the main search page for the HCL. Not only can you select from many different kinds of hardware, a specific vendor, and operating system, but you can also select at what level the products have been approved. Typically you'd select devices that have been approved at the Compatible level to be sure a product will work

	NT Workstation (required)	NT Workstation (recommended)	NT Server (required)	NT Server (recommended)
Processor	486/33 MHz	Pentium 100	486/33 MHz	Pentium Pro
RAM	12	32	16	64
Hard drive	120	150	140	250
CD-ROM	Yes	Yes	Yes	Yes
Video	VGA adapter	Ultra VGA	VGA	Super VGA

Table 2-1.   Windows NT 4.0 Requirements for Intel-based Systems

with NT. Because this web page is updated almost daily, it is the best place to look at it before you purchase any piece of hardware you're going to use on an NT system. You can also find a version of the HCL included with the Windows NT 4.0 Resource Kit.

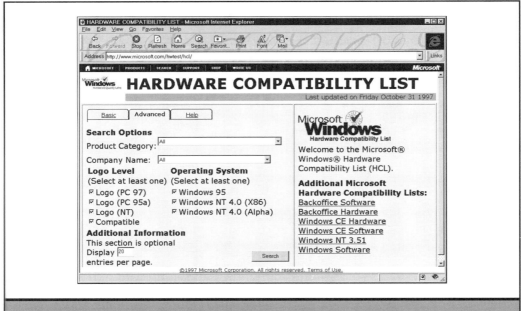

Figure 2-1.   Microsoft provides this HCL search engine on its web site

Figure 2-2 illustrates the result of a search for all compatible ISDN modems for Windows NT from any vendor. The search resulted in a list of four modems. You'll notice on the right that the HCL is somewhat incomplete as it doesn't indicate the model number or modem chipset for the compatible devices. Nonetheless, the HCL is useful and can also be an excellent source for the latest drivers or installation notes. Some searches will turn up drivers for devices you may have already so you can download them to update your system.

The Microsoft Compatibility Tool

In addition to the HCL, Microsoft has created the Microsoft Compatibility Tool. This free tool examines whether the hardware on your computer can support Windows NT Workstation or Server. It identifies PCI, EISA, ISA, MCA, and legacy devices, as well as system resources used by the detected devices. Then it compares the detected devices with the system requirements and HCL to determine whether Windows NT can be installed and whether it will run properly. It also provides a summary of detected hardware and logs the hardware to a file (ntct.txt) on the second floppy disk.

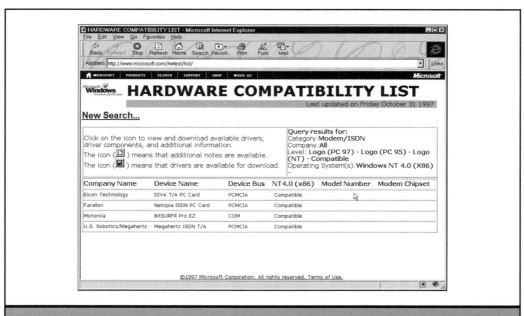

Figure 2-2.   A search for compatible ISDN modems found four devices

Why Use the Compatibility Tool?

Why, you say, would I need a tool to tell me if NT can be run on a system when I can simply try to install NT? You can save yourself plenty of time and frustration by using this tool before you start deploying NT. If you have a large number of workstations to upgrade, try the Compatibility Tool on a prototype workstation before attempting to install NT. Additionally, an NT installation can appear to function correctly even though some hardware incompatibility has caused it to fail services or devices without informing you. This tool can be handy for diagnosing problems that occur during the installation of Windows NT. By discovering right up front the problems you would encounter if you tried to install NT on a system, you know where to look when troubleshooting a system.

How Does the Tool Work?

First, you must download *Ntcomp.exe* from the Microsoft web site (**http://premium .microsoft.com/support/downloads/dp2468.asp**). Running the executable file produces a prompt asking you to provide a set of two blank floppies. The tool uses these to create a set of bootable disks. After the appropriate files are copied to these disks, you simply boot your computer with the first floppy. Once the computer is started, you are prompted for the second floppy. A set of Windows dialog boxes guides you through the hardware detection. These boxes display the results in tabbed windows showing you information on network devices, video, hard drive, and the general system . The computer also logs the results to the second floppy in a file called *Ntct.txt*. Here is a sample of part of an Ntct.txt file after it has examined a 486 DX computer:

```
Hardware Detection Tool For Windows NT 4.0 Beta 2

Master Boot Sector Virus Protection Check
Hard Disk Boot Sector Protection: Off.
No problem to write to MBR

ISA Plug and Play Add-in cards detection Summary Report

No ISA Plug and Play cards found in the system
ISA PnP Detection: Complete

EISA Add-in card detection Summary Report
Scan Range: Slot 0 - 16
Slot 0: EISA System Board
EISA Bus Detected: No
EISA Detection: Complete

Legacy Detection Summary Report
```

```
Drive 3, Total Clusters: 51839
              Available Clusters: 12925
              Sectors per Cluster: 16
              Bytes per Sector: 512
              Available Space: 100MB


System Information
Device: System board
Can't locate Computername
Machine Type: IBM PC/AT
Machine Model: fc
Machine Revision: 00
Microprocessor: 80486DX
Conventional memory: 655360
Available memory: 24MB
BIOS Name: Award
BIOS Version: Award Modular BIOS v4.50G
BIOS Date: 07/14/95
Bus Type: ISA



===============End of Detection Report===================
Enough Processor
Enough Memory
Compatible Video
Compatible Network
Compatible KeyBoard
Compatible Mouse

Adapter Description: ATI Ultra (Mach 8)
Listed in Hardware Compatibility List: Yes

Adapter Description: NE2000 compatible
Listed in Hardware Compatibility List: Yes

Adapter Description: Sony Proprietary CD-ROM Controller
Adapter Device ID: *PNPA02B
Listed in Hardware Compatibility List: Not found-check the latest HCL

Adapter Description: Sound Blaster Adapter or compatibles
Listed in Hardware Compatibility List: Yes

Adapter Description: Joystick/game port
Listed in Hardware Compatibility List: Yes
```

```
Truth Table Output:
Enough memory: 1
Enough disk space: 0
Video card: 1
Keyboard: 1
Mouse: 1
CD-ROM drive: 0
```

The detection algorithm identified everything on this computer as compatible. However, it issued an on-screen warning because I had only 100MB of hard drive space available, and Windows NT needs about 120MB. After I cleared up some hard drive space, installing NT on this system proved successful.

There are some limitations to the Compatibility Tool. It cannot recognize free disk space on NTFS or FAT32 partitions. Also, PCMCIA slots are not powered up, so it is impossible for the tool to compare these cards against the HCL.

Advanced Hardware

Certainly, the systems you build will exceed the minimum requirements outlined in Table 2-1. How much hardware you add to your system depends heavily on the designated role for the computer and your budget. There is no lack of devices for NT in the major categories of upgrades, which include RAM, hard drives, and processors. We will consider each of these areas briefly.

RAM

NT loves random access memory (RAM) and not long ago, RAM was expensive. So expensive, in fact, it was seen as a major impediment to migrating to NT. Now that RAM prices have fallen, it isn't prohibitive to upgrade the RAM to 32MB. Almost everyone can afford to put NT on their desktops. But for servers and specialized workstations such as those used for CAD, 32MB is just not enough. It is typical to see at least 64MB on servers, and it is not uncommon to see servers equipped with 512MB. The same is true for workstations involved in 3D graphics—it is hard to have too much RAM here. It is difficult to come up with a formula describing how much RAM you should have in a machine. The best advice is to start with 32MB on workstations and 64MB on servers, and then move up from there.

NOTE: Get the largest capacity SIMMs you can from the start. For example, if you have eight slots, don't populate all eight slots with 4MB SIMMs to get your 32MB of RAM. Use two 16MB SIMMs. This provides you with an easy upgrade path.

Hard Drives

When Microsoft recommends 120MB of free hard drive space to install NT, it is referring only to the operating system (OS) and nothing else. You'll find that 120MB is enough to install the system, but it is not enough to actually *run* the system. You will almost certainly install other software that will take up space and make NT swell a bit. In addition, you need to have a swapfile (Pagefile.sys) on at least one drive. When the physical RAM is exceeded, this file gives the system the impression that it has more RAM. Typically this file is 50MB or more, even before it is used. Because it is difficult to buy a hard drive that has less than one gigabyte of storage capacity, these restrictions are not so much a problem today. Just remember, do not stick NT into a little cramped space and expect it to run well.

Multiprocessor Systems

If you have an especially demanding application or are expecting many users to use a particular server, you should consider getting a computer with symmetric multiprocessors (SMP). NT 4.0 supports up to fours processors out of the box. You can theoretically obtain support for up to 32 processors from third-party hardware vendors. They have to supply a special version of the Hardware Abstraction Layer (HAL) so that more than four processors can be used.

Although SMP systems seem too good to be true, there are some *caveats*. Never expect to get double your performance by doubling the number of processors. There are stories of systems that actually run slower when a second processor is added. First of all, there is some OS overhead involved with adding more than one processor. Also, code has to be written specifically to take advantage of multiprocessor systems. Given these limitations, there are few applications today that take advantage of SMP systems. One set of applications that uses SMP is the Microsoft BackOffice suite of products. Other examples include certain graphics programs that scale according to the number of processors. One service that uses SMP is WINS. You can expect a 25 percent improvement in WINS performance for each additional processor.

INSTALLING WINDOWS NT—KNOW BEFORE YOU GO

Whether you are about to set up one single NT system or thousands, you must plan ahead for a successful installation. Before installing NT, you should be familiar with certain key components of the computer system and the system's position in your network. You should know whether your system is going to be a workstation or server, how it will physically connect to the network, and how it logically fits into your workgroup or domain.

Installation Overview

Installation of Windows NT can be started from NT boot floppies, the NT CD-ROM, a network drive, or even the computer you are going to install or upgrade to NT. If you do not boot from the NT setup media, you will use either the *winnt* or the *winnt32* command found in the /i386 directory on the Windows NT 4.0 Server or Workstation CD-ROM. The winnt command is run only from DOS, and the winnt32 command is run from within Windows. They are similar in many respects and have the following switches and arguments.

To view all your options, type **winnt /?** at the command prompt:

```
WINNT [/S[:]sourcepath] [/T[:]tempdrive] [/I[:]inffile]
 [/O[X]] [/X | [/F] [/C]] [/B] [/U[:scriptfile]]
        [/R[X]:directory] [/E:command]
```

▼ **/S[:]sourcepath**—Specifies the source location of Windows NT files. Must be a full path of the form x:\[path] or \\server\share[\path]. The default is the current directory.

■ **/T[:]tempdrive**—Specifies a drive to contain temporary setup files. If not specified, Setup will attempt to locate a drive for you.

■ **/I[:]inffile**—Specifies the filename (no path) of the setup information file. The default is Dosnet.inf.

■ **/OX**—Creates boot floppies for CD-ROM installation.

■ **/X**—Prevents creation of the Setup boot floppies.

■ **/F**—Prevents verification of files as they are copied to the Setup boot floppies.

■ **/C**—Skips free-space check on the Setup boot floppies you provide.

■ **/B**—Allows floppyless operation (requires /s).

■ **/U**—Allows unattended operation and optional script file (requires /s).

■ **/R**—Specifies optional directory to be installed.

■ **/RX**—Specifies optional directory to be copied.

▲ **/E**—Specifies command to be executed at the end of GUI setup.

You can see by this extensive list of options that this is a powerful program. For example, it is possible to read the NT files from a network drive, use an unattended install answer file (for example, Unattend.txt), and use a temporary drive in another network location..

Basic Installation Steps

Regardless of how you start the NT install process, you follow the same basic steps:

1. You copy a series of files from the installation medium to a temporary directory or floppy disks.

2. After you reboot the system, a limited version of NT is loaded. This smaller version of NT will get you through the rest of the installation process.

3. NT setup automatically detects your hardware using *Ntdetect.com*. This file identifies devices such as your bus, communication ports, mouse, keyboard, video adapter, SCSI adapters, and any coprocessors. If a device is not detected, you'll have to install it manually later when NT is up and running.

4. The installation will query you about where you want to install NT. Also, if there is a previous version of NT on the system, you have the option of upgrading it.

5. The system reboots into a graphical interface.

6. Next, you must supply information regarding the system and its role in the network environment. For example, you'll have to input the computer's name, what kind of network interface card (NIC) you have, and so on. These questions will be discussed later in the chapter.

7. You have the option of creating the Emergency Repair Disk. This disk is essential for recovery of the system in case of a disaster. Because it is used to recreate the Registry and user database, it is specific for each machine.

8. Installation is complete, so the system reboots. As the system comes up, you go through a normal boot process. You should see a menu of OS choices if you installed NT on a machine with other OSes installed; otherwise you will have only two OS choices. You must press a key, or the new install will load by default after 30 seconds. Both choices boot the same operating system—the newly installed version of NT or the VGA video only version of this installation. The VGA video only choice is for troubleshooting problems with your video settings.

If the installation was successful, you should be able to log on to your new NT system and start customizing it for your specific application. NT has changed the way your system boots and added a number of hidden files. You will find several of these files in the root directory of the boot partition. You can use Explorer or the File Manager to change the hidden attributes of these files:

▼ **Boot.ini**—This text file describes the choices of OSes on your system and indicates where to find them among your hard drives.

■ **Bootsect.dos**—This file only exists if there is another OS on the system, because it is the bootsector of the previous OS. If you select the previous OS from the Boot.ini menu, you will load this file.

■ **Ntdetect.com**—This program runs every time NT is started. It is used to detect the hardware that is present, and this information is later incorporated into the Registry.

■ **NTLDR**—This program is responsible for organizing the loading process.

▲ **Ntoskrnl.exe**—This is the Windows NT kernel.

Workstation, Server, or Server/E?

The decision to install NT Server or Workstation is made prior to installation because each has its own installation media. This should be a relatively simple decision to make; use Workstation for all installations unless you must use services that do not run on Workstation or require more than ten concurrent connections to the system. For example, there are a number of Microsoft products that run only on Server such as RAS connections for more than one user, Services for Macintosh, or the backup and primary domain controller. Also NT Server is tweaked internally to enhance performance for network users. If you want the fastest system for running a single user application such as CAD, you should use Workstation. It is streamlined for use by a single user and configured to run the foreground application the fastest.

If you know you need a server, you still have to make a choice. The standard NT Server has been augmented with new technologies and has been released as the Server Enterprise Edition or simply Server/E. This version is seen as an intermediate step between Server 4.0 and Server 5.0. It is promoted as being appropriate for your mission-critical applications because of the technological enhancements. It uses RAM tuning to provide applications with 3GB of memory compared to the usual 2GB. It also adds native eight-processor SMP support and rudimentary two-node clustering capabilities. Some users say that NT should have had these features as part of the standard Server 4.0; others are willing to spend the extra money now for the enhanced capability.

Standalone Server, PDC Sever, or BDC Server?

Once you have decided on NT Server, you still have to decide if your machine is going to be a standalone server, the primary domain controller (PDC), or a backup domain controller (BDC). This is really an administrative decision that should have been made before installation started. In any event, you have to choose during the installation, and once you make your decision, there is no going back without reinstalling NT. However, a BDC can be promoted to a PDC if needed. The differences between the PDC and BDC will be covered later in this chapter.

FAT versus NTFS

During the first phase of installation (step 4 of the Basic Installation Steps), you will be prompted to designate where to install NT. If you have a File Allocation Table (FAT) partition, you will also be asked if you'd like to convert it to the New Technology File System (NTFS). NT prefers NTFS, but this is not an automatic decision because both file systems have their advantages and disadvantages. Table 2-2 lists some of the differences between FAT and NTFS.

FAT	NTFS
Eight characters in a filename	Up to 255 characters in a filename
Three-character extension	Multiple extensions with many periods
Spaces not allowed	Spaces allowed
Not case-sensitive; case not preserved	Not case-sensitive; case preserved
4GB maximum file size	16 Exabyte maximum file size (>1 billion GB)
Less overhead	Greater overhead

Table 2-2.   Key Differences Between the FAT System and NTFS

NTFS Is Robust

Although NTFS offers more flexibility with file naming and maximum file size, there are even better reasons to move to NTFS. It is a robust file system for file servers because it is recoverable and offers hot-fixing. NTFS is recoverable because it logs all directory and file updates. If the system fails for any reason, NTFS will automatically complete the process started during the interruption. This ensures all changes to the file system are completed. Hot-fixing is also completed automatically by the NTFS drive. If NTFS detects that a sector has gone bad, it moves all data from that sector to a good sector and marks the defective sector as bad—all without the application knowing there was a problem with the disk.

As an added bonus, NTFS has built-in native compression for user data. You can designate the directories or drives on which you want to use compression. Whenever a file is placed in these locations, it is compressed on the fly. The whole process is invisible to the user or application. Naturally, the amount of compression depends on the file type, and using compression adds some overhead which results in a small, imperceptible delay while files are compressed or uncompressed.

NTFS Is More Secure

One of the major design goals for the creation of NTFS was to make the file system more secure—less like DOS and more like UNIX. Windows NT accomplishes this by assigning a security descriptor to each file and storing it as part of the file. This descriptor details who created the file, what users and groups can access it, and at what level. Before an application can open the file, the NT security system checks to see if the user or process has sufficient authority to access the file as requested. In this fashion, only authorized users have access to files. This may not seem important in a small network, but in an enterprise, it is essential.

Sure NTFS is great, but the FAT system isn't all bad. It has much lower overhead and is ideal for smaller drives (200MB). Because the NTFS overhead is too much for the small capacity of a floppy, floppies cannot be formatted as NTFS. Additionally, you must use the FAT system for DOS and Windows 95, or if you need to access the drive from these operating systems and NT. You can always change your FAT system into NTFS without losing data, although the reverse is not true. To change your FAT system into NTFS, simply use the *convert* utility at the command line:

convert <drive:> /fs:ntfs

where *<drive:>* is the letter of the drive you want to convert. If convert can't get exclusive access to the drive, you will have to reboot so the conversion can take place on startup.

NT 5.0 NOTE: NTFS gets an upgrade in NT 5.0. It has new disk quotas, distributed link tracking, and encrypted files. Disk quotas allow an administrator to assign the maximum amount of hard drive space a user can use. Distributed link tracking keeps track of files even if you move them from one computer to another within the same domain. For example, if you point to a file icon, and that file has been moved, link tracking should be able to find it. Finally, nonsystem files can be encrypted and saved to an NTFS volume without user intervention, providing on-the-fly encryption. Note, however, that although NT 5.0 can read all previous versions of NTFS, older NT systems cannot read NTFS version 5.0 volumes.

Queried Information

The following list gives a short description of the prompts and options you will be given during the graphical portion of NT installation. In this example, we assume you are installing a computer to operate as a PDC.

- ▼ **User Name**
- ▪ **Organization**
- ▪ **CD-Key**—Found on your CD-ROM or licensing agreement.
- ▪ **Licensing Mode**—Offered on a per server or per seat basis (see the upcoming section called "Licensing").
- ▪ **Computer Name**—Must be a NetBIOS name, unique on network, and 15 characters or less.
- ▪ **PDC, BDC, or Standalone Server**—You can choose only one of these.
- ▪ **Administrator Password**—Sets the password for the default administrator account.
- ▪ **Emergency Repair Disk**—You will be prompted to create this disk, which is essential for system recovery.
- ▪ **Components**—You can choose to include certain components, such as games and Windows Messaging.

- **Networking**—Initially, this determines how you are connected to the network, either via RAS or wired directly.

- **Install Internet Information Server**—Choose this only if you really are going to use it.

- **Selects Network Adapters**—Searches automatically for adapter cards, or you can select from a list.

- **Network Protocols**—You may select TCP/IP, NWLink, NetBEUI, another protocol from Microsoft (for example, Point to Point Protocol), or third-party software.

- ▲ **Services**—Select the services you'd like to load. Your choices include DNS, DHCP, Gateway for NetWare, RAS, and many others.

After you have answered the preceding queries, you are prompted for the I/O address and interrupt for your network adapter card(s).

If you are not using a DHCP server and have selected to use the TCP/IP suite of protocols, you will be asked to supply an IP address, a subnet mask, a default gateway, and any DNS or WINS address information. At the very least you should supply the IP address, subnet mask, and default gateway. If you do not install a WINS address, you will see a dialog box indicating that at least one interface card has an empty WINS address. Do not be alarmed; this is only an annoying warning.

After you review the bindings, start the network; in the case of setting up a PDC, provide the name of the domain. Select the time zone. Then configure your video adapter—be sure to test your choice before proceeding.

The system copies files to their appropriate locations on your hard drive and sets the security on the system files. Eventually, you will be asked to restart the computer. Then the system will come up—hopefully, without any problems. Table 2-3 summarizes the information needed before going into the installation process.

Unattended Installation

Obviously, if you have tens or hundreds of systems on which you need to install NT, you cannot configure each one manually. Fortunately, Microsoft has created some tools to automate this task. Previously in this chapter, you saw all the questions that you must answer during the installation. You can preanswer these question in an answer file (Unattend.txt), and then at the time of installation give the location of this answer file. To help you create this answer file, the Resource Kit includes a utility called the Setup Manager (Setupmgr.exe), shown in Figure 2-3.

Windows NT Setup Manager has three basic areas: the general questions, the network questions, and the advanced questions. The general area has a series of tabs

General

       User Name

       Organization

       CD-Key

       Computer Name

       Domain or Workgroup Name

       Administrator Password

Networking

       NIC type

       NIC settings

       Protocols

       Services

       IP address

       IP subnet

       IP gateway

       WINS addresses

       DNS addresses

Table 2-3.   Information You Should Have in Hand Before Starting an Installation

covering the basic questions such as computer name and the role of the computer in the workgroup or domain. This is where you set the display settings, time zone, install path, and licensing option if you are installing a server. The network setup area contains settings for the network adapter, protocols, services, and modems, as well as any IP-specific information. If you have installed TCP/IP or are using DHCP, your IP address, subnet mask, and default gateway will be given to you the first time you boot up. The advanced setup area contains settings for nonstandard pointing devices, keyboards, or other hardware that NT may not detect on startup. You can also customize the installation to include your own banner, or set up a splash graphic here.

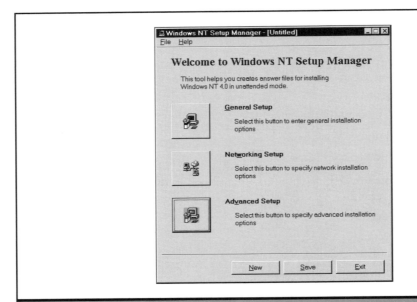

Figure 2-3. Windows NT Setup Manager enables system administrators to install or upgrade Windows NT on computers without having to monitor the process

When you have finished making your changes using the Setup Manager, simply save your settings to a file. Here is an example answer file that configures a workstation to join a domain, use TCP/IP, and set up its modem on COM port 1:

```
[Unattended]
OemPreinstall = yes
NoWaitAfterTextMode = 0
NoWaitAfterGUIMode = 1
FileSystem = ConvertNTFS
ExtendOEMPartition = 0
ConfirmHardware = yes
NtUpgrade = no
Win31Upgrade = no
TargetPath = *
OverwriteOemFilesOnUpgrade = no

[UserData]
FullName = "Joe User"
OrgName = "Acme Fun Toy"
ComputerName = SPINNER
ProductId = "1111-111111"
```

```
[GuiUnattended]
OemSkipWelcome = 1
OEMBlankAdminPassword = 1
TimeZone = "(GMT-05:00) Bogota, Lima"

[Display]
ConfigureAtLogon = 0
BitsPerPel = 8
XResolution = 640
YResolution = 480
VRefresh = 60
AutoConfirm = 1

[Network]
DetectAdapters = DetectAdaptersSection
InstallProtocols = ProtocolsSection
InstallServices = ServicesSection
JoinDomain = ACME
CreateComputerAccount = admin, star1

[DetectAdaptersSection]

[ProtocolsSection]
TC = TCParamSection

[TCParamSection]
DHCP = no
IPAddress = 10.0.5.12
Subnet = 255.255.255.0
Gateway = 10.0.5.1
DNSServer = 10.1.2.1
WINSPrimary = 10.2.20.1

[ServicesSection]
RAS = RASParamSection

[RASParamSection]
PortSections = PortSection1
DialoutProtocols = TCP/IP

[PortSection1]
PortName = COM1
DeviceType = Modem
PortUsage = DialOut
```

To use this unattended answer file, you include a switch in the winnt or winnt32 commands. From the DOS prompt, enter:

winnt /u: <answer file> /s:<source path>

For all other operating systems, type:

winnt32 /u:<answer file> /s:<source path>

Use the */t:<drive>* switch to specify the location of the temporary files.

Licensing

Licensing NT products has always been a confusing endeavor. This is due in part to the number of options that are available. Microsoft needs to license and price products for organizations of all different sizes, so it requires flexibility in its licensing model. It is helpful to remember that a license under Microsoft's plan is not a piece of software; instead it is the right to use a server or client. Under this model, servers and clients are licensed independently.

Basically, you must have one Server License for each server product and one Client Access License (CAL) for each computer connecting to that server. By purchasing NT Server, you are granted one Server License. Windows for Workgroups and NT Workstation do not include a license to access an NT Server. You must purchase a CAL to access file and print services on Windows NT Server. You can deploy CALs in one of two ways: per seat or per server. The most economical option depends on the number of clients and the server features you plan to use.

In the per server option, you buy a license for the server that allows a certain number of concurrent connections. You might have 1,000 users and licensing for 250 users. When 250 users are attached to that server, no additional users will be able to connect.

The per seat option differs in that you buy the right for each client to connect to servers. A client may connect to more than one server. For example, if my workstation has a per seat CAL, I can connect to as many servers as I want, and the server has no restrictions about how many concurrent users are attached.

How do you decide which licensing model is right for you? If your server is used relatively infrequently or always by the same clients, consider the per server option. If your clients access more than one server, it is probably better to use the per seat licensing option. In a mixed licensing environment, things become very confusing and difficult to license properly.

NOTE: A Client Access License is required only when an NT Server is providing basic file and print-sharing services or remote access, not when it is operating solely as a platform for a server application. Client Access Licenses are not required for server access through protocols that don't use basic file and print services. Examples of nonrestrictive use are telnet, FTP, and HTTP.

Removing NT

If you need to remove NT, there is one sure-fire way to get it off your system. Use a DOS diskette to boot the system. Next, use the *fdisk* utility to delete the partition NT resides on. Then create a new partition in its place. Format this partition using the DOS format utility. Now you can install DOS, UNIX, Windows 95, or NT on this partition.

WORKGROUP AND DOMAIN MODELS

Microsoft has created two major models to organize your Microsoft NT Servers and Workstations logically: the workgroup model and the domain model. In the workgroup model each machine has its own user database. Because each computer is autonomous in the sense of the user database and administration, the workgroup model is best for small groups of users, especially those that are somewhat savvy about simple administrative functions such as adding users, sharing drives, and connecting to network printers. System administrators don't particularly like this model, because they must manually configure users and shares on each machine if the users don't do this task themselves. Keeping a large number of machines functioning can be a nightmare. Users must have individual accounts on each machine they use. Allowing users to control administrative tasks such as controlling the user database and shares can also be a security risk.

The domain model has a centralized user database for ease of administration. All user accounts are stored on the primary domain controller (PDC). This makes administration easier because once users have an account on this machine, they can log onto any machine in the enterprise—provided the right to do so has been granted. The PDC, however, has a single point of failure. If this machine goes down, users cannot log onto the domain, although they can still log onto their local machines as if they were in a workgroup. Microsoft created a type of server called the *backup domain controller* (BDC) to cover for the PDC if anything should happen to it. So, already you have two systems that must be running 100 percent of the time in the domain. This is another reason why smaller groups of users do not use the domain model.

Figure 2-4 illustrates the logon sequence for the workgroup and domain models. In this example, user Joe needs an account on every machine in the workgroup. In the workgroup model, he has an account on only one machine and therefore cannot log on to any other machines. In the domain model, he has an account on the PDC, so he can log on to any machine participating in the domain. Notice that in the domain model, traffic is placed on the network. This becomes a consideration when deciding where to place your PDC. Currently, Microsoft recommends no more than 15,000 users per PDC, although this number depends heavily on the power of the computer and the properties of the network to which it is attached.

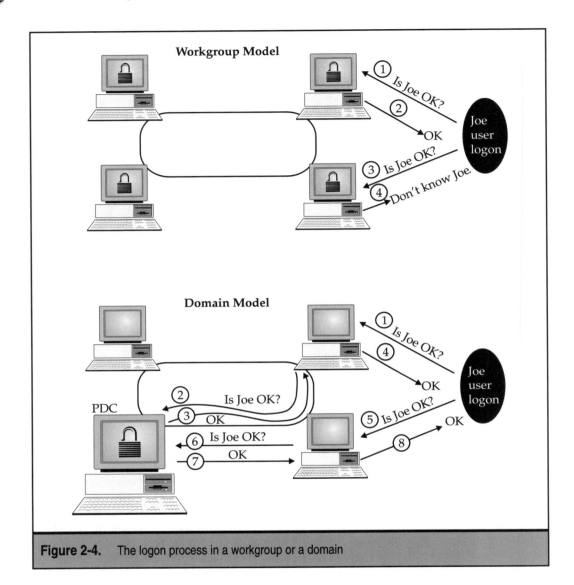

Figure 2-4. The logon process in a workgroup or a domain

Domain Models

Because every network has special needs and can vary greatly in size, Microsoft has defined four different domain models. Each has certain advantages, but it is not necessary to follow the models exactly; they can be mixed into a hybrid to better fit your needs. When considering a model, you should focus on several key issues. The location of users in relation to the PDC is paramount to proper implementation of the domain. Users distant to the PDC must traverse a WAN link, which often can become overloaded. Also, different models allow centralized or decentralized administration. Finally, each domain can only support up to 2,000 servers. The four models are the single domain model, the master domain model, the multiple master domain model, and the complete trust model.

The Single Domain Model

This model, as the name implies, uses a single domain; therefore it has one PDC and one or more BDCs. This is the best model for a single organizational unit that has relatively few users and resources. If there are too many users, user authentication may become sluggish. It is, however, a simple model to administer because everything is centralized, and there are no trusts to manage with other domains.

Trust Relationships

Before we cover the other three domain models, it is important to discuss a concept called the *trust relationship*. Because the remaining domain models incorporate more than one domain, there must be some way to communicate user rights among them if they are to share resources. Basically, you set up a trust relationship between two domains. This link allows the users of one domain access to the other domain.

Trusts can be thought of as one-way—a domain can trust another domain but cannot make other domains trust it. To make a mutually trusting relationship, trust must be set up on both domains. If, for example, domain A trusts domain B, and domain B trusts domain A, you have two one-way trusts and full cooperation between the domains. A user with a valid account in one domain has access to trusting domains. The advantages of trusting relationships are increased user convenience and better use of resources while individual domains are maintained as separate administrative units.

Trusts are set up using the User Manager for Domains dialog box at the PDC of each domain. Figure 2-5 illustrates the interface used to set up the trust.

At the top of this dialog box, you add the name of the trusted domain and a password that is set up at the other domain. This trust relationship is for domain accounts that will be trusted to use resources in your domain. To add your domain to the list of trusted domains on another domain, you have to add a trusting domain. This machine will trust accounts on your domain. Again, you type the name of the domain and include a password that both sides of the trust relationship will use.

NOTE: After a mutual trust relationship has been established, you cannot remove one side of the relationship, and then attempt to reestablish it later. You must remove both sides of the relationship and start again from scratch.

NT 5.0 NOTE: PDCs and BDCs will not be used in NT 5.0. Instead there will be domain controllers (DCs) that synchronize the latest changes to other DCs. Domains and trusts will be managed with the new Domain Tree Management tool.

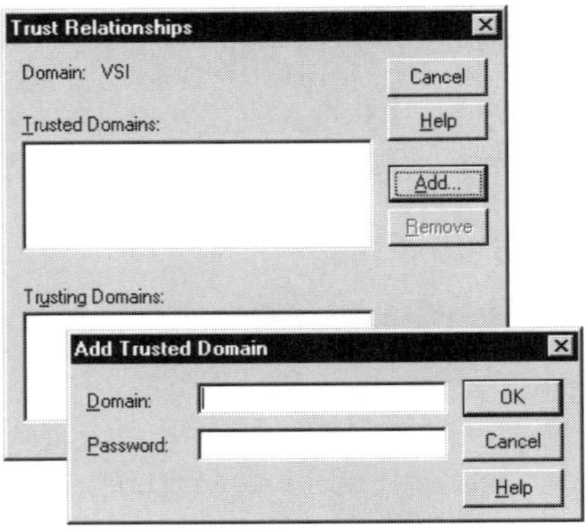

Figure 2-5. Setting up a trust relationship between domains

The Master Domain Model

In the master domain model, there are at least two domains. One domain serves as the master; all users authenticate via this PDC. However, the other domains maintain control over resources such as file- and print-sharing. This is the best scheme for organizations that are divided into units, but do not have so many users (more than 15,000) that they would clog the PDC of the master domain with logon requests. It has the same advantage as the single domain model—there is centralized management.

All other domains trust the master domain; that is, they use the master domain to log on users and pass each user the valid security token. The master domain permits the other domains to trust it. When users log on in one of these other domains, they must select the master domain at the time of logon. Their requests pass through their local domain and onto the master domain where they are validated.

You can set up a BDC to act as the point of user authentication in remote sites. This lessens the burden on the PDC and ensures that users can get authenticated quickly and reliably. Even if the WAN link to the PDC goes down or becomes congested, local users and servers will be able to function normally.

The Multiple Master Domain Model

This configuration consists of more than one master domain and multiple other domains. It is similar to the master domain model except the master domains have two-way trusts between them in the multiple master domain model. This is the best choice for larger organizations that wish to maintain centralized administration but like to have local authority over other resources. This model is slightly more cumbersome to administer because the users are scattered across the master domains. Although a strict hierarchy exists, there are considerably more trust relationships to maintain. This hierarchical structure gives this model its flexibility and scalability. This is a popular choice among mid- to large-sized organizations.

The Complete Trust Model

In this multiple domain model, all domains trust all other domains. Therefore, each domain has its own user database and must administer all its resources, including the users. This is the best model for organizations that are not very large, do not have a centralized MIS department, and can trust all other users in the organization. The major drawback to this method is the number of trusts that must be established and maintained. There are $n \bullet$ *(n-l)* trust relationships in this model, where *n* is the number of domains. For example, if there were eight domains, you would have to take care of 56 different trust relationships.

Domain Monitor

The NT Resource Kit includes a very handy program called the Domain Monitor (Dommom.exe). This administration tool can give you up-to-the-minute information about the status of each domain controller. Figure 2-6 shows the properties listed in Domain Monitor for each domain. In this figure, the remote machine \\TJV is the PDC for the domain VSI. All status indications tell us that the PDC is up and correctly linked to us. If there were any trust relationships with other domains, they would be listed here as well. In this fashion, it is easy to observe from a centralized location the status and trusts among domains. You can set up the Domain Monitor to watch certain domains and give you updates at regular intervals.

Server Manager

Another important administrative tool ships with NT Server and is located in the Administrative Tools directory. It is called Server Manager (Srvmgr.exe) and can be immensely useful for administration of remote machines. Figure 2-7 shows the user interface for Server Manager displaying all workstations or servers that are members of the domain. You can use Server Manager to examine the properties and services of each machine in the domain just as if you were sitting at the machine and examining the properties from within the Control Panel. You can also send a domain-wide message and tell all BDCs to synchronize their account databases with the PDC for that domain.

Use Server Manager when you need to add an account for a computer in the domain. In the example NT installation described earlier, we provided the name of an account and password with sufficient authority to create an account for the computer in the domain at the time of installation. If we had not done that then, we would have to do so now using Server Manager. Whether you have a single domain or many, you'll find this tool essential in administrating your servers.

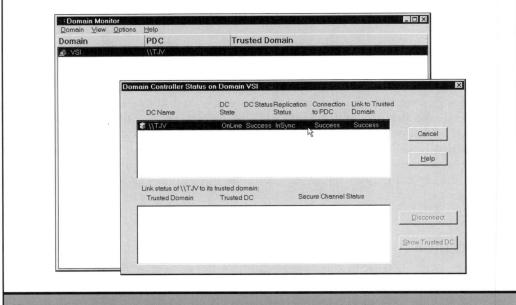

Figure 2-6. The Domain Monitor can view properties of remote domains

NT 5.0 NOTE: The Server Manager tool has been removed in NT 5.0. Its functions are incorporated into the new Directory Management tool.

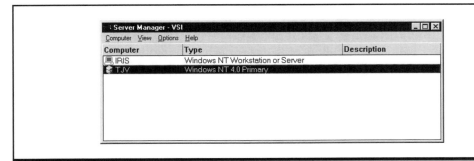

Figure 2-7. The Server Manager tool is useful for remote administration

CD NOTE: It should be apparent that if you have a large NT network, you are going to need help managing it. The tools described in the preceding section can be a tremendous help; however, you may seek additional assistance. There are third-party vendors that have created software tools just for domain administration. Some of these tools are located on the CD-ROM that comes with this book.

USER AND COMPUTER ACCOUNTS

By now you have successfully installed NT on a single machine, or perhaps hundreds. Each machine boots up properly and has all the network and configuration settings appropriate for its role in your network. You have determined how you will logically organize the environment by selecting a workgroup or domain mode. Now you can turn your attention to populating your NT world with users.

System Policy Editor

To use resources within a domain, all computers and users must have an account in that domain or in a trusted domain. One of the best ways to exert control over the computers' and users' desktop, network, and security settings is through the System Policy Editor (Poledit.exe). This tool is found under Administrative Tools in the Start menu. You can customize your default computers and users, or you can specify individual machines, groups, or users. Figure 2-8 shows the interface for the System Policy Editor with options for determining a default computer and user, a specific user and computer, and a global group Domain Admins (which is selected).

NT 5.0 NOTE: The System Policy Editor tool has been removed in NT 5.0. Its functions are incorporated into the new Directory Management tool.

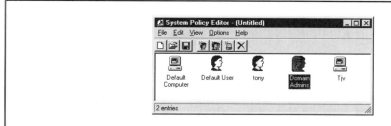

Figure 2-8.   The System Policy Editor allows control over desktop, network, and security settings

The Ntconfig.pol Policy File

Essentially, the System Policy Editor is a user interface for the Ntconfig.pol file, which is read across the network when a computer or user logs onto the domain. This file makes changes to the local HKEY_CURRENT_USER portion of the Registry for changes made to the default user. It makes changes to the local HKEY_LOCAL_MACHINE portion of the Registry for changes made to the default computer. If you include a policy for a specific user, group, or machine, this can also be saved in the Ntconfig.pol file.

When a user logs on to the domain, the Ntconfig.pol file is scanned to see if the user name has a special entry in the file. If not, he or she uses the default user portion of Ntconfig.pol. The same method is applied to the groups to which a user belongs and to machines. A user probably will be part of more than one global group that has an entry in the ntconfig.pol file. When this happens, you can set the priority of policy assignment under Group Priority in the Options menu.

NOTE: When users or computers join the domain, they pull the policy from their logon domain—which may not necessarily be their local domain.

For the Ntconfig.pol file to be successfully propagated throughout the domain, it must be placed in the *systemroot*\System32\Repl\Import\Scripts directory. This is the *Netlogon* share for domain controllers; it is automatically searched for the policy file when a user logs on.

Default System Policies

There are two basic through modes to alter system polices and both use the System Policy Editor. The first method is the policy file. With this method you change the contents of a policy file (such as Ntconfig.pol). When a user logs on, this file is read and alters the user's local Registry. This is an indirect way to alter the local Registry. Changes to policies take effect only after the user logs back on, so that the policy file can be redistributed to the local machine. To enter the policy file edit mode, click on New File or Open in the File menu.

The other method for altering policies is to directly alter the local or remote Registry. Using this mode, changes to the Registry take effect as soon as you disconnect or close the Registry. The System Policy Editor provides a friendly, structured environment to change Registry settings. To enter this mode, click on Open Registry or Connect from the File menu. Be careful when using this mode; you are making changes directly to the Registry just as you would using *regedt32*.

The choice of policies that you can alter in the System Policy Editor is determined by policy template files. These files control which options, check boxes, text strings, and other entries are present. By default two template files are loaded on startup from the %*systemroot*%inf directory. They are Common.adm and Winnt.adm. They provide settings that are common to NT and Windows 95, and settings specific to NT, respectively.

Modifying System Policies

Changing the default setting is easy. Simply double-click on the icon of the group, user, or computer you want to change. The Properties Window for the icon will appear, as shown in Figure 2-9 for the global Domain Admins group. A particular policy can be selected, cleared, or grayed. If a policy is selected, it has a check in its box (as does the Restrict display policy in Figure 2-9). The policy will be implemented, and the setting will be changed in the Registry. If the check box is cleared (empty), the policy will be implemented and the Registry setting will be removed. A grayed check box indicates that the Registry entries will not be modified.

In Figure 2-9 we have changed the settings on the Restrict display policy so that Domain Admins will not see the Screen Saver tab on its Modify Display window. To save the settings, close the Properties windows and click on the Save option under the File menu. The next time a member of the Domain Admins group logs on to the domain, they will not be able to alter the setting for the screen saver unless they are a member of another group that allows such a change and has greater priority in the Group Priority settings under the Options menu.

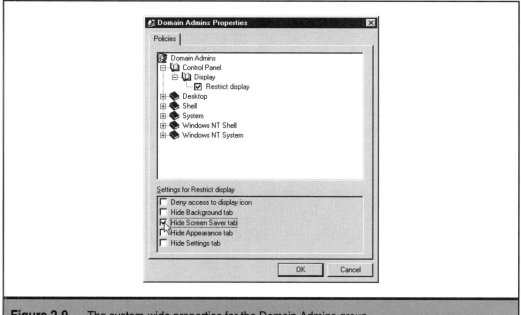

Figure 2-9.   The system-wide properties for the Domain Admins group

Default Users

Without adding even one user, every NT system already has two default users: the administrator and the guest, the most powerful and least powerful users respectively on the system. The administrator account allows a user to perform administrative functions under an account set up specifically for these tasks. It is recommended that administrators use their own accounts for personal use, and then switch to this account for administrative tasks. This ensures against accidental and irrevocable damage to the system or domain. For security's sake, you should rename this account to something a little less conspicuous than *administrator*. You do this through the User Manager, selecting User, and then Rename from the menus. The User Manager is discussed in more detail later in this chapter.

The guest account is provided to allow users who do not have an account on the system to log on and have limited access to resources. Deciding how much access the guest has is up to you. By default, the guest can change environmental settings such as the desktop, but these changes are not saved at logoff. The guest account is installed without a password and is disabled on NT Server by default, for security reasons.

Adding Users

You will probably need to add additional accounts so others (including yourself) can log on to the local system or perhaps the domain. This is accomplished with User Manager (in workgroups) or User Manager for Domains (in domains). Figure 2-10 displays the GUI for User Manager for Domains. User Manager is essentially the same, except it does not have the capability to set global groups and trust relationships.

In Figure 2-10, we see the default accounts and one user account. This account was created by selecting New User from the User menu. This calls up the New User window, as shown in Figure 2-11. You enter the user name, the user's real name, an optional description, and the password for the new user. This seemingly simple window gives you a good deal of control over all aspects of the user's account.

By default, all users are required to change their password upon their initial logon. If this account is for you, you can remove the checkmark in the box related to this requirement and proceed. The buttons at the bottom of the window lead to other windows that control the user's rights and privileges.

▼ **Groups**—You may select in which groups (local and global) the user is a member.

■ **Profile**—You may set the profile (if any) the user should use, the member's home directory, and a logon script.

■ **Hours**—You can set times for each day of the week when this user can log on.

■ **Log on To**—You can designate to which servers the new user may log on. You can select all servers or narrow the list to eight servers or less.

■ **Account**—You can specify when (if ever) the account expires, and whether this is a global (default) account or a local account (for users from an untrusted domain).

▲ **Dial in**—You select this if the user has permission to use Dial Up Networking to dial in to his domain.

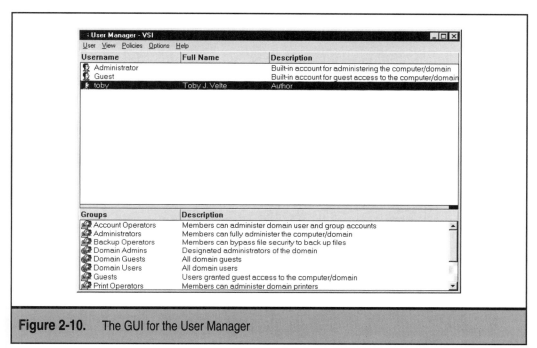

Figure 2-10.   The GUI for the User Manager

NOTE: User names are not case-sensitive, but passwords are.

Once you have created your first user, it is easy to add more users by copying the first entry. Just highlight the user, and select User, and then Copy from the menus. Change the user name and password, and you'll have a new user with the same properties as the first.

If you need to change some aspect of the user or groups of users later, select them manually or collectively. Then choose Select User from the User menu to globally change all of the selected users in one instance.

Users Have Rights and Need Policies

The User Manager houses three very powerful and important policy editors. They are found under the Policies menu and are called Account, User Rights, and Audit. They are used to provide a homogeneous environment for the users, as well as to set some security measures against weak passwords, unauthorized logon attempts, and rights granted unknowingly to users.

The Account Policy editor illustrated in Figure 2-12 gives you full control over users' password properties and account lockout for all users in the domain. It allows you to base password criteria on length and force users to change their passwords after a given time. It can even disallow reusing passwords for a period of time. Account lockout is used mainly to disable an account if there has been a series of incorrect logon attempts. This

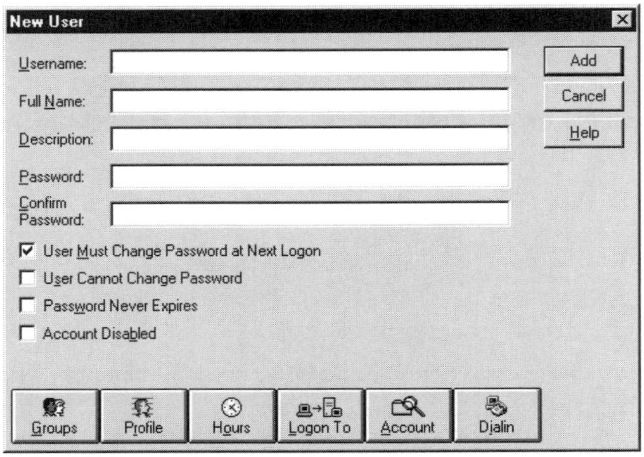

Figure 2-11. Add users with the New User window

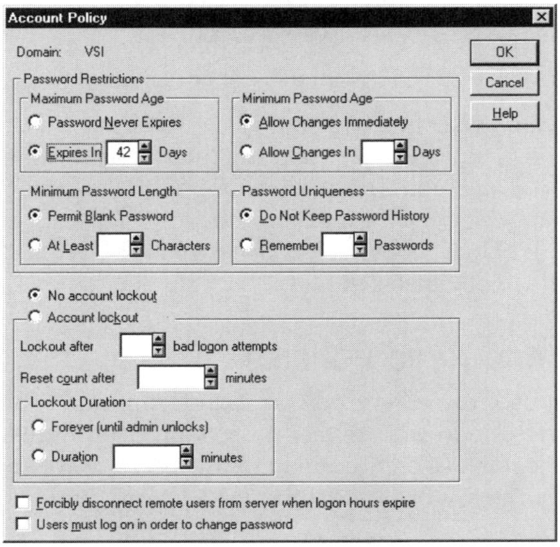

Figure 2-12. Account Policy editor sets properties for all users

security measure prevents unauthorized users from trying repeatedly to guess a password. The settings you choose for both the password criteria and account lockout will depend on how much security you want to impose on the users.

The User Rights Policy editor controls more precisely the rights a user or group may possess. When you select Show Advanced User Rights, you get a list of over 20 rights, ranging from simple rights such as the ability to change the time to more obscure rights like the ability to create a token object. In Figure 2-13 the right to log on locally to the machine is granted to Account Operators, Administrators, Backup Operators, Print Operators, and Server Operators. You can easily add or remove groups or users although you should be aware of the ramifications; many rights may not seem crucial to the functioning of an account but prove to be after you remove them. Be cautious when adding or removing rights because the result may not always be what you intended.

Because the job of the Audit Policy editor is to set which *system* events are to be saved in the security log, this tool seems out of place in the User Manager. The security log can be viewed using the Event Viewer in Administrative Tools. Adding more events to be audited dramatically increases the size of the security log file. If, for example, you decide to audit all successful file and object accesses, you will probably fill up the log file in a few minutes—with information that usually is not terribly useful. However, the size of this file can be restricted in the Event Viewer. Figure 2-14 shows the GUI for selecting events to audit. Failed logon attempts, failed use of user rights, and all restarts are logged here. This information may prove quite useful in troubleshooting a system or sniffing out a potential intruder.

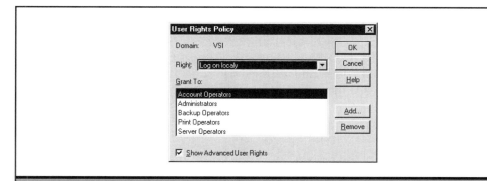

Figure 2-13.   User Rights Policy editor assigns specific rights to users or groups

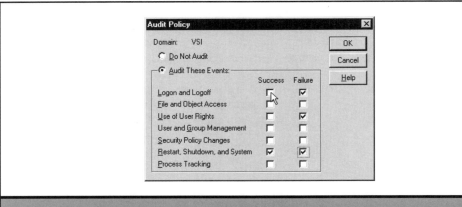

Figure 2-14. The Audit Policy editor configures which events will be logged

User Profiles

Another way to customize Windows NT settings is through user profiles. These settings are created for every user who logs on to a computer for the first time. Compared to system policies, user profiles control more detailed information about the user's environment. They allow users to customize their desktops so that changes they make will be present the next time they log on. If users have roaming profiles, these settings will "follow" them to every computer on the network to which they log on, providing a consistent user environment. If the administrator decides that users should have the same desktop environment each time they log on, mandatory profiles can be used.

Settings

User profiles are contained in a tree structure of folders in the %*systemroot*% Profiles*username* directory and also in a data file called Ntuser.dat. The profile tree structure contains information about shortcuts, printers, recently-accessed files, and other application-specific data. The Ntuser.dat file contains cached information from the Windows NT Registry HKEY_CURRENT_USER. This Registry tree contains information about installed software, environmental settings, and general user-specific information.

User profiles can contain settings for the following items:

▼ **Display**—Background, screen saver, and color scheme

■ **Menu**—Start menu items and desktop icons

■ **Mouse**—Settings for the mouse

■ **Connections**—Network and printer connections

■ **Window Layout**—Window sizes and positions

■ **Explorer**—All user-definable settings for NT Explorer

■ **Help**—All bookmarks in the Windows NT Help System

- **Control Panel**—All user-definable settings made in the Control Panel
- ▲ **Applications**—Windows NT user-specific applications such as the Calculator, Clock, Paint, and Hyperterminal

Local Profiles

There are three types of profiles that allow you the flexibility to control the users' environment or allow them to control their own desktop settings. Local profiles are generated when a user logs on for the first time. The user is given a copy of the profile called Default User. From there, the user can alter settings and expect them to be saved at logoff. Next time the user logs on, the customized profile will be loaded. Local profiles can be used only for that system. If a user has accounts on more than one machine, each machine will have a separate user profile for that user. Changing a setting on one will have no effect on the other profiles.

Roaming Profiles

Roaming profiles allow users to create and maintain a single profile that is used throughout the domain. No matter where the user logs on, the same desktop settings are used; changes are saved and applied at the next logon, regardless of which machine is used.

To give users a roaming profile, you must set up a path to their profile under the Profile button in User Manager for Domains (see Figure 2-11). If you have many users you might have an entry like:*servername**profile path*\%username%. Because you use the environmental variable *%username%*, you can copy this user many times without having to change the name of the profile path. Next you must select the User Profiles tab in the System Properties window of the Control Panel, as shown in Figure 2-15. You can change the type of the profile from local to roaming if a path has been set up for the user in User Manager.

NOTE: If you need to copy a profile from one user to another, use the Copy To button shown in Figure 2-15. Simply copying the Ntuser.dat file and the profile tree structure using File Manager or Explorer will not create the appropriate Registry entries. Windows NT will not be aware nor know how to load the profile.

Mandatory Profiles

Mandatory profiles are a type of roaming profile that cannot be updated by users. Administrators and technical support staff would certainly appreciate it if everyone had the same desktop settings. This consistency would help support staff troubleshoot problems and talk users through problem resolution. Coupled with editing system policies, a mandatory profile can help you exert a great deal of control over the user's environment.

To change a normal roaming profile to a mandatory profile, copy a profile to another account, modify it to fit your needs, and simply change the name of Ntuser.dat to Ntuser.man. When this user (or users, if multiple users are going to use the same profile)

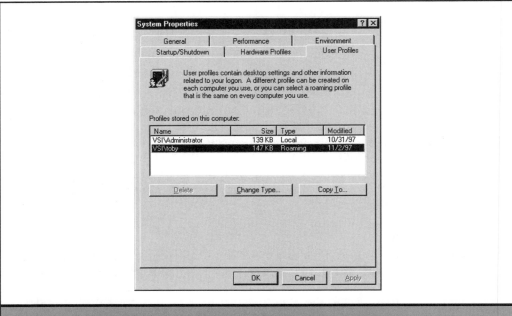

Figure 2-15.   Manage User Profiles within the System Properties window

logs on, your settings will be enforced. Any changes that the users are permitted to make during that session will not be saved to the profile. For future modifications, you can make changes offline on a copy of the profile, and then copy this profile over the working version of the profile.

Slow Connections

When a user first logs on to a computer and uses their roaming profile, it is downloaded from the path set in the user's account to their local machine. The next time the user logs on, the local cached copy of the profile is used so it is not pulled across the network again. If the user makes changes to the profile, it is copied back to the server when the user logs off. For subsequent logons, the local copy is compared to the copy on the server. If the server copy is newer, it is downloaded again to the local machine.

Sometimes a user may be connected to the profile server over a slow connection, or the server may be down. When the local machine requests the profile, it waits for two seconds to get a reply. If it doesn't receive a response, NT prompts the user to use the local copy or continue to wait for the remote copy.

Logon Scripts

Although user profiles can control most aspects of the user's environment, there are times when you need to run a program or a batch file when the user logs on. To do this, enter the path and name of the script in User | Properties | Profile button (see Figure 2-11) in the User Manager for Domains. Because user profiles can specify which network connections to make, you no longer need to include those in the script. However, other operating systems, such as Windows for Workgroups, Windows 95, and LAN Manager clients, don't have user profiles, even though they can take advantage of logon scripts. Another situation in which you'd employ a logon script is for running a certain application. For example, you might want all users to run a virus scan program at logon.

Historically, people have placed script commands in a batch file and run this at logon. You could, for example, have all users mount a shared drive on a server by including the following command:

net use s: \\servername\sharename

Although Windows NT has a somewhat limited scripting language, it is possible to create slightly complex routines. Microsoft has included a number of special logon script variables you can use to create scripts that are general enough to assign to many users. They are listed in Table 2-4.

User Groups

By default, users have no rights. They obtain rights only when an administrator assigns them using the User Rights Policy editor, or by inheriting them by being a member of a group. All users must be a member of at least one primary group (Domain Admins, Domain Guest, or Domain Users). The use of groups alleviates the administrative burden associated with multiple users. NT systems use groups to collectively label users. Users can be members of more than one group, and users can be selected by groups for simple adjustments in rights or policies. There are two major types of groups: local and global.

Script Variable	Description
%HOMEDRIVE%	The drive letter associated with the user's home directory
%HOMEPATH%	The path to the user's home directory without the drive letter
%OS%	The current operating system
%USERDOMAIN%	The name of the domain containing the user's account
%USERNAME%	The name of the current user

Table 2-4. Logon Script Variables

Local Groups

As their name implies, local groups are used only on a single system. Users who are members of local groups have local group privileges only if they are logged on to the local system. Local groups can only contain users from the local user database. Local groups can contain global groups, but local groups cannot contain other local groups. Confused? Here is an example. Let's say there is a local group that gives users special privileges on the local computer. You don't have an account on that computer, but you have an account in the domain and are a member of a global group there. Locally you include this global group with the local group. You now have the local group's special rights but only on that machine.

You create local groups using the User Manager under the User menu. Once you have created the group, you simply add users or other groups. The group is given a unique Security ID (SID) much like users have. The SID is used to identify the user or group and the privileges they have based on what other groups they belong to. When you delete a group, the users are not deleted, only the group and the SID. Unlike users, it is not possible to rename or disable groups.

Global Groups

Global groups provide a way for domain users to access resources across the domain. They are created on the PDC and contain users only from the domain user database. The global group information is transferred to the BDCs just as the user database is. Unlike local groups global groups cannot contain other groups, because they only contain users from the domain. For example, Domain Admins is a group to which you assign users who you wish to have administrative rights. When a new workstation joins the domain, it adds the global group Domain Admins to its local group Administrators. Now all users in the Domain Admins group can administer that workstation. The same thing occurs for domain users and the local group users.

Let's say you have a graphics workstation to which you only want some users to be able to log on locally. The easiest way to accomplish this is to create a global group (on the PDC) and populate it with users. Next, you add this global group to a local group you create on the graphics workstation. You have assigned the right to log on to this local group but not to the local user's group. Now only members of the global group you created (and presumably the Administrator's group) can log on locally.

Migrating from NetWare

If you are in the position to move users over from a Novell NetWare server to an NT server, you can use the Migration Tool for NetWare (Ntconv.exe) that comes with NT Server. This tool allows you to pull account information, files, and folders from an existing NetWare server into a domain on your Windows network. The NT server must have the IPX/SPX protocol running and it must have Gateway Services for NetWare installed. You must have administrative rights on both the Novell and NT server. After the migration, you can look at the log files to verify the translation process.

You start the migration process by selecting a NetWare and NT Server as illustrated in Figure 2-16. You have significant control over how the migration process is carried out. Under User Options and File Options you can specify which attributes are carried over. You can successfully migrate user names, group names, administrative rights, account restrictions, and file system security (only if used with NTFS). However, due to security protection on the NetWare server, you cannot pull user passwords over to the NT domain controller. You have the option of assigning temporary passwords until the users have the opportunity to change them.

NOTE: Before beginning the migration, you should run through a trial migration without committing to the translation. Afterwards, examine the log files to make sure the results are what you intended.

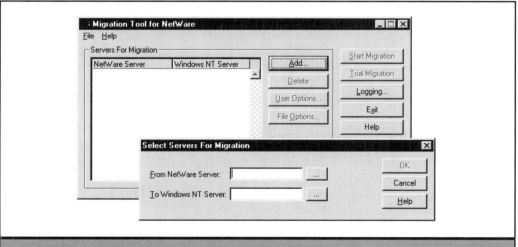

Figure 2-16. Begin NetWare migration by selecting a NetWare Server (source) and an NT Server (destination)

WINDOWS
NT
Professional
Library

CHAPTER 3

Reliability Through Redundancy

Key systems in a network absolutely, positively cannot go down. When they do, hundreds or thousands of users may be unable to perform important business functions. The result is decreased revenues and customers who become irritated with and lose faith in your company. Typically, these systems are servers providing a database or web presence for many users and have significant network traffic associated with them.

Since hardware (and software) components fail over time, one solution has been to create *redundant* systems. In the past, redundancy was quite often a missing feature in both hardware and software products. It was difficult, if not impossible, to build reliable redundant systems. Components were just not designed for redundancy. This is not the case with Windows NT and newer third-party hardware and software. In NT alone, there are integrated features that can provide the kind of redundancy necessary to ensure a high degree of up time. Additionally, software and hardware vendors have created a myriad of products aimed at increasing the reliability of critical systems.

In this chapter we will look at redundant hardware components, such as the configuration of hard disks that make up a RAID system used for immediate data recovery in the case of a single disk failure. We will look at what dual and uninterruptible power supplies can do to keep things running. On a more elaborate scale, we will examine methods used to "cluster" two or more computer systems together to create a fault-tolerant environment for critical applications. Since it is crucial to keep a redundant copy of important data, we'll also look at software that allows you to back up and protect your system and the critical data residing on it.

HARDWARE FAILURE PROBABILITY

Before jumping into solutions for addressing hardware failure, let's examine some of the characteristics of hardware failure. Generally speaking, all parts (especially moving parts), break down and fail at some point. This failure can be due to the decomposition of materials or because of physical wear on the components. System components (such as a hard disk) might be manufactured incorrectly or with defective parts and would subsequently suffer from premature failure. This accounts for the higher rate of failure that occurs when a system is first used compared with later in its life. Most early failures can be eliminated by running the system through a burn-in period. For example, if you are planning on deploying a new disk system, you should run the new hard drives through a period of rigorous reads and writes for perhaps 72 hours before you place the system into production. The same treatment should be applied to a spare disk you keep around in case one disk in the system fails. You certainly don't want to replace a bad disk only to discover your spare failed immediately.

Hardware in Series

Often you will see components rated with a *mean time between failure* (*MTBF*) value. This value represents the manufacturer's estimate of the average time you can expect the device to last before it fails, presumably after the burn-in period. Since many times these numbers come from the manufacturer and are highly subjective, they should only be used for a rough estimate. Nonetheless, MTBF numbers may give you a better idea of how long you can expect a particular component to run.

A system that is made up of components that depend on each other to function is called a system built in *series.* That is, if any component fails, the whole chain of components can't perform its function. Computers can grossly be considered as a system built in series—if, for example, the power supply, CPU, motherboard, hard disk, or network card fails, the system is rendered useless. In a networked environment, the computer depends on every component up to and including the network to function. As you can see, the system becomes more susceptible to failure the more components it has in series. This relationship is defined in the following equation:

Probability of whole system being up = $a_1 \bullet a_2 \bullet a_3 \bullet \ldots a_n$

where a is the probability of a component functioning properly for n number of components. Figure 3-1 illustrates this for ten components in series, each having a probability of being up of 0.90 (90 percent). As you add more devices, the probability that the system will be fully operational decreases. Of course, the components that make up a

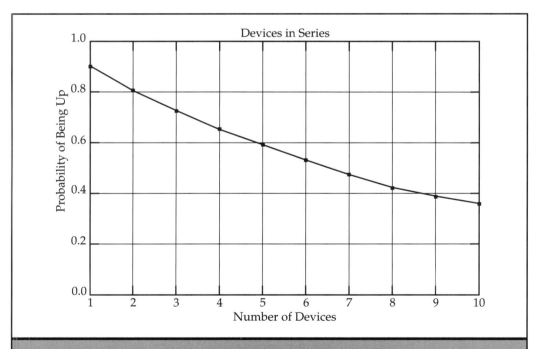

Figure 3-1.   Probability of a system being up as more devices are added in series

modern server have up times well over 90 percent. If they don't, you should be shopping elsewhere. Most vendors will supply the values for reliability to you. The point is that even if the individual components in series have a higher probability of being operational, increasing the number of devices in series will, at least statistically, reduce the system's overall up time.

Hardware in Parallel

Because a computer is inherently serial in design, the solution to increasing the up time of the whole system is to find those components with the greatest probability of failure and run them in *parallel*. For example, you could power a computer with three separate (but parallel) power supplies. If one or two of these devices fails, there will still be one remaining that can sufficiently power the computer. In this mode, the components not required for normal operation (two additional power supplies) are considered redundant. The probability of having at least one of n redundant components up is described by:

$$\text{Probability of being up} = 1-((1-a_1) \bullet (1-a_2) \bullet (1-a_3) \bullet (1-a_n))$$

where a is the probability of being up for each component for n number of components. The value for a is usually the same for each of the redundant components, but this is not necessarily always the case. Figure 3-2 illustrates how adding extra devices increases the up time probability for that device. Each of the ten devices has a probability of being up of 0.90 (90 percent). One of these devices is likely to be up 90 percent of the time. By simply adding another device, the probability of being up goes from 90 percent to 99 percent. This is because you would need both devices to fail at the same time for the system to go down. The practical message here is that you can make great gains in reliability by running two components in parallel, thus having a second component available to assume the role of the failed component.

In the power supply example just discussed, redundant power supplies ensure power will always be available to the computer, but provide no assurance that other parts of the computer won't fail. The strategy taken by many has been to target the components that are most likely to fail and to use redundancy there. This strategy has the effect of increasing the up time of those components, which increases the probability of up time for the system. The next section describes some of those hardware components essential to the functioning of the system and that have the highest rate of failure.

REDUNDANT COMPONENTS

Hardware vendors have created devices that can serve as redundant components to help keep your server up in the event of a failure. These devices are those that are the most likely to fail and include the power being delivered to the computer, the power supply in the computer, the network interface card (NIC), and the SCSI adapter card. Hard disks are also crucial components and are covered in the next section.

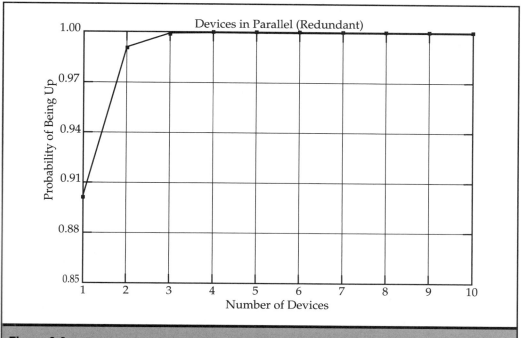

Figure 3-2.   Redundant devices are placed in parallel

UPS

An *uninterruptible power supply* (*UPS*) is an external box containing batteries that powers your computer in the event of power failure. The server's power cord is plugged into the UPS, which is in turn plugged into a standard power receptacle. The UPS monitors the line voltage for any errant fluctuations. If the UPS detects wild fluctuations or no power whatsoever coming from the wall socket, it can power a computer with its batteries for about six to 30 or more minutes. It is a good idea to have UPS protection for all servers and other multiuser devices.

Most server-class UPS devices have a serial cable that connects to your server and can signal it when certain power events occur, such as when the power fails or when the batteries are running low. Since the UPS can support normal functioning of the computer for only a short time, the system should be able to perform a graceful shutdown before the battery power is depleted. A UPS is not a power generator in the sense that it allows for continuous, long-term operation of the system in the event of a total power failure. Power generators serve this function, and are much larger and more expensive devices that you might consider for an entire server room or facility. Most UPS devices are installed as short-term power insurance. Their job is to provide enough power to notify the server and allow it to complete open transactions, close open files, log off users, and, finally, conduct an orderly shutdown of the system, thereby avoiding damage to hardware and data.

Advances in UPS technology have brought more than just power backup. Often UPSes will have circuitry that provides line conditioning that ensures that clean, spike-free power is delivered to your machines. Additionally, some come with the Simple Network Management Protocol (SNMP) support so that you can remotely monitor the status of the UPS and reboot an unruly server. To use SNMP, you have to equip the UPS with a network adapter card (usually proprietary).

NOTE: Since many UPS devices can cut power to a server as well as provide it, care must be taken to monitor the integrity and security of these units.

Configuring the UPS Service

Windows NT has built-in support for UPS devices and can take advantage of many of the advanced features found in these devices.

Follow these steps to install a UPS device:

1. Make sure that the serial port you plan to use for the UPS is properly configured and does not conflict with any other devices. Check to ensure the serial port is installed via the Ports icon in the Control Panel. Then check for conflicts in the NT Diagnostics tool in the Administrative Tools menu item.

2. Make sure that the computer and UPS are powered off.

3. Connect the serial cable from the UPS to the computer on the correct port.

4. While keeping the computer plugged into the wall, power on both the computer and UPS.

NOTE: You should use the serial cable provided with the UPS, because a standard serial cable may have different pin configurations. Without the proper cable the UPS will not be able to communicate with the NT system.

5. You can configure the UPS service using the icon for UPS found in the Control Panel. Clicking on this icon will bring up the UPS service configuration window, as shown in Figure 3-3. You should consult the user's manual that came with the UPS to correctly configure the UPS to work with NT. While reviewing the UPS documentation, check to see if the UPS can support exchanging information with the computer for power failure, low battery alert, and system shutdown. This information will be needed during the next part of the configuration process.

6. From the drop-down list at the top of the UPS window, select the serial port that the UPS is connected to.

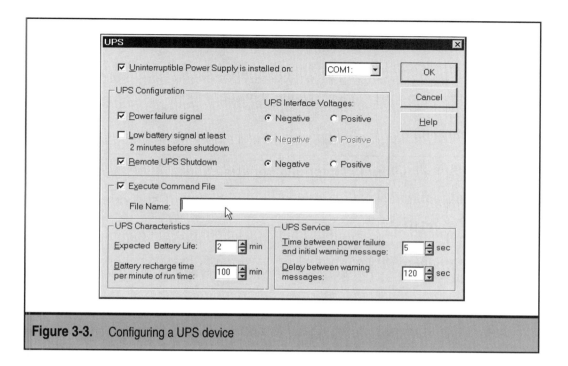

Figure 3-3. Configuring a UPS device

7. If the UPS can send a signal indicating power failure, click on the Power Failure Signal check box, and select the correct polarity of the signal.

8. If the UPS can signal when it is almost out of battery power, select the Low Battery Signal At Least 2 Minutes Before Shutdown check box. Use this feature to get the most up time from your UPS.

9. Select the Remote UPS Shutdown check box if the UPS can support a signal from the computer that tells it to stop providing power to the computer. NT sends this signal indicating it is ready to be powered off, thus saving the UPS battery.

10. Select the Execute Command File check box if you'd like the server to run a script or other program.
You can run a command file to copy important files. The command file must complete its execution within 30 seconds or it will be terminated. Therefore, you should not require user input. The command file must reside in the *Systemroot*\System32 folder and have one of the following extensions: .EXE, .COM, .BAT, or .CMD.

11. Under UPS Characteristics, enter the Expected Battery Life. You should test the UPS (see next section) to get this value before changing the default value. This

value is grayed out if you have configured your UPS to signal two minutes before the battery is expected to run out.

12. Enter how long it takes to recharge the battery. NT assumes the battery has no charge at boot up. A value of 100 indicates that the computer must be on for 100 minutes to charge up one minute of battery support.

13. Under UPS service you can select when and how frequently warning messages are sent to users.

NOTE: The Alerter service must be running for messages to be sent to select users. The Messenger service must be running to send a logoff message to local and network users. If you want to enable these features, check to ensure the services are running by clicking the Services icon in the Control Panel. You should set the service's startup type to Automatic so that the service restarts after the system is rebooted.

14. When you have finished your selections, click OK and you will be prompted to start or restart the UPS service. Click Yes and you'll be ready to test your UPS device.

Testing the UPS

It is very important to test the UPS. The reason you were instructed not to plug the computer's power into the UPS (see the preceding section) is that if the installation is misconfigured, you could terminate the power to the computer without warning. For example, this could occur if the UPS supports remote UPS shutdown and you select the wrong signal polarity, or if you do not have the correct serial cable. Since you have the serial cable connected to the UPS but have ensured that any unpredictable behavior by the UPS won't disconnect the power, you can safely proceed with testing the setup.

With the computer idling, simply disconnect the power plug on the UPS device from the wall socket. If you had selected the Power Failure Signal check box, you should see a message box indicating the power is out. Eventually you would see NT begin to shut down. If you observe during testing that the UPS has functioned correctly, you can power down and plug the computer into the UPS.

NOTE: To maximize your battery time, plug only the computer into the UPS (not the monitor) unless, of course, you need to use the monitor in the event of a power failure.

With the computer plugged into the UPS and the UPS plugged into the wall socket, power up both units. When the system comes up, disconnect the UPS from the wall to ensure the shutdown sequence is appropriate. Check the EventLog files to make sure the shutdown was recorded there.

UPS devices come in a wide range of capabilities. As mentioned earlier, you should get a device that can use the serial port to signal NT of the current power status. If you are planning to deploy several UPS devices, SNMP support can greatly ease the administration of these devices. The other major consideration is the power rating the UPS has. Typically they are rated in volt-amperes (VA). You'll need a UPS capable of supporting the load of the systems attached to it for the time it takes to complete a shutdown. To calculate your requirements, find the voltage and amperage requirements for each piece of equipment. These numbers should be on the component or in its technical specifications. Then multiply the numbers together:

$$VA = volts \times amperes$$

Add all the VAs together for each component to determine your power requirements. Table 3-1 lists some UPS vendors that are known to work with Windows NT.

Dual Power Supplies

The power supply from the wall is delivering 120 or 230 volts AC to your computer. Since the components inside the computer run at 5 or 12 V DC, you need to convert the 120 V AC power to the lower DC voltages. This job is performed by your power supply. Even if you have a UPS in place, the computer may still lose power if the internal power supply fails. Power supplies have the shortest MTBF of all computer-related devices. You should take measures where possible to provide a redundant power supply. Unfortunately, most workstations and low-end servers have a built-in power supply and do not have the capability to add another in parallel. For these systems, you should have an extra power supply on hand in case of failure. This will help you get your system up and running quicker, although it won't prevent down time or loss of data due to an unexpected power supply failure.

Several computer manufacturers now provide the option of redundant power supplies in some server-class machines. Essentially the system has two or more power

UPS Vendor	Capacity (kVA)	Time @ 100% (min)	Price ($US)	Contact
American Power Conversion	0.25 to 16	10 to 12	299 and up	www.apcc.com
Clary	1 to 2	7 to 13	1,600 to 3,000	www.clary.com
Liebert	1 to 24	5 to 15	390 and up	www.liebert.com
Opti-UPS	1	5	200	www.opti-ups.com
Toshiba	1.5 to 50	8 to 25	2,000 to 40,000	www.tic.toshiba.com
Tripp-Lite	0.5 to 5	6 to 17	229 to 4,499	www.tripplite.com

Table 3-1.   UPS Devices

supplies built into the chassis. In the event of a failure, the functioning power supply takes over the duties without missing a beat. You may still need to power off the system to replace the bad power supply, but at least you can do this at off-peak hours.

Multihoming

For enterprise network computers to function, they must be able to communicate through the network to other systems. It is absolutely essential that the network connection is not disrupted for any reason. To end users, a broken network connection has essentially the same effect as powering off the machine—no network, no server.

To ensure the highest network availability for your servers, you can place two network interface cards (NICs) in them. Under NT this is called *multihoming*. Each NIC has its own IP address and may even be connected to different subnets and separate routers, as illustrated in Figure 3-4. This provides for reasonable continuous network access in the event one of the network segments or NICs fails. If a particular path to the server becomes unavailable due to a network outage, there is another path to the server. For example, in Figure 3-4 if NIC 1 connected to the FDDI ring were to fail, the client

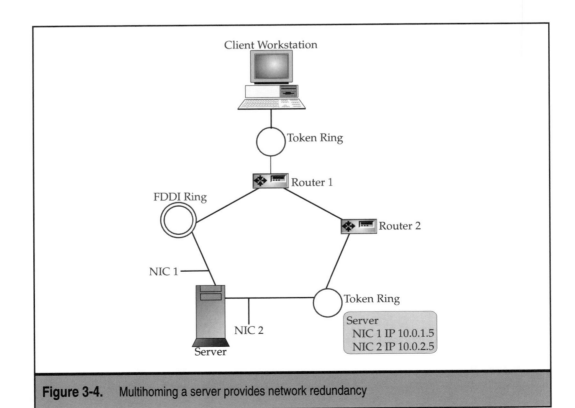

Figure 3-4. Multihoming a server provides network redundancy

could still reach the server by traversing an extra hop through router 2 and connect to the server via NIC 2.

A word of caution: this type of configuration typically uses Windows Internet Naming Service (WINS) or Domain Name System (DNS) to resolve IP addresses, and it doesn't guarantee a connection on the alternate NIC every time the client workstation tries to access the server. The reason is that even though both WINS and DNS are capable of registering multiple addresses under one server name, both will randomly or in round-robin fashion return one of the registered addresses when queried. Should the return address be that of the failed network adapter, the client will receive a "server not found" message or some equivalent indication that the server is no longer available. However, if the client tries to connect again, DNS or WINS may return the address of the functioning NIC. The server will then be available to the client until the next time it queries the name service for the server address.

Host Adapter Cards

As with NICs, the host adapter card that is used to connect the hard disks to the server is susceptible to failure and will certainly bring the system to a halt if it fails. As with the power supplies, it is always a good idea to have a spare adapter card handy in case one fails. But the best solution is to have a second adapter card already in the system. Hardware vendors often sell dual adapter cards to accompany their external hardware disk arrays. Not only does the additional adapter card provide redundancy (see the duplexing discussion in the "Level 1: Mirroring" section), but it can also increase performance by performing multiple disk operations on separate disks in the array.

DISKS

Because hard disks are essential to the function of a server and hold valuable information (even when they are turned off), software and hardware vendors have created methods to maintain data in the event of hard disk failures. Software solutions for data redundancy are less expensive than hardware solutions, although they typically sap CPU cycles and are not as fail-safe as their hardware counterparts. Hardware solutions provide greater protection of data, are usually faster, and scale to larger capacities. Their major drawback is cost, which can be prohibitive.

RAID Levels

A technology called *RAID* minimizes the loss of data due to disk failures. RAID was created by a group of scientists at the University of California at Berkeley in 1987. When they designed the first RAID systems, "RAID" stood for "Redundant Array of Inexpensive Disks." Since then, the "Inexpensive" has been replaced with "Independent," presumably by vendors to avoid charges of false advertising. In any case, the principle remains the same: using two or more disks simultaneously can be faster and more fail-safe than using a single, larger disk. From the discussion of failure probability earlier in the chapter, we know that using two disks in series (if both are required to serve data) is a configuration that is more prone to failure than using a single disk. We also know that using two disks in parallel (one is a copy of the other) is much less likely to result in a data loss compared with using a single disk.

RAID technology offers both serial and parallel solutions at varying levels of coverage. No single RAID level is superior to any other. The RAID level you implement will depend on your needs and budget.

RAID technology can be implemented in software or hardware. In the case of a software implementation, standard drives and controller cards can be used. The RAID software manages all the transactions to the disks. Most hardware solutions are external drive arrays that manage themselves with respect to how the data is stored. To the NT system, the drive array appears as a single drive. Windows NT provides built-in software support for mirroring (RAID level 1) and disk striping with parity (RAID level 5). Most hardware solutions are supported by NT and are recommended over software solutions for speed and reliability.

Level 0: Striping

RAID level 0 is not fault tolerant, because no information is duplicated on the disk system. However, performance is enhanced because the data is *striped* in 64KB stripes across all the disks in the array (see Figure 3-5). Say, for example, you had three drives in your array. When the controller needs to write a 256KB block of data, it writes the first 64KB block to drive 1, the next 64KB block to drive 2, the next 64KB block to drive 3, and the last 64KB block to drive 1. The total available space in the array is the same as the total physical space for all the drives. Because the probability of failure is greater for this RAID level, it is not widely used.

Level 1: Mirroring

RAID level 1 is called *mirroring*, because it maintains an identical twin of the first drive. This configuration is shown in Figure 3-6. Since all data that is written to drive 1 (original drive) is also written to drive 2 (shadow drive), you only get 50 percent of the total capacity of the two drives combined. There is also a slight write performance loss due to the overhead of writing to two drives. However, there is a performance gain on disk reads, and there is very good fault tolerance. A weakness in this design is the controller card, which is a single point of failure. To eliminate the single point of failure here, you can use two controller cards, each responsible for writing to a single drive. This completely duplicates the I/O system and is appropriately called *duplexing*. You should use mirroring if you:

▼ Require a high level of redundancy

■ Demand high read performance

▲ Do not want to deal with the complexity of other RAID systems

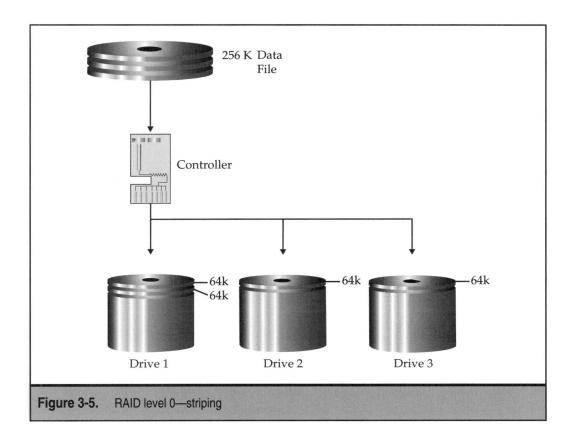

Figure 3-5.   RAID level 0—striping

Level 2

Level 2 RAID uses striping (like RAID 0), but it is performed at the *bit* level. This method used to lay data to the disk requires a good deal of CPU processing and is inefficient. It is thus not widely adopted.

Level 3

Level 3 RAID uses byte striping similar to level 0, but includes a drive dedicated for parity. The *parity* can be thought of as the sum of all the bytes contained in the stripes of the other drives, as illustrated in Figure 3-7. The parity drive provides true fault tolerance, because if any of the other drive fails, the information on it can be calculated by subtracting the bytes in the other stripes from the parity stripe.

The capacity of RAID level 3 arrays can be expressed as a percentage based on the number of drives in the array: $n-1/n$ where n is the total number of drives. Since all drives are involved in every read or write (to calculate the parity stripe), RAID level 3 arrays can

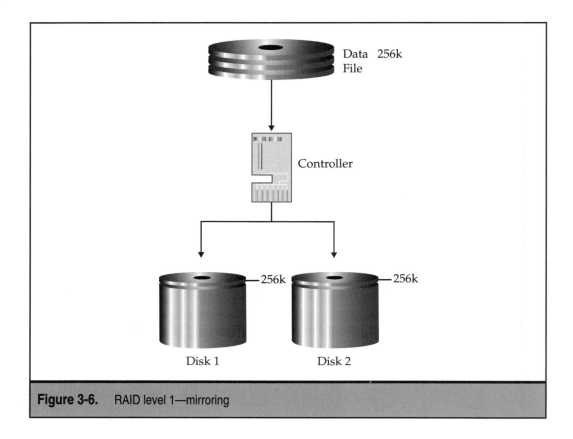

Figure 3-6.   RAID level 1—mirroring

process only one transaction at a time. They are not suited for random access of many small data blocks. These systems are best suited for large sequential requests.

Level 4

Level 4 RAID uses striping at the *block* level to improve efficiency. It dedicates a drive to the parity information like level 3 RAID and thus has the same capacity of RAID level 3 systems.

Level 5

The most popular RAID configuration is level 5 RAID. Here the parity is stored in 64K blocks and placed evenly on all drives, as shown in Figure 3-8. Since the controller can process multiple writes in parallel across the array, RAID level 5 can outperform levels 3 and 4. However, it doesn't perform as well as level 0 or 1 because of the computation used to calculate the parity information.

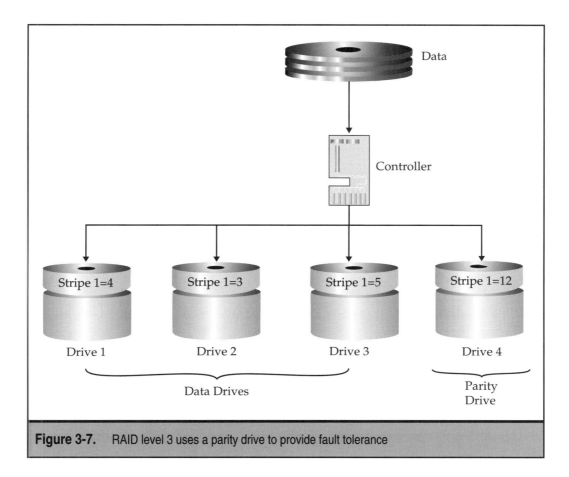

Figure 3-7.   RAID level 3 uses a parity drive to provide fault tolerance

The capacity of RAID level 5 is the same as levels 3 and 4 and should be considered when redundancy is required but you do not have enough money for a mirrored solution or you require the overall larger capacity afforded by arrays as opposed to single, mirrored disks.

Advanced Levels

If you take RAID level 5 and mirror (level 1) the entire disk array and controller (duplexing), you get RAID level 10. This configuration provides excellent fault tolerance and a performance boost. Any single drive in each array or an entire array can fail without data loss. The capacity is reduced to $1–n/2n$ for n number of drives.

If you take RAID level 5 one step further (RAID 5/RAID 5), you get RAID level 55. Just replace each drive in RAID 5 with an array of drives each with its own controller, and

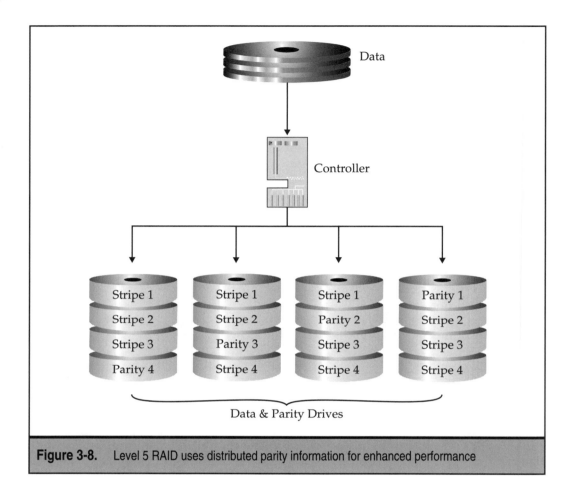

Figure 3-8.   Level 5 RAID uses distributed parity information for enhanced performance

you have massive capacity, excellent performance, and nearly perfect fault tolerance. The ratio of total usable space is the same as in RAID 5 systems ($1-n/n$).

Mirroring

RAID level 1 or mirroring creates a copy of the data disk onto a shadow partition for fault tolerance. Read performance is enhanced because the SCSI controller can perform two read requests at one time. Recovery is quick because you do not need to reinstall NT or re-create a lost disk before the system is fully functional again. Unlike with disk striping, you can use mirroring on the system or boot partition.

NOTE: In NT parlance, the *system* partition holds the hardware-specific information to load NT (for example, NTLDR, NTDetect), while the boot partition holds the NT OS and its supporting files (for example, files in *Systemroot* or *system32* directories).

One major disadvantage of mirroring is that you are only getting 50 percent of the hard disk space you are paying for. In addition, mirroring does not copy the boot sector on the disk, which is then susceptible if it becomes corrupted. Also, if the failure of the disk is due to a software problem (perhaps within NT's disk driver, FtDisk), both disks will be affected. If the disk does fail, you may need to reboot the system to replace it, which translates into down time.

NT Support for Mirroring

Windows NT Server comes with built-in support for disk mirroring. All that is required from you is two disks. The second disk does not need to be physically identical to the first unless you are mirroring the system partition.

NT uses its fault-tolerant disk driver, FtDisk, to keep track of the reading and writing to multiple disks. Normally, FtDisk uses both disks for read operations. In the event of a read failure, FtDisk reads data from the other disk. If there is a write failure on one of the disks, FtDisk uses the remaining disk for all operations.

INSTALLING A MIRRORED DRIVE   You should first prepare two identical hard disks (SCSI systems) by following these steps:

1. Enable the BIOS on the first disk controller, and disable it on the shadow controller (using the SCSI utilities from the manufacturer).

> **NOTE:**   If you are using two controller cards (duplexing), it is much easier to recover from disk failure if you use the same translation on both disks.

2. Format both disks using the controller that has its BIOS enabled, ensuring that each disk has identical cluster and partition geometry.

3. Install NT and any other software you have on the first disk.

Now you are ready to create the mirror set. This is accomplished through the Disk Administrator tool found in the Administrative Tools menu, as shown in Figure 3-9.

1. Click on the original disk, and click on the disk that will serve as the shadow disk while holding down the CTRL key.

2. Click on the Fault Tolerance menu's Establish Mirror option.

3. After the system establishes the shadow disk, click on the Partition menu's Commit Changes Now option.

4. You should create another Emergency Repair Disk and also a boot disk (see Chapter 11), which you may need in case of a disk failure (see "Recovering a Data Disk").

5. Shut down and restart the system.

6. After the system comes up, open the Disk Administrator. You should see the message "Mirror set # [INITIALIZING]." This indicates that the data from the first disk is being copied over to the shadow disk.

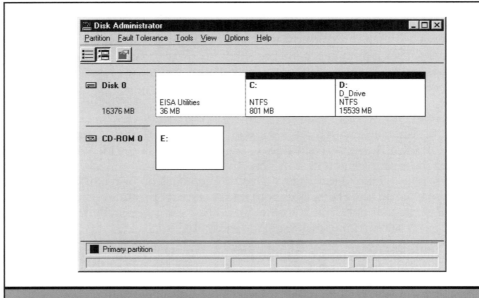

Figure 3-9. Using the Disk Administrator to set up fault tolerance

RECOVERING A DATA DISK When a disk in a mirror set fails, FtDisk orphans the failed disk and uses the remaining disk for all subsequent read and write operations. Users should not be able to detect that a failure has occurred unless they are at the console of the machine with the failed disk.

You should take immediate measures to back up the data, as it is no longer in a fault-tolerant configuration. At the next convenient moment, you should replace the failed disk. The steps you take to do this depend on whether the failed disk was the system partition or a data partition. In either case you start by breaking the mirror set:

1. Use Disk Administrator and select the mirror set.
2. Choose Fault Tolerance | Break Mirror.
3. Confirm your decision.

NOTE: If you do not break the mirror before rebooting, you will see the blue screen of death, because the Registry is expecting to see both disks of the mirror set.

If the disk is a data disk, shut down the system and replace the bad disk with a new, identical disk. Boot up the system, format this new disk, and follow the steps outlined earlier for creating a mirror set.

RECOVERING A SYSTEM DISK   If the failed disk contained the system partition (that is, it contained the boot information necessary to start NT), then you should set the shadow partition as active by selecting the Disk Administrator menu, then Partition | Mark Active. This tells NT that the disk contains the system partition and is bootable. Shut down and replace the disk. Next you will need to make some changes so that NT knows where to find and boot from the shadow disk. We will assume here that you are using two controllers. Recovering with a single controller is a little easier.

One option is to move the shadow disk over to the original controller. You are fooling the controller into thinking it has its original disk back. You will need to change the SCSI ID to that of the original disk for this to work.

A similar option is to leave the disks in their original physical locations but to switch the roles the controllers have been playing. You will need to enable the BIOS on the shadow controller and disable it on the original. This essentially switches the original and shadow disks entirely. You can pick up the mirror set configuration by formatting the new disk and using the Disk Administrator to create the mirror set.

If these methods fail or you don't want to move disks or reconfigure the controller, you can boot the system from an NT startup floppy disk.

NT STARTUP FLOPPY DISK   The NT startup floppy allows you to bypass problems associated with the boot process. This disk must be prepared ahead of time on the system you are going to use it on. You should use this method when the Master Boot Record or the Partition Boot Sector is corrupt, or when you have other problems with the system partition.

First you need to format a floppy from within NT using Explorer, File Manager, or by typing **format a:** from the command prompt. Next you need to add the following files to the disk (they are in the root directory of the system partition and may need to be unhidden):

▼   **NTLDR**—NT boot loader program.

■   **Boot.ini**—Indicates the location of the NT boot files. NT uses the Advanced RISC Computing (ARC) naming convention to find the disk and partition to boot NT. This file will have to be altered to include an entry pointing to the location of the shadow disk.

■   **NTDetect.com**—Used at bootup to detect hardware.

■   **Bootsect.dos**—Only present if you have a dual-boot system. This is the alternate OS boot partition.

▲   **NTbootdd.sys**—Only present if you are using SCSI controllers and the scsi( ) syntax in the Boot.ini file. This file is the SCSI controller driver and may have to be renamed to NTbootdd.sys.

Use the startup floppy by booting from it and choosing the remaining partition to start NT. You should first try to see if you can fix the problem that is causing the remaining disk not to boot. Once you get the system up, format the new disk and continue with creating a mirror set as described earlier.

RAID Level 5

In addition to software mirroring, NT supports a software implementation of disk striping with parity (RAID level 5). It allows you to use from three to 32 disks for the array. Under NT, the data is striped in 64KB blocks to all disks in the array. One stripe is used for the parity information and is distributed evenly across all disks (see Figure 3-8). Because each disk can be read independently, read access is improved compared with a single disk but not to the level of mirrored disks. Nonetheless, you can use more of the overall disk capacity compared with mirrored disks. One downside to a RAID level 5 software solution is that the CPU of the server will be used to calculate the parity information. The software has to read the old stripe and the parity stripe and then compute a new parity stripe before writing it to the disks. This overhead can hinder the performance of your server. Finally, note that you cannot boot from an NT RAID 5 array. This is because NT needs to be running before it can load the necessary software enabling it to recognize the RAID 5 array.

NT Support for Striping with Parity

It is always a good idea to place the RAID array on a separate controller card. The performance increase and redundancy is worth the extra cost. Since the proportion of usable space increases with the number of disks, you will get more capacity by purchasing six 2GB disks compared with four 3GB disks (83 percent versus 75 percent), for example. Remember that with each disk you add, you increase the odds that one of the disks in the array will fail.

NOTE: The system or the boot partition cannot be a member of the disk array.

INSTALLING A STRIPED DISK ARRAY You will need at least three partitions to create a RAID level 5 array. It is best to use independent and identical disks in your array. Although you can use more than one partition on the same physical disk, if the disk fails, two of the RAID partitions will not function and you will lose all your data.

Use the Disk Administrator to create the RAID level 5 array as you did for creating the mirrored set. You begin by selecting three to 32 disks by holding down the CTRL key and clicking on the disks. The size of the RAID partition for each disk is the size of the smallest disk in the array. Although the remaining space is technically still usable, the data stored on the remaining space would not benefit by the RAID configuration. This is yet another reason to buy disks all of the same make and model.

Click on Fault Tolerance | Create Stripe Set With Parity. Disk Administrator will ask you to select the size of the stripe set. You'd typically select the default (largest size) and click OK. All the disks are now given a single drive letter. Note that some of this space will be used for the parity information. For example, if you have four 2GB disks, the maximum size of the stripe set will be 8GB, although 2GB of this will be used for the parity information.

To commit the changes to the registry, click on Partition | Commit Changes Now. You will need to restart NT to initialize and format the stripe set.

When the system restarts, run the Disk Administrator and format the stripe set as either FAT or NTFS. You should see the message "Stripe Set with Parity #N [INITIALIZING]" in the status bar. Once this has completed, you can start using the stripe set.

RECOVERING A FAILED STRIPED DRIVE When one of the drives fails, you should immediately back up the stripe set, as it is no longer fault tolerant. You might notice that disk response is particularly slow. This is because the RAID software must calculate the data on the missing disk. It does this by looking at the stripes on all of the other disks. Use the following steps to replace the failed disk and regenerate the data:

1. Back up the system and shut down.
2. Replace the failed disk with a tested, burned-in disk of the same or larger size.
3. Restart the computer.
4. Open Disk Administrator; select the stripe set and the new disk.
5. Click on Fault Tolerance | Regenerate to start the regeneration process.
6. Quit the Disk Administrator and restart NT.

After you reboot, NT will work in the background to reconstruct the data and parity on the new disk. One major disadvantage of using software RAID level 5 is that you need to power down the system to fix the hard disk. This restriction is removed in some hardware solutions and will be discussed next.

External RAID Arrays

The software RAID solutions outlined earlier are included with NT Server, so all you need to provide is the disk drives. The drawbacks for software solutions are that they only run on NT Server and they are slower than hardware solutions. Also, a software problem may render the fault-tolerant system useless, and software solutions use precious CPU cycles.

Third-party hardware vendors manufacture external RAID arrays of all sizes and capabilities. Some vendors support hot-swappable drives. This enables you to replace a failed drive without powering down the system. Shown next is a table listing some hardware manufacturers of RAID systems that use the SCSI interface and work with Windows NT.

Vendor	Capacity (GB)	Number of Disks	RAID Levels Supported	Price ($US)	Contact
Artecon	12 to 783	9 per enclosure	0, 1, 3, 5	6,500 and up	www.artecon.com
DynaTek Automation Systems	18-144	2-20	0, 1, 3, 4, 5	4,400 to 44,800	www.dynatek.ca
Legacy Storage Systems	4 to 108	8 to 12	0, 1, 3, 5	6,000 to 40,000	www.legacy.ca
nStor	2 to 9	6 to 8	0, 1, 3, 5	11,000 to 31,800	www.nstor.com
Storage Computer	54 to 16,000	12 to 45	0, 1, 3, 5, 7, 10	65,000 to more than 400,000	www.storage.com
Storage Dimensions	Up to 546 per adapter	6 to 12 per adapter	0, 1, 3, 5	5,000 to 35,000	www.storagedimensions .com

Table 3-2.   External RAID Hardware Vendors

CLUSTERING

A *cluster* is defined as a distributed system of two or more computers that can be used as a unified computer resource. This affords the user improved availability, because if one system in the cluster fails, the other can take over the duties of the first. Another advantage of clusters is increased scalability. Clusters make it easy to add components to the collection of computers when the load requires it. You simply take a computer offline to service it, while the cluster continues to attend to the workload. Management is also simplified, in theory, because you can manage groups of systems as if they were a single computer.

Cluster technology is nothing new to the field of computers. UNIX systems have been using clustering for more than two decades and have had fault tolerance, scalability, and global administration during that time. The transition from mainframes to minicomputers to Intel-based PCs has been quite recent, however. The cost of ownership for a cluster of PCs running NT is estimated to be about 20 percent of its UNIX counterparts. Since the cost of UNIX clusters is quite high (usually much greater than $US 100,000) and they are difficult to configure and maintain, administrators are interested in clustering with NT, even though the technology is relatively immature. To this end, Microsoft has created a suite of programs and a set of Application Programming

Interfaces (APIs) for clustering called the Cluster service (code-named Wolfpack) that runs on NT Server. Some third-party vendors decided not to wait for Microsoft and started creating their own clustering solutions.

Types of Clusters

Clustering software comes in two models: the shared disk model and the shared nothing model. In the *shared disk* model, any computer (node) in the cluster can access any hard drive on any of the other nodes. If there is contention for the disk, a Distributed Lock Manager (DLM) will intervene and control access to the resource. The DLM increases network traffic and puts some additional demand on the CPU resources of the cluster.

In the *shared nothing* model, each node uses and owns its own disk resources. If one node requests data belonging to another, it must ask the owner, who in turn passes the desired information back to the requester. In the event of a hardware failure, another node can take ownership of the resources on the failed computer. All NT clustering solutions are of the shared nothing type, and most are made up of only two nodes. There are three basic types of two-node clusters: Active/Active, Active/Passive, and Totally Redundant.

Figure 3-10 illustrates the basic configuration used by many clustering solutions. Two nodes use their own hard drive for the OS and applications, but access the same disk array. They are also connected to the same network segment. Since the network segment is a single point of failure here, you can connect both nodes to another segment via two additional NICs.

The nodes are connected to each other via a crossover cable so they know the status of the other node or so they can keep synchronized. Some vendors use proprietary connection, while others use a basic Transmission Control Protocol/Internet Protocol (TCP/IP) connection over Ethernet.

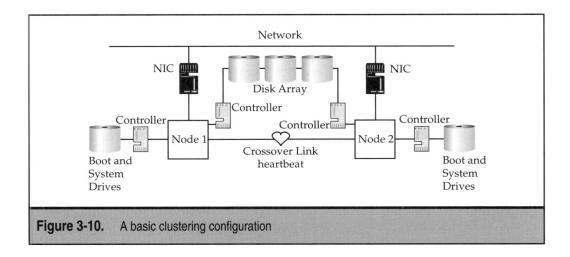

Figure 3-10.   A basic clustering configuration

Active/Active

In the Active/Active model both computers in the cluster serve requests for CPU processing. This is an excellent configuration for getting the most punch for your CPU dollars. Some software solutions even provide load balancing between the two nodes. Presently, however, each node must run its own applications and doesn't share databases (for example, one node runs SQL Server while the other runs Internet Information Server).

The main advantage of two-node clusters is the added redundancy. If one machine fails, the other one takes over the processing workload. In the example illustrated in Figure 3-10, the single node would then run both SQL Server and the Internet Information Server. There is typically a delay of 15 to 90 seconds for this switch to take place. This may be long enough for connections to the now-failed computer to be dropped. Therefore, users connected to the failed server would have to reestablish their connection to the cluster.

Active/Standby

This model is the same as the Active/Active model except that the Standby node sits idle waiting for the first node to fail. The only advantage to these systems is that the software usually has a lower cost. However, you are still buying two nodes and only getting the CPU power of one of them. This method of clustering also requires 15 to 90 seconds of switch-over time.

Totally Redundant

The Active/Active and Active/Standby methods typically use the same RAID drive array running at level 1 (mirroring). In a totally redundant system, every component in the first node is duplicated in a second node. They run the same code simultaneously and are linked together (heartbeat) by use of special clustering software. Although you only use half of the CPU power you have paid for, the switch-over time is less than one second and is virtually imperceptible to users.

Since the two nodes are connected via a 100BaseT network link, the nodes may be located in separate buildings or across campus. If one building should go down, the other will continue without a disruption of service.

Microsoft Cluster Service (Wolfpack)

In 1995 Microsoft set out to bring a software clustering solution to Windows NT Server. This solution is called the Cluster service, but carried the code name Wolfpack for the duration of its development. Currently Wolfpack is available as a stand-alone product for Intel- and Alpha-based systems. Both nodes of a two-node cluster must have the same type of processor. Microsoft checks out hardware vendors' cluster solutions as it does with other hardware and posts compatible devices on the Wolfpack Hardware Compatibility List (WHCL). It is expected that all major PC manufacturers will soon be offering a clustering solution that is compatible with Wolfpack. It is important to purchase a system that is on the WHCL, because many problems with configuring clusters are a result of incompatible hardware.

In addition to the clustering software, Wolfpack also includes a set of APIs for third-party vendors to create applications that can take advantage of the cluster. For example, programmers could make their current application easier to install on a cluster or allow it to scale if more than one node is available in the cluster. Microsoft is planning on using the APIs within Wolfpack to allow their Transaction Server to use the same SQL database on a two-node cluster. They are also updating the applications BackOffice to work within a cluster.

Phase 1

Wolfpack design was implemented in two phases. The first phase of the Wolfpack is called a *fail-over solution*. It uses the Active/Active 2 node model for system redundancy. As mentioned earlier, the two machines run applications, but they cannot run the same instance of an application. When one system fails, the other assumes the first's workload. Therefore, you should plan on using the processors at less than 50 percent utilization each. Otherwise when the second node takes over the duties, you will experience another kind of failure. The server CPU utilization could hit 100 percent. Future applications that take advantage of the Wolfpack APIs will be able to load-balance the workload to better use the processors.

Phase 2

The second phase is called *multiple-node solution*. Phase 2 will enable more than two nodes in the cluster. The reliability of the two-node cluster will still be there. Since the load is balanced among the members of the cluster, true scalability is finally achieved. When the load is too great for the cluster, another node, disk, or additional memory could be added until the load is met. This sort of incremental scalability is highly prized in the ever-changing world of information technology. Ideally, common PCs could be used in the multiple-node solution, reducing the cost of ownership. However, because many clustering solutions use proprietary hardware, the cost can quickly skyrocket.

Third-Party Cluster Solutions

Third-party vendors did not wait around for Microsoft to develop Wolfpack. Therefore some of the products are more mature than Wolfpack. They offer greater functionality and enhanced features compared with Wolfpack, such as using clusters in a heterogeneous environment, including more than two nodes, and including computers running NT Workstation. Some of the hardware solutions use proprietary hardware, which makes it more difficult to scale later by use of standard computers. Some of these systems are even packaged in a single box. However, several vendors have flexible choices for hardware selection and use a proprietary software solution now but are Wolfpack ready. Table 3-3 lists some NT cluster solutions.

Vendor/ Application	Cluster Type	Hardware Implementation	Max Number of Nodes	Dynamic Load Balancing	Price ($US)	Contact
Amdahl/ LifeKeeper	Active/ Active Active/ Standby	Proprietary	3	No	30,720 to 93,737	www.amdahl.com
Cubix/ RemoteServ/ IS	Active/ Active	Any	4,094	Yes	1,875	www.cubix.com
Data General/ NT cluster in a box	Active/ Active	Proprietary	2	No	110,000	www.veritas.com
Marathon Technologies / Endurance 4000	Fault Tolerant	Proprietary	2	No	24,999 not including hardware	www.marathontec hnologies.com
Microsoft/ Wolfpack	Active/ Active Active/ Standby	Any on HCL	Phase 1: 2 Phase 2: ?	Phase 1: No Phase 2: Yes	Not yet determined	www.Microsoft .com
Octopus/ SASO	Active/ Active Active/ Standby	Any	Unlimited	No	1,499 for SASO software	www.octopustech .com
Vinca/ Standby Server	Active/ Standby	Proprietary	2	No	3,995	ww.vinca .com

Table 3-3. Third-Party Cluster Solutions

BACKUPS

Even if you have a redundant array of disks running on a cluster, you still need to back up your data. Often administrators mistakenly think that because they have a fault-tolerant disk system, they don't need backups. Fault-tolerant systems are best at safeguarding against data loss between backups. RAID systems and clusters can protect against loss due to down time. Backups, especially offsite backups, are essential to the protection of your data and should be part of your reliability through redundancy plan.

Media Choices

Tape used to be the only medium used for external backups. Now you can choose from a variety of media formats and configurations. The main differences among the types are the speed of data transfer and total storage size. You will, of course, pay more for a 500GB tape library compared with a simple 4mm DAT drive.

A major consideration is finding a drive that not only stores the vast quantity of data on your systems, but also does so in the window of opportunity you have to execute a backup. This is the time when your servers are not being heavily used and the necessary CPU power and network throughput is available for you to perform your backup. Your backup solution (software included) must deal with this ever-shrinking window.

Tape Media

Tape media have been used for decades to provide reliable copies of important data. They remain the most popular choice today because they have massive storage capacity and relatively low cost per megabyte (compared with hard disks or optical media). New advances in tape technology have increased the capacity of tapes and the speed of the tape devices. Also, hardware vendors have created autoloaders and tape libraries to automate the processing of changing tapes.

4MM DAT   The 4mm Digital Audiotape (DAT) format is the most widely used format today. It has a low profile and relatively large storage capacity. DDS-1 tapes have a capacity of only 2GB, although these are almost extinct now. The next generation of DDS was called DDS-2 and has 8GB of native storage space. Today we have DDS-3 technology—a single tape can hold up to 12GB (24GB with compression) of data, and tape drives can transfer data at a rate of 2.4 MB/sec using a Fast-Wide SCSI-2 interface.

DAT is still used with systems that have a total backup demand less than the capacity of one tape (thus, manually changing the tape is unnecessary). One disadvantage of the 4mm DAT format is that the tape itself is sensitive to read and write operations and can wear out over time. A typical tape can sustain several hundred backups. However, since the header on the tape gets read for every backup operation, a restore of one small file wears out the tape just as much as a full backup or restore.

DIGITAL LINEAR TAPE   The Digital Linear Tape (DLT) format by Quantum uses a half-inch tape, and is faster and more reliable than the DAT format. The capacity of each tape is up to 20GB (40GB with compression), and DLT drives support data rates up to 5 MB/sec. DLT delivers performance advantages over DAT systems by recording and reading multiple channels simultaneously. Compared with DAT, DLT has a lower capacity per unit length of tape, but is better suited for quick reads or writes to the tape. To increase performance and total capacity, tape libraries support multiple drives and hundreds of tapes (see "Autoloaders and Tape Libraries").

ADVANCED INTELLIGENT TAPE   The Advanced Intelligent Tape (AIT) is an 8mm format created by Sony and is more reliable than the original 8mm format from Exabyte. Sony uses a new technique called the Advanced Metal Evaporated (AME) method to create the tapes. The tape has a carbon protective layer that helps the tape withstand the high speeds of the newer drives. Each tape can hold 25GB or about 50GB with compression because Sony has coated the tape with a layer made up of 100 percent cobalt, which doubles the magnetic flux density of the medium, allowing more data to be stored on the tape.

Autoloaders and Tape Libraries

In the enterprise environment you will likely have more data to be backed up than can fit on a single tape. Previously you had to have an army of technicians around to change the tapes. Now machines called *autoloaders* or *tape libraries* do it for you.

Tape autoloaders are used in smaller installations, because they only have one tape drive and usually have fewer than a dozen tapes. You might use autoloaders in a network if it has enough server disk space to fit on one tape, but you want to keep a tape copy for each day of the week. The autoloader would replace the manual operation of changing tapes every day. The performance is the same as with a single tape device, because autoloaders have only a single tape drive.

For larger amounts of data, you will require a tape library. These devices house multiple drives and may use many tapes (100+). Tape libraries are designed for simultaneous reading and writing to multiple drives. To help you fit your backup into the window of opportunity, throughput is increased, because more drives are being used in parallel. In addition, because libraries use multiple drives, you get the benefit of redundancy. If one of the drives should fail, the others will continue to function.

Optical Media

Today, you are not restricted to tape for backup purposes. Optical media has been around for years, but has become affordable only recently. Optical media has certain advantages over tape, such as random access and a longer storage life. Some of the disadvantages associated with optical media, such as small capacity, read-only access, and long access times, are beginning to disappear.

COMPACT DISK RECORDABLE   Initially, CD-ROMs were read-only and were not used for backup purposes. The first recordable CD-ROMs (CD-Rs) cost hundreds of thousands of dollars. Only large corporations or specialty shops could afford them. The cost has decreased significantly since they were first introduced, making their use more common. The capacity is the same as the capacity of standard CD-ROMs (650MB). A limitation of the CD-R technology is that the directory structure must conform to the International Standards Organization (ISO) 9660 file format. This ensures the disk can be read by DOS, Macintosh, and UNIX systems, but imposes a limit of eight subdirectory levels and filenames that must be made up of only uppercase letters, numbers, and underscores. By far the largest disadvantage of CD-Rs is that they can only be written once.

COMPACT DISK REWRITABLE   The rewritable CD-ROM (CD-RW) was developed to address the simple limitation of the write-once CD-ROMs. CD-RWs share many of the other limitations of the CD-Rs, including limited capacity and slow access. The advanced technology used to create the disks renders them unreadable by most CD-ROM drives. Also, the new drives have a higher price tag. Nonetheless, they have enjoyed reasonable success in the marketplace.

DIGITAL VERSATILE DISK   The most recent technological advance in CD-ROM technology has been the Digital Versatile Disk (DVD). It has transformed the CD-ROM into a massive storage media—a single platter can store up to 17GB of data. To achieve this massive storage capacity, the density of the data that can be stored to the disk has been dramatically increased. Researchers and developers have managed to place two layers of data per side. Promoters for this media tout that a single disk can hold video games, data, movies, and the movie soundtrack in four languages.

DVD drives spin three times faster than normal CD-ROMs. This allows them to have a transfer rate of about 10 MB/sec. This new technology makes DVD disks unreadable by standard CD-ROM drives, although DVD drives can read standard CD-ROMs. Currently, DVD drives are read-only. Manufacturers have hinted at creating a rewritable version in the future.

MAGNETO-OPTICAL   Magneto-optical (MO) drives appear in two forms: 3½-inch and 5¼-inch platters. The small disks can hold about 650MB, while the larger disks can fit 2.6GB. Although the drives are relatively expensive, they have fairly short access times. A platter can be placed in the drive and accessed just like a hard disk. Even so, magneto-optical drives are best suited for storing large files that are only accessed occasionally, and the extra delay is not offputting. You can also use them for backing up data; however, the cost of the platters may prove prohibitive.

Like tapes, multiple optical devices can be grouped together for larger operations. A library of recordable CD-ROMs or magneto-optical platters is called a *jukebox*. Although the random access of the optical media decreases the read times, the cost per megabyte is quite a bit more than with tapes.

Open Files

Since enterprise servers run around the clock, there will always be files that are open and in use on the server. Some backup software programs, such as the built-in backup program in NT (NTBackup), cannot back up files when they are open. These files are simply skipped during the backup process. Some of the open files could be part of that mission-critical database or queued data for the corporate e-mail system. It is not always possible to shut down such applications just so you can back them up.

Vendors have recognized this problem, and now many of them employ plug-in software components called *agents* to allow their software to back up open files without disrupting ongoing transactions or jeopardizing data integrity. Some popular agents include those for databases, e-mail applications, and Microsoft BackOffice.

NTBackup and Scheduling

The backup software included with NT is an anemic version of commercially available backup packages. Nonetheless, it is free and can be useful for smaller backup jobs. The current version does not support scheduled backups, making backing up a manual process. To circumvent this problem, you can schedule NTBackup from the command line using the at command (discussed next). By providing the correct arguments in a batch file, you can connect to shared drives on Windows 95 and Windows 3.11 machines, and on other NT systems. For more information about the NTBackup command and its arguments, type **ntbackup /?** at the command prompt.

To schedule the batch file to run at a specific time, use the AT command. The AT command is a command-line program that allows you to schedule the execution of programs or batch files at regular intervals. If you have the NT Resource Kit, you can use the Command Scheduler (Winat.exe) to perform the same task. To automate the backup process:

1. Write a script (batch file) that contains commands to mount network drives.

2. In the script, include commands that instruct NTBackup to add each drive to a tape backup.

3. Schedule when you want the script to run.

Below is a sample script to back up the local machine's C drive and a drive on a remote NT system.

```
1. rem The next line backs up the local C drive.
2. ntbackup backup c: /d "Comment here"/b/hc:on/t normal/l
   "%windir%\LogFiles\backup.log"/tape:0
3. rem The next line mounts and backs up a shared drive on a remote NT system.
4. net use x: \\<workstation>\<sharename> <password> /user:<domainname>\
   username
5. ntbackup backup x: /a/d "Comment here"/hc:on/t normal/l
   "%windir%\LogFiles\backup.log"/tape:0
6. net use x: /delete
```

The second line directs NTBackup to create a backup of the local C drive (ntbackup backup C:\), back up the local registry (/b), use hardware compression (/hc:on), make a normal backup type (/t normal), and write messages to a log file (/l "%windir%\ LogFiles\backup.log").

Line 4 uses the net use command to mount a remote drive. The user must provide a valid user name and password for an account on that remote system. Then line 5 instructs NTBackup to add this drive to the tape. Note that it is not possible to back up registries on remote machines. To fully back up remote NT systems, you should create an Emergency Repair disk, or use third-party backup software that can accomplish this.

The last line of the script disconnects from the remote drive and frees up the drive letter. You can repeat this mounting and backing up process for as many drives as you can fit on the tape.

> ***NT 5 NOTE:*** The new NTBackup program included with NT 5 will support autoloaders and will have the capability of scheduling backup jobs.

Third-Party Backup Applications

When you need to back up more than just the departmental server, you should consider third-party software. The increase in speed, flexibility, and features, such as a backup agent to back up its files while they are open, makes these products worthwhile.

Many of these programs include management tools that allow you to keep track of thousands of tapes and to remotely administer your backup systems. Since these programs are quite similar to each other, we suggest evaluating several before making a decision to purchase.

Some popular third-party backup applications include:

Cheyenne's ArcServe	www.cheyenne.com
Seagate's Backup Exec	www.seagatesoftware.com
Stac's Replica	www.stac.com

Placing a Backup System

When considering the location of a network-based backup server, you should pay special attention to where the servers and their data are located. Even if you have the largest, fastest tape library available, capable of backing up hundreds of gigabytes of data at many megabytes per second, you might still only get a paltry amount of data onto the tape. The bottleneck is not in your new tape device or even in the computer system running it. You probably have placed the tape backup device too far from the data it is accessing, or on a network segment that cannot deliver the data fast enough to the backup device. For example, if your tape drives can write data at 10MB/sec and you are sitting on a 10Mb/sec Ethernet segment, the most data you can provide the backup device is 1.25MB/sec (10Mb Ethernet) in an ideal environment. You should consider placing this device on a faster network segment, such as 100Mb Ethernet or an FDDI ring.

There are several things you can do to reduce network bottleneck:

▼ Place the backup device as close as possible to the data you are backing up. For example, you could place the tape device on the same network segment as the data servers.

■ Multihome your servers and place them on more than one LAN segment. Use the fastest LAN technology you can get, such as 100 Mb Ethernet or the Fiber Distributed Data Interface (FDDI).

▲ Do not even consider backing up over a WAN connection—not only will you overload the WAN link for the duration of the backup, but also the small amount of data you'll get onto tape is not worth the headache.

All these suggestions, when properly applied, should help increase the data throughput to your backup system.

DIRECTORY REPLICATOR SERVICE

Normally you would use the Replicator service to distribute user information to servers throughout your domain. You can also use it to secure against data loss. Basically, you set up an NT Server to push or export directories to other servers or workstations. These directories can contain any information you want to place there. Open files, however, cannot be replicated, so it is best to replicate read-only files. Some possible uses include:

▼ **Copying logon scripts**—If you use more than one domain controller, you should replicate users' logon scripts from the Primary Domain Controller (PDC) to the Backup Domain Controllers (BDCs). Not only does this allow each BDC to provide the script, it allows you to maintain a single source for all scripts.

■ **Mandatory user profiles**—You should replicate mandatory user profiles from the PDC to the BDCs so that the profile can be centrally administrated. This also reduces the amount of network traffic due to downloading the profile at logon.

▲ **Copy frequently accessed files**—Replicate read-only files that are accessed throughout your domain. Placing these files closer to the users will reduce network traffic while still maintaining central administration of the files.

Redundant Databases

Some NT networking applications have built-in database redundancy. They are configured at their installation to share their databases with other systems. These include the Domain Name System (DNS) service, the Windows Internet Naming Service (WINS), and the user database that is copied from the PDC to the BDCs. One networking service that does not have automatic database replication is the database used in the Dynamic Host Configuration Protocol (DHCP) service. You can place a copy of the DHCP database into the export directory of the DHCP server to have it replicated to other systems for redundancy.

Setting Up Import/Export Systems

You can use the Directory Replicator service to copy the contents of a directory to one or several NT Workstations or Servers. You start by setting up the computer that will be sending the data to be replicated (called the *export server*). This computer must be an NT Server, although it does not need to be a domain controller. The computers that receive the replicated data are called *import computers* and can be NT Servers or Workstations. The export server replicates all data in the *Systemroot*\system32\repl\export directory and any subdirectories below it. If you start the Directory Replicator service, this directory is administratively shared as REPL$. Replicated data is placed in the *Systemroot*\system32\repl\import directory on the import computers. By default, logon scripts are placed in the *Systemroot*\system32\repl\export\scripts directory and placed in the *Systemroot*\system32\repl\import\scripts directory on the import computers.

Export Server

Before initializing the Directory Replicator service on the server, you need to log on as an administrator. Make a user account that will be used to run the service. Assign this account to the Backup Operators and Replicator groups, and make sure the password is set to never expire and that this user can log on at all hours. If you use an NTFS partition, the replicator user should have full control rights within the export directories.

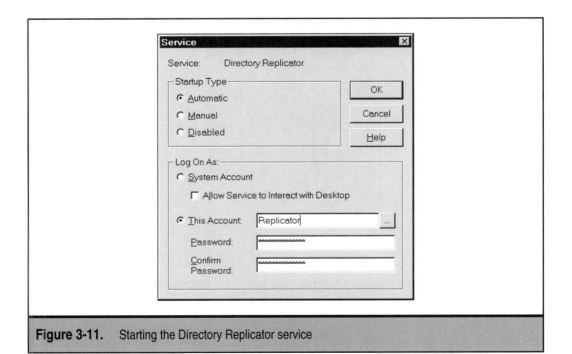

Figure 3-11. Starting the Directory Replicator service

Start the Directory Replicator service from the Control Panel | Services menu. Set the startup type to Automatic. Click on the Account radio button, and enter the name of the user you created to log on as this service, as shown in Figure 3-11.

Configure directory replication by opening the Server Manager and selecting the computer you want to set up directory replication on. Click Properties under the Computer menu item. This will bring up another window that will enable you to fully administer this computer. Click on the Replication button so you can configure the replication settings.

From the window illustrated in Figure 3-12, set the directories you will export or import and the list of import computers you want to grant permission to receive your exported data. Select the Export Directories radio button and verify the path listed. Select an import computer by clicking on the Add button and selecting the computer from the list.

NOTE: You can place locks on files and check the status of the replication by clicking on the Manage button.

It is always a good idea to have the export server also act as the import computer to its own data. This provides you with a local copy of the data in case of accidental removal of the export files. To complete the export/import relationship, you need to configure the import computers.

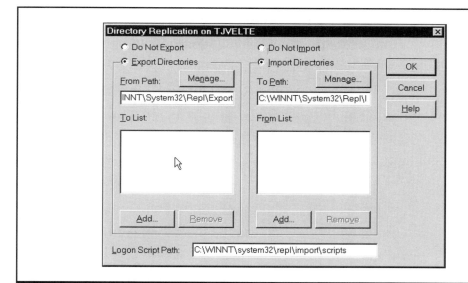

Figure 3-12. Setting the import and export directories

Import System

As administrator, create a user account as you did for the export server (only assign the user to the Replicator group) if the machine does not belong to the domain or to a trusting domain (see Chapter 2). Otherwise, the account you made for the export server should be able to run the Directory Replicator service on the import computer. Again, this user must have full control privileges over the REPL$ directory if NTFS is used.

Set the Directory Replicator service to start automatically using the replicator account you created earlier. We will assume that the import computer is an NT Workstation, although the same procedure is applied to an NT Server. To configure the import computer, open the Server icon in the Control Panel and select the Replication button. This calls up the Directory Replication window, as shown in Figure 3-13. Click on the Import Directories radio button, and then on the Add button to select the source of the files. Choose the name of the server you set up at the export server and click OK. You can check the health of the export/import relationship at any time by clicking on the Manage button on the export server of the import computer.

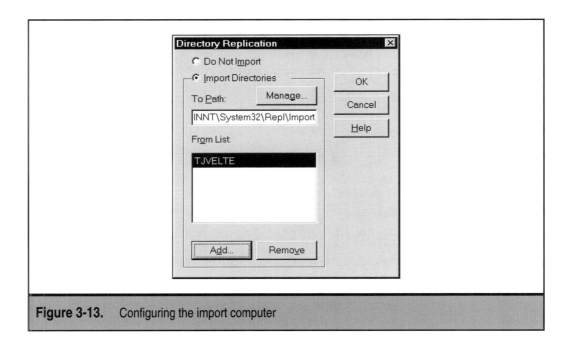

Figure 3-13.   Configuring the import computer

NOTE: NT checks by default every five minutes to see if it needs to copy any changed files to the import computers. To manually change this interval, edit the Registry setting in HKEY_LOCAL_ MACHINE\SYSTEM\CurrentControlSet\Services\Replicator\Parameters. Create a key called **Interval** (REG_DWORD). The data field should contain a number in minutes for the new interval.

CHAPTER 4

Network Administration

On all but the smallest networks, it quickly becomes evident to any system administrator that going around to the console of each system on the network to upgrade software, configure a service, or troubleshoot a problem is difficult—if not impossible. Fortunately, there are numerous tools that can reduce the legwork of network administration. However, these tools are often poorly documented, and detailed information regarding the various network administration applications can be difficult to find. This chapter examines the most useful of the integrated and third-party administrative tools and gives clear examples of their use.

SYSTEMS MANAGEMENT SERVER

Systems Management Server (SMS) is a collection of programs created by Microsoft to ease the burden of administration in an enterprise environment and to help reduce the total cost of ownership of an NT network. It is a large collection of programs brought together under one name. It is beyond the scope of this book to discuss all the capabilities and configuration options of SMS, but we will cover three of its most important and impressive features: hardware/software inventory, software distribution, and remote diagnostics tools.

SMS is organized in a hierarchical structure. At the top is the central site. This site has a SMS system and a SQL database server that stores system-wide information. Beneath this site can be either *primary* or *secondary* sites. A primary site also contains its own SQL database; local administrators can control this site and all sites beneath it in the hierarchy. Secondary sites do not have their own databases, but report inventory and status information to a database higher up the hierarchy.

NOTE: The central site and all primary sites require their own SQL servers. For enhanced performance, it is recommended that the SQL server is a different system from the SMS system.

Using the client/server model, SMS can manage a large number of client computers. Clients run software that allows the SMS to examine their hardware and software configurations. Administrators can present applications for the user to install or force an installation on the remote machines. Administrators may also view clients' desktops and take control of their PC. Obviously, you will have to work out the security and politics of this sort of authority so it is not abused.

A client can be one of many different kinds of workstations including MS-DOS, Windows 3.11, Windows 95, Windows NT, OS/2, and Macintosh. You can use IPX, TCP/IP, NetBEUI, and AppleTalk protocols to communicate with your clients. Not all features are available for every type of client, and you will need an NT Server running Services for Macintosh to reach Macintosh-based clients.

To include clients as part of the SMS environment, the client must first run a batch file. This file is included on the SMS system and is part of a shared drive (\SMS_SHR) residing on the SMS system. The client must make a connection to this share and run the

Runsms.bat file there. This batch file can be run automatically by including it as part of a logon script so your users don't have to do anything to become part of the SMS program. However, you may have to make a few modifications to non NT or Windows 95 clients, depending on what services you plan to offer these clients.

Hardware/Software Inventory

Once the clients are installed, they automatically update the SMS system with their hardware inventory. After the initial client setup, you control how often the inventory is taken. All initial and updated inventory information is stored in the SMS system in the SQL database.

Sites

Figure 4-1 shows the main view for the SMS Administrator GUI. You can see three windows here: the Queries, Sites, and Jobs windows. We will discuss the other windows in a moment, but for now let's look at the Sites window. This windows allows you to navigate through the hierarchical structure of your organization and focus on a single machine.

When you have found the computer you want to learn more about, simply double-click on it, and you will see a window similar to that in Figure 4-2. Here we have

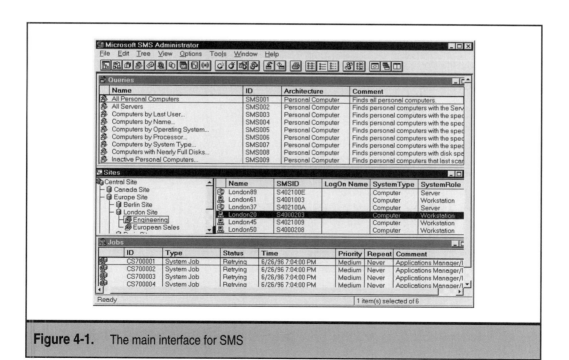

Figure 4-1.   The main interface for SMS

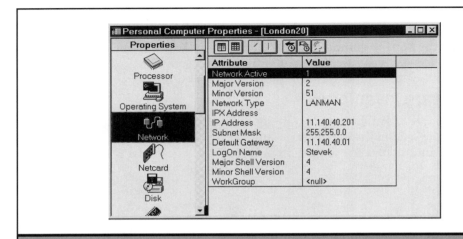

Figure 4-2. Using SMS to get detailed information about a computer

selected a computer in London called London20. On the left of the window is a list of properties we can examine for the computer. They include the following categories:

▼ Identification

■ Workstation Status

■ Processor

■ Operating System

■ Network

■ Network Card

■ PC Memory

■ Video

■ Mouse

■ Services

■ Environment

▲ NT Diagnostics

NOTE: You can also run what SMS calls its Help Desk. This is used to control the computer remotely, reboot it, communicate with the user, or move files to or from the computer. You can also run the NT diagnostics program on the remote computer, the network monitor (see Chapter 12), and NT administrative commands (covered in the Networking Commands section in this chapter).

In Figure 4-2, the network properties are displayed. You can see information about this computer's network settings, although you cannot change values here. Some properties, such as disk drives, may have more than one entry, in which case you can scroll through them to view the attributes of a specific drive.

To inventory software, software auditing must be configured on the client. Then you can monitor software that has been installed on that computer. A newly added property will be listed under the Properties heading when you examine a computer's software inventory. You will be able to view the software's name, the file size(s), the application path, and when it was installed.

Queries

Because you might have thousands of computers in the SMS database, you need some way to select computers other than just by location. Fortunately, SMS includes an interactive query mechanism. You can select computers based on any of hundreds of attributes. Some predefined queries are listed in the top panel of Figure 4-1. You could, for example, search for all servers that are running NT 4.0 but do not have Service Pack 3 installed. This would allow you to create a list of target computers for installation of Service Pack 3. The flexibility provided by the interface creates a very powerful tool to help determine what is deployed on the network and where certain resources are concentrated.

Software Distribution

Software is distributed by sending what Microsoft calls *packages* to the SMS clients you want to install the software. You create a package by bundling all the files that are required to install the application along with any scripts or answer files that will automate the installation. Many Microsoft applications already have predefined packages so you don't have to manually create them.

Creating a Package

Before you can create a new package, you'll need to gather all the files that should be included with the package. Next, check to ensure you have adequate disk space on the site servers that will be distributing the package. You should plan on three to four times the disk space used by the source files. Some of this space is used to compress and decompress the source files. If you have a package definition file (PDF), you should use that to define the properties of the package, otherwise follow these steps to create a package.

1. Open the Packages windows from the SMS Administrator.
2. Choose File | New.
3. In the Name text box type the name of the new package.
4. Add more descriptive text in the Comments box.

5. Choose the appropriate button to define the properties of the package you are creating. Your choices are:

■ **Workstation**—Defines the source location and the command used to install the package on client computers.

■ **Sharing**—Used to control if and how a package is distributed from other servers.

■ **Inventory**—Defines how you want to maintain an inventory on the package.

6. Click the OK button and the package should appear in the Packages window.

Sending a Package

You can view packages by clicking on the Packages window in the SMS Administrator window, as shown in Figure 4-3. To set the properties of the package you double-click on the package. This allows you to control exactly what clients are supported, what commands are run, and where the files for the package are located. You can even set how this package will appear in the inventory list of distributed applications.

To apply a package, simply drag and drop it over a computer or a group of computers in the Sites window. This will call up another window (see Figure 4-4) that gives you control over who will receive the application and how it will be delivered. Here you set the mode of installation, which is usually Custom, Typical, Compact, Complete, or

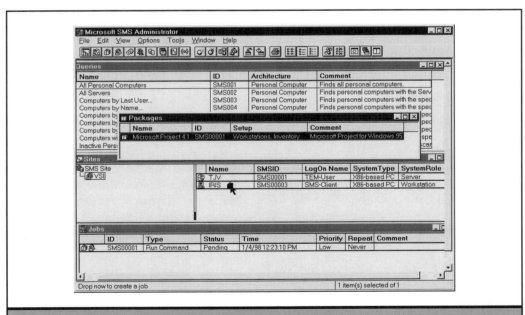

Figure 4-3. Applying a package to a workstation

Uninstall. These choices coincide with the options that are usually available when an application is installed manually. You also set the time and date the package will first be offered to the client. If you don't want to make installation by the client optional, you can force the client to install the package. You can also force installation after a set period of time if the user repeatedly declines the installation offer.

To ease the burden on a SMS system and reduce network traffic, packages are often placed on distribution servers. Distribution servers might be local file and print servers or servers deployed specifically as SMS distribution servers. You can designate which distribution servers will distribute a particular package. After you click OK in the Job Details window, the job will be entered into the SMS job queue. A new job listing can then be seen in the Jobs window. This makes it easy to check the status of each job you start.

Installing a Package

Once the package has been sent from the SMS system or distribution server, the client can install it via the Package Command Manager (part of the SMS client setup). When the client opens this program, a new package will be ready for installation. The user will also be informed if this is a mandatory installation or when it will become mandatory. All the user has to do is click on the Execute button. Unless the package was marked for custom installation (which requires user input), the user is not prompted for any information.

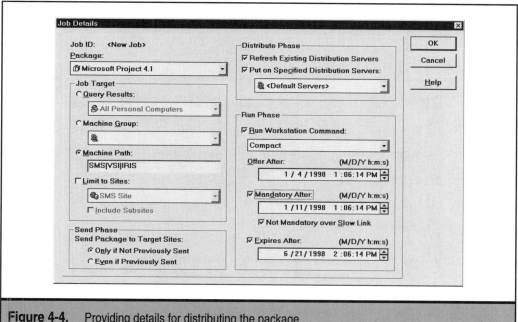

Figure 4-4.   Providing details for distributing the package

The package now moves from the Pending Commands window to the Executed Commands window, as shown in Figure 4-5.

If a package doesn't require user input, you can install it on NT Servers when no one is logged on. This can be accomplished by making the package mandatory to install and running the process in background mode. To run the installation in the background, the package must not write to the console or try to display windows or dialog boxes.

Remote Diagnostic Tools

The properties listed for each computer are actually a powerful set of diagnostic utilities that allow you to troubleshoot problems with that computer. Figure 4-6 displays the diagnostic utilities in the left pane. Four of these utilities (Help Desk, Windows NT Diagnostics, Network Monitor, and Windows NT Administrative Tools) are interactive. Not only can you see the settings for the remote computer, but you can also change many of them just as if you were sitting at that computer. Each of these diagnostic groups has tools that belong to it. For example, clicking on Windows NT Diagnostics reveals eight tools you can use on the remote computer.

Help Desk

The Help Desk has five tools an administrator can use to understand and fix a client's problem. The client must give the administrator certain privileges for the Help Desk to function. These are set at the client under Help Desk Options. The five Help Desk tools are:

▼ **Remote Control**—The administrator can use this tool to view the screen on a remote SMS client and take control of the keyboard and mouse operations. This works for DOS and all Windows-based clients.

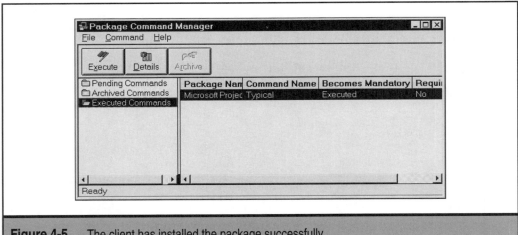

Figure 4-5.   The client has installed the package successfully

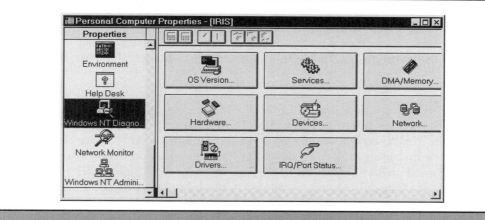

Figure 4-6.   SMS's diagnostic utilities

- **Remote Reboot**— An administrator can use this tool to restart a client's computer.

- **Remote Chat**—With Remote Chat an administrator can have a text conversation with any client. The administrator's text appears in one half of a window and the client's text appears in the other half.

- **File Transfer**—With this tool, an administrator can copy files from the client or place files on the client's system.

- ▲ **Remote Execute**—This utility allows the SMS administrator to run commands on the client's computer. DOS-based commands will open a DOS window for Window-based systems.

Windows NT Diagnostics

The Windows NT Diagnostics tools have the same function as those that appear for this utility in the Administrative Tools program group on standard NT systems. They are:

- ▼ **OS Version**—Details operating system, version, installation date, owner, and service pack level

- **Hardware**—Lists the processor type and BIOS version

- **Drivers**—Lists all the drivers on the remote system and their present status

- **Devices**—Lists the currently installed devices

- **IRQ/Port Status**—Lists the interrupts and physical memory that the ports are using

- **DMA/Memory**—Details which devices are using which DMA channels and lists the memory mapping for the devices
- **Network**—Lists the network identity for the client, basic statistics for the NIC, and the properties of the NIC although it does not detect IRQ conflicts

Network Monitor

The Network Monitor program allows you to capture frames on a network and view their contents. We will cover the Network Monitor more thoroughly in Chapter 12. If you have the appropriate agent installed on the client's computer, when you launch the Network Monitor from the SMS manager interface you can use the client as a remote network monitor. This allows you to capture traffic using the client's NIC.

Windows NT Administrative Tools

The Windows NT Administrative Tools utility has some of the same tools that are available under Administrative Tools in the Programs menu.

- **Event Viewer**—You can open the Event Viewer for the client's computer and view the system, security, or application event log.
- **Server Manager**—You can view and interact with the Server Manager that is running on the client's computer. From here you can view users, file shares, open files, and other server properties.
- **User Manager**—This is the version of User Manager that runs on the local machine as opposed to the User Manager for Domains that runs on the PDC or BDC and authenticates all users.
- **Performance Manager**—This utility allows you to view hundreds of statistics running on the local computer. If you have predefined Performance Manager charts, you can open them and watch the local statistics.
- **Event to Trap Translator**—You can configure SNMP traps that should be sent from the client. These traps can be any event that you deem important enough—from applications to system security to general system functioning.

NOTE: You must be running the SNMP agent on the client and the SNMP service and the SNMP Trap service on the SMS system to be able to catch SNMP traps and incorporate them into SMS.

THIRD-PARTY ADMINISTRATION TOOLS

We will not explore the built-in NT administration tools because we touched on them in Chapter 2, you are probably familiar with them already, and they are somewhat limited when it comes to administering an enterprise. Instead, we will focus on two third-party products you can use to administer an enterprise network full of NT systems.

These two applications do not have the same function. They are used in different areas of enterprise administration of NT networks. The first is called RoboMon; it is an automatic monitoring and alerting program with the capability to perform predefined actions based on specific conditions. The second is called Enterprise Administrator and is used to circumvent some of the limitations inherent in the User Manager for Domains. You may find it useful to use both—whether or not you use SMS.

CD NOTE: Evaluation copies of both applications are available on the CD-ROM enclosed with this book.

RoboMon

RoboMon is an NT monitoring program from Heroix Corporation **(www. robomon. com).** Not only does it monitor many aspects of computers running its software, but it can also intelligently act to correct problems or notify you so you can intervene. Table 4-1 lists the major components of RoboMon.

The brains of the program reside in what Heroix calls *rules*. Rules are small programs that resemble BASIC. RoboMon comes with more than 30 predefined rules that are ready to run. You can use the rules as they are, modify them, or create your own rules. The rules contain the logic that gives RoboMon the capability to perform actions. You run only the rules you want on only the machines you want. This process is controlled centrally.

Central Administration

You must install RoboMon on every client computer you want to administer. Fortunately, RoboMon creates a SMS package so you can easily install it on many machines if you are already running SMS.

Component	Description
Enterprise Manager	Allows you to manage RoboMon centrally
Event Monitor	Displays network-wide events
Rule Developer/Wizard	Contains GUIs for writing or modifying rules
Statistic Builder	Enables RoboMon to monitor all counters that are available to the NT Performance Monitor database (Intel platforms only)

Table 4-1.   RoboMon's Major Components

You use RoboMon's Enterprise Manager to assign rules to specific computers or groups of computers, start and stop rule processes, check the status of rule processes, and modify rule processes on any computer running RoboMon—from anywhere in the network. Figure 4-7 shows the view from the Enterprise Manager console. You can see how you can work your way down through the enterprise to view rule processes on a single computer.

Rules

Rules are usually designed to monitor a specific situation and then take action if specified thresholds are met. For example, you might have a rule that watches a particular server. If the server locks up, the rule can specify to shut down the server and restart it. A collection of rules is called a *RoboMon process*. You run these processes on remote machines, which can be monitored using RoboMon's Event Monitor.

RoboMon can tell if an undesirable situation repeats itself and can take appropriate action. For example, RoboMon can page you if the CPU utilization exceeds 95 percent three times in an hour for a particular machine.

Figure 4-8 displays RoboMon's Rule Developer window. The built-in Paging_Load rule is listed. You can see from the beginning of this rule that it is set to run every 15

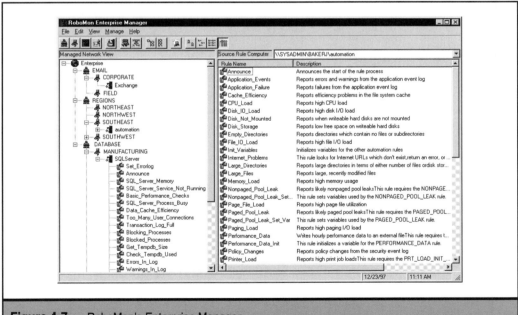

Figure 4-7.   RoboMon's Enterprise Manager

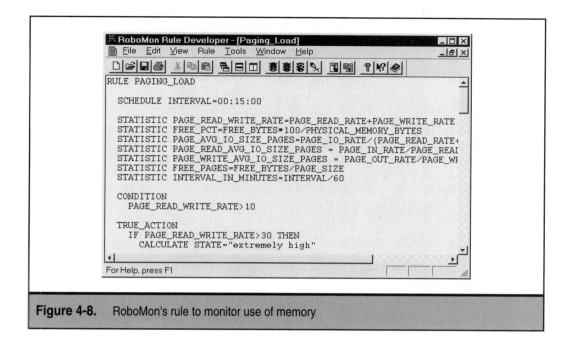

Figure 4-8.   RoboMon's rule to monitor use of memory

minutes. To modify this rule, you simply edit it and save it again. The salient features of this rule are listed in the following code:

```
CONDITION
    PAGE_READ_WRITE_RATE>10

  TRUE_ACTION
    IF PAGE_READ_WRITE_RATE>30 THEN
      CALCULATE STATE="extremely high"
      CALCULATE SEVERITY=1
    ELSE_IF PAGE_READ_WRITE_RATE>20 THEN
      CALCULATE STATE="very high"
      CALCULATE SEVERITY=2
    ELSE
      CALCULATE STATE="high"
      CALCULATE SEVERITY=3
    END_IF
```

If the variable *page_read_write* exceeds 10, the condition is met and action must be taken. A control block calculates how serious this condition is and sets variables (*state and severity*) that it uses later in the rule to notify the Event Monitor. We could add another line that e-mails the administrator when the severity variable equals one. To do so, we add the following line after the CALCULATE SEVERITY=1 line:

```
MAIL USER administrator, TEXT="Hey, I need more RAM"
```

Once we save this rule and apply it to a computer, the administrator will receive an e-mail message if the PAGE_READ_WRITE_RATE exceeds 30.

For this example, we used the unmodified Paging_Load rule and started it on the local machine. We needed to load the system heavily, so it would run out of RAM and start paging to disk. We did this by loading SMS and RoboMon at the same time. The next time the rule was run, pagefile warnings were sent to the Event Viewer displayed in Figure 4-9. There are two windows open in Figure 4-9: the Open Problems window and the Information window. The Open Problems window displays unresolved problems by order of importance. The Information window displays non-critical data about the computers it is monitoring. This data can be quite useful for troubleshooting or tuning a server. To get more information about any particular message, you simply double-click on the message.

Information Overload

You can see that it wouldn't take too many rules to inundate the system with information and problems. It's important to limit the rules to only those that are crucial and to use

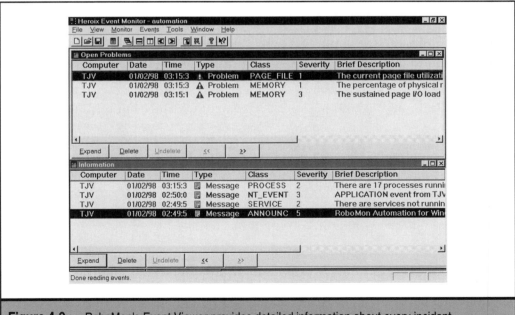

Figure 4-9.   RoboMon's Event Viewer provides detailed information about every incident

them only on those computers that warrant a high level of monitoring. Perhaps you don't want to monitor every user's pagefile usage, but monitoring the Pagefile.sys is a very powerful tool. You could use data from monitoring the Pagefile.sys to say, for example, "Eight of ten of our engineers' desktop systems were accessing their pagefile excessively last week; perhaps we should upgrade the RAM on their computers."

The power of RoboMon stems from the flexibility and intelligence that you can incorporate into your custom rules. One drawback to RoboMon is that you must familiarize yourself with the rule language to create your own rules. However, the extra time it takes to do this may be well worth it if you have many users.

Enterprise Administrator

Enterprise Administrator (EA) from Mission Critical Software **(www. missioncritical. com)** solves a limitation imposed by the built-in User Manager for Domains. By default NT has two kinds of user accounts for administering users. They are the Administrators account and the Account Operators account. The Administrator account is omnipotent and the Account Operator account has many powers, too. However, an enterprise network requires more than two levels of authority. For example, enterprise network administrators want to use the single master domain model for central management and ease of use, but one business unit or division may not feel comfortable having its users and data fall under the control of IS personnel in another division. NT doesn't include enough flexibility for controlling these accounts. This is where EA comes in.

Authority Hierarchy

EA expands on the levels of authority over user accounts by providing a whole new hierarchy of authority for user accounts. EA acts in the client/server mode so all users (clients) get authenticated via an EA server much as is done in a standard NT environment. EA acts as a proxy authentication server to the real user account database (SAM).

NT domain administrators are still the ruling authority in this new model of power. NT domain administrators create Marshals out of ordinary user accounts. The Marshals can create Territories that they can control in their specific areas. Territories may overlap with each other or Marshals can create virtual domains by keeping all Territories separate from each other. Marshals can also create Deputies. Deputies are normal users who have precisely-defined subsets of administration authority within their Territory. The Deputies actually do the administrative work. This hierarchy is illustrated in Figure 4-10.

Client and Server

For the EA model to work, everybody using the domain has to be integrated with EA. Fortunately, EA clients can be NT 3.51 (or later) Servers or Workstations, or Windows 3.11 or Windows 95 or later systems. You can use EA to easily create a SMS distribution package that provides automatic and manual distribution of the client service and is invisible to the end user. The EA server service runs on the PDC and on the BDCs. Clients can use an encrypted pathway to the server during the authentication process.

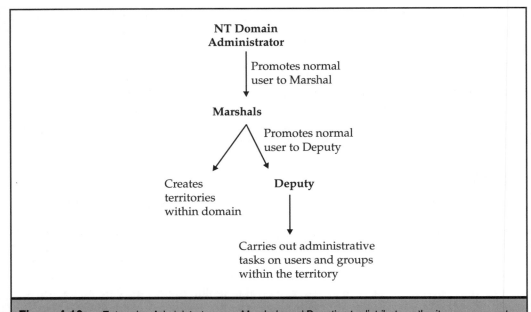

Figure 4-10. Enterprise Administrator uses Marshals and Deputies to distribute authority over accounts

You can control EA from any client if you have the appropriate authority. The GUI is similar to the User Manager for Domains, so using it is easy for users familiar with the standard User Manager for Domains. Figure 4-11 shows the window used for administration. You use tabs to control Territories, Marshals, Groups, and Deputies. After creating at least one Marshal and one Territory, you can create a Deputy to administer the Territory.

For example, I created a new Territory called HQ. Next, I appointed a Deputy to work the Territory. I decided to use the only other person who has an account in this test domain. As shown in Figure 4-12, I gave the new Deputy (my brother) limited rights in this Territory (because I don't trust him fully).

Added Functionality

The capability to distribute authority is a good enough reason to use EA. However, it also offers a number of additional improvements over the User Manager for Domains:

▼ EA comes with a set of commands you can run at the command line to fully automate most of the functions of the GUI. You can incorporate them easily into batch files or scripts.

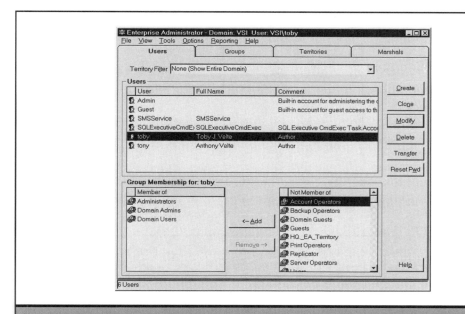

Figure 4-11.   The Enterprise Administrator's user interface

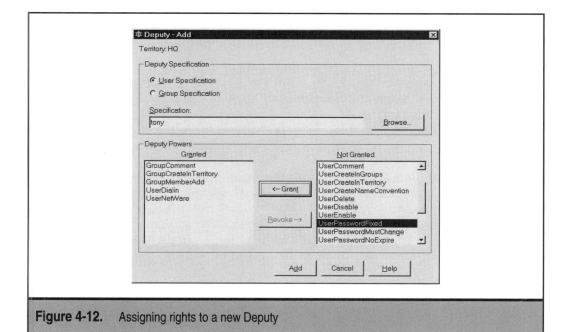

Figure 4-12.   Assigning rights to a new Deputy

- There is great flexibility about enforcing policies for all users. For example, the password strength policy allows you to set the minimum number of uppercase characters required in a password.

- EA offers extensive reporting capabilities. Not only do you see events in the application event log, but you also receive an Access database full of statistics and messages.

▲ You can automatically create home directories and shares for those directories when you create a new account.

EA is a valuable tool to help alleviate the user administration problems inherent in enterprise-wide deployment of NT. It works only in a single master domain model so you may have to make some changes to your domain model before deployment, but this drawback should be weighed against the reduced total cost of ownership that EA provides.

NT 5.0 NOTE: Many of the administrative limitations found in NT 4.0 are removed in the NT 5.0 hierarchy because organizational units (OUs) can be used to divide domains into administrative sectors. Chapter 13 covers this topic in more detail.

MICROSOFT MANAGEMENT CONSOLE

One of the biggest differences coming from Microsoft for administrators is the interface they will use to manage NT systems. Microsoft has eliminated the individual and disparate administrative applications and replaced them with the Microsoft Management Console (MMC) framework. This common framework holds management applications and any third-party applications that are written to its specifications. It is available for NT 4.0 and Windows 95, and will be available for NT 5.0 when it is released.

MMC was created in an effort to make management easier by using an extensible, consistent, and intuitive interface for all the administrative applications. The MMC is a Windows-based multiple document interface (MDI) that resembles Internet Explorer. Because it's just a framework, MMC has no functionality by itself. You need to apply Snap-Ins to give it a purpose. For example, there are Snap-Ins for most of the current administrative tools, such as the Disk Management shown in Figure 4-13.

Snap-Ins are entirely customizable, can be created from scratch, and can even include web-based interfaces. Once you define the MMC with the Snap-Ins you want, you save it as a *tool*. Instead of switching between different applications you can include in your tool only those Snap-Ins needed to perform all elements of complicated administrative tasks within a single MMC Later, you can open that tool and it will have just the Snap-Ins you defined earlier.

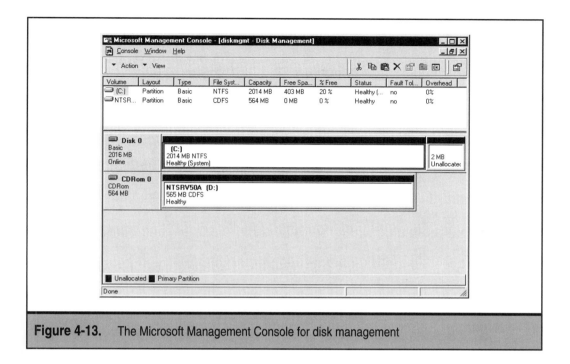

Figure 4-13.   The Microsoft Management Console for disk management

In Table 4-2, you can see that many of the administrative functions that you are familiar with will change with MMC and NT 5.0.

Administrative Task	Before the MMC	With the MMC and Windows NT 5.0
Domain Management		
Manage Active Directory objects	Not applicable	Administrative Tools	Directory Management.
Join a domain tree	Not applicable	Domain Controller Promotion Wizard (*Dcpromo.exe*).

Table 4-2.   Using the MMC in NT 5.0

Administrative Task	Before the MMC	With the MMC and Windows NT 5.0
Manage domain trust relationships	User Manager for Domains	Administrative Tools ǀ Domain Tree Management; right-click on a domain, click Properties, and click the Trusts tab.
Manage site topology and replication of the directory	Not applicable	Administrative Tools ǀ Sites Topology.
Users and Groups		
Manage user accounts and groups	User Manager for Domains	Administrative Tools ǀ Directory Management.
Delegate administrative control to other users	Not applicable	Administrative Tools ǀ Directory Management.
Assign logon scripts	User Manager for Domains	Group Policy Editor Snap-In.
Security		
Manage and monitor system security	Not applicable	Security Configuration Editor Snap-In.
Configure permissions, auditing, and ownership of shares	My Computer or Windows NT Explorer	Administrative Tools ǀ File Service Management.
Configure permissions, auditing, and ownership for directory objects	Windows NT Explorer	Administrative Tools ǀ Directory Management; right-click the object, click Properties, and click the Security tab.
Configure domain security policy	User Manager for Domains	Administrative Tools ǀ Directory Management; right-click a domain, click Properties, and then click Edit under Domain Security Policy.

Table 4-2.   Using the MMC in NT 5.0 (*continued*)

Administrative Task	Before the MMC	With the MMC and Windows NT 5.0
Configure computer security policy for all computers in a domain	System Policy Editor	Administrative Tools	Directory Management; right-click a domain name, click Properties, and then click Choose Policy or Edit under Computer Security Policy.
Configure computer security policy for a single computer	System Policy Editor	Administrative Tools	Directory Management; right-click a computer name, click Properties, and then click Change under Computer Security Policy.
Servers and Resources		
Manage the computers in a domain	Server Manager	Administrative Tools	Directory Management; click the Computers folder under the domain name.
Manage a server's shared volumes, folders, and files	Server Manager and Windows NT Explorer	Administrative Tools	File Service Management.
Publish shares as volumes in Active Directory	Not applicable	Administrative Tools	Directory Management; right-click a container, point at New, and then click Volume.
Manage disk storage and data protection	Disk Administrator	Administrative Tools	Disk Management in the program group.
Monitor and limit disk space use by individual users	Not applicable	The Disk Quotas application; in Windows NT Explorer or My Computer, right-click the NTFS volume for which you want to use quotas, click Properties, and then click Quota.

Table 4-2. Using the MMC in NT 5.0 (*continued*)

Administrative Task	Before the MMC	With the MMC and Windows NT 5.0
Manage server connections and open files	Server Manager	Administrative Tools | Computer Management.
Hardware and Software		
Add hardware to the computer	Control Panel	Control Panel.
Configure devices	Devices option in Control Panel	Administrative Tools | Device Management.
Add and configure network cards	Network option in Control Panel	Hardware Wizard in Control Panel.
Add and configure most network services	Network option in Control Panel	Control Panel | Add/Remove Programs; click the Windows NT Setup tab, click Networking Options, and click Details.
Add and configure Gateway Service for NetWare	Network option under Services tab in Control Panel	Control Panel | Network option.

Table 4-2. Using the MMC in NT 5.0 (*continued*)

Here are some basic instructions to get you started with the MMC. To run the MMC and load a Snap-In, follow these steps:

1. Start the MMC by clicking Start, and then Run. Then type **mmc**. This will display the Console window without any Snap-Ins.

2. On the Console menu, click Add/Remove Snap-In, select Add and choose the Snap-In you want to include. The Snap-In will now appear inside the MMC and is ready for your use.

ZERO ADMINISTRATION FOR WINDOWS

Zero Administration for Windows (ZAW) is an initiative introduced by Microsoft aimed at lowering the total cost of ownership for NT users. As with any other Microsoft initiative, it is not a single product but a collection of software and concepts that are mostly enhancements of previous programs. In this section, we'll discuss the part of ZAW that is available now for NT 4.0 users, and we'll indicate what to look forward to in NT 5.0.

Zero Administration Kit

The Zero Administration Kit (ZAK) is the first real ZAW product to ship from Microsoft. It works with NT 4.0 and can be downloaded from Microsoft at **www.microsoft.com/ windows/zak/.**

ZAK is a set of system policies and scripts that you can use to centrally distribute the NT Workstation OS to client computers. Unlike previous network installations, there are currently two modes, or types, of NT installations you can perform. These modes create two different kinds of NT systems. Both restrict the user from certain parts of the NT operating system. The user is given access only to the parts of NT that the user needs. This policy is aimed at reducing the total cost of ownership, because as we all know, the more access users have, the more likely they will get into something they shouldn't and require help to fix it—which costs money.

NOTE: As with any new application or tool, you should test the product in a lab setting or on a pilot network before deploying it into the production network.

Installation Modes

The two modes of installation are called the *TaskStation* and the *AppStation*. The TaskStation was designed for users who only need access to a single application and not much else. NT boots directly into the application that you select and basically locks out the user from any other aspect of the desktop. This is accomplished using a very restrictive set of policies.

The second mode is AppStation, and although it is also restricted, the user has access to a handful of applications and other aspects of the desktop. The user doesn't have access to system configuration menus or authority to change the desktop environment much. This configuration boots up onto the desktop, but the user only has a limited choice of applications to run.

In all likelihood, your desired workstation modes will not fit neatly into either of these two modes. Fortunately, you can customize them to better suit your needs. This is not, however, straightforward. You don't save much time modifying one of these as compared to creating a system policy the old-fashioned way and applying that to an NT installation (see Chapter 2 for more information).

Distribution Modes

Here is how the ZAK works. You start by building a set of distribution files that reside centrally on a share. You'll need to reserve about 1GB of server disk space for the AppStation installation and a bit less for TaskStation. After you download the ZAK from

Microsoft (*Zak.exe*), you create the installation files by running the *Zaksetup.exe* file from the directory of your choice. For example, if you want to create an installation build for Intel-based clients, start from the /i386 directory that is created when you unpack *Zak.exe*.

A wizard helps you create the installation build. After you have gone through the wizard, some new folders will have been created to hold the applications (NETAPPS), the logon scripts and policies (ZAKADMIN), and the NT 4.0 files (ZAKAPPDIST). Now you need to perform some tasks manually:

1. You must share NETAPPS and the NETSYS folder within the ZAKAPPDIST directory.

2. Create a user group that you will use for the mode of installation. You do this so policies can be applied to the users via the global group. For example, if you are creating an AppStation installation, you should make a user group called AppStation. Don't forget to add users to this group.

3. If you use the Directory Replication service to copy logon scripts, you must manually copy a few files. CopyZakconfig.pol (from ZAKADMIN) to Netlogon and rename it **Ntconfig.pol**. Then, copy the logon script for the mode (found in ZAKADMIN\Logon Script, Applogon.cmd or Tasklogon.cmd) to Netlogon. These files allow your client to find and use the correct policy files.

4. You will need to modify your Unattended.txt file and place it in the ZAKAPPDIST\NETSYS\i386 directory. As a reminder, this is the answer file for NT installation and is different for each machine.

To run the client installation, you must first ensure the client can see the network. Next, have the client run the *winnt* command from your server's \i386 directory like this:

s:\ winnt /u:s:\unattend.txt /s:s:\i386

After you install the first workstation, your work is still not done. You must copy the All Users profile from the client to the NETAPPS\Start Menu folder on the server. Do this for the contents of the \All Users\Start Menu folder and the \All Users\Start Menu\Programs folder. Now, on subsequent installations, the client will have the appropriate menu structure. To test the installation, log on as a member of the global group you created and test the restrictions that are imposed on you.

Remember, this kit is supposed to make things easier and simpler to administer. We'll let you be the judge.

ZAW in NT 5.0

The following set of ZAW software components will be available in NT 5.0. These are a series of loosely related enhancements that provide added functionality with less administrative intervention. For the most part, to take advantage of the enhancements, you must deploy NT 5.0 on all the desktops you want to use the ZAW tools.

IntelliMirror

IntelliMirror is a new caching system that caches network data. Instead of caching frequently accessed disk drive data, as traditional caching programs do, IntelliMirror caches the most frequently accessed network data onto your local hard drive.

When you access the network drive, the system checks to see if your cached version is older than the network version of the file. If it is not, it uses the local copy. This is faster than downloading the network file and reduces network traffic.

If you are disconnected from the network temporarily, you can use the cached copy, and then update the network file once you reconnect. Because you use the Universal Naming Convention (UNC), you use the same name for the file whether you're on the network or reading a local copy. For example, let's say the file is called \\server1\ mydata\myfile.xls. When you are on the network, the UNC name works fine. When you are mobile, you can still use the same UNC name because the cache knows to which file you are referring; therefore you don't have to search around in your directory tree for the file.

Microsoft Installer

Microsoft Installer (MSI) allows unattended, effortless installations. MSI-compatible applications come with an information file that contains all data you typically answer during installation. MSI reads the information file and installs the package without user intervention. Now here comes the fun part.

MSI-compatible applications are "self-healing". This means that if part of Excel, for example, becomes corrupt, it will initiate an installation to repair its broken parts. Because the application has an MSI information file, the entire repair can happen without user input. You can even use the self-healing aspect of MSI to install applications. If you give users a shortcut to the application that doesn't exist, the program will try to repair itself by installing a copy. Naturally you don't want all the users installing applications at the same time, but you could have them install applications to a server and run them remotely.

Server Intelligent Storage

However, you know you can't have all your users install their own private copy of Excel on the server. You need another ZAW tool called *Server Intelligent Storage (SIS)*. With SIS you can set aside part of the storage space on the server to examine each file against the other files and look for duplicate entries. If two files are recognized as being the same, SIS will keep only one copy and make directory entries for the duplicate file. The directory entry links the duplicate file to the actual file. From the users' perspectives, they each have their own private copy of Excel on the server.

Naturally there are some security issues with all these new technologies. These—and many more—problems won't be resolved until NT 5.0 gains popularity and increases its installed base. This is why we recommend testing NT 5.0 in the lab or pilot environment first to assess the risk versus gain.

NETWORKING COMMANDS

Sometimes the flashy GUI administration products just are not adequate. Either their scope is too broad, or they don't focus deeply enough into a specific aspect of management. In other cases, a GUI interface can be cumbersome and slow when you have large changes that need to be executed. Nonetheless, you still have a job to do and need some way to execute it. For these situations, you will often resort to command-line solutions that are customizable, simple, and powerful.

Windows NT has attempted to include a command-line executable for every task you can do within the administrative tools that have GUIs. Although there are commands to do almost everything the GUI applications can do, the commands are somewhat obscure and tedious to use. In this section, we will introduce you to some helpful networking administration commands. Then we will string several commands together to form a custom script you can run once or schedule to run whenever you want.

The Net Commands

The *net* commands are a set of commands you can use to administer users, computers, shared resources, and server services. To get a list of the net commands, type **net** at the command prompt. The syntax of this command is:

```
NET [ ACCOUNTS | COMPUTER | CONFIG | CONTINUE | FILE | GROUP | HELP |
     HELPMSG | LOCALGROUP | NAME | PAUSE | PRINT | SEND | SESSION |
     SHARE | START | STATISTICS | STOP | TIME | USE | USER | VIEW ]
```

To get more information about any particular net command, type **net help <command>** at the command prompt. You can also enter **net hlpmsg** to get more information about NT network messages when all you have is the four-digit NT message number. The messages are usually informative. However, sometimes the messages are of no use whatsoever. For example, if you type **net time** and a time server cannot be located, you will see:

```
c:\>net time
Could not locate a time server.
More help is available by typing NET HELPMSG 3912.
```

So you type:

```
c:\>net helpmsg 3912
```

and see the message:

```
Could not locate a time server.
```

Not terribly helpful. In the following sections, we have broken down the net commands into four groups: user commands, computer configuration commands, server commands, and sharing commands.

User Commands

User commands control user accounts and user groups. Of course, you need to have administrative rights to successfully use the commands. If you want the changes to take effect on the domain user account, you must add the /DOMAIN argument to the following commands. Otherwise the command may take effect only on the local accounts.

NET USER   The *net user* command can create or delete accounts locally or on the domain controller (/DOMAIN). Net user has the following syntax:

```
NET USER [username [password | *] [options]] [/DOMAIN]
        username {password | *} /ADD [options] [/DOMAIN]
        username [/DELETE] [/DOMAIN]
```

If you use net user with no arguments, you will see a list of accounts on that computer. If you create a user with an asterisk (*) for a password, the user will be prompted to enter a password when they first log on. You may use this option in a batch file or script as it would not be prudent to have all the users' passwords in a clear-text file. Some of the options you can use to define the user's account are:

- ▼ **/ACTIVE:{YES | NO}**—Determines whether an account is active.

- ■ **/COMMENT:"comment here"**—Allows a 48-character comment. This comment will appear under the Description heading in User Manager.

- ■ **/COUNTRYCODE:nnn**—Put the country code here if you want NT to use specific language files for messages.

- ■ **/EXPIRES:{date | NEVER}**—Sets the expiration date of the account. If NEVER is used, the account will never expire. Use the mm/dd/yy format to place dates unless your country code uses the dd/mm/yy format.

- ■ **/FULLNAME:"name"**—Enter the full name of the account user.

- ■ **/HOMEDIR:path**—Sets the path for the user's home directory.

- ■ **/PASSWORDCHG:{YES | NO}**—Allows the user to change password if set to YES.

- ■ **/PASSWORDREQ:{YES | NO}**—Sets whether a user is required to have a password.

- ■ **/PROFILEPATH[:path]**—Sets the path for the user's logon profile.

- ■ **/SCRIPTPATH:path**—Sets the path for the user's logon script.

- ■ **/TIMES:{times | ALL}**—Specifies at what times the user can log on. The ALL argument indicates the user can log on at any time (default). Use days of the week for days and the 12- (with am or pm) or 24-hour clock for time notation. For example, if we wanted to add a new user named *joe* and restrict his logon times to Monday through Thursday from 7:00 a.m. to 4:00 p.m. we would enter: **c:\>net user joe /add /times:Monday-Thursday,7am-4pm**

- ▲ **/WORKSTATIONS:{computername[,...] | }**—You can list up to eight computers that you will allow the user to log on from. Use the asterisk (*) to allow the user to log on from any computer.

NET ACCOUNTS   The *net accounts* command can control the account policies for users. Users must be set up prior to using this command. The syntax for the command is:

```
NET ACCOUNTS [/FORCELOGOFF:{minutes | NO}] [/MINPWLEN:length]
             [/MAXPWAGE:{days | UNLIMITED}] [/MINPWAGE:days]
             [/UNIQUEPW:number] [/DOMAIN]
NET ACCOUNTS [/SYNC]
```

Used without any arguments, net accounts will display your current settings for the account properties, for example:

```
c:\>net accounts
Force user logoff how long after time expires?:     Never
Minimum password age (days):     0
Maximum password age (days):     42
Minimum password length:     3
Length of password history maintained:     None
Lockout threshold:     Never
Lockout duration (minutes):     30
Lockout observation window (minutes):     30
Computer role:     WORKSTATION
The command completed successfully.
```

The net accounts command has the following arguments:

- ▼ **/SYNC**—Used only on the domain controller. It forces an update of the accounts database.

- ■ **/FORCELOGOFF:{minutes | NO}**—Sets the number of minutes NT will wait before logging off a user whose account has expired.

- ■ **/MINPWLEN:length**—Sets the minimum number of characters for user passwords (0-14).

- ■ **/MAXPWAGE:{days | UNLIMITED}**—Sets the maximum age (up to 49,710 days) of the user's passwords before they expire. This value must not be less than MINPWAGE.

- ■ **/MINPWAGE:days**—This is the minimum number of days that can pass before users can change their password. This is used to thwart intruders who change the password, and then want to change it back before anyone notices.

- ▲ **/UNIQUEPW:number**—Forces users to use original passwords when their passwords expire. This value can go as high 24.

NET NAME AND NET SEND   The *net name* command simply provides a user with an alias to the system. It has the following syntax:

```
NET NAME [name [/ADD | /DELETE]]
```

It is an alias for the current user. You can send messages to users, computers, or aliases using the *net send* command:

```
NET SEND {name | * | /DOMAIN[:name] | /USERS} message
```

NET GROUP AND LOCALGROUP   The *net group* and *net localgroup* commands affect local and global groups. If used without the /DOMAIN switch, the local groups will be affected. Here is the syntax:

```
NET [LOCAL]GROUP [groupname [/COMMENT:"text"]] [/DOMAIN]
           groupname {/ADD [/COMMENT:"text"] | /DELETE}  [/DOMAIN]
           groupname name [...] {/ADD | /DELETE} [/DOMAIN]
```

You can add or remove users from groups by including the user name after the group name and including the /ADD or /DELETE switches. You can also add or remove groups by using the /ADD or /DELETE switches. If you don't use any switches, you can list the different groups; for example:

```
c:\>net localgroup

Aliases for \\IRIS


-------------------------------------------------------------------
*Administrators    *Backup Operators    *Guests
*Power Users    *Replicator    *Users
The command completed successfully.
```

To add a new group, type:

c:>net localgroup hungryusers /add

And to add a user to this group, type:

c:>net localgroup hungryusers tjvelte /add

To see the members of a group, just type the name of the group; for example:

```
c:\>net localgroup hungryusers
Alias name     hungryusers
Comment

Members


-------------------------------------------
tjvelte
The command completed successfully.
```

Because the net localgroup and net group commands don't allow changing individual permissions or rights, this must still be done manually within the User Manager.

Computer Configuration Commands

The net command also includes commands that are helpful in describing the condition of your computers. Although they do not provide the detail of computer inventory programs such as SMS, they can be gathered within batch files or at the command prompt for immediate viewing.

NET CONFIG   The *net config* command has the following syntax:

```
NET CONFIG [SERVER | WORKSTATION]
```

When you use the SERVER argument, you get a description about the Server service running on the local computer; for example:

```
c:\>net config server
Server Name    \\IRIS
Server Comment
Software version   Windows NT 4.0
Server is active on    NetBT_Elnk31 (0020af74938a) NetBT_Elnk31 (
0020af74938a) NetBT_NdisWan4 (000000000000) NetBT_NdisWan4 (000000000000)

Server hidden    No
Maximum Logged On Users    10
Maximum open files per session    2048

Idle session time (min)    15
The command completed successfully.
```

Using the WORKSTATION switch describes the Workstation service; for example:

```
E:\>net config workstation
Computer name      \\IRIS
User name      toby

Workstation active on      NetBT_NdisWan4 (000000000000) NetBT_Elnk31
(0020AF74938A)
Software version      Windows NT 4.0

Workstation domain      VELTE
Logon domain      IRIS

COM Open Timeout (sec)      3600
COM Send Count (byte)      16
COM Send Timeout (msec)      250
The command completed successfully.
```

NET STATISTICS   The *net statistics* command has the following syntax:

```
NET STATISTICS [SERVER | WORKSTATION]
```

You can generate usage statistics for either the Server service or the Workstation service using the net statistics command. These statistics can be quite useful in troubleshooting. You could write a program that queries computers, and then parses the results. If there were an inordinate number of errors on a computer, the program could alert an administrator. Here is the data the *net statistics workstation* command reports:

```
Workstation Statistics for \\IRIS

Statistics since 5/23/98 1:53 PM

  Bytes received      35616
  Server Message Blocks (SMBs) received      229
  Bytes transmitted      16252
  Server Message Blocks (SMBs) transmitted      228
  Read operations      3
  Write operations      98
  Raw reads denied      0
  Raw writes denied      0

  Network errors      0
  Connections made      2
```

```
Reconnections made    0
Server disconnects    0

Sessions started    3
Hung sessions    0
Failed sessions    1
Failed operations    0
```

NET TIME   The *net time* command synchronizes the internal clock of the computer executing the command with another computer's time. The net time command has the following syntax:

```
NET TIME [\\computername | /DOMAIN[:domainname]] [/SET]
```

You can see the time at any computer in your domain or any domain you can connect with using the /DOMAIN switch. If you want to set the local time to match the time on another machine, use the /SET switch.

Server Commands

The next set of net commands deals with administering computers.

NET START, NET STOP, NET PAUSE, AND NET CONTINUE   *Net start*, *net stop*, *net pause*, and *net continue* all control services on the local computer. The syntax is:

```
NET START | STOP | PAUSE | CONTINUE [service]
```

You can control most of the services that are listed under Services in the Control Panel. You can start, stop, pause, and continue (resume from a pause) services. If you pause a service, it will not respond to new requests until you enter the net continue command. To get a list of services that you can start or stop, type **net help start** at the command prompt. To see a list of services you can pause and continue, type **net help pause**. One of the services you can start is the Messenger service. You might, for example, find it useful to include **net start messenger** in a logon script to ensure users will receive messages from other users or computers.

NET SESSION   The *net session* command lists or disconnects sessions between the local machine (NT Server) and sessions with other computers on the network. It has the following syntax:

```
NET SESSION [\\computername] [/DELETE]
```

Without arguments, you can view all the current sessions:

```
C:\>net sessions
```

```
Computer      User name      Client Type      Opens Idle time
----------------------------------------------------------------------
\\IRIS                       Windows NT 1381  0      02:52:45
\\IRIS        toby           Windows NT 1381  1      00:41:56
\\TJV         SMSService     Windows NT 1381  0      00:10:39
\\TJV         SMSService     Windows NT 1381  0      00:00:28
\\TJV         SMSService     Windows NT 1381  1      07:08:33
\\TJV         toby           Windows NT 1381  0      03:34:47
The command completed successfully.
```

To delete sessions, include the name of the computer and use the /DELETE switch. Leaving the computer name blank and using the /DELETE switch will disconnect all sessions to that server.

NET COMPUTER   The *net computer* command is used only in NT domain architectures. The command adds or deletes a computer from a domain. This command can only be performed from an NT domain controller and has the same function as adding or removing a computer from within the Server Manager administration tool. It has the following syntax:

```
NET COMPUTER \\computername {/ADD | /DEL}
```

Sharing Commands

The following set of net commands helps you manage shared resources. As with most of the other commands, you need to have administrative rights to issue them.

NET SHARE   The *net share* command allows you to make shares on your hard drive available for network users. It has the following options:

```
NET SHARE sharename
    sharename=drive:path [/USERS:number | /UNLIMITED]
              [/REMARK:"text"]
    sharename [/USERS:number | /UNLIMITED]
              [/REMARK:"text"]
    {sharename | devicename | drive:path} /DELETE
```

Some of these options are not intuitive, so they are described here:

▼ **/USERS:number**—This is the maximum number of users that can simultaneously connect to the share.

■ **/UNLIMITED**—Designates that an unlimited number of users can connect to the share.

■ **/REMARK:"text"**—Adds a line of text next to the share.

▲ **/DELETE**—Stops sharing the resource.

Use this command without options to see what shares are present, including the default administrative shares; for example:

```
c:\>net share
Share name      Resource      Remark
-----------------------------------------------------------------------
D$              D:\Default share
IPC$            Remote IPC
C$              C:\Default share
ADMIN$          E:\WINNT      Remote Admin
E$              E:\Default share
print$          C:\WINNT\system32\spool\drivers Printer Drivers
a-drive         A:\
Toonces         C:\!\Toonces
HPLaser         LPT1:      Spooled  HP LaserJet 5P
The command completed successfully.
```

NET PRINT   The *net print* command is used to list the current jobs in a print queue, and the status and the priorities of the job. It has the following syntax:

```
NET PRINT \\computername\sharename
          [\\computername] job# [/HOLD | /RELEASE | /DELETE]
```

For example:

```
E:\>net print \\iris\hplaser

Printers at \\iris


Name    Job #     Size     Status

----------------------------------------------------------------|
hplaser    Queue    0 jobs    *Printer Active*
The command completed successfully.
```

You can also pause, resume, or delete print jobs using the net print command.

NET FILE   The *net file* command allows you to view a list of files being shared on a computer. You can see who has the file open, the permissions on the file, and whether the file is locked. The syntax for the net file command is:

```
NET FILE [id [/CLOSE]]
```

By issuing the command without arguments, you can see a list of the open files and an ID number. You can use this ID number after net file to learn more about its specifics. Using the /CLOSE switch will shut down use of that file.

NET USE   The *net use* command is a powerful and handy command. It is used to connect to resource shares on the network. It can be used, for example, in a logon script to mount remote drives. It can also be used to mount drives to retrieve data or to back up files on those drives. It has the following syntax:

```
NET USE [devicename | *] [\\computername\sharename[\volume] [password |
*]]
        [/USER:[domainname\]username]
        [[/DELETE] | [/PERSISTENT:{YES | NO}]]

NET USE [devicename | *] [password | *]] [/HOME]

NET USE [/PERSISTENT:{YES | NO}]
```

Some of the less obvious switches are:

▼ **/USER**—The authority for the current user is used to connect to the remote drives unless you designate another user with this switch.

■ **/HOME**—This directive connects a user to their home directory as defined in the account record.

▲ **/PERSISTENT**—When followed with the YES indicator, this switch makes the connection every time the user logs on.

NET VIEW   The *net view* command allows you to see the list of resources being shared on a computer. Like most net commands it has a different result if used without arguments. The general syntax is:

```
NET VIEW [\\computername | /DOMAIN[:domainname]]
NET VIEW /NETWORK:NW [\\computername]
```

Without any arguments, you can list all the computers within your LAN as shown here for this simple two-computer network.

```
c:\>net view
Server Name    Remark

---------------------------------------------
\\IRIS
\\TJV
The command completed successfully.
```

Now let's take a closer look at the shares on one of these computers.

```
c:\>net view \\tjv
Shared resources at \\tjv

Share name     Type     Used as     Comment

-----------------------------------------------------------------------
Clients        Disk     Network Client Distribution
share
NETLOGON       Disk     Logon server share
nt40srv        Disk     E:
SMS_SHR        Disk     (UNC)     SMS Site SMS 5/23/98
SMS_SHRC       Disk     (UNC) SMS Site SMS 5/23/98
SMS_SITE       Disk     SMS Site SMS 5/23/98
The command completed successfully.
```

Scripts

It is beyond the scope of this book to discuss the scripting language used in NT in great detail. However, we can get you started with some scripting basics and provide an example of a script you might find useful.

MS-DOS Scripts

Although there are third-party script languages you can use on NT (see Table 4-3), we will discuss the built-in scripting capabilities you already have with NT. NT uses its built-in MS-DOS scripting language. It is small and fast, but the functions are somewhat limited, so you should explore more powerful scripting languages if you have more demanding requirements.

Vendor	Scripting Language	Contact
ActiveState Tool	Perl for Win32	www.activestate.com
Ataman Software	Regina Rexx	www.ataman.com
FastLane Technologies	Final	www.fastlanetech.com
Sun Microsystems	Tcl/Tk	sunscript.sun.com
Wilson WindowWare	WinBatch 97	www.windowware.com

Table 4-3.   Scripting Languages Available for NT

Basically you can place any command-line command in a script. You can use environmental variables so you don't have to customize a script for every user or machine. To get a list of the current environmental variables, type **set** at the command prompt. You will see a list something like this:

```
COMPUTERNAME=IRIS
ComSpec=E:\WINNT\system32\cmd.exe
HOMEDRIVE=E:
HOMEPATH=\
LOGONSERVER=\\IRIS
NTRESKIT=C:\NTRESKIT
NUMBER_OF_PROCESSORS=4
OS=Windows_NT
...
```

Any of these variables can be used within scripts if they are enclosed with the percent symbol (%). The following script is a simple administrative script that gathers some basic information from a machine and saves it to a file.

```
REM This script gathers information and saves it to a text file.
REM First, we place the program in the temp directory.
c:
cd \temp
REM Queries basic information using net commands
REM and saves them to temporary files
net config server > temp1
net config workstation > temp2
net statistics server > temp3
net statistics workstation > temp4
REM This next line uses the environmental variable
REM %computername% to get local information
net view \\%computername% > temp5
REM Copy all temp files to one file located centrally on S drive
copy temp1+temp2+temp3+temp4+temp5 S:\Reports\%computername%.txt
REM Clean up our temp files
del temp1 temp2 temp3 temp4 temp5
REM Let the administrator know the file is ready
net send administrator Report for %computername% done.
```

Although this script only uses a few commands, you can see how easy it is to create a simple script. More advanced scripts incorporate logic blocks, user input, and command-line arguments. Another example of a script is illustrated in Chapter 3. In that example, we used basic script and net commands to run a scheduled backup session.

NOTE: It is very important to test the script as a user with the level of authority that will normally be running the script. Often administrators develop the scripts, and they seem to run fine until users try to run them. When logged on as an administrator, you have more rights than your users. Remember that when you execute a command, you are using the authority of the current user, so your users may run into difficulties when they try to execute the commands.

Scripting in NT 5.0

Windows NT 5.0 offers a new way to write scripts. You use what Microsoft calls the *Windows Scripting Host*. It is a language-independent scripting host for 32-bit Windows platforms. For example, you can write scripts using VBScript or JScript and run them using the Windows Scripting Host. The VBScript and JScript scripting architectures allow much more functionality than the MS-DOS command scripts. However, support is still provided for MS-DOS command scripts. Previously, scripts written in VBScript and JScript had to be embedded in an application or an HTML document.

You run the Windows Scripting Host from either the graphical user interface (*Wscript.exe*) or the command-shell-based host (*Cscript.exe*). This makes it possible to execute scripts directly on the Window's desktop or at the command prompt. The wscript command has the following syntax:

```
wscript [host parameters] [script name] [script parameters]
```

The AT Command

Now that you have created a script, you may want to have the script run automatically using either the Command Scheduler (*Winat.exe*) included with the Microsoft NT Resource Kit or the at command (*At.exe*). The Command Scheduler is a graphical interface for the at command. Although the at command isn't as elegant, you can use it to schedule your scripts if you don't have the Resource Kit. In either case, you'll need administrator rights to submit commands with these utilities.

NT 5.0 NOTE: In Windows NT 5.0, there is a Command Scheduler GUI for scheduling commands included with NT.

Scheduling Jobs

To use either the Command Scheduler or the at command, start the Scheduler service from the Services option in the Control Panel. You will not be able to start this service unless you have administrator privileges. At jobs run under the security context of the Schedule service, not the user requesting the job. The security context of the Schedule service typically runs in the context of the operating system. If your batch file seems to work as intended when you run it from the command line, but fails when it is scheduled, you most likely have not given sufficient privileges to the users you have incorporated into the script to act on your behalf. To allow scheduled jobs to survive a reboot, make sure you set the startup mode of the Schedule service to Automatic.

Let's look at how to schedule a command to run via the at command. Using the Command Scheduler is even easier, but it's good to see how the command really works. The at command has the following syntax:

```
AT [\\computername] [ [id] [/DELETE] | /DELETE [/YES]]
AT [\\computername] time [/INTERACTIVE]
   [ /EVERY:date[,...] | /NEXT:date[,...]] "command"
```

You can use AT without any switches to list the currently scheduled commands. To schedule a job, simply type **AT** followed by the name of the computer you want to run the job on and the date and time you want to run the job. AT has the following additional switches:

▼ **/DELETE**—Cancels a previously scheduled job. You must include the job ID number, which you obtain by listing the jobs using AT without any arguments. If you do not specify the ID number, all jobs on that computer will be deleted.

■ **/YES**—Use with the cancel all jobs directive; see /DELETE.

■ **/INTERACTIVE**—Allows the scheduled job to interact with the currently logged on user. Use this only if the job requires user input. If you don't run a job in interactive mode, and you require user input, the script will hang.

■ **/EVERY:date[,...]**—Schedules the job on specific days of the week or days of the month.

▲ **/NEXT:date[,...]**—Schedules the job to execute only on the next occurrence of the listed days.

For example, let's say we want to schedule a script called *script.bat* to run every Sunday at 1:00 a.m.. We would enter:

c:\>at 1:00 /every:Sunday script.bat

The result would be:

Added a new job with job ID = 1

To view the scheduled job, we can just type:

c:\>at

And the result is:

```
Status ID    Day    Time     Command Line
------------------------------------------------------------
1     Each Su   1:00 AM     script.bat
```

Troubleshooting Scheduled Jobs

The single biggest problem with a malfunctioning script is inappropriately configured user rights. That is why you should test the script using the rights of a typical user. You will also come across a script that doesn't behave if there is user input required during the execution of the script. Because scripts are not displayed unless they are set to run in interactive mode, you cannot tell if the script is waiting for user input or has completed if you don't run it in interactive mode.

You should also ensure that the script is in the path of the system, or you should provide the whole path to the script file. The at command doesn't check to see if the file exists until it tries to execute it.

A great trick to step through or troubleshoot a script is to use the net send command to send yourself messages at different points in the script to make sure it is getting through the file. Scripts can be very powerful although they take time to write and troubleshoot. Future applications should make scripting much easier and more powerful.

CHAPTER 5

Connecting Client Workstations

Windows NT networks support many types of client connections. Although this increases the options for interaction, it also increases the overall complexity of a network. Proper selection and implementation of the various client packages can ensure that your network is reliable and easy to use. As you read in Chapter 4, management of clients in the enterprise is creating the demand for tools that improve the efficiency of setup and maintenance of client computers. Unfortunately, none of these powerful remote management tools can be implemented until clients have been connected to the network. Inevitably, that task requires some hands-on contact with client workstations.

This chapter discusses several client packages, including client support for NT, Windows 95, Windows 3.11, and gateway services for Novell servers. The mechanisms NT uses to support file- and print-sharing will be explained, including the NetLogon service. We will also look at UNIX file-sharing using Network File System (NFS).

CLIENT CONSIDERATIONS

Connecting client computers to NT networks requires two steps: installing and configuring NT client software on the machine, and establishing accounts for accessing resources on the NT network. Although Microsoft and many other vendors provide NT client software for a wide variety of operating systems and network packages, the bi-directional sharing of resources in terms of security and efficiency is not equivalent across all platforms.

The integration of multiple platforms in an enterprise environment is certain to be necessary given new networks are rarely built *in toto*, but evolve from existing systems. The "drawbacks" of having to integrate Windows for Workgroups, NetWare, Windows 95, and Macintosh users on the network can be minimized with careful planning. However, you should keep an eye on utilization and, if affordable, upgrade hardware and software to reduce the diversity of platforms in the enterprise.

Although all the clients just mentioned can be connected to the network, achieving or maintaining the required level of functionality for these clients may be impossible because client performance or security is insufficient. For example, a small DOS or Windows 3.11 workgroup with 486-based clients that need to access NT, NetWare, and UNIX resources could be configured with the entire collection of standard client protocols to provide these services. Unfortunately, the memory demands of the network drivers would leave the clients without enough memory to run applications. The common-sense approach suggests implementing upgraded hardware and operating systems whenever financial constraints permit.

Thin Clients

Full consideration of the best choices for system upgrades is beyond the scope of this chapter, but the classic concept of bringing newer, more powerful machines online is no longer the sole path when replacing antiquated workstations. Although NT has special advantages for security and integration in the enterprise, it also requires considerable system resources that increase the cost per seat. System management is a separate cost factor to consider when choosing what kind of clients to connect. The *thin client* concept has been receiving significant attention as a means of reducing the total cost of ownership, at the level of both hardware and system management.

In many ways the thin client is a return to the idea of terminals running server-based applications. The rationale is to present users with applications that they have become familiar with on their PCs and allow them to have these applications "run" on inexpensive desktop workstations. The application displays its results on the thin client, but the CPU and RAM are located on a server. This permits administrators to easily manage the software and keep a close eye on hardware requirements. In addition, the reduction in overall maintenance through consolidation can save time and money. The clients themselves can also be quite inexpensive. However, the demands on the server increase compared to servers providing predominantly file and print services, so the cost for servers will increase as well as the negative consequences of having the servers go offline.

Microsoft has made a clear commitment to provide thin client technology in its Terminal Server product (formerly code-named Hydra) introduced in beta release at the 1997 Comdex show. The product relies on licensed technologies from Citrix Systems (Winframe), which Citrix has also licensed to a variety of firms who market "Windows terminals". These firms include Insignia Solutions, Inc., Tektronix, and Wyse Technology. There are many other companies seeking different thin client solutions. As with all the issues of enterprise solutions, careful evaluation of the goals of the network must drive the decision process. If many of the client management tools discussed in Chapter 4 (SMS, ZAK, and so on) become more sophisticated, the cost of managing workstations that can function without a server will continue to decline toward the costs *predicted* for thin clients. The best answer is certain to depend on the complex economics of hardware pricing, client licensing, and client support in the enterprise.

NOTE: More information on thin clients can be found in Chapter 9.

NT CONNECTION SERVICES

Creating client connections that work efficiently in the enterprise requires numerous decisions regarding user accounts. If a goal is to have all resources in the network available for a user under a single account and password, NT may accommodate this, but you still have to coordinate account information for other non-NT servers. This may not impose equal security for all resources attached to all client workstations. The NT server process that handles requests for access to resources is the NetLogon service.

For some non-NT users, the connection to an NT network may be a transparent process, but for others, if increased security is implemented, there may be logon changes. Currently, it is not possible to have a single user name and account managed solely within NT if the enterprise incorporates all possible clients. For example, NetWare network servers can be made available to NT network clients, and a single logon user name and password at the NT network client will access both resources once the NetWare account data is entered. The single logon has the appearance of a global user account; however, if the user wants to change their password, they will have to change it on both the NT and Novell systems or keep track of two passwords.

Client Access Licenses

When connecting new clients to NT Servers remember that Client Access Licenses (CALs) are required for the legal use of file, print, and RAS services on the server. Chapter 2 outlined the two choices for licensing, the Per Seat and Per Server options. Refer to that chapter for the consideration of which mode is best suited to your environment.

The License Manager

The License Manager in NT Server is used to maintain the database of licenses, and it can also track the use of licenses for each user. This tool tracks licenses for all of Microsoft's networked products (BackOffice, SQL Server, Exchange Server, and so on) as well as NT Server CALs. Access to server resources requires that there are available user licenses registered in the License Manager. For example, if you have ten Per Server licenses, and an eleventh user with a valid account attempts to log on to the system, they will receive a message that a domain controller could not be located, that they are being logged on from cached data, and that any changes to their profile may not be available. The user will have access to local resources at their workstation, but network drives and printers that are accessed through an NT Server will not be available.

Opening the Licensing icon in the Control Panel allows you to quickly determine which license mode is in effect and how many licenses are present. Figure 5-1 shows the Choose Licensing Mode window. Although it appears to contain the same information that is available through the License Manager, it does not. The number of licenses is entered in the License Manager, and that information is then replicated to the domain controller. The default replication frequency is every 24 hours, and this means that updates to the License Manager would not be seen immediately in the Choose Licensing Mode dialog box. In Figure 5-1 you can see that there are licenses for ten concurrent connections. If an administrator wanted to add an eleventh account to a domain where all the users were connected to the server all the time, an eleventh license would have to be added in the License Manager. The administrator would also have to be sure to replicate the change to the domain controller before the new user would be able to gain access to the server's file, print, and RAS services.

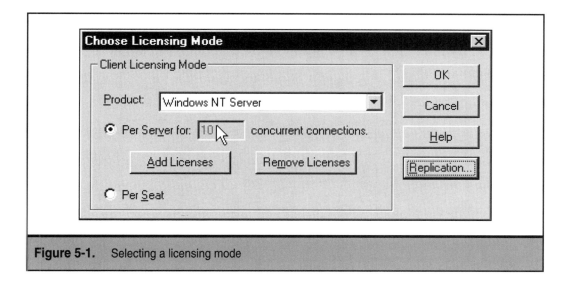

Figure 5-1.   Selecting a licensing mode

NOTE: NT Server has a license logging service that is automatically started upon installation. If this service fails, the License Manager cannot access the license information or replicate it to the enterprise server. Although this is analogous to a failure to synchronize directory database information or information on resources from browsing, the replication of license information does not use server replication and synchronization processes.

Replication

Replication can be forced to occur at a specific time from the Control Panel or the License Manager. Figure 5-2 shows the Replication Configuration window, opened by clicking the Replication button in the Licensing tool on the Control Panel. The same window can be accessed from the License Manager by clicking the Server Browser tab, selecting the server, and right-clicking to obtain the properties for that machine.

You can see that there is a choice to replicate to either the domain controller or an enterprise server. You should select the Domain Controller option if the server is not a PDC or if you do not want the license information to be replicated to a central server. Select the Enterprise Server option and specify its name if the server is a stand-alone server in a domain that is within a larger enterprise. If the server is a PDC and a central management of licenses is called for, selecting the Enterprise Server option will forward the domain licensing information on to that machine. The default replication frequency is every 24 hours and when multiple NT Servers are replicating, there is an automatic delay in the start times for each server to avoid congestion due to simultaneous replication.

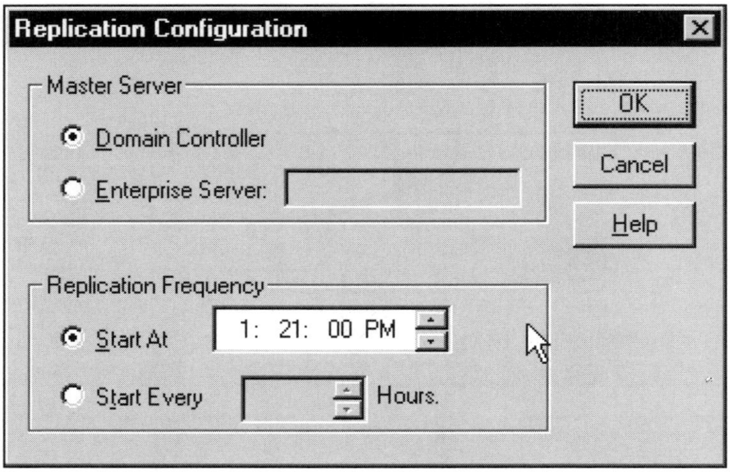

Figure 5-2.   Configuring replication for licenses

Network Browsing Service

You see resources available on the network because of the Browser service. The basic principles underlying browsing are the same across Microsoft's products from DOS to Windows 3.11 to Windows 95 and NT. The Browser service was developed in the context of LANs, not WANs, and this is reflected in the distributed nature of the service and the problems it poses when considering its implementation in the enterprise.

Browser Basics

The concept of browsing was that clients would announce their existence on the network when they started up, and their absence would be noted if they were off the network. Achieving this involved having each client broadcast its presence at some interval. If this were a general broadcast message, it would create a lot of network traffic with the overhead becoming more debilitating as the number of clients increased.

    The solution was to have the clients direct their announcement to a master browser that would maintain a list of the resources on the network. When clients wanted to browse the available resources, they queried the master browser, and when clients shut down normally they announced their departure from the network. The default setting for the Browser service in all Microsoft operating systems is AUTO, which means that every client can potentially become a master browser in its network segment. It is intuitively obvious that under these conditions all the clients in a network segment have to negotiate to designate the master browser, and when the total number of clients increases, the network traffic associated with resolving this is undesirably large. The rationale behind such a system grew out of the issue of what would happen to browsing if the master browser fails. If administrator intervention were required to restore users' ability to see resources on the network, the system would be too brittle.

To avoid overloading the performance of the master browser, Microsoft implemented the strategy in which clients that need to browse for resources query a designated master browser, which replies with the name or names of other machines designated *backup browsers*. These backup browsers have a copy of the master browser's resource list and they provide that information to the clients. The master browser's task is to create the list, designate backup machines (including recruiting new backups if the total number of clients on the network increases), and forward copies of the browse list to the backups and to higher-level browse masters.

NT provides extra control (compared to Windows 95 and Windows 3.11) for defining characteristics of the roles specific machines will play in the browsing service. This makes NT-only networks easier to manage and requires fewer compromises in performance. In mixed client environments, which are the most commonly encountered, judicious control of which clients participate in browsing may permit a more satisfactory compromise between minimal network traffic overhead and a resilient browsing environment.

At the level of implementation, the Browser service relies on two components:

▼   **Browser**—This component is part of the Server service. It maintains the browse list, manages the client's participation in browse functions, and responds to the GetBackupList datagram calls that are central to clients' requests for information on shared resources on the network.

▲   **Datagram Receiver**—This component sends and receives the datagrams regarding browser elections. (We will discuss browser elections later in this chapter.)

It is important to remember that, in the enterprise, successful browsing requires that all clients and servers have the TCP/IP protocol installed and are configured to support WINS or LMHOSTS name resolution (WINS and LMHOSTS are covered in more detail in Chapter 7). Without these features, browsing cannot take place outside of a network segment (that is, across a router).

Multiple Client Browsing Environments

Client workstation contributions to browsing within a network can fall into one of four categories (it should be noted that all categories would be considered browser *servers*):

▼   Non-browser
■   Potential browser
■   Backup browser
▲   Master browser

Windows 3.11, Windows 95, NT Workstation, and NT Server clients can assume any of these roles. The default setting is Potential Browser for Windows 3.11, Windows 95, and NT machines.

CLIENT COMMONALTIES   Non-browsers cannot maintain a list of machines on the network, but they do signal their presence on the network with a periodic broadcast to the master browser. The announcement frequency begins at once per minute and progressively declines to once every 2, 4, 8, and finally 12 minutes. If the master browser is offline, a non-browser computer will not attempt to become a browser. In the enterprise, this might be the preferred setting for most clients, because it will minimize network traffic and streamline browsing. An exception would be in those networks in which clients are turned on and off regularly, because the availability of master browsers and backups will be less predictable. Distributing the capability to browse throughout clients will yield the most robust browser capabilities to whatever mix of clients are on at any given time.

Potential browsers act as non-browsers except when a master browser specifies that the potential browser should become a backup browser, or when no master browser is available; in that case, the potential browser can join in the process called *election*, which occurs to select a new master browser server. Potential browsers are capable of maintaining the browse list needed by clients.

Backup browsers actively maintain a copy of the master browser browse list of the servers and domains. These machines receive directed broadcast requests (the NetServerEnum API calls) from clients that are seeking to obtain a list of shared resources on the network. The backup browser will periodically query the master browser to update its copy of the browse list.

Master browsers receive the directed broadcasts of clients, announcing their existence, and then use the broadcasts to create the browse list for their part of the network. They generate announcements to the domain master browser (DMB) of their own domain, as well as master browsers of other domains. Finally, they monitor the total number of clients in their browse list and the number of backup browsers. If the ratio of clients to backup browsers is too small, the master browsers will elevate potential browsers to backup browsers. This prevents any single backup browser from being overwhelmed with a workload of responding to client browse requests. The master browser will assign a backup browser for every 32 clients on the network segment (for example, if there are between 1 and 31 clients, there will be one backup; if there are between 32 and 63 clients, there will be two backups, and so on).

NT ISSUES   So far we have examined some of the similarities among the different browser clients. Now we will focus on differences among NT, Windows 95, and Windows 3.11 clients.

The browser server status for NT Servers is determined by whether or not the machine is a PDC. When the NT Server machine is designated as a PDC, its Browser service is set to a fifth category, unique to NT—that of a domain master browser (DMB).

Any other NT server machines in the domain can be set to one of the four categories described previously.

To manually configure the browser service in NT, there are several values in the Registry for the key \HKEY_LOCAL_MACHINE\SYSTEM\CurrentControlSet\ Services\Browser\Parameters.

For the *MaintainServerList* value, the possible entries are

▼ **No**—Specifies that the client be a non-browser.

■ **Yes**—Specifies that the client be a browser server. When booted, the client will announce itself and broadcast to determine if there is a master browser in its network segment. If there is, the client requests a copy of the browse list and becomes a backup browser. If there is no master browser, the client forces an election among all clients to choose a master browser. This is the default for an NT Server when installed as a PDC.

▲ **Auto**—Specifies that the client be a potential browser. This is the default for all non-PDC NT Server and NT Workstation machines.

For the *IsDomainMaster* value, the possible entries are

▼ **No**—The default value for non-PDC machines

▲ **Yes**—The default for PDC machines

For the *BackupPeriodicity* value (range 300 to 4,204,967 seconds), the default is 720. This is the frequency with which the backup browser will contact the master browser to update its browse list.

NOTE: If this value is changed, the machine must be rebooted for the change to take effect.

For the *MasterPeriodicity* value (range 300 to 4,204,967 seconds), the default is 720. This is the frequency with which the master browser will contact the domain master browser to update its browse list. When the value is set for the NT Server that is the DMB, it determines the frequency with which the DMB will update its list from WINS.

NOTE: Changes to this entry are implemented without requiring a system reboot.

WINDOWS 95 ISSUES   In Windows 95, the equivalent settings for determining browser server status can be set from the user interface or via the Registry. The settings for non-browser, browser, or potential browser can be chosen from the Control Panel | Network menu by clicking on the File & Print Sharing button and choosing the Advanced tab. The choices for master browser are Disabled (non-browser), Enabled (browser) and

Auto (the default setting, for potential browser). The settings can also be found in the Registry under the key:

HKEY_LOCAL_MACHINE\System\CurrentControlSet\VxNETSUP\Ndi\params.

There is only one subkey of interest in \MaintainServerList where entries of No, Yes, and Auto are allowable. There are no equivalents of the subkeys that allow adjustment of the timing of backup or master browser requests for updates in Windows 95.

NOTE: Both Windows 95 and Windows 3.11 can fully participate in domain browsing, even to the extent of being master browsers. This is valuable if the enterprise contains a network segment on which there are no NT machines. However, for Windows 95 or Windows 3.11 clients to be able to fill this role, the workgroup name assigned to these machines must be the same as the domain name that they will be participating in.

WINDOWS FOR WORKGROUPS ISSUES   Although there is a Registry for Windows 3.11, it has a very different function than the Registry found in NT or Windows 95, and the Browser service is not configured there. Instead, entries need to be made in the System.ini file and the [network] subsection. The MaintainServerList= value can be entered in this section and can have the three entries applicable to Windows 95 and NT. As for Windows 95, the frequency of backup or master browser requests for updates of the browse list cannot be configured in Windows 3.11.

The original browsing service in Windows 3.11 existed prior to NT and, as a result, that original service did not accommodate the concept of DMBs that might exist on a different network segment. To solve this problem, Microsoft includes updated Browser services for Windows 3.11 with the NT Server installation CD-ROM in the \Clients\Update.wfw directory. These files must be installed in Windows 3.11 if those machines are to be able to browse successfully in the enterprise environment. The TCP/IP-32 3.11b protocol located in the\Clients\TCP32WFW directory is also required for correct Windows 3.11 browsing behavior.

BROWSER ELECTIONS   Because of the different browser statuses that clients can be assigned, you need to consider the reasons for these categories and the impact on network performance. For distributed browsing services to function without direct administrative intervention, it is necessary to accommodate the addition or loss of browser servers on the network. This is accomplished by having a browser election held whenever one of three situations occurs

▼   A PDC starts up.

■   A machine designated as a preferred master browser starts up.

▲   A new client starts up and cannot locate a master browser.

Under these conditions, the computer that has started will generate a special datagram called the *election datagram*. This is a directed frame that will go to all clients on the network except non-browsers. The contents of the datagram are the request for an election and the election criterion of the sending computer. You can see when an election has been called because there is an entry in the Event Viewer.

The specific rules for winning elections can be found in the NT Server Resource Kit by searching for *Browser Elections* or reading the MS Knowledge Base article ID # Q102878. Briefly, NT machines are preferred over older operating systems, the PDC has the highest priority and, other things being equal, machines that have been running longer are given preference.

Browsing on the WAN

Browsing in NT networks evolved from the method developed by Microsoft in its first network products. The concept of browsing across routers was not incorporated into those earlier systems designed for browsing among workgroups. For enterprise implementation, browsing must be extended so shared resources anywhere in the organization can be accessed by users.

To gain cross-router browsing capability, NT takes advantage of the properties of WINS to be able to localize all necessary information for routing the NetServerEnum API calls and browsing datagrams (GetServerList, election, and so on) in one place. To avoid enterprise-wide broadcast messages, the browse process employs directed messages. To achieve this, clients must have a way to have specific IP numbers that they associate with the various browser servers, including backup, master, and domain master browser servers. WINS accommodates this need by associating the different types of browser servers with specific NetBIOS names. The last step is to have the clients associate their IP number with their NetBIOS name via a broadcast when they announce themselves on the network, when their status changes (a potential browser is told to become a backup browser by the master browser), or a browser election has been held. A more complete consideration of the mechanisms involved in enterprise-wide browsing via WINS can be found in Chapter 7.

If WINS services are, for any reason, unavailable, it is possible to create an entry in the LMHOSTS file so you can browse across routers. This method has several drawbacks that make it an unattractive method for the enterprise. Microsoft does not guarantee that this technique, which it does not formally support, will be available in Windows 98 or NT 5.0.

NT 5.0 Note: In a Windows NT 5.0-only network, there is no need for WINS because all names are DNS names. Searching for network resources is carried out through a DNS server and the Active Directory.

The display of resources available across domains does not appear in the File Manager, Explorer, or Network Neighborhood when WINS is not functioning. Users can still browse resources, but they must know the domain name and machine name, and be comfortable entering this information from the command prompt using the *net view* command (see Chapter 4). Using LMHOSTS requires being able to place an LMHOSTS file on all machines, and each file will require entries for every client and server on the

WAN. A single, large LMHOSTS file copied to every computer might not pose too great a problem, but if that file must be changed every time a new machine is added or an old one removed, the workload seems unreasonable. A sample LMHOSTS file and a description of the various methods of implementing LMHOSTS is available in Chapter 7.

Enhancing Enterprise Browsing

There are many things to keep in mind when evaluating browsing in the enterprise, and we will enumerate several of the most salient. Keep in mind that any decisions on browsing must be based on the specifics of your particular network configuration. This is not a trivial consideration because it is estimated that approximately 30 percent of daily network traffic can be Browser service announcements, elections, and requests for information. This section covers some of these considerations.

When resources go offline, there is a delay before this information is reflected in browse lists. Depending on where the client is relative to the enterprise and the exact configuration of the timing of browse list updates, it can take many tens of minutes before the loss of resources is reflected in the browse lists. How important this is may depend on how users react when they see a resource on the browse list in the Explorer or File Manager, but then are unable to connect or access that resource. If the lists are updated more frequently, this places a substantial load on network traffic.

The size of the browse list in NT 4.0 can be changed, but for NT 3.51 and earlier, as well as Windows 95 and Windows 3.11, the browse list is limited to 64KB. This limits the maximum number of workstations that can be in a single workgroup or domain browse list to less than 3,000. The exact number will depend on the size of the comments associated with machine names. For a large enterprise, this means that mixed platform environments will be unable to have automatic browsing of every available resource if the total number of computers exceeds 3,000.

Browsing is specific to each protocol (NetBEUI, TCP/IP, and IPX/SPX) operating on the network. This means, for example, that an announcement will be generated repetitively until all protocols have been alerted. Substantial savings can accrue for each protocol that can be eliminated.

If a configuration is chosen to limit the total number of machines that can become browsers, this will reduce network traffic associated with elections. For network segments that do not have a substantial change in the number of clients each day, administrators could configure only the optimal number of backup browsers and have a small (optimal) number of potential browsers as a hedge in case of backup browser failure.

For clients that will not share any of their own resources, the Server service can be turned off. Because users elsewhere in the network do not need to browse that machine, turning off the Server service means that machine will never announce itself to the master domain browser and will not generate periodic announcements. Likewise, the Browser service can also be disabled when not required. If WINS is implemented, access to other resources will be available via the *run* command, however, this requires that the users be knowledgeable enough to use that method to make their connections.

Administrators can gain some insight into the existing traffic generated by the Browser service. The browser will generate a record in the system log when errors and elections occur, and these can be viewed with the Event Viewer. Of greater use are two utilities that are available with the NT Server Resource Kit:

▼ **Browstat.exe**—This command line program can be used to gain insight into the network traffic generated to browser events. You can force an election to occur, and by monitoring the traffic, you can determine if you want to change the configuration of Browser services to minimize the occurrence of elections.

▲ **Browmon.exe**—This graphical tool allows you to view many browsing statistics. An example of this information is shown in Figure 5-3.

Configuring systems for best performance will be labor-intensive without enterprise-wide management tools. You will almost certainly need to change the

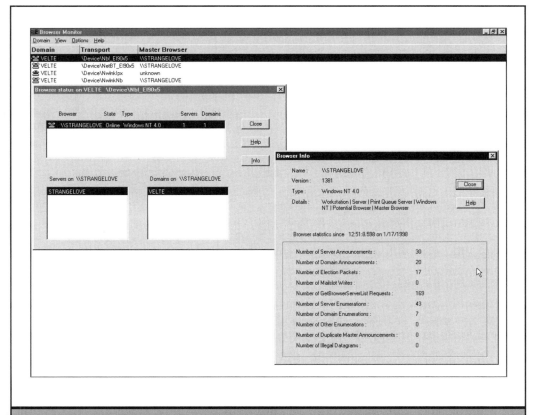

Figure 5-3.   The Browser Monitor can provide detailed information about browser traffic

Microsoft defaults for many implementations because all machines are initially configured by default as potential browsers.

NetLogon Service

The NetLogon service is used by clients to establish a connection with NT Servers. This service is necessary for you to log on to a domain.

NT Clients

On NT client machines, requests by users to log on to their client machine are processed by the Local Security Authority (LSA). Requests for logon to a domain are passed to the NetLogon service, which forwards the request to a domain controller. The NetLogon service on NT Servers passes these requests to the secure domain directory database or passes requests through to a controller in another domain if the requested resources are located in that domain.

The NetLogon service requires the Workstation and Server services. When connecting NT Workstation clients that have been configured in stand-alone or workgroup mode, be certain these services have been set for automatic startup. This can be verified and set in the Services window of the Control Panel. It also requires that the local machine has been set to provide the Access This Computer From Network right, which is set in the User Manager from the Users Rights option on the Policies submenu. Note that the default settings for this right include permission for everyone to have access to the computer. This means that all users in the domain can sit at the client and log on to the domain. This follows the Microsoft practice of having the least restrictive default settings on rights and permissions.

Before the NetLogon service can perform these operations it must first locate the relevant machine (or, machines, in the case of an NT Server NetLogon service). This process is called *discovery*, and it begins as soon as the service is started on bootup. A client NetLogon service will try to "discover" the NetLogon service of the NT Server. If the received user name and password information is in the security database, the machines establish a secure communications channel. If the discovery fails, the NetLogon service on the client will use cached information for the user created from the last logon. This means that the user will be logged on to the client and will have the local privileges that existed at the time of the last logon.

NOTE: When such cached logons occur, any changes in user profiles that have been implemented after the user's last logon will not appear. This includes everything from user permissions to group memberships to Client Access License additions or deletions.

If the discovery is successful, but no user account is found on the domain server, there are two possible outcomes:

▼   If Guest accounts are enabled and no Guest password is set, the user will be logged on as a Guest; otherwise the logon fails.

▲   If the client is attempting to log on to a backup domain controller (BDC), the BDC NetLogon service will pass authentication through to the PDC if that machine is available. This can occur in cases where a user password has been changed at the PDC, but that change has not yet been replicated to the BDC (see more on this in the next section). In this case, the PDC would allow the logon.

NOTE: Clients not running NT Workstation or Server have their access to network resources authenticated by the NetLogon service on the appropriate domain controllers. However, users on these clients have no restrictions on their access to local resources.

NT Domain Controllers

The NetLogon service on domain controllers responds to domain client authentication requests and also establishes secure communication channels with all domain controllers with which it has trust relationships. On startup, the domain NetLogon service will attempt discovery with all trusted domains. If necessary, each domain is polled three times within five seconds of bootup. If the discovery fails in this period, the domain controller will repeat the attempt any time that a request for authentication is received from a client that requires access to resources outside the domain. If no requests are received, the controller will attempt discovery every 15 minutes.

In NT Server, this service receives requests for authentication from clients and passes requests through to trusted servers in other domains when necessary. (See Chapter 2 for further discussions of trust relationships.) This includes both logon authentication as well as requests to access resources (files or printers). If a logged on user seeks to map a network drive outside the domain, the PDC NetLogon service will pass the request to the PDC of the trusted domain, and if the user name and password match the security database in that domain, the request will be honored. If there is a failure, the NT Server will prompt the user to enter a user name and password, thus allowing access if the user has two accounts in different domains, or knows the user name and password of a valid account in that domain.

The NetLogon service is also responsible for synchronizing the security database between the PDC and the BDCs. Modifications to user or group accounts (passwords, group membership, or user or group rights) are stored in a change log (kept in both memory and on disk \%*Systemroot*%\Netlogon.chg). Replicating these changes to the BDC is the responsibility of the PDC's NetLogon service. This is accomplished by the PDC NetLogon service generating a pulse message to which the BDC NetLogon service responds by requesting an update to the directory database. The PDC responds to these requests by sending the contents of the change log to the BDC. This update is called *partial synchronization* because only changes have been replicated between the PDC and BDC. *Full synchronization* is the copying of the complete directory database from the PDC to the BDC. It is required when the BDC is first set up or if the BDC has been offline for too long.

The default size of the change log is 64KB, and once full, new changes bump the oldest changes out of the log file. If the BDC is offline long enough, there will be old changes that will not have been replicated that have been removed from the change log resulting in a mismatch in the account information for the domain between the PDC and the BDC. Full synchronization is required under these conditions. Because a system alert is not normally generated by a failure for correct partial synchronization, you may be aware of the problem only if the PDC is offline and client connections fail when the BDC authenticates logon or resource requests.

Table 5-1 contains the group of Registry values under the HKEY_LOCAL_MACHINE\CurrentControlSet\Services\Netlogon\Parameters key that determine the size of the change log and the timing of requests for replication. The default values are satisfactory unless a PDC must synchronize many BDCs in a domain with heavy network traffic. Increasing partial synchronization frequency increases traffic on the network, but reducing the frequency increases the chance of a loss of synchronization. Increasing the change log size can provide a false sense of security unless you monitor the contents. You

Value Name	Data Type	Range	Default
ChangeLogSize	REG_DWORD	64KB to 4MB	64KB
Pulse	REG_DWORD	60 to 172,800 seconds (48 hours)	300 (5 minutes)
PulseConcurrency	REG_DWORD	1 to 500 pulses	20
PulseMaximum	REG_DWORD	60 to 172,800 seconds (48 hours)	7,200 (2 hours)
PulseTimeout1	REG_DWORD	1 to 120 seconds	5
PulseTimeout2	REG_DWORD	60 to 3,600 seconds	300 (5 minutes)
Randomize	REG_DWORD	0 to 120 seconds	1
ReplicationGov-ernor	REG_DWORD	0 to 100 percent	100
Scripts	REG_SZ	Pathname	NULL
Update	REG_SZ	Yes or No	No

Table 5-1. Registry Settings for the NetLogon Change Log

may think the changes in the security database are few and infrequent so the change log never fills. As long as this is true, partial synchronization will always succeed. However, if the log *does* fill up and you are not prepared for it, problems will arise. Furthermore, the larger the change log, the larger the information needed to be sent to the BDCs, and this again increases network traffic.

NON-NT CLIENT CONNECTIONS

For non-NT clients, different processes take place to allow these workstations to participate in an NT domain. The next section gives a brief description of the steps other clients take to get connected and use resources on an NT network.

MS-DOS, LAN Manager 2.2c, and OS/2 Clients

NT Server includes the Network Client Administrator program in its administrative tools. This program can be used to take the client software that is supplied on the NT Server installation CD-ROM and share it from the CD or from a hard drive on the server. It can also create floppy disks that can be used for a hands-on installation of the client software on DOS, Windows 3.1, or LAN Manager 2.2c servers and workstations. Adding the 32-bit TCP/IP protocol to Windows 3.11 is also supported by the Network Client Administrator. Another feature is that the function of Network Client Administrator can be loaded to non-NT Server machines, including Windows 3.11 and Windows 95 computers. This can avoid burdening a server with the task of making sets of startup and installation floppy disks for configuring clients. You need to make system startup floppy disks in the same format as the operating system that will be used on the client machine. One can always have a multiple-boot DOS/Windows 3.11/Windows 95 machine that can be used for generating the correctly-formatted disks, and then also run the Network Client Administrator to load the data to the floppy disks.

When you open the Network Client Administrator, you may take four actions:

▼ Make a startup disk for DOS or Windows clients.

■ Make a startup disk that will place software on the local hard drive.

■ Copy client administration tools to another computer.

▲ View remoteboot information from clients.

DOS or Windows Startup Disk

When making an installation startup disk for a DOS or Windows client you must be ready to provide the client configuration information and have an appropriately formatted bootable floppy to complete this operation. The first dialog box after choosing to make a startup disk determines the location of the appropriate files to be used, as illustrated in Figure 5-4. The first time the Network Client Administrator is run, the

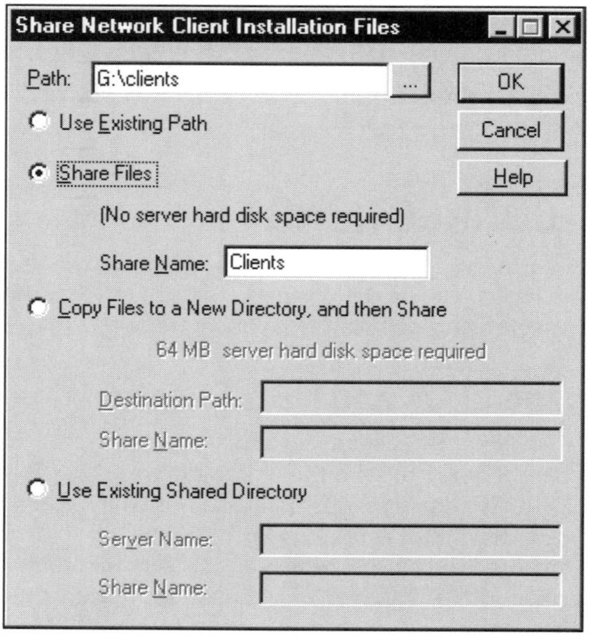

Figure 5-4. Selecting the Share Network Client Installation Files

default location is the NT Server CD-ROM. You can choose to always get the files from there, or place and access them from a hard drive. Once a choice has been made about where the installation files will be kept, the dialog box remembers the location that was last used.

The next dialog box is the Target Workstation Configuration dialog box, which allows you to choose the floppy size, the network client startup to install on the floppy, and the adapter card that is in the client.

Next, you will see the Network Startup Disk Configuration dialog box, as shown in Figure 5-5. It requires you to enter the computer name that has been assigned or has already been in use, the user name, the domain name that the client will be a part of, and the network protocol that will be the primary protocol. The protocol choices are IPX, TCP/IP, and NetBEUI. If the client needs to be able to browse outside its network segment, TCP/IP should be chosen. If TCP/IP is chosen, you can then choose to enable DHCP configuration or directly enter the IP number, subnet mask, and gateway address for the machine.

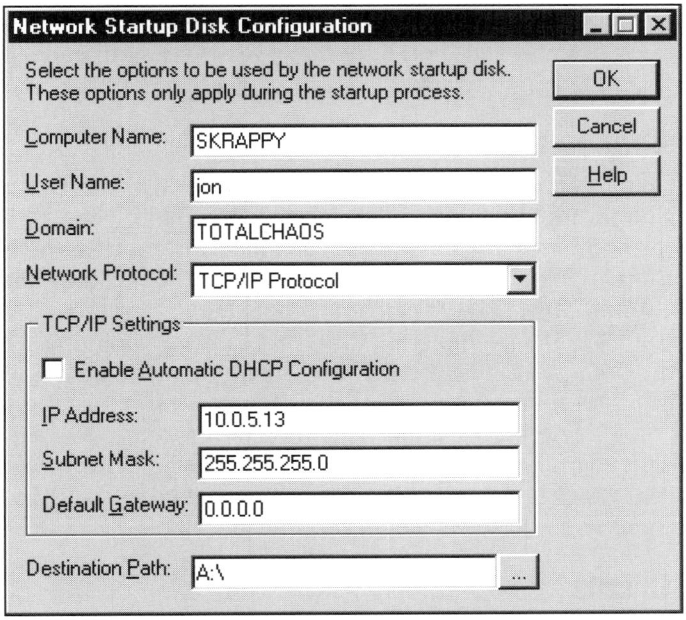

Figure 5-5.   The Network Startup Disk Configuration settings

After accepting this information, you will be prompted to place the disk into the drive. The necessary files will then be copied to the floppy disk. Be aware that the information on the disk assumes that default settings exist on whatever adapter card was specified. If the card has other settings (for example, a different base address or IRQ) you can change the values by editing the appropriate section of the Protocol.ini file. The title of the specific section containing that information will vary from adapter to adapter, so you need to be familiar with the hardware in each client to make the necessary changes easily. Booting the client with this disk in the boot floppy drive will configure the client and connect to the network. It does not, however, install the client software on the local hard drive.

Network Installation Disks

The second task of the Network Client Administrator is to produce disks that can permanently set up the client software on the local hard drive.

When you select the Make Installation Disk Set option you will see the same screen as for making the startup disk that chooses the location of the files needed. Once that decision has been made, you select the client for which you want to have installation disks made. The options on that dialog box include the TCP/IP-32 3.11b protocol for Windows 3.11. The number of disks required for different clients varies, but there is a prompt in the dialog box that tells you how many disks you will need (one for TCP/IP, two for the MS-DOS client, and four for LAN Manager 2.2c for DOS or OS/2).

Copy Administration Client Tools

The third option in the Network Client Administrator is to copy the client tools to another computer. Selecting this option takes you to a dialog box that is very similar to the dialog box for the two preceding options. Its purpose is to specify where the NT tools will be copied. The location is presumed to be an existing network resource, and it requires 16 MB of hard disk space. The contents of the \Clients folder and subfolders from the NT Server installation CD-ROM are copied to the target directory, and the \Srvtools folder is set up as a shared resource. This permits an administrator to run the Windows 95 and NT tools contained in those directories from a non-NT Server machine to avoid using server CPU resources. The folders containing the files necessary to create the startup or installation disks are contained in the shared directory. Unfortunately, the Network Client Administrator tool is not transferred to the target client machine. However, the program can be run via its share on the server if needed.

Remoteboot Clients

The final option in the Network Client Administrator concerns clients that have been set up to boot their operating system off a server, thus the term remoteboot clients. You can view information about the remoteboot client from this menu. You cannot configure remoteboot clients from this dialog box; that task is done via the Remoteboot Manager on the server.

The use of the Network Client Administrator makes it easier to configure LAN Manager and DOS clients if you have never done this before. It is always good to have a source of configuration disks in case of system problems, and this feature makes creation of these tools easy. With the startup disks, you can boot a machine, make a network connection, and then continue the installation from a network drive rather than floppy disks. Still, the system requires a trip to the machine, and that is not as appealing as being able to install or upgrade machines remotely, which is the direction things must go for the enterprise to function in the most cost-effective manner.

Windows 3.11

Connecting existing Windows 3.11 workstations is fairly easy because Windows 3.11 uses the Server Message Block protocol used in NT. NetBEUI is also the default protocol in Microsoft Networking in Windows 3.11. This discussion assumes that Windows 3.11 workstations have Microsoft Networking installed. If there are other protocols in place, such as NetWare or SunPC-NFS, you will have to determine if maintaining these protocols and their drivers is worthwhile after implementing the connection to the NT network. In most cases, access to resources on these other platforms can be provided to the Windows 3.11 workstations via NT Server, and this can free memory in the application-critical 640KB space on these machines. As always, it is recommended that you verify the functionality of this change before making permanent changes to a large number of workstations.

Log On

Before you configure the Windows 3.11 workstations, the first step is to have the user accounts, profiles, and rights in place on the NT Server. Once you have done that, bring up Windows 3.11 and follow these steps:

1. In the Program Manager, open the Network Group and double-click on Network Setup.

2. If the dialog box does not indicate that the Microsoft Windows Networking (version 3.11) is present, click the Networks button and select support for Microsoft Networking. If you have made the decision to eliminate support for other networking platforms, you can remove these at this time.

3. When you are finished, click on OK to return to the main Network Setup menu.

4. If there are disk drives or printers that you intend to share on the NT network, be sure that the main menu dialog box states "You Can Share Your Files And Printers With Others". If it doesn't, click on the Sharing button, and then click on the check boxes indicating that you want to share these resources. Clear these check boxes if you do not want to share Windows 3.11 resources on the network. Click on OK to return to the Network Setup menu.

5. Check in the drivers window to be sure that the TCP/IP-32 3.11b driver is installed. If it is not, it is available on the NT Server CD-ROM in the \Clients\TCP32WFW\Netsetup folder. The Network Client Administrator tool can create a floppy disk for installing this driver, or it can share the installation files over the network.

6. Finally, click on OK from the main Setup menu to begin the installation process for any changes that have been made. You will be prompted to reboot the computer after this. If Microsoft Networking had not been installed before, you will need to reboot now. Otherwise, click on the Continue button.

After choosing to reboot or continue, you continue the configuration in the Network Group | Control Panel.

7. Double-click on Network to open the Microsoft Windows Network dialog box, as shown in Figure 5-6.

8. Verify the computer name. Remember, for Windows 3.11 workstations that are being added to an NT network, the network administrator should verify this

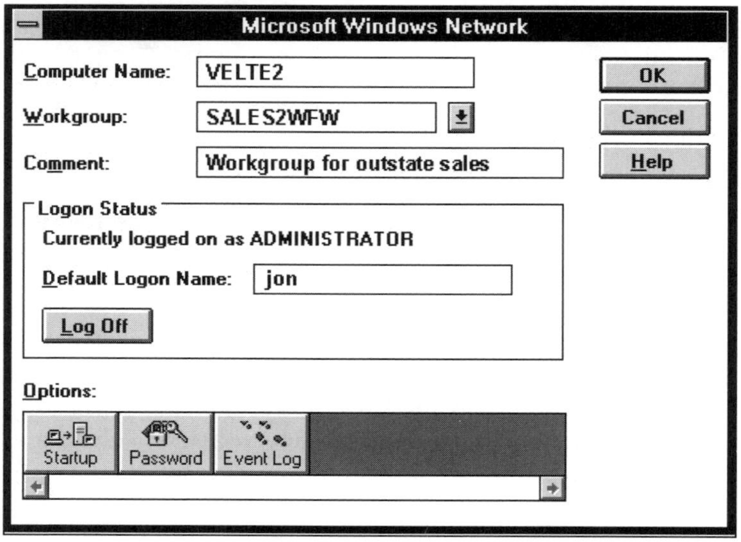

Figure 5-6. Windows 3.11 network configuration window

name so that it does not conflict with any other computer names in use on the network.

9. In the Workgroup box, select or enter the name of the NT domain that the workstation will become a part of. You can also add a 48-character comment.

10. In the Default Logon Name field, enter the user name for the account (or one of the accounts) that has been set up on the NT Server for this computer.

11. Under Options, click the Startup button. This will bring up the Startup Settings window shown in Figure 5-7.

12. Uncheck the Log On At Startup box. Check the Log On To Windows NT box under Options for Enterprise Networking and enter the NT domain name (be sure it is the same as the workgroup name from the preceding screen. Click on Set Password.

13. The next window, shown in Figure 5-8, contains the domain authentication information. The user name and password entered here must match that of the account setup in the NT domain specified, or logon will fail.

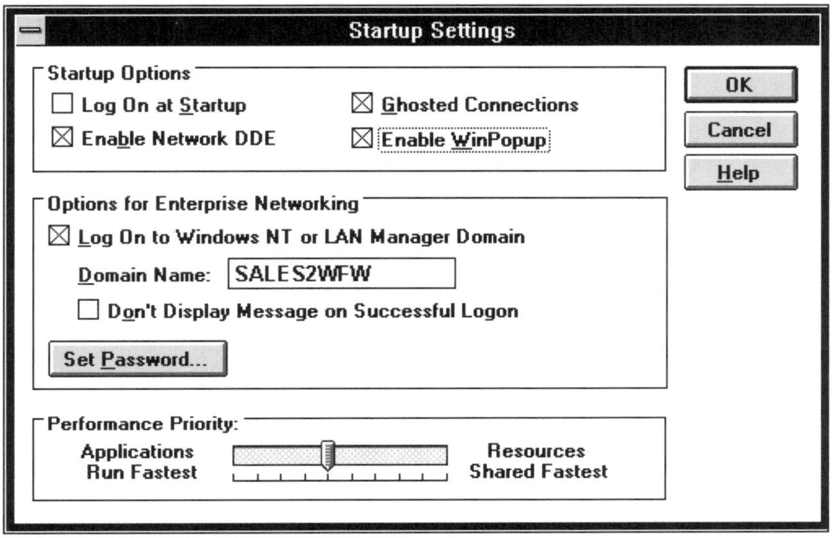

```
┌─────────────────────────────────────────────────────────────────────┐
│  ─                        Startup Settings                            │
│ ┌─Startup Options─────────────────────────────┐   ┌──────────┐       │
│ │  ☐ Log On at Startup      ☒ Ghosted Connections │   OK     │       │
│ │  ☒ Enable Network DDE     ☒ Enable WinPopup     └──────────┘       │
│ └─────────────────────────────────────────────┘   ┌──────────┐       │
│                                                     │  Cancel  │       │
│ ┌─Options for Enterprise Networking───────────┐   └──────────┘       │
│ │  ☒ Log On to Windows NT or LAN Manager Domain    ┌──────────┐     │
│ │                                                   │   Help   │     │
│ │     Domain Name:   SALES2WFW                      └──────────┘     │
│ │     ☐ Don't Display Message on Successful Logon                   │
│ │  ┌──────────────┐                                                 │
│ │  │ Set Password...│                                               │
│ │  └──────────────┘                                                 │
│ └─────────────────────────────────────────────┘                     │
│ ┌─Performance Priority:───────────────────────┐                     │
│ │   Applications    ├──────┬────────────┤  Resources               │
│ │   Run Fastest                            Shared Fastest          │
│ └─────────────────────────────────────────────┘                     │
└─────────────────────────────────────────────────────────────────────┘
```

Figure 5-7.   Setting the startup parameters

This method establishes a domain logon for Windows 3.11 users. It is the most restrictive method for connecting, but it is also the most secure. The restrictions require that users go to the Change Domain Password screen to change their password, but this does keep their logon and network resource account information synchronized. This also

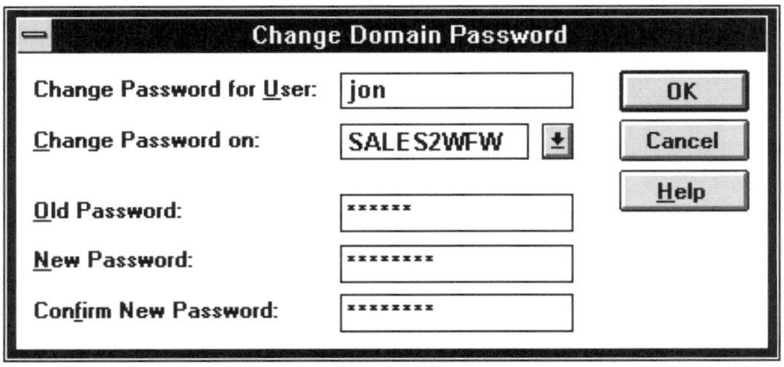

```
┌─────────────────────────────────────────────────────────────────┐
│  ─                  Change Domain Password                        │
│                                                                   │
│  Change Password for User:   [jon            ]   ┌──────────┐    │
│                                                   │    OK    │    │
│  Change Password on:         [SALES2WFW  ][±]    └──────────┘    │
│                                                   ┌──────────┐    │
│                                                   │  Cancel  │    │
│  Old Password:               [******       ]     └──────────┘    │
│                                                   ┌──────────┐    │
│  New Password:               [********     ]     │   Help   │    │
│                                                   └──────────┘    │
│  Confirm New Password:       [********     ]                      │
│                                                                   │
└─────────────────────────────────────────────────────────────────┘
```

Figure 5-8.   Setting the Windows 3.11 password

allows the users to have their profiles and rights managed at the domain level. Windows 3.11 users will be able to connect to network drives and even mount them for reconnection at startup. These connections are made through the File Manager.

NOTE: You can also make network connections from within an application's File Open dialog box. If the File Manager is open when you make such a connection, this new resource will not appear in the File Manager. Closing File Manager and reopening it will display the information created outside the File Manager.

File Shares

Once you have connected the Windows 3.11 workstation to the network, sharing files can be accomplished from the File Manager. Selecting Share As from the Disk menu or clicking on the icon of the familiar hand holding a folder will bring up the Share Directory dialog box. From that window you can share entire drives or directories within drives. As indicated earlier, you cannot have file ownership for Windows 3.11 files as you can for NTFS.

The security for access to shared resources on the Windows 3.11 machine is minimal. A failed logon does not deny the user access to local resources on the Windows 3.11 machine. Furthermore, anyone with direct access to the machine can boot off a floppy disk and have complete access to files. If this is a concern, there are password protection products offered such as the Norton Utilities or Central Point Software Utilities. These methods will prevent easy access to sensitive files, but they cannot prevent a malicious user from reformatting a hard drive. Do not be lulled into a false sense of security when using the domain logon method with Windows 3.11. The usual rule applies: if a resource is sensitive or vital, the machine needs to be physically locked away from unwanted users.

Windows 95

Because Windows 95 represents Microsoft's improved Windows 3.11 product, the same functionality (and unfortunately many of the limitations) applies to Windows 95 that applied to Windows 3.11. Because the Windows 95 GUI was added to NT 4.0, many elements of configuring Windows 95 will be very familiar.

Logon

Clicking on the Network icon in the Control Panel will display the Network Properties window. To connect a Windows 95 workstation to the NT network and set up for domain logon as we did for Windows 3.11, Client for Microsoft Networks must be installed and selected as the primary network logon. Select Client for Microsoft Networks and click on the Properties button. You will see a window similar to Figure 5-9. Check the Log On To Windows NT Domain box and enter the name of the NT domain where the user accounts have been created for users who will log on from this machine.

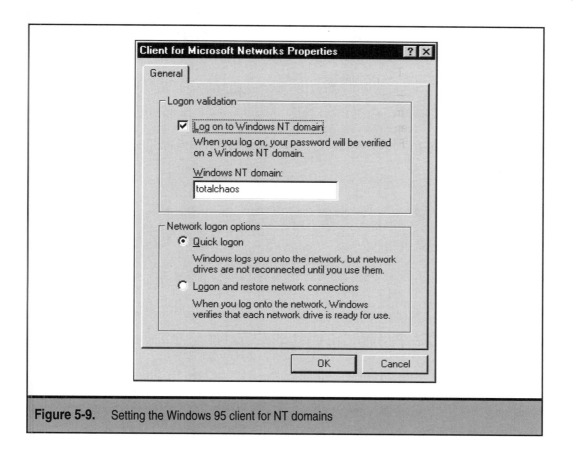

Figure 5-9.   Setting the Windows 95 client for NT domains

The TCP/IP protocol must also be installed and configured correctly for the network. If you intend to share files or printers connected to the Windows 95 machine, you must have the File and Printer Sharing for Microsoft Networks service installed. After you verify the correct TCP/IP, DNS, WINS, and bindings settings, click on OK to return to the Network dialog box and click the Identification tab. Verify the computer name. As with Windows 3.11 workstations, an administrator should verify that the pre-existing Windows 95 machine name does not conflict with existing names on the network. Finally, return to the Network dialog box window and click on the Access Control tab. If you want to have users log on using NT Server domain authentication, select the User-Level Access Control option and enter the name of the domain that will authenticate the user accounts, as shown in Figure 5-10.

Caution is again urged regarding the illusion of security created by having the network logon authentication. If a user simply hits the Cancel button at the network logon, logon is *not* aborted. The Windows 95 client cannot browse resources that depend on a successful logon to an NT domain, but the shares for local resources and nondomain

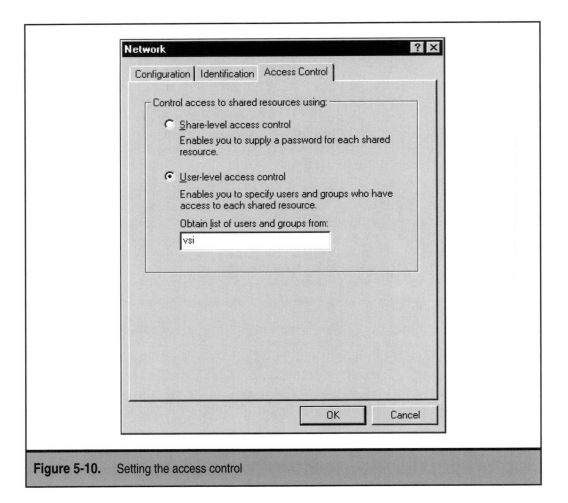

Figure 5-10. Setting the access control

resources (Windows 95 or Windows 3.11, for example) are still available on the network. Changes made to those shares are also propagated to the network. This means that an unauthorized person can sit at a Windows 95 machine and take its shares offline (of course they can also simply reformat an entire hard disk if they want).

NOTE: The preceding information is true for Windows 95 machines in a default configuration. Administrators can substantially reduce users' ability to impact the Windows 95 environment by using System Policies features (via the System Policy Editor, *Poledit.exe*) and mandatory user profiles (creation and configuration of the User.man file). Nevertheless, the reality is that Windows 95 is not a particularly secure system. For a determined user with physical access to a Windows 95 machine, the means to bypass these methods are easily available.

File Shares

Windows 95 shares are functionally identical to Windows 3.11 shares in terms of security. There are, however, some differences in terms of the access given to users who connect to the shares over the network. From the File Manager or Explorer, right-click on the drive or directory to be shared and select Sharing. The next window allows you to select the users who will be given access to the share, and what level of access they will be granted. If you have set up the Windows 95 client for network logon, then the list of possible users is provided from the server that the user logs on to. The access not specified and full control options are self-explanatory, but the custom user rights are a new feature compared to Windows 3.11. With the custom rights method you can independently allow a network user to read and/or write to a directory and, in the example shown in Figure 5-11, create and delete a new file or folder. These users would not be permitted to delete files or directories that another user had previously created, however.

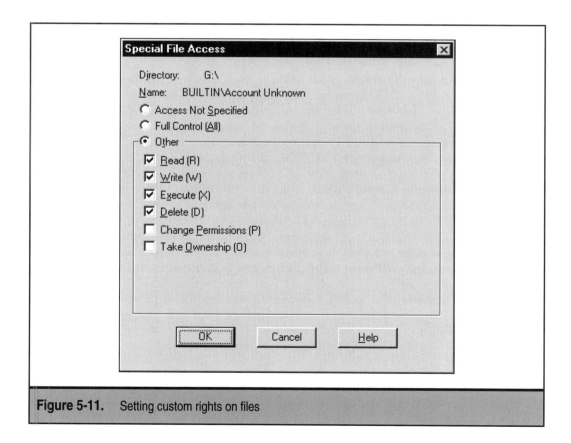

Figure 5-11.   Setting custom rights on files

NT 5.0 Note: In Windows NT 5.0 networks, Windows 95 clients must upgrade via a service pack to be compatible with the new Active Directory name space. NT 4.0 clients should upgrade to NT 5.0 to take full advantage of NT 5.0 features.

SERVICES FOR MACINTOSH

NT 4.0 Server includes well-developed services for giving Macintosh clients access to NT network resources and even allows Macintosh user accounts to be authenticated and managed by NT domain controllers. Many existing Macintosh networks utilize the AppleTalk network protocol running on LocalTalk hardware. Connecting LocalTalk hardware to NT can be accomplished by placing Ethernet cards into the Macintosh clients. This will improve the network speed over LocalTalk, although many older Macs cannot add Ethernet cards. LocalTalk cards are available for machines running NT (be sure to verify the hardware compatibility before buying). Another method is to place a LocalTalk network onto the Ethernet via a LocalTalk/Ethernet router. If this hardware is already in place, no additional hardware or software is required to connect the Macintosh clients.

Installing Services for Macintosh

You install Services for Macintosh (SfM) onto an NT Server by clicking on the Network icon in the Control Panel. Click on the Services tab, and then click on the Add button. Select Services for Macintosh from the Service list and click on OK. Provide the information on the location of the source files and continue. Once the files have been installed on the server, click on the Close button. The bindings are reevaluated, and then the dialog box for Microsoft AppleTalk Protocol Properties opens. Specify the network card, AppleTalk zone, and routing settings, as shown in Figure 5-12, and then click on OK. When you close the Network window you see the typical NT prompt to reboot the machine; however, SfM does not require this. The reboot is not damaging, but it is time-consuming.

After you leave the Network window or restart, you will find two new tools available. In the Control Panel there is a MacFile icon, and in the Administrative Tools folder on the Start menu there is now a File Manager entry. The MacFile icon is for the Macintosh Server service, which will have been started if you performed a reboot. If you skipped the reboot, clicking on the MacFile icon will generate a message indicating the service has not started. Answer Yes to the request to start it. Once the service is operating you will see the MacFile server window, as shown in Figure 5-13; it is similar to the server window for NT.

Logon

Macintosh users must log on to gain access to the volumes created using MacFile (described in the next section) or printers shared on the NT network. If the Macintosh

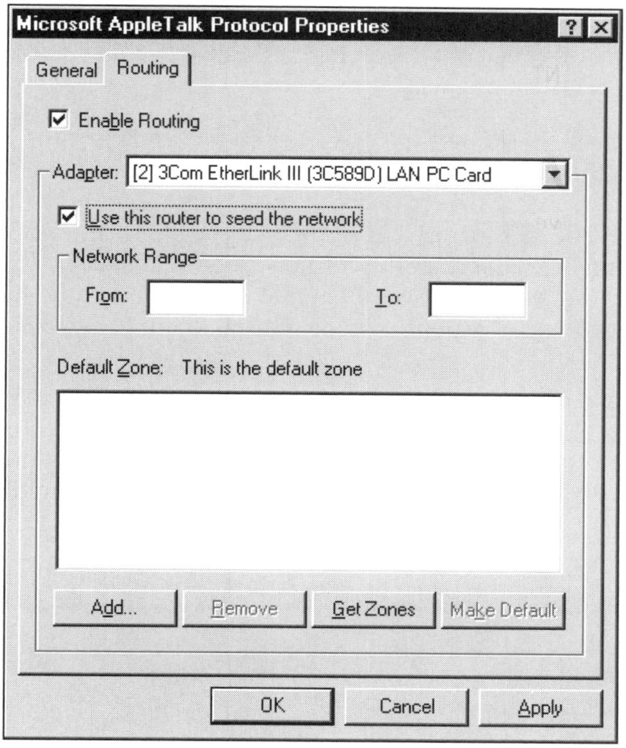

Figure 5-12.   Configuring the AppleTalk protocol

Figure 5-13.   MacFile Properties management window

users have existing accounts within the NT network, these NT accounts can be applied to the Macintosh logon. Macintosh logon can be configured for three levels. These levels can be selected from the MacFile Server icon in the Control Panel by pressing the Attributes button (see Figure 5-14):

▼ **Guest**—Check the Allow Guests To Logon box and clear the Require Microsoft Authentication box. Valid Macintosh users who do not have NT network accounts can access SfM-created volumes. Guest accounts must be enabled on the NT Server that is being logged on to, but a nice feature is that Guest accounts can be enabled for the NT network and disabled for Macintosh users by clearing the Allow Guests To Logon box. You should be sure your organization's security policies allow Guest accounts before considering this option.

■ **Standard AppleShare authentication**—Be sure the Require Microsoft Authentication box is cleared. Macintosh authentication occurs via the AppleShare client software that is located in the Chooser in MacOS. This system employs clear-text passwords with a maximum length of eight characters.

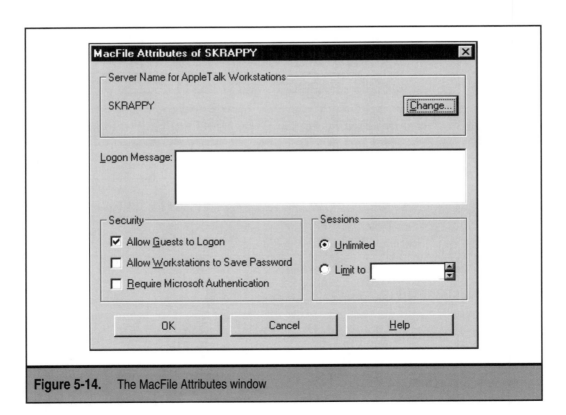

Figure 5-14. The MacFile Attributes window

▲ **NT-based authentication**—Do not check the Require Microsoft Authentication box until the needed files have been copied to the Macintosh client (see upcoming text). Once configured, users will have to use the User Authentication Module (UAM) that Microsoft has included with SfM. Macintosh users must provide their NT user name and password when connecting to the NT Server. This is the standard NT-encrypted password that can be up to 14 characters long. The Microsoft UAM must be configured on the Macintosh client to implement this option. On the Macintosh, select the Chooser, and from the dialog box select AppleShare, as shown in Figure 5-15.

Pick the AppleTalk zone that was chosen when the SfM was installed on the NT Server. This will produce a list of servers in that zone, and you can select the NT Server. Clicking on OK will take you to the logon box, where logon is based on either of the first two methods detailed earlier. Clicking on OK will open the Server dialog box displaying available Macintosh volumes located on the NT Server.

When SfM creates a Macintosh volume, a Microsoft UAM volume is created and will appear in the server list. Select that volume, click on OK, and exit the Chooser. Open the Microsoft UAM volume, which should now be on the Macintosh Desktop. Also open the System folder for the Macintosh and locate the AppleShare folder within it. If there is no

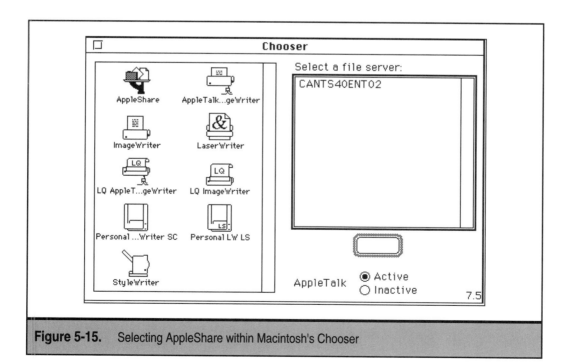

Figure 5-15.   Selecting AppleShare within Macintosh's Chooser

AppleShare folder, drag and drop the AppleShare folder from the UAM volume into the System folder. If there is an existing AppleShare folder on the Macintosh, open the UAM AppleShare folder, select the MS UAM file, and copy it (drag and drop it) into the AppleShare folder on the Macintosh.

This installation produces a change in the Logon dialog box that the Macintosh user will see when selecting to log on to the NT Server. The NT-encrypted user name and password authentication based on their NT account are now used to log on to volumes on the NT Server.

NOTE: The exact appearance of this dialog box depends on the version of MacOS running on the client and how the options for logon are set for the Macintosh server level. Users may or may not see options for Guest and clear-text logons. Even if these are visible, once the Use Microsoft Authentication box is checked from the MacFile Server Attributes window, only the Microsoft UAM logon will be accepted by the NT Server.

Volumes

To create the Macintosh-accessible volumes, open the NT Server's File Manager from Administrative Tools. Select the folder that will become a volume, and then either select MacFile/Create Volume or click on the MacFile–Create Volume icon on the toolbar. Then provide the volume name that Macintosh users will see. The path is filled in with the resource that you select. The password is a security measure *solely* for Macintosh users. It is not the password associated with the logon account for the user, and it is not relevant for NT clients accessing the same directory. You can also specify volume security and the number of users who can connect to the resource.

NOTE: If you create a volume from any folder located on a hard drive larger than 2GB you will be warned that Macintosh OS limitations may cause Macintosh clients to malfunction.

The volume created contains all elements of the directory tree below the topmost level. You cannot create a separate volume for a subdirectory within the directory tree. If you require separate volume names and access privileges, you must place the desired folders in independent directory trees. Furthermore, if you create a volume for a folder, no new volume can be created that would include that volume. You can see an example of this if you try to create a volume for the entire drive that contains the *%Systemroot%* path; you will find that you are told you can't create a volume within another volume. This occurs because the installation of SfM creates a Volume | Microsoft UAM volume in that drive. The following illustration displays a section of a directory tree. In this tree, the folder labeled *MacShare* is a volume. The only folder in the figure that could also be created as a volume is the folder *MacVolumes*. All the other folders are excluded from becoming volumes because MacShare is in their directory tree.

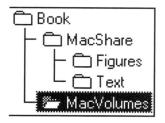

All the information generated in this process is irrelevant for NT clients on the network. The NTFS resources are unaffected by adding the access for Macintosh clients. Furthermore, if access to Macintosh clients is no longer desired, removal of SfM can be implemented. In this situation, the volumes disappear from Macintosh users, but the files remain as directories on the NTFS drives and are accessible to the NT network as usual.

> **NOTE:** Remember that these volumes cannot be created in FAT-formatted resources. When DOS and Windows 3.11 users view the shared volume, NTFS will create a standard DOS "8+3" filename for longer Macintosh filenames (which can be up to 31 characters). If Macintosh users will share extensively with clients using the shorter DOS filename limits, it is wise to have the Macintosh users restrict their filenames to avoid problems with filename recognition. There is a second reason that Macintosh users would be well advised to use DOS filenames. Macintosh users cannot see the 8+3 names that NTFS creates for the long Macintosh names. A Macintosh user who uses both long and 8+3 filenames could be prevented from saving a file with a long name because NT will have already used the 8+3 name. This problem occurs because two unique Macintosh long filenames can both reduce to the same 8+3 name.

GATEWAY SERVICES FOR NOVELL NETWORKS

Given the large installed base of Novell networks, the integration of NetWare resources is an important consideration when implementing NT into the enterprise. Realistically, Microsoft would like to take over Novell's customers and Novell would like to counter NT's surge into its markets. The devotion expressed for one system over the other often has more to do with opinion than experience based on comparative testing of both products' suitability for the tasks demanded. It is not the purpose of this section to determine which product is the most appropriate for general or specific environments or tasks. A description of the integration tools available from Microsoft follows. If you have existing Novell installations you are likely aware of Novell's recent efforts to provide its own NT integration tools (see **www.novell.com/intranetware/ntint**).

You must test for yourself which methods are the most beneficial for your situation. A recommended strategy is to consider what operating system will be the backbone for your network. Whether it is Novell or NT, the client software should be whatever fits best with the overall architecture.

The following sections discuss the NetWare integration tools based in NT Server. NT Workstation has some similar components. Specifically, the NWLINK IPX/SPX protocol is installed by default, and the Client Service for NetWare (CSNW) parallels the Gateway Service for NetWare (GSNW) provided by NT Server. These workstation elements probably would not be selected for implementation in the enterprise environment, where the more elaborate server tools are available.

A final caveat is that care should be taken to stay abreast of patches released by both Microsoft and Novell for all relevant products. Technical support departments must face the realities of keeping their customers functional. This means that solutions to problems are generated in response to known problems, but the complexity of the enterprise means that new, unforeseen problems are likely, especially with the continued rollout of new versions of the operating systems and the existence of varied legacy client systems.

The NWLink Protocol

We will briefly describe the NWLink IPX/SPX protocol (see Chapter 1 for more information on the IPX/SPX protocol), which underlies all of NT's NetWare integration tools. This stack is installed by default with NT Server or Workstation, and it provides the means for NetWare clients using IPX/SPX to access NT Servers. To set up the protocol, click on the Network icon in the Control Panel or right-click on Network Neighborhood and choose Properties. In Figure 5-16, you see the NWLink IPX/SPX Properties window. This displays the internal network number associated with the network adapter card. This value will be 0 unless the server has more than one Ethernet card installed. If there are multiple adapters, each one can be selected, and the internal network number that you want to associate with each adapter can be set. Finally the frame type can be specified. The default setting is Auto, which makes the NT machine examine the network at power-up so that it can determine the type or types of frames that are being used. For example, NetWare 2.2 and 3.1 have a default of Ethernet 802.3, but NetWare 4.0 uses 802.2.

To select manual frame type, press the Add button, which brings up a window, as shown in Figure 5-17. This selection enables a faster response because no time is taken to examine the frames present on the network. If you specify the frame type, you can have multiple manual selections that each have their own network number assigned. This arrangement can be used in combination with multiple network cards in a server to permit selective routing of different frame types, which can improve the throughput of servers. To make this possible, select the Routing tab from the NWLink IPS/SPX Properties window and check the Enable Routing box. You also have to install the Router Information Protocol (RIP) service.

A substantial number of parameters underlying NWLink behavior can be set by editing the Registry. A full description of these parameters can be found in Microsoft article PSS ID#:Q99745, which is available on the TechNet CD-ROM or the Microsoft

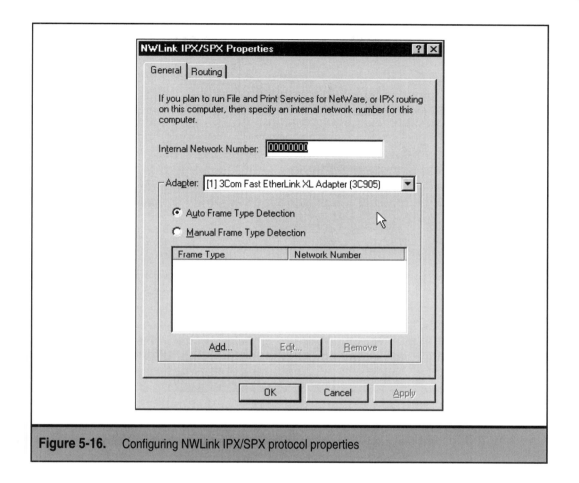

Figure 5-16. Configuring NWLink IPX/SPX protocol properties

Support web site (http://**support.microsoft.com/support**). Remember that the Performance Monitor can look at NWLink-relevant counters for IPX, NetBIOS, and SPX traffic that may be combined with changes to the Registry to achieve specific performance goals.

Gateway Services for NetWare

Installation of Gateway Services for NetWare (GSNW) on an NT Server provides the integration tool that can offer access to NetWare resources for clients on the NT network. As mentioned earlier, network drivers do exist for Windows 3.11, Windows 95, and NT

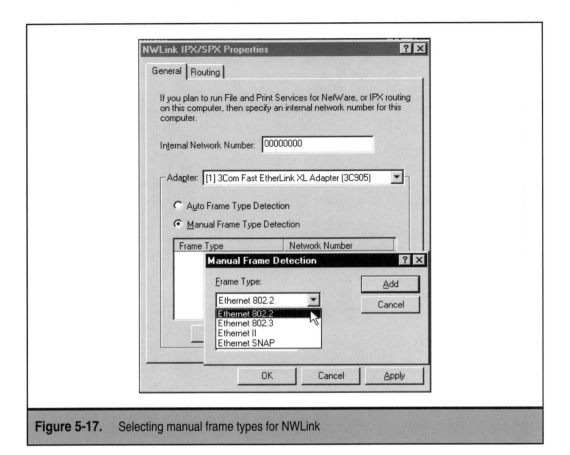

Figure 5-17.   Selecting manual frame types for NWLink

Workstation machines, but providing the service through the NT Server removes the need to maintain the protocols on every client. The administrative load to maintain such functions would be too great in the enterprise, which is why we are not considering those platforms. Another consideration is that GSNW does not work with Novell's IntranetWare.

GSNW has the attraction that clients of NT networks no longer need to have a NetWare-compatible protocol stack running along with the NDIS stack. All requests for NetWare resources are sent through the gateway using standard NT protocols, and the gateway handles the communication with the Novell server. This obviously places the workload squarely on the server and GSNW, and a user familiar with NetWare performance that is migrated to NT may notice the difference.

Double-clicking the GSNW icon in the Control Panel brings up the initial GSNW dialog box, as shown in Figure 5-18. To begin the setup, select the NetWare server that will be the preferred server for the gateway. You can also select tree and context information, determine print options, and have Novell logon scripts run if desired. If the Novell use of drive letters in the logon conflicts with NT, the latter plan can cause problems in NT with drive letter assignments. Users can still connect to all desired resources, map connections, and have those connections restored at bootup by using the File Manager or Explorer instead of the logon script.

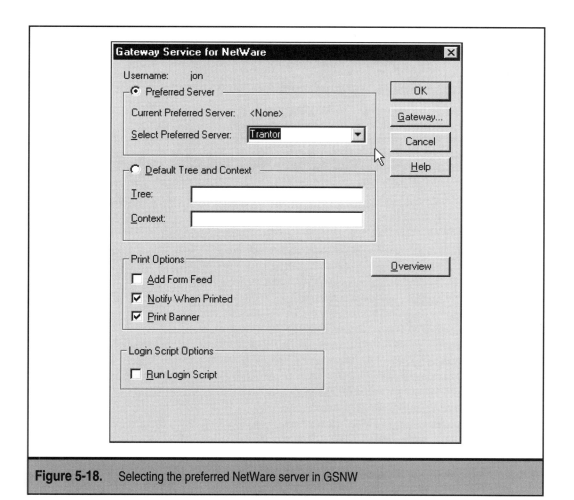

Figure 5-18.   Selecting the preferred NetWare server in GSNW

Once you have made the server selection, click on the Gateway button to bring up the Configure Gateway dialog box, as shown in Figure 5-19. Check the Enable Gateway box and enter the gateway account name and password. This gateway name is what NT clients will see, so employ a naming strategy that will be familiar to users who are also NetWare clients some of the time. Next click on the Add button to designate the NetWare resources that will be mapped to the gateway that has been created.

NOTE: The gateway concept means that all NT clients will access the NetWare resources specified for this gateway through a single user name and password. There may be many enterprise environments that will not accept such an arrangement. At this time, there is no way to avoid this because GSNW accomplishes its task by creating a single share, and all client access from the NT side goes through that point.

The final step is to specify the resources to share through the gateway, as shown in Figure 5-20. In the New Share dialog box, you enter the share name (which will be visible to NT clients), the Novell network path to map to that share name (which will not be

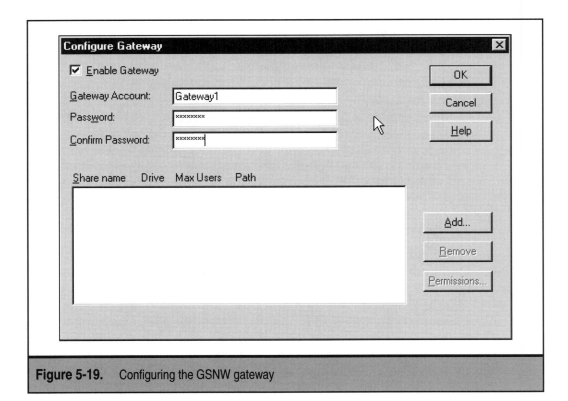

Figure 5-19.   Configuring the GSNW gateway

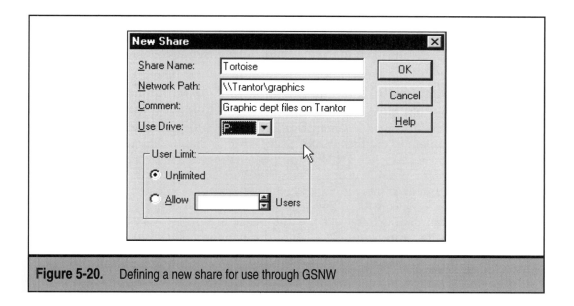

Figure 5-20. Defining a new share for use through GSNW

visible to NT clients), a comment (which can be used to help NT clients recognize NetWare resources that they may know by their NetWare path), and finally a drive letter that the share will be mapped to. Clicking on OK will return you to the preceding menu, where you can repeat the process to make more resources available through the gateway—with the obvious limitation of how many drive letters are free on the server.

NT Server includes an administrative tool called the Migration tool for NetWare. The tool functions in concert with GSNW when you are acting as both the NT administrator and the NetWare supervisor. The program allows bringing NetWare user accounts (minus passwords) to NT. Although this is an appealing concept, it is limited by the failure of user rights to map perfectly from Novell to NT. For example, there are a set of NetWare user rights (grace logons, restrictions on user space, the number of user connections, and requiring logon from specific workstations) which do not exist for NT users. Nevertheless, the Migration tool may offer some attractions, and an administrator can perform a test migration that creates log files that will allow evaluation of the success or failure of the process.

Microsoft has introduced two products that further enhance the chances of migration: the File and Print Services for NetWare (FPNW) and Directory Services Manager for NetWare (DSMN). These products do not ship with NT Server and must be purchased separately from Microsoft. FPNW, as the name suggests, helps to provide support migration by providing access to applications and files for both NT and NetWare clients. When the Migration tool is used in conjunction with FPNW, several of the NetWare user properties that do not normally migrate are now accommodated. DSMN does not require FPNW, but it certainly would be valuable in cases where migration was implemented using FPNW. The DSMN is designed to synchronize dual user information (as well as group information) that will exist during the migration process. This means that the SAM database in NT would be linked to the NetWare bindery security database.

Enterprise Considerations in Novell Integration

Although Microsoft has provided a means to have NetWare resources in the enterprise made accessible to NT clients, enterprise network performance will not be made satisfactory by implementing these tools. Several points create difficulties for network administration and speed when NetWare and NT systems are both present.

Using GSNW may provide user access to NetWare servers, but the work associated with dual sets of user accounts for NT and Novell remains.

In addition, there are considerations regarding the number of protocols your network can support. If your goal is to reduce the number of protocols (TCP/IP, IPX/SPX, and NetBEUI) on your network, you will want to drive the technology in the direction of a single protocol. Even in pure Novell networks, the direction is usually TCP/IP although there may be a few hurdles that Novell has to leap before it will be entirely possible. Many networks support IPX/SPX on the local and wide area networks. The overhead of supporting this protocol is well-known. Service Advertisement Protocols, commonly called SAPs, are "broadcast" throughout the network, consuming router and network resources much like NetBIOS broadcasts do. Additionally, IPX/SPX is not transportable over the Internet; it is tunneled in TCP/IP.

UNIX CONNECTIONS

The long existence of UNIX in networked environments has resulted in a growing number of products that permit the cross-platform sharing of resources between NT and UNIX systems. Sharing files across systems is now easily accomplished and includes the choice of sharing UNIX drives to NT clients, using either the SMB or NFS protocols. We will give a specific example of sharing UNIX via an SMB server and via an NFS server, and then provide a listing of other products that are available. No special endorsement of the products used in the examples is intended. They were chosen due to their popularity and presence in a number of diverse types of organizations. As always, given the rapid changes in software capabilities, you must evaluate which offering is the best product given your specific needs.

File Servers

This section considers the case of making UNIX resources visible and *browseable* by NT network clients. The usefulness is straightforward—users who have UNIX accounts and frequently work on UNIX systems can gain access to their files without having to sit at a UNIX workstation. Likewise, non-Unix users can easily place or retrieve files on the UNIX system to exchange information. However, UNIX applications from an NT client cannot be run using the types of software described in this section. That requires the use of a different type of program, like X-Windows Server, which will be discussed in the next section.

SMB Server

One very popular means of providing NT clients with access to UNIX drives is the SAMBA server package. This freeware runs on UNIX servers and provides NT client access to UNIX mounts. Before you turn away from the concept of using a noncommercial product in the enterprise, you need to know that SAMBA has been in existence for a considerable period and has been widely used in both academic environments (where it was developed) and several large corporate sites. SAMBA is a robust, well-tested, and well-documented software package that is definitely worth considering if your goal is to allow clients on an NT network to read and save files that exist on UNIX systems. Complete information and a download of SAMBA source code can be obtained from the SAMBA web site at http://**samba.anu.edu.au/samba.**

SAMBA is based on the Server Message Block (SMB) protocol that NT uses for sharing files. SAMBA works by creating UNIX support for the SMB protocol. The SAMBA Daemon responds to SMB requests from NT network clients and becomes a server to respond to those requests.

Because SAMBA is a process that is installed entirely on UNIX systems, a UNIX system administrator must install the SAMBA server. The NT system administrator has almost nothing to do when connecting network clients to a SAMBA server. If you are aware of the many various versions of UNIX that may be in use, rest easy, because SAMBA is compatible with all major versions of UNIX (such as products from Apollo, HP, DEC, NeXT, SCO, Sun, and SGI). This section includes a brief description of the requirements for having SAMBA work with NT.

NT NETWORK CLIENT REQUIREMENTS   Although no SAMBA client files must be installed in Windows 3.11, Windows 95, or NT machines, these computers must have the TCP/IP protocol and DNS services running to be able to connect to the UNIX machines to which they will gain access.

NOTE: If DNS is unavailable, the UNIX machine DNS names and IP numbers can be placed in the HOSTS file located in the *%Systemroot%*\System32\drivers\etc directory.

UNIX CONFIGURATION   The SAMBA server configuration is set in the Smb.conf file (typically located in the */etc* directory). This text file has a section structure that would feel familiar to anyone who has edited the System.ini file in Windows 3.11. There are separate sections for each share that will be created that permit setting valid users, read-write privileges, and public access.

There are also two sections that are very important for use in the enterprise environment with large numbers of clients. The *[homes]* section automatically permits users who already have accounts on the UNIX system to connect to their home directories without having to create individual shares for every account. The *[global]* section sets several comprehensive properties of the server. Of greatest importance are the security options that determine the method of authenticating users. Three security modes can be specified in the *[global]* section under the security= entries.

▼ **Security=share**—The *valid users* entry in each share section can specify users and their privileges within that share. This is a relatively insecure method and is limited to users who already have UNIX accounts, so it is a poor method for general access for NT network users within the enterprise.

■ **Security=user**—In this mode, all authentication occurs via the UNIX user accounts. In cases where all NT network clients also have accounts on the UNIX system, this is a secure and efficient system. For enterprises that already have UNIX accounts for every user of the network, this is a viable option.

▲ **Security=server**—This mode is the clear choice when all users do not have or should not have UNIX accounts. In this mode, user access is authenticated through a server other than the UNIX SAMBA server; for example, an NT PDC. This allows a single NT machine to grant access to both NT and SAMBA resources using a single database of user names and passwords. It also has the great advantage of not requiring users to change their passwords on two different systems. When this entry is made in the *[global]* section, the name of the server that will perform the authentication must be added in the *password server=* entry.

NOTE: This name will be the NetBIOS name of the server. For that machine to be found, it will have to be added to the /etc/hosts file on the UNIX system.

A drawback to SAMBA is that it is only useful if your clients use SMB protocols. This includes Windows 3.11, Windows 95, and NT, but not NetWare or Macintosh clients.

NOTE: SAMBA does not yet support encrypted passwords, which NT 4.0 Service Pack 3 requires. As a result, for SAMBA installations, Windows 3.11, and Windows 95 clients can see the UNIX resources, but NT clients cannot. The NT Registry can be edited to permit transmission of unencrypted passwords. In Regedt32.exe select the HKEY_LOCAL_MACHINE tree and go to the \SYSTEM\CURRENTCONTROLSET\SERVICES\RDR\PARAMETERS subkey. Add the new value EnablePlainTextPassword and specify the Data Type as REG_DWORD. Set the data value to 1 and exit the Registry editor.

NFS Servers

NFS represents a different approach to providing cross-platform file access between UNIX and NT. NFS does not use the SMB protocols. It relies on two methods to provide the file access across PC-based and UNIX systems. The communication between the server machines and clients employs Remote Procedure Calls (RPC) functioning at the session level. The actual data transfers are achieved via External Data Representation (XDR) protocols that handle the translation across operating systems and computer hardware platforms. However, to the NT network user, there is little functional difference between NFS and SAMBA. UNIX resources are browseable, and data can be read or written to UNIX resources if the permissions are set to allow this.

NT NETWORK CLIENT CONFIGURATION   Unlike SAMBA, NFS client software must be installed to provide the file-sharing services. This is because the RPC and XDR protocols are not built in to the Microsoft network platform as is SMB. Although this may seem to be a disadvantage, the only complication arises at the level of Windows 3.11 machines because of the need to use memory resources to load the network drivers for NFS. If Windows 3.11 machines must also load protocols for other networks, such as NT and NetWare, the computer may not have enough memory left over to run applications. Otherwise, the third-party NFS software client packages for PCs typically provide for easy installation.

This requirement for installing NFS client software also has the advantage that NFS for the Macintosh exists and there is even an NFS gateway for NetWare, although it has some drawbacks in terms of performance compared to full NFS client installations. The bottom line is that more platforms have NFS support than SAMBA support.

User authentication is typically handled by the NFS client on the PC via a logon window that will accept a user name and password that is used to check against the UNIX accounts database. If the logon is authenticated, there can be a series of mounts of UNIX resources that can be preconfigured by the user. This is similar to the Reconnect At Logon option for network drives in Microsoft networking. Any requests for connecting to new resources will invoke a comparison of the user name and password that were entered at logon with the user permissions for the shared resource. The mounted NFS resource will appear as a new drive letter in the File Manager or Explorer just as with NT shares, NetWare server resources, or SAMBA shares.

It is possible for only the NFS Daemon on a UNIX system to stop operating. When this occurs, a client is unable to view files on the UNIX system, but it is not always clear that the failure to connect is due to a problem at the client or the server. It used to be that a failure of the NFS Daemon would hang the client if it requested resources, but this is not always the case in recent versions of the NFS client software. When connections cannot be made, you need to be sure that the NFS Daemon is running and that the resources have been exported (see next section) by the server.

UNIX CONFIGURATION   NFS can be considered the mirror image of SAMBA in that there is less work to be done by the system administrator because NFS is the standard method of file transfer used on UNIX systems. The UNIX administrator must configure the resources to be shared. This process should be given considerable thought because it is easy to produce a rather haphazard NFS organization that is subject to more frequent failures. Most UNIX systems are designed to have the NFS server come online when the UNIX machine is booted—if the server has been set up to provide what are called *exports*.

Exports are resources that are physically located on one or more computers. The list of these resources are placed into the /etc/exports file.

The general steps to make a UNIX resource available involve creating the correct entries in the /etc/exports file. Once that is done, the resources are made available by invoking the command (whose exact form will vary across UNIX systems) that activates the exports. The contents of the /etc/exports file include the path name of the resource to be shared and can also include information regarding access privileges (such as read-only, or which workstations are permitted access).

Applications Servers

We will briefly mention methods that can allow applications-sharing across platforms. You can get more information by contacting the vendors listed in Table 5-2 (which is only a representative listing of vendors). The X-Windows packages were developed in the UNIX environment to provide a common graphical interface for applications and had nothing to do with the Windows family of products from Microsoft. X-Windows programs have been ported to run under Microsoft Windows and with these programs, any UNIX application that will run under X-Windows can now be run from an NT network client.

The capability to run Microsoft Windows applications on UNIX workstations is gaining more attention as the power of PC-based machines has increased to challenge that of RISC workstations. Many UNIX users frequently use PCs, and they want to stay at their UNIX machines and run the same programs for word processing, and so on. UNIX systems have achieved this using either hardware or software.

PC emulation software running on the UNIX workstations was the first method used to provide a hardware-independent way to bring Intel-based applications to the UNIX world. Two well-known packages are SunPC from Sun Microsystems, Inc. and SoftWindows from Insignia Solutions, Inc. Both systems achieve their goal, and they have improved as newer versions have been produced. However, all such methods impose a substantial CPU overhead on whatever UNIX hardware is running the emulator. If users are accustomed to running their spreadsheet on a fast PC, they will find the performance of the UNIX emulation to be noticeably slower.

One consequence of the emergence of the thin client concept (see the earlier section, "Thin Clients") has been the creation of application server software that will support more than just Microsoft clients for NT Servers running the new Terminal Server package. Citrix Systems, Inc. has (to date, in beta form only) an add-on component to Terminal Server called pICAsso. This software allows DOS, Macintosh, UNIX, and web browser clients to run Windows applications that are made available through the NT Terminal Server. Further consideration of thin clients can be found in Chapter 9; however, suffice it to say that the speed of NT applications executed on an NT terminal server and displayed on a UNIX machine is determined by both the speed of the network connections and the number of clients accessing the terminal server.

One hardware solution offered by some UNIX hardware vendors involves having an Intel processor board that can be added to provide support for Microsoft Windows. In the real world, you will most often find a UNIX box sitting next to a PC as the most cost-effective solution.

Company	Product Name	Product Type	Web Site
Citrix Systems, Inc.	pICAsso	NT applications add-on to Microsoft's Terminal Server; supports multiple-platform clients	www.citrix.com
Digital Equipment Corporation	Excursion	X-Windows server	www.digital.com
Distinct Corporation	Distinct NFS X/32	NFS	www.distinct.com
Frontier Technologies Corporation	X Server Suite	NFS and X-Windows server	www.frontiertech.com
FTP Software, Inc.	InterDrive	NFS	www.ftp.com
Hummingbird Communications, Ltd.	eXceed/NT	NFS and X-Windows server	www.hummingbird.com
Insignia Solutions, Inc.	SoftWindows	PC emulation for UNIX	www.insignia.com
Intergraph Corporation	DiskShare and Disk Access	NFS server and client	www.intergraph.com
NetManage, Inc.	XoftWare/32, Chameleon32/NFS	NFS and X-Windows server	www.netmanage.com
Sun Microsystems, Inc.	SunPC	PC emulation for UNIX	www.sun.com/desktop/products/PCCP/sunpc/

Table 5-2. UNIX Utility Vendors

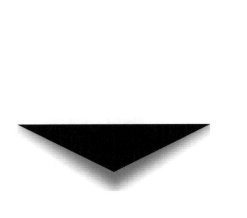

CHAPTER 6

Domain Name System

As a network increases in size, naming services become increasingly more important to the overall function of the network. This is especially important in TCP/IP-based networks. Naming services provide us humans with a translation of an IP address to a people-friendly naming convention. Without naming services, we would have to remember the IP addresses of all the servers and other devices we need to use. Our only other option would be to maintain a local file on every computer that mapped a name to the IP address of every other device we plan to communicate with. Try to imagine what it would be like to surf the Web using IP addresses instead of the **www.*easytoremembernames*.com** convention made available to us by DNS. Naming services also allows hosts to be moved to different locations on the network. This is because moving a server to a new network subnet requires that its IP address be changed. In an environment configured to use DNS, the move only needs to be recorded once in the nameserver. If an environment uses locally configured IP to name files, every workstation would need to be updated with the server's new IP address. Client workstations configured to use a naming service need no reconfiguration as long as they have the address of a name server, assuming they normally use the file server's name when establishing a connection.

On TCP/IP-based networks, the Domain Name System (DNS) and the Windows Internet Naming Service (WINS) play an important role in keeping the servers, printers, and workstations communicating with each other. In this chapter we will discuss the Domain Name System and its features and functions, as well as how to install and configure the Microsoft DNS service. Although we will look more closely at WINS in the next chapter, we will look here at how DNS and WINS can work together to create a dynamic name service. Finally, we will cover DNS planning and look at the future of DNS.

INTERNET DOMAINS

DNS domain naming is hierarchical. All domains originate from the root domain (unnamed) to a top-level domain (for example, COM, NET, and ORG) to a second-level domain (for example, MIT, UMN, HP, and INTERNIC) to (optionally) a subdomain(s) and finally the hostname. The resulting name identifying an FTP host in a marketing department might look like this: ftp.marketing.company.com. At the top of this hierarchy of names is the root, from which the top-level domains branch. They were created to break down the Internet domain into separate meaningful groups. The top-level domains are COM, EDU, GOV, MIL, NET, ORG, INT, and two-letter country codes derived from the countries listed in ISO-3166.

NOTE: You can easily find a listing of the country codes by running an Internet search with the keyword ISO-3166. *A good listing can be found at **www.eexpert.com/_gp_dng.htm**.*

Figure 6-1 illustrates the top-level and second-level domain structure. Although the figure has one second-level domain example under each top-level domain, there are countless others. Below the second-level domains are subdomains and hosts. It is up to each second-level domain owner to define the structure below their domain.

Top-Level Domains

The top-level domain structure, although hierarchical, is still rather flat even though there are millions of hosts. This is because there are few top-level domains under which secondary domains can be located. The COM top-level domain has an extraordinary number of second-level domains directly under it that are not organized by additional subcategories. Hindsight might have led us to define several second-level domains below COM, perhaps breaking down the domains by business type, and then allowing registrations below them. This extended hierarchy can be seen in some country domains where second-level domains are organized into logical domains under which the registered domains are entered.

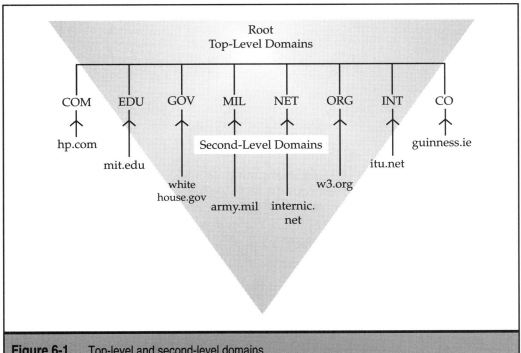

Figure 6-1.   Top-level and second-level domains

Table 6-1 lists the top-level domains and a brief description of their intended use.

Top-Level Domains	Description
COM	Intended for use by companies or commercial entities. This top-level domain has grown substantially in recent years. There have been discussions on whether COM should be broken down into multiple "top-level" subdomains.
EDU	Intended for use by educational institutions. This top-level domain has also grown substantially in recent years. Once open to all educational institutions, use is now confined to four-year universities and colleges. Other educational entities, such as K-12, high school, and two-year community colleges, are registered in the appropriate country domain.
GOV	Intended for use by government agencies. As with COM and EDU, this top-level domain has also seen its registrations increase. Its use is now confined to U.S. federal government agencies. Other governments and their agencies, as well as U.S. state and local government agencies, are now registered in the appropriate country domain.
INT	Intended for use by organizations established by international treaties. You cannot register in this domain unless you comply with the requirements found in RFC 1591.
MIL	Intended for use by the United States military. Second-level registration for the MIL domain is handled by the DDN Registry at nic.ddn.mil.
NET	Intended for use by network providers. This includes NIC and NOC hosts. Your ISP might have a second-level NET domain that it uses for its own infrastructure equipment, for example.
ORG	Intended for use by organizations that don't clearly fit into one of the other categories. For example, many noncommercial organizations use ORG.

Table 6-1.   Top-Level domains

Top-Level Domains	Description
Country (US, FR, UK, IE, DE, and so on)	Intended for a variety of uses as defined by the top-level domain owner. Each country defines and manages the structure of its respective domain. The managing entity may have a geographical structure like the top-level domain US, which breaks down the domains by state and locality. The US domain also has made accommodations within each state domain for schools not qualified for the EDU domain, state government entities, libraries, museums, and other similar entities. More information on the US domain can be found in RFC 1480.

Table 6-1.   Top-Level domains (*continued*)

Second-Level Domains and the InterNIC

Now that you know the basic structure of the top- and second-level domains, you'll have to get one for your organization if you don't already have one. Before submitting a registration request you should check to ensure that the domain is not already registered. You can find out if a name is taken and register second-level domains underneath the COM, EDU, ORG, NET, and GOV domains through the Internet Registry at the InterNIC. There are several ways to complete the registration process. Perhaps the simplest way is to request the domain from your Internet service provider (ISP). Your ISP will contact the InterNIC and process the domain request on your behalf.

Another option is to register the domain directly with the InterNIC. There are instructions and templates at **www.rs.internic.net/rs-internic.html** that help you through the registration process, and provide information on maintaining your registration. Currently, the InterNIC charges $US100 for the initial registration, which is valid for two years. About 60 days before the two years are up, the InterNIC will send a renewal form for the next year. Each successive year after the initial two-year period costs $US50. If you lapse, you will lose the registration and will have to reregister the domain—if it is still available.

If you handle the registration yourself, note that you must provide the InterNIC with at least two name servers that list your domain.

Often, in large organizations, the administrative and billing contacts change over time. Even the location of the organization may change. For that reason, you should make sure that a procedure exists to keep your contact information up-to-date. You can always change the contact information for yourself by using the web pages at InterNIC.

NOTE: If there is a dispute between two or more parties for a domain name, the InterNIC does not help decide who has the rights. It only provides contact information to the parties involved. Also, having registered a domain name doesn't give you any trademark status. It is up to the requester to ensure that the name doesn't infringe on an existing trademark.

Using Whois

If you need to find a contact for a particular domain or verify information for your own domain, you have several options. One is to access the whois database via a web-based query. This can be found at **www.rs.internic.net/rs-internic.html.** Another option is to telnet to **internic.net**. At the prompt, type **Whois** to enter the whois database. In both the web form and the telnet session, enter the second-level domain name for which you would like to search. Whois will search for and return any information that matches your search string. Additional search parameters, as well as a tutorial on the various methods of accessing whois, are located at **www.rs.internic.net/tools/whois.html.**

DIGGING INTO DNS

In order to keep things simple for us humans, DNS does a lot of background work. DNS takes on the mammoth role of managing the complex and translating it into something we can use. As with most systems designed to make something simple out of something complex, the background functions are inherently complicated. Let's look at the concepts behind DNS. You need to know them well to plan and deploy DNS in your NT environment.

Zones

A zone is a defined area of the DNS name space. One (or more) particular DNS host is responsible for each zone. The records for a zone are stored in a zone file. The concept of a zone can be tricky to grasp, but it is really very simple. Picture a zone as a coin sitting on a small piece of paper. The paper is a domain, like hp.com, in which sections are broken down into several subsections, or subdomains. The coin sits on top of the paper and covers a portion of the paper's surface. The zone is responsible for covering an area of the domain (just as the coin covers a section of the paper) and acts as the authority for that section of the domain. Adding additional coins is necessary to fully cover the paper. The converse is true for zones; each area in the domain structure must have a zone server defined to provide DNS service. Figure 6-2 illustrates how zones fit into a domain.

Note that the hp.com zone doesn't include the subdomains under it. Although you can have a zone that includes a domain and subdomains below it, you can also delegate the responsibility to other zones residing on other DNS servers. Reasons for doing so could include network topology, geographical, or business organization considerations. For example, Widgetron is a company that has two very distinct divisions that rely on the corporate IS to manage their DNS. Recently, one division built a capable IS staff; now it is

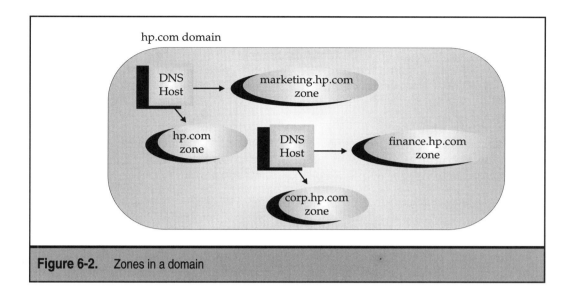

Figure 6-2. Zones in a domain

constructing a new data center. This division has requested more control over the DNS. Because corporate has only one domain, widgetron.com, it cannot give this division control over its part of the DNS without giving it control over the entire domain. However, by creating a subdomain under widgetron.com (called div1.widgetron.com) and listing the division's new DNS server as the name server for the domain, corporate IS can allow the division to administer div1.widgetron.com without impacting the entire widgetron.com domain.

Domains and Subdomains

Domains are a defined area of the name space that provide a logical grouping for subdomains and hosts. By organizing hosts into domains and subdomains, DNS can manage a large number of hosts in a distributed manner while using a naming convention that we humans can understand. There may be many subdomains underneath a second-level domain. For example, domain.com could have finance.domain.com and corp.finance.domain.com to further organize hosts. Subdomains are managed by their respective organizations, allowing the organization to define and manage as many subdomains under their registered domain name as they see fit. However, it is wise to plan your domain structure carefully and take administrative functions into consideration.

Name Servers

There are several different types of name servers. A *primary* name server has the information for its zones located locally on the server. The primary name server is the authoritative server and administration point for its name space. A *secondary* name server receives its zone information from the zone master server (which can be either a primary or secondary server) via a periodic zone transfer. Instead of updating the DNS files on the secondary server manually, the zone transfer function occurs automatically. To a DNS client, a secondary name server is assumed to be as authoritative as a primary name server.

Name Resolution

Name resolution is where "the rubber meets the road". A client host (which could be another DNS server) or workstation initiates the process by sending a query to the DNS host. There are three types of queries used in name resolution.

Recursive Queries

A recursive query is sent from a requester, usually a client workstation, to a DNS host. The client sends a hostname and domain and expects the DNS server to respond with an IP address for the host. The DNS server responds with the requested information or a message that the information doesn't exist on the server. A recursive query is also used between DNS servers when exchanging information using the forwarder function.

Iterative Queries

An iterative query is usually between DNS servers. A name server sends an iterative query to another server when looking for a name server that can resolve a client request. It expects the queried name server to send back information about name servers that it knows about that might be able to resolve the original client request.

Inverse Queries

An inverse query is a reverse address-lookup request. The DNS server or client sends an inverse query when trying to determine the name associated with a particular IP address. This is the opposite of a recursive query. The client sends an IP address and expects the DNS server to respond with a hostname and domain.

Forwarders and Slaves

Forwarders provide an important function when you are using DNS on a corporate network that is connected to the Internet. An internal DNS server for company.domain. com, for example, can be configured to use another DNS server, typically one running on a firewall, that is specifically designated as a forwarder. When the internal DNS server receives a query for information outside the internal zone(s), it communi- cates with the forwarding server. The forwarding server in turn communicates with name servers on the Internet and returns the information to the internal DNS server. If no information is found, the internal server attempts to communicate with name servers other than the forwarder. This mode is called the *nonexclusive mode*. An example of this mode can be seen in Figure 6-3.

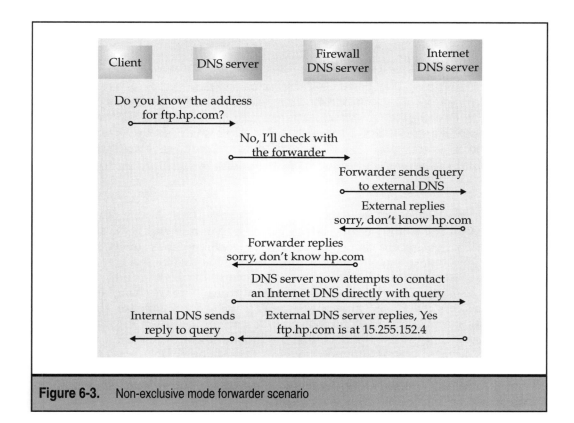

Figure 6-3. Non-exclusive mode forwarder scenario

The other mode, called *exclusive mode*, follows the same process but does not attempt to communicate with name servers other than the forwarder. DNS servers configured to use only forwarders are called *slaves*. When a slave cannot resolve a query, and its forwarder(s) is also unable to resolve the query, the slave server does not attempt to communicate with other name servers; instead it sends a message to the client indicating that the information cannot be found.

Database Files and Resource Records

The database (DB) files and its associated resource records (RR) form the "guts" of a DNS server. They contain all the configuration parameters and DNS information necessary for the DNS server to do its job. Initially, the files and records seem complicated. Indeed they are, but after you have worked with them awhile, you become familiar with their specific functions. In fact, if you use the DNS Manager tool, manipulating these files directly is unnecessary. Even so, it is recommended that you understand the nature of the files—not to mention that regardless of the interface used to modify resource record values, you still need to understand what they do.

> **NOTE:** In Microsoft DNS Server, DNS information, including startup parameters and zone information, is kept in the Registry after the first system reboot when the service was installed. If you want to use the original boot file, you must edit the HKEY_LOCAL_MACHINE\SYSTEM\CurrentControlSet\ Services\DNS\Parameters area of the Registry and delete the value EnableRegistryBoot. This is not recommended unless you have a specific reason for doing so. Once the value is deleted you will loose all zone additions and changes made using the DNS Manager tool.

Zone File

The zone file contains information about a particular zone. This file includes the Start of Authority (SOA) record for the zone, which indicates that the server is the authority for the domain. The SOA record contains several values including the primary name server DNS name, and the refresh and retry values for secondary name servers to use when contacting a master server.

There is also a serial number that is incremented when there are changes in the zone. Secondary servers check this value periodically. If the serial number on the master is greater than the serial number of the zone data copy it has, the server will initiate a zone transfer to refresh its database. Another important SOA record value is the time-to-live interval (TTL), which sets the minimum amount of time another DNS server is permitted to cache the data returned to it during a query of the first server. This ensures that the cached data remains on the server for only a limited time, preventing old, inaccurate information from being passed back to a client.

Cache File

The cache file contains information on the root name servers for the Internet. The cache file is used by the local name server to "refer" lookups outside its authoritative domain to valid root servers who can then assist in finding the DNS server that is the authority over a particular domain. You can view and download the current file via FTP at at **ftp://rs.internic.net/domain/named.cache.**

Reverse Lookup File

The reverse lookup file allows the DNS to work backwards, by returning a hostname when a resolver sends an IP address. This function has often been used as a security mechanism by allowing a host on the network to reverse look up the name of the computer requesting a connection. If the name associated with the IP address matches what the host has in its security database, the requesting computer is allowed access. This function doesn't work when you are using DHCP because a workstation's IP address is subject to change. In a WINS-enabled network, this limitation can be circumvented by integrating WINS and Microsoft DNS as described later in this chapter.

BIND Boot File

The BIND boot file is simply a configuration file for Berkeley Internet Name Domain (BIND) based DNS servers.

It specifies:

▼ The local directory where other DNS files can be found

■ The location of the cache file

■ The domain that the server has authority over (primary and secondary)

■ A list of servers with zone information for primary and secondary servers

▲ A list of forwarders that are available to attempt recursive queries

NOTE: In Microsoft DNS, the preceding information is stored in the Registry rather than the BIND boot file.

Name Server Record

Located within the zone file, the name server record lists the name servers for a particular domain so that other name servers know where to go when they need to look up a name in that particular domain.

Host Record

This record is also located in the zone file. The host record defines the location of static, hostname IP address entries for a zone. When a DNS server receives a request to resolve a hostname to an IP address, the host record is read and the IP address value returned.

Mail Exchange (MX) Record

The MX record lists the hosts that handle mail for a particular domain or host. There can be multiple mail hosts listed in the MX record. The resolver tries servers by selecting the MX server with the lowest preference number in the list, and then moves to the server with the next highest preference number. In this manner, e-mail can be forwarded to a primary mail server in your organization. If the server is down, it can be forwarded to another e-mail server. If that server is down, mail might then be forwarded to an e-mail server at your ISP until it can be sent to your primary or secondary mail server.

Canonical Name (CNAME) Record

The CNAME resource record defines an alias (nickname) for the official (canonical) hostname. There are several situations in which one or more CNAME records are useful. One situation is when you are changing a hostname for a device. You can create a CNAME record for the new host record that has the old hostname so that users can still use either. Also, because the use of multiple CNAME records allows multiple hostnames to be resolved to a single IP address, CNAME records allow a single host to be known by several names such as ftp.domain.com, www.domain.com, gopher. domain.com, and so on. This can be helpful when you want a single server to be known by different names that represent the different services that it may provide. For example, a single server could be known as ftp.skippy.com and www.skippy.com so that users can easily find the server by the service that it provides.

Pointer Record

The pointer record contains a static mapping of an IP address to a hostname for reverse lookups. It is a sort of mirror image of the host file. The IP address is listed in reverse order and has in-addr.arpa appended to it; so, for example, the pointer record for skippy.domain.com at 10.5.31.101 is 101.31.5.10.in-addr.arpa IN PTR skippy.domain.com.

DNS, WINS, AND RFCS

Although you might feel like you live in a Microsoft world and even assumed that WINS would handle all of your name service needs, take a closer look. If you play a role in keeping a large network running, you definitely know of a UNIX host or two, and perhaps you have a mainframe with a brand new IP stack. We'd also be willing to bet that some of the intranet servers that have been popping up around the network are running Linux or some other flavor of UNIX. Unless your company did a complete conversion to new Windows 95 or NT desktops, you probably have a few DOS or Win 3.11 desktops running LanWorkplace or some other non-WINS-aware stack. Larger networks also tend to be connected to the Internet via a dedicated circuit and firewall so that TCP/IP desktops have access to the web, Internet e-mail, and FTP file transfers.The point is that there are plenty of reasons to run DNS on your network. Not the least of which is that Microsoft has said that when Directory Services becomes a reality, it will use DNS to allow clients to find directory servers. Later, clients will be able to break the NetBIOS over IP chains and use DNS as the dynamic naming service of choice.

DNS and WINS

Because Microsoft used NetBIOS over TCP/IP (NBT) as the foundation of Microsoft networking, mechanisms for managing naming services that didn't fit into the DNS architecture had to be constructed. The development of WINS was driven by the shortcomings of running a broadcast protocol (NetBIOS) over IP. We will discuss WINS in the next chapter but before we get there, we will look at how Microsoft DNS can use WINS.

The Microsoft DNS Server can be configured to use the WINS database to resolve NetBIOS name queries. Essentially, it can act as a front end to a WINS database, allowing DNS clients to query the DNS server. The WINS server can be configured to query the WINS database if it can't find the address in its host database. If WINS finds the entry, it returns an address to the DNS server. The DNS server sends the address to the client. This allows a DNS client to find a WINS registered host. This is an important feature for NT-based networking, which we will talk about more in the "Integrating DNS with WINS/DHCP" section later in this chapter.

Microsoft DNS RFC Support

Although Microsoft DNS offers integration with WINS, which is a nonstandard implementation to the DNS server, Microsoft DNS is based on standards that have been adopted by the computer industry. Microsoft DNS supports the following RFCs: 1033, 1034, 1035, 1101, 1123, 1183, and 1536.

Although the RFCs can make for some pretty dry reading, if you are serious about thoroughly understanding DNS, you will want to take a few hours to review them. Table 6-2 lists some of the more interesting DNS-related RFCs.

There are other RFCs that have information related to DNS; they can be found by searching the InterNIC's Internet documentation page at: **www.ds.internic.net/ds/ dspg0intdoc.html.**

RFC	Title
1033	Domain Administrators Operations Guide
1034	Domain Names—Concepts and Facilities
1035	Domain Names—Implementation and Specification
1101	DNS Encoding of Network Names and Other Types
1123	Requirements for Internet Hosts—Application and Support
1183	New DNS Resource Records (RR) Definitions
1480	The US Domain
1536	Common DNS Implementation Errors and Suggested Fixes
1794	DNS Support for Load Balancing
1883	Internet Protocol, Version 6 (IPv6) Specification
1886	DNS Extensions to Support IP Version 6
2050	Internet Registry IP Allocation Guidelines
2065	Domain Name System Security Extensions

Table 6-2.   DNS-Related RFCs

INSTALLING AND CONFIGURING MICROSOFT DNS

Aside from the complexities inherent in the DNS protocol, installing and configuring Microsoft DNS is straightforward. Nonetheless, it would be a good idea to set up a Microsoft DNS server where you can install and configure it with the intention of getting familiar with it before attempting an installation on the production network.

Installing Microsoft DNS Server

The first step when installing the DNS server is to make sure you have accurate information configured in your server's TCP/IP stack. The installation pulls the current host name and domain from the TCP/IP configuration. If you don't have the information already configured, enter it and reboot before you install this service.

Next, click on the Network icon in the Control Panel or right-click on the Network Neighborhood desktop icon and select Properties. Click on the Services tab to make sure the server is not already installed. Then click on the Add button. Select DNS Server from the list and click on OK. Enter the location of the NT Server files and click on Continue. After the files have been copied and DNS Server is displayed in the Service listing, click on Close and restart the server. After installation, the DNS files are located in the <%Systemroot%>\systems32\DNS directory.

Configuring DNS Server

Installing the DNS service is easy and if you've done your planning, configuring the service isn't much harder. To manage and configure DNS, click on DNS Manager in the Administrative Tools menu. This brings up the interface you use to configure the DNS server (see Figure 6-4).

Domains and Zones

The next step is to add the local DNS server by clicking on New Server under the DNS drop-down menu. Enter the DNS server name as it appears in your TCP/IP configuration. The local server will appear under the server list in the left window of the Manager Tool. Double-click on the local server to view statistics and zones for the new server. Figure 6-4 shows the new server Toonces as it looks before any configuration. As you can see, there are also other DNS servers listed in the manager. If you have other Microsoft DNS servers, you can also manage them remotely from the DNS Manager.

The next step is to create a zone by right-clicking on the server and selecting New Zone from the menu. This brings up a dialog box as seen in Figure 6-5, allowing you to set the zone type.

You have the option of selecting either a primary or secondary zone type. In a primary zone the server is the master server for the zone, and the zone information is stored and maintained locally. In a secondary zone the server gets a copy of the zone information from a master server via a zone transfer.

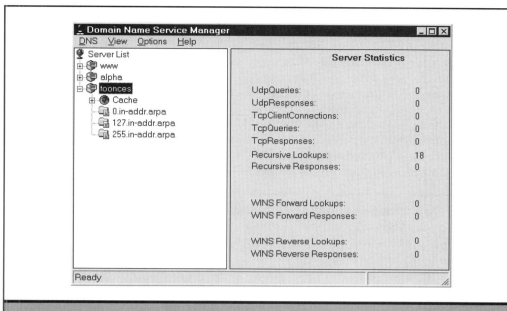

Figure 6-4. DNS Manager view of a new server

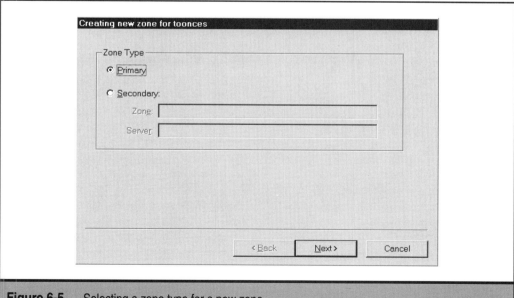

Figure 6-5. Selecting a zone type for a new zone

If you select Secondary, you must enter the zone as it is defined on the master server and the IP address of the master server. If the zone is listed under another Microsoft DNS server in the DNS Manager, you can also drag the small hand icon to the zone, and the zone name and address will be filled in for you, as seen in Figure 6-6.

If you are creating a new primary zone, select Primary and click on Next. The resulting dialog box requires that you enter the zone name and the name for the zone database file, as shown in Figure 6-7.

Once you have entered the zone name and database file name, click on Next. The next dialog box indicates that the necessary information to create a new zone has been entered, and that it is ready to proceed when you are. Click on Finish to complete the creation of the new primary zone. Repeat the process for any additional zones for the DNS server.

NOTE: The Registry keys for each zone are located under HKEY_LOCAL_MACHINE/SYSTEM/ CurrentControlSet/Services/DNS/Zones. Each zone is listed below this key and has a type key REG_DWORD that indicates whether the DNS is a primary (1) or secondary (2) server for the zone.

The next step in configuring the DNS server is to add any subdomains under the new zone(s). To do this, right-click over the zone and select the New Domain menu item. In

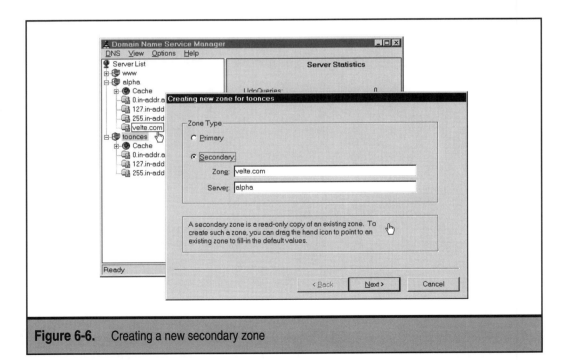

Figure 6-6. Creating a new secondary zone

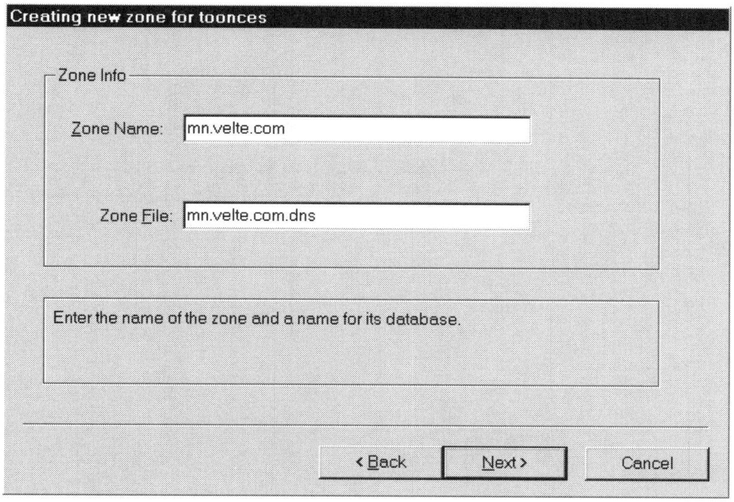

Figure 6-7.   Creating a new primary zone

the New Domain dialog box, enter the name of the new domain and click on OK. The new domain is added below the parent domain in the DNS Manager Server List window. Once all the new domains have been added, you can proceed with the task of entering new hosts and records. This can be accomplished by right-clicking on the domain you want to edit, as seen in Figure 6-8, and selecting either New Host or New Record.

When adding a new host, you are asked for the hostname and the host IP address. In addition, there is a check box that can be selected to create a new pointer (PTR) record for the host entry to enable reverse lookups. If you select New Record, as shown in Figure 6-8, you can add new resource records, including the same record ("A" record), using the Add Host selection. In the New Resource Record dialog box you can add a variety of record types. Table 6-3 lists the most commonly-used record types.

Once you have established your zones, domains, and subdomains, most of the remaining administrative tasks are associated with adding, deleting, and changing resource records. Be careful not to permit the addition or deletion of zones, domains, and subdomains as part of the day-to-day administration of the server. Identify a small group of people who have a good understanding of DNS and your network as the only people authorized to add zones, domains, and subdomains. Your DNS structure can get ridiculously over-complicated and thus prone to failure if you allow "too many cooks in the kitchen."

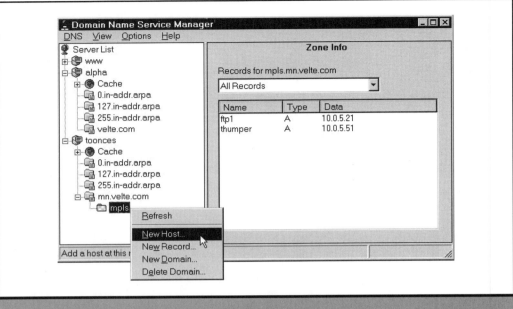

Figure 6-8. Adding hosts and resource records in a domain

Record Type	Description
A Record	Address Record is used for host entries in a particular domain. This record is added when adding new host entries into the domain.
CNAME Record	Canonical, or Alias Record, is used for adding additional host name entries to an existing hostname. Adding an alias for a host allows it to be known by multiple names.
MX Record	Mail Exchange Record is used to define a mail exchanger for the domain that will accept or forward e-mail sent to user@domain.com. The preference number allows multiple servers to be prioritized so that the server with the lowest preference number receives mail messages. Multiple entries enable mail messages to be held by a server with a higher preference number until the server with the lowest preference number is available.

Table 6-3. Common record types

Record Type	Description
PTR Record	Pointer Records are used when the DNS server is asked to perform a reverse lookup. It allows a server or workstation to send an IP address and receive the DNS name associated with that address.

Table 6-3.   Common record types (*continued*)

Integrating DNS with WINS/DHCP

As mentioned earlier, Microsoft DNS can be integrated with WINS. Because DHCP clients can register with WINS, DNS gets "pass-through" access to the WINS registrations. Figure 6-9 outlines the process a workstation would use to resolve an address not found in DNS but found in WINS.

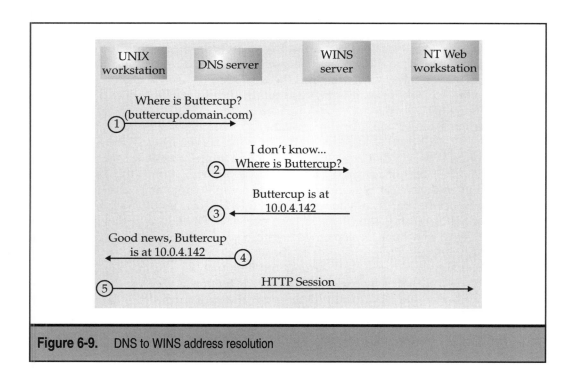

Figure 6-9.   DNS to WINS address resolution

1. A UNIX workstation wants to view a web page on an NT workstation named *Buttercup*. The UNIX workstation sends a query to the DNS server asking for the IP address of Buttercup (buttercup.domain.com).

2. The DNS server checks its host records in the zone file but doesn't find a record for Buttercup. The DNS server, configured to use WINS resolution, asks the WINS server if it knows the address for Buttercup.

3. The WINS server checks its database and because the NT workstation uses DHCP and WINS, its IP address and NetBIOS name Buttercup are dynamically registered with the WINS server. The WINS server responds to the DNS server's request by sending the IP address for Buttercup.

4. The DNS server, in turn, replies to the UNIX workstation's query with Buttercup's IP address.

5. The UNIX workstation can now contact Buttercup and browse the web pages on it.

Before this can happen, you must configure the DNS server to use WINS resolution for the zone. This is accomplished via the DNS Manager by right-clicking on the zone you want to configure. Select Properties from the menu and click the WINS Lookup tab. Check the WINS Resolution check box and enter the address of at least one WINS server, as illustrated in Figure 6-10. If you have more than one WINS server, use the Move Up and Move Down buttons to specify which WINS server is contacted first. In most cases, you should put the closest WINS server at the top of the list to maximize response time.

The other checkbox, Settings Only Affect Local Server, is used to change the read-only setting on specific fields in the secondary server zone file received from a master server, allowing you to manually modify fields in the zone file.

Clicking the Advanced button brings up the Advanced Zone Properties dialog box, as shown in Figure 6-11.

The check box allows you to enable the submission of the DNS domain as a NetBIOS scope when the DNS server sends a request to the WINS server. Instead of the DNS server asking the WINS server "What is the IP address of Buttercup?", the DNS server would ask "What is the IP address of Buttercup.companydomain.com?". The WINS server would read Buttercup as the NetBIOS machine name and companydomain.com as the NetBIOS scope. We suspect that hardly anyone checks this box. Use of a NetBIOS scope is strongly discouraged by Microsoft, especially if you are using DNS. The option is there for organizations that may have implemented NetBIOS scopes and need to use the option so that NetBIOS names in different scopes can be uniquely identified by DNS.

The Cache Timeout Value sets the amount of time that the information returned in a particular query can be cached in the DNS server for reuse without the DNS server having to resubmit the query to the WINS server. The value defaults to ten minutes but

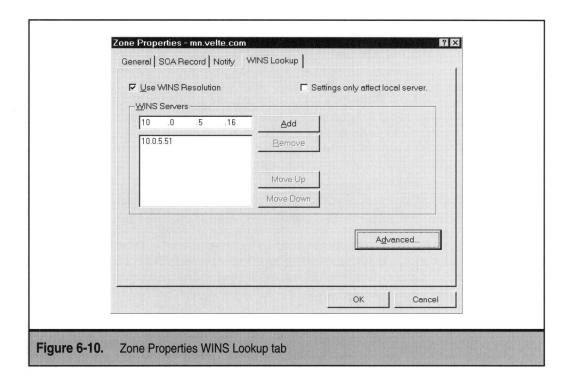

Figure 6-10.   Zone Properties WINS Lookup tab

can be set for more or less time depending how often the WINS information changes. If you have an extremely high number of updates to WINS, the value should be set lower. If your WINS environment is mostly static, infrequently registering new names, you could set the value higher.

The Lookup Timeout Value is used to set the amount of time the DNS server should wait for a response from the WINS server. The default is one second. If your closest WINS server resides over a slow WAN link that has periods of high utilization, or your WINS server is running at high utilization, you may need to set this value higher. However, if this value needs to be increased to anything over a couple of seconds, you should probably examine your network architecture and the number and placement of your WINS servers.

Another configurable feature is the WINS Reverse Lookup. It allows a DNS server to perform a reverse lookup for a client against a WINS database. To enable this feature, configure the in-addr.arpa zone properties under the WINS Reverse Lookup tab. To enable, check the Use WINS Reverse Lookup check box and enter the DNS host domain associated with the in-addr.arpa zone.

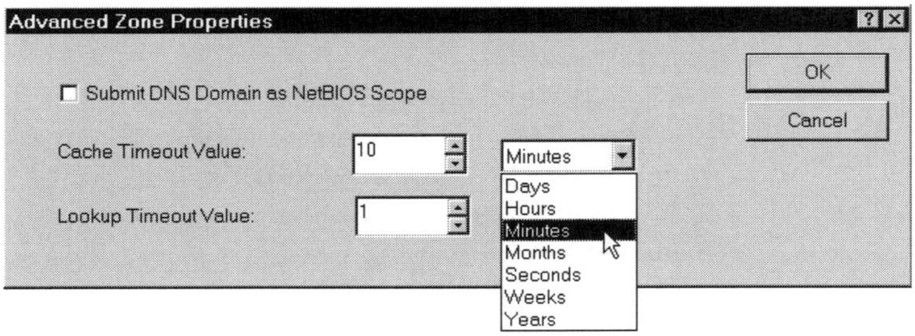

Figure 6-11.   Advanced Zone Properties configuration window

Special Configuration Items

A couple of interesting features not unique to Microsoft DNS are the round-robin lookup and the DNS Notify features. Round-robin provides load balancing and DNS Notify allows you to further tune how your DNS servers communicate with each other.

Round-robin Lookup

Another configurable DNS function is round-robin lookup. It is essentially the opposite of the CNAME function. A CNAME record allows you to define multiple hostnames for a single IP address. The round-robin technique allows you to define multiple IP addresses for a single hostname or alias. To accomplish this, follow these four easy steps:

1. Create multiple host entries, one for each replicated server.

2. Add a CNAME record for each host entry, where the Alias Name is the name you want all of the servers to be known as (it should be the same for all servers).

3. In the For DNS Host Name value, enter the first hostname to be part of the round-robin configuration.

4. Repeat adding CNAME records for all of the hosts to be included in the round-robin configuration.

Round-robin entries are useful in situations where you have multiple servers that are replicated, such as web servers. Round-robin performs basic load balancing functions by sending back all of the addresses for a particular hostname in order, from the top of the list to the bottom. Usually the client uses the first address sent by the server. The next client to query DNS is sent the next address in the list. In this manner, traffic can be balanced over multiple servers.

The catch with round-robin load balancing is that although round-robin helps load balance traffic to multiple servers, it is not aware of the state of the servers. If one of the servers crashes, round-robin continues to direct traffic to it each time the IP address of the server gets to the top of the list. The client tries to contact the downed server, but the connection fails. If the client retries, there is still a chance that it will get the downed server's address. Only adding more servers to the round-robin list decreases the odds that the client will get the downed server. Nonetheless, round-robin offers more fault tolerance than a DNS reference to a single server and is very useful when your web (or other type of server) utilization increases to the point where you need multiple servers.

DNS Notify

Although this function was not found in earlier implementations of DNS, DNS Notify can be useful and is available in Microsoft DNS. DNS Notify tells a master server to notify secondary servers that the zone has changed, and that they should request a zone transfer. Configure DNS Notify in the Zone Properties dialog box under the Notify tab. This process is independent of the normal zone transfer interval the secondary server uses to periodically update its zone file. If you are not having any problems with the zones (that is, the secondaries are out of synchronization), then you probably don't want to trigger zone transfers every time the zone information changes.

However, if you want to control which servers are allowed to request and receive a zone transfer, select the Only Allow Access From Secondaries Included On Notify List checkbox. When it is enabled, the primary will only send zone transfers to the secondary servers in the Notify List. This feature can increase the security of your internal DNS by preventing zone transfer requests being processed and sent to an unauthorized party who may be interested in looking at the host records and other information in the file.

DNS Client Configuration

The process for configuring a TCP/IP client to use DNS varies, depending on the client operating system or the TCP/IP stack. Most configurations consist simply of placing the name of the DNS server in the correct box.

Manual Configuration

We'll use Windows 95 as the client in this discussion, but most other clients can be configured in a similar fashion. For DOS-based clients, the configuration for DNS is usually in the Protocol.ini, Net.cfg or some other text file usually located in a network driver directory. Other clients may have a utility that you can use to enter DNS information. A quick look at the network client documentation for a particular client package should give you the necessary information on configuring the client for DNS.

To configure a Windows 95 client, right-click on the Network Neighborhood desktop icon and select Properties from the menu. At the Configuration tab scroll down the Installed Components list until you get to the TCP/IP component(s) associated with a network interface. Double-click on the TCP/IP component to bring up the TCP/IP Properties window. Click on the DNS Configuration tab to display the DNS configuration options, as seen in Figure 6-12.

Select Enable DNS and enter the workstation's hostname if it is not already filled in. Next, add your DNS servers, making sure that the logically closest DNS server is listed first. The first DNS server in the list will be tried first; the next one will be tried only if the first DNS server fails to respond. In the Domain Suffix Search Order box enter the subdomains that will be searched to resolve name queries.

For dialup connections, you may have DNS servers provided to you in the dialup documentation, but more frequently the client simply needs to be configured to get the IP information (including DNS servers) from the dialup server.

Automatic Configuration

Clients can be configured automatically to use specific DNS servers if you have the workstations configured to use DHCP. The DNS configuration, as well as other workstation configuration parameters, can be defined in a DHCP scope and passed to the workstation when it acquires a DHCP lease.

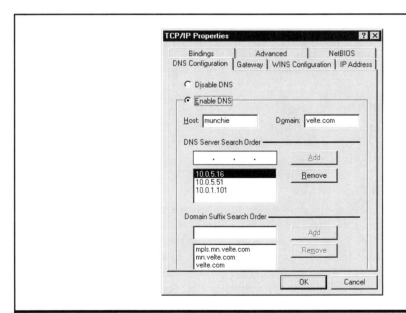

Figure 6-12. Windows 95 DNS client configuration window

For new installations, you can specify in the Unattended.txt file the TCP/IP configurations for the new workstation, including the name of DNS servers (see Chapter 2 for more information).

After you have completed the configuration, you will need to reboot the computer for the configuration to take effect.

Managing DNS

There are several tools provided with or integrated into NT 4.0 that you may find useful when administering DNS.

DNS Manager

Your primary interface with the DNS service is the DNS Manager application installed with Microsoft DNS. Although we have already covered the tool as part of the setup and configuration process, there are some additional features you will find useful in managing DNS servers. DNS Manager allows you to manage local and remote DNS servers using the same interface. This is particularly useful because you should always have multiple DNS servers to manage. Each of the servers added to the management console appears every time the manager is started, and you can manage all of the DNS-related functions on a remote server as easily as on the local one.

NT 5.0 NOTE: In NT 5.0 the management tool interface is contained within the Microsoft Management Console (MMC). Although this interface is new to NT users, the functionality is the same as in NT 4.0.

DNS Statistics

The DNS Manager tool also provides information for each of the servers opened in the management console. The statistics found here are very useful in determining how each DNS server is doing. Keeping up on the statistics allows you to be proactive in your planning. The statistics can tell you when one server is substantially busier than the others, allowing you to shift the load to another server before a crash occurs.

The WINS information can be helpful as well. For example, when using DNS to WINS lookups, you might be surprised at the number of WINS forward and reverse lookups and responses. If there are too many, or if there is a large gap between lookups and responses over a short period of time, you might have a problem with a network link or WINS server. By staying proactive, you can keep ahead of problems.

NSlookup

Nslookup is used to display resource records on a DNS server. A command-line implementation of Nslookup is provided with NT. There are also freeware and shareware implementations of Nslookup that use command-line and GUI interfaces. The NT Nslookup is started by entering **nslookup** at the NT command prompt as follows:

nslookup *[-option ...] [hostname] [server]*.

You can enter multiple options separated by a hyphen. *[hostname]* should be replaced by the name or address of the computer whose address information you want to ascertain. *[server]* identifies the name server you are querying. If *[server]* is left blank it will revert to the default server(s). A summary of the available commands can be displayed by entering **help** or **?** at the Nslookup interactive prompt.

Logging

Although DNS doesn't write large amounts of data to system logs, it does report on significant DNS events such as when the DNS service was started or stopped and when zone transfers have been completed. It also logs DNS database file errors and other DNS errors. It doesn't hurt to start the Event Viewer to peruse the logs once in a while, even if everything seems to be running fine. The information in the log files can let you know about a problem before your users become aware of it, and it can also help you determine tuning and configuration parameters that optimize your networking environment.

INTEGRATING DNS INTO A DIVERSE NETWORK

Designing and implementing DNS on a large network requires careful planning. Part of this process should include a detailed review and documentation of the existing network infrastructure. You should assess at least the following items:

▼ The total number of nodes on the network
- The number of remote locations
- Locations with local TCP/IP-based servers
- The capacity and reliability of WAN circuits
- The topology of network backbones
- The type of Internet connectivity
- The type of firewall(s) used to secure the network
- The geographical and business layout of the organization
- The number and type of private external connections to other organizations
- The configuration of RAS services for remote-dial users
- The NT domain architecture
- The existing WINS architecture
- The staff available to support DNS
- The type of client workstations on the network
- The availability of DHCP and the number of nodes using it

■ The TCP/IP addressing scheme currently in place

▲ The availability of DNS servers at your ISP

You should have all this information together before you begin designing a solution. Once you do, you can use the information to help answer a few key questions and make some important decisions. Let's look at some of the major issues.

Domains

Defining the domains and subdomains has a lasting impact on the network. Having too many subdomains and DNS servers becomes difficult to manage and the domain becomes very difficult for your users to navigate. Too few and you may run into capacity issues.

A number of factors need to be taken into consideration before deciding on a domain architecture: the number of nodes, the number of remote sites with servers, the available bandwidth between larger sites, the way your company is organized to support IS infrastructure, and the way the company is organized geographically. These factors drive a decision to define a single domain for the entire organization, or to break the domain into subdomains.

We have seen very large, geographically-diverse networks with a single domain run quite well. Management has decided to keep the domain structure simple for administrative reasons, or because it gives them the ability to incorporate future technologies or improvements into the infrastructure easily. We have also seen smaller networks that have their domain broken down into subdomains by region. They have several regional offices with small satellite offices connected to them. This type of organization of subdomains around geographical regions worked quite well for them. If you already have a single domain and were thinking about changing it, you might want to wait until NT 5.0 is generally available. You will probably want to reconsider how your domain is structured under NT 5.0. If you don't have to make major changes to your domain for any particular reason, hold off until you have had a chance to look at the next release of NT. Refer to Chapter 13 for more information.

Redundant DNS

Remember that you should have two DNS servers for each zone, a primary and a secondary (both can host more than one zone however). Available support, network topology, and environment will dictate where you place them. DNS servers should always be placed in a secure environment with reliable power and network connectivity. A common configuration is to have one primary server and two or more secondaries located in different physical locations for fault tolerance and disaster recovery. DNS server distribution has one rule: Don't put all your eggs in one basket. On a network that relies on the availability of DNS, failure is not an option. If DNS doesn't work, the whole network might as well be down. Workstations that rely on DNS won't be able to tell the difference. Figure 6-13 illustrates the deployment of primary and multiple secondary servers in well-protected data center environments. In addition, a caching server is deployed at the large site containing local TCP/IP-based servers. The clients are configured to use the two secondaries, but not the primary when resolving. This is done to reduce the load on the primary so that additional secondaries can be added to the environment as required.

If the load on the secondaries increases to capacity, additional secondaries and/or caching servers can be deployed without wholesale modification of the environment.

Load Balancing

Load balancing DNS traffic across several DNS servers can be accomplished in several ways. In an environment where most of the workstations have statically-defined IP addresses (that is, addressing information has been manually entered into each workstation), you need to make a conscious effort to configure workstation DNS entries so that an equal number of workstations are configured to use each of the servers. In an environment where DHCP is commonly used, you can balance DNS server usage by alternating which DNS server is listed as the default DNS host in the DHCP scope definition. This strategy, coupled with periodic monitoring, helps ensure that your servers are evenly loaded and helps you assess when you need to add another one.

Caching Name Servers

Caching name servers can be a valuable addition to the network infrastructure, especially in large networks that make extensive use of Wide Area Networks (WAN). A caching server looks like a DNS server to the client. However, a caching server does nothing more than the following tasks:

▼   Receives a query from a client.

■   Checks its cache for the information.

■   If it doesn't find the information in its cache, the caching server queries a DNS server.

■   Receives the information from the DNS server.

▲   Sends it to the client and stores the information in its cache.

The next time a client requests the same information, the caching server returns the information without contacting the DNS server.

A caching server can reduce WAN traffic by keeping redundant queries on the local network instead of on the WAN. A caching server doesn't receive zone transfers, which further reduces WAN traffic. You should consider caching servers in sites where you have a large number of TCP/IP clients and you observe large amounts of DNS traffic on the WAN. You might also deploy a caching server in sites where you have local TCP/IP servers and TCP/IP clients but no DNS primary or secondary servers. These clients can likely use the caching server to resolve addresses of local servers even if the WAN is down.

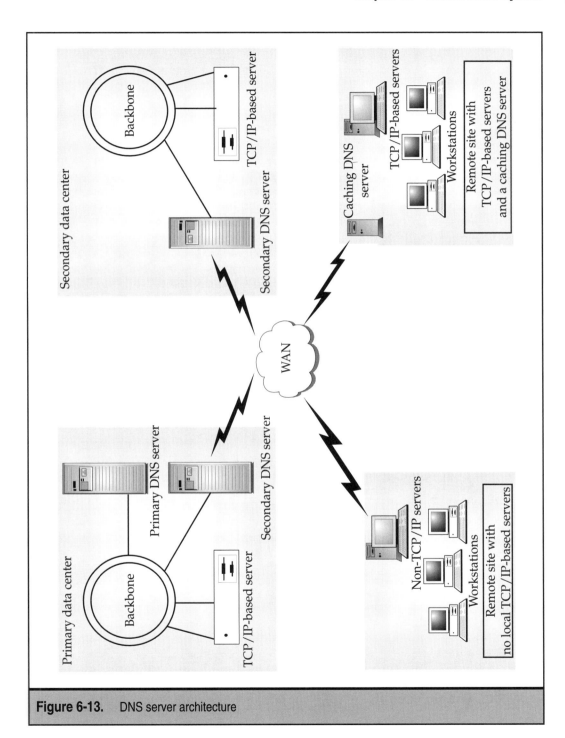

Figure 6-13.   DNS server architecture

You should note that caching DNS can pose a challenge when a client is configured to use a caching server and is resolving a hostname with multiple IP addresses. The address rotation function of round-robin DNS can be defeated if the cache is not flushed frequently.

TRACKING DNS EVOLUTION

There are some exciting changes on the horizon for DNS that need to be taken into consideration when planning any major changes to an existing DNS architecture. Many weak areas in DNS are beginning to see improvements. Secure authentication will be incorporated into DNS as will dynamic host registration. Enhancements to the TCP/IP protocol promise to add functionality and security. Enhancements to DNS, TCP/IP, and Directory Services will all play a role in how we use networks in the future. The implications of incorporating these technologies are wide-ranging but the ability to create a dynamic environment with integrated security is exciting. It is a challenge to be able to support network devices that have a high degree of mobility while verifying users are who they say they are via secure authentication. Couple this with network-wide logon and the capability to perform end-to-end encryption while economizing on network bandwidth consumption, and you have a very tall order. However, it's a goal worth shooting for. Let's look at some of the new developments bound to impact how we use DNS.

IPv6 (IPng)

Although there are many new features in the latest proposed version of TCP/IP, known as IPv6, the most notable changes for DNS are the following:

▼ A new resource record type has been defined so that a domain name can be mapped to a 128-bit IPv6 address.

■ A new domain has been defined to support lookups based on the new address.

▲ According to RFC 1883, IPv6 will allow for expanded addressing capabilities, header format simplification, improved support for extensions, flow-labeling capabilities, and authentication and privacy capabilities.

These new features mean DNS was not forgotten when IPv6 was developed. DNS will be able to incorporate the new, larger TCP/IP addressing structure and take advantage of IPv6 capabilities in the future.

Dynamic DNS

Perhaps one of the biggest proposed changes to DNS is the addition of the dynamic update functions. A client machine using DHCP can register its hostname with DNS much as it can do with WINS today. This allows DNS to populate its hosts tables not only with static host entries, but also with host entries or workstations that have their IP addresses dynamically assigned at bootup using DHCP.

Secure DNS

RFC 2065 outlines new extensions to the DNS protocol that provide a level of security not present in the current version of DNS. DNS Protocol Security Extensions to the DNS provide data integrity and authentication services to security-aware resolvers or applications using cryptographic digital signatures. The digital signatures are stored in secured zones as resource records. Another very important feature is the capability of Secure DNS to store authenticated public keys in the DNS to support public key distribution service and general DNS security. Finally, security extensions allow optional authentication of DNS protocol transactions, which is particularly valuable in DNS server-to-DNS server communication.

Incremental Transfer

Another proposed addition to DNS is the Incremental Transfer Protocol (ITP). ITP uses the DNS Notify function to let secondary DNS servers know there is a change in their zone database. Instead of sending the entire zone file to the secondary, Incremental Transfer Protocol sends only the portions of the zone file that have changes. This reduces the amount of traffic between servers and allows an increase in the propagation of zone information to the secondary servers.

Future Role in Microsoft Networking

What does all this mean to Microsoft networking? It appears that DNS will be playing a much larger role in Microsoft networking with the introduction of Active Directory to be released along with NT 5.0. NT 5.0 domains will map directly to the DNS name space. DNS will eventually replace WINS as the name server and locater for NT directory services. Take a look at Chapter 13 for more information about the role of DNS in NT 5.0.

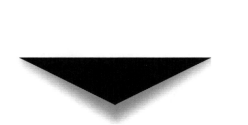

WINDOWS
NT
Professional
Library

CHAPTER 7

WINS and DHCP

Windows Internet Naming Service (WINS) and Dynamic Host Configuration Protocol (DHCP) play different roles in the enterprise network, but they can be configured to work together to help you create a very dynamic and manageable network environment. WINS, like DNS, is a naming service that maps names to IP addresses. DHCP provides a mechanism for automating the assignment of important IP information in order to configure network devices such as workstations and printers. Both WINS and DHCP server services are available with Windows NT Server. The WINS service is available to all Microsoft-based network clients and WINS-compliant non-Microsoft clients. DHCP is more prevalent, and there are many non-Microsoft clients that work with a Microsoft DHCP server, including many IP-enabled Apple computers and printers, Hewlett-Packard and other print servers, and several UNIX operating systems with standards-based DHCP client network stacks.

In this chapter, we will look at the evolution of WINS, how it is installed and managed, and how to integrate it into the network. Then we will look at the underpinnings of DHCP, cover its installation and management, and discuss how DHCP can be integrated into the network. Finally, we will look at configuring the services to work together, and we will examine a few different network scenarios that illustrate several common configurations.

WINDOWS INTERNET NAMING SERVICE

Windows Internet Naming Service (WINS) provides dynamic registration and mapping of NetBIOS names to IP addresses. Basically, a WINS server sits on the network and listens for WINS clients requesting to join the network or requesting the IP address of another WINS client already on the network. During the registration process, a WINS client queries the WINS server to see if it can use a particular NetBIOS name on the network. WINS checks to see if any other computer has the name registered. If not, WINS allows the computer to register the name. The WINS server stores the name along with the IP address of the client. During later conversations with the WINS server, a computer may ask WINS where a particular resource (for example, a server or printer) bearing a unique NetBIOS name is. If the requested resource is registered with WINS, or if a static entry for the resource exists in the WINS database, the WINS server replies to the request with the IP address of the resource. The client can then establish TCP/IP-based communications with the resource.

As explained in Chapter 1, NetBIOS is a session-level interface that can be used over a variety of transport protocols. NetBIOS is responsible for locating resources on the network, establishing connections to the resources, managing the sending and receiving of data between resources (for example, nodes and application peers), and managing the termination of the connections. The particular feature of NetBIOS we are interested in here is how NetBIOS manages the registration of NetBIOS names and how NetBIOS names are resolved.

The NetBIOS School of Broadcasting

In a broadcast-based network (using a nonroutable transport protocol like NetBEUI) each node is able to hear all the other nodes when they broadcast on the network. When a new node wants to join the network, it broadcasts the name it intends to use to all the other nodes on the network in a process called *registration*. Every node on the network receives the new node's broadcast announcement that it intends to use a particular NetBIOS name. If none of the other nodes has any objections, the node begins communications using the NetBIOS name.

Once several nodes are running on the network, they will inevitably want to communicate with each other. To do so, a node broadcasts its desire to communicate with another node by sending a broadcast packet. All the nodes examine the packet to see if it is intended for them. Once the intended recipient recognizes the broadcast, it can send an acknowledgment that it is on the network and ready to communicate directly to the original node. At that point, the two devices can establish a session and communicate without broadcasting.

Figure 7-1 illustrates a broadcast domain (A) consisting of four workstations on a Token Ring, which is connected to a router and a second broadcast domain (B) consisting of two servers connected to another interface on the router. All the nodes on the LAN segment A can establish communication sessions among themselves but cannot communicate with the two servers located on LAN segment B. This is because broadcasts are typically not allowed to propagate through a router. In the illustration, the dashed line indicates the router blocking the broadcast traffic between the two segments. Because the server broadcasts on segment B are not forwarded to the workstations on segment A, the workstations cannot "see" the servers and cannot communicate with them.

In a small network, this method of dynamically registering and resolving unique names among nodes works well and is easy to maintain. However, as a network grows, the amount of broadcast traffic necessary to support the management of the name space increases. Each node has to listen to all the broadcasts. This increases overhead on each node and on the network. Routers must be configured to bridge NetBIOS traffic; otherwise nodes on different subnets cannot communicate with each other. In addition, relatively low-bandwidth wide area network connections have to carry broadcast traffic in this scenario.

Enter NetBIOS over TCP/IP (NBT). NBT allows NetBIOS sessions to work over TCP/IP-based networks, including the Internet. The challenge is getting the NetBIOS interface to map to the IP address so that TCP/IP can be used. Once NetBIOS name-to-IP address mapping is established, NBT nodes can communicate using the standard TCP/IP network interface.

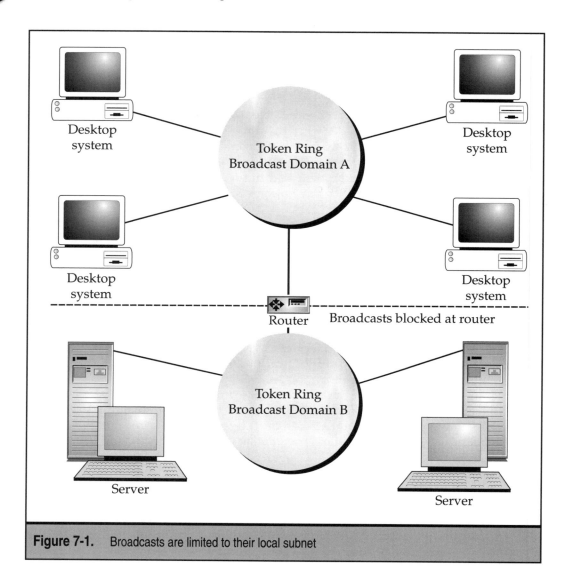

Figure 7-1. Broadcasts are limited to their local subnet

NOTE: NBT accomplishes broadcast name resolution using UDP port 137. In most routed networks, UDP broadcasts are not forwarded by the routers, so name resolution is limited to the local subnet. Although many routers can allow you to forward UDP broadcasts on specific ports, great care should be used and all other alternatives should be weighed before you even consider the option of allowing broadcasts. Allowing broadcasts on large routed networks can increase network and administrative overhead.

If you don't allow UDP broadcasts through your routers and don't use WINS, there are only two ways to accomplish name resolution on a routed, IP-based network: use the LMHOSTS file or use DNS.

LMHOSTS

To address limitations placed on broadcasting by TCP/IP, the LMHOSTS file was created to allow name resolution of resources on remote networks using TCP/IP. The LMHOSTS file is a text file that maps NetBIOS names to IP addresses, providing a mechanism for a node to resolve names without broadcasting. The file is located locally on the node and is not updated dynamically. To allow a computer to resolve a name using the LMHOSTS file, the name and address must be entered manually into the file.

Maintaining the LMHOSTS file on each individual workstation can quickly become a time-consuming task, even on a small network. Every time a new resource, such as a server, is added you must update the LMHOSTS file on all machines. With the original implementation of the LMHOSTS file, each computer that required access to the new server needed to have a local copy of the file updated. With the introduction of LAN Manager 2, extensions were incorporated into the LMHOSTS file that enable a systems administrator to enter a pointer to a LMHOSTS file located elsewhere on the network. This allows the file to be centrally located and administered.

When all the local LMHOSTS files are configured to include the contents of the central file, management of NetBIOS to IP address mappings can be much easier. The LMHOSTS file is usually located in %*Systemroot*%\system32\drivers\etc. Let's look at the contents of an LMHOSTS file located on a remote computer that has a few local name-to-address entries and pointers to two (primary and backup) remote LMHOSTS files located on a central server.

```
#LMHOSTS file for toonces (IP 10.0.5.33) - Last modified 3/27/98

10.0.17.10     thumper    #PRE    #DOM:vsi       # Proxy server
172.16.4.55    ws005      #PRE    #DOM:uscorp    # Tully NT Wks
172.16.4.56    ws006      #PRE    #DOM:uscorp    # Tully 95 Wks
10.0.5.99      fred       #PRE    # central LMHOSTS file
10.0.5.178     barney     #PRE    # Alternate LMHOSTS file

#BEGIN_ALTERNATE
#INCLUDE \\fred\pubshare\lmhosts
#INCLUDE \\barney\pubshare\lmhosts
#END_ALTERNATE

#Comment to indicate end of LMHOSTS file
```

The example file uses several keywords that perform special functions: The first keyword, *#PRE*, is used to force the entry to be read and preloaded into the NetBIOS name cache. If #PRE is not used, the entry will not be read until the broadcast and WINS resolution methods have failed. This keyword is generally used when commonly- accessed resources are not in the local broadcast network, and WINS is either unavailable or the remote resource is not registered in WINS. However, the #PRE keyword must be used for server entries referenced in the #INCLUDE statements; otherwise the #INCLUDE statement will be ignored and the centrally-shared LMHOSTS file will not be read.

NOTE: In Windows NT machines, only the first 100 #PRE entries are read in the LHMOSTS file. If you want to preload more than 100 entries, add a DWORD value MaxPreLoads to the HKEY_ LOCAL_MACHINE\SYSTEM\CurrentControlSet\Services\NetBT\Parameters key in the Registry. Enter the desired number in the newly-created MaxPreLoads DWORD value.

The next keyword, *#DOM,* is used in conjunction with the #PRE keyword to specify the domain in which the referenced NetBIOS name entry exists. This allows the domain name to be preloaded into the cache along with the NetBIOS name and facilitates browsing and logging into remote domains, assuming you have an account.

The #INCLUDE keyword allows a remote LMHOSTS file to be used to resolve NetBIOS names. When a lookup using broadcast and WINS fails, the local LMHOSTS file will be read. If the desired entry doesn't exist in any entry above the #INCLUDE entry, the contents of the LMHOSTS file on the share of server referenced after the #INCLUDE keyword will be searched for a mapping. Typically, multiple #INCLUDE entries are used to provide access to a backup copy of the LMHOSTS file should the first server in the list be unavailable. When the centrally-managed LMHOSTS file is used, customization of the local file should be kept to a minimum. The central LMHOSTS file should contain all the necessary entries so that administration can be kept as simple as possible.

NOTE: To enable clients to access a shared central LMHOSTS file using the INCLUDE function, you must add the share name to HKEY_LOCAL_MACHINE\SYSTEM\CurrentControlSet\Services\ LanManServer\NullSessionShares.

You can also replicate a centrally-administered LMHOSTS file using the Replicator service in NT. However, this method only works for replication between NT-based workstations and servers. Replication methods are outlined in Chapter 3.

If you use or are planning to use DHCP, you might as well forget about using the LMHOSTS file for anything except special situations. With DHCP, IP addresses are dynamically-assigned and therefore subject to change at any moment. Attempting to keep up with the registrations would be fruitless. For that reason, Microsoft WINS and DHCP are engineered to work together.

Using DNS to Resolve NetBIOS Names

An alternative to using the LMHOSTS file is to use the Enable DNS for Windows Resolution option, as shown in Figure 7-2. It's available in recent implementations of Microsoft TCP/IP stacks.

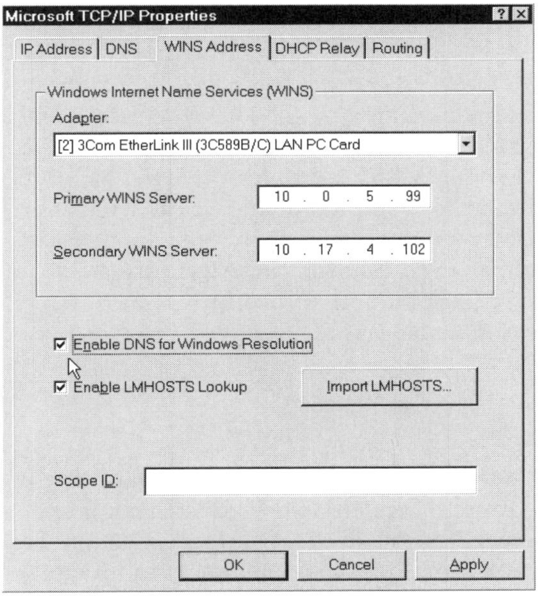

Figure 7-2.   Enable DNS for Windows Resolution

Enable DNS for Windows Resolution will only be effective if the NBT clients on your network are able to take advantage of this feature. In addition, the NetBIOS names must be carefully managed. Without WINS, they will not be dynamically registered. When using DNS to resolve NetBIOS names, there are some other limitations that you should consider. First, the NetBIOS name must match the DNS hostname. To accomplish this, you will need to assign all clients a unique machine name, and then enter the machine name as the hostname in DNS. Because the NetBIOS name space is flat, you are limited to using a single DNS domain for name-to-IP address mapping. This is because the NBT client expects to see a single flat name space. Name resolution requests are sent to the DNS using this assumption.

NT 5.0 NOTE: In NT 5.0 networks there is no need for WINS because all computer names are stored in the Active Directory name space, which is not flat. You can read more about this name space in Chapter 13.

To get a clearer idea of how it works and why this limitation exists, let's look at how a name resolution is processed. For example, let's say a NetBIOS application on the client is looking for a NetBIOS node named *hrserver*. Because the client is configured to use DNS for Windows Resolution, a DNS query is constructed using the NetBIOS name *hrserver* appended to the domain name *company.com* as entered in the client's DNS configuration. The result is that the client sends a standard DNS query to the DNS server that asks, "What is the IP address of hrserver.company.com?" The DNS server responds, "The IP address for hrserver.company.com is 10.0.5.17." When the client receives the response from the DNS server, it strips off the domain name and tells the NetBIOS interface, "The IP address for hrserver is 10.0.5.17." As you can see, the NetBIOS interface doesn't care about anything other than the NetBIOS name. It can't make any distinction between company.com and another domain name; therefore you are forced to enable this feature using a single DNS domain. In addition, because IP address assignments will be statically defined in DNS, you will not be able to use DHCP in this scenario. This creates yet another compelling reason to use WINS.

WINS ESSENTIALS

Before implementing WINS, it is necessary to understand the underlying architecture and specific WINS concepts. There are two high-level components to WINS: the WINS client and the WINS server. The WINS client performs two functions. It registers with the WINS server when it first comes up on the network, and it queries the WINS server for IP-to-NetBIOS name resolution. The WINS server receives and processes WINS client registrations and queries and communicates this information to other WINS servers by replicating its database in a process called *replication*.

Name Registration, Renewal, and Release

The first time a WINS client communicates with the WINS server is upon initialization of the TCP/IP stack. The client initiates the process by sending the WINS server a name registration request. The WINS server receives the request and checks its database to see if the name is already registered. If not, the registration is accepted and written to the database to be used during subsequent lookups by clients. While the client is running, it will periodically contact the WINS server to renew its registration, ensuring that it continues to keep its registration with the WINS server. When a workstation shuts down, it will contact the WINS server to release the registration, making it available for registration by the same client later or for another client when the entry in WINS has expired. Let's look more closely at the details behind registration, renewal, and release.

Registration

After a client boots and the TCP/IP stack has initialized with either a DHCP-assigned or static IP address, a name registration request is sent to the primary WINS server. The WINS server reads the request and chooses whether to accept or reject the request depending on several factors, including whether or not the name already exists in the WINS database. If the name already exists, the WINS server checks to see whether or not the IP address of the requester is the same as the one in the WINS database.

If the name is already registered and marked active, and the IP address of the requesting client is different, the WINS server will send a message to the IP address in the database. This sequence starts with a wait for acknowledgement (WACK), which tells the client to wait for the server to follow up with a name query request. If the client responds, the WINS server tells the first requesting client that the name is already registered. This process is done to ensure that there are no duplicate names on the network.

Once the WINS server has determined whether or not to honor the registration request, it will send the client a positive or negative name registration response.

Renewal

To help keep the WINS database from getting cluttered with unused names, a client's name registration has a limited life. During the registration process, the client is told that the name has a specific time to live (TTL). This is also called the *renewal interval*. The client keeps track of the renewal interval, and when half of the renewal time has passed, the client will register itself with the WINS server again. If the client fails to register once during the renewal time, the WINS server releases the registration.

NOTE: NT clients will renew a registration when half of the renewal interval has passed; other clients may renew at different times during the renewal interval.

Release

There are two types of name release. The first type, called *explicit release*, happens when a client is shut down normally. During the shutdown process the client will send a name release request, and the server will mark the entry as released in the database. The second type, called *silent release*, occurs when the client is abruptly shut off and is not able to send a name release request to the server. In this case, the registration expires when the renewal interval has passed without the client attempting to refresh the name registration.

Node Types

Name resolution can be accomplished by several different methods. One or more methods is used by different client TCP/IP implementations. Windows NT-based systems can use any of the node types depending on how the client is configured. By default, WINS clients are configured as h-node. Table 7-1 lists the node types along with a brief description.

NOTE: You can use the command-line IPCONFIG /ALL command in NT to display the TCP/IP configuration. The node type will also be displayed. In Windows 95, you can use the graphical program *Winipcfg.exe* to display IP information including the node type.

Node Type	Description
B-node	Broadcast node. Communicates using a mix of UDP datagrams (both broadcast and directed) and TCP connections. B-nodes can communicate with each other only within a broadcast area but normally cannot communicate across routers in a routed network. Note that b-node generates broadcast traffic, and every node in the broadcast domain has to examine every broadcast, consuming network and node resources.
P-node	Point-to-point node. Communicates using directed UDP datagrams and TCP connections. P-node uses local or remote NetBIOS name servers. Note that if the NetBIOS name server is unavailable, p-node will not be able to communicate with other local or remote nodes.
M-node	Mixed mode node. M-node is like p-node, which uses the b-node method of broadcasting first. If the broadcast is unsuccessful, p-node point-to-point communication with the name server is used. M-node generates broadcast traffic, but is able to use name servers across routers. M-node can communicate using b-node within the local broadcast domain if the name server is unavailable.
H-node	Hybrid node. H-node is a combination of b-node and p-node functionality like m-node, but h-node uses point-to-point communication first. If a name server is not accessible, h-node will revert to b-node broadcasts. During this time, h-node continues to poll for the name server and returns to point-to-point communication when one becomes available.

Table 7-1. WINS Node Types

Name Query

Name queries are sent by client end nodes. In a broadcast network, a name query is accomplished by broadcasting a name query request to all listening nodes. With WINS, the name query request sent by the client is directed to the primary WINS server as defined in the client's network configuration parameters. If the primary WINS server does not reply, the client will send the query to the secondary WINS server. Depending on the specific WINS client implementation, the client may take additional steps to resolve the name. The WINS clients in Windows 95, Windows for Workgroups version 3.11, and NT versions 3.51 and newer will also use the secondary WINS server if the primary WINS server can't find the requested name in its database.

With the Microsoft client, the name resolution process can incorporate many methods of name resolution. As shown in Figure 7-3, it is possible for the client to try everything from the local cache to the WINS server to LMHOSTS files and finally DNS. For example, if Client A were configured as an h-node with a primary and secondary WINS server, and the Enable DNS For Windows Resolution and Enable LMHOSTS Lookup options were checked, the client would step through several methods to perform a name query to resolve Client B.

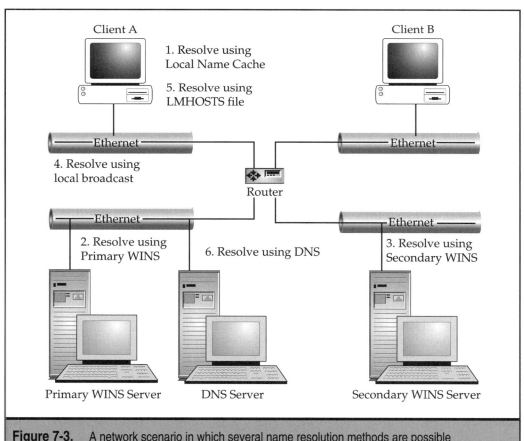

Figure 7-3. A network scenario in which several name resolution methods are possible

The following list is a step-by-step example of the name resolution process:

1. The client begins by checking its local NetBIOS name cache. If the name was recently resolved, it will still be in the cache and the client uses the cached information.

2. If the name is not found in the cache, the client sends a name query request to the primary WINS server.

3. If the primary WINS server is offline, or if it replies with a negative name query response, the client sends another name query request to the secondary WINS server.

4. If the secondary WINS server is offline, or if it replies with a negative name query response, the client will broadcast a name query request.

5. If the client still gets no positive name query response, it will perform a lookup against the LMHOSTS file.

6. If the entry is not in the LMHOSTS file, the client will attempt a DNS lookup before finally giving up.

This impressive effort doesn't guarantee that the query will succeed, but it certainly increases its chances.

Replication

We will look at how replication is *configured* later in this section. For now, we will cover the basic concepts of WINS database replication.

Although a single WINS server could probably manage the NetBIOS name service for all but the largest networks, you probably wouldn't use just one. First and foremost, it would not be wise to place all your eggs in one basket. Anyone having the opportunity to witness a catastrophic failure of the WINS service on a WINS-reliant Microsoft network will tell you that when WINS is down, the network is down. Furthermore, there are design considerations that drive the installation of multiple WINS servers. If the network is spread across a large geographical area connected by leased-line WAN connections, you will likely have at least two WINS servers—each in different regional hubs to spread the load and provide protection against a disaster.

To keep multiple servers synchronized, WINS employs database replication. WINS databases are replicated between partner servers in an organized fashion. Servers that exchange WINS database entries with each other are called *replication partners*. There are two types of replication partners: push and pull. A pull partner requests WINS database entries from another server. A pull is set to occur at specific intervals or when an update notification is sent to the server by a push partner. A push partner sends update notifications based on specific events (to be discussed later). The primary and secondary WINS servers for a client must be push/pull partners with each other, as illustrated in Figure 7-4.

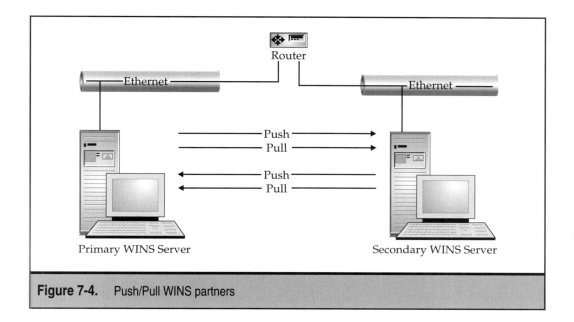

Figure 7-4.   Push/Pull WINS partners

It is recommended that all WINS servers on the network be push/pull partners so that the name space is consistent. Figure 7-5 shows the WINS Manager configuration dialog box for establishing push and pull replication between WINS servers.

NOTE: Because the RFCs regarding WINS only define the client-to-server relationship of WINS, Microsoft WINS servers and other WINS servers will not communicate with each other. In a multiple WINS server environment, where different implementations of the WINS server exist, there is a high likelihood that the entire name space will not be consistent or manageable.

WINS Proxy Service

The WINS Proxy Service is useful if you have b-node-only clients such as older versions of OS/2 on your network. Placing a WINS proxy on local broadcast domains, as shown in Figure 7-6, allows b-node clients to see if a NetBIOS name has been registered in WINS.

The proxy listens to the local network broadcasts. When a b-node client broadcasts a name registration request, the proxy forwards the request to the WINS server. The WINS server checks for a name registration. If the WINS server finds a registration, it will tell the proxy to send a negative name registration response to the b-node client. This function helps prevent duplicate names on the network. Note that the proxy only queries the WINS server; it cannot perform name registrations on behalf of the client, nor will the WINS server store name registrations for b-node clients. To register b-node clients so they

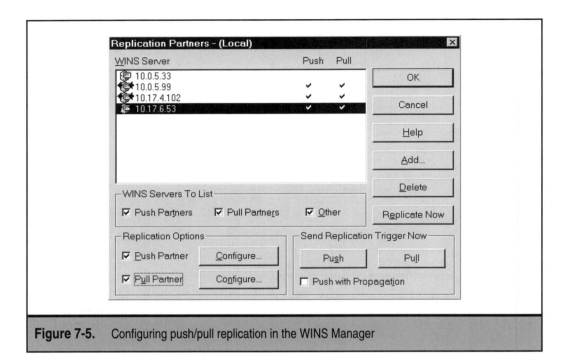

Figure 7-5.   Configuring push/pull replication in the WINS Manager

are accessible to clients from outside the local subnetwork, you can create static mappings in the WINS database for them.

NOTE: At least one but usually no more than two WINS proxy agents need to be placed on every local subnet where you have b-node-only clients needing access to resources outside the subnet.

A proxy can also respond to name query requests from b-node clients attempting to look up NetBIOS names. In order to avoid responding to requests made to other nodes on the local broadcast domain, the proxy server compares its network address to the address of the query. If they match, it will not respond to the broadcast. This keeps the proxy from responding to name resolution activity local to the broadcast domain. However, if the address is found in the proxy server's remote name cache or on the remote WINS server and is not part of the local broadcast domain, the proxy will respond to the client with the resolved name. This function allows b-node clients, typically designed before WINS even existed, to take advantage of the name resolving function of WINS without ever knowing WINS resolved the name. Essentially, the client is tricked into believing the proxy server is just another b-node.

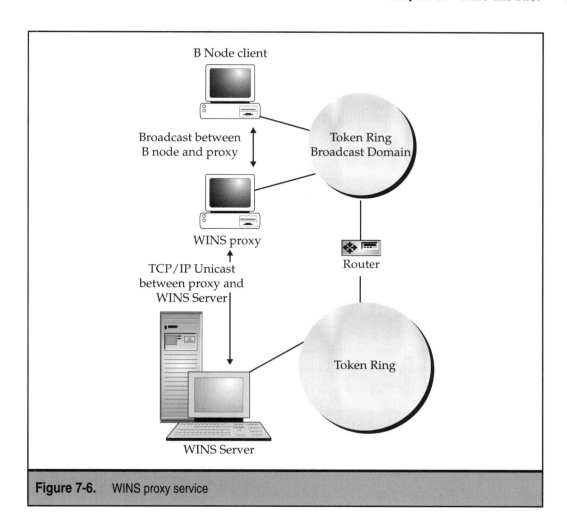

Figure 7-6. WINS proxy service

INSTALLING AND CONFIGURING MICROSOFT WINS

Installing the Microsoft WINS server is as simple as it gets. On the other hand, con-figuring WINS requires a bit more effort.

Installing Microsoft WINS Server

Before you proceed with installing the WINS server, make sure you are logged on with administrator privileges. Installing WINS is done by either right-clicking on the Desktop Network icon and selecting Properties from the drop-down menu or opening the Control Panel and double-clicking on the Network icon. At the Network dialog box, click on the

Services tab. This shows all the network services currently running on the server. If the Windows Internet Name Service is listed, it is already installed. You can check if the service is running by double-clicking on the Services icon in the Control Panel and scrolling down to view the WINS service. If it is running, proceed to the "Configuring WINS" section of this chapter.

To proceed with the installation, click on Add. Select Windows Internet Name Service from the list and click on OK.

In the next dialog box, you will be prompted for the path to the NT Server i386 directory (for Intel installations). Once you have entered the correct path, click on OK. After the necessary files have been copied, close the Network Services installation dialog window and restart the server. Once the server has restarted, make sure you reapply the latest service pack to complete the installation.

Configuring WINS

To configure WINS, click on Start | Programs | Administrative Tools | WINS Manager. The main view of the WINS Manager, as shown in Figure 7-7, displays a split window with WINS Servers on the left and Statistics on the selected server on the right. To add

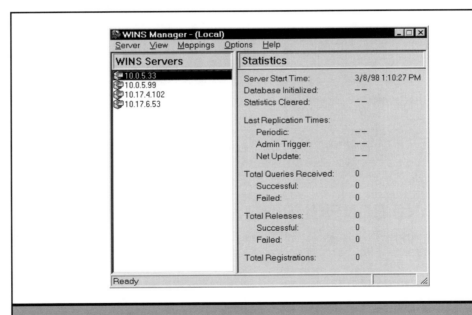

Figure 7-7. WINS Manager main window

additional WINS servers to the view so that they can be managed, click on Server | Add WINS Server, and then enter the IP address of the server to be added. Once you have added all of the WINS servers to be managed, click on the server you want to configure.

From the WINS Manager, select Server | Configuration. This action brings up the WINS Server Configuration window shown in Figure 7-8.

Much of the configuration of your WINS server can be accomplished here. In addition, there are parameters that will help you tune WINS in your network. Table 7-2 describes each of the configuration items found in the Configuration Window.

The next step in configuring WINS is to establish replication partners. This is done in the Replication Partners window shown in Figure 7-9.

In all but the smallest networks, there should be at least two WINS servers to provide, at a minimum, fault tolerance from server hardware or software failure. As we mentioned earlier, the method of synchronizing databases on multiple WINS servers is called replication. Replication partners are those WINS servers that have a push, pull, or

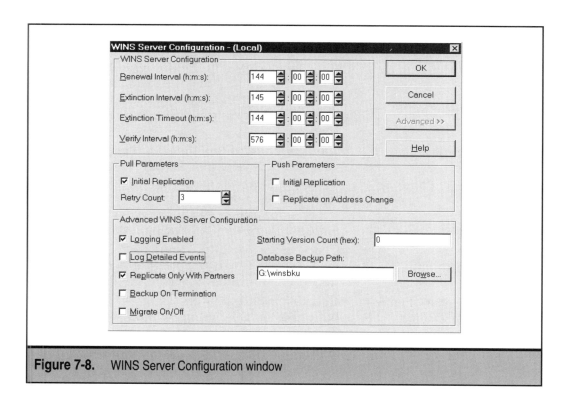

Figure 7-8. WINS Server Configuration window

Configuration Parameter	Description
Renewal Interval	Specifies how long a client has to refresh its name before the name will be released. Microsoft WINS clients refresh halfway through this interval (three days), which allows a client to maintain its registration through a weekend. The default is six days (144 hours).
Extinction Interval	Specifies the time from when an entry is marked released to the time the record is marked as extinct. The default is six days (144 hours).
Extinction Timeout	Specifies the time from when an entry is marked extinct to the time the record can be scavenged from the database. The default is six days (144 hours).
Verify Interval	Specifies the time interval that will trigger a WINS server to verify that old names owned by another WINS server are still active. The default is 24 days (576 hours).
Pull Parameters, Initial Replication	Checking the Initial Replication check box causes the WINS server to pull database replicas when the WINS server has been stopped and restarted or when a replication parameter has been changed.
Pull Parameters, Retry Count	Specifies the number of times an attempt will be made to a partner to pull database replicas. The value should be approximately three times the replication interval specified in WINS Manager | Replication Partners | Replication Options | Pull Partner | Replication Interval parameter.
Push Parameters, Initial Replication	Checking the Initial Replication check box causes the WINS server to notify push partners of the database status when the server is started.
Push Parameters, Replicate on Address Change	Checking the Replicate on Address Change check box causes the WINS server to notify push partners whenever an address changes in a database record.

Table 7-2.   WINS Server Configuration Options

Configuration Parameter	Description
Logging Enabled	Checking the Logging Enabled check box causes the WINS server to log database changes.
Log Detailed Events	Checking the Log Detailed Events check box causes the server to conduct detailed logging. This option is resource intensive and is generally enabled only when debugging problems.
Replicate Only With Partners	Checking the Replicate Only With Partners check box forces the WINS server to replicate with push/pull partners only. If the check box is disabled, the WINS server can replicate data from any unlisted WINS server.
Backup On Termination	Checking the Backup On Termination check box enables an automatic backup of the WINS database whenever the WINS server service is shut down. Note that this feature will not perform this backup when the system shuts down unless you stop the WINS service before shutdown and give the backup time to complete.
Migrate On/Off	Checking the Migrate On/Off check box enables the server to treat static and multihomed records in the database as dynamic so they can be overwritten by a new registration. This allows the gradual migration of non-WINS clients with static entries to WINS clients of the same name with dynamic entries.
Starting Version Count	Specifies the highest version ID for the database. The value can be increased when you are recovering from a corrupted database. You set the value higher than the highest value of all the other servers. The database will be re-replicated to the partner servers. The current value for any managed server can be viewed by selecting a specific server in the WINS server window and selecting View	Database in the WINS Manager.
Database Backup Path	Allows you to select where WINS will keep regular backups of the WINS database.

Table 7-2.   WINS Server Configuration Options (*continued*)

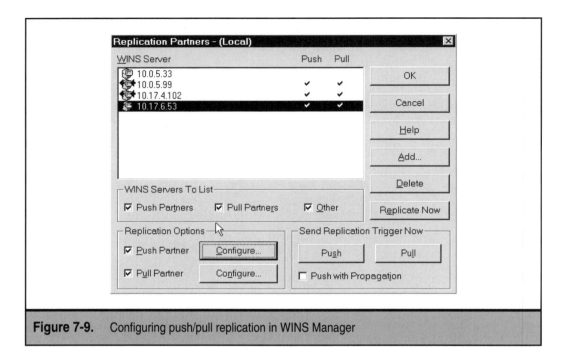

Figure 7-9. Configuring push/pull replication in WINS Manager

push and pull relationship with each other. Table 7-3 describes each of the configuration items found in the Replication Partners window.

The WINS Manager | Options | Preferences window contains additional configuration parameters that modify the way the WINS server and the WINS Manager

Configuration Parameter	Description
WINS Server	Displays a list of servers that are replication partners of the server being configured. The checkmarks indicate whether the server is a push partner, a pull partner, or both.
WINS Servers To List	Filters the WINS Server list. Checking a selection allows servers with the specific relationship to be displayed in the WINS Server list.

Table 7-3. Replication Partners Configuration Parameters

Configuration Parameter	Description
Replication Options, Push Partner	Allows you to specify push partnerships with the highlighted server in the WINS Server list. Clicking on the Configure button brings up a Push Partner Properties box that allows you to define the update count. The Update Count parameter sets how many local updates can be processed before push partners are notified of the changes.
Replication Options, Pull Partner	Allows you to specify pull partnerships with the highlighted server in the WINS Server list. Clicking on the Configure button brings up a Pull Partner Properties box that permits you to define the start time and replication interval. The Start Time parameter lets you to set the time when replication should start. The Replication Interval parameter allows you to set how often replication will happen. On fast LAN connections, the replication interval should be set to 5 to 15 minutes. For replication over WAN connections, the replication interval should be set for 30 minutes. If the WINS environment doesn't change much, the interval could be longer.
Send Replication Trigger Now	Clicking the Push or Pull Send Replication Trigger Now button causes the WINS server to send a replication trigger to the WINS server selected in the WINS Server list. Checking Push with Propagation tells the selected WINS server to propagate the replication trigger to all of its replication partners.
Replicate Now	Causes the WINS server to start the replication on demand.

Table 7-3.   Replication Partners Configuration Parameters (*continued*)

behave. You can select how you want the WINS Manager to display the WINS servers listed in the Address Display section. You can also change the Server Statistics refresh rate or disable Auto Refresh altogether. Table 7-4 describes each of the configuration items found in the Options | Preferences window.

Configuration Parameter	Description
Address Display	Address Display controls how address and name information is displayed in the WINS Manager. This also determines how a connection is made to remote WINS servers. If you select IP Address Only, WINS Manager uses TCP/IP to connect to the WINS server(s). If you select Computer Name, WINS Manager uses named pipes to connect to the WINS server(s).
Server Statistics	Select Auto Refresh to enable the manager to automatically refresh the Server Statistics at the time interval entered into the Interval box.
Computer Names	Select LAN Manager-Compatible if you want computer names to conform to the LAN Manager naming convention. This is the default because Windows NT conforms to the LAN Manager convention.
Validate Cache Of "Known" WINS Servers At Startup Time	Causes the WINS Manager to try to contact all the WINS servers in the WINS Server list every time you start the manager.
Confirm Deletion Of Static Mappings And Cached WINS Servers	Warns you every time you delete a static mapping or the cached name of a WINS server.
Pull Partner Default Configuration	In the Start Time box you can enter a default value that will be suggested for every new pull partner you add. In the Replication box you can enter a default value that will be suggested for every new pull partner you add.
New Push Partner Default Configuration Update Count	In the Update Count box you can enter a default value that will be suggested for every new push partner you add.

Table 7-4. WINS Preferences Window

WINS Registry Settings

WINS stores its configuration information in the Registry. There may be times in which you need to modify one or more parameters that are not in the WINS Manager. Some WINS Registry parameters are listed below. A word of caution, be careful when modifying the Registry. One mistake and you may damage your server. Have your system and Registry fully backed up, and make sure you have a current Emergency Repair Disk before you manually edit the Registry.

The Registry keys are located in the HKEY_LOCAL_MACHINE\System\CurrentControlSet\Services\WINS\Parameters key.

The specific keys and a description for each are listed below:

▼ **DbFileNm**—This defines the path name to the WINS database file. The default is *%Systemroot%*\System32\WINS\WINS.MDB.

■ **DoStaticDataInit**—When set to 1, the WINS server initializes the database with records from the files listed in the DataFiles subkey. When set to the default of 0 the initialization will not occur.

■ **LogFilePath**—This defines the location for the WINS server log files. The default setting is *%Systemroot%*\System32\WINS.

■ **McastIntvl**—This defines the number of seconds between WINS server multicasts to other WINS servers. The default is 2,400 seconds.

■ **McastTtl**—This defines the multicast time to live. TTL limits the number of hops that the multicast is allowed to travel on the network before it is dropped. The TTL can be from 1 to 32; the default is 6.

■ **NoOfWrkThds**—This defines the number of threads the WINS server can use. Although the range is from 1 to 40, the default is 1. If you have more than one processor, the default is one thread for each processor.

■ **PriorityClassHigh**—When set to the default of 0, the WINS service runs like other services. When set to 1, the WINS service will be in the high-priority class. Services running in lower classes will not be able to preempt the WINS service.

▲ **UseSelfFndPnrs**—When set to the default of 0, the server will not automatically find and configure other WINS servers on the network as push/pull partners. If set to 1, the WINS server will try to find and configure other WINS servers as push/pull partners.

The Registry keys for replication partners parameters are located in the HKEY_LOCAL_MACHINE\System\CurrentControlSet\Services\WINS\Partners key:

▼ **PersonaNonGrata**—This defines WINS server IP addresses that you want to block from replicating with the local server.

▲ **Pull\<IPAddress>\MemberPrec**—This defines the WINS server replication preference level. The default of 0 sets the server to low preference. Changing the value to 1 sets the server to high preference.

THE IMPACT OF WINS ON THE NETWORK

When implementing WINS on a network, try to stick with the default parameters unless you have identified a good reason not to and understand the implications of changing them. Most of the WINS parameters will work just fine as they are. However, you will need to modify the replication intervals between WINS servers depending on where they are placed on the network. As a general rule of thumb, you should set the replication interval at 15 minutes when replicating over a LAN connection, 30 to 60 minutes over a local WAN connection, 60 to 90 minutes over a domestic WAN connection, and 2 to 12 hours over an international WAN connection.

If you need to ensure that WINS is synchronized across your entire network very quickly, you must use lower interval times. We will look at two scenarios: WINS on a LAN and WINS on a WAN. Because we don't have a compelling reason to change them, we will leave the Renewal Interval, Extinction Interval, Extinction Timeout and Verify Intervals parameters at their default settings. To tune the replication traffic for the network connection type, we will be modifying the Push Update Count and the Pull Replication Interval parameters as necessary for the environment.

Local Area Network Implementation

You might be tempted to use only one WINS server when your network consists of LANs in a single building or LANs in a campus environment where high-speed fiber connects the LANs. Spare yourself the future headache of hearing all your users complain at the same time when the single WINS server crashes or the network segment it is on experiences problems. You should try to place two servers in geographically separate areas, even if they are in different buildings only 200 meters apart.

You want to make sure at least one of the servers is operational at all times. For example, if a power failure takes out one location, you want to have a server in another location that is still functioning and keeping people happy. With that in mind, Figure 7-10 illustrates a two-server WINS implementation. Because the servers are connected to each other via LANs, they have plenty of available bandwidth to communicate with each other. The router in the illustration could be one or several routers, and the link between the servers may span across a campus network consisting of several different buildings.

WINS server A and WINS server B are configured as push/pull replication partners with each other. Because they are connected by a high bandwidth network connection, replication can occur frequently. We could configure the servers to replicate every 5 to 15 minutes and every 5 to 15 record changes. This would keep convergence of the WINS database under 15 minutes for the entire WINS environment.

Wide Area Network Implementation

When wide area networks (WANs) are involved, it is much easier to justify multiple WINS servers. WANs usually have limited available bandwidth and although WAN connections can be very reliable, they are arguably not as reliable as local LAN

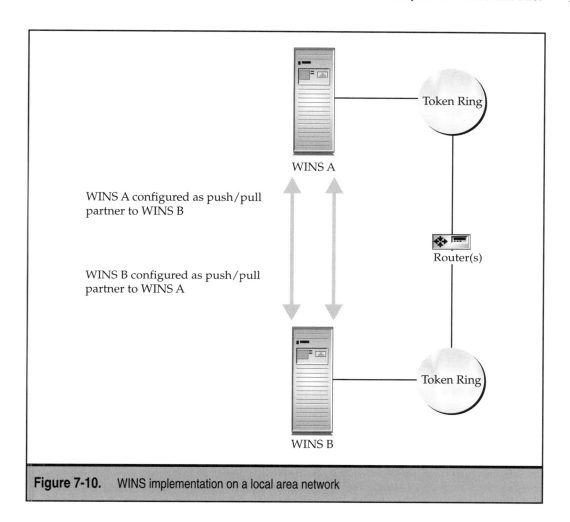

Figure 7-10.   WINS implementation on a local area network

connections. The challenge with WANs is to keep the WINS environment synchronized without consuming substantial WAN bandwidth with replication traffic.

A WAN environment is illustrated in Figure 7-11. There is a LAN network (perhaps a whole campus) on one side of the WAN and another LAN on the other side. There might also be additional local WAN connections from either campus to other facilities using the network.

Because there are a large number of users (let's say 6,000) in both campus environments, two local WINS servers are deployed on each side of the WAN. To keep the utilization balanced over the local servers, half of the WINS clients have local WINS AA or BB as their primary WINS server while the other half of the WINS clients have local WINS A or B as their primary WINS server. In other words, clients in campus A would be

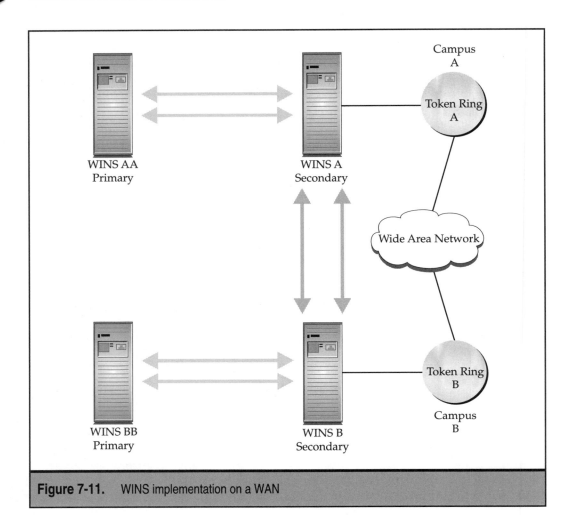

Figure 7-11. WINS implementation on a WAN

configured to use WINS A or AA while clients in campus B would be configured to use WINS B or BB. In the client configuration, the secondary server is always the other local WINS server.

Because we have LAN connections between WINS servers A and AA and we also have LAN connections between WINS servers B and BB, the local pairs are replication partners as illustrated. WINS A and AA are configured as push/pull partners that replicate every 10 minutes and 10 changes. WINS B and BB are also configured to replicate every 10 minutes and 10 changes.

However, the WAN link is heavily utilized and we don't want to add more traffic to it by replicating unnecessarily. Because we know that the users on campus A usually access servers and other resources located on campus A, and that users on campus B usually access servers and other resources on campus B, we are fairly certain that we can keep people happy as long as WINS converges in less than an hour. To calculate the maximum allowable replication time between WINS A and WINS B over the WAN, we add the maximum replication time between AA and A to the maximum replication time between B and BB. In this case, we would have 10 + 10, or 20 minutes. We then subtract the number from the maximum allowable convergence time to get the longest allowable replication time between A and B while still keeping us under our 60-minute goal. In this case, we would subtract 20 minutes from 60 to arrive at 40 minutes.

We can now configure WINS A and WINS B as replication partners with a replication time of 40 minutes and 60 changes. We set the record count higher to ensure that it doesn't force more frequent replication. The maximum time it would take for a record to be propagated from WINS AA to WINS BB is 60 minutes.

DYNAMIC HOST CONFIGURATION PROTOCOL

The Dynamic Host Configuration Protocol, commonly referred to as DHCP, is used to automatically configure workstations, printers, and other IP devices over the network when the devices initialize. Ranges of IP addresses are allocated by a systems administrator and entered into the DHCP server in pools called *scopes*. A scope can contain all or part of a range of addresses in a subnet.

IP clients are configured to use DHCP to request IP information from the DHCP server when booting. When the client contacts the DHCP server, the server responds with IP information appropriate for the device. The server gives the client an IP address lease, meaning that the client has the right to use the address for the time specified in the lease. A lease time is usually anywhere from a few minutes or hours to days or months depending on the specific network and client requirements. Clients will also communicate periodically with the server during the lease period to negotiate a renewal for the lease before it expires.

Properly implemented, DHCP can be a very useful tool in helping manage a large TCP/IP network. As users and their workstations become increasingly more mobile, keeping the IP addressing information on the workstation becomes more of a challenge. It is very difficult for an average user to understand and configure IP information on a workstation. For example, let's say there is a user who travels to several locations within the organization with a laptop computer. The user removes the laptop from its docking station and travels to another company location to work on a project. Upon arrival, the user connects the laptop to a network port in the temporary office space. Without DHCP, the user would need to track down a LAN administrator and ask the administrator to reconfigure the laptop with a new IP address and default gateway, and perhaps different DNS and WINS server addresses. Without this information, the laptop would not be able to communicate with any TCP/IP-based resources on the network. If the network were designed with DHCP servers providing IP information for each user subnet, the laptop would be able to boot and get all the IP information necessary for the user to begin TCP/IP network communications without having to manually reconfigure the laptop.

DHCP Overview

There were several key design goals established when DHCP was being developed. First is that DHCP clients should get all the IP configuration parameters from the server. Once implemented, there should be no manual configuration required. In addition, there should be no user involvement; the entire process should occur automatically. Also, to create a high-performance and fault-tolerant environment, a DHCP client should be able to send out a DHCP request and have the capability to handle and choose from several replies. This allows multiple servers to be online to support DHCP requests.

Caching Clients

One of the most important issues you will face with an enterprise DHCP implementation is that of caching by DHCP clients. Clients can store their previous IP information and use it after a reboot. In large networks, the base of installed client software may be very diverse. You will probably have many different types and versions of desktop operating systems that have different implementations of the DHCP client. The standards specify that the DHCP client software should be able to retain the client configuration even when the client reboots; this is accomplished by the client storing a DHCP cache file on the local workstation. When the workstation reboots, it should check the contents of the cached file, check its lease to make sure it has not expired, and be able to use the configuration even if a DHCP server is not immediately available. A common problem is that some implementations of the DHCP client do not support caching and need to communicate with the DHCP server every time the workstation is rebooted.

Here is a good example of why this is a problem. Your DHCP server is at a remote location and the WAN connection is broken. A user running an application that accesses information across the WAN experiences a problem that locks up the workstation or otherwise causes the user to reboot the machine. With a caching DHCP client, the workstation reboots, uses the cached information, and makes a note to check with the server later, because it can't contact the DHCP server now. However, the user can still access other IP hosts and resources.

If the client reboots, doesn't have a local cache file, and cannot contact the DHCP server, the workstation will try several times to contact a DHCP server. It fails and typically generates a DHCP error message. Now, the user cannot access any IP resources, even if they are in the same building or on the same subnetwork. This user will become upset and frustrated. Multiply that by several hundred users and you will have what appears to be a major network outage (and a major pain in the neck). The point is to make sure your DHCP client software can successfully cache DHCP information between reboots and function in the absence of a DHCP server before you roll out DHCP to the client workstations.

DHCP Compatibility

Two other design goals for DHCP are that it should not interfere with current implementations of network protocols and that network devices that do not use DHCP can still communicate on the network. A good example of these devices are hosts and workstations whose IP addresses are statically configured by design or because they do not support DHCP. Therefore, DHCP has to support static address assignments. For example, some programs have software keys that are configured to only recognize machines with a certain IP number. If the address changes, the program won't run. DHCP scopes can also be configured to exclude specific ranges of IP addresses, allowing statically addressed devices to use the addresses in the excluded range without interference from the DHCP service.

DHCP is based on the Bootstrap Protocol (BOOTP) but adds much more functionality to it. The notable differences between the two are that DHCP can lease an address to a client for a specified time period whereas BOOTP cannot. When a client gets an IP address via BOOTP, it has that address indefinitely or until it is manually reassigned and the client is reinitialized. The other major difference is the capability of DHCP to provide IP configuration information beyond the basic IP address, subnet mask, and default information provided by BOOTP. DHCP is also backward-compatible with BOOTP. DHCP servers can honor BOOTP client requests.

As far as backward compatibility is concerned, DHCP is RFC-compliant with the BOOTP relay agent. This gives DHCP the capability to use industry-standard mechanisms to forward-broadcast BOOTP packets across routed networks. Many routers can be configured to act as a BOOTP relay agent. In addition, the Windows NT TCP/IP stack also includes a feature enabling it to act as a BOOTP/DHCP relay agent. The agent can be configured in the Network | TCP/IP Properties | DHCP Relay tab as shown in Figure 7-12.

The relay agent is configured with addresses of DHCP servers on the network. The agent itself resides on a different subnet from the DHCP servers. When clients on the subnet begin broadcasting as part of their search for a BOOTP or DHCP server, their broadcasts are blocked by the router. However, the listening relay agent on the subnet is able to hear the broadcasts and forward them through the router to a DHCP server. With router and computer-based relay agents available, a DHCP server should not have to be placed on each subnet. DHCP is described in RFC 2131, and related information can be found in the RFCs listed in Table 7-5.

NOTE: DHCP client-to-server communication uses UDP port 67. DHCP server-to-client communication uses UDP port 68.

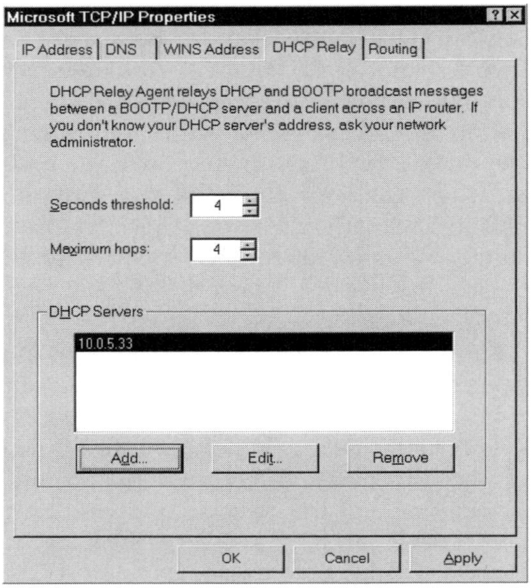

Figure 7-12. DHCP relay agent properties

RFC	Title
1533	DHCP Options and BOOTP
1534	Interoperation Between DHCP and BOOTP
1541	Dynamic Host Configuration Protocol
1542	Clarifications and Extensions for the Bootstrap Protocol
2131	Dynamic Host Configuration Protocol (Obsoletes RFCs 1531 and 1541)
2132	DHCP Options and BOOTP Vendor Extensions
2241	DHCP Options for Novell Directory Services

Table 7-5. DHCP-Related RFCs

DHCP Address Allocation Process

Communication between the client and the server consists of an exchange of several different packets that establish where the client is and what it is asking for, and help determine which server will honor the client's requests.

The following two tables summarize the DHCP messages used in the process. Table 7-6 contains the messages that a client sends to a server. Table 7-7 outlines the messages that a server sends to a client.

Client Message	Description
DHCPDISCOVER	The client broadcasts a DHCPDISCOVER message in an attempt to locate a DHCP server. When a DHCPDISCOVER message is received from a client, the server selects an address from a DHCP scope to offer to the client and sends a DHCPOFFER message to the client. The process of selection is to first use the client's current address if there is one. Next, the server will offer the client's previous expired or released address, if it's available. If configured, the client can also specify a particular address. The server will honor that request if the scope definition includes the address, and the server allows the client to request a particular address. If none of the preceding steps is an option, the next available address in the scope will be allocated. Note that the server determines the right scope to use by examining the source address of the message, which is usually forwarded by a relay agent.
DHCPREQUEST	When a DHCPREQUEST message is sent by a client and contains a *server identifier* option in the message, the client is responding to a DHCPOFFER message from a server. Otherwise the message is from a client verifying or extending a lease for a particular address.
DHCPDECLINE	The client sends a DHCPDECLINE message in response to a DHCPOFFER message sent by the server. The client sends a DHCPDECLINE message to let the server know that it believes the offered address is already in use.

Table 7-6.   Client to Server DHCP Messages

Client Message	Description
DHCPRELEASE	A DHCPRELEASE message is sent by a client to indicate that it no longer needs the address. Typically this message is sent from a client that is performing an orderly shutdown. The message can also be from a client that is performing a release and renewal, which is usually done as part of a troubleshooting process by the user or an administrator.
DHCPINFORM	When a client sends a DHCPINFORM message, it is usually requesting special configuration parameters. The server replies by sending a DHCPACK message back to the client with the information.

Table 7-6.   Client to Server DHCP Messages (*continued*)

Server Message	Description
DHCPOFFER	The server sends a DHCP offer in response to the DHCPDISCOVER message sent by a client. Several servers may respond to a client. The client is responsible for selecting which DHCP server it will use. The selected server will receive a DHCPREQUEST message from the client.
DHCPACK	The server sends a DHCPACK message to the client. It contains the IP address assigned by the server and additional configuration parameters as defined in the subnet scope.
DHCPNAK	A server sends a DHCPNAK message to the client to indicate the client's network address is incorrect. This usually happens when a client has relocated to a new subnet or when the lease has expired.

Table 7-7.   Server to Client DHCP Messages

To better understand how DHCP works on the network, let's look at a standard DHCP conversation between a client requesting a lease and the server leasing the address. We assume that the client is located on a different subnetwork than the two available DHCP servers. The router has been configured as a BOOTP/DHCP relay agent and will forward the broadcast messages from the client's LAN to the remote DHCP servers.

1. The client broadcasts a DHCPDISCOVER message on its local subnet.

2. The router, acting as a DHCP agent, forwards the broadcast DHCPDISCOVER message directly to the DHCP servers.

3. Both servers reply with a DHCPOFFER message directed to the router acting as a DHCP agent.

4. The router receives the DHCPOFFER messages and broadcasts them on the client's subnet.

5. The client receives the DHCPOFFER messages from both DHCP servers and selects one to send a DHCPREQUEST message to. The message is broadcast so both servers will receive it. However, the message includes a server identifier so that the servers can tell if the client is responding to them.

6. Because the client doesn't have an IP address yet, the router again forwards the client's broadcast to both servers.

7. The DHCP servers read the DHCPREQUEST packet and determine if the request was intended for them.

8. The server is identified by the server identifier in the DHCPREQUEST message from the client. It reserves an address for the client and responds with a DHCPACK message containing the configuration parameters.

9. The router broadcasts the DHCPACK to the client.

10. The client receives the DHCPACK message with configuration parameters. The client checks the parameters and notes the duration of the lease specified in the DHCPACK message.

The client is now configured.

NOTE: If the client detects that the address is already in use, it will send the server a DHCPDECLINE message and will start the whole process over again. Also, if the client moves to a different subnet and sends a request to use its old address, the DHCP server(s) will respond with a DHCPNAK message, triggering the client to start the entire process from the beginning.

INSTALLING AND CONFIGURING DHCP

As with WINS, installing DHCP is quick and very simple. Before installing DHCP you should verify that you have configured the server with a static IP address on the interface where you plan to enable DHCP. After installation, the base configuration of DHCP goes quickly. Most of the effort will be in adding and maintaining DHCP scopes on the server.

Installing Microsoft DHCP

Before you proceed with installing the DHCP Server service, make sure you are logged on with administrator privileges. Installing DHCP is done by either right-clicking on the Desktop Network icon and selecting Properties from the drop-down menu or opening the Control Panel and double-clicking on the Network icon. At the Network dialog box click on the Services tab. This shows all the network services currently running on the server. If the DHCP Server service is listed, it is already installed; you should check if the service is running by double-clicking on the Services icon in the Control Panel and scrolling down to view the DHCP service. If it is running, proceed to the "Configuring and Managing DHCP" section of this chapter.

To proceed with the installation, click on Add. Select Microsoft DHCP Server from the list and click on OK.

In the next dialog box, you will be prompted for the path to the NT Server i386 directory (for Intel installations). Once you have entered the correct path, click on OK. After the necessary files have been copied, close the Network Services installation dialog window and restart the server. Once the server has restarted, make sure you reapply the latest service pack to complete the installation.

NOTE: You can start and stop the DHCP server in the Services Manager found in the Control Panel. You can also start, stop, pause, or continue the DHCP service from the command line by entering **net [start, stop, pause, or continue] dhcpserver**.

Configuring and Managing DHCP

Administering a DHCP server is done using the DHCP Manager tool found in the Start | Programs | Administrative Tools | DHCP Manager menu. When you start the manager, you are presented with a DHCP Servers list on the left and an Option Configuration window on the right, as seen in Figure 7-13.

Server Properties

You should configure the server properties first. Make sure the Local Machine is selected in the DHCP Servers list, and then click on Server | Server Properties to open the Server Properties window shown in Figure 7-14.

Under the General tab there are two configuration items. The first is Enable DHCP Logging. Although you can use the log file for troubleshooting, it is also very handy for getting a peek into what is going on behind the scenes. Enabling this option and checking the logs periodically allow you to spot potential problems (such as a client that is renewing its lease every minute).

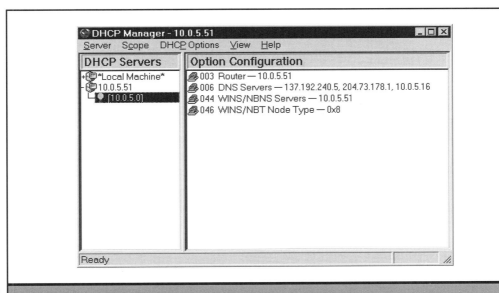

Figure 7-13.   The DHCP Manager tool

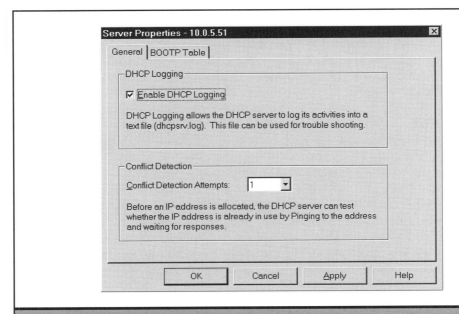

Figure 7-14.   Server Properties window

The other configuration item under the General tab is Conflict Detection Attempts. This new feature was introduced with NT 4.0 DHCP Server. If you don't have any problems with duplicate IP addresses, it probably isn't necessary to enable this feature. It will just increase the amount of time it takes a client to get a lease. However, if you aren't sure whether you have duplicate IP address problems or you know you do, this option should be enabled. Although it can help reduce the occurrence of duplicate addresses on your network, you shouldn't rely on it to solve your addressing woes. If you are getting duplicate addresses on the network, you should be looking carefully for the source of the problem. It could be that Bob in Accounting decided to set up his own DHCP server on the network, or that your users have taken to assigning their own IP addresses (we've seen it happen). In any event, enabling the option can help keep things stable while the problem is being investigated.

NOTE: The Microsoft DHCP Server Activity Logfile (Dhcpsrv.log) is located in the *%Systemroot%*\system32\dhcp directory. The log provides information including:
When the log was started, stopped, or paused
If a new IP address was leased, the IP and MAC addresses of the client and the client name, if available
If a lease was renewed or denied, the IP and MAC addresses of the client and the client name, if available
When an IP address was discovered to be already in use on the network
When requests were denied because all of the available addresses were allocated
If a BOOTP request was given an address, the IP and MAC addresses of the client

The other Server Properties tab, BOOTP Table, allows you to configure the DHCP server BOOTP functions. You can specify Boot Images, Filenames, and File servers to provide BOOTP client support.

Creating Scopes

Now that the Server Properties configuration is complete, we can get down to the business of creating a pool of available IP addresses or scopes. To open the Scope Properties window, click on Scope | Create. The IP Address Pool properties in the window, as shown in Figure 7-15, allows you to define the address pool start and end addresses, the subnet mask, a range of addresses to be excluded, and any individual addresses that you want to exclude from being assigned by DHCP.

Lease Duration is the second set of properties in the Scope Properties window. Setting this to unlimited is not recommended. The server will permanently assign addresses and may eventually exhaust the entire scope. You can accomplish essentially the same thing by defining a very long lease duration. The lease duration Limited To number can range anywhere from one minute to hundreds of days. There are many factors that go into selecting a lease duration, including the amount of acceptable traffic generated and the degree of sensitivity that your clients have about a DHCP server being available to renew a lease. If the lease is very short, say 10 minutes, every client will contact the DHCP server

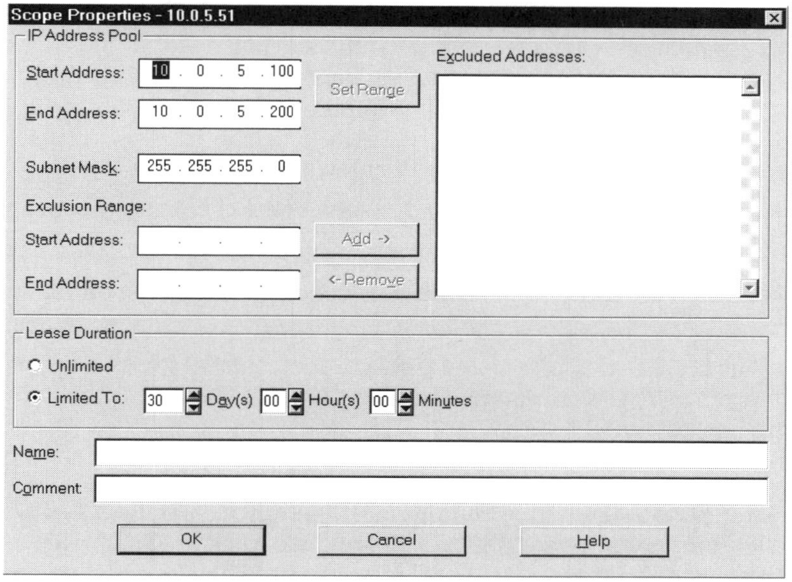

Figure 7-15. Creating a DHCP scope

at least once during that time frame to renew the lease. If the DHCP server goes down during that time frame, clients would not be able to renew their leases and would stop using their IP addresses. If the lease is very long, there is a good chance that leases will be reserved with the server long after the client has left the network. Having unused leases wastes IP addresses. Generally speaking, leases of 10 to 30 days work well for most environments.

NOTE: You can add reserved addresses for clients that can't negotiate a lease or need a fixed address by opening the Scope I Add Leases window and manually entering the IP address, the unique identifier and the client name. This is normally used for BOOTP clients.

The final two configuration items, Name and Comment, allow you to give the scope a meaningful name and add a comment. You could name the scopes by location and use the comment field for a local contact name and number.

Scope Active Options

Once you have created the scope, you must activate it. But before you do so, there is one more step to configuring the scope. Make sure the new scope is selected then click DHCP Options I Scope.

This brings up the DHCP Options: Scope window, as shown in Figure 7-16. You must select several Unused Options, add them to the Active Options list, and configure the Active Options values.

On a routed network with DNS and WINS servers, you must activate and configure the following options:

▼ **003 Router**—Specifies the default IP gateway address

■ **006 DNS Servers**—Specifies the DNS servers the client should use

■ **044 WINS/NBNS Servers**—Specifies the WINS or NetBIOS name servers

▲ **046 WINS/NBT Node Type**—Specifies the client node type for name resolution

NOTE: The DHCP Global option is used to set active options for all scopes. A good candidate for a Global option in an NT environment would be option 046 WINS/NBT Node Type because it should be active in all scopes in an NT network. The DHCP Defaults option allows you to enter default values for options so that you don't have to enter an option value every time you create a new scope.

Add these options to the Active Options list, highlight each option, and edit the value appropriate to your environment. When you are done, click on OK.

Now you can activate the new scope. This is accomplished by selecting the new scope and clicking on Activate in the Scope menu.

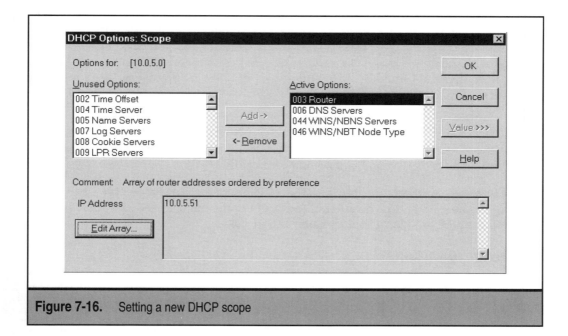

Figure 7-16.   Setting a new DHCP scope

Viewing Active Leases

After a period of time, the scope will accumulate active leases. These can be viewed by double-clicking on the scope or by highlighting the scope and selecting Scope | Active Leases from the drop-down menu. Either method will bring up the Active Leases window for the scope, as illustrated in Figure 7-17.

In the Active Leases window, you will see scope usage statistics and individual client properties. Clicking on the Properties button allows you to configure the client's IP Address, Unique Identifier, Name, Comment, and Lease Expiration Date options.

Superscopes

With network switching equipment entering the mainstream, large logical network segments are possible. However, depending on how the IP addressing has been set up, you may have a limited number of available IP addresses to use for DHCP clients on each physical network segment. Superscopes allow multiple subnets and their associated scopes to exist on a single physical subnet and to be managed as a single logical unit. You should consider superscopes before you start increasing the number of users on a given subnet beyond the number of available IP addresses for the subnet. Since it is usually very difficult to alter your IP addressing scheme after it has been implemented, you may need to configure your router interfaces to act as the gateway for multiple subnets. If your routers can accommodate this, you can effectively increase the number of IP addresses

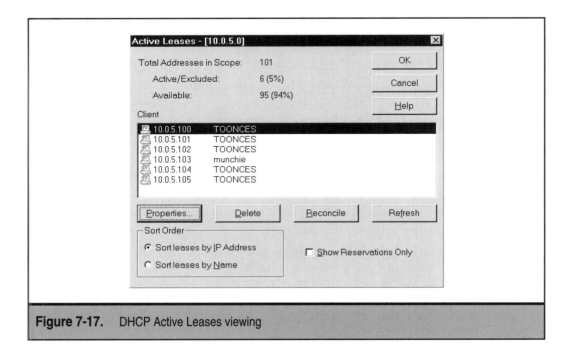

Figure 7-17. DHCP Active Leases viewing

available on that interface. This feature of DHCP will allow you to assign superscopes for the segment that consists of multiple child scopes. The child scopes represent the subnets that you want to have appear as one logical scope.

DHCP Registry Settings

Like WINS and most other NT services, DHCP stores its configuration information in the Registry. There may be times when you need to modify one or more parameters that are not in the DHCP Manager.

The Registry keys are stored in the HKEY_LOCAL_MACHINE\Systems\ CurrentControlSet\Services\DHCPServer\Parameters subkey. Making changes to anything except the RestoreFlag subkey will require you to restart the server.

Some important DHCP Registry parameters are listed here:

▼ **APIProtocolSupport**—Defines the protocol the DHCP server will use. The default of 0x1 sets the server to use Remote Procedure Calls (RPCs) via TCP/IP. When set to 0x2, the server uses RPC over named pipes. A setting of 0x4 forces the server to use RPC over Local Procedure Calls (LCP); a setting of 0x5 allows the server to use RPC over TCP/IP and RCP over LPC. If you want the server to use all three (TCP/IP, named pipes, and LPC), set the key to 0x7.

■ **BackupDatabasePath**—Defines where the backup DHCP database is stored. The default is %*Systemroot*%\System32\DHCP\Backup.

■ **BackupInterval**—Defines the backup interval. The default is 60 minutes (0x3C).

■ **DatabaseCleanupInterval**—Defines the interval to wait before expired client records are deleted from the database. The default is 24 hours, which is defined in the key as 864,000 (0x15180) minutes.

■ **DatabaseLoggingFlag**—When set to 1, logging is enabled (default).

■ **DatabaseName**—The default database name is DHCP.MDB, but you can change the name in this key.

■ **DatabasePath**—Defines where the DHCP database files are located. The default location for the files is %*Systemroot*%\System32\DHCP.

▲ **RestoreFlag**—Setting the parameter to 1 forces a DHCP database restore from the backup copy.

Security Issues

One of the biggest security problems on a network using DHCP is that unauthorized or rogue DHCP servers can be installed on a subnet. A rogue DHCP server could send clients duplicate IP addresses, disrupting communication on the network. More malicious activities could also be conducted. The rogue DHCP server could send clients a false gateway, thereby redirecting traffic to a different router. Clients could be configured to use a false DNS server that redirects them to an Internet host set up to capture logon IDs and passwords, right through the firewall!

> **NOTE:** Sometimes a rogue DHCP server is set up by somebody who doesn't know better. When problems start occurring, the individual is never around to correlate the installation of their server with the recent network problems. To help identify problems associated with rogue DHCP servers, the Microsoft NT 4.0 Resource Kit includes a utility that can listen for DHCP packets on a subnetwork. The *Dhcploc.exe* is a command-line executable that will beep and send alert messages when it detects unauthorized DHCP servers.

Another security issue brought about by DHCP is the increased difficulty in tracking suspicious user activity on the network. When IP addresses are statically defined, it is fairly easy to track down the offending workstation and the offending user. Because DHCP assigns IP addresses dynamically, a workstation's (and user's) IP address can change. The only way to trace an address back to a particular workstation is to shuffle through the DHCP logs. On a large network this can be difficult, if not impossible, particularly if some time has passed since the incident occurred.

DHCP NETWORK COMPONENTS

Let's look at how DHCP servers, clients, and relay agents would appear on a network. The network in Figure 7-18 has two DHCP servers, DHCP A and DHCP B. There is also a workstation configured as a DHCP relay agent (proxy). There is one standard DHCP client, one BOOTP client, and a workstation with a manually-configured IP address.

In this example, the DHCP servers are configured so that each server has half of the LAN's addresses for its scope. DHCP A has the first half of the IP address range, and DHCP B has the second half. Should DHCP A crash, DHCP B can process requests until DHCP A comes back up, because it has half of the LAN subnet addresses available to lease.

DHCP A and DHCP B have an exclusion range so clients such as the statically-configured IP client can use fixed addresses. The DHCP servers are also configured to support the BOOTP client. They have a boot image name, a file name, and the address of the file server where the files are located. When the BOOTP client boots, DHCP provides the information necessary for the client to boot (boot image) to the client.

The relay agent forwards the BOOTP and DHCP requests through the router (which is not configured to forward BOOTP/DHCP) to the two DHCP servers.

This is a common scenario; all the clients are rarely able to use the same services on the network in the same manner. Special devices like the relay agent or a specific router configuration help incorporate many diverse systems into the network using TCP/IP to help create a homogeneous network. DHCP employs several mechanisms so that it can provide functionality without impacting devices that cannot use DHCP. DHCP also

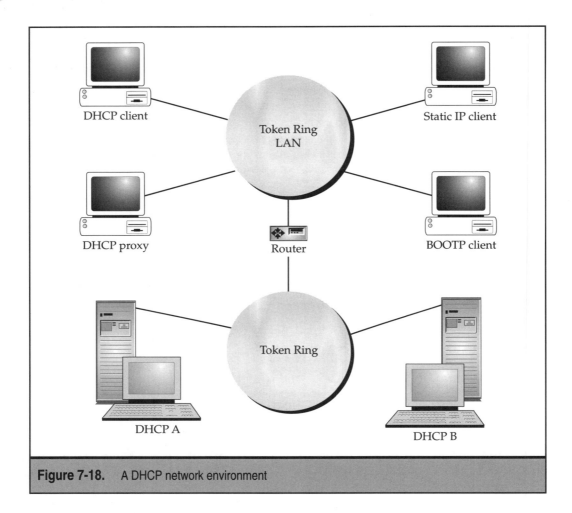

Figure 7-18. A DHCP network environment

provides client compatibility to older technologies like BOOTP so that multiple services don't have to be maintained on separate machines.

AN IMPORTANT NOTE ON DNS, WINS, AND DHCP

Many clients may depend on the services being available (DNS, WINS, and DHCP) all the time. It is critical that you design them to be high-availability services right from the start. In the planning phase, make sure you communicate this to others in the organization. Executives, managers, systems engineers, and systems administrators need to be aware how critical these services are to the operation of the network. Naming and addressing services can greatly reduce administration costs and end-user frustration. They can bring value to the organization by allowing the network environment to be flexible and scalable. However, high-availability systems are also expensive. Although your organization can get tremendous value by having the services, you need to ensure that everyone involved in acquiring, implementing, and supporting the services understands the costs associated with them.

WINDOWS
NT
Professional
Library

CHAPTER 8

Internet Services

The technologies that comprise a complete Internet/intranet solution for organizations are evolving at a rapid rate. Changing standards and an increase in the number of products available make designing and implementing an enterprise solution challenging. Programming languages, protocols, and security are just some of the subjects that need to be understood before building a solution for your organization.

Because the focus of this chapter is Internet Services for Windows NT, we will narrow our discussion down to special issues related to implementing this service on NT. Microsoft's Internet Information Server (IIS) is included as part of the Windows NT 4.0 license and is well integrated with the NT operating system, so we'll start there. We will cover the installation and configuration procedures and take a closer look at IIS features and functions. Then we will examine add-on applications and other components that can be used to greatly enhance server functionality and security.

Proxy servers speed up Internet/intranet access by caching frequently-accessed world wide web (WWW) content. A proxy server can also help secure your network and protect your servers from unauthorized access. We will discuss how to install and configure Microsoft's Proxy Server and look at specific configuration issues. Additionally we'll see how the Microsoft Proxy Server can function as a firewall. In the last section, we will walk through several enterprise integration scenarios that will help you design a scalable solution for your enterprise.

NOTE: For the purposes of this chapter, except where indicated, Internet and intranet can be used interchangeably. This is because an intranet, generally speaking, is really just a private or semi-private Internet. TCP/IP services are used similarly whether you are on the Internet or a private TCP/IP intranet.

INTERNET INFORMATION SERVER

The Internet Information Server provides integrated HyperText Transport Protocol (HTTP) and File Transfer Protocol (FTP) services. IIS also has add-on components and third-party applications (available via download from Microsoft at **www.microsoft.com/iis**) that extend its capabilities beyond the basic Internet services. These capabilities include e-mail, security, and site management tools.

Microsoft designed IIS to take advantage of the NT domain or active directory organization of user accounts, so that additional user databases are not required when using authentication or when administering the server. This feature is of particular value when you already have a large number of user accounts in your NT domain. Another notable feature of IIS is that it is tightly integrated with the NT operating system and NTFS. It interacts with several standard server administration tools such as the Event Viewer, Performance Monitor, Simple Network Management Protocol (SNMP), and Systems Management Server (SMS) allowing enhanced troubleshooting and management.

IIS also supports the Internet Server Application Programming Interface (ISAPI). With ISAPI, it is possible to create programs that manipulate data coming into the server or data being sent back to the client. ISAPI is used to create connectors to other servers (for example, database servers) via Open Database Connectivity (ODBC) service.

Planning the Installation

Building a capable, reliable, and secure web site takes careful planning. You should begin by identifying what you want to accomplish with your site. If your content is fairly static and is maintained by a small group of individuals, the basic server setup suffices. If you need to have dynamic content and create web pages on the fly, a database is necessary. If your site is going to contain a large amount of information, you should consider a searchable interface so that your users can get to the data they need quickly.

Software Components

The following list breaks down some of the basic and additional software components that can be incorporated into IIS to help you create a site server that meets your objectives.
   For starters you need:

   ▼   A server class system (see following section for specifications)

   ■   A network interface card

   ■   A network connection to your LAN

   ■   A WINS server or a local LMHOSTS file on every client (intranet)

   ■   An Internet connection to your ISP (Internet)

   ■   At least one registered IP address (Internet)

   ■   Private or registered internal IP addresses (Intranet)

   ■   A DNS server (internal DNS server(s) *and* at least one external DNS server provided by your ISP is recommended)

   ■   NT Server 4.0 or 5.0

   ▲   IIS (NT 4.0 Service Pack 3 or better, or NT 5.0 with IIS 4.0 or better)

   This allows you to set up a basic IIS service and start creating web pages (WWW) and host document and data stores for retrieval (FTP). It also allows you to set up a searchable collection of documents and data using the Gopher service (IIS 3 only).
   For advance functionality from IIS you may incorporate:

   ▼   Active Server Pages (ASP)

   ■   NetShow

   ■   Index Server

   ■   Java Virtual Machine

- FrontPage server extensions
- FrontPage client software
- Seagate Crystal Reports
- SQL Server
- SNA Server
- Exchange Server
- ▲ Office 97

Because of the explosive growth in Internet-based activity, additional components for IIS are being developed and existing functionality is being refined at a rapid pace. You can get the latest information on Microsoft IIS at **www.microsoft.com/iis.** Another place to look for Microsoft Internet products like browsers and authoring tools is:

www.microsoft.com/internet.

Hardware Requirements

Most software products for NT list base and suggested memory requirements, as well as other hardware requirements in their documentation. It is wise to consider hardware requirements before you install the software, or you may come up embarrassingly over-budget when you backpedal to upgrade your server. Table 8-1 shows the minimum hardware requirements for a basic IIS system.

Hardware	Minimum	Suggested
Processor (Intel)	486/66MHz	Pentium 150 or better
Processor (RISC)	150MHz Alpha	200MHz Alpha or better
Memory	32MB	64MB or better
Disk Space	50 to 100MB	500MB or better
Video	VGA 640 × 480	SVGA
CD-ROM	2× Speed	6× Speed or better
Network Adapter Card	10Mb Ethernet 4Mb Token Ring	100Mb Ethernet 16Mb Token Ring
Dial-up Adapter (for Internet dial connections)	28.8Kb/sec	28.8Kb, 33.6Kb, 56Kb, ISDN

Table 8-1. IIS Hardware Requirements

It's a good idea to check the Windows NT Hardware Compatibility List (HCL) before purchasing hardware. You should note that some of the latest hardware may not be on the list yet because of the delay between testing and releasing the newest version of the HCL. The latest HCL information can be found on the web at **www.microsoft.com/hwtest/hcl**. There is also more information on this topic in Chapter 2.

Even if you are trying to stick to a budget, don't become too parsimonious when purchasing hardware. Hardware problems undermine your hard work and can consume a large amount of your time. Use server and peripheral systems known to be reliable from manufacturers that have good warranties, support, and quick turnaround on repairs. Don't forget to consider the other servers your company owns. Having several servers of the same model can help justify spare parts and possibly a spare server that can be configured as a stand-in if one server fails. Chapter 3 offers more information on designing redundancy into your server(s) if uninterrupted up time is a requirement.

MEMORY   Of all the different components that make up a server, the one that can make a big difference for a relatively small investment is memory. When you have a system that is constantly swapping memory to disk, you have an expensive machine that is not performing up to its potential.

NT Server running IIS was designed to provide the basic WWW services: HTTP and FTP, using a very efficient 400KB of RAM. However, additional server services and other applications such as SQL Server or Exchange can consume quite a bit of memory. Without enough memory and the right hardware, your server may be very limited in the number of sessions it can support concurrently. Coming up even 1MB short of the necessary amount of memory may greatly reduce server performance.

Microsoft recommends that after you ensure that you have enough memory to run NT and all the services and other applications, you should make sure you have at least 256KB of memory for each concurrent user. With memory being fairly inexpensive, it is a good investment to add even more than your calculated requirement. It should be noted that in enterprise environments, you should seriously consider running services like SQL Server and Exchange on separate servers, because in addition to having an appetite for memory, they are also processor-intensive.

Placement Considerations

Building a solution that integrates effectively into your network requires that you examine your existing infrastructure. Where is the best location for your IIS server? If you have a full data center equipped with UPS or generator backup, and multiple points of entry for network connections, consider placing your server there. Of course, you'll need occasional access so you can hard reset the servers (if necessary) and conduct regular tape rotations. If you work in a location that is remote from the data center, you must have a staff there who can unpack, install your server into a rack, connect it to a network port, and power it up.

It is always tempting to place your server close to where you usually work. You can walk into the server room, see the server, and run tape backups; and—assuming you live close to your job—you can drive in at night to reboot the server if it crashes. All personal conveniences aside, in any environment where your server is critical to a business function, you need to make sure the following requirements are met:

▼ The server is physically secure.

■ It is regularly backed up.

■ The backup medium is rotated to an off-site facility.

■ The server has a reliable power supply such as a UPS.

▲ The network connections are reliable and have enough capacity to meet demand.

Although you are probably proud of your new baby, you need to send it out in the world with good support. In an enterprise environment, you are probably responsible for developing and integrating new technologies into a variety of systems that serve your business. You may not want to make a career out of managing day-to-day operations on every system you design and build. The point here is you should make sure that you have planned for the ongoing support of the servers and services you develop.

Figure 8-1 illustrates typical locations for Internet and intranet web servers. The Internet web server is located between the firewall and a proxy server/firewall in the demilitarized zone (DMZ). Additional security and filtering can take place at the initial router connecting to the Internet. The intranet server is protected from the outside by the firewalls but offers quick access for local users.

Installing IIS

Before you begin an installation, make sure you have the necessary software to install version 3.0 or better. IIS version 2.0 ships with NT 4.0; installing Service Pack 3 upgrades IIS to version 3.0. From there, you can download and install the additional components of IIS 3.0 as needed for your particular installation.

You can think of version 3.0 as an enhanced version of 2.0. The basic package is the same except IIS 3.0 is designed to integrate the additional components into a cohesive and manageable package.

IIS 4.0 is part of the NT 4.0 Option Pack and installs over previous versions but should not be installed over any beta versions of IIS 4.0. The initial challenge with IIS 4.0 has more to do with getting the necessary installation files than anything else. There are more than 70MB of CAB files and other installation files in the NT 4.0 Option Pack. When planning an IIS 4.0 installation, order the CD-ROM for a fee or plan to spend several hours (minimum) downloading the NT 4.0 Option Pack.

First-Time Installation

As noted earlier, there are several versions of IIS. We will look at both IIS 3.0 and IIS 4.0, because there are a few reasons you might use IIS 3.0 instead of IIS 4.0. One reason is that IIS 3.0 provides the Gopher service and IIS 4.0 does not. If you need or desire to have

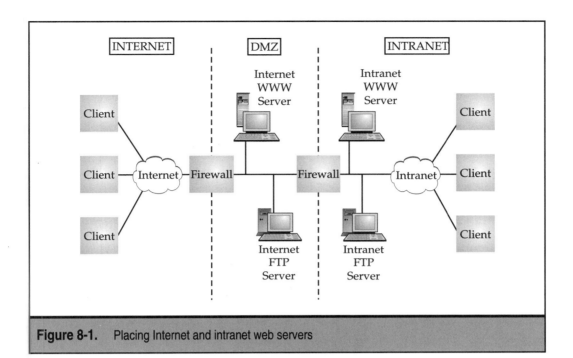

Figure 8-1.   Placing Internet and intranet web servers

Gopher running, you must use IIS 3.0. Also, you might use IIS 3.0 if your web and FTP needs are fairly simple. Finally, IIS 4.0 requires more horsepower and runs better on Pentium-based systems. If you are running your server on a 486-based machine with limited memory and it is working well, you may find that upgrading to IIS 4.0 pushes your machine over the edge. We have both versions running and have observed a noticeable increase in swapfile activity (a sure sign that more memory is needed) on the IIS 4.0 system. In any event, carefully evaluate your needs against your existing hardware, and plan for necessary upgrades if you want to start running IIS 4.0 with additional components.

If you don't have IIS installed on your server, start in this section. If you have installed IIS already but have not yet upgraded via a service pack to IIS 3.0, proceed to the section entitled "Upgrading IIS 2.0 to IIS 3.0". If you have already completed both steps, you can proceed to the section entitled "Configuring IIS 3.0". If you are planning to install IIS 4.0, proceed to the section entitled "Installing IIS 4.0 (NT 4.0 Option Pack)".

NOTE: If your server already has FTP or WWW services running, you must disable them prior to installing IIS. It may be possible to start these services later by changing the ports that the services run on. Check the services' configuration options and documentation for more information.

As with most services running on NT, installing IIS is a straightforward process. Either right-click on the Desktop Network icon and select Properties from the pull-down menu or open the Control Panel and double-click on the Network icon. At the Network dialog box (see Figure 8-2) click on the Services tab. This shows all the Network services currently running on the server. If the Internet Information Server is listed, it is already installed and you should proceed to the "Configuring IIS 3.0" section of this chapter.

To proceed with the installation, click on Add. A list of other services that are not installed on your system appears. Select Microsoft Internet Information Server from the list and click on OK.

In the next dialog box, enter the path to the NT Server i386 directory (for Intel installations). Setup assumes this directory is on a CD-ROM. However, we recommend keeping a copy on your hard drive for easier retrieval. For example, you might enter **C:\NTSRV\i386** if you have a copy of the files on your hard drive. Once you have entered the correct path, click on OK. On NT 4.0, the next dialog box is entitled Microsoft Internet Information Server 2.0 Setup (see Figure 8-3). Note that you are installing version 2.0 at this time. This should remind you to reapply the most recent NT Server 4.0 Service Pack (SP3 or better) after the IIS 2.0 installation to upgrade IIS from version 2.0 to 3.0.

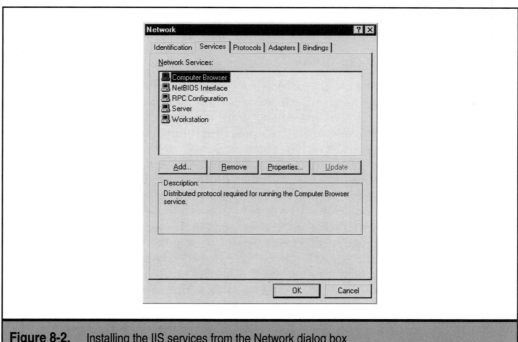

Figure 8-2.   Installing the IIS services from the Network dialog box

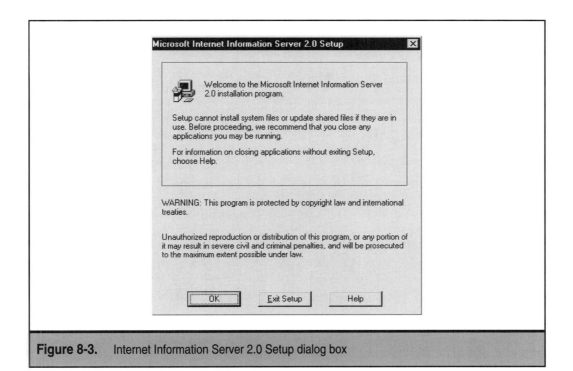

Figure 8-3. Internet Information Server 2.0 Setup dialog box

SELECTING IIS SERVICES Close any other applications that are running and click on OK to proceed. At this point, you are presented with a dialog box offering all the options available. Select the options you will be using by clicking on the appropriate check boxes, as shown in Figure 8-4.

The following services are available for installation:

▼ **Internet Service Manager (ISM)**—This tool allows you to manage services running on local and remote machines. Its functionality is not limited to the base IIS services (WWW, FTP, and Gopher). You can also manage Microsoft Proxy services and other related services installed on the server with the ISM tool.

■ **Internet Service Manager (HTML)**—This HTML-based version of the ISM tool allows you to manage IIS services and configure various service properties from remote locations. This tool is useful when you want to check or change service properties over a dialup session, for example. Note that you cannot start or stop services using this version of the ISM tool. If you could stop the WWW service, you would promptly disconnect yourself because the HTML version of the ISM relies on the WWW service to run.

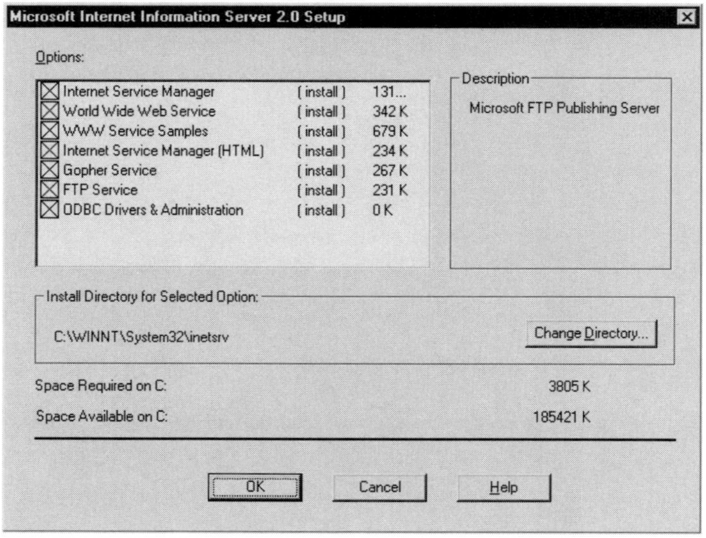

Figure 8-4. Choosing IIS options

- **Gopher Service**—The Gopher protocol is a simple search-and-retrieve protocol originally developed at the University of Minnesota. A Gopher client can download files and move within a directory structure, as well as link to other Gopher servers. Install this service only if you plan to use the Gopher hierarchical system of organization.

- **FTP Service**—Selecting this option installs the IIS FTP service. This version of the FTP Service replaces the one that is available on the NT 4.0 Server CD. Make sure that you have removed the earlier version before installing the new one.

▲ **ODBC Drivers & Administration**—Installs Open Database Connectivity (ODBC) drivers Check this option if you will be logging on to an ODBC database or if you want to build database access into your web applications.

If you are not sure which services you need, you might want to select all the options. Services such as the Gopher and FTP services can be stopped and removed later if you determine you do not need them. However, if you are certain you don't need a particular service, don't install it. Aside from consuming system resources, unmanaged services can be a potential security hole.

NOTE: For additional security, review the services bound to your server's network adapters and unbind any that are not needed.

REMOVING IIS SERVICES   If you have already installed some of the services and want to add or remove options, you can determine the status of a service by clearing the check box next to the option. If Remove appears in brackets next to the option, it is already installed. If Remove does not appear, the option is not currently installed. The Internet Service Manager is automatically selected if you choose to install any other options except ODBC Drivers & Administration. The Internet Service Manager can be installed without the other options if you do not plan to run Internet services on the local machine but want to administer IIS services on remote machines. Additionally, you can install the Internet Service Manager (HTML) interface to the server manager if you want to use a web browser to perform most administrative functions.

PUBLISHING DIRECTORIES   Once you have selected the options you want to install, click on OK. The next dialog box, Publishing Directories (see Figure 8-5), is used to select the root directories for the WWW, FTP and Gopher services. If any of these services were not selected for installation, they will be grayed out. When you accept the default directories, all the files that will be published for that service are placed in the directory you

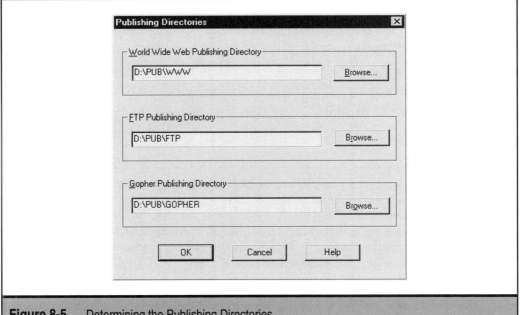

Figure 8-5.   Determining the Publishing Directories

designated. If you have already set up files to be published or shared, for example **C:\PUB\FTP**, enter the full path to that directory. Because we like to keep the OS partition separate from the data partition, we set the root for each service as **D:\PUB\WWW, D:\PUB\FTP,** and **D:\PUB\GOPHER** respectively.

NOTE: You are not allowed to specify network shares as root directories during the installation. However, if you want to use shares on another server, select the defaults during installation. Later, you will be able to set the service roots to shares on other systems (virtual shares) using the Internet Service Manager tool.

If the directories have not been created already, setup will ask if you want to create them. If you specified existing directories and received this prompt, you should go back and check your entries. If you haven't already created the directories, click on OK.

SELECTING ODBC DRIVERS   If you chose to install ODBC drivers, the next stage of setup prompts you to select from the available ODBC drivers. Select the drivers you plan to use and click on OK. If the selected drivers have been installed already, and they are older than the drivers from the NT 4.0 installation, they will be updated. If you already have newer drivers installed, setup will ask if you want to replace the newer drivers with the older ones. If this occurs, click on No and setup will proceed with copying files. Once setup has copied the necessary files, the installation is complete. A dialog box indicating that setup was successfully completed is displayed. Click on OK to return to the Network Services dialog box, and then click on Close.

Make sure all applications are closed and restart the system. Once the system has been restarted, you can complete the installation by applying the latest service pack to upgrade IIS 2.0 to IIS 3.0.

Upgrading IIS 2.0 to IIS 3.0

Upgrading IIS 2.0 to 3.0 on NT 4.0 is as simple as acquiring the latest service pack (SP3 or better) and installing it.

NOTE: As with any system level software, be careful when you apply a new service pack. A service pack can fix problematic bugs and close security holes, but it can also cause problems. Test any new service pack on a non-critical server first. Give yourself time to "kick the tires" on the new service pack by running all your applications as you would on a production server (see "Regression" in Chapter 12). Once you have tested the service pack and are ready to install it on production servers, give yourself plenty of time to deal with unexpected problems.

When you run the service pack, a Welcome dialog box is displayed. If this is your fist time installing the service pack on the server, follow the dialog box's advice and update the emergency repair disk (ERD) and run a backup. If there is a problem later, you may be spared the task of reinstalling NT, all your applications, and any local user accounts. If you have already installed the service pack and are rerunning it to update the system, you should still update your ERD and perform a full backup.

Before applying a service pack, we recommend the following steps:

▼ Use the *Rdisk.exe /s* command to update the Emergency Repair Disk.

■ Make sure you have a full system backup including the Registry files.

■ Disable all third-party drivers and services except those required to boot up the system (for example, drivers for a drive array controller card).

■ Verify that you have the most current versions of third-party drivers and services.

▲ Read the service pack release notes carefully; some bugs and incompatibilities are explained there.

Once the ERD has been updated and a full backup performed, click on Next. Read the Software License Agreement and click on Yes if you accept the terms. If you don't agree with the terms, click on No to exit setup without installing the service pack. Clicking on Yes brings up the next setup dialog box, which asks you to select between installing the service pack or uninstalling a previous installation of the service pack. Click on Install, and then click on the Next button.

The next dialog box (see Figure 8-6) prompts you to decide whether or not you would like to create an Uninstall directory. We recommend that you do if you have the space on your hard drive (approximately 40MB). When setup creates an Uninstall directory, you can run the service pack setup and select Uninstall. This causes setup to restore all your systems files to the state they were in prior to applying the service pack. If you don't have the space, you should probably review your hardware configuration and acquire more hard drive space.

Click on Next to proceed with the installation. If you want to change any of the setup parameters, do so now by clicking on Back and making any necessary changes. Once you are ready, click on Finish to install the service pack. Once setup has completed the application of the service pack, a dialog box (see Figure 8-7) indicates that the system must be restarted.

Once the system is restarted, this installation of the service pack is complete, your IIS version 2.0 has been upgraded to 3.0, and you can proceed to the configuration section.

NOTE: If you are curious about the contents of the service pack executable, running the executable with a /x will extract all the service pack files to a directory for your perusal.

Configuring IIS 3.0

Once installed, IIS is managed with the Internet Service Manager (ISM) tool. You can use it to start and stop the IIS services on local and remote IIS servers, allowing you to centrally administer any number of servers. Let's look at the tool now.

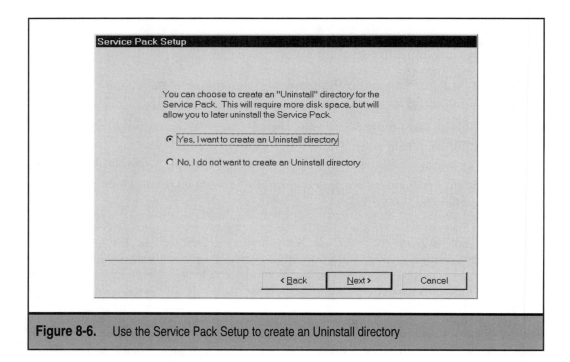

Figure 8-6. Use the Service Pack Setup to create an Uninstall directory

To start the IIS ISM, click on Start and select Internet Service Manager from the Programs | Microsoft Internet Server menu. After launching the IIS manager tool, take a look at the services listed and verify that they are running as in Figure 8-8.

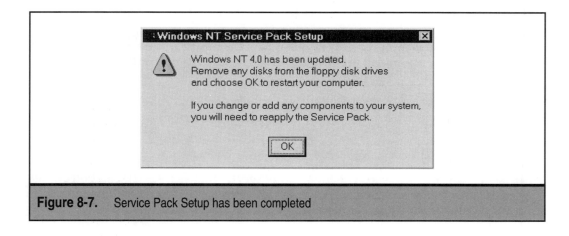

Figure 8-7. Service Pack Setup has been completed

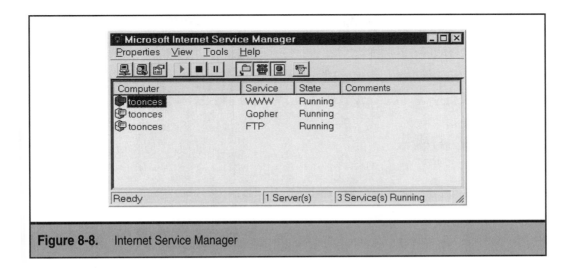

Figure 8-8. Internet Service Manager

Right-mouse click on any of the listed services to activate a menu that allows you to start, stop, pause, and edit the properties of the service. The Properties menu item has the same functionality. If you have remote servers, they should also be accessible from this tool. If they are not listed, go to the Properties menu and select Find All Servers; IIS will search for other IIS sites on your network.

If you already know the name of a server and would like to manage it, go to the Properties menu, select Connect to Server, and enter the name of the server you want to manage. Assuming that you have administrative privileges, you can manage any IIS server on your network in this manner.

If you installed the IIS manager for HTML, you can perform the same administrative functions, but you cannot use this interface to start, pause, and stop services. You can go directly to the HTTP tool by entering **www.<*computername*>/iisadmin/default.htm** into your browser URL address box. This will bring you to the main administration screen, as shown in Figure 8-9. From here, administrative functions can be performed much as they would be in the standard IIS ISM tool.

For additional information, you can go to the IIS default page (see Figure 8-10). It has plenty of information on IIS features and functions. It includes online documentation, and if you chose to install them, sample pages. If you have an Internet connection, there are links to take you to even more information on the web. It is a great place to learn more about what is possible with IIS.

Configuring the WWW Service

Configuring the WWW services is done by double-clicking on the WWW Service option listed in the ISM main screen, and then selecting Properties. You can access the IIS online

Figure 8-9. The HTTP IIS manager tool

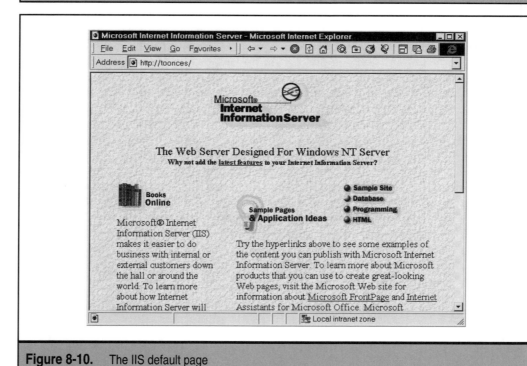

Figure 8-10. The IIS default page

configuration information directly with your browser at **www.<*computername*>/ iisadmin/htmldocs/03_iis.htm**. This section of the online documentation describes how to configure the various WWW services step-by-step.

Some of the properties you may want to adjust are:

▼ **Connection Timeout**—Users are logged off if they have no activity within this period. Shorten this time to eliminate users who hold the connection open without actually retrieving any information.

■ **Maximum Connections**—This number represents the maximum users that can be connected at once to your WWW server. Keep this in line with what your hardware and network connections can support.

■ **Anonymous Logon**—If you would like non-domain users to access your WWW server, you must allow anonymous logons.

■ **Username/Password**—This account controls access to the web pages. Restrict the privileges of this account to allow access only to resources you are willing to share with all users.

▲ **Password Authentication**—If you do not allow anonymous users, you should require users to have a password using the Windows NT Challenge/Response method to provide the most secure method of authentication. Unfortunately, the only WWW browser capable of the Challenge response is Microsoft's Internet Explorer 2.0 (or higher). In other instances, you need to allow clear text authentication.

VIRTUAL DIRECTORIES AND SERVERS   You have more options for creating directories to store your Internet pages than you had during the initial installation. You can create *virtual directories* that can be on the same computer or located remotely. To the user, a virtual directory appears as a subdirectory of the root Internet directory.

If you would like to run more than one web site from a single computer, you can create *virtual servers* within IIS. Users access two web sites believing that each web site is sitting on its own box. In reality, both web sites are being run on the same machine.

Both virtual directories and virtual servers are easily installed via the Directory Properties window for the WWW service, as shown in Figure 8-11. To call up this window, click on the Add button in the Directory tab from the WWW Service Properties window.

To create a virtual directory, follow these steps:

1. Add the path to the virtual directory.

2. Click on Virtual Directory.

3. Enter the alias of the directory. This is how the directory will appear to users.

4. If the directory resides on another computer, enter the user name and password that will be used to access this share.

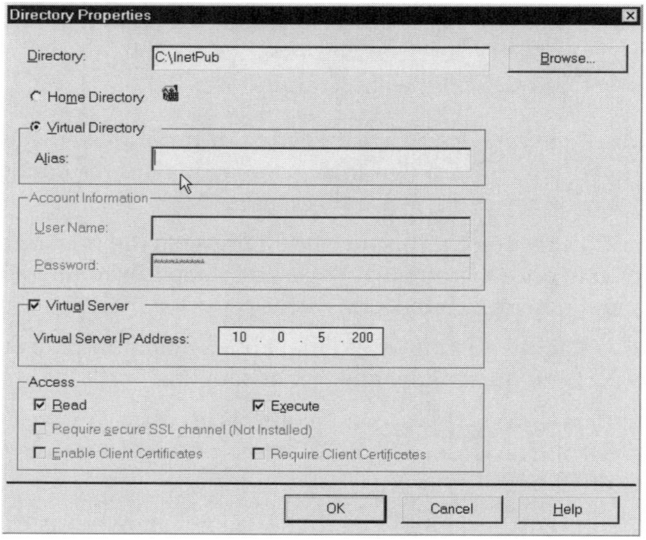

Figure 8-11. Creating a virtual directory or virtual server

5. Select the level of security you want to impose on the users. Typically read-only access is sufficient. If there are executables on the server, such as Java, ActiveX, or CGI scripts, you must allow for execution. The Require Secure SSL Channel option is enabled only if you have installed the Secure Socket Layer on your computer.

6. Click on OK to finish the creation of the virtual directory.

To set up a virtual server, follow these steps:

1. Click on Add in the Directory's tab.

2. Type the directory for the root of WWW service and select Home Directory.

3. Click on the Virtual Server box.

4. If the directory will reside on a remote machine, enter the user name and password to access this share.

5. Indicate the IP address for this web site.

6. Click on OK to complete the install of the virtual server.

7. Repeat these steps for each virtual server for this computer.

NOTE: After adding a virtual server, you must add the new IP address to your network adapter card. This is accomplished within the network setup. Go to Network Properties | Protocols | TCP/IP Protocol | Properties | Advanced. Then click on the Add button in the IP address window and enter the new IP addresses and subnet masks.

You can set up to five additional IP addresses per network card installed via the network configuration options. You can create more entries by editing the Registry. Use a Registry editor such as *regedt32.exe* to add additional IP addresses and subnet masks:

1. Start *regedt32.exe* and navigate to the following registry subkey:

   KEY_LOCAL_MACHINE\SYSTEM\CurrentControlSet\Services\ <Adapter Name>\Parameters\Tcpip.

2. Double-click on the IPAddress value.

3. In the Multi-String Editor dialog box, type each additional IP address on a new line, and then click on OK.

4. Double-click on the SubnetMask value.

5. Enter each additional subnet mask on a new line in the dialog box as you did for the IP address, and then click on OK.

6. Exit *regedt32.exe* and restart your computer.

LOGGING The WWW configuration allows you tremendous control over which events are logged and how they are logged. In addition to letting you log accesses to ordinary text files on a daily, weekly, or monthly basis, or until the log file reaches a particular size, you can export the log files to an SQL/ODBC database.

You will probably use other applications to read your log files and to create statistics for web usage so that they may be posted on web pages. Often these statistics are used to determine what kinds of users are accessing the web server and what they are interested in. Also, the logs can be invaluable when trying to determine the culprit of a security breach. There are many third-party tools available that can facilitate the management of logs. A list is available on the Microsoft IIS web page.

NOTE: The log files get quite large if your server is well-used. Nonetheless, it's a good idea to place them on a remote machine so they can be read even if the server has been compromised.

ACCESS CONTROL Obviously security is a concern and you want to do everything in your power to raise the level of security without hindering access to your legitimate users. IIS includes some limited security features you can employ, although you should certainly explore other options, as discussed in Chapter 10.

With the IIS you can grant or deny access to specific computers using the Advanced tab in the Server Properties window. If you wish to control access of users on the Internet, you might deny access to a particular address or group of addresses that may be misusing your site. However, if you have a private intranet, you might want to grant access to users of a specific subnet, for example the users of the 10.0.5.0 subnet. To do this, you click on the Granted Access radio button, and then the Add button. Enter the IP address (with a zero at the end to signify all users of that subnet) and the subnet mask used there, for example: 10.0.5.0 and 255.255.255.0.

Another option in the Advanced properties window is to set a limit on how much network traffic the Internet services can use. This might be important to you if you don't want the web server to use all the available throughput on the local segment or all of the servers' network bandwidth allocated for web services.

Configuring the FTP Service

This service has many of the same configuration options as the WWW service so we will only expound on those that are different. In the Services tab there are many options that are independent from the other services but have the same effect. These options include connection timeout, maximum connections, and whether or not to allow anonymous users.

One interesting check box is Allow Only Anonymous Connections. You should select this box if you allow anonymous connections. Otherwise, when legitimate users log on they will be forced to supply their password via clear text, which exposes them to capture. Allowing only anonymous connections ensures no passwords are sent over the network but makes your site available to all.

The FTP service allows you to display a message to your users when they log on and log off, or when the maximum number of users sessions has been reached. To configure these messages click on the Messages tab.

The Directories tab allows you to configure virtual directories as you did for the WWW service, although you cannot create virtual servers. You also get the option of displaying the directories in either the DOS or UNIX convention.

The logging and advanced features of the FTP service are similar to the WWW Service and should be configured to fit your needs.

Configuring the Gopher Service

The Service tab has the same options as the services we've discussed already, but again they are independent from them and should be configured separately. The Directories tab has the same functionality as it did in configuring the FTP server. Although you cannot create virtual servers, you can create virtual directories. As with the other two services, you have complete control over logging via the Logging tab, and limited access control via the Advanced tab.

Additional IIS 3.0 Components

Let's look at a few of the additional components available to enhance your Internet Information Server. Discussion of these components could fill entire books. With that in mind, we will look at the features that offer enhancements you are likely to use immediately.

Active Server Pages

Active Server Pages (ASP) is available in IIS versions 3.0 and 4.0. It allows you to mix HTML and scripts using a variety of authoring programs to create new web pages on the fly. Active Server Pages extends the functionality of the basic web server by making it much easier to build dynamic, web-based applications. It provides support for the execution of ASP scripts which can be written in VBScript, JavaScript, and JScript as well as other scripting languages. Additionally, ActiveX server components written in C++, Visual Basic, and Java can be incorporated into an Active Server Page. There are also prewritten objects that can be used to build a complete web application with little or no programming necessary. ASP includes several standard objects that can be used in developing web applications.

In short, ASP scripting is used to generate HTML on the fly. Here is how it works. When a client workstation running a browser hits the IIS server and opens an ASP document, a script is run. The script generates the HTML code based on user input, type of browser, content of "cookies" stored on the client, and so on. As it executes, it may query a database and place the data in a table to be sent back to the client in the HTML stream. Because the server processes requests, executes applications, receives the results, packages them, churns HTML code, and sends it to the browser, it needs to be a very powerful system. If your server is going to be an "active" server, make sure it is has plenty of processing power.

ActiveX Data Object (ADO)

The ActiveX Data Object is a component that enables connectivity to ODBC or OLE-DB databases. With it, a web application can be built that can read and store data in a variety of databases including SQL Server, Access, Informix, Sybase, and Oracle.

NetShow

The NetShow server provides streaming audio and video content over the network. It also supports multicasting of audio content, which allows the server to send a single, directed broadcast (multicast) to multiple users. This allows many users to listen to the same audio stream without the server having to send out a separate audio stream to each workstation. NetShow provides streaming media output, which permits the client to start listening to or viewing the content as the data flows into the workstation. Without streaming media support, the client would have to wait until the entire file containing the audio or video content was completely transferred to the client before it could be replayed.

NOTE: Great care should be taken when implementing any high-bandwidth application servers on the network. Audio and video data streams generate a substantial amount of network traffic and should be located where high network utilization will not interfere with other critical network traffic.

Index Server

Index Server is a single server search engine for IIS. It can be downloaded from the Microsoft web site as a free component of IIS. Index Server can automatically build a full text-searchable index of your web that is accessible from any browser. In addition to full indexing of text and HTML web pages, Index Server can index Microsoft Office documents. It can even recognize and index office document properties like author name, document title, and keywords, as well as other standard and custom properties. Index Server respects all NTFS security attributes. It will not display a restricted document in a search unless the user is authorized to read it.

In an enterprise environment, you may want to set up a central search server. The Index Server can be set up as a search server with the indexes of other servers' files stored on the central server.

FrontPage Server Extensions

Microsoft FrontPage extensions can be installed on the IIS server so that a FrontPage client can publish content directly to the IIS server (as opposed to using FTP or writing to a share). This is a very handy feature when you have many people authoring content on the server. You can set each user's rights and allow users to publish only to the areas where they have the authority to publish. In addition, the FrontPage authoring tool allows users with limited authoring experience to start publishing without extensive handholding.

Crystal Reports

A limited version of this very popular Seagate software product is available for IIS. It can automatically build reports from the contents of the IIS log files. The reports can be exported into HTML format dynamically so that your reporting is always current. You can purchase the full version from Microsoft for additional functionality. Go to the Microsoft web site for more information.

IIS 4.0 (NT 4.0 Option Pack)

At the time of this writing, the NT 4.0 Option Pack with IIS 4.0 had just been released from beta. However, to get you started, we will cover the installation process and discuss some of the new features found in this release.

Installing IIS 4.0 (NT 4.0 Option Pack)

Whether you have a previously installed version (IIS 2.0 or 3.0) or are starting fresh, you should ensure that you have the latest service pack installed. If you have already installed an alpha or beta version of IIS 4.0, you must uninstall it before you install the final version.

NOTE: You must have installed Internet Explorer version 4.01 [version 4.72.2106.5] or better before you attempt to install the NT 4.0 Option Pack.

To begin, click on Setup from the installation directory located on the CD-ROM, a local drive, or a shared directory on the network. If you don't have IE4.01 or better, setup informs you that you need to install it. If you have installed IE4.01, setup continues.

NOTE: If you have installed Microsoft Proxy Server 2.0, you will be notified that you have to rerun the Proxy Server setup after you have completed the IIS 4.0 installation.

Because Gopher is no longer supported in IIS 4.0, if you have the Gopher service running, setup gives you the option of removing the service or exiting setup. Clicking on OK removes Gopher and displays the welcome screen, as shown in Figure 8-12.

Click on Next, read the End User License Agreement, and click on either Decline to quit the install or Accept to proceed. If you are upgrading from an older version of IIS, an Upgrade Only/Upgrade Plus window appears.

Selecting Upgrade Only allows you to perform a "standing" upgrade. It essentially upgrades only the options you have already installed; it doesn't give you the option of installing any new components. Upgrade Plus allows you to select additional uninstalled and new components. Selecting Upgrade Plus allows you to see the options and select those that you want to install; the components you already have running under your old version are checked. Many of these components are new to IIS. Combined into a single product, they provide an impressive suite of capabilities.

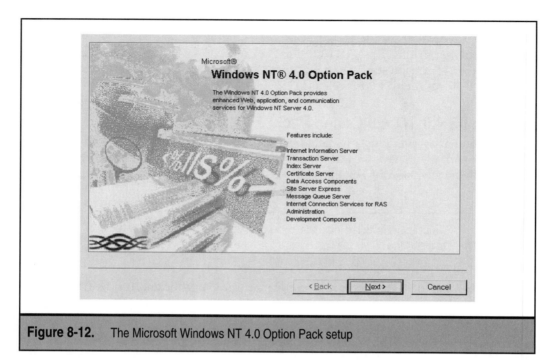

Figure 8-12. The Microsoft Windows NT 4.0 Option Pack setup

You have the option of installing the following Microsoft components and sub-components:

▼ Certificate Server

■ FrontPage 98 Server Extensions

■ Internet Connection Services for RAS

■ Internet Information Server

■ Data Access Components

■ Index Server

■ Management Console

■ Message Queue

■ Script Debugger

■ Site Server Express 2.0

■ NT Option Pack Common Files

■ Transaction Server

■ Visual InterDev RAD Remote Deployment Support

▲ Windows Scripting Host

Once you have selected the options you wish to install, setup will prompt you for various configuration parameters depending on which components you have chosen. At this point, setup copies the necessary files. Upon completion, reboot your server to complete the installation.

New IIS 4.0 Features

There are numerous new features in IIS 4.0. One of the most important is the integration of Microsoft Transaction Server. It brings reliable application services to the web. It does so using what Microsoft calls Transactional Active Server Pages to support multiple actions, like database writes, with the actions committed together. If the actions cannot be committed together, the Transaction Server will back out of the transaction to insure the data is always consistent. In other words, if part of a database transaction fails the Transaction Server can back out of the entire transaction. This is a key feature for financial applications and other database applications.

IIS 4.0 also includes new and improved tools for site management and content analysis. Most notable is Microsoft Site Server Express, a tool that provides information about site usage patterns and how the site is structured. Other management improvements include integrated server management via the Microsoft Management Console and improved web-based administrative capabilities. Also new is the X.509 digital certificate server and an improved search engine.

Getting More Information

More information on the NT 4.0 Option Pack can be found at **www.microsoft.com/iis/**. If you have the installation files already, make sure you read the product documentation found in the *DriveLetter*:**\NTOptionPackSetupFiles\iisread.htm**.

MICROSOFT PROXY SERVER

Proxy Server's primary function is to provide caching of frequently-accessed Internet data. A proxy server is typically located between the client and the host on the Internet, as shown in Figure 8-13. Caching data can save use of the slower WAN connection for data that hasn't been downloaded to your site. Because proxy servers can be configured to block certain ports or users, they also provide some security.

Microsoft Proxy Server provides a very robust collection of features that are well-suited to networks with mixed workstation operating systems. It ships with proxy support for web, WinSock, and SOCKS protocols. MS Proxy Server provides several features that you should look for in a proxy server:

▼ CERN-compliant applications (for example, WWW, FTP, and Gopher)

■ Secure Socket Layer (SSL) 2.0 and SSL 3.0

■ Network News Transport Protocol (NNTP)

■ Internet Relay Chat (IRC)

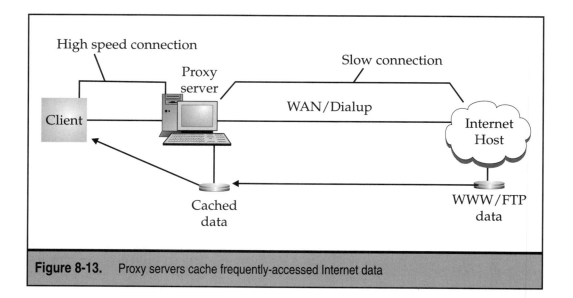

Figure 8-13. Proxy servers cache frequently-accessed Internet data

■ Post Office Protocol 3 (POP3)

▲ Simple Mail Transfer Protocol (SMTP)

NOTE: When planning a proxy server installation, start with the minimum recommended hard drive space (approximately 100MB), and then add a minimum of 1MB for each WWW client accessing the server. For example, if you have 100MB for the base cache, and you have 200 clients who will be using the proxy server, you need a minimum of 300MB of drive space for the cache. Of course, your proxy server and your users won't complain if you add more than the recommended minimum.

SOCKS Proxy Service

Microsoft Proxy Server supports SOCKS version 4.3a. It works with Windows, Macintosh, and UNIX client workstations, although it has been incorporated into the server primarily to support UNIX and Macintosh systems. SOCKS Proxy Service allows client workstations to run telnet, FTP, Gopher, and HTTP through the proxy server. It uses the TCP component of the TCP/IP protocol. It supports neither applications that rely on UDP nor Novell IPX.

As with other proxies, SOCKS allows client workstations to connect to the internal side of the proxy server; the server then manages the connections on the external side out to the Internet. There is no user-based authentication, thus no way of controlling access based on users or groups. Instead, client identification is based on IP addresses. If you are using DHCP to assign client IP address information, you will have to allow whole blocks of users at a time. Because a combination of the WinSock and Web Proxy services can perform the same function for clients while maintaining user-based access control, you will probably want to limit access to the subnetworks or specific address ranges where non-WinSock-enabled clients exist.

WinSock Proxy Service

Microsoft Proxy Server includes a client package that allows WinSock applications to run through the proxy server. It works with almost every application that is compliant with WinSock version 1.1. To a WinSock application, the WinSock proxy client looks like a standard WinSock interface. Behind the scenes, the client redirects the WinSock API calls to the proxy server. The proxy server in turn communicates with the external host and returns the information to the client workstation. Because the client sits below the actual application using WinSock, a variety of applications can be run, such as mail clients, telnet, newsreaders, Internet Relay Chat, and even newer applications like NetShow and RealAudio.

NOTE: The WinSock proxy client is only compatible with Windows-based client workstations running Windows 3.11, Windows 95, or Windows NT.

Because the WinSock Proxy Service supports authentication between the client and the server, you can control access by user ID or user group. You can control access for particular users and groups by enabling or disabling specific ports (which control the types of services available). Both inbound and outbound connections can be managed to this level of granularity. In addition, you can apply filters that control access to specific web sites by domain name or IP address.

Web Proxy Service

Far and away the most popular service of Microsoft Proxy Server is the Web Proxy Service. This is because the Web Proxy Service is the only service of the three that can provide HTTP- and FTP caching. It can also proxy HTTP, HTTP-S, Gopher, and FTP traffic to and from any CERN-compliant browser running on any operating system that the browser supports.

Like the WinSock Proxy Service, it can provide user, group level, and anonymous access through the proxy server. You can further control the access, permitting or denying it by protocol.

A firewall-like feature of the Web Proxy Service is the server's capability to allow reverse proxying and reverse hosting for web publishing. The proxy can police requests from the external side of the server into the internal network, or you can place your web servers on the internal side of the proxy server and tightly control access to them.

Installing and Configuring Microsoft Proxy Server

The first step in installing Proxy Server is to acquire the installation files. A complete 30-day evaluation version can be downloaded from the Internet or run from a CD-ROM from Microsoft. It should be noted that much of the configuration of Microsoft Proxy Server is done during the installation process. The remaining configuration steps are outlined in the Managing Microsoft Proxy Server section. You should be familiar with the product and your network before you attempt to install the server.

You will need the following information before installing Microsoft Proxy Server:

▼ The registration number from the CD or a trial registration number

■ The type of clients accessing the proxy server (for example, NT i386/Alpha, Windows 95, or Windows 3.x)

■ The client-side protocol (for example, TCP/IP, IPX)

▲ The IP address ranges on the internal side of your network when using TCP/IP

NOTE: If you intend to cache information, you must use a hard drive on the local server; you cannot cache to a network drive. Before the installation, you should also make sure the drive or drives you plan to use are NTFS-formatted and have enough free space available for the cache.

Once you have the installation executable, run it from the local or network drive or CD-ROM. Setup will unpack some temporary files and bring up the Proxy Server Setup welcome dialog box.

The next dialog box requires you to enter the registration number or "CD-Key" number before installation can proceed, as shown in Figure 8-14.

Enter the registration number that shipped with your CD or, if you are installing an evaluation version downloaded from the web, enter the registration key listed in the download site documentation.

The next dialog box returns a product ID number. Although you can view the number in the About box of the ISM tool, you should write it down. If you have purchased the product and ever need to call for support, you may be asked to provide the number.

Click on OK to proceed. The next dialog box prompts you for a location to install the program. Accept the default or select a folder suitable for your configuration.

Next, click on the Installation Options button. This opens the Installation Options main dialog box, as shown in Figure 8-15.

The installation options include:

▼ Install Microsoft Proxy Server

■ Install the Administration Tool

▲ Install Documentation

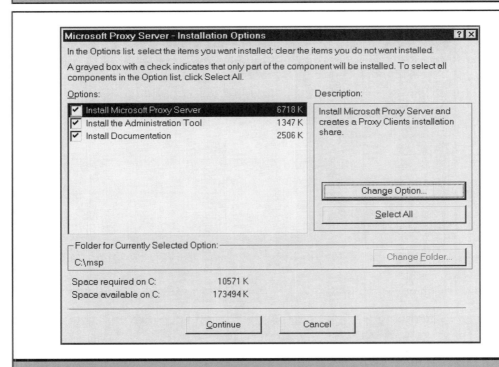

Figure 8-14. Entering the Proxy Server CD-Key registration number

Figure 8-15. The Proxy Server Installation Options main dialog box

You will probably want to install all these options. Clicking on Change Option when Install Microsoft Proxy Server is highlighted will open another installation dialog box, as shown in Figure 8-16.

Besides allowing you to choose whether or not you would like to install the server, this dialog box allows you to select whether you want to install proxy client shares for Windows NT Intel/Windows 95, Windows NT Alpha, and Windows 3.x machines. The shares allow client workstations to run the SOCKS proxy client installation from the server share for their particular operating system. Note that clients do not need the proxy client software to access web HTTP and FTP through the Microsoft Proxy Server. Once you have made your selections, click on the OK button to proceed with the install.

If you are not running the network service IPX SAP Agent, you are notified that the service is required to support client workstations that are using IPX but not TCP/IP. If you plan to have only IPX clients use the proxy server, you must make sure the SAP agent is installed and running. To accomplish this, go to the Network properties | Services | SAP Agent, and install as you would any other network service.

The next dialog box (see Figure 8-17) allows you to configure the proxy server cache drives. Remember, if you want the proxy server to cache information to the hard drive, it

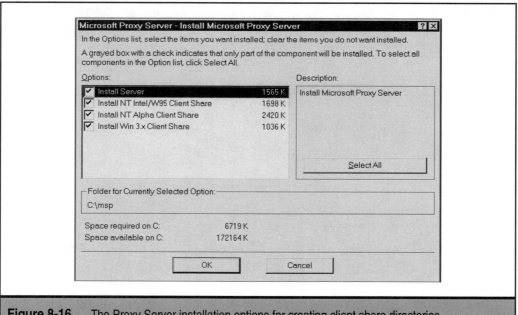

Figure 8-16.   The Proxy Server installation options for creating client share directories

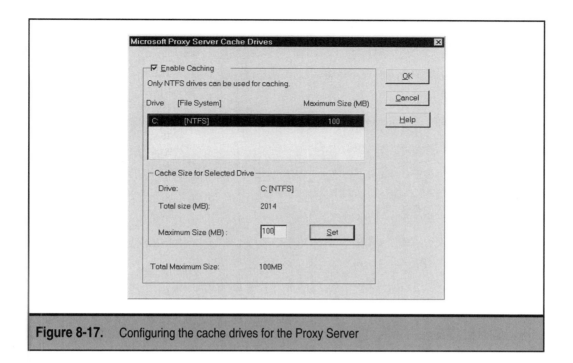

Figure 8-17.   Configuring the cache drives for the Proxy Server

must be an NTFS drive. You can also modify the drive properties later in the Properties menu for the Web Proxy Service from the Proxy Server manager tool.

Now you can select which drive or drives you want to use for caching proxy data. Additionally, parameters for the maximum cache size for each cache drive are defined here. Once the cache drives have been configured, click on OK to continue.

The next step in the configuration is to define the IP addresses that are on the internal side of the network. The proxy server needs to know what addresses are valid on the internal side of the proxy so it can properly route traffic. Once the internal addresses are specified, all other addresses are excluded and thought to be on the external side of the proxy server. Configuration of the addressing parameters is accomplished in the Local Address Table Configuration dialog box shown in Figure 8-18. Here you specify the range of IP addresses within your network that you would like to permit access to the Internet.

You can imagine that entering all IP address ranges for an enterprise could consume the better part of a day. Instead of manually entering the internal address ranges, you can automatically generate a local address translation table based on parameters selected in the Construct Local Address Table dialog box shown in Figure 8-19. If you use one of the designated private address blocks (10.x.x.x, 192.168.x.x, 172.16.x.x-172.31.x.x) you should

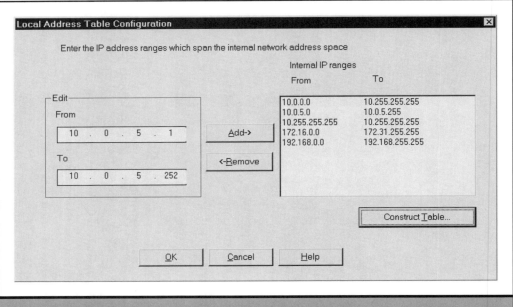

Figure 8-18. Configuring the Local Address Table

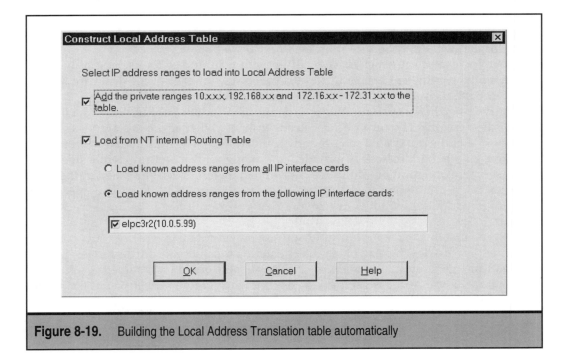

Figure 8-19. Building the Local Address Translation table automatically

check the Add the Private Ranges box so that the local address table (LAT) will include these addresses.

You can also select the Load from NT Internal Routing Table box so that the LAT will include addresses found in NT's routing table. If you select this parameter, you should manually select the interface cards that you want the LAT construction process to use. Select only the interface card(s) on the internal side of your proxy server. Exclude the interface card(s) on the Internet side of your proxy server. The other option is to allow the LAT construction process to build the LAT using the IP routing table associated with all interface cards. However, if you choose to do this, you must remember to remove the Internet-side addresses from the LAT. After verifying that the LAT contains only internal network addresses, proceed by clicking on the OK button.

The setup and configuration process continues with the Client Installation/ Configuration window shown in Figure 8-20. If you chose earlier to create proxy client installation shares, some of the parameters that the client installation will use can be set here. In addition to defining how WinSock Proxy clients will be able to connect to the WinSock Proxy Server, several key browser-related functions can be set under the Properties button.

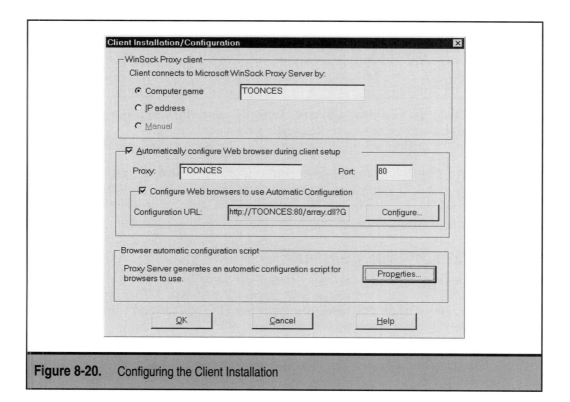

Figure 8-20. Configuring the Client Installation

The WinSock Proxy client can be configured to connect to the proxy server using the server name or its IP address. For example, if you had several proxy servers in an array (see "Arrays" in the next section), the DNS could be configured so that it had several IP addresses for the host entry "Toonces". Then several proxy servers could be set up to service requests sent to the hostname Toonces thereby increasing fault tolerance and reliability. If you have a DNS host on your internal network, there is really no reason to use an IP address. You should configure the WinSock Proxy clients to connect using the server name.

You also have the option of defining whether the client installation routine checks the client for an installed web browser. If one is found, the client setup routine can configure the browser to use the proxy server. This feature is especially useful when converting users from direct Internet access to proxied Internet access. The proxy client setup can find and reconfigure the browser to use the proxy server automatically, an especially handy feature when you have hundreds of clients or clients scattered across a number of locations.

The newest web browsers allow you to take automatic configuration one step further. They can be configured to point to a URL that contains an automatic configuration script. This script can configure the browser to properly use the proxy server. The script can be changed on the server, instead of having to make the change in the client web browser configuration.

In addition, you can configure the browser to only use the proxy for intranet sites by specific addresses and domains. You would do this so that intranet servers are accessed directly without going through the proxy server. Once the client configurations have been set, click on OK. Setup will display an Access Control dialog box.

NOTE: One of the most notable features of many NT-based proxy servers is the capability to authenticate and maintain access control using NT domain user accounts.

The Access Control dialog box allows you to enable or disable access control for the Web Proxy and WinSock Proxy services based on users and groups. Select the users and groups you would like to give access. Once you have finalized your selections for access control, click on OK and the installation finishes.

Managing Microsoft Proxy Server

Management and configuration of the services is done via the Microsoft Internet Service Manager tool. It can be accessed via the Start menu | Programs | Microsoft Proxy Server | Internet Service Manager. The same program can also be accessed from the Internet Information Server menu. The services on the local machine are listed.

NOTE: If you want to administer services on remote machines, click on the Internet Service Manager | Properties menu and select Find All Servers to view all available servers or Connect to Server to administer a specific server. Be aware that you cannot discover the WinSock Proxy Service on remote machines when you select Find All Servers; to do this, you must use the Connect to Server item using the server name.

Once you have connected to the server you want to manage, you should see the three proxy services: SOCKS Proxy, WinSock Proxy, and Web Proxy. From there you can left-click on a particular service to start, stop, and access the Properties dialog box. Each proxy service has several specific tabs used to configure the services. The three proxy services have two service properties tabs in common. They are the Service and Logging tabs. All three services also have a Permissions tab, but its usage under the SOCKS Proxy is different than it is under the WinSock and Web proxies. Let's look at some of the more significant configuration parameters.

Shared Services

The Shared Services items are located in the Services tab of the proxy server's Properties window. These configuration options are shared by all three proxy services.

SECURITY   The first tab, Packet Filters, lets you activate and configure packet filtering on the external interface. When checked, you can control the IP packet types allowed through to the internal interface. This tab allows you to block incoming packets from specific hosts, addresses, or even fragmented block packets. Additionally, you can block packets destined for a particular server service on the internal network based on the TCP/IP port they use. Exceptions can be added or modified for allowing specific services, like DNS, Ping, or other applications requiring specific ports through the proxy.

The second tab, Domain Filters, allows you to set the default access to Internet sites as either Permit All or Deny All. Once set, you can add domain names to the Except box to create a list of sites that are either allowed (if you chose the default Deny All) or blocked (if you chose the default Permit All).

The third tab, Alerting, can be configured to monitor network traffic in the external interface when packet filtering is enabled. Alerts can be written to the NT EventLog and/or sent to an e-mail address via a SMTP mailer.

The fourth tab, Logging, allows you to set a variety of logging options. You can set the logging to be regular or verbose. For offline analysis of the log file, you can choose to have the log write to a file or an SQL/ODBC database.

ARRAYS   An array is a logical group of proxy servers. The servers communicate among each other via a predefined port. The benefit of having proxy server arrays is that they can work together to balance the traffic load, and allow the proxy service to be fault-tolerant.

If the array members are configured to be synchronized, you can send configuration changes out to all of the servers in the array by making the changes on one server.

AUTODIAL   The autodial feature setup for the Microsoft Proxy Server is accessed via the Autodial button located in the Service tab of any of the three services' Properties dialog boxes. It enables Microsoft Proxy Server to dial on demand using a RAS Phonebook entry. This is very useful if one of the Proxy Server services must establish a dialup connection to the Internet. If configured, dial-on-demand is used for all client traffic using the SOCKS and WinSock proxies. For the Web Proxy service, dial-on-demand is invoked only if the proxy server cannot locate the requested information in its cache.

PLUG-INS (WEB PAGE)   Clicking the Plug-ins (Web page) button launches your default browser and, assuming Internet access, connects to **www.microsoft.com/proxy/plugins/ vendors2.** The site has a number of third-party plug-ins and compatible software, including firewall, antivirus, content filtering, and reporting tools.

Common Services Configuration

The services' configuration buttons are located in the Services tab of the proxy server's Properties window.

CLIENT CONFIGURATION   The Client Configuration window is used to modify the client setup routine used to configure client workstations as discussed in the "Installing and Configuring Microsoft Proxy Server" section of this chapter.

LOCAL ADDRESS TABLE   The Local Address Table can be viewed and modified here. If you recall, the LAT is used to specify all the internal IP addresses on your network, thereby excluding the external addresses. The information is necessary because it tells the proxy server which way to route packets.

SERVER BACKUP   This option sets the directory where the backup file should be saved. It allows you to change it from the default if you need to do this.

SERVER RESTORE   This option restores the proxy server configuration from the backup file. A partial restore only restores non-machine-specific parameters, which is useful if you have another server that you wanted to quickly reconfigure as a stand-in. A full restore recovers all server parameters.

SOCKS Proxy

Unique to the SOCKS Proxy Service, the SOCKS service's Permissions tab contains a table that allows you to permit or deny access based on domain/zone, IP address, subnet mask, destination, port number, or TCP service name.

WinSock Proxy

The WinSock Proxy Service Protocols tab allows you to define the WinSock applications that are allowed to run through the proxy. Each protocol can be edited and its parameters modified based on port, TCP/UDP, and inbound/outbound access.

The service's Permissions tab allows you to define whether users or groups of users are allowed through the proxy. You can set up access control for all protocols or configure access control on a protocol-by-protocol basis.

Web Proxy

The service's Caching tab allows you to enable or disable disk caching of HTTP and FTP data. You can set specific cache parameters, including the size of the disk cache file(s) and cache expiration policy, as well as advanced caching parameters that allow you to fine tune the server caching.

The service's Routing tab is used to configure the Web Proxy Server to redirect client requests either through an array, to another upstream proxy server, or to the Internet.

The service's Publishing tab allows you to configure the Web Proxy Server to look like a web server on the external side when it is actually proxying the web traffic to an internal web server.

MAKING THE CONNECTION

Incorporating complex technologies into a network is always challenging. Introducing new technology into a large-scale enterprise network environment poses additional challenges. The issue of scalability is sure to be among the first to surface. What works well for a dozen nodes doesn't always work well for a hundred, a thousand, or ten thousand nodes.

The complexity in connecting your web server to the network or Internet is often an overlooked issue. Serious consideration must be taken in deciding how to connect your users. With a myriad of acronyms and choices it is often confusing to determine what exactly you need. You don't want to put a small pipe in front of your new server, making it useless, but you don't want to pay for extra bandwidth that isn't used.

Connecting to the Internet

If you do not have an agreement with an Internet Service Provider (ISP) or an existing connection to the Internet, you will want to find an ISP that fits your needs. Some of the questions to ask your prospective ISP are:

▼ How many hops are you from a major backbone?

■ What are the different types of dedicated access you offer?

■ What is the setup charge for different services?

▲ What are the monthly charges?

The fewer the number of hops the ISP is from a major backbone on the Internet, the faster the service and the fewer points of failure between the Internet and your client workstations. It is also important to choose an ISP that offers connections of greater bandwidth than what you need now. This way, it is relatively easy to upgrade in the future without having to change ISPs. Aside from monthly access charges, be sure to verify the installation charges. They tend to vary wildly from ISP to ISP. For many ISPs, a good deal of their money comes from installation charges.

Most ISPs offer you a variety of speeds and connection types. The slowest and most common is the dialup 28.8Kb/sec analog line. This account is primarily targeted for the single-user population. This service is for dialup only and does not work for a server you want up on the Internet all the time. Some ISPs have come up with creative options such as dedicated single or multiple "bonded" 28.8Kb/sec connections. However, to host even a marginally popular web site, you will need more bandwidth than 28.8Kb/sec modems can provide.

Integrated Services Digital Network (ISDN) can be configured to connect when the user dials out to the Internet or as a full time connection to the Internet. The dedicated ISDN sometimes isn't really "on" all the time. Instead, your ISP dials you when a packet arrives that is destined for your network. With ISDN, call setup only takes a few seconds whereas conventional modems can take much longer. The same thing happens when someone on the inside of your network sends a packet out to the Internet.

One data channel of a basic rate interface (BRI) ISDN line can move data at 64Kb/sec. Two "bonded" data channels can move data at 128Kb/sec. In either scenario, you pay your phone company to have the ISDN line (roughly $40 per month), and then pay your ISP for the access. The access charge can vary depending on how many hours you use it, or the charge can be about $300 per month for unlimited hours.

Figure 8-21 illustrates connecting a web server and a proxy server to the Internet via a dialup connection. Clients access the Internet through the proxy server before they reach the modem.

In the enterprise, you probably have more users than can be supported by a single ISDN line. To meet these demands, phone companies and ISPs have solutions that can scale to meet your needs. One approach is to purchase a leased-line connection such as a T-1 (1.544Mb/sec). A leased line offers 7x24 connectivity to the Internet and provides speedy Internet access for a large number of users. A single T-1 for example, can support access for several hundred to thousands of users. If a T-1 is too expensive for your implementation, the phone company can break it up for you and let you use only a portion of it. This is called a *fractional T-1*.

An example of connecting to the Internet using a leased line is illustrated in Figure 8-22. Clients access the Internet by going through a proxy server and a router.

Another option is to purchase a connection that uses packet- or cell-switching technology. Frame Relay, for example, can scale from 56Kb/sec to 1.5Mb/sec per line. An advantage of Frame Relay is that you can burst above the committed information rate (CIR) if there is available bandwidth for the traffic on the Frame Relay network. For higher bandwidth requirements, ATM can scale from 155Mb/sec to 622Mb/sec.

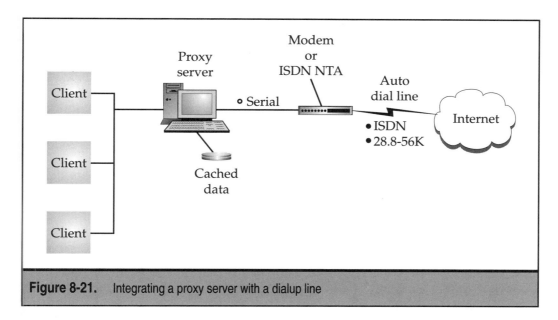

Figure 8-21. Integrating a proxy server with a dialup line

Naturally, the more throughput you get, the more you pay. Table 8-2 illustrates some of the different connectivity options. Of course, the number of users that each type of connectivity can support varies tremendously, depending on how active the users are.

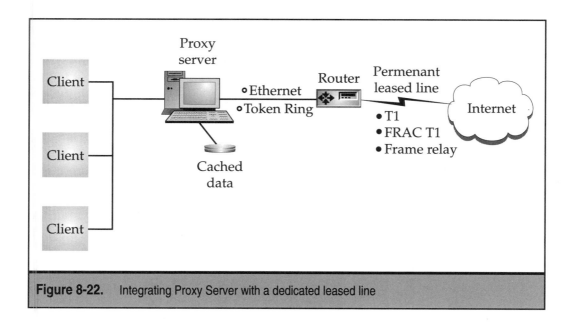

Figure 8-22. Integrating Proxy Server with a dedicated leased line

Type	Bandwidth	Estimated # of Users	Relative Cost
Modem	9.6Kb/sec	1	1
Modem	28.8Kb/sec	1 to 5	1
ISDN	64Kb/sec	5 to 10	3
ISDN	128Kb/sec	5 to 50	5
T-1 (DS1)	1.54Mb/sec	50 to 500	10
T-3 (DS3)	45Mb/sec	4,000+	100
ATM	155 to 622Mb/sec	10,000+	200+

Table 8-2.   Relative Connectivity Costs

The relative costs listed in Table 8-2 are compared to the costs of a typical 28.8Kb/sec connection. If, for example, a 28.8Kb/sec connection costs you $20/month, expect to pay about $60/month for a 64Kb/sec ISDN line and $200/month for a T-1 line.

Throughput Requirements

With all these options, and the rapid changes in network technologies, it is hard to know exactly what to purchase. It is especially difficult if you haven't had a server up before to gauge utilization. Nonetheless, there are some "back-of-the-envelope" calculations you can perform to get a rough estimate of the demand that will be placed on your web server.

First, you need to know the general size of the data users are going to be pulling from the server. Go to your default web page—the one that everyone who logs on to the site will load. Add up all the items on that page. Do the same for a couple other pages. Add all these sums together to get the average number of bytes that a typical user is going to request per session. For example, let's say that you have an initial page that contains 200KB, and two others have a size of 300KB and 250KB, respectively. Your total is 750KB per session. To give the measure some element of time, pull the pages down yourself and see how long you take to examine the material. If you spend about two minutes pulling down and looking at the pages, you can estimate that an average session takes two minutes and transfers 750KB.

Now you need to estimate how many users will be accessing the site during its busiest time. In this example, you estimate that there are ten concurrent users at 9:00 a.m., the busiest time of day for this server. So your demand is:

$$10 \times 750KB/120 \text{ sec} = 62.5KB/sec$$

This value is in bytes and because throughput is usually measured in bits we need to multiply this number by 12 (8 bits in a byte + 4 bits for overhead). Thus, our demand can be expressed as:

$$62.5 \times 12 = 750Kb/sec$$

You might want to consider a T-1 line or a fractional T-1 line. If this rate of hits is sustained, you certainly want to meet the demand. If this is only a transient peak, you should consider a Frame Relay link that can temporarily burst above the data rate of the line. Another alternative is to reduce the size of each page by using text wherever possible, decreasing the size of your graphics, and reducing the number or size of loadable modules, such as Java applications. Additionally, reorganizing your site to reduce the amount of time it takes for users to find what they need can reduce the overall server and network load.

Bottleneck Avoidance

Somewhere in the design of your web server architecture lies a bottleneck. It is the single reason why your pages don't appear more quickly on the clients' computers. Finding the bottleneck can be very difficult. One useful tool is the Performance Monitor that is built into Windows NT. You can easily monitor memory usage, disk swapping, network throughput, and processor utilization. See Chapter 11 for more information on how to use the Performance Monitor.

You can use the Network Monitor tool to see if the bottleneck resides on the network connection from your server to your users. If, for example, you are only able to pass 500Kb/sec on your T-1 connection, and everything in your PC indicates that the bottleneck is not within the PC, you should contact your ISP. The bottleneck may be located somewhere on the ISP's network.

If, on the other hand, you have purchased high-end equipment and optimized your system only to find the demand is just too great for it, you should consider adding more machines to serve the web pages. If there isn't an obvious dichotomy to split the servers into more than one web address, consider having more than one server use the same fully-qualified IP address name (for example, **www.microsoft.com**) but have different IP addresses. You can have the DNS server randomly assign a different IP address when a request comes in for the IP name. The problem with this approach is that the DNS server doesn't know how busy each server is or when one goes down so there is no true load balancing.

Alternatively, you can use a load balancing router such as the Equalizer from Coyote Point Systems or the LocalDirector from Cisco Systems. These hardware solutions can detect a downed server and can load balance among the servers to provide the best performance.

Management Tools

How do you know how many hits per minute you get, or what users are retrieving from your web site? You can scour the log files and try to make sense of them, or you can use a management software tool that can do these tasks and much more, such as find references to nonexistent pages or simulate hits. Some web management tools for NT are listed in Table 8-3.

Product	Contact	Price ($US)
SiteSweeeper	www.sitetech.com/sitesweeper	230
net Analysis Pro 3.0	www.netgenesis.com	2,500
EBT DynaBase	www.ebt.com	2,500

Table 8-3. Web Management Tools

WINDOWS
NT
Professional
Library

CHAPTER 9

Routing and Remote
Access Service

Today the capability computers have to communicate with each other is unprecedented, as is the amount of work you can accomplish with them. Computers are getting cheaper, lighter, and more powerful. At the same time, applications are being developed to help users do more with computer technology from any location that has a phone line. Because of the proliferation of portable computer technology and true network-enabled applications, remote access connectivity to the corporate network has become a business requirement.

Establishing a reliable and secure remote access point into the network is an extremely challenging project. Over time, a higher percentage of users will be accessing the network remotely. Remote users will need clear documentation and training on how to establish a dialup connection, properly log on, navigate the network, and use applications remotely. The dialup facility will need to provide connectivity by use of phone lines and modems, or a connection to a third-party vendor who provides the modem pools and routes the traffic back to the network. In addition, the environment has to be monitored and managed carefully to ensure that every remote access point of entry is secure. This chapter is about building a remote access solution for your corporation.

RAS IN THE ENTERPRISE

Windows NT Server provides options that help make remote access a manageable and functional part of the enterprise network. With NT's Remote Access Service (RAS), you can create a scalable environment where remote users can access the network from almost anywhere. In this chapter we will focus on designing, installing, and managing the Remote Access Service from the client to the transport and finally to the server services that connect to the corporate network. Because the Internet plays an important role in remote dialup access, we will focus on the use of TCP/IP for remote access connectivity. Additionally, we will examine the use of RAS as a method of connecting remote offices to the corporate network. Throughout the chapter, we will discuss important security issues that arise when you're connecting remote users to the network.

There are many transport options for enabling remote access. The most common method is dialup access directly to the remote access server through a modem. We will also discuss two other methods of enabling remote access connectivity.

The first is the use of an Internet service provider (ISP) for dial-in facilities. An ISP can provide a virtual private network (VPN) on public Internet lines. Users dial into the ISP using the Point to Point Tunneling Protocol (PPTP). The traffic is then transported over the Internet to a (PPTP) RAS server connected to the corporate network.

The second method of remote access connectivity is to use what we will refer to as a private service provider (PSP), such as CompuServe. A PSP can provide the modems that your remote users dial in to. The traffic is then transported over the PSP's private switched network by use of ATM and X.25 to a RAS server connected to your corporate network. ISPs and PSPs enable you to stretch the RAS modem connection far from your

RAS servers. Many offer a point of presence (POP) in cities throughout the world, allowing remote users to dial into local modem pools instead of using long-distance or toll-free phone lines.

Clients and Servers

Windows NT 4.0 Remote Access Service can be divided into two components: the client and the server. The client is found in the home or on the road, so it typically dials the server or an ISP/PSP to initiate a connection. The remote-dialer software used to dial RAS server or ISP/PSP is called Dial-Up Networking and is managed via the Dial-Up Networking interface found in the Accessories menu. The NT RAS server components are managed by the Remote Access Administrator interface found in the Administrative Tools menu. If you have Routing and Remote Access Services (RRAS) installed, RAS server administration is performed by use of the Routing and RAS Admin Interface found in the Administrative Tools menu after you have installed the RRAS components.

NOTE: RRAS, code-named "Steelhead," is an updated NT service that combines the functionality of NT RAS service with the Multi-Protocol Router NT service. The service provides unified support for remote access dialup, remote office connectivity and routing, and Virtual Private Networks (VPN) via the Point to Point Tunneling Protocol (PPTP), each of which we will discuss in this chapter.

Because both the client and the server components of RAS ship with Windows NT, and client packages ship or are available for Windows 9x and Windows 3.x, no additional software purchases are necessary to enable basic and secure dialup services. Also, because most nonMicrosoft RAS clients either include or support software for Microsoft RAS, dialup access can be established for little more than the cost of modem hardware, phone lines, and of course, your time. Figure 9-1 illustrates a single RAS server dialup solution. In this example, a RAS server can be accessed via a standard phone line or through ISDN. Additionally, the RAS server has a connection to the LAN/WAN and the Internet.

By purchasing additional hardware such as modem banks (discussed later in this chapter), you can construct larger dial-in facilities using NT RAS Server. For even higher-capacity dialup services, multiple NT servers can be deployed to allow for a larger number of simultaneous users and to provide a high level of fault tolerance. You might even consider placing RAS servers in different physical locations as part of a disaster recovery strategy. Figure 9-2 illustrates a multiple RAS server dialup solution.

In Figure 9-2 there are two RAS servers: East and West. The remote clients have been configured so that they can selectively dial either one. Should one server fail, the other is still available to accept connections. To ensure full availability, each server should be capable of supporting your entire user base at any time. This means that each server should be running at a maximum of 50 percent capacity during normal operation. Having a backup server is useless if only half your users can connect—just ask the half that can't connect.

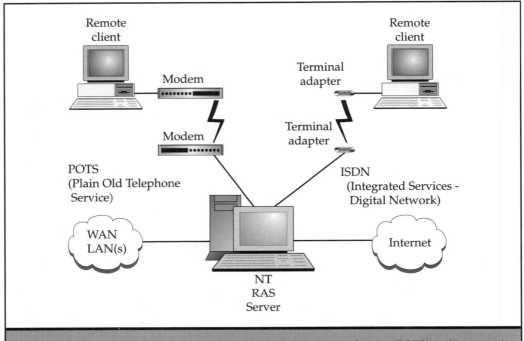

Figure 9-1. A single RAS server can support Plain Old Telephone Service (POTS) and Integrated Services Digital Network (ISDN) connections

Remote Node and Remote Control

A common misconception about remote access is that the remote users will have access to all of their applications no matter what computer is used when dialing in. It seems that people tend to view RAS as a turn-key method for them to remote control their office computer from their home computer or laptop. Although NT RAS can enable remote control, it is not automatically provided. There are many third-party products available that enable remote control connections over NT RAS that perform well for many applications. However, NT RAS simply provides a network connection—a remote node—that can be used, among other things, for remote control software sessions. Remote control is an adaptation of the remote node connection that streamlines itself to better use the slow links typically encountered while connecting remotely. Let's take a quick look at the differences between remote node and remote control.

Remote Node

Remote node can be thought of as a relatively slow LAN or WAN network connection. Although it is nonpersistent, RAS provides a true network connection. You can map drives, connect to and share printers, access databases, and use other network devices

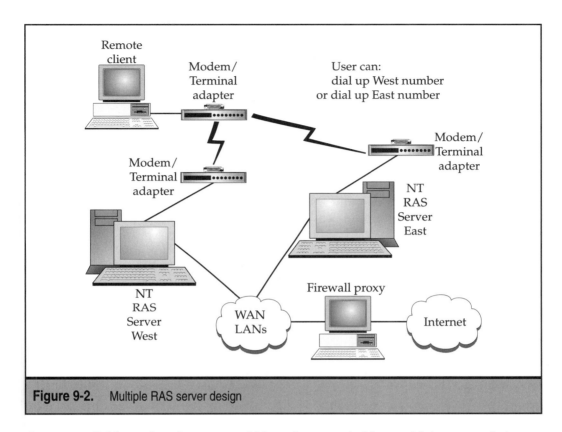

Figure 9-2.   Multiple RAS server design

that are available, such as fax servers. Although you probably wouldn't want to do it, you can also execute applications like Word or Excel from a mapped drive on a remote file server. Once the connection process is complete, the only difference between a LAN connection and a remote node connection is that a remote note connection is much slower than a LAN connection. This is where the limitations arise.

Many applications run from a file server over the LAN have executables and associated files that exceed several megabytes in size. Executing a 1MB file on a LAN would take a couple of seconds over a shared Ethernet connection. Executing that same program from a file server over a remote node connection would take anywhere from 30 seconds to several minutes or longer, depending on the application and your connection. A simple remedy to this situation is to install the application on the local computer and run it from there, allowing it access to necessary data (presumably smaller than the application) over a mapped drive via the remote node session.

Remote Control

Remote control is broken down into two parts: the host side and the client side. Remote control uses the network that a remote node connection provides to send a redirected screen from the *host* machine residing locally on the network across the dial connection to the *client* where the screen is displayed. The client sends keyboard and mouse data back to the host. The result is remote control of the host machine by use of the client's keyboard, mouse, and monitor.

You might want to use remote control when it is not practical to install the application on the remote machine, or the application uses so much network bandwidth that it cannot run over a slow RAS connection. A very good example of a program that would require remote control is the LAN-based version of cc:Mail, which many organizations have in place today. It was designed to be used in a LAN environment, so it maps a drive on a server so it can access the mail file. When it reads and writes to the mail file on the server over the LAN, performance is acceptable. When it reads and writes to the server over a remote node drive mapping, performance is painfully slow (to be fair, Lotus Notesmail using TCP/IP works well over a remote node connection). Applications such as cc:Mail and other applications designed to run over LANs are prime candidates for remote control environments when they must be used by remote users.

With remote control applications like PC Anywhere, the host can only run one session per client. For every client dialing into a remote control session, you need to provide one remote control host for it to connect. With remote control applications like WinFrame, you can run multiple concurrent client sessions on a single remote control server. You may save a few dollars on hardware purchases, although the server will have to be capable of running multiple users and will therefore require more horsepower than single-user machines. Multiple processors and 4MB to 8MB of RAM per concurrent user are recommended by Citrix, the developers of WinFrame.

Thin Client Technology for NT

Thin client technology is not really new. For the most part, remote control packages for single machines and for OS/2 servers and X-Windows could be called thin client because the application runs on the remote machine and only video, keystrokes, and mouse data are transmitted between the client and the host.

Thin clients for NT consist of a multiuser NT environment capable of effectively running around 2 to 15 (although we have heard of as many as 60) concurrent users on a server. Citrix licensed the right to develop a multiuser version of the NT operating system that could provide concurrent remote control sessions on a single NT server. The server and client can communicate via TCP/IP or IPX by use of Citrix's proprietary protocol called the Independent Computing Architecture (ICA). Packaged inside the network protocol, ICA is specifically designed and optimized to send screen information and keystroke and mouse movements between the server and the client. Published tests and experience have proven that WinFrame, using the thin-client paradigm, can effectively provide high-density remote control sessions at a very acceptable level of performance and manageability.

In the next section we will take a closer look at the new breed of remote control software commonly referred to as superthin client servers.

Superthin Client Technology for NT

The superthin client concept shaves a few pounds off the thin client concept. How? By specifying that nothing but the bare minimum be running on the client the superthin server provides the bare-bones client with its windowed environment and its applications. The client's machine only needs to be concerned with booting up and running the superthin client. This client is capable of connecting to, viewing, and sending keystrokes and mouse movements to the server.

Windows NT Hydra, like WinFrame, is made up of three key components: the client, the server, and the protocol used to communicate between the two. Like WinFrame, Hydra runs on an enhanced version of the NT operating system (in this case NT 4) that allows concurrent user sessions to run on the server. The client can run on Windows NT, 95, and 3.11. Support for other platforms is implied and should include Mac, UNIX, and NetPC devices. The protocol that it uses is different from the ICA protocol used by Citrix. Microsoft has chosen to use the same protocol used for another Microsoft product called NetMeeting. The protocol, called T.Share/T.120 Remote Protocol, is based on International Telecommunications Union's (ITU) T.120 protocol. One notable feature of this protocol is that it can support encrypted sessions.

One common thread with WinFrame and Hydra is that Microsoft and Citrix are jointly cooperating on the development of a new Hydra-based technology for Windows NT Server 4.0 and future versions. In addition, Citrix will develop pIcAsso, a server add-on that provides support for the ICA protocol so that existing and future ICA WinFrame clients will be able to run sessions on a Hydra server.

RAS PROTOCOL PRIMER

RAS clients have the option of using one of several protocols when connecting to a RAS server. Certain nonMicrosoft clients may be limited to a particular protocol, but an NT RAS server can usually be configured to support them. For installations where there is an opportunity to select the remote client's operating system, newer is almost always better. It's no surprise that Windows 95 and Windows NT 4.0 allow for easy dialup network installation and configuration when connecting to an NT RAS server. Many of the latest nonMicrosoft client packages can use the Point to Point Protocol (PPP) to connect to an NT RAS server and subsequently to the corporate network using an extension to their "native" (i.e., IP, IPX, NetBEUI) LAN protocol.

NOTE: If possible, select only one protocol for use in your dialup solution. Running additional protocols reduces the overall throughput of the RAS connection. Also, management and problem resolution headaches can be avoided by sticking to the minimum number of required protocols. When you're choosing a dialup protocol, we strongly recommend using TCP/IP, unless you have a specific reason not to do so. TCP/IP is a reliable, scalable, open protocol that has withstood the test of time.

One of your goals should be to minimize the number of protocols in use on your network while maintaining the functionality your users require. When you're looking for opportunities to streamline the number of protocols, RAS should not be overlooked. Keeping things simple means they are easier to manage. When your network is easier to manage, the unavoidable problems are much simpler to resolve. Binding multiple protocols to a RAS session when perhaps only one is needed adds additional traffic overhead to an already slow network connection.

Setting RAS Protocols

Defining the protocols that will be in use on any given dialup session can be done at the server by selecting only those necessary to support your users. The clients can also limit the protocols by selecting only the protocols that they need. For example, you may need to have TCP/IP and IPX available on your network, but only some of your users need to use IPX to remotely access a Novell file server. You can enable TCP/IP and IPX on the RAS server, configure all remote clients with TCP/IP, and add IPX to only those remote clients needing access to the Novell file server. By limiting users to only the protocols they need, everybody can access TCP/IP databases and e-mail, and browse the intranet and Internet—only those needing Novell connections actually have the overhead of IPX on their dialup connection.

Besides the network layer protocols IP and IPX (see Chapter 1), there are many other protocols that make up a successful RAS connection working at other layers in the OSI network layer model. Figure 9-3 illustrates where common protocols and transport methods are used as part of the remote access connection.

Each of the protocol and transport methods is described next. They are grouped in three sections: "Network Protocols," "Connection Protocols," and "Transport Methods."

NOTE: In NT versions 3.5 and above, PPP support for TCP/IP, IPX, and NetBEUI is provided. Before NT 3.5, the only RAS protocol available was Microsoft's nonroutable NetBEUI or AsyBEUI.

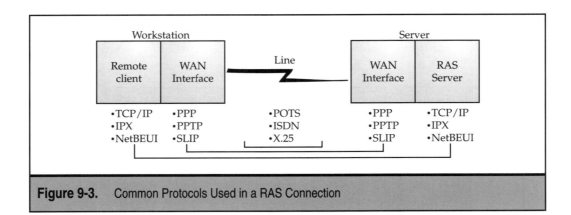

Figure 9-3. Common Protocols Used in a RAS Connection

Network Protocols

As you may recall from Chapter 1, network protocols such as TCP/IP, IPX/SPX, and NetBEUI are used as the basis for network communication. Using PPP over RAS can support TCP/IP, IPX, and NetBEUI individually or can allow for any combination of the three to be used concurrently.

In RAS, these protocols are used as the foundation of the dialup networking connection. Any of the three can be encapsulated in the Point to Point Protocol so that it can be transmitted across the RAS link. As we discussed in the remote node section, this transparent passing of the network protocols "fools" the remote computer into thinking it is directly attached to the network, when it is really connected over analog or digital telephone line. We will briefly cover each protocol as it relates to RAS in the following section. More general information about network protocols can be found in Chapter 1.

TCP/IP

The Internet uses the suite of protocols called TCP/IP as its transmission protocols. All Internet service providers offer support for TCP/IP, usually via PPP or Serial Line IP (SLIP). Even when you're connecting to a private network, TCP/IP is a good choice, because TCP/IP is routable, robust, and in well-designed networks, fault-tolerant. Also, it can be firewalled or filtered, making it an excellent choice for use in external connections where security is important. What's the catch? The underlying infrastructure is complicated and challenging to implement so that it is scalable and fault-tolerant as well as easy to use.

Dynamic Host Configuration Protocol (DHCP), described in Chapter 7, can automate the configuration of IP information on the client. You should configure the TCP/IP clients to use server-assigned IP addresses. Whenever possible, you should configure your RAS servers to use DHCP to allocate IP addresses and define the DNS and WINS servers that the clients should use. In addition, the DHCP server should be used to assign addresses for DNS and WINS name servers. That done, you will be free to make changes to your network topology, addressing, and name-server environments without having to worry about manually updating information on remote clients because the information is pushed from the server to the client each time they log on. The changes can be made in the DHCP scope(s) defined for the remote clients and will be automatically used next time they log on.

For example, let's say that you have four RAS servers that collectively support 400 remote clients. Your remote clients may dial in to any one of the four servers. You recently had two instances in which the DNS server, located on the WAN, was unavailable because of a network outage that in turn affected your TCP/IP-based remote users. To increase the availability of DNS, you have decided to add another DNS server to the network and put it in the same building as your RAS servers. For your remote users to take advantage of the new server, you need to make sure that their remote client TCP/IP configuration is set to use the new DNS server as the primary server and one of the old DNS servers as the secondary server.

If you use hard-coded information, you will need to manually reconfigure each remote machine. You may be able to create a script, a disk, or instructions to help make the changes, but any way you look at it, it will not be easy to reconfigure 400 client machines. If your clients are configured to use server-assigned information, you simply make the changes in the appropriate DHCP scope. The new DNS server will be used by the remote clients the next time they dial in, and every subsequent session until you change it.

If you need to examine TCP/IP configuration parameters on the client you can use the command-line executable IPconfig.exe included with Windows NT, or the GUI-based *WNTIPCfg.exe* included with the Windows NT Resource Kit. For Windows 95-based machines, use the Winipcfg.exe GUI-based executable. The command-line utility allows you to view the IP address, subnet mask, and default gateway for each adapter bound to TCP/IP as well as to release and renew DHCP leases. The GUI-based utility adds more information about the current TCP/IP configuration. The information includes IP address(s) of WINS servers and DNS servers as well as additional information about the status of DHCP leases.

IPX/SPX

IPX/SPX is a proprietary protocol suite developed by Novell for use in its networking products. Because of the large install base of Novell networks, IPX/SPX is in use worldwide on many networks both large and small. Although it is optimized for LANs, it is routable and runs well over WANs and dialup connections when properly configured. Configuring IPX/SPX for dialup networking requires little effort, there are no naming services, and addressing is handled when the protocol is installed.

Be aware when using IPX/SIPX in enterprise networks that the protocol relies on broadcasts using the Service Advertisement Protocol (SAP) to inform devices on the network about what servers, printers, and other services are available for use. In larger networks, SAPs can become unwieldy, consuming network bandwidth and adding processing overhead to network routers and other devices. Because of this, many larger organizations will filter SAPs from network segments where they are not needed. When a SAP is filtered from a workstation, that workstation will no longer be able to identify the service or server associated with the SAP, and will not be able to connect or make use of it. Thus, when planning IPX-based RAS connectivity, you will need to verify that all necessary SAPs are routed to the RAS server so that the remote client can access servers and other services.

NetBEUI

Windows NT NetBEUI is based on the NetBIOS Extended User Interface (NetBEUI) protocol. It is a very simple protocol that is designed for small (by today's standards) LANs that required nothing more than file and print services. It is very easy to configure RAS to use NetBEUI, and in small installations where the connection requirements are limited to file servers and printers, it works well. However, broadcasts are an undesirable characteristic of the protocol. In larger networks, use of the protocol may result in a flurry of broadcasts called a *broadcast storm*.

Connection Protocols

Connection protocols are used to provide the support necessary to set up and carry on a remote communication session between the remote client and the RAS server. Once the session has been established and the necessary information such as addressing, name registration, location of name servers, and location of gateways has been ascertained, the connection protocol works at the data link layer of the OSI model (layer 2) and carries the network protocols (layer 3) over the dialup connection. These protocols provide error control, compression, and encryption for the link.

Point to Point Protocol (PPP)

The Point to Point Protocol suite (PPP) is a collection of industry standard protocols called Link Control Protocols (LCP) and Network Control Protocols (NCP). They provide standardized encapsulation over point-to-point connections. Because PPP works across multiple OSI layers, it can also provide mechanisms that allow for assignment of IP addresses and related information, link configuration, error detection, network layer address negotiation, and data compression management.

RAS multilink PPP allows you to combine two or more communications links in a single dialup session, increasing the available throughput. You can combine analog and ISDN links connecting the remote client to the RAS server. Of course, you'll need additional modems at both the client and the server to service the additional lines.

Point to Point Tunneling Protocol (PPTP)

Windows NT Server 4.0 adds support for the new Point to Point Tunneling Protocol (PPTP). PPTP creates a private, encrypted "tunnel" for any type of packet from the remote client to the PPTP server. PPTP makes it possible to use IP, IPX, NetBEUI, and other protocols over the Internet or over any IP, IPX, or NetBEUI network. The multiprotocol encapsulation feature allows a client with PPTP configured for its RAS port to connect to the server in a secure fashion over the Internet with the added functionality of being able to wrap other protocols into an IP packet. With PPTP, it is possible to use the Internet as you would a private WAN.

NOTE: Windows 95, Windows NT, Macintosh, and Windows 3.11 clients are able to take advantage of PPTP with the addition of third-party software.

Serial Line Internet Protocol (SLIP)

Serial Line IP (SLIP) has been commonly used for TCP/IP point-to-point serial connections since the 1980s. In most cases, SLIP is used when you're dialing into a UNIX host or into a server connected to the Internet. Most ISPs now offer PPP as an alternative to SLIP. Because it doesn't support additional features like addressing, error detection, or compression, there is little reason to use SLIP unless you have no other alternative. But if your ISP uses a SLIP-based UNIX host or a router and you have an assigned IP address, SLIP can be quickly and easily configured.

Transport Methods

Transport methods use physical layer protocols to send data in frames in point-to-point communication. Although the function of the method is the primary concern of communication carriers, you should be aware of the different methods in use today.

Plain Old Telephone Service (POTS)

Standard telephone services primarily use analog signals for voice transmission, and are the most common transport for dialup networking. Modems allow transmission of data over the analog medium of the telephone system, providing remote connectivity to almost anywhere there is telephone service. Although uncommon in the United States, there are some areas where the analog service is multiplexed to the point where line quality is so poor that modems and even fax machines cannot establish a connection over the link. In any event, good service is so prevalent that it makes it very likely that a remote user will be able to dial into a RAS server from almost any location.

Integrated Services Digital Network (ISDN)

The Integrated Services Digital Network (ISDN) is a digital version of POTS. However, ISDN doesn't need a modem because it can handle a digital signal directly. It uses a device called a Network Terminal adapter type 1 (NT1) to manage the transmission of data over ISDN channels.

There are two bearer B-channels that can transfer data at 64KB each. ISDN also has a third channel called the delta or D-channel for signaling and line control. The D-channel is not typically used for data transfer, but is responsible for overhead tasks such as setting up a call from one ISDN adapter to another.

There are two ISDN protocols: Basic Rate Interface (BRI) and Primary Rate Interface (PRI). BRI uses both of the B-channels and the D digital channel. PRI ISDN uses T-1 data circuits that contain 24 of the B-channel, 64KB/sec lines. One of the channels is reserved for the D-channel and handles signaling and line control. ISDN adapters are becoming relatively inexpensive and are available at many computer stores. Make sure you consider purchasing the same brand (get the same model if possible) as the ISDN adapter at the other end, because ISDN is notoriously difficult to configure even when both adapters are the same brand.

X.25

X.25 has been around since the 1980s and is still in use. Although there are faster, lower-cost alternatives to X.25, it is widely available and may be the only choice in certain areas. X.25 works by sending and switching packets over a defined network path. It uses devices called Packet Assembler/Disassemblers (PAD) that do just what the name implies: take data, assemble it into X.25 packets, and send it across the network. At the other end, the PAD disassembles the packets in the same sequence in which they were originally assembled. X.25 can be used for RAS communication by using address information provided to you by your carrier.

CONFIGURING RAS CLIENTS

Although you will certainly not be going around configuring RAS on all your clients' workstations, you should be intimately familiar with the procedure, because decisions made at the time of installation greatly affect throughput, security, and the functionality of RAS. Also, you will most likely need to document the installation process for users or educators to disseminate throughout your corporation. You should work through a client installation, and ensure all settings and scripts are optimized for your environment. RAS provides client support for most common operating systems including:

▼ Windows NT (3.5 or newer) Workstation and Server

■ Windows NT (3.1) Workstation and Server

■ Windows 95

■ Windows for Workgroups

■ Novell NetWare

■ UNIX

■ OS/2

■ DOS LAN Manager

▲ Macintosh OS

Installing Dial-Up Networking

Installing and configuring Dial-Up Networking (DUN) on a Windows NT 4.0 Server– or Workstation–based computer is completed as follows: Select Start | Programs | Accessories | Dial-Up Networking. You can also invoke the DUN interface by clicking on the My Computer desktop icon and then clicking on Dial-Up Networking. This method is illustrated in Figure 9-4.

From here, you will be prompted to type the location of the Windows NT 4.0 installation files. Enter the path to either the CD or a local drive in which the contents of the \i386 directory have been copied.

Installing a Modem

If you have not installed a RAS-capable device, the Remote Access Setup program asks if you would like to install a modem. Select Yes to start the modem installer. This will

Figure 9-4. Selecting Dial-Up Networking from the My Computer window

invoke a window asking if you want to try to detect the modem or if you will select it from a list, as shown in Figure 9-5. If you know the make and model of the modem and have verified that it works, we suggest you select it from the list or provide a disk from your modem's manufacturer. If you are unsure of your modem type and port configurations, you can have the installer attempt to detect your modem.

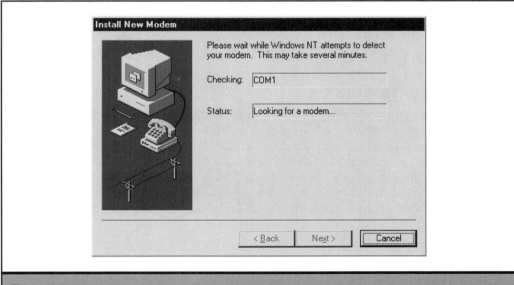

Figure 9-5. Searching for a new modem during modem installation

Detecting a Modem

If you decide to have the installer detect your modem, it will display a dialog box indicating that it is searching for your modem on all available ports. Be patient, it can take awhile. Sometimes NT will detect a modem that doesn't exist in your machine. It is usually best to reject this choice and select your modem from the list. If you experience any errors, chances are good that you have a hardware conflict. Examining the Port configuration from the Control Panel and using the NT Diagnostics tool in the Administrative Tools menu may yield valuable information in solving hardware conflicts.

If you choose to select your modem from a list or if you have a disk with the modem driver files on it, you will be presented with a dialog box offering many modem types and speeds. Select your modem from the list, or insert the modem disk and click the Have Disk button. If you have a modem that is not listed and have no disks from the manufacturer, you might be able to get your modem to function by selecting a generic modem, as illustrated in Figure 9-6. Select Standard Modem Types and the top speed your modem is capable of handling.

Once you have set the properties for your modem, click the Finish button, and then click on the Dialing Properties button. This will bring up a window (shown in Figure 9-7) that allows you to customize your dial settings according to your location. You can specify dial location, outside line, calling card, call waiting, and tone/pulse dialing settings. Later when you are using RAS, you simply choose your location, and all these settings will be

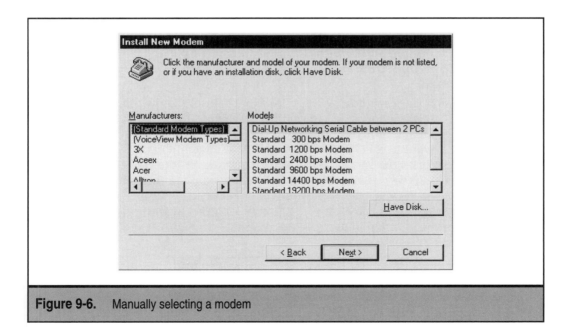

Figure 9-6.   Manually selecting a modem

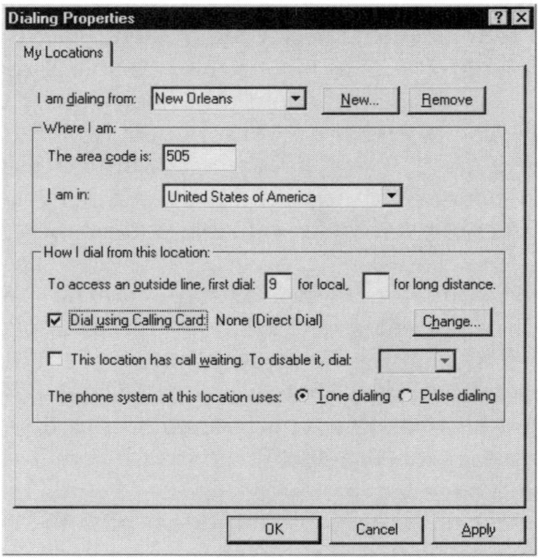

Figure 9-7. Setting modem dialing properties

recalled. Once you have configured your dialing properties, click OK. You will then be asked if you would like to configure RAS for your new modem; click Yes.

Modem Dialup Properties

In the list of RAS-capable devices, select the new modem and click the Configure button. The Configure Port Usage window will appear. Here you select how the RAS device will be used. You can select whether it can dial out, receive calls, or both. Usually a RAS device acts as a client and only dials out, or acts as a server and can only receive calls.

For DUN, you want to check Dial Out As A RAS Client and make sure that Receive Calls_As_A_RAS Server is unchecked. Click OK, return to the device configuration window, and click on the Network button. This will call up another window similar to Figure 9-8. Select the dial-out protocols you will be using to communicate to your RAS server. You can select up to three protocols, but must select at least one. Click OK and then click the Continue button in the device configuration window to proceed with your installation of the RAS client.

NOTE: The protocols that are currently installed on the machine are selected by default. If you want additional protocols, you will need to install the protocol(s) from the Network icon in the Control Panel.

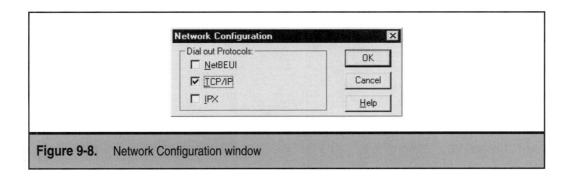

Figure 9-8.   Network Configuration window

When everything has been installed and configured, a Network Settings Change dialog box will be displayed. You will be prompted to restart your computer so that your new device and its setting can be initialized.

Make sure you have closed any open applications, and click Yes to restart the system so that changes can take effect. Once the system has been restarted, select Start | Programs | Accessories | Dial-Up Networking. As described earlier, you can also invoke the DUN interface by clicking on the My Computer desktop icon and then clicking on Dial-Up Networking. This will bring up the Dial-Up Networking main window.

Adding Phonebook Entries

Now let's add a new phonebook entry to test the configuration. Select an existing phonebook entry from the list, click the More button, and select Edit Entry And Modem Properties from the list, or click the New button to create a new entry, as shown in Figure 9-9.

Setting the Phonebook Entry

Clicking on the New button calls up the New Phonebook Entry window. This is a multitabbed window that provides a single interface for the configuration of many properties that define phonebook entries. The Basic tab allows you to create or modify the phonebook entry name and to add a descriptive comment for the connection. Additionally, a phone number and alternate phone numbers are added in this screen. If you have multiple RAS-capable devices, make sure you have selected the one you wish to use for this entry in the Dial Using list. If there are no entries to choose from, you will have to return to the modem install procedure and add a device.

You can also modify several modem configuration parameters by clicking the Configure button. If you are having trouble making a connection to your RAS server, this is one place to look. If the modem is dialing but not negotiating a connection, it sometimes helps to lower the initial connection speed. After that, try unchecking the Enable Modem

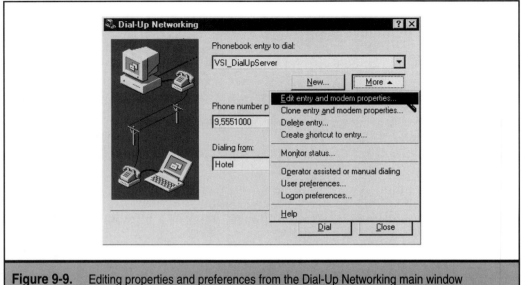

Figure 9-9. Editing properties and preferences from the Dial-Up Networking main window

Compression check box. If the negotiation still fails, try unchecking the Enable Error Control and Enable Hardware Flow Control check boxes.

NOTE: To ensure configuration changes have taken effect, you should completely close and restart DUN.

Setting the Server Properties

The Server tab, shown in Figure 9-10, allows you to define the type of server you will be connecting to with this client. When using DUN to connect to an NT 4.0 RAS server, you should select the "PPP, Windows NT, Windows 95 Plus, Internet" entry. You should select "SLIP: Internet" if you are dialing into an Internet service that does not support PPP. The Server tab also has check boxes for enabling software compression and PPP LCP extensions. Refer to the documentation from your ISP on whether to use them. In most cases, when you are connecting to an NT 4.0 RAS server, you can enable both parameters. As with compression and error and flow control settings, the software compression and PPP LCP extensions should be at the top of your list of culprits when you are troubleshooting a new dialup connection.

The Network Protocols check boxes and the TCP/IP Settings dialog box are also accessible from the Server tab. Select the protocol(s) used by the server. There is no need to check them all if you only need one or two. Selecting protocols that are not configured for use on the server will not benefit you. Additional protocols increase the overhead on the connection and can slow it down.

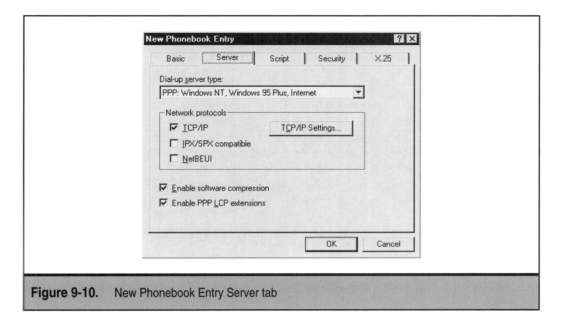

Figure 9-10.   New Phonebook Entry Server tab

Using Scripts to Automate Connection

The Script tab (see Figure 9-11) allows you to select a script that can automate your logon to the remote server. Because NT RAS Server doesn't require special scripting, you won't

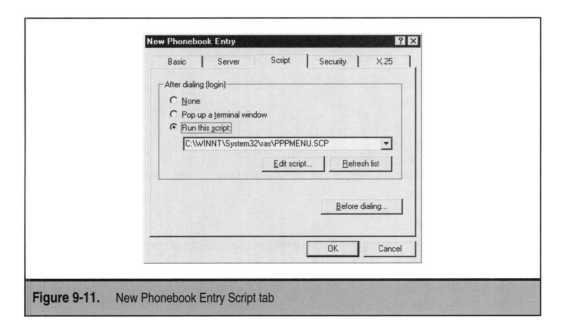

Figure 9-11.   New Phonebook Entry Script tab

need to select a script when dialing directly into an NT RAS server. However, if you use an ISP or another network provider that requires you to log on to a RAS server that doesn't use NT authentication, you have two options.

Switch.inf Scripts

The first option is to use a script embedded in the Switch.inf file. The default Switch.inf file is installed along with RAS and is located in the *%Systemroot%* system32\ras directory. It is well commented and has several sample sections to help you create a script suited to your needs. There is also a detailed description of the Switch.inf file in the Rasphone.hlp that is located in the *%Systemroot%*\system32 directory. Shown next is a simple Switch.inf file used for connecting to the CompuServe network. Remarks are set off by a semicolon (;) and are not read when the script is executed.

```
;Win NT 4.0 Switch.inf for CompuServe Network Dial
;[Cserve] is the name of the script
[Cserve]
COMMAND=
COMMAND=<cr>
COMMAND=<cr>
OK=<match>":"
     LOOP=<ignore>
     COMMAND=+<cr>
OK=<match>":"
     LOOP=<ignore>
     COMMAND=hostname<cr>
OK=<match>"UIC:"
     LOOP=<ignore>
     COMMAND=loginID<cr>
OK=<match>"assword:"
     LOOP=<ignore>
     COMMAND=password<cr>
OK=<ignore>
; End of script
```

This script is straightforward and gets through the logon process quickly and without user input. *Commands* are instructions that are sent to the host computer. For example, the line

```
COMMAND=password<cr>
```

sends the text *password* (put your password here) followed by a carriage return. The OK command is input from the server that the client is waiting for before acting. In the lines

```
OK=<match>":"
LOOP=<ignore>
```

the script is waiting for the text ":" to appear before moving on to the next lines of the script. The LOOP=<ignore> line ensures that all other input from the host is ignored until it sees a colon. Typically, writing a script from scratch requires a lot of trial and error. As a troubleshooting tool you should select Pop Up A Terminal Window and enter your text manually there to get the correct order of commands to send and strings to search for, so you can use them in your script.

Scripting Command Language Scripts

The second option, Dial-Up Scripting Command Language (SCL), is supported by Windows NT and Windows 95. Because it can be used on both platforms, it is probably better to use this language when developing scripts that you plan to distribute on multiple platforms. Shown next is a sample SCL script that can be used for connecting to CompuServe.

```
;Script for CompuServe Network
proc main
set port databits 7
set port parity even
transmit "^M"
waitfor "host name:"
transmit "CIS^M"
waitfor "UIC:"
transmit $USERID, raw
transmit "^M"
waitfor "Password:"
transmit $PASSWORD, raw
transmit "^M"
set port databits 8
set port parity none
endproc
```

Like the Switch.inf file, the script is quite simple, but it gets the job done. With SCL it is possible to create scripts that are interactive and that have error handling routines incorporated into them. The Dial-Up Scripting Command Language is described in more detail in the Script.doc file located in the \%*Systemroot*%\system32\ras directory.

Security Settings

The security configuration options for authentication and encryption are illustrated in Figure 9-12 and provide the following functionality:

▼   **Accept Any Authentication Including Clear Text** —Permits the client to request any authentication. This setting may pass an unencrypted password over the link using plain ASCII characters. It is possible for someone with

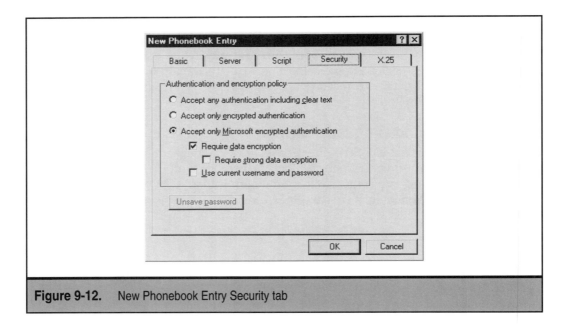

Figure 9-12.   New Phonebook Entry Security tab

physical access to the network to conduct a packet capture and "sniff" the logon sequence to capture the user name and password.

■ **Accept Only Encrypted Authentication** —Requires the client to request that the authentication be encrypted, thereby protecting the logon sequence from prying eyes.

▲ **Accept Only Microsoft Encrypted Authentication** —Requires the client to request authentication using MS-CHAP only. If this option is selected and the server supports it, you can require the client and server to use encryption for data passing between them for the duration of the session.

Table 9-1 outlines the logon security options for RRAS.

Let's look at the various options available when you're authenticating to an NT RAS server.

Password Authentication Protocol (PAP)

PAP is the simplest form of authentication that you can use between the client and the RAS server. The authentication process is not encrypted; the user name and password are transmitted in the clear and could be viewed by anyone with physical access to the wire. Because there are secure alternatives, this option should not be used unless there is some reason that the client and the server cannot use a more secure method. In a Microsoft environment, there is really no reason that PAP should be needed.

Authentication and Encryption Policy	Microsoft Client Available Options	Non-Microsoft Client Available Options	Server Authentication and Encryption
Accept any authentication including clear text	PAP, SPAP CHAP MS-CHAP	PAP CHAP	PAP, SPAP CHAP MS-CHAP
Accept only encrypted authentication	SPAP CHAP MS-CHAP	SPAP CHAP	SPAP CHAP MS-CHAP
Accept only Microsoft encrypted authentication	MS-CHAP	MS-CHAP	MS-CHAP

Table 9-1.   Authentication and Encryption Matrix

Shiva Password Authentication Protocol (SPAP)

Shiva is a very popular remote access solution, and you may have clients in the field that are using the Shiva client software. If you are building an NT RAS dialup solution, you can use SPAP to support these Shiva clients. SPAP is considered more secure than PAP because it encrypts the passwords as they travel across the wire. It can be considered relatively secure, although you should consider upgrading the remote clients to a client that supports CHAP or MS-CHAP when time permits.

Challenge Handshake Authentication Protocol (CHAP)

CHAP is an industry standard protocol that supports encrypted ID and password authentication. This keeps the authentication traffic from being viewed while it travels between the client and the server. In addition, CHAP uses a three-way authentication process. The server sends a challenge to the client; the client responds with an encrypted value that the server verifies. Once the value is verified, access is granted. Then the server periodically revalidates with the client to ensure that the client is real and not a played-back data stream. Curiously, CHAP stores the ID and password in the clear, which makes the information accessible to someone with physical access to the server. Still, most of the risks of the authentication process reside in the initial authentication process. If your servers are properly secured and monitored, the protocol can be considered secure.

Microsoft Challenge Handshake Authentication Protocol (MS-CHAP)

MS-CHAP is the best authentication protocol available for use with Microsoft clients authenticating to an NT RAS server. MS-CHAP is a Microsoft proprietary version of

CHAP, but uses the RSA MD4 standard. It uses a one-way hash function that makes a 128-bit string from a random variable-length string. The procedure produces a checksum for the message that makes the message virtually impossible to decrypt if you don't know the checksum. In addition, MS-CHAP uses the RSA RC4 algorithm to support encrypted traffic during the entire RAS session. The 128-bit version is available in the United States and Canada, while the 40-bit version is the highest allowable for export to other countries.

User Callback

You can configure more user-defined options under the User Preferences selection at the DUN main window. Four user preference tabs appear. The Dialing tab allows you to set the redial properties when a busy line is encountered. The Callback tab (see Figure 9-13) allows you to use this option if it has been set up beforehand on the server and it is offered to you. Therefore, if you are using the callback function, you would have had to provide a callback number to the administrator of the RAS server for the server to reach you—unless you are given the right to pass your callback number to the server at the time of connection.

Callback is often used to incur long-distance charges at the server side. For example, if you were dialing in from home and your RAS server were in another area code, you could configure the RAS server to call you back at home every time you dialed in. This would be useful if your company doesn't allow you to expense your phone bills.

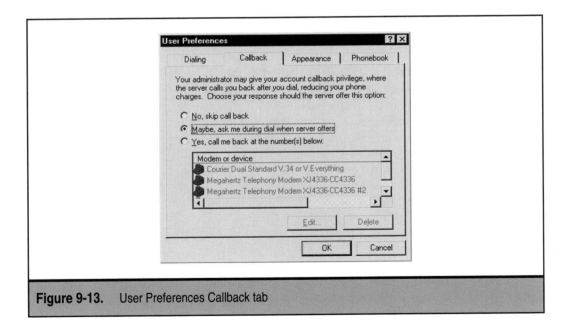

Figure 9-13.   User Preferences Callback tab

Monitoring the Connection

From the Appearance tab you can configure many informational displays. You can set what information is displayed during the connection process and what information is gathered from the user at the time of connection. Many of these indicators are quite useful in troubleshooting a RAS connection problem.

The Dial-Up Networking Monitor is accessible from the Control Panel or from the Monitor Status selection in the DUN main window. The DUN Monitor is illustrated in Figure 9-14. The Status tab provides device and connection statistics for each RAS device installed. Here you can watch basic network statistics being generated, such as bytes in or out and amount of compression. The most helpful information is in the Device Errors section. The different types of errors are enumerated here for your RAS device.

You can also use the Dial-Up Networking Monitor to hang up active connections. If you have more than one device connected, you can hang up a specific device if you want to use it for another call.

The Summary tab was designed to manage multilink as well as single connections. Here you can see how each line is being used and even identify which users are passing traffic through each line of your multilink connection.

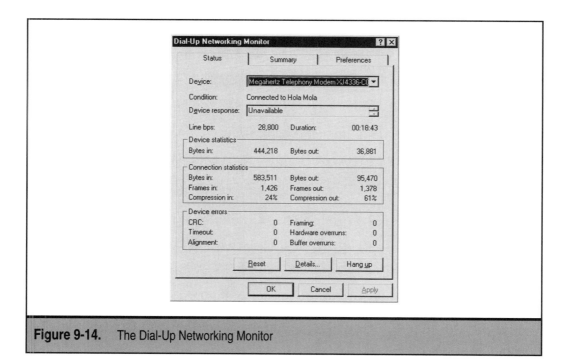

Figure 9-14.   The Dial-Up Networking Monitor

INSTALLING THE RAS SERVER

Installing and configuring Remote Access Server for Windows NT 4.0 is initiated by opening the Control Panel and clicking on the Network icon. This will open the Network configuration window and display five tabs: Identification, Services, Protocols, Adapters, and Bindings. Click on the Services tab, and verify that Remote Access is not listed in the Network Services area. This is illustrated in Figure 9-15.

1. After verifying that the Remote Access Service is not already installed, click the Add button and select Remote Access Service from the list, as illustrated in Figure 9-16.

2. Click OK and enter the location of your Windows NT \i386 directory. After the necessary files have been copied, you will be prompted to add a RAS device. If you already have the device installed, select it from the list and click OK. If you need to add a new RAS device, click Install Modem or Install X.25 PAD in the Add RAS Device window.

3. If you need to install a new modem, the modem installer will guide you through the process. It is the same process as you used earlier to install DUN for client access. Once you have installed and selected a RAS device, you will

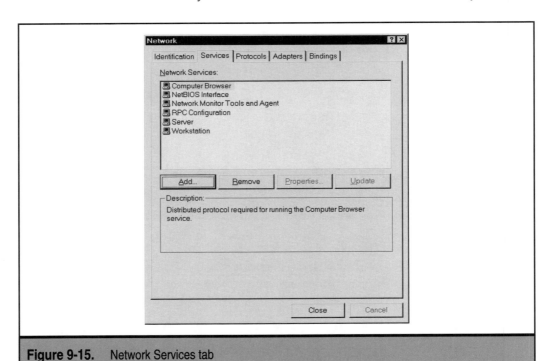

Figure 9-15. Network Services tab

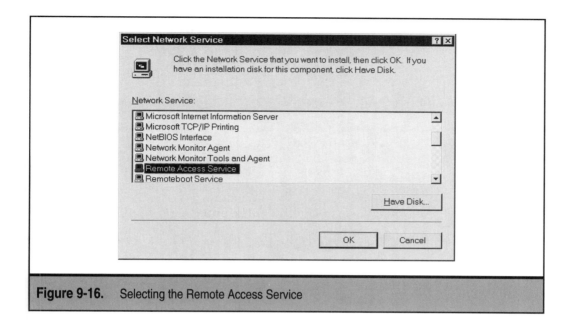

Figure 9-16.   Selecting the Remote Access Service

need to configure port usage for dial-out only. You bring up the Configuration Port Usage window by clicking on the Configure button in the Remote Access Setup window as illustrated next.

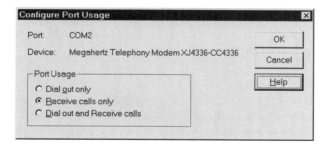

Configuring Network Protocols

The next step is to open the Network Configuration window and modify the Server Settings as appropriate for your server. The Network Configuration window (see Figure 9-17) allows you to define the protocols and settings that will be available to clients.

NetBEUI

For NetBEUI, you have few configuration options. You can select whether you want to allow remote NetBEUI users access to the entire network or to restrict their access to just

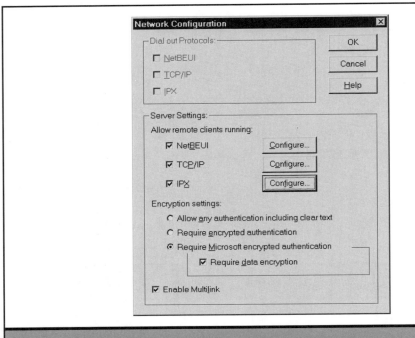

Figure 9-17. Network Configuration for a RAS server

the RAS server. This option is available for IPX and TCP/IP as well. Restricting access to the RAS server is a way of keeping users confined to a single machine set up for remote users. This restriction keeps the server from routing traffic to the rest of the network and keeps network traffic away from remote users.

IPX/SPX

When you're configuring IPX for RAS, several IPX network parameters must be specified. The RAS server acts as the SAP agent for the remote clients and must forward the SAPs over the remote link. Doing this requires that the server has an IPX network address for the remote side of the server. You can configure the server to assign each remote workstation with its own IPX network number, making each remote IPX session appear as if it were on a separate network segment, or you can have the server assign the same network number to every remote workstation.

Unless you have a specific reason for assigning different network numbers, it's a good idea to configure the server to assign the same network number to all IPX clients. This limits the size of the routing table that the server has to parse. You can also choose whether you want the server to allocate network numbers automatically or from a set range. If you are doing any type of filtering on your network or you assign IPX network numbers in accordance with predefined standards, you can use this feature to define the starting number of a range of network numbers for your remote clients. Figure 9-18 illustrates the default IPX network settings.

TCP/IP

When configuring RAS for TCP/IP, you need to make sure you have the proper IP addressing information for your server. In addition, you should verify the presence of any DHCP servers that might be available on your network. If a DHCP server is available, a scope can be defined on the DHCP server for the remote clients. The RAS server can then use the DHCP server to dynamically assign IP addresses to the remote clients when they connect. More information on DHCP is available in Chapter 7.

If you do not have a DHCP server, you can define a pool of static addresses to be assigned to remote clients when they connect. You can also allow the remote client to specify its address as long as it's a valid address on the RAS server subnet. However, DHCP and static address pools work so well that there is rarely a reason to add complexity by allowing clients to specify their addresses. Usually a remote client will require a specific address only when the client is running an application that uses the IP address as a way of validating who the user is. Figure 9-19 illustrates the default TCP/IP configuration.

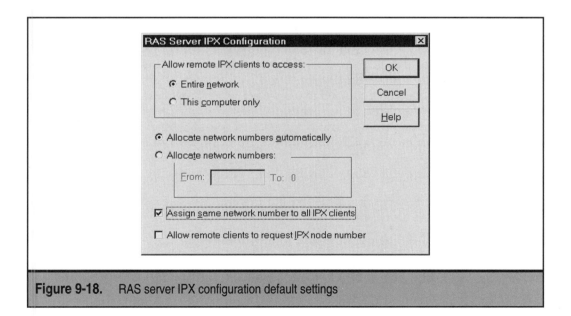

Figure 9-18.   RAS server IPX configuration default settings

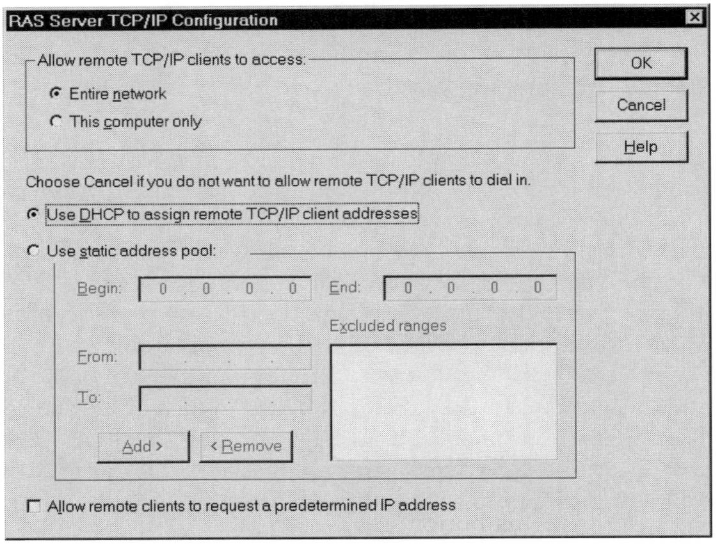

Figure 9-19. RAS server TCP/IP configuration default settings

Once the network components are configured, click Continue and specify the location of your \i386 directory when prompted. After the system has copied any necessary files and installed additional protocols, you will be rewarded with a dialog box indicating that you have successfully installed RAS.

But you aren't done yet. You need to close the Network window and click OK when asked if you would like to restart the computer. Once the system has rebooted, you can proceed to the Remote Access Admin application found in the Start | Programs | Administrative Tools menu.

Managing RAS

The Remote Access Admin interface is straightforward and easy to use. It allows you to manage multiple RAS servers and view important server information. At a glance, this tool provides a listing of multiple RAS servers (if you have more than one in your domain), the up/down state of the servers, the total ports available on the server, and the ports currently in use. You can use the interface to view servers in a local domain as well as other domains (assuming you have administrator rights). See Figure 9-20 for a view of a very small RAS server collection.

Double-clicking on a server brings up another window listing all the communication ports, active users, and the date and time the dialup connection started. From there you

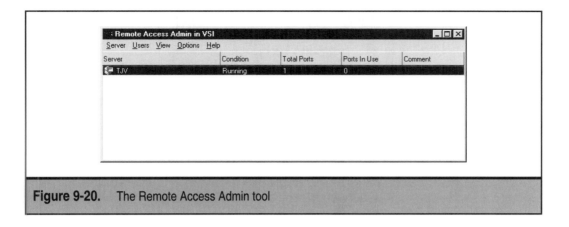

Figure 9-20.   The Remote Access Admin tool

can drill down even further to view information about individual communication ports (see Figure 9-21).

Clicking on the Port Status button brings up another window that allows you to browse through the RAS ports. You can view important information, such as the current modem condition, line condition, port speed, connection statistics, device errors, and name and addressing information about the remote client. Figure 9-22 shows an inactive port waiting for a call.

The Remote Access Permissions window is used to grant user dial-in permissions on the server. In addition, each user can be configured for no callback, callback set by caller,

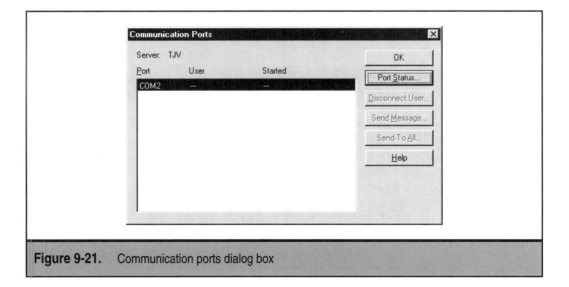

Figure 9-21.   Communication ports dialog box

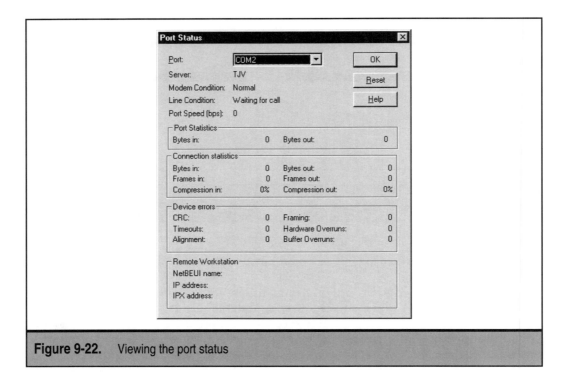

Figure 9-22.   Viewing the port status

or have a callback number defined. The Remote Access User window presents information about a particular user currently dialed in. From this window, you can disconnect the user, send a message to a particular user, or send a message to all users currently dialed in.

Internet Connection Services for RRAS

A fairly new addition to the ever-growing collection of RAS client and server software is Microsoft's Internet Connection Services for RRAS. It's really more of a collection of applications and wizards that you can use to greatly enhance a new or existing NT 4.0 RRAS implementation because it doesn't modify your RRAS installation.

Internet Connection Services includes a customizable dialer you can distribute to your dialup client, and the wizard to configure and build it. It also has a server-side application, Connection Point Services, that "pushes" an updated dialup phonebook to your remote users, giving them the latest information on pooled and dedicated dialup facilities. Finally, it includes the Internet Authentication Service that integrates with RAS and your NT user database, and allows you to retain your existing account database.

CD NOTE: On the CD-ROM you will find software you can use to help manage RAS and to troubleshoot modem problems, including Remote Access Manager by VirtualMotion and Timbuktu Pro by Netopia.

ENTERPRISE CONSIDERATIONS

Determining the enterprise solution that best fits your needs can be very challenging for several reasons. First, it is impossible to determine the usage requirements of your users if there is no solution in place. Even if you have something working right now, you will need to gather statistics over time to accurately predict your needs. Second, the kind of data users send over the RAS connection can change dramatically with little warning. For example, if users who typically send text versions of reports within e-mail messages suddenly were to switch to attaching Word documents of the same reports, the size of the transfer could double. This is not a result of a new application or new users, just simply user behavior. Third, because of the variability inherent with the interaction of computer systems and third-party hardware, there is no easy recipe for determining how much of a system you will need to satisfy your users' demands.

Before You Roll Your Own

Before you request a sundry of servers and equipment so you can build the ultimate remote access solution, you should consider some of the alternatives that third-party vendors can provide. We will briefly cover the alternatives to buying a truckload of modems and installing them in your server room.

Using an Internet Service Provider

The first alternative is to consider using an ISP. Contracting with a regional or national ISP can give your users access to hundreds or thousands of modems, and you won't have to reset them at night. Depending on your needs, an ISP could provide your users with roaming accounts so they could dial in from Boston on Monday, Minneapolis on Tuesday, and San Francisco on Wednesday.

The infrastructure scenario would look like that shown in Figure 9-23. Your ISP provides you with access to modems that allow your users to dial in and connect to the Internet. Your client machines are configured with Windows 95 running TCP/IP and the PPTP client software installed and configured using a client installer that you or your ISP wrote. You have a T-1 from your ISP connected to a backbone area on your network. The point of access is protected by a firewall with TCP ports 1723 and IP protocol 47 allowed through the firewall to the PPTP server.

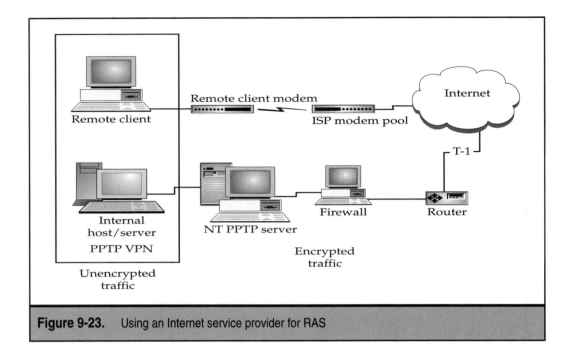

Figure 9-23. Using an Internet service provider for RAS

NOTE: You can use RRAS as a packet filtering firewall. If you do, you will need to configure the following filters so that PPTP traffic is allowed through to your PPTP server:

Input Filters
>   Source packet filter for port 1723
>   Destination packet filter for port 1723
>   Packet filter for allowing protocol 47

Output Filters
>   Source packet filter for port 1723
>   Destination packet filter for port 1723
>   Packet filter for allowing protocol 47

Behind the firewall you have a Windows NT 4.0 server with RRAS configured as your PPTP server. The server is configured to only accept PPTP VPN traffic; it takes the encrypted traffic originating from the remote client, decrypts it on the inside of your PPTP server, and sends the traffic on your internal network. Return traffic is encrypted by the PPTP server and sent out through the firewall. It travels onto the Internet through the encrypted VPN back to the remote client.

This scenario allows you to use the Internet as a wide area network while outsourcing your modem headaches to an ISP, although you may still have to manage the firewall, the PPTP server(s), and the associated security.

Using a Private Service Provider

The other option is the use of a private service provider (PSP) to provision modems and network connectivity back into your network. A good example of a PSP would be CompuServe Network Services. They provide local-dial modem access throughout the world and send your traffic across their switched network to a host or hosts connected to your network. They manage the modems and servers and maintain a help desk for connection-related dial problems. An infrastructure scenario using a PSP like Compu-Serve would look like that shown in Figure 9-24.

In this example, your PSP provides you with access to modems that allow your users to dial in and connect to their private network. Your client machines are configured with Windows 95 running TCP/IP, IPX, or NetBEUI. The client software is installed and configured by an installer program that your PSP prepared for you. You have up to 512KB of bandwidth using X.25 circuits from your PSP into your facilities. They are connected to four NT 4.0 RAS servers by use of Eicon X.25 cards. The point of access onto your network is on the Ethernet interface on the RAS server. A firewall stands between the RAS servers and your network. It is configured to allow authorized traffic through and to deny all other traffic.

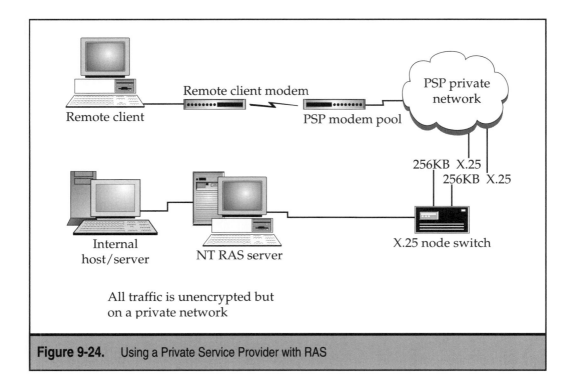

Figure 9-24.   Using a Private Service Provider with RAS

The PSP manages all the circuits and hardware for you, letting you manage the user accounts. The client dials into a local number, they are authenticated once to gain access to the private network, and then the traffic is routed across the PSP private network to a specific RAS server. The user is authenticated again, and the traffic is then passed through the RAS server onto the internal network.

This scenario also allows you to use the PSP network as a wide area network, while outsourcing your modem headaches. In addition, you don't have to worry about maintaining the server OS or hardware, or about monitoring the status of the incoming circuits—they do all that for you. You are left managing the user accounts and helping with problem resolution when it appears that a remote client problem may be related to the network. The amount of operational overhead can be dramatically reduced, especially in environments where there is a very high volume of RAS traffic.

Office to Office Connectivity Using RAS

Although you can configure RAS so that multiple users could use a single modem connection, you should be very careful about that type of connectivity. Bandwidth is so limited that just a couple users could easily bring the link to a crawl. In all but the smallest remote offices, other alternatives, such as small dedicated routers using ISDN, make more sense than using dial-on-demand RAS. However, let's take a look at a situation where using dial-on-demand RAS would be an effective solution to a connectivity problem in a small, remote office.

In this example, the main corporate headquarters of a company is located in the center of the region. Most of the company's regional offices have more than 100 users each, so they use dedicated 56KB to T-1 sized circuits (via Cisco 2500 series routers) to establish a 7x24 routed WAN back to corporate headquarters.

The problem: Whenever the corporate people decide to look into a new regional market, they set up a small office in the area staffed with an "advance" team of financial and market analysts (four to seven people). They spend about two to three months in a small office in the area conducting research. They usually move in quickly and need connectivity so that they can exchange e-mail, documents, and spreadsheets with headquarters.

In response to these needs, you set up a small server that acts as a RAS dial-on-demand server as well as a small file and print server in the remote office. It could be configured with two modems using MultiLink to give them an acceptable amount of bandwidth for file transfers. Because you already have a few remote access servers at corporate headquarters to support dialup users, the server is configured to use the same facilities. The remote team gets a rapidly deployable, portable network with WAN access at a reasonable cost. Once the decision has been made to open a regional office, the dial-on-demand solution can be used until staffing has been completed and a more permanent solution can be implemented.

Hardware Scenarios

The best way to begin to develop a RAS solution is to estimate the number of users you expect to be connected at the peak usage and the expected throughput demands of each user. Naturally, the users are limited at an upper bound by the connection type. Most likely, users don't use all of the offered throughput 100 percent of the time.

Next look at solutions that are in place serving users. You might have another division in the company that has already connected its users with RAS. This is a great place to start trying to gauge your system. Here are some basic guidelines for three different-sized organizations.

Small Site

In this example, there is a small organizational unit with up to 50 employees. You need to provide dialup support for a small number of users when they are traveling or working from home. They might have 28.8KB/sec modems. Their primary use is to transfer small files and check their e-mail.

Because you think the site may grow in the future, you should probably start with fast modems connected to an eight-port serial adapter connected to a 486 with 24 to 32MB of RAM. Because of the slow speeds of the dialup connections, the data coming from the users is not likely to overload the CPU. In the future, you could double the number of modems to the computer without much worry of having to upgrade the server.

Medium-Sized Site

For medium-sized sites, we will assume about 500 users. As with all sites, some users want to dial up using modems. Additionally, there are power users who connect via ISDN. The users conduct file transfers, check e-mail, and may run remote access software. They have tremendous fluctuations in their traffic demands, and thus your solution should support the erratic throughput requirements. Let's also assume that your peak concurrent sessions will not exceed 24 POTS dial sessions and ten ISDN dial sessions in the near future.

At a minimum, you should have one system powered by a Pentium-class processor with 32 to 48MB of RAM. You should use multiport serial adapters connected to modem concentrators that support eight to 18 modems each. You will also need external BRI ISDN adapters connected to your server by an ISDN interface adapter.

Large Sites

For this exercise, we will assume a large site is 1,000+ users. If your site has many more than 1,000 users, you can scale this paradigm by duplicating the basic system, perhaps for divisions within the company. You will almost certainly be supporting file and print sharing from servers within the organization. There may be e-mail, Internet access, and the use of applications over the RAS connection.

To support this load, you should use modem pools that can support 60 or more analog connections. Also, you will need PRI ISDN adapters. These devices are typically proprietary devices that have a single, concentrated connection to the computer. The server should be a fast Pentium computer with one to four processors, depending on the user load and other duties it may perform. For example, if you also use the RAS server as a user authentication device, you'll need to take that into account when estimating the necessary processing power. The server should have 64 to 128MB of RAM.

Once you have purchased a system and put it in place, you should allow a test group of users to try it out. You can closely monitor the usage of the RAS server using the Performance Monitor (see Chapter 11). Some key indicators to watch include:

▼ 100 percent of modems used for any length of time

■ 100 percent CPU utilization

■ Extensive disk swapping

■ Modem errors such as CRC errors indicate a poor line quality

▲ Serial overrun errors that indicate the computer can't keep up with the incoming data

Based on the results from the test group, you should make any necessary changes/additions, and test again to make sure problems have been resolved. Then deploy your solution to the rest of your users, and continue to monitor the RAS servers for the above-mentioned problems.

Vendors

There are many vendors who can provide computer systems and software to help keep your dialup solution functional, scalable, and manageable. Some products provide high-volume dialup services allowing extensive connectivity to IP-based networks and the Internet. Others offer solutions that enable remote node and remote control in a single package. Table 9-2 lists vendors who sell client and server solutions that work with Windows NT.

Modem Options

Planning a large-scale, dialup solution that provides concurrent access for a large number of users requires many modems and the line capacity to handle the network traffic. Although you can use high-density serial cards and modems attached directly to your RAS servers (see Table 9-3), you may want to consider outsourcing your modems.

There are vendors who can provide your users with dial access via a local call from hundreds, if not thousands, of locations in major countries throughout the world. They provide the inbound POTs and ISDN lines as well as the modems at their facilities. From

Company / Product	Clients Supported	Client Software	Connection	Price ($US)	Contact
Attachmate / Remote LAN Node Plus	Windows, OS/2, Windows NT, DOS	Remote control, remote node	Modem link, Internet	$596	www.attachmate.com
Avalan Technology / Remotely Possibly 32	Windows, Windows NT	Remote control	LAN link, modem link, Internet	$169–$399	www.avalan.com
Markham Computer / NetSupport Manager	Windows, Windows NT, DOS, OS/2	Remote control	LAN link, modem link, Internet	$149	www.mcc-usa.com
McAfee / Remote Desktop 32	Windows, Windows NT	Remote control	LAN link, modem link	$79	www.mcafee.com
Stac / ReachOut	Windows, Windows NT, DOS	Remote control	LAN link, modem link, Internet, wireless	$189	www.stac.com
Symantec / PcAnywhere32	Windows, Windows NT	Remote control	LAN link, modem link, Internet, wireless	$149	www.symantec.com
Tactica / Caprera	Windows, Windows NT, OS/2, UNIX	Remote node	LAN link, modem link, Internet, wireless	$1500 per server	www.tactica.com

Table 9-2. Remote Access Server and Client Software

their network, a high-speed connection can be extended to your network, completing the connection and allowing your users access.

Table 9-3 lists some vendors who specialize in providing hardware/software solutions for dialup connectivity on Windows NT. All support normal modem connections as well as ISDN connections.

Company / Product	Clients Supported	Max Dialup Ports	Client Software	Price ($US)	Contact
3Com / OfficeConnect Remote Access Server 1000	DOS, Windows 3.x, Windows 95, Windows NT, OS/2, MacOS, UNIX	600	None	14,995 to 120,000	www.3com.com
Ascend Communications / Max 4004	DOS, Windows 3.x, Windows 95, Windows NT, OS/2, MacOS, UNIX	96	Remote node	$15,500	www.ascend.com
Citrix Systems / Citrix Winframe	DOS, Windows 3.x, Windows 95, Windows NT, OS/2, MacOS, UNIX	255	Remote node, remote control	5,995 per 15 users	www.citrix.com
Comtrol / InterChangeVS 1000	Windows 3.x, Windows 95, Windows NT	256	Remote node, remote control	2,495	www.comtrol.com
Cubix / AccessServ / IS	DOS, Windows 3.x, Windows 95, Windows NT	64	Remote control	3,500 and up	www.cubix.com
Perle Systems / Perle 833	DOS, Windows 3.x, Windows 95, Windows NT, OS/2, MacOS, UNIX	8	Remote node	1,795 and up	www.perle.com
Shiva / LanRover / Plus	DOS, Windows 3.x, Windows 95, Windows NT, OS/2, MacOS, UNIX	72	Remote node	11,900 and up	www.shiva.com

Table 9-3. Remote Access Servers

ROUTING AND RAS (RRAS)

RRAS (formerly code-named "Steelhead") provides an extensible platform for multiprotocol routing and internetworking. Businesses can use RRAS for LAN-to-LAN routing and remote site connectivity over wide area networks , or over the Internet via VPN connections. Other advantages include client-to-server and server-to-server Point-to-Point Tunneling for virtual private networks , demand-dial routing, Microsoft Point-to-Point Compression (MPPC), IP and IPX packet filtering, and PPP Multilink Channel Aggregation.

NT 5.0 NOTE: In Windows NT 5.0 RAS is installed as a component of RRAS and shares a common management console.

RRAS is an additional component of RAS and is available now from Microsoft as a free download at **www.microsoft.com/communications/routing&ras.htm**. You will also find excellent documentation there about the use and configuration of RRAS. RRAS has the following advantages and features:

Advantages

▼ Integrated with the NT Server operating system

■ Unified routing/remote access service solution

■ Not as difficult to use and configure as traditional routers

■ Works with most standard PCs and NICs

▲ Has APIs so developers can create custom routing solutions

Features

▼ Network protocols including IP and IPX

■ Routing protocols including RIP (Routing Information Protocol), SAP (Service Advertising Protocol), and OSPF (Open Shortest Path First)

■ Remote administration using graphical user interface

■ Command-line interface with scripting

■ Demand-dial routing to connect remote LANs

■ PPTP server-to-server for secure virtual private networks

■ Remote Authentication Dial-In User Service (RADIUS) client support

▲ Packet filtering for security and performance

NOTE: IP packet filtering features in RRAS include filtering on TCP Ports, UDP Ports, IP protocol IDs, ICMP types, ICMP codes, and source and destination addresses. IPX packet filtering features in RRAS include source address, source node, source socket, destination address, destination node, destination socket, and packet type.

RRAS supports MultiLink, PPTP, Dynamic Host Configuration Protocol (DHCP) Relay Agent, Windows Internet Name Service (WINS), and Domain Naming Service (DNS).

Although these new features enhance RAS, perhaps the greatest attraction of RRAS is that it is integrated within NT and is intimately tied to RAS. Additionally, RRAS is much easier to configure and implement compared with stand-alone routers.

Installing the RRAS Upgrade

When you install RRAS in NT 4.0, it replaces NT's RAS software and adds its new features. Before installation you should have installed the NT Service Pack 3 or higher. Next you must delete any of the following services that are installed on your NT server, because RRAS replaces them.

▼ RAS
■ RRAS (beta 1)
■ RIP for Internet Protocol
■ RIP for NwLink IPX/SPX
■ SAP Agent
▲ BOOTP/DHCP Relay Agent

When you remove RAS, you will delete all your existing RAS configuration files, so you should take precautions to save those files you may need later, such as the Switch.inf or Modem.inf files. Nonetheless, you will still have to start the installation of RAS over when you install RRAS.

Because the initial beta of RRAS was so volatile, we recommend serious consideration before implementation, or testing RRAS on a spare system before putting it on a critical machine. Later you can migrate your existing installation over to the test lab or production environment.

You should install the appropriate protocol or services listed in Table 9-4 *before* installing the RRAS upgrade if you want them to be available within RRAS.

The last step before beginning the installation is to ensure all your network hardware adapter cards are correctly installed and functioning.

To start the installation, double-click on the executable file you have downloaded from the web. There are three related components available for installation, as illustrated in the following illustration.

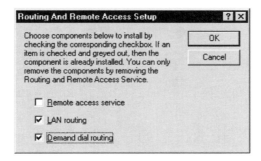

▼ **Remote Access Service** —Replaces RAS

■ **LAN Routing** —Supports LAN-to-LAN routing and LAN-to-WAN routing

▲ **Demand Dial Routing** —Enables NT to connect to non-persistent links such as modems as users request access to remote resources

After selecting the components of RRAS you wish to install, you are prompted with a few routing configuration options. Then you must restart the server. After your system reboots, you can complete the configuration of the routing services or monitor the routing using the new Routing and RAS Admin tool.

RRAS Administration

RRAS is intended for use by system administrators already familiar with routing protocols and routing services. Through the Routing and RAS Administration tool, administrators can manage routers and RAS servers in their network. The RRAS Administration tool is added to the Administrative Tools menu in NT Server. It has a tree view on the left displaying the installed network and routing components of the Routing and Remote Access Service. The list in the right window displays the interfaces for a selected protocol, as illustrated in Figure 9-25.

If You Use	Install This Service or Protocol
IP routing	TCP/IP protocol
IPX routing	NWLink IPX/SPX–compatible transport
SNMP management	SNMP service

Table 9-4.   Items to Be Installed Before RRAS

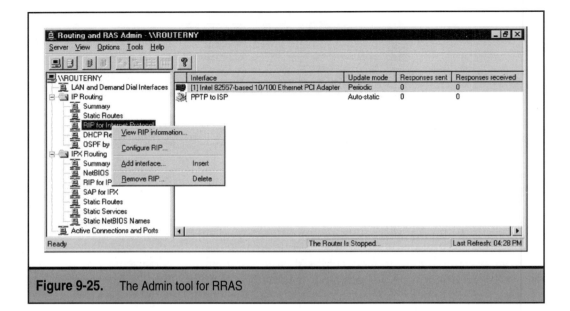

Figure 9-25. The Admin tool for RRAS

You can use the RRAS Admin tool to configure components such as protocols or interfaces by right-clicking on the desired object. It is also useful to view routing tables whether they are static or generated by use of networking protocols. Of course, you can use the GUI for other routing administrative duties such as:

▼ Adding routing protocols and interfaces

■ Adding a demand-dial interface

■ Deleting or disabling interfaces

■ Administering RAS servers

■ Viewing RAS Servers in a domain

■ Granting dial-in permissions to RAS clients

■ Adding and deleting static routes

■ Adding and deleting packet filters

■ Adding local host filters

▲ Adding PPTP filters

RRAS can be used to replace a traditional router in many situations. Because it is a new product, care should be taken when planning the installation of RRAS routers in place of traditional router products—especially when you need high throughput. For example, RRAS can process about 40,000 packets per second, while average stand-alone routers can process up to millions of packets per second. RRAS is better suited for smaller remote sites as described in the remote office scenario.

CHAPTER 10

Security

There is a growing interest in using Internet, intranet, and extranet connectivity to enhance the flow of information to customers, vendors, employees, and key business partners. Because of the increased level of interaction among networks, computers, and their users, security should be placed high on your list of priorities. Whether you are building a new network or server, or upgrading an existing environment, including security in your plans can reduce risks and save additional effort and money later. Also, if you have discovered lax security in your existing networks or servers, you can always improve it. Even though security risks can be well-hidden in the complex technology on networks today, a little education and diligence can help you ferret out most of the major risks and address them.

In this chapter, we look at some of the most pressing security issues faced by administrators of enterprise networks. We examine security fundamentals, outline how to determine the correct level of security, and review basic security policies that should be incorporated into your environment. We look at firewalling and NT security from the network perspective. The operating system section covers the C2 Configuration Manager tool in the NT Resource Kit, user authentication, file systems, and more. Finally, we explore emerging technologies by looking at the IPSec (IP Security) standard and virtual private networking (VPN).

SECURITY ESSENTIALS

Building and maintaining a network is technically challenging, and adding security to the equation doesn't make things easier. If you're like most IS professionals, you're probably putting in at least 45 hours of work a week. We'd be willing to bet that you spend even more of your personal time reading books like this and educating yourself on relevant, work-related subjects. Of course, there are always other things to do with your free time. Worrying about network security on the 46th hour of your week might not rate very high on the list, especially if that 46th hour conflicts with a 9:00 a.m. tee time on a beautiful Saturday morning or with quality time spent with the kids. However security is a serious issue, and a lot of the information on your network is a major business asset that needs to be carefully protected.

If you want to do a good job of keeping critical information secure, and you have the responsibility to do so, make sure security is a recognized part of your everyday job. Doing this should help ensure that you have the time to properly address security issues on a regular basis. Remember that for security efforts to be effective, everyone from application developers to network administrators to managers and users should understand that they have a role in maintaining the overall security of the environment. You can start by educating your organization on security fundamentals. If your organization has an IS security department, join with its members to help define, refine, and update network and server security policies.

To get off on the right foot, you must establish a foundation for security that includes making the effort to understand your existing environment, answering key questions, and creating well-defined policies and operational procedures. From there you can implement many of the technical aspects of security quite easily. This section is intended to get you going by identifying the basics so you have a solid foundation for implementing some of the more complicated components of a secure environment.

Key Questions

Being able to answer the following questions will help you establish a baseline that you can use when constructing a balanced security design. Before we get started, take a few minutes to answer these questions as they relate to your organization. Note that "information" refers to data stored on systems, as well as the applications required to view and manipulate the data.

▼ **What information is critical to the organization?**
Critical information is information your organization requires to function properly. It may include product design information, e-mail communications between officers of the organization, legal documents, organizational charts, employee information, or financial data. Besides the information itself, the integrity of applications that are critical to business functions should be considered. Don't forget that information about your network, such as network and host addressing, router configurations, DNS/WINS servers, remote access servers, firewalls, and other information systems assets should also be regarded as critical to the organization.

■ **Who owns the information?**
Every bit of information should have an owner. This may not be the creator of the information but somebody else who has custodial responsibility for how the information is handled. Your organization may not clearly identify who is ultimately responsible for different parts of the overall information asset. However, before you effectively implement security, you need to identify owners or push for individuals to step forth and take ownership. You cannot keep information secure without these definitions.

■ **Who needs access to the information?**
Determining who needs access to the information can be challenging, especially in large, distributed environments. Owners or custodians of the information should already have lists of authorized users. However, when information is going to be made generally available, on the Internet for example, you must consider that many users will need access. Always document who needs access, what they will be accessing and why they will be accessing the information. This documentation should also support a business case; that is, granting access to information should support the objectives of your organization.

■ **Where is the information stored?**

If you don't know where it is, you cannot secure it. By locating the information and understanding how it is stored and used, you can implement methods of controlling access to it and ultimately protecting it. Keep in mind that although information might be saved to a file server, it might also be stored elsewhere, such as in a workstation cache file. Browsers typically cache web content on the workstation, and unless configured not to do so, may cache information from secure sessions on the local hard drive. Physical security also plays an important role in ensuring that information remains secure. This means having the capability to control physical access to resources like servers and network equipment.

■ **What would be the impact if the information were stolen, corrupted, or unavailable?**

This can often be a hard answer to pin down, unless an incident occurs. However, arriving at a realistic and supportable impact estimate is critical in determining how much security is enough. If information, such as catalog type content on an external web server, is deleted or damaged, it may be sufficient to have a minimal level of security coupled with regular backups of the site. Corrupted or stolen accounts receivable data, on the other hand, would likely have a much greater impact on operations; therefore they may dictate that you invest more heavily in securing the information.

▲ **How long can the organization operate without access to the information, and at what cost?**

Determining how long an organization can operate if information is destroyed or otherwise inaccessible is very important. Survival of the organization hinges on honestly assessing what information and resources are so critical that not being able to use them for a period of time would force the organization out of business. This type of analysis is common in disaster recovery planning. If loss of specific resources (or access to them) for hours, days, or weeks impacts the organization to the point that it can no longer continue to do business, a major effort should be taken to protect those resources.

Too Little Vs. Too Much

As with any other investment in technology, security investments can be under or over applied. If you don't invest in a solid, well-designed security environment, losses due to security breaches may cost the company a substantial amount more than the preventive costs. If you get into security overkill or mismanage your security environment, you may spend more money on security infrastructure and management than the value of the information you are trying to protect. For security to be effective, you must know what you have and understand the reasons why it needs to be secure. Resist the temptation to act impulsively when making decisions about security. If you make decisions before you analyze the requirements carefully, you risk making mistakes.

Determining the right amount of security for your environment boils down to risk versus cost. There is a lot behind the subject of risk assessment and management. We will focus on the key concepts and look at what you can do to quickly determine where your information may have the highest levels of exposure.

The overall cost associated with securing your network and its resources (data, applications, servers, workstations, and so on) should be less than what the cost would be if the network were compromised and data destroyed or altered. That doesn't imply that security can be done "on the cheap". In fact, when you examine security breach scenarios, you may find that it costs much more to suffer a loss of information than you originally would have estimated. For example, in systems where financial data is critical, such as brokerage systems, altered programs that process stock transactions could result in a loss of millions of dollars in a matter of minutes. In companies where confidential customer data is stored, such as credit card or insurance companies, public posting of the information on the Internet could severely damage the company's reputation, costing untold dollars in lost business and lower stock prices.

The following list identifies common security risks.

▼   Denial of service

■   Destruction of systems or data

■   Loss of confidentiality

■   Undetected modification of data

■   Information theft

■   Unauthorized use of systems

▲   Financial data manipulation or theft

After examining the possibilities and reviewing the likelihood that an event will occur, you are probably going to want to make some changes immediately. But before you begin looking into how you will acquire funds to increase the security level of your network environment, do your homework and planning. This way, you can present the risks and a plan to apply security measures in a sensible, cost-effective manner.

Policies

The creation and ongoing management of security policy is the most important factor in securing information successfully. The security policy is a clearly-defined set of rules that is formed from the results of the risk analysis. It should address all the areas that have been identified as important based on exposure. It can include the following areas:

▼   Remote access

■   Virus detection and prevention

■   Server installation and configuration

- Backups
- User account creation and management
- Password rules
- Application development and use
- Software licensing
- Network management
- Cable plants
- Physical security
▲ System administration

If you don't already have a set of policies, you should make it a priority to create one. Because there can be rather complex legal aspects to a security policy, we will not address the entire process here. Many books outline how to develop a good security policy for your organization. However, you can start creating a policy document by following this sample outline:

1. Indicate an implementation date and any revision dates.
2. State and support the organization's business objectives.
3. Clearly and accurately describe the environment.
4. Communicate the results of the risk assessment.
5. Identify whom the policy affects.
6. Clarify areas of responsibility for implementation and management.
7. Identify who will enforce policy and how.
8. Identify approval authorities.
9. Define procedures to be used for managing access.
10. Outline appropriate and inappropriate uses of your information assets.
11. Procure top-level management sign-off.

Once you have a policy, you must make sure that stakeholders (management, users, and so on) understand the policy and are properly educated on its functions.

Goals

Security practices and principles are objectives and guidelines that determine what your security policies are and how they are implemented and managed. Practices and principles should be focused around the following goals:

▼   Reduce risk

■   Lower security-related expenses

■   Reduce or eliminate legal liability

■   Increase user confidence

■   Improve customer perception of reliability and security of information

▲   Balance security and usability

Expectations

Before you can get what you want, you must define your expectations. At a minimum, a good security infrastructure must be able to do the following tasks:

▼   **Authenticate**—Before being granted access, a user should be uniquely identified via the logon process. Guest accounts should not be used or even allowed. If users are manipulating secured data on your systems, you should be able to positively identify each user based on their logon identification.

■   **Track accountability**—You must be able to track who has done what to secured data. Logging needs to include identification of users and information about how they have manipulated secured data.

■   **Control access**—Users should be able to access the systems and information to which they have rights. Unauthorized users should be prevented from using network and server resources and from denying access to authorized users.

▲   **Protect data**—Data requiring security should have controls that prevent unauthorized reading and copying. In addition, there should be controls that allow only authorized individuals to alter or remove the data.

Remember, if you cannot justify your security decisions and explain them to everybody in simple terms, you risk alienating your users and management. They will be far less likely to cooperate with your IS department if they think security efforts are really just a thinly-veiled attempt to acquire more control over what they do. Try to involve everybody in the planning process and help educate them on the issues. If users don't understand why security is important, they will show you that they are remarkably adept at finding ways around almost everything you implement.

Now let's take a look at some specific technologies that you can use to secure your enterprise network. Keep in mind all the general strategies discussed previously, so when you go to implement these security features, they will have maximum impact.

IMPLEMENTING FIREWALLS

When an organization connects its network to an untrusted network that it doesn't have any control over, the organization risks having a user on the untrusted network access resources and data on its network. If the untrusted network is the Internet, and there is no protection between the two networks, millions of people have access to resources and data on the organization's network. This situation is usually unacceptable to organizations. To address this risk, organizations can deploy a firewall. This barrier to the internal network can be as simple as a basic filter on an ISP's router. It can also be a sophisticated blend of barrier routers (screening routers), application-layer firewalls running on UNIX, NT, or another machine type, backed by an additional screening router. In either configuration, the goal is to protect the trusted network from the unknowns on the untrusted network.

Usually, one side of the firewall connects to the external (untrusted) network, and the other side connects to the internal (trusted) network. Figure 10-1 illustrates a basic firewall implementation on a network.

Although some firewalls accommodate other protocols, the most common protocol supported by firewalls is TCP/IP; therefore, we will focus on firewalling TCP/IP traffic. Varying degrees of protection are provided by different types of firewalls. Two basic

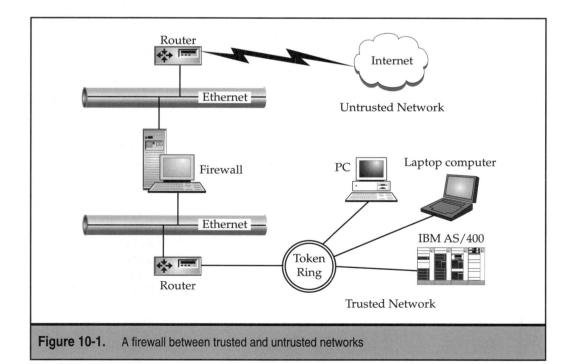

Figure 10-1. A firewall between trusted and untrusted networks

types of firewalls are commonly used in TCP/IP environments: packet filtering firewalls and proxy firewalls.

Packet Filtering

Although many software-based firewalls employ packet filtering, it has traditionally been employed on routers. Regardless of the platform, packet filtering concepts remain the same.

A packet filtering firewall may consist of several different components, including access control lists or filters that allow specified traffic to pass through (based on IP addresses and ports) while dropping all other traffic. This is done as the traffic is examined by the router. The router looks at the address information in the header of TCP/IP packets and, based on internal routing tables, directs the packets to the appropriate router interface. The router makes routing decisions based on information statically configured into the router or on information it has received from other routers on the network (see Chapter 1 for a review). When filters are added to the router configuration, it is possible to control what can pass through the router. This effectively turns the router into a firewall.

Sets of filters are typically referred to as *access control lists* and are entered directly into the router configuration; therefore, it is very important that the router is carefully secured and monitored on a regular basis. Because many routers are configured using telnet and do not employ encrypted password authentication (passwords can be observed using a protocol analyzer), passwords should be changed frequently on routers, especially those that function as firewalls. If your router supports higher levels of authentication, such as the Remote Authentication Dial-In User Service (RADIUS), you should look into implementing them. Other tips include disabling SNMP on the router if you do not need it, and restricting telnet access to the router by IP address or subnet if your router allows this.

What Access Lists Do

Access lists filter network traffic by controlling whether routed packets are forwarded or blocked at the router's interfaces. Your router examines each packet to determine whether to forward or drop the packet, based on the criteria you specified within the access lists. For example, in Cisco routers, access lists can be defined to filter packets based on the source or destination address of the traffic, a specific upper-layer protocol, or other information. It is recommended that you use router access lists as a basic measure of access control of your network even if you have another firewall located behind it. The basic rule for configuring access lists is to deny everything, and then selectively permit what you want.

The following text is an example of Cisco router access list commands as applied to a portion of the router configuration used to control access to various services.

```
access-list 101 permit tcp 0.0.0.0 255.255.255.255 192.12.13.2 0.0.0.0 eq 23
(permits access to a communications server at 192.12.13.2)
```

```
access-list 101 permit tcp 0.0.0.0 255.255.255.255 192.12.13.100 0.0.0.0 eq 21
access-list 101 permit tcp 0.0.0.0 255.255.255.255 192.12.13.100 0.0.0.0 eq 20
(permits access to an FTP host at 192.12.13.100)

access-list 101 permit tcp 0.0.0.0 255.255.255.255 192.12.13.100 0.0.0.0 gt 1023
access-list 101 permit tcp 0.0.0.0 255.255.255.255 192.12.1.100 0.0.0.0 gt 1023
access-list 101 permit tcp 0.0.0.0 255.255.255.255 192.12.1.101 0.0.0.0 gt 1023
access-list 101 permit udp 0.0.0.0 255.255.255.255 192.12.13.100 0.0.0.0 gt 1023
access-list 101 permit udp 0.0.0.0 255.255.255.255 192.12.1.100 0.0.0.0 gt 1023
access-list 101 permit udp 0.0.0.0 255.255.255.255 192.12.1.101 0.0.0.0 gt 1023
(permits TCP and UDP connections for port numbers greater than 1023 to specific
hosts)

access-list 101 permit tcp 0.0.0.0 255.255.255.255 192.12.12.100 0.0.0.0 eq 53
(permits incoming Simple Mail Transfer Protocol (SMTP) e-mail to 192.12.13.100)
```

There is much more to properly configuring a router as a firewall, and router vendors differ in their specific configuration commands, but the preceding example should give you an idea of how the filters look and work within a router. You will certainly want to find individuals trained on the specific brand of routers to configure them for optimal security.

Proxy Firewalls

A proxy firewall acts as a relay and brokers traffic "on the fly" based on specific IP protocols and ports. A proxy firewall can also perform address translation between the internal and external networks. This allows the entire internal network to be represented as a single IP address on the external side, concealing information about internal hosts from prying eyes on the external side.

Because proxying requires that the firewall understands the underlying protocols (FTP, telnet, HTTP, etc.), special software is required. This means that proxy servers usually run on systems similar to a standard server. The underlying operating system is typically UNIX, or more recently, NT. The firewall software controls the flow of network traffic between the internal and external network interfaces. Proxy servers sometimes require that the client workstations are specifically configured to use the proxy services. However, as proxy servers evolve, more of them support transparent proxying for most common IP protocols and do not require client-side configuration.

NOTE: Chapter 8 includes an overview of Microsoft Proxy Server version 2.0.

Using Firewalls

As we discussed earlier, firewalls are used to separate and protect your trusted network from untrusted networks. Untrusted networks might include the Internet but could also include customer and vendor networks, or even other networks within your organization. When an organization connects to other untrusted (customer, vendor, or external company) networks, the "traditional" view of a single firewall connecting to the Internet can be expanded to include additional firewalls. Figure 10-2 illustrates a scenario with multiple firewalls to multiple untrusted networks.

These additional firewalls are typically used to control access between segments of a corporate wide area network (WAN). This type of security requirement is on the rise in larger organizations as they grow through acquisition. Use of firewalls is always recommended when an organization cannot trust the other side of the internetwork. The "better safe than sorry" rule of thumb is that you should not trust any remote network. This includes networks within the organization unless you are 100 percent comfortable that they adhere to the defined security policies. If you cannot be certain that policy is being adhered to in the organization's marketing network, for example, you should implement a firewall.

Newly-acquired businesses initially have a higher level of autonomy and highly-varied levels of security. Because their security policies may not meet the parent corporation's requirements and they may have connections to other untrusted networks, the new network environment should be considered untrusted as well. This fact should not hinder appropriate connectivity, however; incorporating a firewalled WAN connection between the parent company and the new company can enable communication without putting the parent networks at risk.

You should note that firewalls cannot protect against attacks from the inside. Many reports over the years indicate that more than 50 percent of all attacks come from the inside of the network and are carried out by current or previous employees and contractors. This means that although firewalls play a very important role in securing your information, firewall deployment should not be the end of your security efforts. You still need to maintain good host security and user authentication within your internal network. You should also be monitoring your publicly accessible servers (WWW, FTP, etc.) for intrusions from the inside as well as the outside.

The Scoop on TCP/IP Ports

TCP/IP communications rely on IP addressing and ports to identify the type of services used in communicating between two hosts. Applications use different reserved and non-reserved port assignments to "listen" for incoming requests from other hosts. Port numbers range from 1 to 65,535 and represent logical rather than physical ports. Ports 1 to 1,023 are reserved for specific, standardized server applications. Ports above 1,023 are

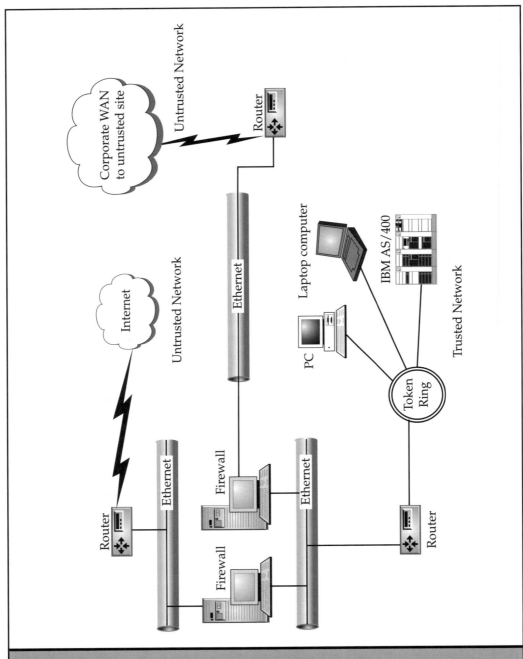

Figure 10-2. Multiple firewalls to multiple untrusted networks

used when an application dynamically assigns a communication stream between the client and the server to one of the open ports. Table 10-1 lists some of the more common reserved ports (RFC 1060).

To protect your NT network, firewall your connection to the Internet and make sure that you block access on the following ports:

▼   137/tcp NETBIOS Name Service (netbios-ns)

■   137/udp NETBIOS Name Service (netbios-ns)

■   138/tcp NETBIOS Datagram Service (netbios-dgm)

■   138/udp NETBIOS Datagram Service (netbios-dgm)

■   139/tcp NETBIOS Session Service (netbios-ssn)

▲   139/udp NETBIOS Session Service (netbios-ssn)

NOTE: Unless you have external Exchange servers that need to connect to Exchange servers inside your network, you should also block port 135 which is used as the Remote Procedure Call (RPC) port mapper. Recently-documented attacks have used this port to crash or disable servers.

By blocking these ports, you effectively eliminate all Server Message Block (SMB) access through the firewall to your internal servers. Because NT supports several types of networking, however, you still have to pay attention to the standard TCP/IP services (FTP, HTTP, and SMTP) as they can be a potential target if they are misconfigured and accessible from the external network. Verify that these standard services are run under an ordinary user account rather than the system account.

Firewall Vendors

Many firewalls are on the market today. Some are better than others at performing specific functions. Some can be considered more secure (a matter of considerable debate among vendors), and others can be considered faster. Before selecting a firewall, have a clear idea of your particular requirements, including an estimate of the number of concurrent users and sessions, required throughput while filtering or proxying, and a list of other needs specific to your environment (including your budget). Table 10-2 contains a list of some (certainly not all) of the more popular firewall systems.

NT SECURITY ISSUES

There have been countless debates on whether or not NT is really secure. The truth is NT—and all other operating systems that incorporate network connectivity—are insecure if not properly configured and managed. You cannot get around it. Although there are differences between Novell, UNIX, and NT when it comes to security, each has one major security element in common. This element dramatically impacts how secure

Application	Port	TCP/UDP
echo	7	TCP/UDP
ftp-data	20	TCP
ftp	21	TCP
telnet	23	TCP
smtp	25	TCP
time	37	TCP/UDP
name	42	TCP/UDP
whois	43	TCP
domain name server (DNS)	53	TCP/UDP
bootp	67	UDP
tftp	69	UDP
gopher	70	TCP
http	80	TCP
finger	79	TCP
pop3 (mail)	110	TCP
portmapper/sunrpc	111	TCP/UDP
nntp (news)	119	TCP
ntp	123	UDP
NetBios name	137	UDP
NetBios datagram	138	UDP
NetBios session	139	TCP
snmp	161	UDP
snmp-trap	162	UDP
rexec	512	TCP
rlogin	513	TCP
shell	514	TCP
syslog	514	UDP
RIP	520	UDP
UUCP	540	TCP

Table 10-1.   Some Reserved TCP/UDP Ports

Firewall Product Name	Company	URL	Telephone Number
Firewall-1	Checkpoint	www.checkpoint.com	(800) 429-4391
Eagle	Raptor Systems	www.raptor.com	(617) 487-7700
Borderware & Sidewinder	Secure Computing	www.sctc.com	(800) 692-5625
Blackhole	Milkyway Networks	www.milkyway.com	(408) 566-0800
BorderGuard	NSC	www.network.com	(612) 424-4888
Secure Network Gateway	IBM	www.ibm.com	(800) 426-2255
CyberGuard	Cyberguard	www.cyberguardcorp.com	(800) 666-4273
Labyrinth	Cypress Consulting	www.cycon.com	(703) 383-0247
ANS Interlock	ANS Communications Inc.	www.ans.com	(800) 456-8267
Private Internet Exchange (PIX)	Cisco Systems, Inc.	www.cisco.com	(800) 553-6387
Digital Alta Vista Firewall	Digital Equipment Corporation	www.digital.com	(800) 344-4825
Gauntlet Internet Firewall	Trusted Information Systems, Inc.	www.tis.com	(888) 847-3477
Watchguard Security Management	WatchGuard Technologies, Inc.	www.watchguard.com	(800) 682-1855

Table 10-2.   Firewall Products

the operating system is once it's installed. The element, as you might have guessed, is the people involved with configuring and managing the system. Although some components of NT are difficult to secure because of the way NT is designed, configuration and management of the server is the largest factor in system security.

Keeping this in mind, let's look at what you can do to set up and maintain a secure NT Server environment.

TCP/IP Filtering

In Windows NT 4.0, you can filter TCP/IP traffic on TCP and UDP ports, and IP protocols entering the machine's network interfaces. The configuration of filtering is not very forgiving or self-explanatory unless you are experienced in IP filtering. If you activate the filters, you need to know the ports and protocols of all TCP/IP services the machine requires to do its job. This can be difficult to determine unless you understand all the TCP/IP services required by your system. Table 10-1 can be helpful in identifying ports needed by specific services. To enable the filters, open the Network Properties window, select the Protocols tab, highlight the TCP/IP protocol, and click on the Properties button. From there, select the IP Address tab and click on the Advanced button. In this window, check the Enable Security checkbox and click on the Configure button. This will bring up the TCP/IP Security dialog windows, as shown in Figure 10-3.

Select the adapter for which you want to apply the filter(s). Remember, if you check the Permit Only option, you will block all IP traffic except what you explicitly allow when

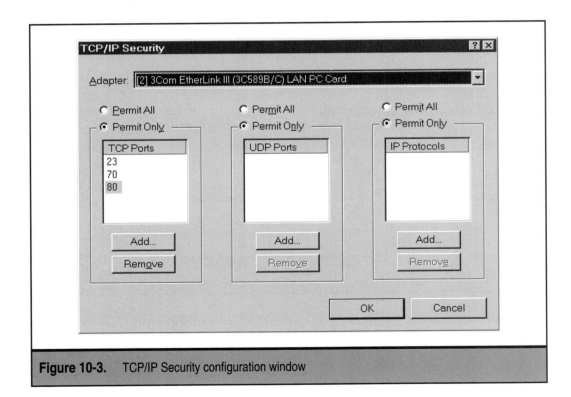

Figure 10-3.   TCP/IP Security configuration window

adding ports or protocols. For example, to block all TCP traffic through the selected interface except web traffic, select Permit Only (TCP) and click on the Add button to add ports or protocols. In the dialog box, enter **80.** This will block all TCP packets except those on port 80. This can be repeated for other ports as needed. When you have finished, click on OK until you return to the main dialog box.

FTP and WWW Service Security

The two services that you will most likely allow anonymous access to are the FTP and WWW services. If the server is on the Internet, you can never be sure who will be logging on and what their intentions are. It may be obvious to you that you shouldn't put private or proprietary information where it will be accessible to anonymous users. But even if there is no other information on the server, you still want to maintain the integrity of the data you are making available to these users. If security is lax, someone might be able to alter the data, introducing a virus or false information. Subsequent users will be accessing this manipulated data. At a minimum, you need to ensure that this doesn't occur. However, most servers have at least some private information on them that you don't want anonymous users accessing. This is especially true of FTP servers with individual user accounts and directories and WWW servers with active content such as those used to collect information input from different users. There are several steps you can take to limit anonymous users to areas of the system specifically set up for anonymous access.

FTP Services

The FTP service included with NT 4.0 uses the local guest account as the default anonymous user account. If you installed IIS 3.0 or later, the FTP and WWW services use a special account named IUSR_*computername,* which was created specifically for the service. If you don't have IIS 3.0 or later, you can still tighten security by changing the anonymous account from guest to one that has no unnecessary privileges or memberships in privileged groups. Either way, you should create a separate NTFS partition for the FTP home directory.

As part of the configuration process, make sure that the FTP anonymous account doesn't have any rights on other partitions and is not a member of any groups with rights to other resources on the server.

WWW Services

The WWW service can be more challenging to secure depending on what you have running on the WWW server. To begin with, you should implement the recommendations made for the FTP service. On top of that, you should pay close attention to directories accessible by the anonymous account IUSR_*computername.* Executables, GCI, ASP, and other scripts have all been used to perform unauthorized activities on WWW servers, so you should make sure to examine the rights of the anonymous account in the directories where they are located and set the permissions to read-only and execute (RX). The flip side of securing WWW services happens on the client. When you secure your server, you are also protecting the clients accessing your server from Java and ActiveX code that someone may have placed on your server. You should make sure that permissions for these areas are read-only for anonymous users.

Securing Servers

We know that NT-based WWW/FTP and firewall servers connected to the Internet or other untrusted networks should be carefully configured. Let's take a look at the steps you should take to ensure that only needed services run on the server and that only needed protocols are bound to the network interfaces. Be careful when making these changes and test the resulting server to make sure the security is functioning as expected.

The following checklist recommends guidelines for securing a server.

▼ Remove all protocols except TCP/IP.

■ Remove the WINS client network bindings on any externally-exposed interfaces (leave the TCP/IP binding).

■ Use a router with an access list to filter out all unneeded protocols and ports.

■ Filter all TCP/UDP and IP traffic using the Advanced Security dialog box, as described earlier in this section.

■ Disable the guest account.

■ Allow only necessary user accounts on the server.

■ Use long, mixed-character passwords and force changes regularly.

■ Remove all unneeded shares, such as those created by SNA server and SMS.

■ Disable all unneeded services.

■ Use NTFS and check permissions carefully.

■ Create a separate volume for each service (FTP, WWW, and so on).

■ Validate the accounts under which the services are running. Instead of using the system account, create accounts that give the services only the permissions they need.

■ Enable audit logging.

▲ Monitor the security audit log regularly.

NT 5.0 NOTE: In NT 5.0, there is a new version of NTFS (Version 5.0), which supports file encryption on the disk for added security.

Restricting Anonymous User Access

NT 4.0 Service Pack 3 includes a mechanism that allows you to remove the capability for anonymous logon users to connect to the Registry remotely. Once the service pack is installed, anonymous users cannot remotely connect to the Registry and access the data there. In addition, the service pack creates a group called *Authenticated Users*, which is similar to the Everyone Group, in which anonymous logon users cannot be members. This restricts the ability of anonymous logon sessions, which can be manipulated so that system security can be compromised.

Strong Encryption of Password Information

NT 4.0 Service Pack 3 adds the capability to use strong encryption techniques that protect the Security Account Manager (SAM) information. The information could be compromised by members of the administrators group. To prevent easy decryption of passwords, even by administrators, strong encryption of account password derivative information is employed. The strong encryption secures account information by using a 128-bit random key to encrypt password data. To use the strong encryption you must run the *Syskey.exe* utility. Note that even if you do not enable strong encryption, the risk of eavesdropping does not exist for logon passwords. They are never transmitted "in the clear" over the network; a challenge-response protocol is used instead.

NOTE: FTP and telnet passwords are transmitted in the clear. Passwords and data are transmitted in clear text and may be discovered or "sniffed" anywhere on the network between the client and the host, including parts of the network at your ISP.

Common Network Vulnerabilities

Aside from the basic vulnerabilities outlined earlier, new security holes continue to be found. Many can be closed by careful configuration of the systems, routers, and firewalls. Other vulnerabilities may be addressed in the latest service pack. However, holes are found in between service packs, and not all fixes are included on the service packs. For these reasons, you should be monitoring Microsoft's Security Advisor web site for the latest information and security patches. The site contains security information and patches for the NT operating system, Office, Internet Explorer, Internet Information Server, Microsoft Proxy Server, and other Microsoft products.

NOTE: You can protect your systems against these and other vulnerabilities by getting the appropriate patches for your NT operating system version and the most recent service pack installed on a particular system. The patches, service packs, and documentation can be found at **ftp.microsoft.com/bussys/winnt/winnt-public/fixes/usa/**. The international versions of these files can be found on the directory above the /usa directory. The Microsoft Security Advisor site, **www.microsoft.com/security**, also has information about recent fixes as well as other security information.

If you have other software and hardware products, you should also look for resources that help you monitor their current security issues. Some of the more recently identified vulnerabilities have shaken many administrators. Some are a potential threat to the information on your network, while others interrupt access to services on your network and servers. The latter are called *denial of service* attacks, and they seem to be a popular nuisance attack on servers connected to the Internet.

The latest of these attacks, referred to as the teardrop and teardrop2 attack, can crash NT Workstation and NT Server versions 3.51 and 4.0. This is achieved by sending specially corrupted UDP packets to the target. There are a couple of denial of service attacks that involve sending UDP packets to port 19 (chargen) using a false (spoofed) source IP address or by piping commands. Network bandwidth can be consumed in this manner, and if the server is running DNS, it is possible to cause a DNS outage or even a system crash. You should note that UDP attacks can be thwarted by filtering all UDP traffic at the router, or, in NT 4.0, by configuring the TCP/IP service bound to the network interface as described in the "TCP/IP Filtering" section earlier in this chapter.

CD NOTE: The CD-ROM includes many links to security related sites. Many of the sites include information on newly identified vulnerabilities, and some offer security bulletins that allow you to receive that latest information via e-mail.

Passwords

Passwords function as the key to the lock on the door of your information assets. The password can be guessed easily if it is too short or if it is the name of your dog or some common word. If it is written on a note under your keyboard or in a notebook, it can be discovered. You should configure your user accounts to use longer, mixed-character passwords, configure the system policies to force frequent password changes, and educate users on the mistake of writing down passwords. However, if you are over zealous and make users change their passwords too frequently, they will be forced to use passwords that are easy to remember or discover (and easy to crack).

NOTE: Password settings are controlled in the User Manager for Domains administrative tool. This tool is described in more detail in Chapter 2.

Password Filtering

NT 4.0 Service Pack 3 includes a password filter called *Passfilt.dll.* It allows you to increase password strength by enforcing stronger rules. Additionally, custom password filter DLLs can be written to implement different password rules. After the service pack is installed, it is located in the *%systemroot%*\system32 directory. To use it for your domain, install the service pack on the primary and backup domain controllers or copy it from another server to the domain's primary domain controller.

After the file is in place, make sure the following Registry setting exists. If not, add it:

HKEY_LOCAL_MACHINE\SYSTEM\CurrentControlSet\Control\Lsa
Value: Notification Packages
Type: REG_MULTI_SZ
Data: Passfilt.dll

After installation, the following password policy will be in effect.

▼ Passwords cannot contain the user's name or full name.

■ Passwords must have a minimum of six characters.

▲ Passwords must have characters from a minimum of three of the four classes shown in Table 10-3.

Audit Trails and Logging

A major component in managing a secure environment is the audit trail. Because all auditing in NT is disabled by default, you have to manually select which events you want to audit. This is accomplished in the User Manager | Policies dialog box, as shown in Figure 10-4.

The resulting log information can be read using the Event Viewer | Log | Security dialog box. However, before you enable all sorts of auditing, you should establish a few things:

▼ Which machines you want or need to audit.

■ What you want to audit (users, files and objects, systems processes, etc.)

▲ How long you want to retain the logs (audit events are written to the security log and viewed using the Event Viewer).

Depending on your hardware, auditing may have an impact on system performance. In most cases, you shouldn't notice a performance hit. Nonetheless, auditing too many events will quickly fill up your log files. It is best to choose carefully those events you feel are most critical. The following events are important to watch:

▼ Logon and Logoff—Failure

■ User and Group Management—Failure

▲ Security Policy Changes—Success and Failure

Class	Characters
English upper-case letters	A, B ...Y, Z
English lower-case letters	a, b ... y, z
Westernized Arabic numerals	0, 1 ... 8, 9
Nonalphanumeric characters	!%&...

Table 10-3. Valid Password Characters

Audit Policy

Domain: VELTE.COM

[OK]

[Cancel]

[Help]

○ Do Not Audit

● Audit These Events:

	Success	Failure
Logon and Logoff	☑	☑
File and Object Access	☐	☐
Use of User Rights	☐	☐
User and Group Management	☑	☑
Security Policy Changes	☑	☑
Restart, Shutdown, and System	☑	☑
Process Tracking	☐	☐

Figure 10-4.   User Manager Audit Policy window

It is also possible to place audits on NTFS files using the File Manager. Highlight a file or directory, and then click on the Security menu item and Auditing. You can select to audit different types of access to the file or directory, including read, write, delete, and execute.

CD NOTE: Many vendors specialize in creating software that monitors audits and sends alerts to an administrator. One of the most popular of these programs, Kane Security Monitor by Intrusion Detection, Inc. is on the enclosed CD-ROM.

Backups

No discussion about security would be complete without mentioning backups. One can hardly think of a better way of getting a substantial amount of information that can be removed from its original site that could be browsed at leisure. Once a backup has been made, it needs to be protected as well as, if not better than, the source of the backup. The main reason is that most backup mediums are very portable and are capable of containing a substantial amount of information. A stolen backup tape restored to an unauthorized user's system could be examined at great length without the user running the risks that are associated with illegitimate activities while online. You should make sure that your backup medium is kept in a secure location such as a safe or locked cabinet and that access to it is limited to authorized administrators. When rotating backups offsite, use a trusted backup service or a trusted administrator to move the tapes to a secure offsite storage location.

Another issue to consider regarding backups is the account used to perform the backups. This account typically has access to the entire file system. If the account is compromised, an unauthorized user has access to the directories and associated data being backed up. Because of this, you should treat the backup account as you would an administrator account. Make sure to include the use of long passwords and check the logs regularly.

Remote Access Security

Remote access is one mode of transport that should be very secure. Think about it: your sites might employ a number of physical security measures to ensure that unauthorized individuals are not walking around the workplace. Your organization probably has locked file cabinets to protect confidential files. There are locked server and wiring rooms; there may even be security guards at front desks. All these measures are taken to keep prying eyes from gaining access to information and equipment. Well, what if there were a way for unauthorized individuals to sneak past the guard desk and move around the building rummaging for information without being seen—not even by the office snoop. If you allow remote access to the network, there is a way for this to happen. All it takes is an improperly secured system configured to allow dial-in access.

There are many reasons to allow remote access, but if you don't need it, don't allow it. If you do allow remote access, make sure that you pay careful attention to how it is configured. The following is a list of things you can do to increase the level of remote access security.

▼ Use the strongest level of authentication.

■ Use session encryption.

■ Firewall your RAS servers.

■ Enable and enforce time-of-day restrictions.

▲ Enable auditing.

Auditing within NT allows you to track certain system events in a log file. To enable RAS auditing, change the following Registry key to 1: HKEY_LOCAL_MACHINE\ System\CurrentControlSet\Services\RasMan\Parameters\Logging.

You can find more information about remote access in Chapter 9.

C2 Configuration Manager

The NT Resource Kit includes the C2 Configuration Manager tool, which can help you quickly check and set several security parameters from the C2 Configuration Manager interface. The National Computer Security Center (NCSC) is the U.S. government agency responsible for developing guidelines and procedures to use when implementing and maintaining system security. It has defined different levels of security for different types of computers. Windows NT has been successfully evaluated by the NCSC at the C2 level as long as it is not connected to a network. The reason for this is that the C2 rating was written to define security standards for non-networked systems. However, using C2 measures, such as those in the C2 Configuration Manager, go a long way toward increasing the strength of your systems in the face of an attack.

You start the C2 Configuration Manager by selecting Resource Kit | Configuration | C2 Configuration. The main window, shown in Figure 10-5, displays an icon indicating C2 compliance status, the security feature, and the current setting of the particular features. Most of the features can be quickly configured to C2 standards by double-clicking on the feature, and then clicking on the C2 button in the resulting dialog box

The C2 Configuration Manager can save you a lot of time. With many security features, you have to figure out which Registry settings to change or add to properly secure the system. The C2 Configuration Manager automates the manipulation of the Registry parameters for many key configuration items.

EMERGING TECHNOLOGIES

Over the last 20 years, the need for remote computer systems to communicate with each other has increased dramatically. The Internet has been used by schools, government

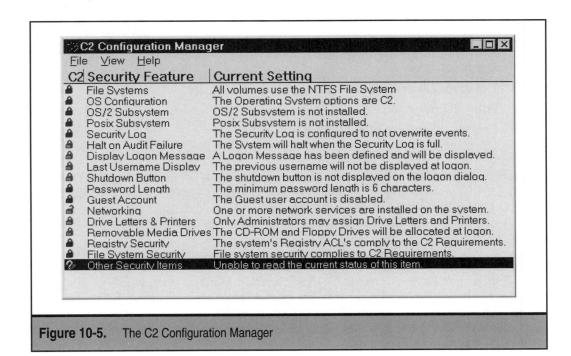

Figure 10-5. The C2 Configuration Manager

institutions, and more recently, commercial organizations to facilitate computer-to-computer communications using the TCP/IP protocol.

In the past, with the exception of some government agencies, most organizations transmitted data over the Internet "in the clear". With protocol analyzers, it's possible to view the contents of packets as they pass through the Internet. The Internet is becoming a popular choice for those wanting to communicate with others because it's easy and inexpensive. However, as more people use the Internet and more business is conducted on it, the need to enhance security and privacy becomes imperative.

For example, company XYZ wants to transmit its payroll file to a payroll processing vendor using the Internet. Unfortunately, a few dishonest people are out there on the Internet. They may be waiting to catch credit card numbers as they fly by, or they may have been hired by a competitor to get information from XYZ's payroll file. If the information is sent out in clear text on the Internet, someone with bad intentions may be able to capture the information without leaving home. Worst of all, XYZ might never know they have been robbed!

The good news is technologies are being established by Internet standards committees to help safeguard your data. A variety of hardware and software vendors are already developing products around these new standards. One of the most important of those standards is IP Security (IPSec). The class of products expected to be built around this standard will enable organizations to create standards-based virtual private networks (VPNs) over dial connections, private and semiprivate networks, and the Internet. The technologies will enable organizations to create trusted networks using encrypted tunnels through untrusted networks. The tunnels, consisting of encrypted data, can be read by a protocol analyzer but not interpreted. In this section, we will look at IPSec standards and VPN technology.

IPSec

IPSec is the set of protocols being developed by the Internet Engineering Task Force (IETF) to support secure exchange of packets at the IP layer. IPSec is expected to be adopted as a standard during 1998. Initially, the IETF planned to release IPSec with the next generation of IP, known as IPv6. It opted to release IPSec separately because of the strong need for a standards-based set of security protocols for use on the Internet.

Because IPSec operates at the network layer (layer 3), it can provide secure transport capable of supporting any application that uses IP. IPSec uses public key encryption using the ISAKMP/Oakley protocol.

IPSec provides three main areas of security when transmitting information across a network:

▼ Authentication of packets between the sending and receiving devices

■ Integrity of data when being transmitted

▲ Privacy of data when being transmitted

The standard combines several technologies and standards that form a complete solution for securing information over a network:

▼ Support for Diffie-Hellman key exchange

■ Support for public-key cryptography

■ Incorporation of several data encryption algorithms

■ Incorporation of traditional and keyed-hash algorithms for packet authentication

▲ Integrated capability to use digital certificates to authenticate the caller

Although there are several options for IPSec communication, the most common scenario (called IPSec tunnel) works like this:

1. A standard IP packet is sent to the IPSec device with the expectation that the packet will be encrypted and routed to the destination system over the network.

2. The first of the two IPSec devices, which in this case would probably be either a firewall or a router, authenticates with the receiving device.

3. The two IPSec devices negotiate the encryption and authentication algorithms to be used.

4. The IPSec sender encrypts the IP packet containing the data, and then places it into another IP packet with an authentication header.

5. The packet is sent across the TCP/IP network.

6. The IPSec receiver reads the IP packet, verifies it, and then unwraps the encrypted payload and decrypts it.

7. The receiver forwards the original packet to its destination.

Central to IPSec is the Internet Security Association Key Management Protocol (ISAKMP/Oakley). Although the keys can be configured manually, this mechanism allows the exchange of public keys and communication with a digital certificate authority when setting up a secure session between two devices, and it is much more manageable. Once the authentication is complete, IPSec allows the use of many different encryption algorithms, including DES.

All these standards contribute to the development of technologies that will support standardized virtual private networks.

Virtual Private Networking

Virtual private networking allows organizations to use semiprivate and public networks such as the Internet as though they are private and secure networks. Although there have been many implementations of VPN technology, those based on IPSec promise to offer interoperability with other vendors. This will allow organizations to establish VPNs between each other without requiring that they use the same brand of firewall or router.

VPNs use encryption and encapsulation technology to create a secure tunnel over a variety of transmission mediums. VPNs use IP tunneling (encapsulation) that subsequently transports encrypted packets. The encapsulated packets travel through the Internet just like their clear-text siblings. Once they reach their destination, they are decrypted and sent along to the intended recipient.

Authentication technology is used to make sure the session between the two devices is authorized. Microsoft's Point to Point Tunnelling Protocol (PPTP) enables organizations to create dialup VPNs. Cisco and other router vendors have offered products that support the tunneling of data across the Internet and other networks. More recently, they have added various methods for encrypting the contents of the tunneled packets, so that true VPNs can be established. Firewall vendors have also integrated tunnels with encryption into their products. All these products are poised to reshape how we use the Internet, and free us from the limitations on where we can compute.

Organizations will be able to replace or supplement costly private network bandwidth and perhaps use the bandwidth on the Internet access they already have. With PPTP VPN technology for dialup access, an organization can outsource the management of modems and dial access equipment to their ISP. If the ISP has a national or international presence, traveling remote users can dial into a local ISP point of presence, avoiding the cost of long distance and 800-number calls. VPNs allow you to reduce network management responsibilities, but remember that you will still need to provide support and management for the VPN software, hardware, and configuration.

Organizations can also use VPNs to link remote LANs across the Internet or any other IP network. Virtual VPNs are flexible, multipoint connections that can be set up or closed down quickly. Because firewall vendors plan to include IPSec VPN technology, organizations will be able to set up and tear down VPNs between internal and external organizations on an as-needed basis. These technologies will be instrumental in facilitating rapid deployment of communication channels between individual users and large organizations alike.

WINDOWS
NT
Professional
Library

CHAPTER 11

Tuning and Troubleshooting

In what seems more art than science, network and server tuning can and should be part of the daily tasks of managing an enterprise NT network. Where network performance management is science, tuning and troubleshooting could be considered art. Proper design and maintenance can help keep your network from being an artist's rendition of a network. If you rely on last-minute troubleshooting and cobbled-together solutions, your network will take on the appearance of a Salvador Dali painting. It will become nothing more than a confused and twisted rendition of reality, unpredictable and chaotic.

The true poetry of performance tuning and troubleshooting lies both in methodical planning and careful execution. In this chapter we will examine the basic philosophy of tuning and troubleshooting as well as provide real solutions to common tuning and troubleshooting issues.

TUNING NT SYSTEMS

Tuning is an ongoing process that changes as quickly as the network. Ideally, properly-maintained networks are continuously monitored to ensure the utilization of components falls within an acceptable range. In addition, keeping an eye on application development goals and objectives can keep you ahead of the performance curve. Knowing what plans (application rollouts and the addition of new users, servers, and WAN sites) are being made can allow you to tune the network before performance becomes an issue. Adding higher performance network equipment such as routers, switches, and faster transport protocols like FDDI and Fast Ethernet are all a part of the overall performance tuning that should be done to keep the network at peak performance. You should always be looking for opportunities to use existing and new technologies.

The Seven Habits of Highly Effective Tuning

There are several key areas that need to be considered before you start tweaking individual network and server components.

1. **Know your network**—Having accurate documentation of your network, including up-to-date network diagrams that include specific information about network equipment, network topologies, network protocols in use, protocol addressing, WAN links, server and user LAN segments, and administrative contact information is absolutely critical. Without accurate information about the overall network, you will not be effective in keeping performance acceptable in the long run, especially on large, dynamic networks in which there are high levels of change occurring.

2. **Baseline your network**—To get anywhere, you need to know where you are coming from. Baselining your network gives you an important point of reference when you begin to look for opportunities to maximize performance. You can combine information from tools such as network analyzers and server

tools like Performance Monitor. Using the collected information allows you to build a picture of the average capacity of your network.

3. **Keep it simple**—Keep your tuning efforts within reasonable and understandable parameters. In enterprise networks, many people are involved in building, maintaining, and tuning the overall network environment. If you must make what would be considered nonstandard changes to your network and server parameters to successfully tune your network, make sure to document those customized solutions completely.

4. **Keep the network as flat as possible and resist "seat-of-the-pants" engineering**—As larger networks evolve, resist the temptation to hang hubs off hubs and add additional routers that hang off user LAN network segments, for example. This nesting of network components creates single points of failure that may not be well documented and are likely to be difficult to manage. You also increase the likelihood that you and others will spend additional time troubleshooting, which leaves you with less time to spend planning for the future needs and requirements of your users. There are also security issues associated with allowing "seat-of-the-pants" engineering on the network. An undocumented router hanging off a remote part of the network can be a wide-open door to unauthorized individuals.

5. **Reduce unnecessary administrative network traffic**—Keeping the number of network layer (and higher) protocols low is one way to reduce the level of unnecessary traffic on your network. Monitoring "administrative" traffic like SNMP polling, WINS replication, DNS zone transfers, and server-to-server traffic will allow you to make intelligent compromises in the name of tuning. For example, you may need to adjust the SNMP polling intervals of remote equipment so that you can use more of a WAN link for user traffic.

6. **Stop (or at least curtail) network abuse**—A very important but often overlooked opportunity in tuning the network is to make sure users are not abusing the network. On every network, there are always users (and sometimes administrators) who don't seem to understand that the network is there to support other users that have legitimate business to conduct over the network.
Access to the Internet seems to compound the problem. Inappropriate use of the network can be found everywhere. Some examples include users who constantly surf the web for non-business purposes or initiate large file transfers to download the latest Homer Simpson sound bites during peak business hours. In some cases, your users may not know better. They may not understand the impact of downloading and running that nifty new screen-saver that makes use of streaming content from the Internet to display sports scores. Other abuses may include the occasional Doom or Quake server that appears on the network, but many problems come from the improper placement of legitimate servers on the network. Make sure that file, print, and

other servers are given appropriate points of connectivity onto the network so that system administrators are not tempted to put servers on user segments. You may need to simply inform your users and define usage policies. You can also implement or enable Internet access control using proxy servers or set up filters to restrict access to only those services that support legitimate business needs.

7. **Partner for proactive planning**—Always work to identify ways in which users and application developers can use the network more efficiently. Helping your users help you is an ongoing effort that can yield great rewards over time. Create an environment in which users, application developers, workstation and server administrators, and network administrators have an opportunity to communicate on a regular basis.

Performance Monitor

Having the right information about the current state of your systems and the network is critical when conducting performance tuning and troubleshooting problems. In this section, we will take a closer look at the Performance Monitor application included with NT.

When tuning your NT network, it can be invaluable to have detailed information about the operating system, workstation and server hardware, peripherals, network interfaces, and other software services. Windows NT includes a mechanism designed to gather statistics based on information provided by various software components running under NT. The information generated by these components is collected by the Windows NT Performance Registry. The Registry serves as a mechanism to provide performance data to Win32 applications via the Win32 API. There are standard NT performance measurements defined and written to the Performance Registry by default. Additionally, programmers can create a DLL that writes performance data for other drivers and services to the Performance Registry. This allows other Win32 applications to read the data. Windows NT Performance Monitor executable (*Perfmon.exe*) is a Win32 application that allows you to view the data in the Performance Registry.

Performance Monitor Fundamentals

The Performance Monitor (Perfmon) icon is located in the Administrative Tools folder. When Perfmon is first started (see Figure 11-1), it is in an inactive state; thus it is not monitoring anything. Don't be deceived by its diminutive appearance; Performance Monitor is a very powerful tool. The amount of information that Performance Monitor can access is staggering. A little exploration using the tool can give you information about the state of your machine, help you find bottlenecks, and show you where to tune for performance. This section will provide you with an overview of the tool. An in-depth examination of Performance Monitor and its underpinnings is available in the Windows NT Resource Kit's *Optimizing Windows NT* documentation.

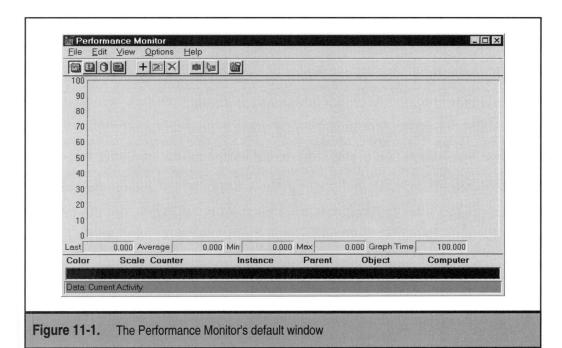

Figure 11-1. The Performance Monitor's default window

Performance Monitor is best understood by thinking of it as an application with four discrete tools referred to as *views*. These tools allow you to visually display, perform actions on, store, and generate reports on data read from the Performance Registry. These four views are described in Table 11-1.

All these views read information about local and remote systems. The information is organized into computers, objects, instances, and counters.

▼ **Computers**—Represents the local or a remote machine of which there are many objects. This distinction allows you to easily view multiple computers with Performance Monitor.

■ **Objects**—Represents a physical, logical, or software component associated with a particular computer. Each object may have more than one instance and contains a number of counters relevant to the object.

■ **Instances (of an object)**—Can be created for each physical, logical, or software component. If there are two processors in the computer, there are two instances of the Processor object. When objects and their associated counters have multiple instances, you can monitor the counters associated with each individual instance separately. In some cases, you have the option of displaying counter data that is based on the total values of all instances.

▲ **Counters**—Represent meaningful and measurable information defined within an object. For example, the Processor object has several counters, one of which is %Processor Time (the %Processor Time counter represents the percentage of time the processor is busy executing non-idle threads). Another counter is Interrupts/sec (the number of device interrupts the processor is handling per second). There may be many counters defined within an object.

> **NOTE:** Before you can view counter data from physical and logical disk objects, you must turn on the disk counters (start the DiskPerf service). This is done at the command line by entering **diskperf –y**. If you need to start the disk counters on a remote system, enter **diskperf –y \\computername**. You will need to reboot the system before the counters will be active. To turn off the counters, enter **diskperf –n**.

You can view which computer, object, and counters you want to read in any of the four views. After selecting a computer, you will see a list of objects available on that computer. Figure 11-2 shows a portion of the drop-down object list for the computer TOONCES.

View	Description
Chart	Displays selected counter data as an in-line graph, or a histogram formats.The two display options are called Gallery settings. You can select either display option in the Options │ Chart Menu (CTRL–O).
Alert	Allows you to create alert events based on counter thresholds. Alerts can be set to perform actions based on when a counter exceeds or drops below values specified by a user. Actions include notification to network users using the Alert and Messenger services and can also be set to execute an application as defined in the Run Program on Alert box in the Alert Entry and Add to Alert windows.
Log	Allows you to create or open an existing log file and write object data to the file. You can use the log to create reports in the Report view. You can also export the log as .TSV and .CSV text formats (tab- or comma-separated values) for use in applications such as Excel.
Report	Allows you to list objects and their associated counter data in a report using values derived from current activity or from a log file.

Table 11-1. Performance Monitor Views

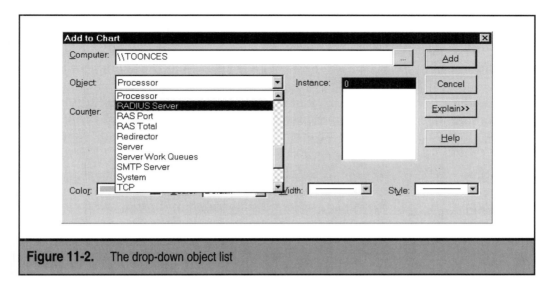

Figure 11-2.   The drop-down object list

Some of the objects in the list were added when particular programs were installed on the computer. Others can be added through a manual process. In addition, Windows NT has a number of objects that are available by default; they are listed in Table 11-2.

To get started with Performance Monitor, we will create a chart that displays useful information about three different computers on the network. We will point out some of the Performance Monitor features along the way.

Chart View

In Figure 11-3 we selected the Chart view and clicked on the Add button on the tool bar to bring up the Add to Chart window. We then selected TOONCES and selected the highlighted Processor object. We kept the default %Processor Time counter and chose a bar/line color of Black. We left the scale at the default of 1.0, and increased the line width one notch so it was more visible. We kept the line style at the default solid line. Because TOONCES only has one processor, instance 0 is the only instance we can select. If TOONCES had two processors, we could choose between instance 0 or 1. Before clicking on the Add button to add this counter to the chart, we clicked the Explain button so we could get a detailed description of the highlighted counter–%Processor Time.

We continued to add two more Processor Time counters, one for a computer called *ALPHA* and another for a computer called *WWW*, so we could look at the processor utilization of three computers on the same chart. After letting Performance Monitor run for a while, we had a comparison of the processor utilization of the three computers, as shown in Figure 11-4.

To change the Gallery view of the display from a line graph to a histogram, open the Chart Options dialog box by selecting Options | Chart from the menu, or by clicking the Options button located on the right-hand side of the toolbar, or by using the shortcut key

Object	Function/Description
Cache	File system memory cache information including cache hits.
LogicalDisk	Logical drive information including disk read-write times, transfer rates, and free space measured in megabytes.
Memory	Physical memory information including committed bytes in use and page reads-writes.
Objects	Software objects that provide information about operating system events, processes, semaphores, threads, and so on.
PagingFile	Page file usage and usage peaks.
PhysicalDisk	Physical disk information including disk read-write times, transfer rates, and disk queue length.
Process	A software object that allows you to set counters to monitor the behavior of selected applications or the total of all running applications.
Processor	Hardware processor information; counter data specific to the Pentium processor can be monitored by installing the Pentium counters available on the NT Resource Kit.
Redirector	Network redirector information including bytes received/sent, connections, file reads-writes, packet data, and network errors.
System	Includes counters that provide general system information including Registry quotas in use, total processor time, systems calls, and system uptime.
Thread	Provides information about threads as a total or within a particular process.

Table 11-2.   Default Objects

CTRL + O. Besides allowing you to change how the chart is displayed, Chart Options lets you select whether or not you want the legend, value bar, grids, and labels to be displayed. You can also define the vertical maximum number to be displayed on the left-hand side of the chart. You can also change the update interval time or set it to manual if you want to take attended readings.

As with the other views, Chart view can be set up for a wide variety of counters, which can be read in real time or from previously-saved log files. The uses for the Chart view range from quick performance spot checks to long-term analysis of data. The

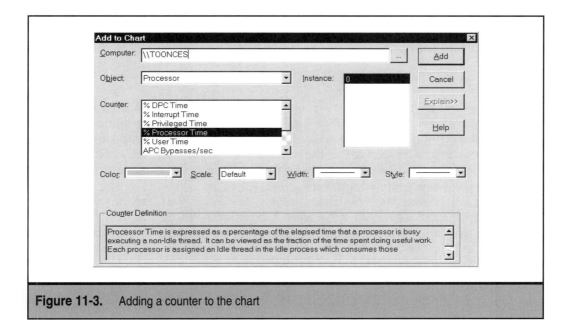

Figure 11-3. Adding a counter to the chart

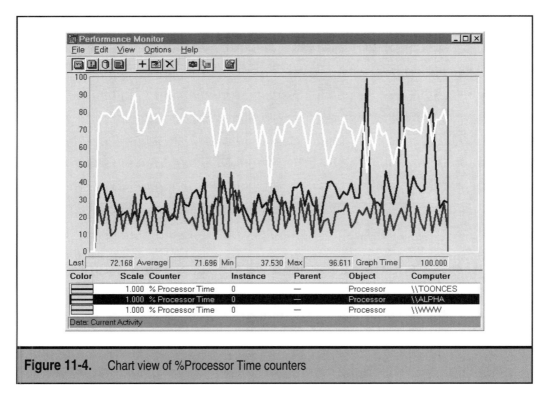

Figure 11-4. Chart view of %Processor Time counters

information bar below the graphs provides last, average, minimum, and maximum data on the selected counter. When capturing to a log file, this information is stored and can be read later.

Alert View

This view is helpful when you want to monitor specific counters but don't want to sit and watch a graph all day. You can set thresholds and have Performance Monitor send you a message if the threshold is exceeded. For example, you might monitor the free space on a logical disk and have an alert sent if the free space falls below a specific value. You can also specify a command-line executable that will be run if the monitored counter falls above or below the predefined threshold.

Adding alert counters is done in the same way as it was in the Chart view. Click on the Add Counter button or select Edit | Add to Alert from the menu. Figure 11-5 illustrates three alerts defined in the Alert Legend. The Value column lists the counter threshold that needs to be exceeded before triggering an alert event. Note that the greater than symbol (>) to the left of each value indicates that the counter value must be greater than the value listed. If the less than symbol (<) were there, it would indicate that the alert

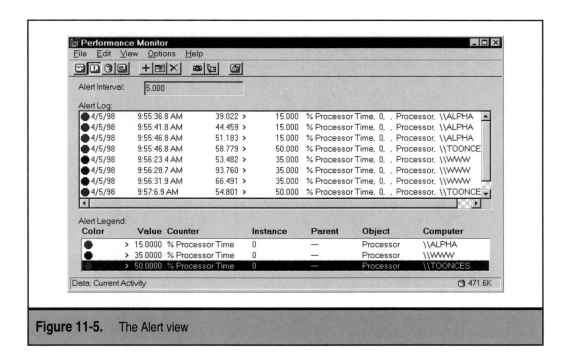

Figure 11-5.   The Alert view

counter is configured so that the counter value must fall below the value listed before an alert event would be triggered.

The remainder of the Alert view display is dedicated to the Alert Log. Every time a threshold is exceeded, an entry is displayed in the Log view listing that includes the following information:

▼ Predefined alert that generated the entry

■ Time of the alert

■ Counter value with a greater than or less than symbol

■ Threshold value

■ Counter

■ Instance

■ Object

▲ Computer

In order to have Performance Monitor send an alert message, it must be configured to do so. The defined Net Name must be a registered NetBIOS name, and the Alerter and Messenger services must be running on an NT system (or WinPopUp on Windows 95 and WFWG systems) for the message to be delivered. You can register a NetBIOS name at a specific computer such as "bobalert" by entering **net name bobalert /add** at the computer's command prompt. Once the name is registered, the alerts will be displayed on that computer.

The Alert Options dialog window (see Figure 11-6) is used to define several settings including the following options:

▼ The view switches back to the Alert view when an alert event has occurred.

■ The alert event logged into the Application Log so it can be read with the Event Viewer.

■ The alert event sends a network message to a specific network name listed in the Net Name dialog box.

▲ The Update Time option set to Manual Update or Periodic Update at a defined interval.

Log View

The Log view allows you to capture object data at specified intervals for review and analysis at a later time. Any of the other views can read the log file and perform their specific functions as if the logged data were being generated in real time. For each object selected, all the counters associated with the object are written to the log. To write data to a log you must add objects to the Log view. This can be accomplished by pressing the CTRL + I shortcut key combination, or by selecting Edit | Add to Log from the menu when in the Log view. This action will bring up the Add to Log dialog window, which will

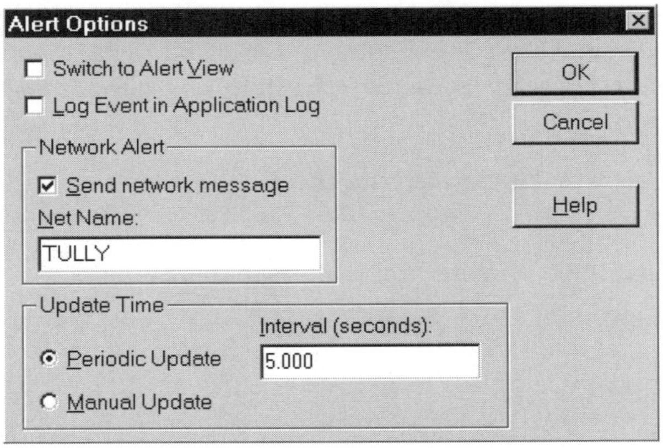

Figure 11-6.   The Alert options window

allow you to select computers and objects to log. Once you have added the objects you want to log, open the Log Options dialog window and specify a location, log file, and Update Time settings.

Be careful when setting the interval; some objects can generate a large amount of data in a very short time. If the interval is short and the object is writing a large amount of data to the log, you might run out of hard drive space in a matter of minutes. Once these parameters are set, click on Save, and then click on the Start Log button and close the Log Options dialog window. At this time, the Perfmon will begin capturing data for all the displayed objects (see Figure 11-7) and will allow you to monitor the log file size.

To stop the log, open the Options dialog window and click on the Stop Log button. To view the logged data, select one of the other views (Chart, Alert, or Report) and click on Options | Data From and select the path and filename of the log file. Each tool reads the data as if it were being collected in real time.

Report View

The Report view is similar to the Chart view in that its function is to display counter information. It differs in that it displays the information in a tabular list organized by computers, with objects and counters listed below each server. The values are aligned on the right-hand side of the report, with multiple instances in successive columns to the right. The addition of counters is done in the same way that counters are added to the Chart view. Figure 11-8 illustrates the layout when several counters have been selected for the report.

The Report view Options dialog window has only one option. You can define the Update Time Periodic Update interval or select Manual Update. You cannot print your

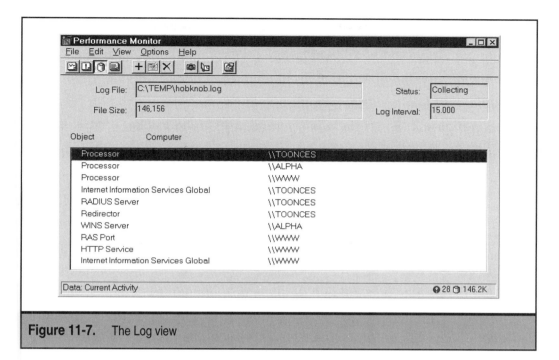

Figure 11-7.   The Log view

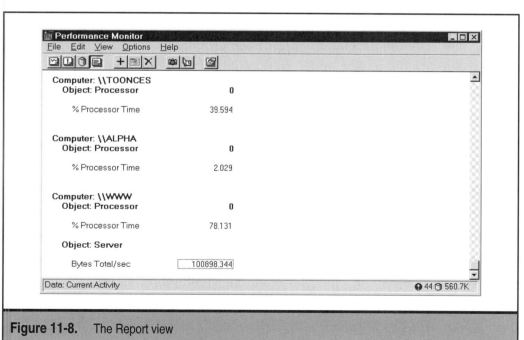

Figure 11-8.   The Report view

reports from the application, but you can export them to a file and open them in a spreadsheet application such as Excel. From there you can print the report or further manipulate the data. With a little bit of tinkering it is possible to generate some attractive and meaningful charts and graphs.

Performance Monitor Shortcut Keys

For your reference, Table 11-3 includes a complete list of shortcut key combinations for use in Performance Monitor.

Shortcut	Description
CTRL+C	Toggle to Chart view
CTRL+A	Toggle to Alert view
CTRL+L	Toggle to Log view
CTRL+R	Toggle to Report view
CTRL+O	Display Options dialog window (based on current view)
CTRL+M	Toggle to display the title and menu bars (also achieved by double-clicking on the Perfmon workspace)
CTRL+T	Toggle to display the toolbar
CTRL+S	Toggle to display the status line
CTRL+P	Toggle to Always on Top
CTRL+U	Trigger Update Now function
CTRL+E	Display the Input Log File Timeframe selection window
CTRL+B	Add log file bookmark comment
CTRL+W	Save workspace settings for all views
CTRL+F12	Open File command (based on current view)
SHIFT+F12	Save File command (based on current view)
F12	Save As command (based on current view)
BACKSPACE	Toggle to the currently-selected counter in Chart Gallery Display
TAB	Add to Chart, Alert, Log, Report (based on current view)
F1	Help

Table 11-3. Performance Monitor Shortcut Keys

Performance Monitor Files

It takes quite a while to set up Performance Monitor to perform different tasks. You can save specific configurations in settings files, and you can also define a default configuration that is read every time you start the program. Table 11-4 lists the default settings for file extensions as well as other default extensions used by Performance Monitor.

NOTE: Saving your workspace as _Default.pmc in the working directory will cause Performance Monitor to start up with your workspace settings, configuring all views as they were when saved. Interestingly, if you save the file with a .PMW extension, Performance Monitor does *not* automatically start up with your workspace settings.

Performance Monitor Registry Parameters

The first time you run Perfmon, the Perfmon subkey is added to the Registry, and several default entries are made. Registry information for Performance Monitor is stored in HKEY_CURRENT_USER\Software\Microsoft\PerfMon.

▼ **CapPercentsAt100**—The default value is 1. This defines a display cap of 100 percent by default. If Performance Monitor reads a value higher than 100 percent from the Performance Registry, and the default value of 1 is set, Perfmon will be limited to displaying a value no greater than 100 percent.

■ **DataTimeOut**—The default value is 20,000ms (20 seconds). This parameter specifies how long Performance Monitor will wait for data from its data collection thread. If data is not returned within the specified time period, a value of 0 will be displayed. The default should suffice unless you are gathering data remotely over a slow link.

Perfmon File Extensions	Description
.PMW	Stores workspace settings for all views
.PMC	Stores Chart settings
.PMA	Stores Alert settings
.PML	Stores Log settings
.PMR	Stores Report settings
.LOG	Default log file extension
.TSV and .CSV	Export log file formats

Table 11-4. Performance Monitor File Extensions

- **MonitorDuplicateInstances**—When set to the default value of 1, Performance Monitor will display more than one instance of an object with the same name. For example, if two copies of *Notepad.exe* are running, both processes will be displayed individually.

▲ **ReportEventsToEventLog**—The default value of 0 keeps Performance Monitor from logging error and warning events to the Application Log in Event Viewer when it cannot retrieve data or the data is unreadable. If set to 1, it will log the events.

NT Network Tuning

In a client-server environment, network bottlenecks usually reside in the network hardware or at the servers (provided there are no malfunctioning components). Performance Monitor can be used to help locate the bottleneck so you can take corrective measures. Perfmon can also be used to indicate where to take proactive action to plan for future growth.

Network Performance

When monitoring network performance you need to pay special attention to how the network segments are being utilized and how the servers are holding up to the demand placed on them. The two services you can focus your attention on are

▼ **Workstation service (Redirector)**—The Redirector (RDR.sys) transmits requests on the network destined for servers.

▲ **Server service**—The Server service (SRV.sys) receives the incoming requests and passes them up to the server.

NOTE: Although you can change Registry settings to tweak the performance of NT systems, NT's autotuning often does an adequate job. Changing Registry settings is risky because the widespread effect is usually unknown–you may be doing more damage than good.

THE REDIRECTOR SERVICE The Redirector service helps connect clients to servers. Presumably the bottleneck is not going to be at the client, although this is not always the case. You can observe how much data is leaving the client by looking at the Bytes Total/sec counter. If this value (summed for all clients on a network segment) approaches the capacity of the segment, you will likely encounter a network bottleneck. For example, if the network segment is capable of 10Mb/sec, you will at best only get 1.25MB/sec (10,000,000 bits divided by 8). In reality you'll be lucky to sustain 80 percent of this value because of network overhead and collisions (see Chapter 1).

To get a more accurate picture of the network utilization, you can use the Network Monitor (see Chapter 12). This program will tell you the present percent of utilization and the packet distribution based on type. Remember, on collision-based networks, warning lights should be going off in your head when this value exceeds 60 percent.

When there is a delay to get packets on the network, the Current Commands counter increases beyond the number of NICs installed on the computer. This counter describes the length of the queue for packets waiting to get on the network segment. In this case, the bottleneck could be the network or the server.

THE SERVER SERVICE   The Server service receives requests for work. When it can no longer keep up with the demand, it denies the requests and generates an event in the Work Item Shortage counter. If this counter increases continually, you have a serious bottleneck forming at the server. This is probably due to a dearth of resources at the server. You can check the number of users by looking at the Logon Total, Logon/sec, or Server Sessions counters.

You should also watch the Pool Nonpaged Failures and Pool Paged Failures counters. They record the number of times memory allocations from either the physical memory or the paged memory has failed, usually due to insufficient resources. The ramifications of running low on memory can be devastating. Either add more physical RAM or increase the size of the page file.

Capacity Planning with Performance Monitor

Once you have put out all the fires for the day, you should start thinking about using Perfmon to help prevent future fires by predicting where to add capacity. The best approach is to monitor some key counters on as many servers and segments as you can. You can use Perfmon's automatic reporting functions to help you with this task. Some key counters to watch are listed in Table 11-5. These counters cover the essential bases, including the network segments, memory, hard drive space, and processor utilization on servers. Don't watch too many counters else you will become inundated with data, and your log files will quickly fill up.

Object	Counter
LogicalDisk	%Free Space
Memory on servers	Pages/sec
Network segments	%Network Utilization, Total bytes received/sec
Paging File	%Usage Peak
PhysicalDisk	%Disk Time, Avg. Disk Queue Length
Processor	%Processor Time

Table 11-5.   Perfmon Counters for Capacity Planning

You might want to watch the counters and place alerts on some of them. For example, you could have Perfmon send you an alert if the %Free Space on a server's disk dropped below 10 percent or if the %Network Utilization exceeds 60 percent on a crucial Ethernet segment.

> **NOTE:** As mentioned earlier in the chapter, to monitor disk counters, you must type **diskperf –y** at the command prompt and reboot. There is a slight hit on disk performance when the counters are activated (less than 1 percent). To turn off the counters, type **diskperf –n** at the command prompt.

To keep track of all this data, you can store it in log files. You'll probably want to write a script or program that can parse the log files and glean only the most useful data for presentation. Another alternative is to use a pair of programs included with the NT Resource Kit: *Datalog.exe* and *Perf2MIB.exe*.

The Datalog.exe program allows you to capture the data found in the logs and forward it to a data store for use later. It runs as a service, so you don't have to be logged on to use Datalog. To learn more about Datalog.exe, review your NT Resource Kit documentation about Monitor.exe and Datalog.exe.

The Perf2MIB.exe program allows you to create SNMP MIBs out of your Perfmon data. Network management software can then be used to query the computer for this information. More information about MIBs and SNMP can be found in Chapter 12. Check your NT Resource Kit documentation for information on how to use Perf2MIB.exe to set up an MIB.

TROUBLESHOOTING

Problems that prevent proper service of your NT systems can arise from many different areas in the enterprise network. For example, if a client cannot access the data on a server, there could be a problem in any of the following areas:

▼ Client computer's network configuration

■ User's authentication

■ Services failed on the client's computer

■ Client software bug or malfunction

■ Network hardware including NICs, cabling, routers, hubs, and switches

■ Server's software, services, or network configuration

▲ Server's hardware including processor, memory, power, and hard drives

It is the administrator's or support professional's job to resolve issues like this and make sure they don't happen frequently. In this section we will discuss the general attack strategy and some useful tools you can use to resolve problems in your NT network.

Problem Resolution

Because problems can occur at many different levels in the network, it's good to have a procedure to follow so that you can quickly resolve the issue. The following steps can be applied to most network problems.

Define Problem

The first thing any support personnel should do when a user reports a problem is to do their best to define the problem. Very often users will report very vague statements like, "My program doesn't work" or "The network is down." They do this because they don't fully understand all the components involved with the network or because that is what someone told them the problem was before.

If you are dealing with a naive user, you must be clever to define the problem. For example, you may have to ask the user to try to run other programs to see if they are affected. You could also check with other users to see if they are experiencing similar or different problems.

Once you have exhausted every means possible to define the problem, or you think you have a grasp of the situation, you should document the incident for use later.

Locate Problem

Locating the problem can certainly be the most difficult step because failures can occur anywhere in the network. It is sometimes helpful to start by cutting the network in half and determining in which half the problem resides. For example, in our client-server problem, you don't know if the problem resides with the server or the client. You should start by determining this. Can the client use another system to successfully communicate with the server? If so, you can focus your attention on the client's computer or local segment. In a network, it's good practice to first examine the problem to see how many users are affected. If you can eliminate the server or the network segment where the server operates, you can categorize this problem as less critical than if many users are denied service.

To help determine the location of the problem, you can use many tools. For example, you can consult with any probes or management stations you may have deployed to see if they are reporting any unusual behavior. You can use a network analyzer (see Chapter 12) to view network traffic. If you find that the problem resides at the level of workstations, numerous applications, such as the Event Viewer (see the section "Event Viewer," later in this chapter), can pinpoint the problem.

Review Changes

If the system used to work properly (i.e., this is not a failure of a new application, feature, and so on), you can take a shortcut to finding a solution. Review all changes that have taken place since the system was known to function properly. From this information you may be able to determine the cause of the problem. This is where good documentation is so valuable. You might ask

▼ Was anything added or removed from the network or computer?

■ Have you started using a new transaction or function?

■ Were any servers or services (such as DHCP) added to the backbone?

■ Did anybody make changes to applications, systems, or the physical surroundings?

▲ Did you notice the problem at a particular time of the day, week, or month?

Sometimes you'll get lucky and stumble across the answer to your problems right away by checking to see what has changed recently. You might not determine the answer right away, but often these questions point you in the right direction.

Attempt to Fix the Problem

By this stage you have defined the problem and learned of any changes that have taken place recently. Now you need to take action to correct the problem. This might be as simple as replacing a cable or rebooting a system to see if a service restarts properly. It may get quite complicated. In these cases you must replicate the problem in a test network that is separate from the production network. It is often best to change one thing at a time and retest the system. Changing many things may solve the problem but may also introduce more problems.

After several unsuccessful attempts you may need to return to the first stage or subsequent stages to gather more information. When you believe you have solved the problem, you should test it, perhaps first on the test network, and then in the environment where the problem was first noted.

Diagnostic Tools for NT

Now we are going to focus on some useful tools that are part of Windows NT or part of the NT Resource Kit. These tools are primarily used in the *locate problem* or *review changes* stages of problem resolution, as described in the preceding section.

Built-in Tools

Windows NT comes with a plethora of built-in tools that you can use to troubleshoot and resolve problems. We are going to focus on a few key tools here, although you should feel encouraged to explore the Administrative Tools menu for other useful applications.

HARDWARE DETECTION TOOL (NTHQ) The Hardware Detection tool (NTHQ) is a program you boot into to inspect your hardware. It is not automatically installed with

NT, but can be found on your NT product CD-ROM. To install and use it, follow these steps:

1. Insert a blank 3.5-inch floppy into the drive.
2. From within NT, go to the NT product CD-ROM *Support\Hqtool* directory.
3. Run the Makedisk.bat program.
4. Reboot the system with the NTHQ floppy disk in the drive.

When your system reboots, the NTHQ program will automatically load and inspect your computer for:

▼ PCI devices and resources

■ ISA Plug and Play devices and resources

■ EISA and MCA devices

▲ Legacy devices and system components

The results of the detection process are recorded in the NTHQ.txt file.

You can use this information as a hardware inventory for the machine. It is also useful for troubleshooting startup problems. If you are having difficulty starting NT, running this program will indicate which devices and resources are detected and used. You might find, for example, that a particular device is not responding and is preventing NT from starting.

WINDOWS NT DIAGNOSTICS   The Windows NT Diagnostics program is one of the first places you'll look to define and determine the cause of problems. It is started via the Programs | Administrative Tools | Windows NT Diagnostics menu item. It has the following nine tabs, each full of information.

▼ **Version**—Contains information about the version of NT, Service Pack level, processor level, and registered user. You might check this to see what build you are using without having to reboot.

■ **Resources**—Lists the use of resources such as IRQs, I/O ports, DMA channels, memory used by devices, and discovered devices. This is an excellent place to look for potential conflicts of resources.

■ **System**—Provides detailed information about the system BIOS and CPU. It's easy to check here for BIOS version information without having to reboot.

■ **Display**—Contains vendor-provided information about the video card and the video driver. Check here to see what NT thinks of your video hardware.

- ■ **Environment**—Lists environmental variables that pertains to all users; another button (Local User) selects variables that pertain only to the currently-logged on user.

- ■ **Drives**—Lists the drives available to the local computer.

- ■ **Memory**—Details information about the use of the physical RAM installed on the computer. More information can be found here than in the Task Manager. Get information about kernel memory, threads, processes, and handles, and see how the page file is being used.

- ■ **Network**—Contains information about the local network environment and the NIC, and statistics about network traffic.

- ▲ **Services**—Lists the services and devices on the local machine along with their current status. You can also check the properties of each service or device to learn more about how it runs under NT and its dependencies. This can be very useful in troubleshooting a failed service.

The Network tab is illustrated in Figure 11-9. In this view you can see basic information pertaining to the network environment and the current user. By clicking on

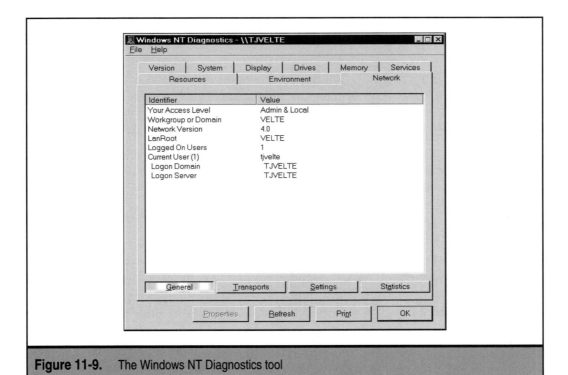

Figure 11-9. The Windows NT Diagnostics tool

the Transports, Settings, or Statistics buttons, you can see more information about the NIC, and how much and what kind of traffic has occurred recently on the local subnet.

EVENT VIEWER   If the NT system that is giving you trouble is running, you should try to locate the problem by looking through the logs using the Event Viewer. The Event Viewer contains three different sets of logs:

▼   **System**—Monitors system components such as device drivers.

■   **Security**—Tracks changes to the security system and alerts you to possible security breaches such as failed logons. What is recorded here depends on the settings in the Audit section of the User Manager. If you audit too many events, you'll quickly fill up the log with useless information.

▲   **Application**—Records events by applications. Programs can be set up to record information in this log.

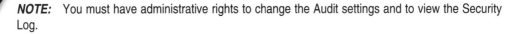

NOTE: You must have administrative rights to change the Audit settings and to view the Security Log.

The Event Viewer records events in a chronological order with the newest or oldest listed first depending on the View settings. You can also filter for specific events or search the entire log for matches to your query.

Figure 11-10 illustrates the System Log for the computer TJVELTE. The three types of events shown here are informational (*i* symbol), warning (*!* symbol), or critical (stop sign). You can tell a lot by looking at this window. In Figure 11-10, you can see that there is a recurring problem associated with the Remote Access Manager that appears to be causing problems with the Service Control Manager.

To get more information about any specific event, double-click on it or use the menu View | Event Details. Doing so on the *RemoteAccess* event brings up Figure 11-11. The upper panel gives a short description of the problem, which can be quite useful. Sometimes it displays suggestions to resolve the problem as we see in this figure. In the bottom panel, data contained for the event can be viewed in binary (the Bytes option) or as DWORDS (the Words option). Not all events generate data. Most often, data is generated from within an application and stored in the event for debugging purposes, so you are most likely to come across data in the Application Log.

Resource Kit Tools

If you don't have the Windows NT Server Resource Kit, you should purchase it without delay. It is an absolute requirement for anyone working with NT at the administrative level. It contains an abundance of utilities you can use to help manage, configure, and design your NT enterprise network. We will focus on some troubleshooting tools that are included with the kit. All tools described here can be accessed in the Programs | Resource Kit 4.0 | Diagnostics directory.

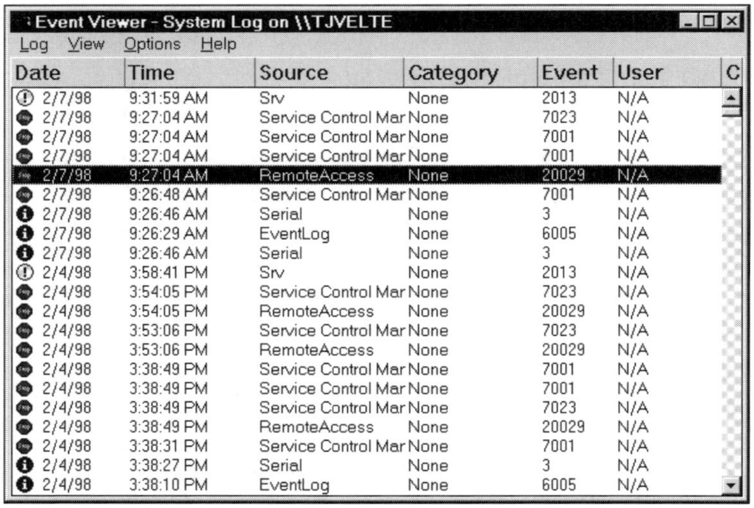

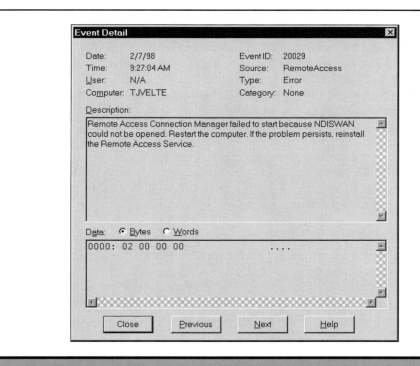

Figure 11-10.   The System Log

Figure 11-11.   Detailed information about a specific event

NOTE: The Resource Kit and other sources of help are discussed in more detail in Appendix C.

DOMAIN MONITOR   The Domain Monitor utility is useful for gaining a high-level view of the domain or domains in your organization. You can select a domain to watch and instantly check its status. This tool is especially useful when you are trying to troubleshoot authentication or trust issues.

Domain Monitor will attempt to seek out the PDC, any BDCs, and down-level computers in the domain. It will indicate whether the machine is functioning as part of the network or is somehow disconnected. You can also check the replication status of the PDC and the BDCs. The status of the replication can be InSync, InProgress, or ReplRequired.

▼   **InSync**—Indicates all controllers are synchronized.

■   **InProgress**—Tells you a replication is under way.

▲   **ReplRequired**—A replication is required because the controllers are out of synch.

Figure 11-12 illustrates two domains that have serious problems–the PDCs for each domain cannot be located. This means there are two NT computers that say they belong to a domain but neither can locate the PDC for its respective domain. Because the PDCs cannot be found, there is no information about the trust relationships they may have with each other or other domains.

You can check the trust relationships between domains here by double-clicking on a domain or choosing Domain | Properties. For any domain, you can list the trusted domains and the status of the link to them. You can see the status of the secure channel that links the NetLogon service of one domain to another domain so that user authentication can take place across domains.

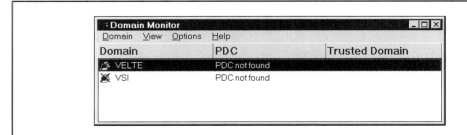

Figure 11-12.   The Domain Monitor checks the validity of domains

> **NOTE:** If your domain contains many computers, you probably should not run this utility over a slow WAN link because it will take considerable time to send information about the entire domain to you.

NET WATCH Net Watch allows you to keep track of network connections for any computer on your network. You can list and monitor the following types of connections:

- ▼ Manually shared drives
- ■ Default shares
- ■ Shared printers
- ▲ Named pipes

Figure 11-13 shows an example of the connections and shares currently on the workstation called IRIS. Even though this is a remote workstation, you can manage the shares or create new ones from this interface. In addition to the remote management functions, you can watch (in real time) the connections being made to the shares. You can see who is using what resource at any time.

This tool is handy for troubleshooting problems related to making connections to resources. It's possible to see if a share is available and whether a user is attached to it.

BROWSER MONITOR The Browser service enables Windows computers to know the names of resources in its environment. There is usually one master browser per network

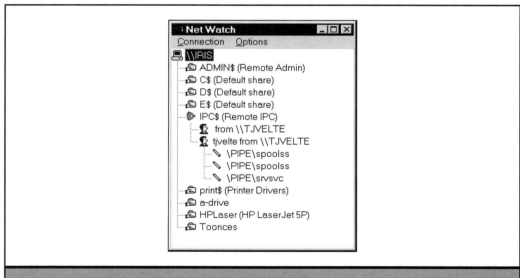

Figure 11-13. Net Watch keeps track of network connections

segment and any number of backup browsers or potential browsers. Browser systems keep track of resources that are available so that every machine doesn't need to be constantly broadcasting in search of resources. The master browser tells the other computers to query it when it needs to know what resources are out there. This is what happens when you attempt to browse your network neighborhood, for example.

Deciding which system is going to be the master browser is a collective decision that the computers make through an election process. Because of this process, you don't inherently know which system is the master browser. More information about the Browser service can be found in Chapter 5.

The Browser Monitor tool can tell you who the master browser is for any domain you can connect to. Figure 11-14 illustrates the Browser Monitor for the domain VELTE. The name of the computer acting as the master browser, along with the transport device that it's using, is listed. For more information about the master browser, you can double-click on the domain or select Domain | Properties. This will bring up another window that details many statistics about the master browser and the Browser service such as:

▼   Number of server announcements

■   Number of domain announcements

■   Number of election packets

■   Number of GetBrowserServerList requests

▲   Number of illegal datagrams

When this tool is coupled with the Event Viewer, you can get a grasp on most browser-related problems. For really tough problems you must also use the Network Monitor to capture traffic on the network (see Chapter 12) and explore the contents of packets.

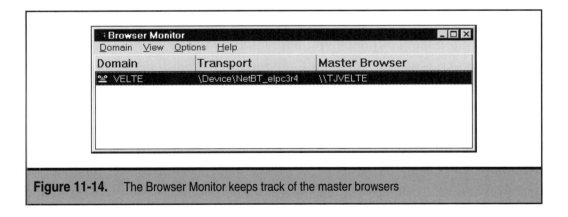

Figure 11-14.   The Browser Monitor keeps track of the master browsers

TCP/IP Troubleshooting

To successfully troubleshoot an NT enterprise network, you'll need to familiarize yourself with a good set of TCP/IP troubleshooting tools. Table 11-6 lists some command-line tools that are already part of NT. Some of them have been explained in previous chapters, but we'll cover *arp, ipconfig, ping,* and *tracert* in detail here.

ARP

The Address Resolution Protocol (ARP) allows computers to make connections to other computers at the physical layer. Even if you use a NetBIOS or TCP/IP name for

Command Line Tool	Description	For More Information
arp	Allows you to view and modify the Address Resolution Protocol table	This chapter
ipconfig	Displays the current TCP/IP configuration and allows you to update or release configuration values	This chapter
nbtstat	Displays the NetBIOS over TCP/IP connections, reloads the LMHOSTS cache, and determines the registered name and scope ID	Chapter 1
net statistics	Lists basic statistics about TCP/IP traffic	Chapter 4
nslookup	Queries DNS servers for host aliases, services, and record information	Chapter 6
ping	Sends echo requests to target workstations	This chapter
route	Used to add, change, or view the current route table	Chapter 1
tracert	Determines and lists the hops to the target workstation	This chapter

Table 11-6. TCP/IP Command-line Tools

computers, the name must be converted to the media access control (MAC) name of the NIC in the computer. When a computer first tries to connect to another workstation, it must broadcast with ARP to determine the MAC address. Once the NT system learns the MAC address, it uses that address to communicate with the other workstation. The computer then stores the IP-to-MAC address conversion in its ARP table.

The *arp* command allows you to view and modify the ARP table. This can be very handy when you are trying to troubleshoot name resolution problems. The arp command has the following syntax:

```
ARP -s inet_addr eth_addr [if_addr]
ARP -d inet_addr [if_addr]
ARP -a [inet_addr] [-N if_addr]
```

▼ **-s**—Adds the IP address (inet_addr)-to-Ethernet MAC address (eth_addr) to the ARP table. The IP address should be in the standard four-octet format, and the Ethernet address should be six hexadecimal values separated by dashes.

■ **-d**—Deletes the entry designated by the Internet address.

▲ **-a**—Displays the current ARP table. If you include an IP address, then only that computer's IP-to-MAC address mapping will be shown.

The [if_addr] argument is used to specify an IP address other than the default one. If we just want to view the current ARP table, we can type **arp –a** at the command prompt. Here is the result on a small network with two other computers:

```
Interface:    10.0.5.13 on Interface 2

Internet Address     Physical Address     Type
10.0.5.10            00-20-af-74-93-8a    dynamic
10.0.5.15            00-60-97-8e-6e-3c    dynamic
```

IPConfig

The *ipconfig* utility is a great place to start troubleshooting your TCP/IP problems. It is used to describe the current TCP/IP settings on a computer. The ipconfig command has the following syntax:

```
ipconfig [/all | /release [adapter] | /renew [adapter]]
```

Used without any arguments, ipconfig displays the most basic TCP/IP settings including the IP address, subnet mask, and default gateway for each network adapter card. You can use the following arguments with ipconfig:

▼ **/all**—Displays more than the basic TCP/IP configuration data. You can also see the information about name servers the computer uses.

- ■ **/release**—Releases the IP address for the specified adapter if the adapter uses DHCP.

- ▲ **/renew**—Renews the IP address for the specified adapter if the adapter uses DHCP.

For example, if you type **ipconfig /all** at the command prompt, you'll see something like:

```
Windows NT IP Configuration

        Hostname . . . . . . . . . . : iris.velte.com
        DNS Servers . . . . . . . . : 10.0.5.51
                                      10.0.5.16
                                      10.4.128.113
        Node Type . . . . . . . . . : Broadcast
        NetBIOS Scope ID. . . . . . :
        IP Routing Enabled. . . . . : Yes
        WINS Proxy Enabled. . . . . : No
        NetBIOS Resolution Uses DNS : No

Ethernet adapter Elnk31:

        Description . . . . . . . . : ELNK3 Ethernet Adapter
        Physical Address. . . . . . : 00-20-AF-74-93-8A
        DHCP Enabled. . . . . . . . : No
        IP Address. . . . . . . . . : 10.0.5.10
        Subnet Mask . . . . . . . . : 255.255.255.0
        Default Gateway . . . . . . : 10.0.5.51
```

Using this simple command can give you a good deal of information about the TCP/IP configuration. Check to make sure the subnet mask is not *0.0.0.0*. This indicates a conflict between the IP number and another system on the subnet. If everything looks good here, you should proceed to use the *ping* utility to check end-to-end connectivity.

Ping

The *ping* command sends an Internet Control Message Protocol (ICMP) echo packet to a target workstation. The target workstation should respond immediately. This tells you both workstations are functioning properly and a route exists between them. Because a network breakdown can occur anywhere between you and the target workstation, it is best to follow the following procedure:

1. Ping the local loopback address. If there is a reply from this address, you know TCP/IP is installed and configured on the local computer.

    ```
    ping 127.0.0.1
    ```

2. Ping the local IP address to verify that it is configured correctly and not in contention with another computer.

    ```
    ping IP_address
    ```

3. Try pinging the address of the default gateway. This will determine whether you can reach your closest router (this is necessary to reach computers on different subnets).

    ```
    ping IP_address_of_gateway
    ```

4. Ping the address of the target workstation that is located on a subnet connected to your subnet via a router. This will determine whether your traffic can pass through a router.

    ```
    ping IP_address_of_host
    ```

5. Now try to ping the same target workstation using its fully-qualified domain name. If this fails, but step 4 works, you have a problem with name resolution, not network connectivity. From here you should ensure DNS systems are available, the HOSTS and LMHOSTS tables are accurate, and WINS is also functioning and configured properly.

    ```
    ping IP_name of host
    ```

The ping command has the following syntax:

```
ping [-t] [-a] [-n count] [-l size] [-f] [-i TTL] [-v TOS]
    [-r count] [-s count] [[-j host-list] | [-k host-list]]
    [-w timeout] destination-list
```

Some of the arguments you can use with ping are

▼ **-t**—Continues to ping the specified destination until interrupted (CTRL+C).

■ **-n** *count*—Pings *count* number of times, and then quits.

■ **-l** *size*—Sends packet of *size* bytes to specified host.

■ **-f**—Sets Don't Fragment flag. If this flag is used, the packets will not be broken up by network devices.

▲ **-w** *timeout*—Sets the timeout value in milliseconds. The default is 750ms. You can increase this value for remote systems that are separated by slow WAN links.

Tracert

The Trace Route (tracert) troubleshooting tool is used to determine the path packets take between two endstations. It works by sending out a packet with a time to live (TTL) value of one. Routers typically reduce the TTL by one and send the packet on its way. However, if a router reduces a packet's TTL to zero, it sends the packet back to the sender as expired. When this happens, the sender can learn information about the router. Tracert does this for the first router, and then adds one to the TTL and sends out another packet. This packet travels as far as the second router and expires. The router returns the packet and information about itself. This process proceeds until the target workstation has been reached or the maximum number of hops has been exceeded.

The *tracert* command has the following syntax:

```
tracert [-d] [-h maximum_hops] [-j host-list] [-w timeout] target_name
```

> ▼   **-d**—Prevents resolving address-to-host names

> ■   **-h** *maximum_hops*—Sets the upper limit on the total number of hops the trace can take in search of the target workstation

> ■   **-j host-list**—Sets loose source route along host-list

> ▲   **-w** *timeout*—Sets the timeout in milliseconds for each hop

You use tracert by simply typing **tracert** followed by the target workstation. In the following example the target machine is only five hops away.

```
C:\>tracert host.company.com

Tracing route to host.company.com [10.0.5.12]
over a maximum of 30 hops:

  1    230 ms   210 ms   220 ms   routerwan.company.com [10.0.34.72]
  2    220 ms   230 ms   221 ms   routera.company.com [10.0.21.4]
  3    240 ms   221 ms   210 ms   routerb.company.com [10.1.5.132]
  4    230 ms   220 ms   221 ms   routerc.company.com [10.0.23.6]
  5    230 ms   221 ms   210 ms   host.company.com [10.0.5.12]

Trace complete.
```

Boot Problems

One of the most frustrating problems with NT is when you can't boot the system. Because NT won't even come up, all of the NT-based tools are useless. The first thing you must do is get NT up and running again so you can determine why it failed in the first place. Most often NT fails to start because of severe hardware failures or misconfigured files. The former problem should be addressed with the NTHQ tool described earlier; the latter problem will be covered here.

Before troubleshooting booting problems, you should acquaint yourself with the different stages of the boot process. There are two basic stages to the boot process: the *boot* phase and the *load* phase. The boot stage loads platform-specific components. The load stage loads Windows NT components such as drivers and services. Both Intel and RISC-based systems have these two stages. However, the files and processes used to boot into an Intel or RISC system differ slightly. Table 11-7 lists the key files for Intel systems, and Table 11-8 lists the files used by RISC systems.

Boot File	Description
Boot.ini	This text file describes the choices of operating systems on your system and indicates where to find them among your hard drive partitions.
Bootsect.dos	This file exists only if there is another operating system on the system, because it is the bootsector of the previous operating system. If you select the previous operating system from the Boot.ini menu, you will load this file.
NTDetect.com	This program runs every time NT is started. It is used to detect the hardware that is present, and this information is later incorporated into the Registry.
NTLDR	This program is responsible for organizing the loading process.
NTOskrnl.exe	This is the Windows NT kernel.

Table 11-7.   Files Required to Boot *Intel* Systems

The Intel Boot Phase

The following stages take place when booting NT on Intel-based systems.

1. Once the computer is turned on, it runs through the Power On Self Test (POST) routine.

2. After the boot device is selected (from setting the BIOS), the Master Boot Record (MBR) is loaded, and the program there is run.

Boot File	Description
Osloader.exe	Organizes the loading process much like NTLDR does on Intel machines.
NTOskrnl.exe	This is the Windows NT kernel.
NTBootdd.sys (some SCSI systems)	Present only on systems that boot from a SCSI partition on which the adapter BIOS is disabled. It is the device driver NT uses to access the hard drive.

Table 11-8.   Files Required to Boot *RISC* Systems

3. The MBR determines the active partition, and the boot sector found there is loaded into memory.

4. On NT partitions, the NTLDR program is loaded. At this stage the official NT boot sequence is initiated.

5. NTLDR prepares the processor to run in a 32-bit flat memory model. NTLDR also creates the appropriate minifile system so that NT can load files from FAT, NTFS, or HPFS file systems.

6. NTLDR loads the Boot.ini file and displays the boot loader menu (operating system choices) to the user.

7. If the user selects a non-NT operating system, Bootsect.dos is loaded. If NT is selected, NTDetect.com is loaded.

8. NTDetect.com checks the hardware and reports back to NTLDR for future inclusion in the Registry. At this stage, the screen is black and progress dots appear as NTDetect.com scans the hardware.

9. NTLDR loads *NTOskrnl.exe* and provides it the information obtained about the hardware through NTDetect.com. Next, the load phase commences.

The boot phase for RISC-based systems is only slightly different from the Intel process. For RISC systems, the resident ROM firmware is responsible for finding a bootable partition. Once this is done, the firmware checks to ensure the partition is supported by the firmware. If it is, the firmware checks the root of the file system's directory for the *Osloader.exe* program. If the firmware finds the program, it will pass control over to the program along with a list of the available hardware on the system.

Then *Osloader.exe* takes control of the boot sequence and subsequently passes control over to the NT kernel (*NTOskrnl.exe*). The functionality provided to Intel systems by NTLDR is not needed in RISC systems because these functions are taken care of by the firmware. Then, like the Intel process, RISC systems enter the load phase. Both platforms follow the same basic plan within the load phase.

The Load Phase

The load phase is comprised of four components: the kernel load phase, the kernel initialization phase, the services load phase, and the Windows NT subsystem start phase.

THE KERNEL LOAD PHASE   This stage is initialized as soon as *NTOskrnl.exe* is loaded. This stage occurs when NTDetect.com has completed its analysis of the hardware on the system. (There is still a black screen, but all progress dots have been printed.) It immediately loads the driver for the hardware abstraction layer (HAL), which acts to shield NT from hardware-specific nuances.

NOTE: To view which drivers are being loaded, simply enter **/sos** after the NT entry in the Boot.ini file. For example:

```
multi(0)disk(0)rdisk(1)partition(1)\WINNT="NT Workstation
  Version 4.00" /sos
```

Next, the Registry is scanned for drivers and services that must be loaded. They are listed in the Registry under HKEY_LOCAL_MACHINE\SYSTEM\CurrentControlSet\ Control\ServiceGroupOrder. The drivers are loaded but not initialized yet.

THE KERNEL INITIALIZATION PHASE   Now the screen goes to its familiar shade of blue, and the build number and processor information are listed at the top of the screen. The kernel is initialized as are the drivers that were loaded in the preceding phase. This is the area most likely to encounter problems because it can be difficult to load drivers successfully if a configuration has been corrupted somehow. There are four level of errors that can be generated at this stage:

▼ **Ignore**—At this level, NT ignores the error and proceeds with the boot sequence.

◼ **Normal**—NT ignores the error and proceeds with the boot, but it also generates an error.

◼ **Sever**—If you are using the LastKnownGood configuration, the boot sequence ignores this error and continues with the boot process. If you are not using the LastKnownGood configuration, the system will reboot and use the LastKnownGood configuration.

▲ **Critical**—A critical error will fail the boot sequence and most often generate what is known as "the blue screen of death".

THE SERVICES LOAD PHASE   This phase starts the Session Manager (SMSS.exe), which runs the programs that are listed in the Registry under HKEY_LOCAL_MACHINE\ SYSTEM\CurrentControlSet\Control\SessionManager\BootExecute. If a drive has been set to be converted to NTFS or to be checked, it will do so now. Then it creates the Pagefile.sys file and loads the required subsystems, as listed in the Registry under HKEY_LOCAL_MACHINE\SYSTEM\CurrentControlSet\Control\SessionManager\ Subsystems\Required. However, the only required subsystem is Win32, by default.

THE WINDOWS NT SUBSYSTEM START PHASE   *WINLogon.exe* and *LSASS.exe* start when the Win32 subsystem is initialized. These programs provide the Logon dialog box. Although you can log on at this point, NT is still loading services that are marked for automatic load. Two of these services are the Workstation and Server services.

Registry Settings for Boot Information

The Registry stores all the configuration settings used during the bootup process in the HKEY_LOCAL_MACHINE\SYSTEM hive, as illustrated in Figure 11-15. There are usually several sets of configuration files listed, such as:

▼ **Clone**—A temporary storage area for the current bootup sequence. If the boot-up is successful (that is, a user was able to log on), these setting are copied over to another control set such as ControlSet001 and referred to as the LastKnownGood configuration by the Select subkey (see Figure 11-15).

■ **CurrentControlSet**—Stores the Registry values for the current system configuration. If changes made to this configuration result in a failed boot, the contents are copied over to another control set such as ControlSet002.

■ **ControlSet00x**—Contains the settings for the boot configurations. One of these will be the LastKnownGood configuration, and the others may be failed configurations. The role each plays is defined by the Select subkey.

▲ **Select**—This subkey defines how each configuration will be used. In Figure 11-15, the current control set and default is set to ControlSet001, and the LastKnownGood configuration is set to ControlSet002. Thus, if I select the LastKnownGood configuration next time I reboot, ControlSet002 will be used.

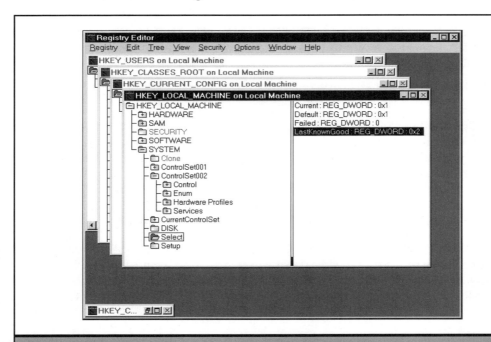

Figure 11-15. The Registry stores the boot information

Problems in the Boot Process

As you can see, there are many possible steps that can fail in the boot process. In this section, we will address problems with the boot phase and the load phase.

BOOT PHASE PROBLEMS   If the failure is in finding the correct boot files (boot phase), you can always use a boot disk to start the system and replace or repair the missing or damaged files. A boot disk has a copy of the essential boot files and a Boot.ini file you can customize to point to an active NT partition. Creating a boot disk is covered in Chapter 3. When you have boot phase problems you will see the following types of errors:

```
BOOT: Couldn't find NTLDR
Please insert another disk
```

or

```
Windows NT could not start because the following file
is missing or corrupt:
\<winnt root>\system32\ntoskrnl.exe
Please re-install a copy of the above file.
```

LOAD PHASE PROBLEMS   If your boot problem is in the load phase of the boot process, first try to start NT using the LastKnownGood configuration. If you still receive a critical error that presents itself in a blue screen of death, try other configurations if available. If none of these work, try to repair your NT system using an Emergency Repair Disk (ERD).

THE EMERGENCY REPAIR DISK   The Emergency Repair Disk (ERD) can repair missing or corrupt NT files necessary to boot NT, including the Security Account Manager (SAM) database, disk configuration information, Registry settings, and software information. Each ERD is unique, so you'll need to make one for every machine (unless machines are identically configured). To create an ERD, type **rdisk /s** at the command prompt. You will be asked to insert a blank floppy disk, and after a few minutes, you will have a custom ERD.

To use the ERD, start a normal NT installation. After NT Setup has found your previous version of NT, you will be asked if you want to repair this version of NT. Select Yes. You will be prompted for the ERD, and then the NT product media shortly thereafter.

NOTE: When you use the ERD, you place the system in the state it was in when you made the ERD. This may have undesirable effects on the Registry including user account settings such as users and passwords. This is why it is important to make an ERD every time you make significant changes to the NT system.

If the repair process doesn't work or you don't have an ERD, you can still access the files stored on the debilitated NT system. One way is to install another copy of NT on the same system (use a different directory for the *systemroot*). Then you'll be able to see your old files, although you may have to change the permissions on the files from Account Unknown to your user if you were using NTFS. Another way is to remove the hard drive and place it in another NT system, and then mount the drive on that system.

Considering how unfriendly NT becomes if there is a problem with the boot sequence, it is best to keep a boot disk and an ERD on hand to save yourself time, aggravation, and possibly your data.

NT 5.0 NOTE: With NTFS version 5.0, you can encrypt data on the hard drive. This may prevent you from recovering your data by installing another NT operating system or moving the hard drive to another NT system.

CHAPTER 12

Network Testing and Capacity Planning

More and more network administrators and managers are realizing the utility of testing their networks. By proactively examining your network, you can better visualize the traffic on your network and avoid potential disasters. Additionally, testing the behavior of a network-based application prior to rolling it out can help ensure that the rollout will be a success. The large costs of rolling out a major application drive the need for testing and validation. Properly testing before deployment offers rewards beyond peace of mind. Avoiding the major expense of backing out of a large-scale deployment should be all the reason you need to make sure testing is part of the plan. This chapter covers the benefits of different types of network testing and outlines the steps you need to take to determine the general health of your network.

Because the network exists to provide applications a means of communicating, we will introduce some tools that can be used to analyze and monitor network-based applications for planning or troubleshooting purposes. We will also discuss how to evaluate applications in a laboratory setting and on the production network. Finally, we'll show you how to integrate the topology of your network and the traffic associated with it into a model, so you can run simulations to determine how to correctly configure and manage your network.

BENEFITS OF TESTING

Although network *monitoring* using both simple and sophisticated tools has been prevalent for decades, the benefits of proactive network *testing* using the same or similar tools are just now being realized. A network administrator and manager will reap great rewards by investing resources in network testing. With proactive testing, you can expect reduced down time, better network performance, quicker deployment, higher user satisfaction, and more efficient use of your employees' time and the company's resources.

Be Proactive Not Reactive

The rapid growth in the deployment of technology has put the administrator in a fire-fighting, reactive mode, responding only when some device or some service goes down. One benefit of network testing is the ability to plan or forecast the behavior of the network to reduce the number of problems in the future, placing you in a proactive mode. Because the size and complexity of networks does not appear to be subsiding, it is even more important that you turn from a reactive mode to a proactive mode. The cost associated with application down time is simply too great not to adopt proactive planning.

It is evident that corporations are using their networks to support important and critical business functions. High availability, reliability, and performance of the network are critical for the modern business to be successful. Proactive planning is the best approach to meet these high demands.

Costs and Benefits

By testing the network before deploying a new piece of hardware or software, you can ensure that it will be able to support the increased traffic load. You will also be able to gauge what limitations exist in an application. When you deploy the application, it will work as expected, and you will be able to monitor its consumption of network resources. When the application resource consumption starts approaching the limitations on the existing network, you can take action before a problem arises. The result is increased up time and user satisfaction.

A more frustrating and potentially more costly problem found in many networks is the insidious *network slowdown*. When the network goes down, you are probably made painfully aware of the failure within minutes. You react swiftly to bring it back up because of the loss incurred each minute the system is down. However, if the network were to become 10 percent slower over time, you or the users might not notice. If they did notice and told you, the situation might not make your priority list because you have seemingly more important problems to fix. Nonetheless, this kind of loss can be more costly than a single outage, as illustrated in the following table. For example, if you have 100 operators processing orders at one per minute, and the profit is $1 per order, your total profit is $100 per minute. In the event of an outage that lasts one hour, you loose $6000. If your employees can take orders at only 90 percent of the usual rate because of a slowdown, your losses are $96,000 for every month that the network is subject to this slowdown.

Full Functionality	Outage (1 hour)	Slowdown (10%, 1 month)
Loss $0	$6000	$96,000

Another cost benefit from testing is the leverage it gives you when you need to deal with a vendor. By testing a product ahead of time, you become familiar with the product and how it works in your environment. You can ask the vendor to address certain limitations of the product before you sign for it. For example, you might insist on proof that a product can deliver on its promise before you purchase it. The only way to know if it will perform up to its specifications is to place it in your production environment or a laboratory environment and run tests. Having extensive knowledge about the application allows you to negotiate confidently with a vendor.

You can also define hardware requirements while testing. It is very difficult to determine how much bandwidth or how much server power you need if you don't clearly understand how the equipment will perform. You don't want to spend money for a quad Pentium processor machine when a single processor model will do the job. You don't want to pay for a point-to-point T1 circuit when a 256KB/sec frame relay connection provides all the necessary throughput. Testing and modeling can predict how much hardware you need for the job and help you make forecasts for the future.

Testing Complements Management

Network testing does not replace network management. There is a role for each and they work together to create a more efficient system. Testing before deployment increases user satisfaction, network up time, and the ability to grow without as many problems as usually accompany introduction of a new hardware component or software upgrade.

Management tools are still an integral part of a network administrator's resources. For example, management tools can report the average use of a link to the administrator, who can use this information to determine what load level to use when testing a new application. Figure 12-1 illustrates the interaction of the different tools an administrator might use for network administration. New software or hardware is tested in a controlled environment, and this information, plus information about the existing network, is used to plan the new product's deployment. Network monitoring tools are still used to troubleshoot problems as they arise.

For example, new hardware or software is selected for possible deployment on the network. The product is run through a testing process that may include examining the protocol(s) it uses, how it uses them, the bandwidth it consumes while processing a transaction, or other variables. The next step, planning, takes the results of the testing and assembles a plan for deploying the product. The deployment occurs, and management

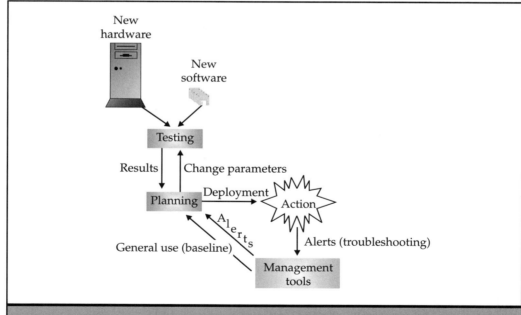

Figure 12-1. Management and testing work together to optimize network efficiency

tools monitor the product's actual behavior and compare it to its expected behavior based on the test data. If the product behaves as expected, the testing was accurate. If the product does not behave as expected, modifications to the testing process must be made.

Capacity Planning

Computer systems are becoming more distributed in nature. More applications are run in the client/server mode. Many clients access servers for crucial and timely information. Some enterprise applications are widely distributed (for example, e-mail, group organizers, and database applications such as Lotus Notes). Push technology and the information on the Internet are both distributed in nature; data sent from the server to the client may traverse many networks. All these applications increase the amount of traffic on a network. Add this load to your ever-growing, more traditional applications, such as DB2 and SQL databases, and file and print servers, and you place a mammoth load on your existing network infrastructure.

This increased load causes network slowdown and sometimes outages. Typically in the past only a few people were affected by a network outage. These days nearly every person in the corporation depends on the network to do their job. For some, an outage may be an annoying inconvenience, but for others, loss of access may translate into a loss of revenue or customers.

"OK", you say, "I'm sold; sign me up for large capacity lines to all users. Maximum bandwidth for everybody, no matter what the cost." Well, although your WAN carrier and hardware vendors will not protest, this approach is a tremendous waste of money. As mentioned earlier, testing and planning can help you determine what throughput you need to meet the demands of the applications. Additionally, testing allows you to predict more accurately your needs for the future and develop the most cost-effective solution before disaster strikes.

GOALS OF TESTING

Testing is not done solely for the sake of testing. You'll find that you have a particular set of criteria that you need to test against. You cannot efficiently test everything there is to test about any given application. You need to focus on the items most likely to impact rollout success or failure. It is imperative that you start by clearly defining your test objectives: What is it specifically that you want to know? In other words, what questions do you want answered. Some possible questions might be:

▼ Is a 64KB/sec line going to cause excessive network delays?

■ Does the redundant NIC work if the other fails?

■ How many users can run this application concurrently?

■ Does this new version of software work with our other applications?

▲ Can the external RAID drive deliver on the promised throughput?

Next you should examine different testing scenarios to determine their value in answering your question. This should be carefully planned. Is the test going to unequivocally answer the question you have put forth? Could the test be confounded because of your methods of testing. Are there any other experimental designs that you could use? You need to stay focused on answering the question—simplicity reigns. In the following sections, several different testing objectives are described, and their potential applications are discussed. You will want to start with one of these objectives in mind, although you will note that these objectives overlap a good deal.

Throughput

Throughput testing is used to find bottlenecks in systems. Bottlenecks can include the server's hard drive system, the NIC, the LAN, routers, hubs, the WAN link, and the corresponding hardware on the client's side. The focus here isn't to optimize code within an application, but rather to determine the throughput for each step in the process of using the application. Values are typically in Kb/sec. Usually the bottleneck is located on the LAN or WAN, but this is not always the case.

Through application analysis you can determine the minimum throughput requirement before users begin to wait excessively for the application to respond. Further analysis reveals the location of the excessive delay. Usually a delay is introduced as more users start using the application, or unrelated network traffic is added. Because of the importance of application testing, it will be discussed in more detail later in this chapter.

Reliability

Reliability testing ensures the hardware or application functions an acceptable percentage of time. You could load an application onto your test network and run it continuously for three days, monitoring it for errors the entire time. If no errors are detected, you might increase the load until errors start to appear. Sooner or later components will begin to fail. You probably don't have time to thoroughly test every component, although it is quite useful to know the limits of every piece of hardware and software used in your network.

You might find reliability testing important for product comparison or as part of an acceptance test (see "Acceptance" later in this section). Also, you can use reliability testing to determine the mean time between failures (MTBF), and then use this value to help determine your redundancy strategy (see Chapter 3).

Functionality

You use *functionality* testing to verify that all the features of an application perform as desired. You observe how the application runs for a user. Typically, the application designer performs all these tests while designing and debugging the application. However, once you stick the application on the test network and increase the load, interesting things can occur.

You will want to load the test network to match the production network as closely as possible. You might use functionality testing to evaluate a product, before deploying a new version of an application, or if you need to troubleshoot a program that is causing errors on the production network.

Regression

Regression testing addresses the performance and functionality of a new software version or a hardware upgrade. This is different from functionality testing in that you are not testing the new features; instead you are testing the same features that were in the older version. Functionality testing should take place prior to regression testing. New versions of software fix old bugs, but they can introduce new bugs that may be worse than the old ones. Frequently the bugs in the software that is in production have been handled with a workaround or a patch. This is why deploying a new version will sometimes introduce more problems than it fixes. Some examples of items that might warrant regression testing include:

▼   A new router operating system code

■   A new release of Microsoft Office

■   A new network interface card

▲   A new version of an in-house application

Again you should test the applications or hardware in an environment that is as close as possible to the production network (see "Laboratory Network", later in this chapter). Place a load demand on the device or software that it is likely to encounter in production. Frequently administrators only have time to read about the product, install it on one or two machines, and observe it there before making a decision about whether or not to adopt it. When it comes time to deploy, the administrator cannot be certain how it will work when loaded with more users. It is vital for a company to adopt new technology, including new versions of software. However, doing so without careful planning can be very disruptive to the organization.

Acceptance

Acceptance testing is perhaps the last testing you will perform before you deploy a new application or hardware into the production network. This occurs when you have everything in place, and you are checking to make sure everything performs as planned. Outside contractors or consultants often provide a Service Level Agreement (SLA) that guarantees a certain throughput or other measure of quality. Acceptance testing measures the quality of service (QoS) to make sure it is up to the established level.

You should make the test network as realistic as possible. Try to use the same hardware and OS versions that are in use in the production network. You might even consider bringing in a few seasoned users so that you can get their feedback. They will know how the application worked before. Almost certainly they will tell you if things have improved or not.

Use this type of testing before signing off on hardware or software purchases if you are given the opportunity to evaluate them. This is your last chance to evaluate the new product before it goes into production, so be very careful before sending it out into the production network.

TESTING YOUR NETWORK

At this point you might have a pretty good idea about what it is you'd like to test. Before running tests, you should be aware of the different protocols, tools, and methods of analysis that are commonly used to test networks.

This section describes the Simple Network Management Protocol (SNMP) briefly and introduces you to remote network monitoring (RMON) so you can better understand how to gather data about your network traffic. Next, you'll learn about the software and hardware tools that you can use to gather this information. Then we'll show you how to construct a controlled laboratory environment to test applications, and we'll run through an example of an application test from start to finish. We'll finish this section by describing how to reduce the information into more meaningful units so you can make sense of it all.

Network Monitoring Standards

Standards organization groups such as the Internet Engineering Task Force (IETF) serve to ensure that there are standards for network monitoring. These standards are typically published as Requests for Comments (RFCs) and subsequently adopted by vendors so that their products comply with the standards and work with other vendors' products, including applications. This means that all devices in your network do not have to be from the same manufacturer. Also you don't need an entirely separate system to monitor hubs versus routers, for example, just because they are from different vendors.

The following sections provide a short description of the most popular standards for network monitoring. There is some overlap among them, and you will quickly see that a combination of them will likely fit your needs best.

NOTE: A great place to download and learn more about RFCs is at the InterNIC site *www.internic.net/ds/rfc-index.*

SNMP and MIB

The Simple Network Management Protocol (SNMP) is the most popular method to monitor network nodes. This IP-based protocol uses the connectionless User Datagram Protocol (UDP) for transport and operates at the OSI application layer. For virtually any network device to be considered manageable, it must be SNMP-compliant. These devices range from routers and hubs to uninterruptible power supplies and network probes. Software agents found on workstations use SNMP to query network devices. Network devices respond using the SNMP.

SNMP-2 is a major revision of the original SNMP and is covered in RFCs 1902 through 1908. SNMP-2 contains all the functionality of SNMP but addresses many performance and security concerns present in SNMP. For example, you can use encrypted management passwords in SNMP-2.

SNMP devices work as follows:

1. A workstation uses SNMP to query an SNMP-capable device for specific usage information, such as how much traffic has passed through the device in a given period of time.

2. The SNMP device receives the request, verifies that the supplied password is valid, and searches its Management Information Base (MIB) for the requested data.

3. The SNMP device uses SNMP to return the information to the requester.

All the information that can be reported by a particular device can be found in its MIB. The MIB is a structured database of information pertaining to that node. The MIB is updated dynamically so when you make a request, you get statistics for the immediate condition. Because each managed device is SNMP-compliant, it knows how to respond to standard queries issued by the network management protocols.

Some managed devices have private MIBs as extensions to the standard ones. These extensions provide additional, proprietary information that can only be obtained using the vendor's management software or other third-party management software that can read the extensions. Recently, there has been a recommendation called MIB-2 that supersedes the standard MIB with a number of new monitoring objects.

RMON

Remote network monitoring (RMON) is a set of SNMP-based MIBs that defines network monitoring devices used for diagnosing local area networks at the physical and data link layers (layers one and two of the OSI model). Network management stations query management agents using SNMP as their method of accessing MIB information about a device.

The original RMON (RFC 1271) defines nine groups of Ethernet diagnostics:

▼ **Statistics**—Contains basic traffic data (such as throughput) for each interface on the RMON agent.

■ **History**—Records periodic statistics for later retrieval from a management station.

■ **Alarms**—Takes samples from the statistical group and compares the values with predefined thresholds. If a value exceeds a threshold, an alarm or trap is generated and sent to the management station.

■ **Hosts**—Maintains statistics for each host station on the network based on the host's MAC address.

■ **Host Top N**—Keeps a list of the top hosts in a given statistical group, such as the top 10 hosts based on generating network traffic.

■ **Traffic Matrix**—Provides a table of the source and destination stations for conversations. If a new conversation is recorded for a pair of workstations, an entry is added to this matrix.

■ **Filters**—Stores any filters you use. You could add a filter to watch only traffic going to a specific host, for example.

■ **Packet Capture**—Essentially acts as a buffer for packets once they flow through a defined channel.

▲ **Events**—Controls the specifics about the generation and notification alerts.

An RMON agent might be a standalone probe that is installed onto a network segment and whose only function is to gather statistics and report them to a management station. Sometimes RMON agents can be part of another network device such as a router or a switch. These are called *embedded RMON agents*.

Basically an RMON agent tracks and analyzes traffic and gathers statistics. A management station periodically requests these statistics from the agents. This is somewhat different than SNMP devices, which typically don't do their own statistical analysis. SNMP devices provide data that has not yet been assimilated and reduced by statistics, which requires more frequent and larger network transfers. The benefit of using RMON agents is that less data is transferred across the network, and the management station doesn't have the burden of calculating the statistics.

RMON-2

The second generation of RMON is called RMON-2 (RFC 2021). It defines network monitoring and gathers statistics at the network and application layers. Unlike the original RMON, RMON-2 can not only monitor its own segment, but also monitor other segments through routers. The functionality of RMON-2 does not include monitoring of the physical and data link layers, and therefore it is not a replacement for the original RMON. RMON organized its MIB into nine groups describing how traffic flows at the level of the frame (physical and data link layers). RMON-2 uses the following eight groups to describe how traffic flows in packets (network and application layers):

▼   **Protocol Distribution**—Records percentage of traffic based on the network protocol, such as IP, IPX, and Appletalk.

■   **Address Mapping**—Identifies hosts based on MAC addresses and Ethernet or Token Ring addresses.

■   **Network Layer Host Table**—Records packets, errors, and bytes per network layer protocol.

■   **Network Layer Matrix Table**—Tracks conversations between two hosts based on the network layer protocol.

■   **Application Layer Host Table**—Records packets, errors, and bytes based on the application, such as cc:Mail, ping, and HTTP.

■   **Application Layer Matrix Table**—Tracks conversations between two hosts based on the application.

■   **Probe Configuration**—Enables remote configuration of probe settings, such as how and where error traps are sent and how to download new software.

▲   **History** — Uses customized filters to track specific hosts or applications and store statistics based on the filter settings.

One disadvantage of RMON-2 is that it is CPU- and memory-intensive. It is estimated that RMON-2 can demand two to five times the resources used by RMON. This has two implications. First, if you have an embedded RMON-2 agent, you could be loosing a good deal of the processor power and memory to the monitoring agent. This additional overhead may impact the ability of the device to perform its primary task. Second, you may need to make a substantial upgrade in hardware and software for your system to function with RMON-2. You may even have to upgrade to a newer device. You'll have to decide if the cost is worth the added functionality. If, for example, your network monitoring is for troubleshooting, you can probably get by with RMON. If you need to analyze your network application by application, you must have RMON-2.

RMON-3

In the works is a new standard of network monitoring called RMON-3. This new addition caters to the WAN. For example, a new MIB will be created that deals exclusively with frame relay characteristics such as errors like the Forward Explicit Congestion Notification (FECN) and Backward Explicit Congestion Notification (BECN).

Currently, WAN probes are proprietary and don't work with each other. One example is Enterprise RMON by NetScout Systems Inc. It's expected that much of Enterprise RMON will be submitted to the IETF and eventually will be adopted as the RMON-3 standard.

Tools

Collecting network traffic doesn't require any special hardware other than a computer and an NIC that operates in promiscuous mode (many standard cards do). You do need, however, special software for capturing data or communicating with SNMP or RMON agents. You often see network analysts carrying around special devices they use to troubleshoot the network. Underneath the rugged case lies a standard PC with a standard NIC—albeit more than one NIC typically.

For the sake of simplicity we are going to break these network monitoring devices into two groups: network analyzers and network probes. Naturally there is overlap with what these devices do. Your enterprise will probably use both because they serve specific needs common to all networks.

Network Analyzers

Network analyzers, or protocol analyzers as they are sometimes called, are used primarily for troubleshooting, although as you'll see, they can be quite handy for other purposes. They excel at recording information at the lowest layers in the OSI model, the physical and data link layers. They don't usually use the RMON standards for reporting, but they may contain SNMP support for remote management.

TROUBLESHOOTING   Analyzers are the devices that are often found in rugged cases, because they are often called in when there is a problem on a network, and then taken away when the problem is resolved. They are used to get a snapshot of the traffic occurring on the network at that moment. For example, you can use an analyzer to see instantly if there are a great number of frames on the network with errors caused by an errant NIC or computer. You can also look inside a frame and see its contents (although you will be disappointed by what you see most of the time).

Here is an example of when you would use an analyzer. Let's say you are called in to examine a network because users are complaining that it is very slow, and users are not doing anything unusual to cause an increase in traffic. You connect the analyzer to a LAN segment and instantly see that there is an enormous number of broadcast frames on that segment. You determine that they are Novell SAPs originating from Novell servers on the other side of the country. With a little investigative work, you find out that someone has turned off a filter on a router that was used to block the SAPs. Once the filter is activated again, the number of broadcasts goes down and users experience the throughput they once had.

OTHER USES   Because you cannot gather statistics about how network protocols are used on the network over a long period of time, you usually don't leave analyzers in place for very long. Nonetheless, there are other uses for analyzers than just troubleshooting.

Most analyzers can record network traffic and play it back to the network at a later time. This can be quite useful when you want to test how other systems react to a specific request and you want control over the request. Additionally, you can generate traffic to stress test your systems and determine at exactly what level of traffic they break down.

Because you can filter traffic based on host or destination addresses, analyzers can be used to capture a single traffic conversation between two machines. This point will be expounded on later when we analyze a new application prior to deployment.

THE MICROSOFT NETWORK MONITOR   As mentioned earlier, all you need to analyze the network traffic is a standard PC, a NIC, and some software. Fortunately NT comes with a network monitoring tool that can be installed from the Services tab in the Network configuration window. It is called the Network Monitor. There are two components that can be installed. The first is called the Network Monitor Agent. This is available with NT Workstation and Server. Once installed it allows a Microsoft Network Monitor Tool (running on NT Server) to monitor the traffic that the agent sees. The other component, Network Monitoring Tool, is only available on an NT Server. When both components are installed on an NT Server, it is called the Network Monitor Tools and Agent. The agent is also installed with the tool on NT Server so you can see traffic associated with that Server.

NOTE: The Network Monitor Tools and Agent that ships with NT Server only allows you to capture packets that are originating from or destined to the local machine. To capture packets headed for other machines, install the Network Monitor Tools and Agent included with the Systems Management Server (see Chapter 4).

The Microsoft Network Monitor is a powerful network analyzer. It can track information up to the network layer, perform filters on stations or protocols, and conduct packet analysis. To start the Network Monitor, click on Network Monitor in the Administrative Tools menu. You will be prompted to select an agent if your local agent is not running. To connect to an agent running on another system, click Capture, and then Networks from the menu. Then, select the name of the computer running the Monitoring Agent. Note that you will need to have administrative rights on both machines to do this.

Once the Network Monitor has connected to an active agent you will see the main Capture window. Click on the Capture button (looks like a play button) and watch the statistics start to accumulate, as shown in Figure 12-2.

This multiframe window contains a plethora of information on the utilization of the network. Packets are continuously sent to a buffer (user-defined) until the buffer fills up. Then the newly-arrived packets overwrite older packets. You can watch the statistics change over time or stop the capture to view individual packets.

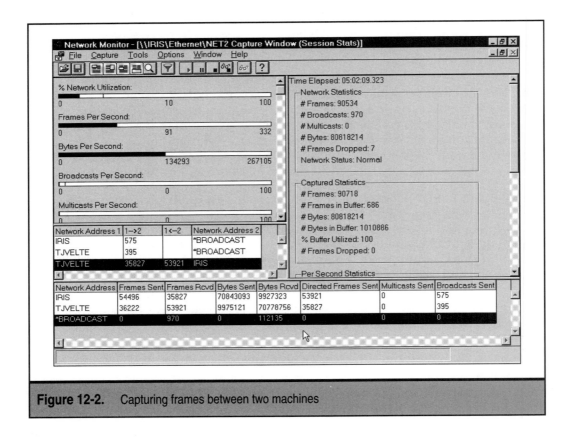

Figure 12-2. Capturing frames between two machines

From the Capture menu, click the Stop and View item. This will end the capture and bring up the packet analysis window, as shown in Figure 12-3. Double-clicking on a particular frame will open it and display its contents for you.

A tremendous amount of detail can be gleaned from the analysis of the Network Monitor at the general statistics level and at the individual packet level. It is well worth your time to investigate this application. Other third-party solutions are listed in Table 12-1.

Network Probes

Network probes very often can provide detailed network information much like an analyzer, but they typically don't provide single packet analysis. However, they can do much more when it comes to monitoring the general health of the network because they do not suffer from the myopia inherent to analyzers. They can analyze the network traffic at the network and application layers using RMON-2.

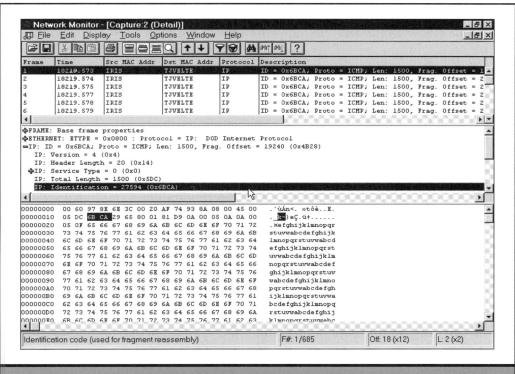

Figure 12-3.   Packet analysis using the Network Monitor

Company/ Product	Solution Type	LAN Protocols	WAN Protocols	Generate Traffic	Price ($US)	Contact
Cinco Networks/ NetXRay	Software	Ethernet, Token Ring, FDDI, LocalTalk	None	Yes	995	www. cinco. com

Table 12-1.   Third-Party Network Analyzers

Company/ Product	Solution Type	LAN Protocols	WAN Protocols	Generate Traffic	Price ($US)	Contact
Digitech Industries/ WAN900	Software and hardware	Ethernet, Token Ring, FDDI	RS-232, RS 449/442. V.35, T-1, FT-1, X-25, Frame Relay, ISDN, SMDS, ATM, DDS, E-1/FE-1, DS3	Yes	Starts at 5,000	www. digitechinc. com
LANQuest /Frame Thrower	Software and hardware	Ethernet, Token Ring	None	Yes	1,595 to 2,795	www. lanquest. com
Network General/ Distributed Sniffer System	Software and hardware	Arcnet, Ethernet, Token Ring, FDDI, LocalTalk	RS-232, RS 449/442. V.35, T-1, FT-1, X-25, Frame Relay, ISDN, SMDS, ATM	Yes	Starts at 11,500	www. ngc.com
RadCom/ RC-155-c ATM Traffic Generator/ Analyzer	Software and hardware	Ethernet, Token Ring, LLC, SNAP, Token Ring Mac	ATM	Yes	17,500	www. radcominc. com
Xyratex/ Gigabit Ethernet Protocol Analyzer	Software and hardware	Ethernet, Fibre Channel	None	Yes	Starts at 25,000	www. xyratex. com

Table 12-1.   Third-Party Network Analyzers (*continued*)

    Probes can be PCs with probe software installed on them, or they can be separate
hardware devices that are smaller than PCs and have no monitor or keyboard attached to
them. Either way, they sit quietly attached to the network gathering predefined data. All
administration is done remotely, via a serial port connected to the back of the probe or on
the probe console if there is one available. As you can imagine, probes usually have
relatively permanent homes compared to their worldly cousins—the analyzers.

THE PROBE HIERARCHY   Because they aren't moved around much, you'll need to have a fair number of probes deployed throughout your network if you want to keep an eye on the entire network. To ease the management problems associated with distributed monitoring devices, the probes usually are set up to report to a midlevel management station, which is simply a workstation with management software loaded on it.

The probes are smart so they are capable of gathering data, running statistical analysis on the data, and then sending only the important numbers back to the manager station. Typically you have a manager station for every 10 to 15 probes, depending on the volume of traffic the probes must crunch. A higher-order manager periodically queries the midlevel managers for probe information. It's this higher-order manager that must assimilate all the data and produce meaningful data sets and graphs in a timely fashion.

ADVANCED USES   Probes and their corresponding management software can be very powerful network management tools. Not only can you see the kind and volume of traffic that exists on any segment where you have a probe, you can also learn a great deal about different properties of the stations on that segment. For example, you can tell what percentage of traffic is going to the web (and where), and you can also tell which machines are turned on. This is accomplished through the management station, which knows about all the machines that the probes can see, and can then use SNMP to get information about its current status from each machine.

Probes offer an excellent way to determine which nodes are on your network and examine their physical and logical organization. This information can be fed into a modeling tool so you can run *what if?* simulations (see next section) on a realistic representation of your network.

PLACEMENT   In all likelihood you will not be able to place probes on every segment in your network due to budget constraints. Therefore you must determine the best possible locations for placing probes. Because you will not be able to see every aspect of the network, you should try to maximize traffic capture and minimize probe count. It can be helpful to view the network logically, especially with some traffic data (perhaps captured via SNMP or RMON) to determine these sites.

Basically, you want to place probes at sources or sinks of traffic. You might, for example, have an FDDI ring that has 20 servers attached to it. Naturally, this is an appropriate place for a probe because a lot of traffic is going to be traversing the FDDI ring.

NOTE: Probes usually cost much more for faster LAN protocols such as FDDI (versus Ethernet).

Although the probe market has been traditionally dominated by UNIX probes and UNIX management software, there are a large number of new offerings now ported to

NT. Table 12-2 lists probes that work with NT, including HP's newly ported OpenView product called the Network Node Manager.

Laboratory Network

If you don't have a test lab, you will want to put one together so you can:

▼ Reproduce problems in a controlled environment

■ Evaluate new products or versions of software before placing them into production

▲ Examine an application without the usual background traffic or with a controlled background load

To start, you should establish the lab's scope and objectives. For example, you may be asked to build a lab to address year 2000 problems, or to evaluate new applications for network demands before they are put into production. From your testing goals, you can create a list of hardware you'll need. For many questions you'll need each piece of hardware that is found in the production network and is related to the problem. For troubleshooting questions, it's a good idea to have on hand a previous version of the hardware/software, the current version, and the planned next version.

Environment

It is best to have a dedicated room for the lab. It offers heightened security and the psychological impression that the room is for testing and not day-to-day maintenance of

Company/Product	Solution	Price ($US)	Contact
Ascend/NetClarity	Software	9,900 for eight probes	www.ascend.com
Bay Networks/ StackProbe	Software and hardware	5,500 to 12,000	www.baynetworks.com
Compuware/ EcoScope	Software	3,000 to 12,000 per probe	www.compuware.com
HP/Network Node Manager for NT	Software	4,995 for 250 nodes	www.hp.com/openview
NetScoutSystems	Software and hardware	1,495 for software; probes 2,995 to 14,995	www.netscout.com

Table 12-2. Third-Party Probes for NT

the production network. How much space will you need? As a rough estimate, plan one square meter for each computer in a tiered or rack-mounted environment. If each system is on a desktop, plan for three square meters for each computer. Large routers and other oversized equipment take up about 1.5 square meters each. In addition, plan for 50 square meters of work and storage space for every 15 square meters taken up with equipment.

The test lab should be properly cooled and heated by a system designed to ensure minimal temperature fluctuations. If humidity is a problem, include a unit that can constantly maintain low humidity.

Another major concern is power. Naturally you have to abide by the local safety and electrical laws. Do what you can to ensure clean, stable power for your systems. Uninterruptible power supplies can do a lot to filter power and prevent the destructive effects of brownouts and blackouts (see Chapter 3). As a general rule, provide a separate 20-amp circuit for every dozen computers with monitors. Large routers, switches, and hubs can demand much more power so they should be on separate circuits.

Hardware

Based on the test questions you are interested in answering, you created a list of hardware you will need. Then you acquired the appropriate space including heating, cooling, power, and security. One other aspect of the design should be addressed before purchasing anything—cabling. Cable management should be an integral part of your design process. You can use colors, labels, and symbols to identify different components of the network. Of course, you must document your strategy and make sure lab users are aware of the meaning of the colors and symbols. It goes without saying that you should keep the cables tied down so the lab is neat and uncluttered. You can use clips or re-adjustable tie-downs if you need to change connections often—as is the case in a testing setting.

LAN EMULATION   Figure 12-4 illustrates a lab configuration to test a new client/server application for use on the LAN. A router separates two network segments. On one segment resides the server running the test application, an analyzer/traffic generator, and a client workstation. The other segment has an analyzer/traffic generator and another client workstation. In this configuration you can test the application's performance on the segment local to the server, and then test performance across a router.

You can use the analyzers/traffic generators to measure the latency and processing time of the server and workstations (see next section for details). You can also use them to generate traffic and test the client/server application under heavy loads. This configuration is easy to manipulate; you can easily alter it to meet your current testing requirements.

WAN EMULATION   Figure 12-5 illustrates a relatively simple layout to test applications over WAN links. Also, this is a good setup for examining problems related to routers

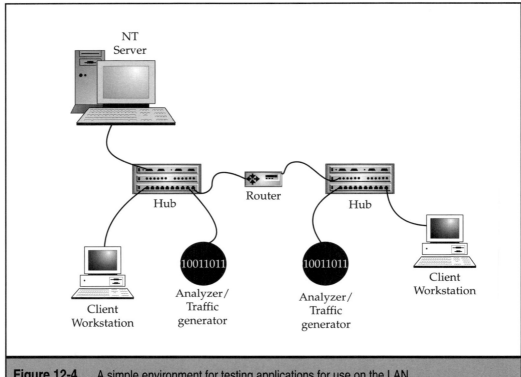

Figure 12-4. A simple environment for testing applications for use on the LAN

allowing access or sharing routing tables, for example. You can use real WAN links such as Frame Relay or purchase WAN emulators that allow you to dial in the speed of the emulated WAN link. WAN emulators allow you much more flexibility in testing different speeds for the WAN links.

With this configuration, you can test applications as they pass through one or two WAN links, or you can test them via the LAN link. Simply by shutting down Router #2, traffic flowing from segment B to segment C must pass through two WAN links. If Router #2 is on, this same traffic pattern will pass through WAN #1 and Router #2 if the routers are configured correctly to get to segment C. To test traffic passing through no WAN links, you set up traffic to flow from segment A to segment C.

As you can see, this design is extremely flexible especially because each segment has its own hub; therefore you can attach many devices temporarily without having to rearrange the network design or change the router configurations. You can use the analyzers/traffic generators to monitor the application or create loads on each segment. Once you decide which segments are going to communicate with each other for the test, you can move the probes around to monitor those two segments. This way you don't need a probe for every segment in the lab.

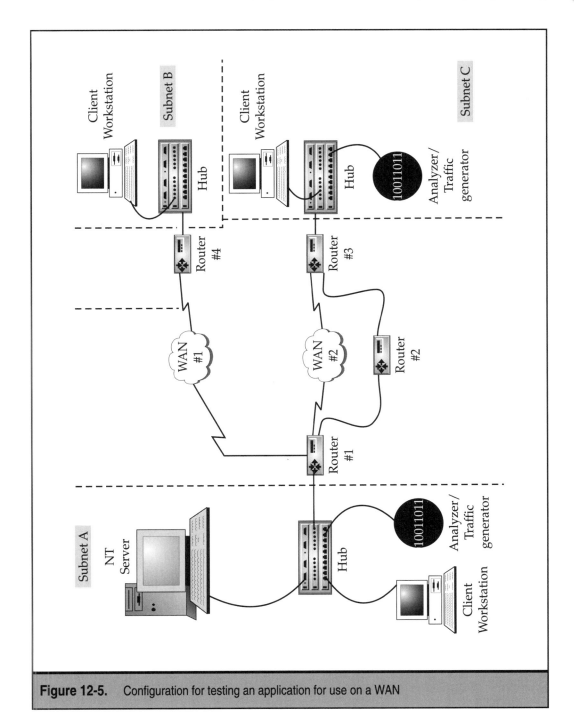

Figure 12-5. Configuration for testing an application for use on a WAN

Testing Applications

Whether you are troubleshooting a slow application on the production network or analyzing a new application before deployment, the basic technique is the same. For our purposes, we will assume you are assessing an application before deployment on the production network so we can conduct our tests in a lab setting. We will also assume that the application has passed functionality and regression testing. This means that the application does what it has been promised to do and doesn't introduce any new bugs in the process. You now need to conduct throughput testing and acceptance testing to ensure user satisfaction on the network.

Network Setup

For this exercise we will use a simple test network, as illustrated in Figure 12-6. The cloud shape represents a WAN link, a router connection, or perhaps other devices that emulate the production network. If you are testing on your production network, just replace the cloud with all devices in your network between the client and server computers. At one end of the test network is an NT Server, and at the other end is a client workstation. You'll also notice that there are network analyzers on each network segment. They will be used to monitor the conversation and record precisely when packets leave and arrive at the two computers.

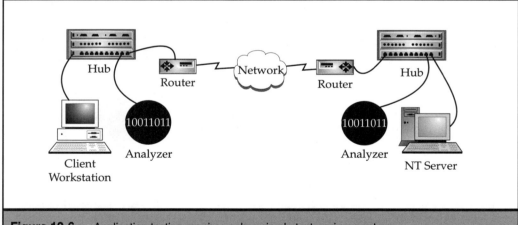

Figure 12-6. Application testing requires only a simple test environment

Running the Test

Here is how to run the test:

1. Configure the analyzers to only capture packets from the client and server computers.

2. At the same time, enable the analyzers to start capturing packets.

3. Use the client to request information from the server.

4. Stop capturing when the conversation is complete.

5. Repeat these steps for each different kind of request (that is, requesting a record, depositing a record, changing a record, and so on).

When you are finished, you will have a collection of analyzer trace files that holds the packets for each type of transaction. It is essential that you keep track of which files belong to what transaction and which analyzer. You will examine each trace file to determine the number of packets travelling in each direction, the number of bytes in each direction, and delays at each computer and on the network. All you need for this is a simple spreadsheet and some patience. Table 12-3 illustrates a spreadsheet with ten conversations. The start and stop times, the application name, its protocol, the host and destination address, and packets and byte count for traffic on both directions is listed.

Start Time	Stop Time	Application	Protocol	Host A	Host B	#Pkts (A->B)	#Bytes (A->B)	#Pkts (B->A)	#Bytes (B->A)
"11/20/ 1997 13:30:54"	11/20/ 1997 14:00:53"	"cc:Mail"	"IPX"	"Novell_ Client1"	"Novell_ Server34"	922	79,377	922	108,908
"11/20/ 1997 13:31:24"	"11/20/ 1997 14:00:33"	"WWW (Web)"	"IP"	"[132.207. 129.164]"	"[132.157. 182.24]"	95	38,130	70	7,245
"11/20/ 1997 13:32:50"	"11/20/ 1997 14:01:22"	"Novell Print Services"	"IPX"	"Novell_ Server41"	"Novell_ Server34"	88	6,394	88	24,417
"11/20/ 1997 13:30:11"	"11/20/ 1997 14:00:04"	"Telnet"	"IP"	"[132.189. 30.4]"	"[132.15. 244.152]"	29	9,354	44	4,562

Table 12-3. A Sample Spreadsheet Showing 10 Conversations

Start Time	Stop Time	Application	Protocol	Host A	Host B	#Pkts (A->B)	#Bytes (A->B)	#Pkts (B->A)	#Bytes (B->A)
"11/20/ 1997 13:32:26"	"11/20/ 1997 14:00:32"	"Oracle"	"IP"	"[132.143. 57.83]"	"[132.40. 215.61]"	675	337,690	831	54,314
"11/20/ 1997 13:30:14"	"11/20/ 1997 14:02:03"	"FTP"	"IP"	"[132.143. 53.83]"	"[132.40. 215.61]"	0	0	7	403
"11/20/ 1997 13:31:42"	"11/20/ 1997 14:01:19"	"Telnet"	"IP"	"[132.129. 30.4]"	"[132.111. 244.152]"	29	9,354	44	4,562
"11/20/ 1997 13:32:38"	"11/20/ 1997 14:00:07"	"FTP"	"IP"	"[132.193. 57.83]"	"[132.80. 215.61]"	675	337,690	831	54,314
"11/20/ 1997 13:31:53"	"11/20/ 1997 14:01:13"	"cc:Mail"	"IPX"	"Novell_ Client3"	"Novell_ Print- Server2"	6,387	490,376	6,383	395,974
"11/20/ 1997 13:30:41"	"11/20/ 1997 14:00:43"	"cc:Mail"	"IPX"	"Novell_ Client39"	"Novell_ Client21"	2	169	2	130

Table 12-3. A Sample Spreadsheet Showing 10 Conversations (*continued*)

Analyzing the Results

Now we will introduce a number of variables that will help us keep track of the different numbers:

▼ **Pkt**—The size of the packet (bits, b)
■ **BW**—The bandwidth of the network connection (b/sec)
■ **RT**—The round trip network delay (seconds, sec)
■ P_c—The processing time of the client (sec)
▲ P_s—The processing time of the server (sec)

Figure 12-7 illustrates (schematically) a typical traffic flow for a single conversation. The client initiates the conversation by requesting information. It sends a request packet to the server, which arrives, after some network delay, at the server. The server does some internal processing for a length of time (P_s) and sends out a reply to the client. It arrives at the client after a network delay. The client performs a processing task for a given length of time (P_c) and the process begins again. If we add the two network delays together you get the total round trip delay (RT). These numbers are useful in describing the properties of the application.

You can measure all of these delays because the analyzers record and time-stamp each packet as it moves by. Note that you would only be able to calculate the one-way network delay times if the two analyzers were time-synchronized with each other. Here is the problem: If the first analyzer is some unknown seconds ahead of the second analyzer, you cannot determine exactly the length of the one-way network delay. This is because there are two unknowns: the offset time and the network delay.

You can determine the round trip delay of the network by the following method. First record the *total* round trip delay from the client analyzer. It records when the request packet went out and how long it took until the reply was seen coming back. Then subtract the processing time of the server from the total round trip delay to determine the round-trip *network* delay. To calculate the server processing time just record when the request was seen at the server (from the server analyzer) and subtract that value from the time the reply was seen leaving the server.

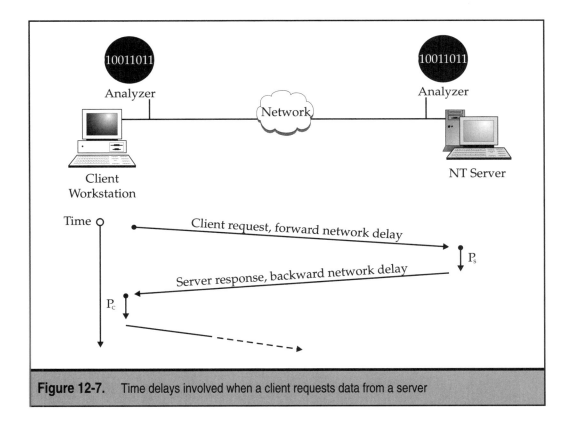

Figure 12-7.   Time delays involved when a client requests data from a server

Now what do all these number mean? How can you use them? First of all, we should better define the processing times of the client and server, P_c and P_s. Because we are measuring the processing time based on when packets enter and leave the computers, the measured processing time also includes the time it takes for the computer to put and read the packet on the wire. This is 2×Pkt/BW. It is multiplied by two because each packet experiences this delay when it is sent and received. To get the correct client and server processing times, we must subtract these delays as follows:

▼ $P_c = P_{c(measured)} - (2 \times Pkt / BW_c)$

▲ $P_s = P_{s(measured)} - (2 \times Pkt / BW_s)$

It is useful to define another variable called the *application rate (AppRate)*. It describes the rate at which the application is running in bits per second and is defined as:

$$AppRate = \frac{Pkt}{RT + P_c + \dfrac{2Pkt}{BW_c} + P_s + \dfrac{2Pkt}{BW_s}}$$

This equation is used for a single request and reply, although a typical conversation consists of many more packet transfers. Nonetheless, a single packet exchange is indicative of the conversation as a whole. Obviously, one of the goals in designing an application and the network it runs on is to minimize the AppRate. To do this, it seems natural to make the numerator large and the denominator as small as possible. This is true, but the packet size is found in both locations. Here are a couple of general rules to help increase the AppRate:

▼ For the Application Designer:

■ Decrease the client and server processing time, P_c, P_s

■ Reduce the number of packets used

■ Make the packet larger (Pkt) instead of having many small packets

▼ For the Network Designer:

■ Increase the bandwidth (BW) to reduce the time it takes to place and read data from the wire

■ Reduce the network delays (RT) as much as possible

Conducting application analysis as outlined here helps pinpoint where in the AppRate equation major delays are introduced. Very often the delay is found on the network (RT), and this variable is very complicated. Further analysis must be taken to discover where the bottleneck lies in the network. In any event, at this point you would have eliminated the application, the client computer, the server computer, and their immediate network connections as the source of delays.

SIMULATING YOUR NETWORK

Simulation is the process by which you create a software model of your network and subject it to different designs or traffic loads to see how well it functions. As networks grow, the devices and connections that comprise them make understanding them as a whole untenable. It becomes impossible to predict with any accuracy how one traffic demand will affect another part of the network. There are simply too many devices, too many routes, and too many traffic conversations going on simultaneously.

The solution is to construct a model of your network piecemeal. All models operate under the axiom "garbage in, garbage out". To build a model of your network that considers every aspect of the network and the traffic it carries is to build your network again. A model must include certain simplifications and assumptions. The trick is knowing what aspects can be simplified without compromising the model. This section outlines the simulation process and helps you understand where to make those simplifications.

Preparing to Simulate

In the preceding application analysis you accurately determined the network requirements of an application so the users experience minimal delay. However, this was conducted in a test environment without all the nuances of the real production network. You need to know how the application will behave as the application data traverses the production network, which may consist of many routers, switches, WAN links, and certainly other applications competing for the available bandwidth.

The next thing you need to do is test the application in a simulation to predict its behavior on the production network. But before you can run a single simulation, you must create a representation of the production network.

Topology

The topology of the network refers to both the physical devices that comprise the network and the logical settings. Consider this the framework for your model. Later you are going to lay traffic conversations onto this framework.

Some physical devices that must be included in the representation of the network are:

- ▼ Routers
- ■ Computers
- ■ Switches
- ■ WAN links
- ■ LANs
- ▲ Point-to-point connections

Some logical parameters that must be considered are:

▼ Interface settings on routers

■ LAN speeds

■ WAN speeds

■ Router capabilities (such as backplane speed)

■ Routing protocols

▲ Naming conventions

Fortunately, there are programs that can discover the physical and logical settings on your network. Most of these programs use SNMP to query the devices. Sometimes you need to provide a list of routers and their corresponding IP addresses. Other programs need only the address of a seed router. The discovery program learns what it can from the router's MIB ands then asks the router who its neighbors are. From there it steps through the entire network, learning about routers, interfaces, and devices on each network segment.

Many times, simulation programs do not include a discovery tool; they import the topology from other network monitoring tools as described previously. In any event, you have just realized the first benefit of simulation—network documentation. Building the topology of your network has the added benefit of creating an inventory of the most important devices on the network and their settings.

Traffic

The "blood" of any network is the ephemeral traffic that courses over links and through routers to its final destination. That is why it is absolutely essential to emulate the traffic in as much detail as is computationally possible. There are two basic levels on which to model the traffic: the byte baseline and the application profiles.

BYTE BASELINE   Baselining is the process by which you record the amount of traffic that is on the network over a period of time. This information can be obtained from RMON devices because it is not concerned with network or application layer details. All you need to know is how many bytes have passed per second over your links or through your devices. This level of reporting provides you with percent utilization for your links, and this information can be quite useful in its own right.

Because you only receive information about bytes and not about network protocols or applications, you cannot discern one program's traffic from another. Therefore, byte baselining has limited value for simulations, because you are interested in how individual applications behave on the network.

APPLICATION PROFILES   An alternative to baselining is to use probes that are capable of detecting information from passing packets about the network protocol and application that generated the packets. These probes usually use RMON-2 or their own proprietary methods to gather this information. Although the probes are quite good at picking out what network protocol a packet is using (for example, IP, IPX, or DECnet), they need to be configured manually to identify many of your applications (for example, Word, telnet, or CAD). However, once this is complete, you can identify every traffic conversation on the network. Here is some of the data that can be extracted:

▼ Network protocol

■ Application name

■ Source computer

■ Destination computer

■ Number of packets in each direction

■ Number of bytes in each direction

■ Latency for application

▲ Duration of conversation

Looking at your traffic at this level is very useful. You can check latency for applications to see if they are meeting a minimum quality of service. You can see how much throughput is being used by which applications. Because you know the source and destination of every traffic flow, you can tell where your web traffic is going, which users are using which resources, and so on. You may simply want to analyze this information for its utility, but we are going to use it here to complete our description of the model network.

Data Reduction—Meaning from Mayhem

As you can imagine, if you have multiple probes capturing conversations on your network, you will get thousands of conversations per minute. This amount of traffic will bog down even the largest machines running simulations. The best way to deal with the large number of conversations is to remove or consolidate them.

REMOVE DUPLICATE CONVERSATIONS   The first method to reduce the number of conversations is to eliminate duplicate conversations. Because you have multiple probes located on the network, there is a possibility that two probes will capture and record the same conversation. When you collect the conversations from all the probes, some conversations will be represented twice if you don't consolidate the same traffic conversations.

Typically, the workstations that act as probe managers perform this consolidation for you so you are not erroneously counting traffic twice. If they don't, you'll have to create a utility that looks at each conversation that has identical attributes and deletes one of them.

REDUCE CONVERSATIONS   There are two parts to reducing the number of valid (not duplicate) conversations. The first part eliminates conversations that are too small to have a significant impact on the network traffic. For example, you may find that about 40 percent of your conversations make up less than one percent of the total traffic. This is because these conversations have very few packets and very few bytes. But because they are still a conversation, they register in the simulation and can use up precious resources there.

The second aspect uses consolidation to reduce the number of overall conversations. In other words, conversations that have the same source, destination, and application can be lumped into a single conversation. All packets and bytes are added so no traffic load is lost. Typically, you also have a time criterion, so you only consolidate conversations that are close to each other in time. Eliminating small conversations and consolidating the remaining conversations can reduce your number of conversations by 40 to 70 percent.

Simulators

Now you have a topological map of the network and a collection of application conversations that use this framework. The next step is to run simulations. Simulators are software packages that have typically run on powerful UNIX workstations in the past. They usually cost $40,000 to $100,000 each and require training to use. Because of the cost and complexity of simulation tools, many companies contract with a firm that specializes in this type of work. The firm may provide the tools used in gathering the data and running the simulations.

Simulators usually use an analytical or a discrete approach to modeling the traffic. The analytical approach is usually much faster because it makes more assumptions about the traffic before running a simulation. Discrete-event simulation analyzes each packet to determine its behavior. It can be argued that the analytical method is just as accurate as the discrete event method. Because of the long simulation time involved in using the discrete event method, it is recommended to use a simulation tool that employs the analytical method for larger networks (more than 50 routers).

NOTE: Modeling can be very deceptive if you do not fully understand the variables that go into a prediction. The simple "garbage in, garbage out" rule applies especially to simulations.

Before running a simulation, you should, of course, have a specific question in mind. Some of the questions you could ask fall under two major categories: change analysis and fault tolerance. Here are some "what if?" questions you could ask for each category:

▼   Change Analysis:

■   Change or add WAN links or LANs

■   Change or add routers

■   Change routing protocols

■   Move servers

■   Move users

■   Add or remove an application demand

For fault tolerance you will ask how failure of specific devices or groups of devices will negatively affect application demands.

▼ Fault Tolerance:

■ Fail network devices

■ Fail LANs

■ Fail WAN links

■ Fail facility

■ Fail city

Answering these questions will help you in areas such as capacity planning, rollout validation, disaster recovery, and lifecycle management. You can obviously have a lot of fun with simulators, so let's jump in and look at two simulators we can use to create our own "what if?" scenarios.

COMNET Predictor

COMNET Predictor is an analytical modeling tool from CACI (**www.caciasl.com**). CACI also sells a discrete-event modeling tool called COMNET III. COMNET Predictor runs on NT and is intuitive and quite easy to install. We will go through a simple simulation here on a lab network we built from scratch. Alternatively you can import your topology from third-party sources such as:

▼ HP OpenView

■ Cabletron SPECTRUM

■ IBM Netview for AIX

■ Digital POLYCENTER

■ Castlerock SNMPc

■ CACI SIMPROCESS

▲ NAC MIND

In our example, we added traffic demands by hand because the network was simple. In real life, you'll need to capture them with probes and import them into COMNET Predictor using one of the following sources:

▼ Network General Expert Sniffer

■ Network General Distributed Sniffer System

■ Axon Network LAN Servant

■ Frontier Software NETscout

■ HP Netmetrix

- ■ Wandel & Golterman Domino Analyzer
- ▲ Compuware EcoScope

Figure 12-8 illustrates our hand-made test network in a logical view. There are two LAN segments separated by a WAN link. There is an NT Server and Workstation on each LAN. You can see the network building tools on the left side of the screen. Creating a network is as simple as clicking on the network item (such as LAN or Server) and dropping it into the main window. You connect devices with links and later define their characteristic by choosing from a predefined list (such as T-1 or ISDN connection) or customizing your own specifications.

You can see we have two different models of Cisco routers in our test network. The simulation tool is familiar with the capabilities of the routers and will include them in the simulation.

In Figure 12-9, you can see five traffic demands that were placed manually. They indicate the origin, destination, application, protocol, and rate for each. You can pick applications from a predefined list or create your own as we did here for cc:Mail. In a simulation of the production network, there may be thousands of conversations listed in this window. Of course, you would import them from probes.

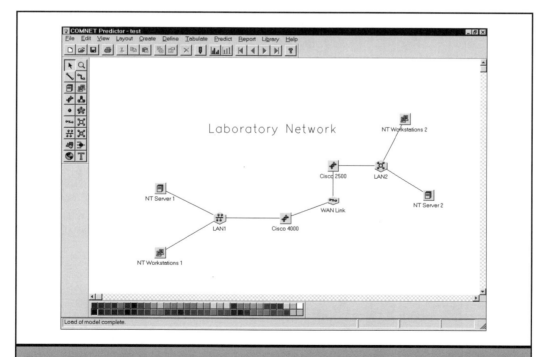

Figure 12-8. COMNET Predictor's main window shows a logical view of our network

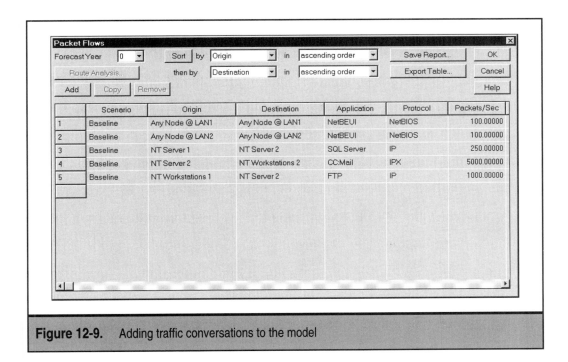

Figure 12-9.   Adding traffic conversations to the model

Finally we are ready to run a simulation. We simply click on the Run Simulation icon (stoplight) and the simulation is under way. Because this is a simple network with few demands, the simulation is over in a fraction of a second.

Numerous reports can be generated that look at utilization, forecasting, and network failures. Figure 12-10 is a report showing the percent utilization for each device or LAN in the network. We told Predictor that we expect a 10 percent growth in traffic each year. Predictor calculated the use of each device or LAN and projected its use for the next two years. From this report, we can see that we might want to keep an eye on our WAN link. You could easily change the throughput of the WAN link and run another simulation.

NetMaker XA

NetMaker XA is a UNIX-based modeling tool from Make Systems **(www.make systems.com).** It is IP-centric and focused on modeling WAN links. It models application conversations from LAN to LAN. It can model protocols other than IP, although you may have to make a table mapping the non-IP protocol machines to their IP addresses (IPX servers to their IP subnetwork, for example).

NetMaker has its own built-in discovery tool that gathers from the routers information about their interfaces and connections to other routers, WANs, and LANs. You can display the discovered network in a number of different views. Figure 12-11 illustrates a sample network displayed in a geographic view. There is an icon for each

Network Resource Analysis				✕

Resource type [Nodes and Links ▼]   Perf. measure [Util % ▼]   [Help]   [Cancel]

☐ Bottlenecks   ☐ Max 1-way if full-duplex   [Save Report...]

☐ Warnings and alarms   Rank method [descending order ▼]   [Export Table...]

in the rank year   Rank year [2 ▼]   Top N [5]   [Top N Chart...]

	Nodes and Links	Year 0 Util %	Year 1 Util %	Year 2 Util %
1	WAN Link	32.55	35.81	39.39
2	LAN2	31.75	34.92	38.42
3	Cisco 2500	15.63	17.19	18.91
4	LAN1	12.74	14.02	15.42
5	Cisco 4000	8.33	9.17	10.08
6	NT Server 2	0.63	0.69	0.76
7	NT Server 1	0.03	0.03	0.03
8	NT Workstations 1	0.00	0.00	0.00
9	NT Workstations 2	0.00	0.00	0.00

Figure 12-10.   A COMNET Predictor report giving percent utilization for each network device or LAN

router. The WAN links are drawn in color to signify their throughput. You can zoom in or out to any level of detail you want.

You can also display the network logically as shown in Figure 12-12. This is called a *link-based layout*; it places routers with the most WAN links emanating from them at the center of the diagram. All routers and LANs are displayed here with their labels on them for identification. This diagram is quite useful in determining the optimal placement for probes.

In this example test network there are already a number of conversations mapped to the network devices, so we don't need to import them or create them from scratch. Normally you can import traffic conversations using one of the many popular third-party probes.

For our simulation, we elected to fail the WAN links one at a time so we could see which application demands would fail. In Figure 12-13, the WAN Link option is selected and the start and finish times of the simulation are set.

Clicking the Go button starts the simulation, failing one WAN link at a time and determining which application conversations would fail. The results are shown in Figure 12-14.

For each WAN link (*r-at01, r-ny01* for example), the failed demands are listed on the right. For the first four WAN links that were brought down, no applications were left unsupported. This is due to the fact that either no demands were using that link or there was an alternate or redundant route for the demand to take. On the other hand, bringing

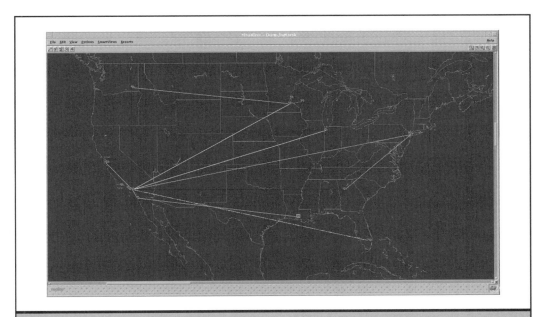

Figure 12-11.   NetMaker XA can display your network based on where the sites are located geographically

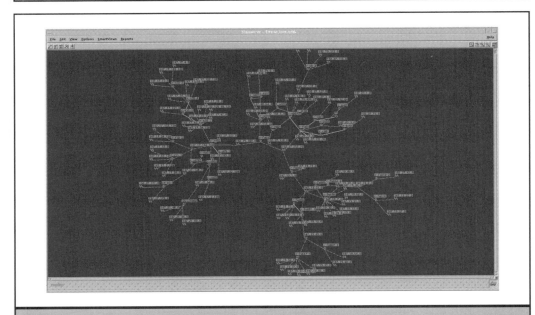

Figure 12-12.   A logical representation of our test network

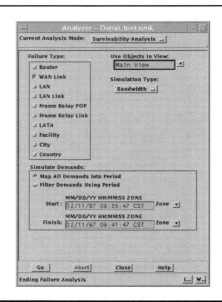

Figure 12-13. Setting up a simulation to fail WAN links

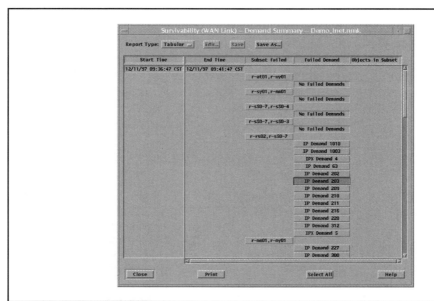

Figure 12-14. The results of failing WAN links

down the link *r-rs02, r-s50-7* resulted in 13 failed conversations. From this simulation, you may want to add a redundant route for these demands.

Lifecycle Management

Conducting simulations is a very important part of lifecycle management for your network. Simulations should be carried out often, as there are usually many changes to the ever evolving topological and traffic makeup of the network. Figure 12-15 illustrates how the different stages of simulations fit into lifecycle management and lists their benefits.

Creating a topological map of your network allows you to take inventory of all the devices that can be discovered using SNMP. By conducting traffic analysis you learn about the utilization on the LAN and WAN links as well as network devices. You can also see how long users have to wait for applications to respond, which may be part of a quality of service contract. Running the simulation allows you to answer many "what if?" questions to help validate the rollout of a new application or hardware. It also helps you plan your capacity for future growth and determine your plan in case of network failures.

A simulation is neither the starting point nor the end point for your network design questions. If anything, you'll learn that running simulations incites your curiosity and generates more questions than it answers. Along the way you will certainly appreciate the complexity of the network and gain more of an intuitive sense of how all the components work together.

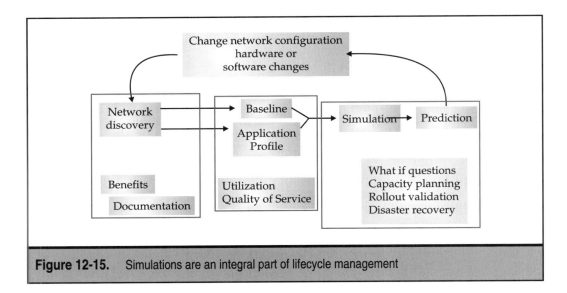

Figure 12-15.   Simulations are an integral part of lifecycle management

CHAPTER 13

Planning for NT 5.0

Not since NT was first introduced has there been such a radical change to Microsoft networking. Up to NT version 4.0, Microsoft has been padding the features in all its operating systems to make them more functional in larger networks. They have had to create services such as WINS or integrate services such as DNS and DHCP to accommodate larger networks. Finally in NT 5.0, Microsoft has made substantial changes to the underlying structure of NT networks.

NT 5.0 introduces a whole domain structure along with new user administration and file-sharing capabilities, just to name a few of the enhancements. Obviously, we cannot cover all the new features in NT 5.0 here. We are going to focus only on the organizational aspects of converting your NT 4.0 network to an NT 5.0 enterprise. We'll start by highlighting the differences in the installation of NT 5.0 compared to NT 4.0, and then discuss some of the key technologies that are introduced in NT 5.0. Next you'll see how to start planning your new domain tree. Finally, we'll finish the chapter by creating a simple two-domain network using NT 5.0.

NOTE: Currently, NT 5.0 is in the beta stage. We do not encourage use of beta software in your production environment. However, it is not too early to start planning your NT 5.0 migration. If possible, you should first run a practice migration to NT 5.0 in a laboratory environment.

UPGRADING SYSTEMS

The installation/upgrade path from Windows operating systems to NT 5.0 is nearly the same as it was for NT 4.0. However, there are a few notable exceptions, including the capability to upgrade Windows 95 directly to NT 5.0. This will allow Windows 9x machines, for the first time, to upgrade to NT without having to go through a new installation. Nearly all user configurations and preinstalled applications will be available within NT 5.0 after the upgrade.

You start the installation process with the *winnt.exe* (from a DOS prompt), or *winnt32.exe* executables from within any version of Windows (see Chapter 2 for more information about installing NT). Some of the command-line switches have changed, so you should type **winnt /?** at the command prompt for more information.

System Requirements

A new minimum level of required hardware comes with the new version of NT. Table 13-1 lists the new system requirements for NT 5.0 Workstation and Server running on Intel machines. These, of course, are the minimum requirements recommend by Microsoft. Personal experience suggests that you should augment the RAM significantly above these minimum requirements. Otherwise you will likely observe excessive memory-to-disk paging, which will make your machine run sluggishly. NT 5.0 Workstation supports two processors natively, and NT Server supports up to four processors.

	NT 5.0 Workstation	NT 5.0 Server
CPU	486/66 MHz	Pentium 133
Hard Drive Space	274 MB	286 MB
RAM	24 MB	32 MB

Table 13-1.   Recommended Minimum Requirements for NT 5.0

File Systems

As with previous version of NT, you have a choice of several different file systems. During installation, you can chose the FAT and NTFS systems, or the new FAT32 and NTFS version 5.0 formats. Use the following guide to help you choose your file system:

▼ **FAT**—If you need to support Windows 3.x, DOS or Windows 9x on the drive, you must use the FAT system. If you format a drive that is 2GB or larger using the FAT system, it will be formatted as the FAT32 system.

■ **FAT32**—If you have Windows 9x and don't need to support Windows 3.x or DOS (or older versions of NT) on that drive, choose the FAT32 file system.

▲ **NTFS**—If you choose to format the drive as NTFS, NTFS version 5.0 will be used. NTFS 5.0 is not currently supported by NT 4.0, but it is expected that a future service pack will allow NT 4.0 to see NTFS 5.0 drives. You can see all versions of NTFS with NT 5.0, however.

NTFS 5.0 offers several features in addition to those of the standard NTFS that ships with NT 4.0:

▼ File encryption on the disk

■ Capability to add disks to volumes without rebooting

■ User disk quotas that allows you to restrict space for users

■ Distributed link tracking points to the new location when you move a file

▲ Fully compatible with Distributed File System (Dfs)

Dual-boot Installations

If you have Windows NT, Windows 3.x, or Windows 95 installed on your computer, you have the option of upgrading the existing operating system or installing a new copy of

NT 5.0 alongside it. If you choose to install a new copy of NT, you will have at least two operating systems on your machine you can boot into upon startup. This is called a dual-boot system.

NOTE: You cannot upgrade from Windows 98 to NT 5.0 beta 1 unless you use the command-line switch **/#u:Win98**. *This bypasses the block that prevents upgrading Windows 98.*

To have DOS or Windows 9x as an alternate operating system, you must have at least one partition formatted in the FAT type. These operating systems should be installed prior to the NT installation. It is highly recommended that you place NT on its own partition. Although the operating system resides in its own directory, if you install multiple copies of NT on the same partition, NT will write to the same Program Files directory that is used by the other Windows 9x or NT operating systems. NT may write over some files there or change the permissions on some important files, which might prevent booting into an alternate operating system.

New Workstation Options

During the installation of NT 5.0 Workstation, you will be given the option of selecting what role the workstation will play. The four modes of setup are Typical, Portable, Compact, and Custom.

▼ **Typical**—This mode asks the least amount of questions and automates most of the installation, discovery, and configuration of your devices and other components. This is the recommended mode for standard setups.

■ **Portable**—New to NT are options for portable computers. Now there is support for options specific to laptops, such as power-saving modes and hot-swappable PCMCIA cards. You should check the Hardware Compatibility List (HCL) to see if the laptop's power-saving mode is supported.

■ **Compact**—This mode is for a typical installation with no optional components installed. Use this mode when disk space is a concern.

▲ **Custom**—This option is for advanced users who want maximum control over the installation process.

Two Server Types

In NT 4.0 there were three choices for server types: primary domain controller (PDC), backup domain controller (BDC), and stand-alone server. Because the concept of the BDC goes away with NT 5.0, the two choices you have with NT 5.0 are domain controller (DC) or stand-alone server.

A DC is an NT Server that participates in the domain by keeping a copy of the account database and sharing it with other DCs. Unlike previous versions of NT, you can promote a stand-alone server to a DC without reinstalling NT. To promote a system to a DC, you use the Domain Controller Promotion wizard (*dcpromo.exe*). Later in the chapter, we'll use this tool to promote a couple of ordinary servers to DCs.

DOMAIN ORGANIZATION

Although there are many changes and enhancements to NT 5.0, the organizational changes to the domain models will have the largest impact on the NT enterprise network. The previously-defined domain models (see Chapter 2) become, in many ways, obsolete. The concept of a PDC and a BDC gives way to a single type of NT Server that holds the user account database (domain controller).

The changes to the domain organization will allow NT to be more scalable because it can handle more objects in a network more efficiently than previous versions of NT. This should also allow easier management and reduce the total cost of ownership. Microsoft has addressed the limitations of NT in the enterprise in version 5.0. At the core of these changes is the new Active Directory that is incorporated into NT 5.0.

Active Directory

Active Directory (AD) is a directory of objects in a domain or a collection of domains. AD keeps track of objects (users, directories, printers, computers, and so on) in a data model that is based on the popular X.500 data model. It is hierarchical in nature and quite unlike flat-file directories such as the Registry. For example, instead of keeping the Security Account Manager (SAM) database in the Registry (flat file), this information is contained within the AD. This enables up to about 10 million entries as opposed to the roughly 40,000 maximum users you can fit into the Registry-based SAM.

Active Directory is both the service that provides the information contained in the database and the database itself. If a user wants to know a particular property or attribute of an object, for example, the full name of a user, they need to know some information about the user (such as the user's logon name) and use that to query the AD database. The client would probably use the Lightweight Directory Access Protocol (LDAP version 2 or 3 is supported) to communicate with the AD server, and the server would subsequently look up or determine the result and send this back to the requesting client. If the client doesn't know the exact name of the user, they can specify what they do know, and the AD will return all matches. Because the hierarchy of the AD is the same as that of the organization of the enterprise, searches are intuitive.

NOTE: Presumably, Windows 9x clients will be able to take advantage of Active Directory by upgrading through a service pack. NT clients will need to upgrade to NT 5.0 to take advantage of all features present in the AD.

Schema

An important part of the AD is the *schema,* which is the objects and their attributes within the AD. The schema defines the containers that will be present in the AD and where in the tree they can be found. No two ADs need the same set of containers, so the schema is very specific to each AD. However, if you have several domains that are in the same enterprise, it is important that they share the same schema; otherwise they will not be able to understand the entries in other Active Directories.

When a user or application does not find an object that fits its needs, it can extend the schema, provided it has sufficient privileges. If you need to add a new object, you must have administrative rights and give the object at least one attribute. You can add attributes to existing objects, but you must define them. For example, if you add a text field attribute to an object, you must define the maximum size of the field.

To reduce the amount of time the AD must search through objects to find a match, you can add indexes for an object. An index is a presorted list of the different members of an object based on a particular attribute. If you had a user object, you might want to create an index based on the last-name attribute because this attribute is most often used for searches and can be unique among different users.

Global Catalog

An enterprise may consist of many domains organized in a hierarchical fashion that is reflected in the structure of the Active Directory. This enterprise may span continents and be separated at times by small-throughput links. AD allows you to start a search of the directory at the root and proceed down through all the domains until the search finds a match. This is helpful when you don't know the exact location of an object but do know some of its attributes.

Searching from the root of the AD tree is inefficient and sometimes impractical for some users. To alleviate this burden on the root, you can configure some NT Servers to contain a *global catalog* (GC). The GC contains a partial replica of the Active Directory. It follows the schema but does not hold all the attributes for an object. It might, for example, hold only the user's last name, e-mail address, and phone number for the user object. These attributes are presumably the ones used most frequently in searches. This allows you to examine a local source that will, in most cases, give you the location of the object you are looking for.

You can configure servers to act as GC servers via the Site Replication Manager. This is an MMC tool found in the Start | Programs | Administrative Tools | Sites Topology menu. From here you select the site, and then right-click on the NT Server you want to hold the GC. Under Properties, select Global Catalog Server and click on OK.

The global catalog is generated automatically as part of the Active Directory replication process (see "Replication," later in this chapter). Placement of GCs should be done thoughtfully. Updated records are copied to them, which will generate additional network traffic between servers. Having to query a GC across the WAN creates network traffic and can waste precious WAN resources. A balance needs to be struck between having a local GC or using a GC in a remote location. As a general rule, there should be one GC at each site unless the site is very small and the replication traffic is greater than the query traffic to the next closest GC.

Sites

A *site* in Active Directory parlance is a part of the enterprise network that is comprised of one or more subnets (that is, an independent network segment comprised of a set of IP addresses in TCP/IP networks). These subnets must be connected to each other with 10 Mb/sec throughput or better to belong to the same site. A domain has the same meaning as it does for previous-version NT networks. A site, therefore, may contain only part of a domain or more than one domain. Typically, a site is a geographic location, either a building or a cluster of buildings. If multiple buildings are connected via a high-speed link, they are considered to be at the same site.

The site is entered into domain controllers because they use this information to help you find the closest server provider. This information is also used during replication. NT 5.0 automatically determines which AD servers are in the same site and which are located outside this site. NT 5.0 replicates database information more frequently to servers within a site.

Domains

The Active Directory is comprised of one or more NT domains. In the AD model, all objects are contained within domains. Like domains in previous versions of NT, they are the security boundary for a network. Each domain has its own security policies and trust relationships with other domains. The security policies include how strong the passwords must be, as well as other user account parameters. Each user is given a Security ID (SID), which includes the name of the domain.

TRUSTS   In NT 4.0 you had to manually and explicitly set up a complex array of one-way trusts between domains. Now transitive trusts are set up automatically when a new domain joins a collection of domains (called a tree—see next section). This eliminates the need to set up and maintain a large number of explicit trusts. The trusts are hierarchical just as the domains are. However, administrative rights are not transitive by default. This means that an administrator in one domain does not have administrative powers in another domain by default.

These trusts use the Kerberos security protocol to communicate between two domains. You can still establish one-way trusts for special security situations or to connect with NT 4.0 domains.

TREES   A collection of domains that share the same name space, global catalog, and schema is called a *tree*. Each domain has a Kerberos trust linking it to its parent domain.

Figure 13-1 illustrates a simple NT tree consisting of three domains. The names of the domains are *root.com, division.root.com,* and *group.division.root.com.* You can see that they share the same name space and follow the standard DNS format. Each domain has at

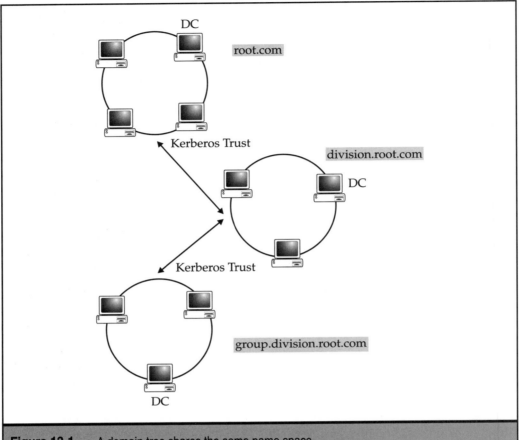

Figure 13-1. A domain tree shares the same name space

least one domain controller, and transitive Kerberos trusts are established at the time of creation for each of the domains.

The division.root.com domain is a child domain of the root.com domain, and the group.division.root.com domain is a child domain of the division.root.com domain. It is important to build and migrate to the NT 5.0 model by starting from the topmost or root domain and work down through the tree. You can add a child domain to any preexisting domain, making the tree model highly flexible.

FORESTS   You can join domains that do not share a common name space to create a tree. A *forest* is a set of domains that share a common schema and global catalog but not the same name space. In Figure 13-2 there are seven domains that belong to three different

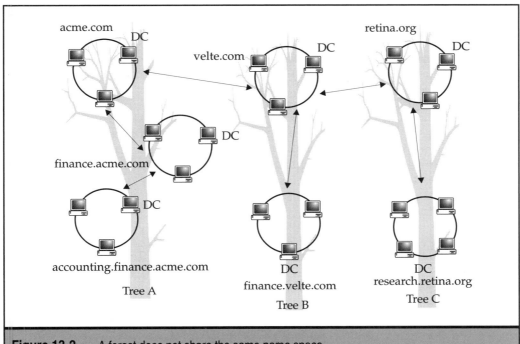

Figure 13-2.   A forest does not share the same name space

trees, which together comprise a single forest. The trees trust each other with transitive hierarchical Kerberos trust relationships. By default, the trust relationships are formed by the tops of the trees. The trusts can be created to form other pathways and altered for security measures.

One of the advantages of the tree and forest organization is that it is quite easy to rearrange the forest structure when the needs of an enterprise demand it. For example, you can easily make the following changes:

▼   Add a domain to a tree

■   Remove a domain from a tree

■   Rename a domain

■   Merge trees in a forest

▲   Rearrange trees and forests

You can do these things without having to reinstall NT. However the parent domain-to-child domain relationship still holds under these rearrangements. If you rename a parent, you will rename all its children domains. The same goes for deletions; deleting a parent domain will delete its children. You don't actually delete domains; you just eliminate their trust relationship with the tree. The deleted domains remain intact, but they are unable to use resources within the tree or forest.

MULTIMASTER REPLICATION   NT 5.0 uses *multimaster replication* within domains. Instead of having one central database for the domain that is replicated to subordinate domain controllers (as is done in NT 4.0), NT 5.0 treats all domain controllers as peers. You can update a record on any domain controller and expect that it will update all domain controllers after some time. Replication is passed from one DC to another only when there is new information, and only the information that has changed is sent to the replication partner.

To tackle the issue of having information change on one DC while it is being changed on another, domain controllers use timestamps and an *update sequence number* (USN) to keep track of which DC was updated first. A USN is a 64-bit number that is advanced when a change is made to the Active Directory. Each DC keeps track of the USNs of its replication partners. When a replication is called, the DC requests all changes that took place since the last time it received an update, and then resets its USN for each of its replication partners.

If a DC attempts to update another DC with different information, both DCs first check their USN, and whoever has the largest (most recent) number will win and be replicated. If the numbers are the same, timestamps are used to determine which change was most recent. This is why it is important to keep all computers, especially DCs, synchronized to a standard clock.

By default, replications are called every ten minutes within the same site. To ensure a smooth replication, the Active Directory creates a logical ring topology of all DCs within a site. The replication proceeds around the ring until it reaches the starting DC. You can change the ring order or the topology to another configuration, such as a star, if you want.

Replication to other sites within the domain usually does not occur as often. This interval can be set up by the administrator.

Organizational Units

Domains can be subdivided into separate administrative boundaries called *organizational units* (OUs). In Chapter 4, we discussed some of the administrative problems with the NT 4.0 domain architecture. Basically, not all users in a domain can or should be under the control of a central administrator. As we saw in Chapter 4, third-party vendors have addressed this problem by delegating authority to smaller units within the domain. That is, in effect, what Microsoft has done in NT 5.0.

Various administrative tasks can be doled out to local authorities in an OU so the central administrator does not have to deal with the day-to-day changes, such as resetting a password for a user.

OUs can be nested within other OUs so you can express the level of control you desire. OUs do not partake in any replication and do not require any special machines to serve as their controller. This allows you to cheaply (no need to buy another computer) and easily parse a domain into manageable subunits. Depending on how your company is organized, you might make each division its own domain and each group within that division its own organizational unit. Because it is really a way to mark administrative boundaries, you should let your administrative requirements guide you.

DNS

Windows NT 5.0 domain names follow the convention of the DNS naming scheme. In fact, DNS is intimately connected with Active Directory and NT 5.0. You saw in Chapter 6 how NT uses DNS as a name resolution service. In NT 5.0, DNS also serves to resolve the location of the LDAP-based Active Directory objects. There must be at least one dynamic DNS server installed in order for Active Directory to function properly.

Active Directories contact the local dynamic DNS server and publish their own record as a Service Resource Record. This way other computers can find Active Directories just by knowing the domain name and querying DNS. Therefore, if a client uses Active Directory and wants to see what another domain contains in its AD, the client only needs to point to the domain name and an AD will be contacted automatically.

NOTE: WINS is used as a name locator in NT 4.0 networks. In NT 5.0 networks, WINS is not required unless NT 4.0 or other down-level clients are still active.

Although Microsoft recommends using its NT 5.0 DNS server, you can use any DNS server that meets the following criteria:

▼ Supports SRV Records (RFC 2052)

■ Supports dynamic DNS (RFC 2136) for full functionality

▲ Uses BIND version 8.1.1 or higher

You are not required to use the same DNS zone name as the name of the domain, although it will make administration much simpler. For example, the naming convention might be as follows:

NT 5.0 Domain	research.velte.com
DNS Zone	research.velte.com
Client	my-pc.research.velte.com

Try to get a DNS server at each site unless a site has few users. This will reduce network traffic (DNS queries) and provide quicker response times for clients trying to obtain names from the DNS server. For larger, more centralized corporations, it might make sense to have fewer zones, because there is less replication traffic to keep all the zones updated.

Distributed File System

Another feature that is being deployed currently to enhance the scalability of Windows networks is the Distributed File System (Dfs). Dfs allows you to collect network shares and reshare them as a single share on an NT Server. This allows you to bring together a large number of disparate shares and place them in a single name space. Users no longer have to mount each share on different machines with a new drive letter, because all the shares they need will be under a single share on a Dfs server. The Dfs server doesn't actually house the shares; they still remain on the computers where they were before. Dfs organizes the shares so they appear as a single drive.

Dfs is built into NT 5.0, so there are no additional components to install. Currently, Dfs can be installed as a service on NT 4.0 machines. An NT 4.0 workstation can act as a client to a Dfs server but cannot itself host a Dfs share. An NT 4.0 server can host a single Dfs share and can also act as a Dfs client. There is an upgrade path for Windows 95 machines to be able to act as Dfs clients. Here is how Dfs works.

Creating a Dfs Root

First you create a share on an NT Server. You might call this "public" or "d-drive". Next, use the Dfs Administrator tool found in the Programs | NT 4.0 Administration Tools menu, as shown in Figure 13-3. From here you can configure and manage any Dfs on your network if you have administrative rights. You must create the root of the Dfs using a preexisting share. In the example, we'll use the one we just made. It will be known as the root of this Dfs.

Now we can begin to add more shares to the root of the Dfs. This is done through the Dfs Administration tool under Dfs | Add To Dfs menu item. This will call up another window resembling Figure 13-4. From here you can map a directory off the root Dfs to a share located on another computer. The remote shares can be on any NT machines, Windows 9x machines, and even Windows 3.11 computers. They can be either the FAT or NTFS type.

NOTE: Some shares have restrictions on the number of connected users that are honored within the Dfs. For example, NT Workstation shares only allow up to ten concurrent connections. This restriction holds true while it is part of a Dfs root as well.

Advantages of Dfs

Because Dfs maps the physical location of the shares into a single name space, the location of the data stored on shared drives becomes transparent to users and applications. Other than being much easier to organize and search, this has several ramifications. It is possible to create redundant drives. Let's say, for example, that you have two shares

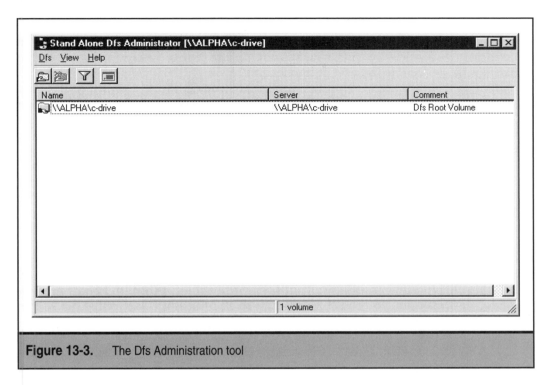

Figure 13-3.   The Dfs Administration tool

located on separate servers that are identical in content and are read-only for normal users. You could map both shares to the same location in the Dfs. This is called an *alternate volume.*

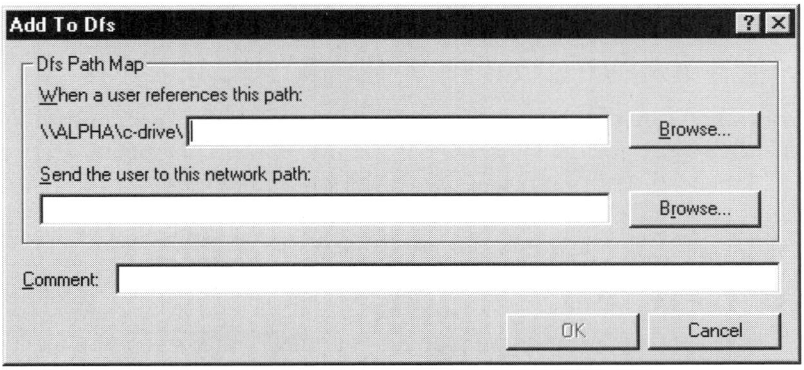

Figure 13-4.   Adding shares to a Dfs volume

Alternate volumes can be used for redundancy. If a user is accessing one of the volumes and it crashes, the application will time out, and upon reconnection it will be restored to the identical but alternate volume. In the best of cases, the switch to the alternate is transparent to the user or application.

Alternate volumes can also be used for load balancing. When a user requests data from that particular name space on the Dfs, they will be given access to one of the two alternate volumes, thus distributing the traffic between the two. If Dfs is used with Active Directory, the user will be given the logically closest share because the AD is aware of sites and will forward the request to the share that is at the same site as that of the user.

Here are a couple examples of where using the Dfs is practical. First, you can create a Dfs share consisting of only file systems that you want to have backed up. Then you can tell your backup software to connect to a single Dfs share and back up the whole thing. You avoid having to hunt down and connect with multiple server shares. You must ensure the shares are in their original position if you need to restore data from the backup media.

Another example of using Dfs effectively is using Dfs on a web server. You might have a central home page that links to a page or set of pages for each department. Instead of allowing all departments access to your server and allowing them to update it when they have new material, you could create a Dfs share on the web server that has shares located in each department. The shares that comprise the Dfs share are managed by the different departments that contribute the the web page. Thus, you have your root home page and all the different departments located in the next directory. The departments don't have to relinquish their security rights to you, and you don't have to relinquish yours to them.

Connecting to Dfs Shares

Connecting to a Dfs share is as easy as connecting to any other share. You simply provide the Universal Naming Convention (UNC) name of the Dfs server, followed by the Dfs share name of the root, and then any subsequent paths. For example:

*ServerName**Dfs_ShareNameRoot**Path**FileName*

Security is taken care of by the usual methods in NT via Access Control Lists that are maintained at the source of the share, not at the Dfs share. This means there is no other security mechanism to set up or configure to use Dfs.

MIGRATING TO NT 5.0

It is not too early to start planning your conversion to NT 5.0. Even if you feel you are just getting NT 4.0 out the door, there are things you can do now to ensure an easy migration later and reduce disruption of service common to a new deployment. First, we'll discuss how to organize your new enterprise network and how NT 5.0 deals with both centralized and decentralized network topologies. Then, we'll cover how the migration will take place. Lastly, we'll go through a simple two-domain setup, highlighting the differences in NT 5.0 compared to NT 4.0.

Enterprise Organization

Because you have a hierarchy of domains in a tree and a hierarchy of organizational units within domains, you have a two-tiered system with NT 5.0. This two-tiered system allows the NT 5.0 enterprise to be very flexible. Depending on how your enterprise is organized politically, geographically, and logically, you can create custom NT 5.0 network designs that fit your needs.

The domain controllers are at the focus point of any domain. Previous versions of NT forced you to decide whether a machine was going to act as a domain controller or not at the time of installation. To promote a normal server to domain controller status required a new installation. Now, a normal NT Server can be promoted to act as a domain controller by using a simple utility (*dcpromo.exe*).

The beta release of NT 5.0 does not support demoting DCs to stand-alone servers, so the promotion process is one way. In future releases you will be able to promote and demote domain controllers whenever you want without reinstalling NT. This is because the directory service that is the domain controller is just another service that can be installed or uninstalled. This service is called the Directory Service Agent and whether or not it's running determines if the server is a domain controller. It does not appear in the Services' MMC because it can only be altered via the Domain Controller Promotion wizard. This flexibility allows you to create or change existing domains quickly.

Domain Examples

Let's examine two different domain structures that serve different needs. For each of the examples we will assume there is a large organization that has offices in the United States, France, and Australia. Our job is to figure out how to organize the NT enterprise and to determine how much bandwidth it needs to connect these three disparate sites.

Example of a Centralized Domain

The first design is the single domain model. Here all three sites are under the same domain. There is a domain controller at each site to ensure fast logons and easy updates.

When an administrator creates a new object in France, for example, the entire object is copied to the other two domain controllers at the other sites. If the administrator changes a property, only the change is propagated to the remaining sites.

To help control the administrator rights in this model, we create three organizational units, one for each site, and assign specific rights to administrators there. After some thought we determine that this model has too much network traffic, so we try something else.

Example of a Decentralized Domain

In this example, we create a separate domain for each site. The domains are all part of the same tree and thus share the same name space. They have transitive trust relationships among them. Now, when an object is created or updated, only the local domain controllers are affected. There is still some residual overhead on the network because data about the tree structure is sent to all member domain controllers. Nonetheless, this model incurs little network traffic and allows all members access to tree-wide resources via Kerberos trust relationships.

If the users query the directory in another domain, significant network traffic may occur. To alleviate this burden, a machine hosting the global catalog is positioned at each site. Now when a local user sends a query for information about a nonlocal object, the global catalog can provide some information about the object. If more information is requested, it can provide the exact location of the object. The number of queries that are sent across the WAN is reduced because the global catalog knows about all the objects in the tree.

There is some network overhead in maintaining the GC, so we will have to monitor whether there are enough queries to justify having the GC present locally. In all probability, there is an advantage to having the GC.

Converting from Existing Domain Structures

Table 13-2 is useful in converting from your existing NT domain structure to a new NT 5.0 domain structure. Important points to keep in mind are the political and geographical status of the organization and how centralized or decentralized you want your enterprise. The new structure can be more flexible than previous designs, but you will make decisions at the onset that will have a long-lasting impact on your network.

NT 4.0 Domain Model	NT 5.0 Domain Strategy
Single Domain	Create a single domain with multiple domain controllers (DCs), and then add organizational units (OUs) to support administrative needs. Connect to other trees to make a forest of limited trusts when a separate name space is used.

Table 13-2. Converting NT 4.0 Domains into NT 5.0 Trees and Forests

NT 4.0 Domain Model	NT 5.0 Domain Strategy
Complete Trust	This model is totally decentralized, so make separate domains for each current domain. Connect them into a tree or forest depending on the name space and type of trust relationships you want among domains.
Master Domain	You can either create a single domain and subsequent OUs for each of the previous domains or create a tree with parent and child domains. In either case, you should start upgrading at the top and work your way down the tree.
Multiple Master Domain	If you can agree on who is going to control a single master domain, make a tree, child domains, and OUs. If you must have equal control over all domains, create a forest of domain trees. The latter approach may require more administration due to trust relationships and the trees not sharing the same name space.

Table 13-2.   Converting NT 4.0 Domains into NT 5.0 Trees and Forests (continued)

Upgrading Servers

There is a tremendous amount of planning for any enterprise involved in migrating to NT 5.0. However, once you have decided on an NT enterprise design and created an upgrade plan, at some point, you will actually start converting your existing NT 4.0 domains to the new NT 5.0 structure.

The steps to upgrading your domains can be broken down into three primary steps. First, you will almost certainly upgrade a primary domain controller to a new NT 5.0 domain controller. Then, you will create or upgrade other domain controllers to NT 5.0 domain controllers. When all domain controllers are converted to NT 5.0, you will switch the domain into an all Active Directory mode to take advantage of all NT 5.0 technologies.

Step 1–Upgrading the First PDC

Converting an NT 4.0 domain almost always starts at the top with the PDC. This is because the domain can then immediately join a tree if one exists, and administrators can use the administrative tools to create AD objects (such as OUs). Also, when other members of the domain are upgraded, they will have a domain to join.

Once the PDC is converted to an NT 5.0 DC, it will still be able to function with NT 4.0 BDCs, clients, and other NT Servers. Although it migrates the Security Account Manager (SAM) database from the Registry to the directory store, it still presents this information to down-level clients as a flat file. It can still authenticate users and maintains all the functionality it had before the conversion.

A safe approach is to take a copy of the PDC offline and upgrade that machine in a controlled environment. Run it through its paces there. If everything looks okay, bring it up on the production network and prepare to turn on the other copy of the PDC or promote an NT 4.0 BDC if anything goes wrong. Once you have a stable NT 5.0 DC online, you can proceed to the next step.

> **NOTE:** The migration process almost always should occur from the top down simply because new NT 5.0 systems can then join a forest, domain, or tree immediately.

Step 2–Creating More Domain Controllers

In this phase, you will add more domain controllers so you have redundancy at the level of the Active Directory. You should still maintain an NT 4.0 BDC just in case something goes wrong with the NT 5.0 DCs. If something bad does happen, promote the NT 4.0 BDC to the PDC and revert to the NT 4.0 domain.

The domain controller that used to be the PDC for the NT 4.0 domain is still regarded as such for the NT 4.0 system. It uses the old protocol for replication with BDCs but also uses the newer protocol for replicating the AD with its NT 5.0 domain controller partners.

Step 3–Going Native

Once you have converted all the BDCs to NT 5.0 DCs, and you are sure you never want to add another NT 4.0 domain controller, you can switch the domain from the mixed mode over to native mode. When the network is in native mode, the multimaster replication for the Active Directory is used. Also, clients can benefit from transitive trusts. This means that they can see resources all over the tree.

Creating an NT 5.0 Tree

In this example, you'll start with two NT 4.0 domains that have a trust relationship, and you'll end with a single NT 5.0 domain tree consisting of two domains—a parent domain and a child domain. You'll change the names of the domains to conform with the new DNS name space.

A real migration is much more complicated, but this example will help you understand what is involved in a migration. In real life, you'll probably want to do the first migration offline on test machines with copies of your real PDCs.

Getting Started

The basic process follows these steps:

1. Upgrade the NT 4.0 PDC to an NT 5.0 stand-alone server.
2. Add the DNS service.
3. Configure the DNS service.
4. Promote the server to a domain controller.
5. Repeat for all domain controllers.

NT 5.0 is so heavily dependent on DNS as its name server and locator that you must have a DNS server already functioning to correctly upgrade a system to NT 5.0. Because the DNS server can be anywhere, including the same computer, you must add the DNS service before promoting the server to DC status.

After all domain controllers have been promoted, you set the properties of the domain to native to take full advantage of the Active Directory and inherent trust relationships.

To start the conversion, place the NT 5.0 CD-ROM into the PDC. This brings up a splash screen and a prompt asking if you want to upgrade to NT 5.0 at this time. Click on No and choose to install NT instead of upgrading. If you attempt to upgrade NT on a PDC, a DC will be created. In the beta release of NT 5.0 you cannot demote a DC to a stand-alone server, so you will *install* NT from scratch instead of *upgrading* your NT system. This is because you need to start with a stand-alone server, and then promote it to DC status. Once you have elected to install NT, the familiar installation process will begin by copying files to your hard drive.

Continue with the installation as you would normally. When prompted for the type of NT Server to install, select the Stand-Alone Server option. When prompted to supply networking information, click on TCP/IP Protocol, and then include your statically-defined IP number. In the DNS section, add your machine's IP number to the list of DNS servers. Continue with the installation until you have completed the process and have rebooted.

DNS Setup

Before adding the DNS service, you should know the DNS name of the domain you are going to use. It could be something like *company.com.* Because the child domain will incorporate its name as part of the top-level domain, a name of a child domain might be known as *finance.company.com.*

ADDING THE DNS SERVICE   To add the DNS service, follow these steps:

1. Add the DNS service via Control Panel | Add/Remove Programs | Windows NT Setup | Networking, and then click on the Details button. Select Microsoft DNS Server and click on OK.

2. You will be prompted to verify that you indeed want to configure DNS now. Click on Yes to proceed.

3. Select a private DNS server and click on Next.

4. Select a root server and click on Next.

5. Select the Add A Forward Lookup Zone option and click on Next.

6. Select Primary so it can accept dynamic updates and click on Next.

7. Enter the name of the zone and click on Next. (This is normally the name of the Active Directory, for example, velte.com.)

8. The default name is appropriate, so click on Next.

9. Do not select the Add a Reverse Lookup Zone Now option unless you are experienced with DNS and want to configure one. Click on Next.

10. Click on Finish to close the DNS wizard.

CONFIGURING DNS FOR DYNAMIC UPDATES   Now you have installed and configured DNS for your system. All future configurations of DNS will be through the DNS plug-in for the Microsoft Management Console, which is called the DNS Manager. You must use the DNS Manager now to enable dynamic updates on the forward lookup zone. Open the DNS Manager by selecting Start | Programs | Administrative Tools | DNS Management.

From within the DNS Manager expand the DNS server object, and then the Forward Lookup Zones folder. Right-click on the zone you just created (velte.com in our example) and click on Properties, as illustrated in Figure 13-5.

A tabbed window will appear. Click on the General tab and select the Allow Dynamic Update check box, as shown in Figure 13-6. This concludes the configuration for DNS; now you are ready to promote this server to a domain controller.

Domain Controller Promotion

The promotion process is started by typing **dcpromo** at the command prompt. This invokes the Domain Controller Promotion wizard (*dcpromo.exe*). Because you are creating the top-level domain controller, all you need to know is the name of the new domain.

We will get more involved in the steps of the wizard when we discuss promoting the second domain, because that promotion is slightly more complicated. But for now, you

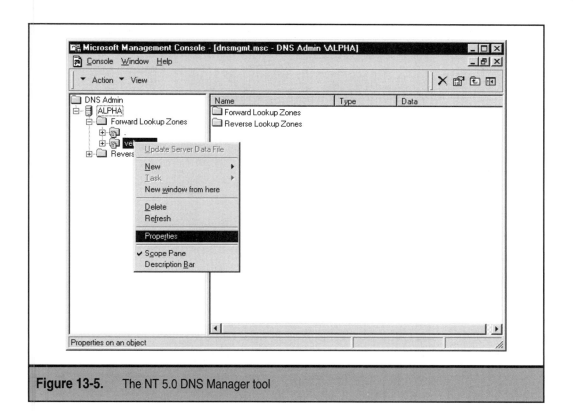

Figure 13-5.   The NT 5.0 DNS Manager tool

need to promote your first domain controller. After starting the wizard, you will be prompted to enter the name of the new domain (velte.com in this example). Do so and select the Create A New Domain Tree option. Shortly thereafter you will be prompted to continue with the promotion process. Click on Next, and you are on your way. After a reboot, the NT 5.0 DC should come up with no errors. If the DNS is not functioning properly, you will see a barrage of messages shortly after bootup about not being able to find a DNS server.

Now you are going to create another domain called *research.velte.com*. This domain is going to be a child domain off our first domain, velte.com. To start, upgrade this NT 4.0 Server to NT 5.0 stand-alone server status. Then add the DNS service as you did before on the previous domain. However, this time configure the DNS to serve the research.velte.com domain.

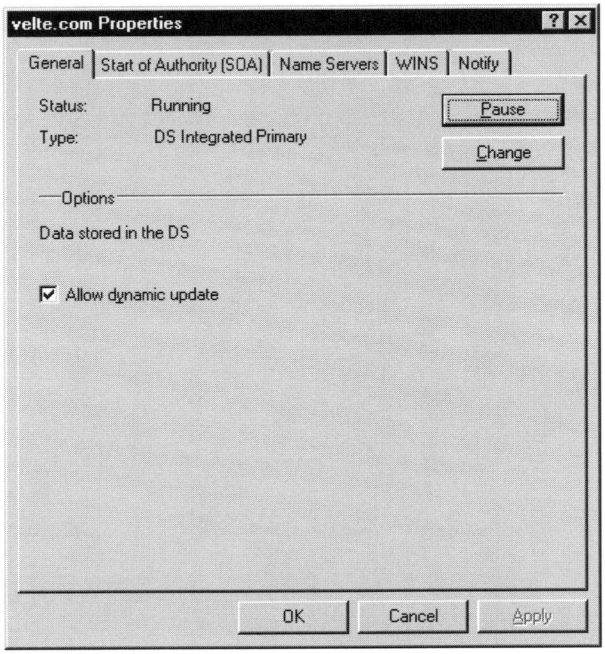

Figure 13-6.   Configuring DNS for dynamic updates

Now start the DC Promotion Wizard and enter the name of the new domain. Instead of creating a new domain tree, click on the Join A Domain Tree option and type the name of the parent domain, as shown in Figure 13-7.

The next step is to set up the trust relationship with the parent domain. As shown in Figure 13-8, you must supply an account with administrative rights in the parent domain to allow a link to be formed. If you have problems with this step, it is likely that the parent domain could not be found. Check your DNS setup and confirm that the parent can be located from this machine.

Click on Next and proceed with the promotion by approving your selection and clicking on Next. This should initiate a successful promotion of another domain controller.

To check whether the promotion is successful and the tree is intact, use the Domain Tree Manager. On your newly-promoted child domain you can call up this tool from the Start | Programs | Administrative Tools | Domain Tree Manager menu. As you can see

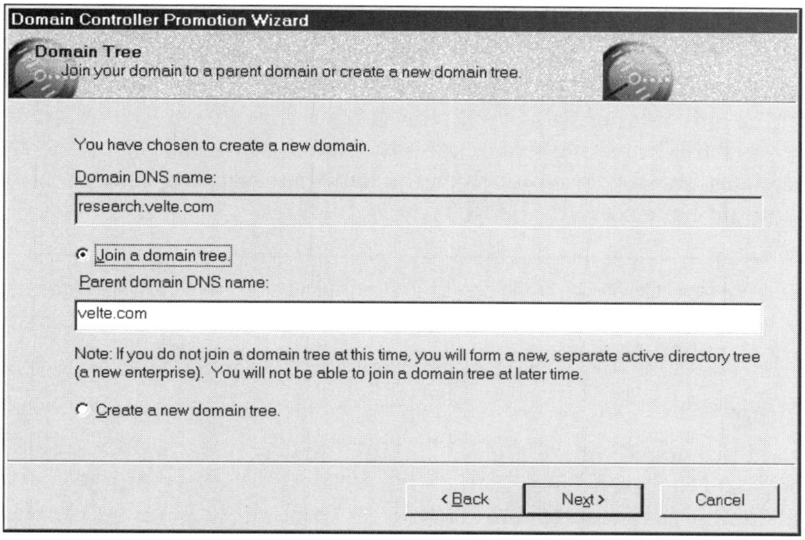

Figure 13-7. Joining a domain tree

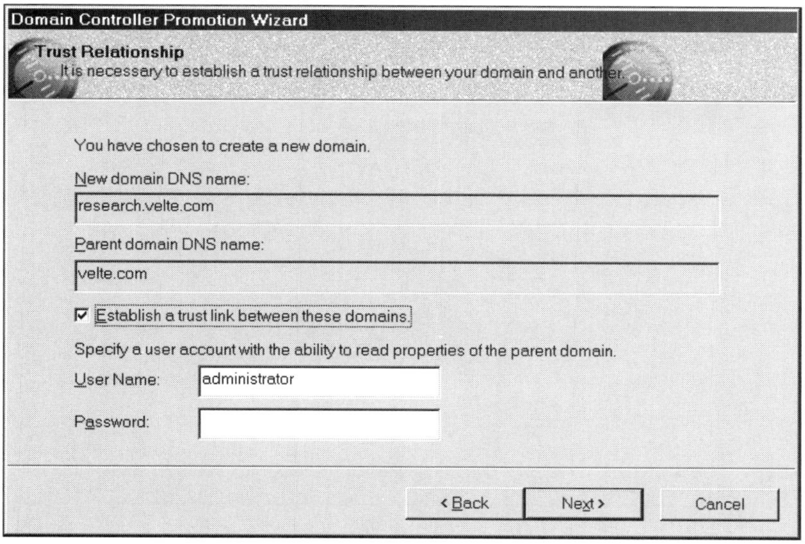

Figure 13-8. Setting up the transitive trust relationship

in Figure 13-9, the parent domain, velte.com, is listed at the top, followed by the newly-created child domain, research.velte.com.

If you right-click on the new domain, and then click on Properties, you can check the trust relationships. Doing this brings up a window similar to Figure 13-10. From here you can see that the only relationship is with the domain called *velte*. That relationship is one of a parent, and the transitive trusts are established. If we had done the same on the top-level domain, the figure would have looked the same, but instead of VELTE and Parent, we would have seen RESEARCH and Child.

NOTE: The NetBIOS names of the domains are still used along with the DNS names of the domains (that is, VELTE and velte.com, and RESEARCH and research.velte.com). This is to ensure down-level compatibility with NT 4.0 systems.

Going Native

As mentioned previously, there are certain advantages to setting the network mode to native as opposed to mixed. They include the capabilities to use multimaster replication and have all members of a tree browse resources throughout the tree. "Go native" only if you are sure you are not going to add more NT 4.0 domain controllers.

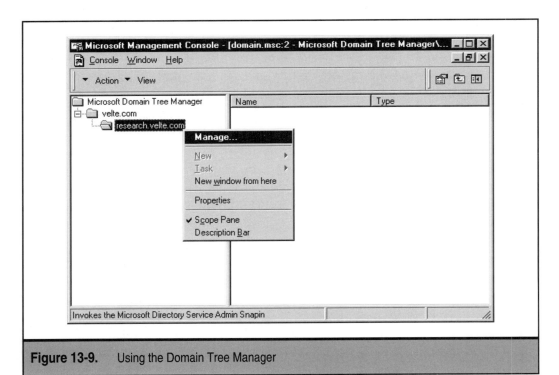

Figure 13-9. Using the Domain Tree Manager

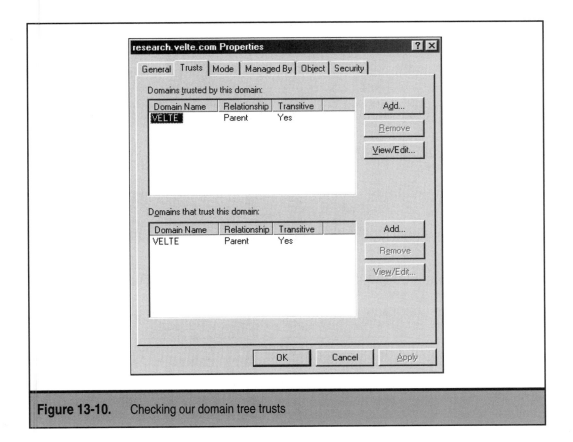

Figure 13-10.   Checking our domain tree trusts

To make the switch to native, you must have administrative privileges. Go to the Domain Tree Manager and right-click on the topmost domain. Then click on the Mode tab illustrated in Figure 13-11. Click on the Change To Native Mode option and click on OK. (In our example there are no options available because we have already gone to the native mode, and once you choose native mode there is no going back.)

Making the Move

Migrating to NT 5.0 will be an arduous task for any enterprise, so is it worth it? Because so many enhancements to NT 5.0 bring it, finally, to the enterprise level, the answer is "Yes". As any enterprise administrator can attest, many problems with NT stem from its

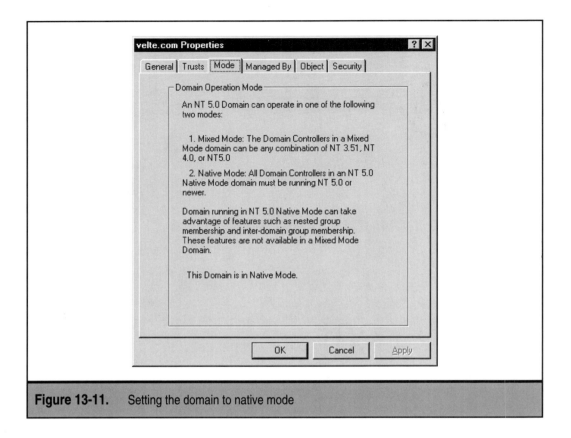

Figure 13-11. Setting the domain to native mode

inability to properly scale to a large enterprise environment. To recapitulate, by using NT 5.0 an enterprise will gain the following advantages:

▼ Tight integration with the Internet and Internet technologies

■ Easier and more flexible enterprise organization

■ More refined administrative control over users and objects

■ Greatly enhanced structure of network objects in the Active Directory

▲ Increased security and ease of trust management

However, this conversion must be planned with great care. To assure the minimal amount of down time, Microsoft has built-in backward compatibility into NT 5.0. Thus you can migrate at your speed and avoid doing a complete overhaul all at once.

APPENDIX A

Year 2000 Problem Identification and Resolution

W e are rapidly approaching the turn of the century, the year 2000. This date brings with it an issue that some fear will have severe repercussions. Many devices in operation today cannot distinguish between the year 1900 and the year 2000. This is because many computer programs use only a two-digit representation to identify years. The dd/mm/yy and mm/dd/yy formats are quite common in computer programs. These applications assume that the years being represented are in the 1900s and only the last two digits need to be variable. The bug occurs when math is performed on these dates. For example, a computer program can properly calculate the time between 12/31/98 and 12/31/99. However, it cannot understand that 12/31/00 doesn't (or may not) mean 1900. The result of the calculation of years between 12/31/98 and 12/31/00 could be -98 years or 98 years if the system incorrectly assumes that the *00* stands for 1900. However, if *00* means 2000, the correct answer is two years. This problem is so severe in some systems that there is tremendous concern about system crashes when 1999 becomes 2000.

The practice of using a two-digit date became commonplace in the early days of computer programming when memory was extremely expensive and anything that could be done to save memory was a good thing. This is no longer true; memory has become cheap, and the amount of memory saved by using a two-digit representation for the year is insignificant. Most programs written in the last several years are capable of using a full four-digit representation for years. Retrofitting all the legacy systems still in place today is a monumental task. The information in this appendix will try to summarize what the year 2000 problem is, what is affected, and how to develop a plan to reduce your exposure to the year 2000 problem.

WHAT WILL FAIL?

Defining exactly what will fail has been debated for quite some time and will continue right up to the tick of the clock as the century turns. Computers may delete files or records from storage as being too old. Telephone systems may shut down if they perceive time as moving backwards. Systems that need periodic maintenance will request it and may shut down until it is received. Inventory systems may assume that perishables are too old to be used and reorder large quantities of replacements. Programs that use day-of-week calculations will also be effected. The first day of the year 2000 is a Saturday; the first day of the year 1900 was a Monday.

There is no limit to the kinds of problems that can occur because computers and microprocessors are in almost every part of our lives. Some experts believe that most of the affected programs can be found and fixed—at least the ones that will cause serious problems. Some believe it's an impossible task to root out all the systems that use a two-digit representation of the year. These systems run everything from the computer on your desktop to the power plants and water processing systems we all need to survive. So who is right? Only time will tell, but much time and effort is now being spent to minimize the potential catastrophes that may be right around the corner.

Microsoft states that all its current products are year 2000-compliant, although some earlier versions do have some issues. Microsoft publishes a complete list of the products that it is aware of having year 2000 compliance issues, along with what the specific issues are, on its web site. You can look at Microsoft's site at **www.microsoft.com/cio/ articles/RELATED_Y2K_LINKS.htm.**

Mainframes and Midrange Computers

Mainframe and midrange computers constitute the largest number of legacy systems. This is where most problem applications reside. Operating systems, system software, and application programs have been developed on these platforms for many years. "Old" programming languages, such as COBOL '74, that don't support four-digit years are still around today. Newer versions of most of these outdated software packages are year 2000-compliant, but not all. In some cases, a revision to an application to make it year 2000-compliant may involve an upgrade to the programming language it's written in, or even an upgrade to the operating system that the host runs on. These upgrades can be very tricky and expensive.

Personal Computers

The issues with personal computers (PCs) are the same as with the larger host systems, although not as rich a legacy exists here. Most of the operating systems and applications that run on these systems have been developed more recently, while year 2000 awareness was growing. That's not to say the problem with PCs isn't large. The sheer number of these devices installed today creates an enormous undertaking in a year 2000 compliance initiative. In the mainframe environment, changes to a system or application are centralized. In the desktop environment, a change to an application may involve thousands of upgrades. If a hardware upgrade is required to support the year 2000 compliance initiative, the expense and effort can become enormous.

Network Infrastructure

At first glance, the network infrastructure seems less affected by the year 2000 problem in the enterprise. The job of the network infrastructure is to simply get data packets from point A to point B, right? For the most part, that's true. There are many time-sensitive components to the network, however. Issues with the network infrastructure and year 2000 compliance appear to be more with the management systems for these components and some of the services that are becoming more and more a part of the network infrastructure. Features like DNS, DHCP, and WINS fall into this category. Even firewalls, file and print services, remote access services, and directory services are becoming just another part of the network infrastructure. All these elements need to be considered for year 2000 compliance.

Embedded Systems

An *embedded system* is a computerized device that is incorporated into some larger piece of engineering equipment or industrial product. Embedded systems can be found almost anywhere, from the telephone on your kitchen wall to the power plant that supplies electricity to your city. The problems associated with these systems seem to be the most difficult to define or, at least, size up. They are also the systems that incite the most doom and gloom among journalists and visionaries. Some of the things that contain embedded systems are

▼ Telephone systems

■ Global positioning equipment

■ Fire alarms

■ Security systems

■ Power generators

■ Hospital equipment

■ Meteorological equipment

■ Telemetry

▲ Radio control systems

PLANNING A YEAR 2000 PROJECT TO PREVENT DISASTER

As you can see from the preceding information, this is a very complicated issue with disastrous implications. In order to limit the risk to your business, it is very important to properly plan for the year 2000. The following sections give you some ideas that will help you develop a year 2000-compliance plan for your organization.

Building the Project Plan

The year 2000 project plan will serve as the framework for you to successfully test and deploy year 2000-compliant components on your production network. There are several steps that should be taken in developing a project plan for the year 2000 problem. First, identify all the business systems that are likely to be affected by the problem. Then prioritize those systems and deal first with the ones that are most likely to negatively impact your business. Next, develop a plan to resolve the year 2000 issues that you've identified. These solutions need to be implemented and verified in a testing lab environment before they are put into the production network. You'll also want to be sure there is no "year 2000 virus" introduced into your production systems.

When you're satisfied that the solutions you've tested in the lab are sound, you should first implement them in a production pilot. Roll out the components into the production network when you're comfortable with the results of the pilot. Continue monitoring these systems after rollout to ensure they are working properly.

Estimating Costs

The cost of implementing a year 2000 compliance project can be very high. One of the first things that must be done as soon as you've identified the systems that must be upgraded is to estimate the costs of implementing the plan. If you're the year 2000 compliance project manager, show these costs to management as soon as possible. Without the commitment of senior management, you will be unsuccessful in your efforts. That commitment must include the financial and human resources required to implement the plan you've developed.

The costs to implement your year 2000 project may include some or all of the following expenses:

▼   Licensing fees for new, year 2000-compliant software

■   Hardware upgrades to run the newer versions of software

■   Creation of a year 2000 test lab (space, hardware, software, and so on)

■   The human resources to develop the year 2000 compliance plan

■   The human resources to develop the changes required

■   The human resources to perform the testing

■   The human resources to implement the compliant components into production

▲   The human resources to monitor the results and verify that there is no negative impact

Identifying and Selecting Resources

In a large corporation with an enterprise network, a year 2000 compliance project will require an enormous amount of resources, both human and financial, as we demonstrated in the preceding section. To a certain extent, it may involve every person in the corporation. It may be best to break the overall project into smaller subprojects to make the task more manageable. The specific breakdown will vary depending on the structure of your organization. Some potential subgroups are listed here.

▼   Mainframe hardware and applications

■   Distributed hardware and applications

■   Technical infrastructure

- Testing coordination
- Legal
- Finance
- ▲ Corporate communications

Internal Resources

Once you've defined the structure of your project team, you need to designate resources to manage it. These can be a core group of individuals responsible for the different areas involved. Each area can then break down the project into even smaller tasks and assign resources to accomplish those.

For example, you could have an overall year 2000 project office. This office would consist of players representing all the major components. If one of those components were the technical infrastructure, it could be broken down into mainframe hardware and software, non-mainframe hardware and software, telecommunications infrastructure, and technical vendor compliance. Each of these areas would need to be assigned a resource that is accountable for the delivery of that piece of the overall project. Very large organizations may need to break those components down even further in order to make them manageable.

As you can see, the resource requirements can become very large. It can be a difficult task to procure these resources because the project will cost a lot but will generate no revenue. A well-documented and thought out plan that outlines the risks associated with this issue will be a tremendous asset in gaining support for this effort.

External Assistance

It may become necessary to look at external resources for help because of the enormous amount of resources and the skills required to run a project of this scope. Numerous companies are springing up doing nothing other than year 2000 compliance projects. Many companies are marketing tools to aid in testing for year 2000 compliance. For example, data-aging tools can help verify that applications that have been modified for year 2000 compliance still function properly, and tools that "find and fix" date-sensitive code in applications are becoming commonplace. Just go on the Internet and do a search on "year 2000 tools", and you'll find hundreds of companies advertising their wares.

You may also want to consider bringing in consultants to assist in the development of your year 2000 project plan. Many companies don't have the skills required to develop or implement a project of this type. Outside consultants can use the knowledge they've gained by working on this problem in other places. This can help reduce the learning curve for internal resources to become knowledgeable in year 2000 issues, as well as reduce their workload. Like the year 2000 tools mentioned earlier, you'll have no trouble locating external resources willing to assist you with your year 2000 project.

TESTING AND CERTIFICATION

Year 2000-compliant systems have been defined as: "Application systems that are capable of correct identification, manipulation, and calculation using dates outside of the 1900 to 1999 year range and have been tested as such." The key words here are "tested as such." Without proper testing of the solutions you have implemented, you may be putting your production systems in jeopardy. The following sections cover some basics in building and implementing a test plan to verify your solutions are sound before they are put into production.

The Y2K Lab

In order to test your solutions you'll need a test environment. This test environment must contain all the components you've identified in your plan as potentially being affected by the year 2000 problem. It must include all the systems and all the possible configurations in your production environment that you expect to have in place at the turn of the century. This includes the logical components of your infrastructure as well as the physical. It should resemble your production systems and network infrastructure as much as possible. You may already have a test lab that you can use in part for year 2000 testing. It will, no doubt, need to be enhanced if you want to do a thorough job of year 2000 compliance testing.

By this point, you should have an inventory of all the network infrastructure hardware and software, host systems, and applications you currently have. As part of your planning, you should determine what will still be around in year 2000. Some hardware may be obsolete and replaced by then. Some applications will be replaced by others. Many versions of operating systems will be upgraded. All these decisions should be made, or at least considered, before you determine how the year 2000 test lab will be equipped.

Once you know what you need to build, you'll need to acquire the assets to build it. Again, you'll need the commitment of senior management to supply the resources.

Depending on the number of different configurations you'll need to support, you may want to consider devices such as hot-pluggable drives with preconfigured environments. Using these devices will expedite the testing process once you get started. If one test requires a server running Sybase and the next requires DB2, or one needs a workstation running Windows 95 and the next requires Windows NT, you could save yourself a lot of time by using shortcuts such as these.

Vendor Certification

Your vendors should be a significant resource in your year 2000 planning. You'll need to work with vendors to verify that their products are year 2000-compliant, and if they aren't, find out their plans and timeframes for making them year 2000-compliant. In fact, you should have each vendor supply you with a certification letter stating that its product is year 2000-compliant. You may even want to include a list of year 2000-compliant parameters that you want vendors to certify their equipment against. Ideally you should get documentation of the testing methodologies used to certify equipment, but you may find significant resistance. It never hurts to ask.

Running Y2K Tests

We've talked in high-level terms about what year 2000 compliance means. In order to develop a test plan, we'll need to put more specific meaning to it. The following list outlines a few of the parameters that can be considered crucial for year 2000 compliance. This list can be used as a guideline and enhanced for your specific situation. You can get more testing parameters from any number of sources, including vendors, consulting firms, and the Internet. The high-risk dates referred to in this listing are 12/31/1999, 01/01/2000, 02/28/2000, 02/29/2000, and 03/01/2000.

▼ Does the product always utilize a four-digit date in date-related functions or operations?

■ Does the product permit entry and display of four-digit dates?

■ Does the product handle mathematical calculations properly in aged data containing the high-risk dates?

■ Does the product sort dates properly when 19xx and 20xx are both included?

■ Does the product accurately compute the proper day of the week when dealing with a high-risk date?

■ Does the product properly perform backups and restores when crossing high-risk date boundaries?

■ Does the product correctly insert a row in a database keyed on a date field?

■ Does the product correctly calculate time differences between dates that span high-risk dates?

▲ If the product performs a leap-year calculation, does it handle the year 2000 as a leap year?

The Testing Approach

The testing phase should be broken down into manageable sections, just like your overall plan. The first step should be to test each product individually to see if it can properly execute year 2000 processing in its current environment. This can be done using tools that will age your data. Then you can test to verify that the product meets the criteria you've decided is important for your organization and applicable to your environment. This step would be considered *unit testing*.

Once you have completed the unit testing, it's time to test the products in an environment that allows the dates (in all the components of the system) to be advanced beyond 12/31/1999. For example, you could test an application running on a set of servers by advancing the dates on all the systems.

The final phase of your testing would be to run an *end-to-end test,* which combines all the elements that have been tested individually up to this point. This would include desktops with all the year 2000-compliant systems and applications, the network infrastructure with all its components, the host systems (both server- and mainframe-based) and all their systems and applications, and all the tools that you use to monitor and maintain all these components. This part of the testing can become extremely complicated and difficult. You may want to limit this type of testing to the products that you deem critical to your business.

Contingency Plans

So you've done an outstanding job of building your year 2000 project plan. You've rooted out all the non-compliant systems and applied the proper fixes to them. You've tested them all and implemented them into the production network. There's nothing left to do but sit back, relax, and wait for the clock to strike midnight on 12/31/1999, right? Wrong! Given that this is an issue we've never had to deal with before, the odds that something has been overlooked, or that something won't act quite the way it did during testing are higher than we'd like them to be. Someone with a computer in a field office could be running some bootleg software that you never knew about that could introduce a bug into your network. Or perhaps someone dials into your network or connects via the Internet and affects something you didn't expect. It would be wise to have a contingency plan in place.

So how do you develop a contingency plan for something you aren't even aware of? You can approach this issue in a couple different ways. If you have backup systems available for any of the products in your network, get them ready for use in case they are needed. Many times this could be nearly impossible, but it warrants some consideration.

You could also put a plan together to disable any parts of the network that cause problems when these critical dates arrive. This is the divide-and-conquer method. Shutting down a bridge or router to isolate an affected area would be one way to do this. This could be done simply by disabling a port on a hub, if you can identify the source of the problem.

Finally, be sure you have access to the personnel who are capable of finding and fixing any problems that occur. Their names are probably on the long list of key contributors that were involved in the year 2000 project all along. All the internal resources, external resources, and vendors who have been involved should be very familiar with your environment and will be best suited to jump in and fix things that may have been overlooked. During the entire project you should be building a call tree that lists these people.

WHERE TO FIND MORE INFORMATION

The information presented here doesn't even break the surface of the year 2000 issue. If you're involved in a year 2000 project, a plethora of information is available to help you. Many books and articles have been written on the subject. Year 2000 web pages contain information about everything from technical and legal issues to chat lines and third-party support.

WINDOWS
NT
Professional
Library

APPENDIX B

Enterprise IP Management

Managing the complex world of IP internetworking and the services necessary to keep an IP-based network healthy is a tremendous challenge. This appendix looks at three products that can help you address the challenges of managing the IP infrastructure in an enterprise network environment.

WHY IP MANAGEMENT?

Business, government, and educational institutions are moving aggressively toward the deployment of applications that can function on the corporate intranet as well as on the Internet. Government and educational institutions have used TCP/IP for decades, and many businesses have established TCP/IP as the protocol of choice on their networks. Even more businesses are moving to standardize on TCP/IP as the need to interconnect corporate networks with each other and the Internet grows. The proliferation of distributed, mission-critical applications is driving the need for a managed, high-availability TCP/IP infrastructure. In these environments, coordinated, reliable IP management is becoming increasingly important.

We will look at several IP management products that are designed to replace or enhance your existing IP management tools, such as those that ship with NT Server. If properly deployed, these products can help simplify the management of complex TCP/IP networks while reducing administrative overhead and increasing overall reliability.

IP Management Challenges

Effectively managing IP addressing is one of the biggest challenges in networking today. Many organizations have moved to standardize on TCP/IP as their primary network protocol. Most organizations have traditionally assigned and managed IP addressing in router interfaces and servers, but the process of moving IP out to the desktop has dramatically increased the number of IP addresses in use. It has always been challenging to track and manage IP addresses, but the sheer volume and complexity introduced by large-scale IP deployment has made the task an administrative nightmare for network administrators and managers. To address these challenges, especially at the workstation, DHCP has been deployed. The catch is that the increased use of DHCP has shifted much of the management burden from tracking statically-configured IP addresses to managing a mission-critical DHCP service.

Because the use of TCP/IP has increased tremendously, another pressing challenge has been the management of DNS. DNS management becomes more of a challenge as the number of hosts registered with DNS increases. The move, add, and change activity in larger, dynamic networks pushes manual DNS management approaches to the limit. To make IP management even more difficult, many applications (directory services, Internet, intranet, thin client, and so on) depend on reliable and accurate responses from DNS. When peer-to-peer networking is used with DHCP, you must dynamically tie together DHCP and DNS. As they leverage IP technologies in their network infrastructure, organizations of all sizes can potentially benefit from IP management.

Traditional IP management tools consisted of several discrete components and might be considered crude compared to what network managers have at their disposal today. The most common components were static DNS (to provide IP name services) and BOOTP (to provide host IP address assignment, default gateway, and, in some cases, boot images over the network). Management of these components was accomplished by manipulating configuration files either manually using a text editor like *vi* or through relatively-disjointed user interfaces. In early versions of NT Server, DNS and DHCP/BOOTP services were not even included as part of the server operating system.

It wasn't until NT Server 4.0 that Microsoft included what could be considered a functional and reliable DNS service designed to run on NT. In NT 4.0, DNS and DHCP services are included. They are generally considered reliable, and function well under most circumstances. There are some limitations that can be overcome by good network design, but they can pose a challenge when trying to manage the services on a day-to-day basis. However, in many smaller networks, the basic services have proven cost-effective, reliable, and fairly easy to manage.

In larger networks, nodes may be dispersed among many remote sites. Also, move, add, and change activity might be high, and organizational issues may drive the need to distribute management of the IP infrastructure in a more granular fashion. In these cases, third-party IP management tools should be considered.

NT 5.0 Note: Microsoft plans to provide a better level of integration and an improved management interface for the DNS and DHCP services in NT 5.0. At the time of this writing, however, the third-party IP management tools offer a measure of integration and additional functionality not currently included with NT Server. Also, the third-party IP management vendors represented here have a substantial installed base, and their products are expected to evolve to take advantage of emerging technologies, including those introduced with NT 5.0.

Cost Vs. Benefit

Because it is not always practical to hire additional staff when the number of nodes on the network increases, network managers need to look at ways of enabling their existing staff to become more efficient in their IP management tasks. Integrated IP management tools can help keep the IP management staff from increasing at the same rate as the node count.

A general rule of thumb is to allocate one full-time staff person per 4,000 managed IP addresses. With a good IP management tool and properly-trained staff, you should be able to effectively manage the IP environment with half as many administrative staff members as compared to an environment that doesn't have an integrated management tool. Of course, these figures can vary depending on the specific needs of an organization, the volume of changes that occur on a regular basis, the network environment, and other factors. You can achieve additional efficiency when most moves, adds, and changes are handled by DHCP and Dynamic DNS.

You should also note that regardless of the efficiencies obtained with an IP management tool, when move, add, and change activity is high (perhaps due to a major rollout of services like DHCP), a temporary increase in administrative staffing must be considered for the duration of the rollout.

Another major benefit to implementing an IP management tool is the opportunity to reduce service (DNS, DHCP, etc.) downtime. An IP management tool can increase the quality of management and level of control over the environment. This can contribute to a dramatic reduction in service outages. When IP services such as DNS and DHCP are unavailable on an IP-based network, a majority of the IP-based applications will cease to function properly. When an outage has been determined to cost the business money in lost revenue or employee downtime, keeping the services operational at all times becomes very important. The IP management tools discussed in the following section can help keep downtime to a minimum by offering the following benefits:

▼   Reducing the opportunities for human error by assigning administrative rights to specific job functions and by providing an organized, logical user interface.

■   Enabling the database of address information to be written to more than one physical server, perhaps one placed in another location on the network.

▲   Allowing multiple, redundant systems to be deployed across the network while still allowing the systems to be managed from a common management console.

Finally, the IP management tools discussed here enable an organization to implement Dynamic DNS (DDNS) services in conjunction with the DHCP service. Dynamic DNS allows nodes on the network that have acquired their IP addresses via DHCP to register their hostname in DNS automatically.

NOTE: This function of DDNS is similar to the dynamic name registration capabilities in NBT-based nodes that use WINS. Although WINS and DNS can be configured to provide dynamic name registration, the function is limited to nodes that are WINS-aware. In this scenario, non-WINS nodes still require their hostname to be entered manually into DNS if other IP nodes on the network must be able to connect to them using the node hostname.

With DDNS and DHCP, many of the management tasks are performed automatically. A node can be moved to another segment on the network and be up and running without having to manually reconfigure the workstation or manually update the DNS host table. This feature can quietly save a company money in reduced downtime experienced by users as they wait for a LAN administrator to reconfigure their workstation and a network administrator to manually change their DNS host entries. Network printers and other DHCP-enabled devices can also be moved to different network segments without requiring the devices to be reconfigured manually.

Key Features

A number of features are important when evaluating IP management products. Table B-1 outlines many key features of three highly-rated IP management applications: QIP, NetID, and Meta IP.

CD NOTE: For your convenience, evaluation versions of the IP management products listed here are on the CD-ROM included with this book. Note that the complex nature of IP management is reflected in the applications themselves. Each manufacturer uses a different mix of database engines and unique user interfaces, and each has integrated security. Although the products strive to simplify IP management, they are unlikely to be immediately intuitive unless you have had experience working with IP management software. To avoid frustration, carefully review all the *readme* files and installation notes prior to installation. Better yet, if you have Internet access, take the time to browse these vendors' web sites for detailed product information and the latest versions of their evaluation software.

	QIP 4.0	NetID 3.0	Meta IP 3.1
Manufacturer	Quadritek Systems, Inc.	Bay Networks, Inc.	MetaInfo, Inc.
Client Interface Options	Windows NT/95, X terminal (XR11 and Motif), and Secure Web	Web (Java/Frames), Windows NT 4.0/95, and Solaris 2.5	Web (Java)
Supported Server Platforms	Windows NT 4.0, Solaris, HP-UX, and AIX	Windows NT 4.0, Solaris 2.5, and HP-UX 10.x	Windows NT 4.0
Remote Management Capability	Via all client interface options	Via all client interface options	Web
Supported Database Engines	Sybase 11.x and Oracle 7.x	Sybase 11.0-11.4 and Oracle 7.x	ODBC-compliant database such as Microsoft SQL Server
Supports DDNS	Yes	Yes	Yes

Table B-1.   IP Management Product Features

	QIP 4.0	NetID 3.0	Meta IP 3.1
WINS Integration	No (Feature integrated into QIP Enterprise 5.0)	Yes	Yes
BOOTP Support	Yes	Yes	Yes
Redundant DHCP	Split scope only (Fully redundant in QIP Enterprise 5.0)	Yes — Primary/Backup	Yes — Primary/Backup
BIND version(s)	4.8.x, 4.9.x, and 8.1.x	N/A (8.1.1 in NetID 4.0)	4.9.x and 8.1.x
Year 2000-Compliant	Yes	Yes	Not determined
Product Target Market	Small, medium, and large organizations	Small, medium, and large organizations	Small, medium, and large organizations
Contact	www.quadritek.com	www.baynetworks.com	www.metainfo.com

Table B-1.   IP Management Product Features (continued)

Information regarding these products is updated on a regular basis; we will look at currently-shipping product highlights. Where applicable, features of new versions likely to be shipped in the near future will be mentioned. To get the latest information on any of the products, refer to documentation located on their respective web sites. The web site URLs are listed in Table B-1.

QIP 4.0

QIP 4.0 was designed specifically with large networks in mind. As with the other IP management products, the IP information in QIP is stored in a central Sybase or Oracle database. QIP supports cross-platform integration, allowing services and the database to reside on a mix of UNIX- and NT-based systems. This allows an organization to leverage existing server hardware when deploying QIP. The latest features include year 2000 compliance, as well as BIND 8.1.x DDNS, security, and support for incremental zone transfers. Additional features of value to enterprise environments include integrated support for groupings of subnets, Open Shortest Path First (OSPF) route summarization information, Variable Length Subnet Masking (VLSM), and the Classless InterDomain Routing (CIDR) protocol.

The QIP 4.0 user interface, shown in Figure B-1, can provide two different views:

▼   A network view for standard IP management administrative functions

▲   A network modeling view to assist with network planning and design

The interface supports granular, user-based access levels so that authority over domain and subdomain IP address moves, adds, and changes can be defined for individual administrators. The following services are managed via this interface:

▼   **QIP DHCP**—Supports standards-based DHCP and BOOTP requests.

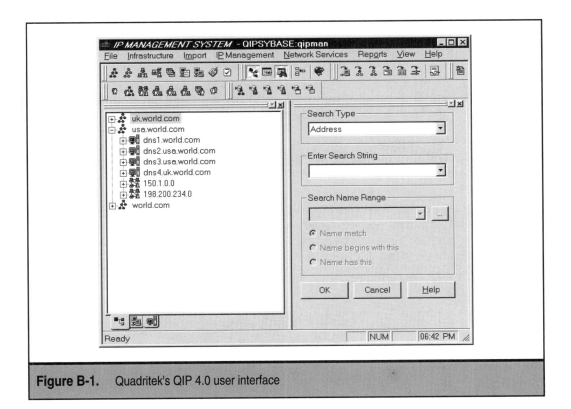

Figure B-1.   Quadritek's QIP 4.0 user interface

▲ **QIP DNS**—Supports DDNS using QDDNS, a proprietary version of DDNS. Quadritek has offered a commercially-available DDNS that was developed before the standards were officially accepted. Quadritek has stated that the next release of QIP will incorporate the standards-based DDNS.

In QIP Enterprise 5.0, the product will support database replication and DHCP fail-over. Both features further strengthen the product's high-availability position.

For an added measure of fault tolerance and overall system reliability, each of the components (QDHCP, QDDNS, the QIP Enterprise Server, BOOTP, and so on) can operate independently of the other services. QIP also updates both primary and secondary DDNS/DNS servers during normal operation to ensure accurate information on all the servers and to prevent assignment and lookup failures should a server go down. The servers can be scheduled to synchronize with each other based on a specific schedule.

Other notable features include an open architecture that links easily through APIs to other applications, including HP's OpenView network management software. This open architecture also incorporates customizable routines, allowing the assignment of IP names and addresses in accordance with specific company standards. QIP also includes command-line executables that enable other applications to interact with the QIP database.

NetID 3.0

NetID 3.0 consists of several components that are managed via an administrative user interface called the NetID Tool Set, as shown in Figure B-2 and described next.

▼ **Server Manager**—This service communicates between the DNS and DHCP servers and the database (Sybase or Oracle). The Server Manager's job is to make sure the information between the servers and the database is kept current.

■ **DNS Server**—This service supports DDNS and DDNS reconfiguration, which allows immediate updates to server policy and zone structure. This allows the information to be propagated to all of the servers quickly so that DHCP information is available in DNS very quickly.

■ **DHCP Server**—This service supports standards-based DHCP and BOOTP requests. The user interface also provides detailed DHCP statistics.

▲ **Web Gateway**—This service supports NetID Tool Set access into the NetID database.

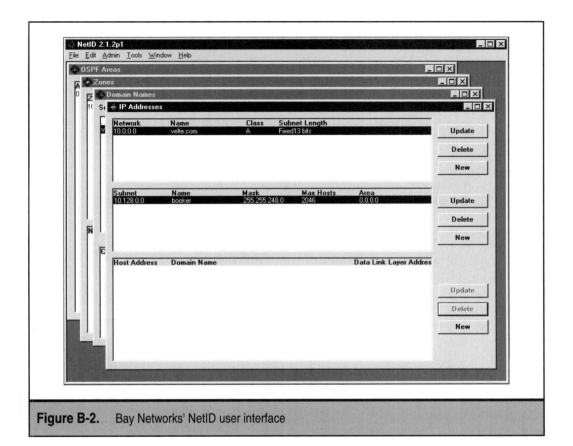

Figure B-2.   Bay Networks' NetID user interface

The NetID interface has several customizable database fields that allow entry of user-defined information. The fields allow you to keep track of information such as location of the subnet.

NetID's distributed architecture enables it to scale from small networks with one thousand hosts and a few DNS and DHCP servers to large networks with hundreds of thousands of IP addresses and hundreds of DNS and DHCP servers. NetID stores information in a central Sybase or Oracle database that multiple users access using the NetID Admin tool or Web Gateway. The Admin tool provides an overall view of your IP address and DNS architectures and a common management platform for both dynamic and static addressing and all your DNS and DHCP servers.

NetID DNS servers retrieve their configuration information from the database on startup. Any changes to DNS information made through the Admin tool or by DHCP servers are automatically and incrementally pushed out to the DNS servers, eliminating the traffic associated with zone transfers. NetID DNS servers are based on standard BIND code and interoperate with any BIND-compliant name server.

NetID DHCP servers provide standards support for both DHCP and BOOTP. DHCP servers also obtain their configuration from the NetID database and are updated incrementally with any configuration changes made automatically. The DHCP servers write information about all outstanding leases to the database so they can be viewed from the Admin tool.

NetID addresses the challenge of DHCP fault tolerance by incorporating a primary and backup DHCP server strategy. The scopes are defined on both the primary and backup servers serving the same address ranges. The servers are configured to communicate using a direct server-to-server protocol. If the primary server fails, the backup server detects the failure, and then begins honoring the DHCP requests until the primary server is back online.

NetID lets you create custom fields to track user-defined information against IP addresses or subnets. Custom fields can be used to track information such as user name, phone number, billing codes, and location against an IP address.

One of the biggest implementation challenges is populating an IP management tool with your existing host, subnet, and DNS information. NetID imports DNS zone information files, UNIX host files, and custom files. The custom file import lets you import user-defined file formats such as spreadsheets containing subnet and host information.

Another notable feature is NetID's support for VLSM. VLSM is often used in networks where limited IP address space requires economic use of the available addresses. VLSM allows you to match the subnetwork size to the number of required hosts, making more efficient use of your overall address space. Using the NetID administrative interface, subnets can be partitioned and joined. The subnet masks are automatically calculated, eliminating the common errors associated with VLSM design and architecture.

Finally, NetID has a feature that allows hostnames to be generated automatically in accordance with administrator-defined naming standards. With it, you can let NetID generate the hostnames using your corporate naming standard. This reduces human error and increases standardization.

CD NOTE: The CD-ROM contains version 2.1.3 of NetID, not the latest 3.x version. This is because the interface for 2.1.3 and 3.0 are virtually identical. The advantage of using version 2.1.3 is it includes an integrated database—the installation creates an SQL database and installs the user interface against it. Installing the evaluation product (3.x) from the web requires you to have your own Oracle or Sybase database and configure NetID to connect to it—a difficult hurdle for most users. To get an evaluation copy with Oracle, contact Bay Networks and request an evaluation CD-ROM.

Meta IP 3.1

The Meta IP/Manager and Admin tool form the foundation of Meta IP. The IP/Manager component stores configurations for the DNS and DHCP services. This interface is shown in Figure B-3.

All user interactions with Meta IP are accomplished using a Java-enabled browser, as shown in Figure B-4. As with the other IP management tools, IP/Manager allows you to administer the DNS name space from any location that has TCP/IP access to the server.

Concerns about the security of the browser-based communication between the server and the Java client have been addressed by incorporating a form of encryption MetaInfo refers to as a "hybrid protocol" for Java applets to server communications. In addition, administrative access to the IP/Manager server is protected by user name and password authentication. The server can also be configured to restrict access based on IP address, hostname, or domain name.

The product consists of the Meta IP/Manager, which manages the following three components:

▼ **DNS Server**—The server is based on BIND 8.1.1 and provides support for DDNS, WINS, and IPv6. The server also supports DNS security extensions.

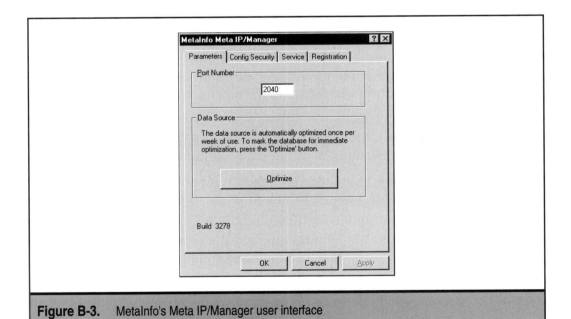

Figure B-3. MetaInfo's Meta IP/Manager user interface

■ **DHCP Server**—The server supports all standard DHCP options. DHCP
   configuration is managed via the management interface, which generates the
   necessary server configuration files for each managed DHCP server.

▲ **Load Balancer**—This product enables the distribution of traffic across multiple
   servers. The Load Balancer manages server pools and can direct traffic to
   underutilized servers and away from crashed servers.

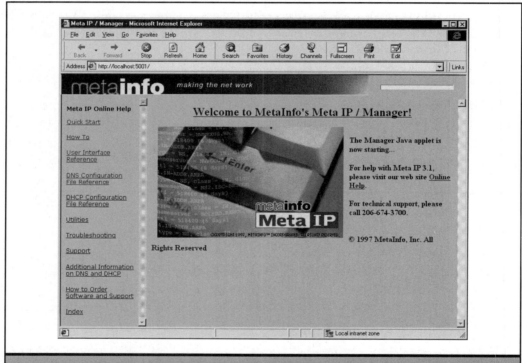

Figure B-4.   MetaInfo's Meta IP/Manager Java-enabled web user interface

WINDOWS
NT
Professional
Library

APPENDIX C

Windows NT Resources
— Where to Get Help

A t some point in the future you may come across a perplexing problem with your NT network that you cannot resolve easily. You'll ask your colleagues, friends, and technically-skilled pets for help—to no avail. You will have to seek a solution using other resources. This appendix lists some excellent sources where you might find solutions. Solutions can be found through direct interaction with other people, in the case of user groups and newsgroups, or through Internet or database searches, such as those found on Microsoft's TechNet or Knowledge Base.

ONLINE HELP

Perhaps the most overlooked resource is the one that sits in front of you all day. More and more user and administrator documentation has moved from the traditional paper-based documentation to documentation and other resources installed on your computer or integrated into the application itself. You can find help at the command prompt, the locally-installed HTML, TXT, PDF, DOC, and other files, and through the help menus built into Windows NT.

Help Books

The first place you should look for help is in the global help books found in the Start menu and shown in Figure C-1. These books contain highly-detailed information on many subjects. You can search by a book's subject, key words using the Index tab, or ordinary words using the Find tab. In Figure C-1 you can see that all NT commands are listed alphabetically. Clicking on the command brings up a short description of the command.

Command-line Help

Sometimes you need more detailed information or do not want to wade through the help books' hierarchical organization to find your topic. You can get immediate information on Windows NT commands from the command prompt using the *help* command. To use the help command you simply type **help** followed by the command; for example, typing **help help** provides information on using the help command.

```
C:\>help help
provides help information for Windows NT commands
HELP [command]
command - displays help information on that command
```

However, not all commands are supported by the help command. To get a list of commands that are supported, type **help** without any arguments. To get help on commands that are not supported by the help command, type the *command* followed by **/?**. In nearly all cases, this will give you a listing of how to use the command and its arguments. Some commands (such as ping, tracert, and telnet) expect an address or other

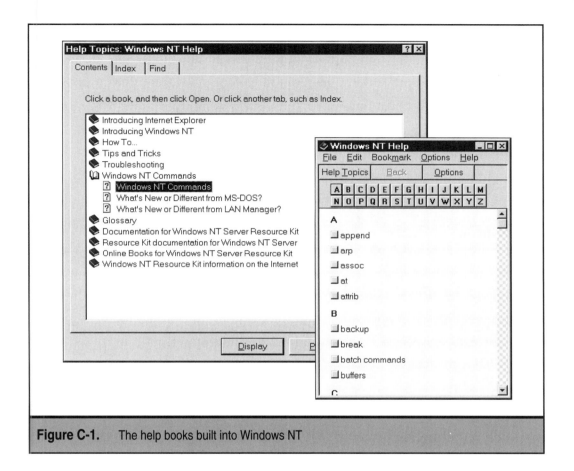

Figure C-1.   The help books built into Windows NT

argument to follow the command. They attempt to resolve the **/?** and report an error. To get help on these commands, enter **-?** right after the command. For example, let's say we want help information on the tracert command. Below is what happens when you type **help tracert**, then **tracert /?**, and finally **tracert -?**.

```
E:\>help tracert
This command is not supported by the help utility. Try "tracert /?".

E:\>tracert /?
Unable to resolve target system name /?.

E:\>tracert -?

Usage: tracert [-d] [-h maximum_hops] [-j host-list] [-w timeout] target_name
```

```
Options:
 -d                 Do not resolve addresses to hostnames.
 -h maximum_hops    Maximum number of hops to search for target.
 -j host-list       Loose source route along host-list.
 -w timeout         Wait timeout milliseconds for each reply.
```

Additional Files

In many cases, an application will include locally-installed documentation files. These files may be installed automatically or selected when running the application's installation routine. They can usually be accessed via an additional icon or menu selection in the application's program group. If there are no additional icons installed along with the application, a search of the application's installation or working directories for files with the following extensions can often uncover additional documentation.

▼ **HTM, HTML**—HyperText Markup Language files, viewable using a web browser

■ **TXT, ASC**—ASCII-based text files, which usually include version-specific information and discuss specific installation issues

■ **DOC**—Microsoft Word-based files, which usually include version-specific information and discuss specific installation issues, but may also include full application documentation

■ **WRI**—Microsoft Write-based files, which usually include version-specific information and discuss specific installation issues

■ **PDF**—Adobe-based files, which usually include version-specific information and discuss specific installation issues, but may also include full application documentation

▲ **HLP**—Additional Windows help files, which may not be readily accessible through the application interface but include application-specific information

TECHNET

Although Microsoft is parsimonious with technical support by telephone, it does provide more information than most users know what to do with in the form of the TechNet CD-ROMs. Microsoft packages current technical information, support patches, drivers, and programs onto three CD-ROMs, which are published every month. You can sign up to receive a year's worth of CD-ROMs for a very reasonable fee (approximately $US300 for single users and $US700 for unlimited users). Every month you will receive three CD-ROMs packed with the following features:

▼ More than 150,000 pages of current technical information

■ 14 resource kits

■ All recent service packs

■ Knowledge Bases on many subjects

■ The entire software library from Microsoft (current active library)

■ Sample software

▲ Current drivers and patches

If you are serious about supporting NT or just want the most recent NT software, you should subscribe to Microsoft TechNet. Most of the software is not fully licensed, but you will certainly be given the opportunity to evaluate it. Figure C-2 illustrates the search capabilities included with TechNet. For more information about TechNet, explore **www.microsoft.com/technet.**

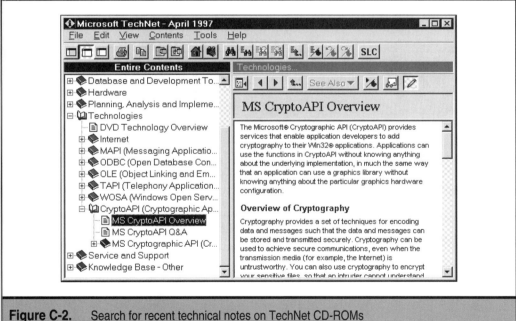

Figure C-2.   Search for recent technical notes on TechNet CD-ROMs

MICROSOFT ONLINE SUPPORT

Although Microsoft is not in the business of giving away free technical support over the phone, they do provide a number of resources online. Microsoft allows you to access many free resources on its web servers that may help you resolve your problems.

One of the best places to look at Microsoft is the Support Online site (**www.microsoft. com/support**). You may have to register with Microsoft to gain access to what Microsoft calls *premium content*. Although registering is free and accomplished relatively quickly, you are asked all sorts of information that you may not be willing to provide. Once registered, you can enter a question or set of keywords to search through their databases. Your query will be carried through hundreds of megabytes of technical notes and Knowledge Bases in search of matches. Many times, your question or problem will be matched to a similar one, and you can see how that problem was resolved. Figure C-3 illustrates the support query page where you enter your questions.

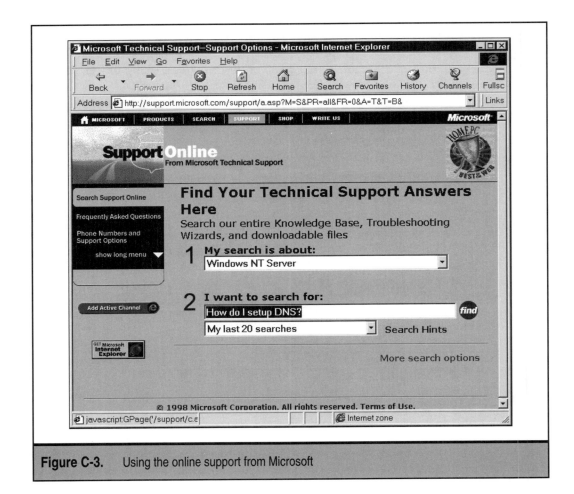

Figure C-3. Using the online support from Microsoft

You can search by using either keywords (the default) or what Microsoft calls *natural language*. If you search using natural language, you should phrase your question in the form of a sentence such as, "How do I configure the Registry?" To use natural language, you must click on More Search Options, and then select Natural Language.

When you are looking for more comprehensive support for your enterprise, you might want to check out Microsoft's enterprise support options (**www.microsoft. com/enterprise**). Here you can read about phone support packages and consulting services offered to large organizations.

INTERNET SOURCES

There is an abundance of information about Windows NT on the Internet. The problem is there is a lot of garbage that gets in the way when looking for truly useful information. If you set your sites on a few of the links listed in Table C-1, you may cut out some of the unnecessary garbage and reduce your overall search time. There are two major groups of links listed here. The first is Resource Links, which invariably lead to more links and focus on NT-related information. The second group of links is Print Material. These links point you toward publishers of books and magazines. These sites are also full of NT-related information and information on how to obtain the sites' publications. Most magazines publish much of their material on their web sites.

CD NOTE: These links and many more can be found on the enclosed CD-ROM.

Name	Type	Link
Resource Links		
Microsoft's FTP site	File Repository	ftp.microsoft.com
Beverly Hills NT Resource Center	Resources, File Repository	www.bhs.com
Jumbo NT Archive	File Repository	www.jumbo.com/pages /windowsnt
European MS WinNT Academic Centre	Resources, Information, File Repository	emwac.ed.ac.uk
Worldwide Association of NT User Groups	Resources, User Groups	www.wantug.org

Table C-1.   NT Resources on the Internet

Name	Type	Link
Association of Windows NT System Professionals	Resources, User Groups, Information, File Repository	www.ntpro.org
Print Material		
Osborne/McGraw-Hill	Books	www.osborne.com
Microsoft Press	Books	mspress.microsoft.com
Duke Press	Books	www.dukepress.com
Wiley	Books	www.wiley.com
Macmillan Computer Publishing	Books	www.mcp.com
Windows NT Magazine	Magazine	www.winntmag.com
Back Office Magazine	Magazine	www.backoffice.com
Enterprise NT Magazine	Magazine	www.entmag.com
Windows NT Systems Magazine	Magazine	www.ntsystems.com
Windows Magazine	Magazine	www.winmag.com
Info World	Magazine	www.infoworld.com
Network World	Magazine	www.nwfusion.com

Table C-1. NT Resources on the Internet (*continued*)

NEWSGROUPS

Newsgroups are discussion groups in which you can carry on conversations with users throughout the world on a particular topic. Unlike chat rooms, the discussions do not happen in real time; rather you post a message, and users can read it and respond to it if they desire.

Getting Started

There are thousands of newsgroup topics, so they are narrowed down to a relatively specific subject. For example, one newsgroup on Windows NT is called *comp.os.ms-windows.nt.misc.* Here is how newsgroups are used. A user posts a message (an essay, a question, or any piece of text) to the newsgroup. The message gets distributed all over the world through *news servers.* News servers keep copies of the messages and replies, and other users read the posted messages. If another user wants to reply, they simply select the initial message and reply to it using their news reader software. Then their message is posted to the news servers located throughout the world. Each newsgroup can have many hundreds or thousands of users associated with it. Therefore, it can be challenging to keep up with the volume of information provided in newsgroups.

The first thing you'll need to do is to get the news reader software. Most web browsers ask if you'd like to install a news reader when you first install the browser. Otherwise, you can add the news reader component later by going to the browser's add-on component site and selecting the news reader. There are also separate news reader software programs that work quite well and are available for free on the Internet.

Using Newsgroups

After you get your news reader functioning, you'll need to point it at a news server so it can start retrieving posted messages. News servers are often inside corporations (for example, news.company.com) or are located at your ISP on the Internet. Because there are thousands of newsgroups, your news server may not subscribe to them all. To get a list of newsgroups, check out **www.liszt.com/news**. Your news reader software should let you select from the available newsgroups, and you can start reading and posting messages immediately, as shown in Figure C-4. You can also see some of the newsgroups related to Windows NT in this figure.

NOTE: There is a certain amount of decorum expected when posting to newsgroups. Newsgroup users are not particularly tolerant of novices and their mistakes, so it is best to read a little bit about the proper etiquette to use. You might check out **bell.ucs.indiana.edu/kb/menu/usenet** for more introductory information.

People often use newsgroups to post their specific problem in hope that some guru will read it and answer promptly. The disadvantage is you may have to wait a long time before you receive an answer, and you can't always trust the answer. But it is free after all.

NT USER GROUPS

For a more personal experience, you can join a local NT-users group. These groups are located all over the world and are usually started by individuals who have a strong interest in NT and the BackOffice suite of products. They typically hold monthly meetings and get together to talk about new products, problems, or upcoming NT events.

Perhaps the greatest advantage to user groups is that the people you meet there will have similar interests and problems. Thus, the contacts you build there may prove invaluable. Some user groups have hundreds of users, while others number only about a dozen. To find an NT user group near you, look at the web site of the Worldwide Association of NT User Groups (WANTUG) at **www.wantug.org**.

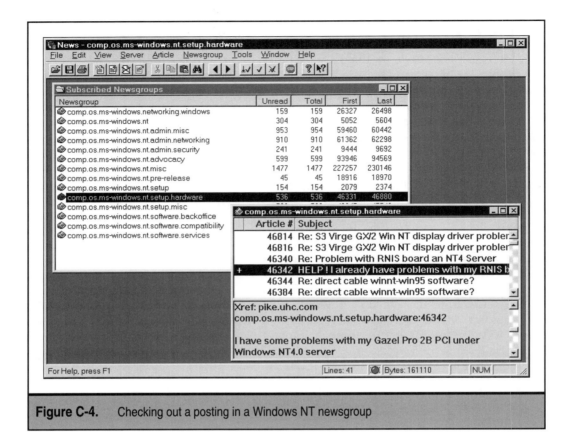

Figure C-4. Checking out a posting in a Windows NT newsgroup

NT RESOURCE KIT

No review of NT resources would be complete without a discussion of the NT Resource Kit. The Resource Kit should be in every NT administrator's tool chest. Its wealth of utilities and technical information helps administrators, power users, and programmers configure, troubleshoot, and tune their NT systems.

For the Windows NT 4.0 version, the Resource Kit is offered as two separate products, one for NT Server and one for NT Workstation. Although both contain many of the same utilities and documentation on the CD-ROM, they each have specific enhancements for different needs. The NT Server Resource Kit is for network administrators who set up, administer, and support Windows NT Server-based networks. The NT Workstation Resource Kit is for power users, application developers, and administrators of smaller networks because there is less information about networking NT systems.

The NT Server Resource Kit includes the following books:

▼   *Windows NT Server Resource Guide*

■   *Windows NT Server Networking Guide*

▲   *Windows NT Server Internet Guide*

The only book that comes with the NT Workstation Resource Kit is *Windows NT Workstation Resource Guide.*

The *Windows NT Workstation Resource Guide* is included on the CD-ROM in the NT Server Resource Kit. The CD-ROM contains many utilities, including utilities in the following categories:

▼   **Batch Tools**—Perl 5 and Regina REXX

■   **Computer Administration and Configuration Tools**—C2-level security, automatic logon, Command Scheduler, run application as a service feature, time zone editor, and a uni- to multiprocessor conversion utility

■   **Computer and Network Setup Tools**—Profile setup and Setup Manager

■   **Computer Diagnostic Tools**—Crystal Reports Event Viewer

■   **Desktop Tools**—Multiple desktops, animated cursor editor, image editor, and the soft input panel

■   **File Tools**—File and directory comparison, file compression and expansion, and a text file viewer

■   **Internet and TCP/IP Services and Tools**—SMTP and POP mail server, IP configuration tool, and uuencoder/decoder

■   **Network Diagnostic Tools**—PerfMon MIB builder, Net Watch, Disk Probe for hard drives, Browser Monitor, Dependency Walker, Domain Monitor, Network Watch, Process Viewer, and SNMP Monitor

■   **Registry Tools**—Online Registry help

■   **Server Administration Tools**—DHCP Relay Agent, remote console, and Service Monitor application

■   **Tools for Developers**—Sixteen Posix tools such as *vi, ls,* and *mv*

▲   **User Account Administration Tools**—Tools to control floating profiles and copy user groups

Also included on the CD-ROM is a series of help books, including an online copy of the books included with the kit, the Hardware Compatibility List, and an overview of all the tools included in the kit.

Microsoft updates the resource kits periodically with supplemental CD-ROMs. These CD-ROMs contain the latest versions of helpful utilities, additional tools, and hundreds of megabytes of valuable information taken from TechNet. For more information about the resource kits check out **mspress.microsoft.com/RESLINK/**.

APPENDIX D

About the CD

The CD-ROM that accompanies this book contains over 300MB of applications you can use to help secure, manage, and maximize your NT systems. We have reviewed and tested each application and think they will be valuable utilities for your NT toolkit.

The interface that accompanies the contents on the CD-ROM was tested on IE 3.02 and higher and Netscape 4.0. You will get the best results using IE 4.0 and Netscape 4.0 or higher. You can, however, search the CD-ROM from the File Manager or the Windows Explorer if you prefer. Some applications require contacting a reseller to obtain a temporary license key. We have made every attempt to identify which programs require this and who to contact to enable your trial version. Most programs are fully functional 'as is', however, there are a few evaluation copies that will time out after 30 days or so.

ADMIN TOOLS

The CD-ROM contains 24 admin tools, including domain management, security, disk, and clustering applications.

Enterprise Administrator

Enterprise Administrator is a tool that can help create security boundaries within a single-master-domain model. You can read more about this powerful application in Chapter 4.

Kane Security Monitor

This security monitoring application is a 24-hour realtime Windows NT security guard. You can configure it to notify you via e-mail or pager if certain security events are detected.

Kane Security Analyst

This is the companion product to the Kane Security Monitor. It searches for security violations and reports them to an administrator. Use KSM to evaluate your systems and pinpoint systems that are most vulnerable to security violations.

Storage Resource Manager

This application is a browser-based, domain-wide disk and user management tool.

Pukka Software

The Domain Admin tool from Pukka Software allows the management of users, groups, servers, RAS, directories, networks, printers, and disks.

Winquota Manager

This is a freeware program that allows you to set disk usage quotas. Note: You must get a freeware version of the security program Pretty Good Privacy (PGP) before this application can be used.

RoboMon

RoboMon is automated problem detection and correction software for NT, UNIX, and open VMS. RoboMon can detect and correct system and application problems proactively and can be managed from a central location. RoboMon is described in more detail in Chapter 4. You will need to contact Heroix, Inc. for a temporary license key to install RoboMon.

Convoy Cluster

Convoy Cluster is a software-only clustering solution for TCP/IP based servers. The software on the CD-ROM allows you to create a floppy disk that you take to each workstation you want to be part of the same cluster. After a short installation, the machine can then act as part of your cluster.

Administrator Assistant Tool Kit

You'll find an excellent set of tools that facilitates security management of NT-based networks.

Fortress-NT

An application designed to help you protect your system's security and resources.

LAN Licenser

Enterprise-wide license management and control. This powerful application will help you keep track of software that is located throughout your enterprise. You must call at 888-NT-UTILS or e-mail **ntsales@sunbelt-software.com** to get a key for the evaluation copy.

Print Manager Plus

Print Manager Plus centrally manages printers and queues in your enterprise.

XLNT

XLNT is a powerful command language for automation of NT system management tasks. You must call at 888-NT-UTILS or e-mail **ntsales@sunbelt-software.com** to get a key for the evaluation copy.

Trusted Enterprise Mgr.

This powerful application allows you to create a manageable hierarchy of users/groups to administer domains. You can delegate your simple system management tasks to others.

AutoLogon

AutoLogon changes the Registry settings so that a user is automatically logged on the next time the system restarts. You can enable and disable AutoLogon any time you want.

BlueScreen

BlueScreen is a screen saver that not only authentically mimics a Blue Screen Of Death, but will simulate the blue screen seen during a system boot, complete with a fake chkdsk of disk drives with errors! It cycles between different blue screens and simulated boots every 15 seconds or so.

ERD Commander

ERD Commander is a utility that enables you to boot NT off of a floppy disk in order to access and repair a dead NT installation. It is a command-line shell that runs off of a set of NT boot disks, giving you full access to non-bootable NT systems with a robust set of familiar command-line file manipulation tools including copy, rename, delete, move, and xcopy.

NTFilemon

NTFilemon is a Windows NT device driver/GUI combination for NT 3.51 and NT 4.0 that logs and displays all file system activity on a Windows NT system.

NTFSDOS

NTFSDOS is a DOS-based network file system driver that is able to recognize and mount NTFS drives for transparent access. It makes NTFS drives appear indistinguishable from standard FAT drives, providing the ability to navigate, view, and execute programs on them from DOS or from Windows, including from the Windows 3.1 File Manager and Windows 95 Explorer.

NTRegmon

NTRegmon is a device driver/GUI combination for NT 3.51 and NT 4.0 that displays all Registry activity taking place on a Windows NT system in real-time.

NTSID

NTSID is a program developed to change a computer's SID. It first generates a random SID for the computer and then proceeds to update instances of the existing computer SID it finds in the Registry and in file security descriptors, replacing occurrences with the new SID. Carefully read the documentation at **www.ntinternals.com/ntsid.htm** before using.

NTSync

NTSync directs the operating system to flush all file system data to disk in order to ensure that it is stable and won't be lost in case of a system failure, thereby preventing any modified data present in the cache from being lost.

NTUndelete

NTUndelete is a utility that integrates silently into NT 4.0's existing Recycle Bin to provide full protection of files deleted from anywhere. NTUndelete also provides a filtering dialog box that allows you to prevent files of specific extensions, such as editor backup files and temporary files, from being sent to the Recycle Bin.

VolumeID

Although NT's built-in Label utility lets you change the labels of disk volumes, NT does not provide any means for changing volume IDs. This utility, VolumeID, allows you to change the IDs of FAT and NTFS disks (floppies or hard drives).

DIAGNOSTIC TOOLS

The CD-ROM contains 11 diagnostic tools, including network system and health evaluation tools, benchmarking applications, and logging/alerting tools.

NetScan

NetScan Tools brings many classic UNIX network client utilities to a Windows GUI environment. It includes support for Name Server Lookup (NSLOOKUP), Ping, Traceroute, Finger, Whois, Time Sync, Daytime, Quote, Chargen, Echo, Ident Server, Winsock Info, services and protocols database checks, and NetScanner.

Net.Medic

Net.Medic sits on the user's desktop and acts as a powerful agent, gathering and reporting on the user's network and application experience. You can easily customize the application to report on events in great detail or just give you a snapshot of the health of your network environment.

Nbench

Nbench is a benchmarking utility that reports on the following components: CPU, L1 & L2 cache, disk speeds, and memory.

BalanceSuite

This utility will help you eliminate network I/O bottlenecks and arm yourself with NIC fault tolerance. You must have Service Pack 3 or higher and a hotfix downloaded from Microsoft for the application to run. See the program's documentation for more information.

PerfMan

PerfMan is an NT performance management tool with powerful functions.

LogCaster

LogCaster is an advanced Eventlog management and alerting tool.

Contig

Contig is a single-file defragmenter that attempts to make files contiguous on disk. It's perfect for quickly optimizing files that are continuously becoming fragmented, or for files that you want to ensure are in as few fragments as possible.

CPUMon

CPUMon is an advanced performance measurement tool. Its GUI/device driver combination makes the wide range of processor performance counters present on the Pentium, Pentium Pro, and Pentium II easily accessible.

NTHandleEX

NTHandleEx is a GUI/device driver combination that shows you information about which handles and DLL processes have been opened or are currently loaded.

WinObj

WinObj is a must-have tool if you are a system administrator concerned about security, a developer tracking down object-related problems, or just curious about the Object Manager namespace. WinObj is a 32-bit Windows NT program that uses the native Windows NT API (provided by Ntdll.dll) to access and display information on the NT Object Manager's name space.

NTRecover

NTRecover is an advanced Windows NT "dead-system" recovery utility for x86 NT installations. Using NTRecover, NT machines that fail to boot because of data corruption, improperly installed software or hardware, or faulty configuration can be accessed and recovered using standard administrative tools, as if the machines were up and running.

IP UTILITIES

The CD-ROM contains seven IP utilities. Meta IP, NetID, and QIP are all discussed in Appendix B.

Meta IP

Meta IP is an IP management tool that consists of the IP/Manager and Admin interfaces. The IP/Manager component stores configurations for the DNS and DHCP services. All day to day user interactions are accomplished using a Java-enabled browser. The DNS server is based on BIND 8.1.1 and provides support for DDNS, WINS, and IPv6. The server also supports DNS security extensions. The DHCP server supports all standard DHCP options.

NetID

NetID is an IP management tool. Version 2.x is included on the CD-ROM because it installs with an integrated database and doesn't require the full Oracle database installation. If you want to evaluate the product using the Oracle database, you can request a full-evaluation copy from Bay Networks. Since the user interface has not changed much from NetID 2.x to 3.0, the demo located on the CD-ROM offers a good look at the user interface. NetID Supports DNS, DDNS, and DHCP. The product stores information in a central Sybase or Oracle database that multiple users access using the NetID Admin Tool or the NetID Web Gateway.

QIP

An IP management tool, QIP allows for the management of DNS and DHCP and uses a central Sybase or Oracle database. It supports cross-platform integration (UNIX and NT based), BIND 8.1.x DDNS, security, and incremental zone transfers. Additional features include integrated support for groupings of subnets, OSPF route summarization information, VLSM, and CIDR.

QIP Subnet Calculator

The Quadritek Subnet Calculator is a simple tool for determining the most appropriate subnet masking for a given network. It has the ability to calculate the total number of subnets, the total number of hosts, and the boundaries of each subnet given the network address and the subnet mask.

IP Calc

IP Calc is a freeware subnet calculation tool that computes Network ID, Subnet ID, and Host ID information. It supports CIDR/Supernetting and displays both dotted decimal and dotted hexadecimal.

Big Brother

Big Brother is a program designed to monitor your IP-network activities. Just add hosts, routers, etc. to its graphical interface by specifying an IP address or hostname.

Hostname

Hostname is a very simply utility that takes either an IP address (e.g. 209.98.7.238), or a hostname (e.g. **www.velte.com**), and performs a translation into its inverse form. For example, if you pass Hostname an IP address, you'll get back a hostname, and if you pass it a hostname it will give you the corresponding IP address. Hostname runs under Windows 95 or Windows NT.

RAS UTILITIES

The CD-ROM contains five RAS utilities that enhance remote access management and enable remote control of NT systems.

RAS Pro

This shareware utility allows you to gain more administrative control over your Dial Up Networking solutions.

Timbuktu

This program is a remote control application or service that allows you to remotely control another computer even through a reboot.

Virtual Motion

Virtual Motion's Remote Access Manager adds a powerful layer of resource management, access control, and usage accounting to the native Windows NT RAS. You will need to get a key from Virtual Motion to use this product. Please see the documentation on the CD-ROM for more information.

RAS Manager

RAS Manager allows you to automatically control and track your RAS resources.

Remotely Possible

Remotely Possible is a complete remote control solution that is very fast.

MISCELLANEOUS UTILITIES

The CD-ROM contains 11 miscellaneous utilities, including defrag, memory optimization, data mirroring, and batch command tools.

Diskkeeper Light

This is the popular disk defragmenter for NT. Use it to reduce your disk access time.

ER Disk

This utility allows you to create Emergency Repair Disks for remote machines—very handy in the enterprise.

Event Admin

Event Admin can consolidate your Event Viewer logs from multiple machines for easy viewing.

EZ Clean

EZ Clean allows you to watch the changes that are made to your Registry or file systems when you install a new application.

RAMCharge

Supercharge your NT system throughput. If you have not installed the Psapi.dll as part of NT Service Pack 3, you will need this DLL in the *%Systemroot%*/system32 directory to run RAMCharge. Versions for both NT Server and Workstation are included on the CD-ROM.

SuperDisk NT

Create a RAM disk on any system capable of running Win NT. There are two versions here: one is for Intel systems with less than 128MB of RAM and the other is for alpha systems with less than 128MB of RAM. You will need a license key to run this program. Please view the documentation on the CD-ROM for more information.

SmartBatch 32

SmartBatch 32 is a management and monitoring application that watches unattended processing on Windows NT.

Octopus HA+

This program provides real-time LAN/WAN data mirroring. Note that when you license Octopus, you need two copies so you can install both the source and target nodes. For demo purposes, you can install the same demo copy on both systems. Also: You will need to call Sunbelt at 888-NT-UTILS to receive your evaluation password.

Media Mirror

Media Mirror is an application that provides fault tolerance for your backup tapes. Call 888-NT-UTILS or e-mail **ntsales@ntsoftdist.com** to get your key for the evaluation.

SuperCache NT

This utility can increase your disk performance between 500 and 2000 percent. You will need a key to run this application. Please see the documentation that comes with the product on the CD-ROM for more information.

UltraBac

UltraBac is fast and very feature-rich backup support program for LANs.

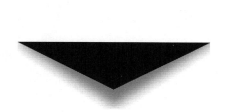

Index

References to figures and illustrations are in italics.

▼ A

acceptance testing, 445-446
access control lists, 381-382
Account Policy editor, 79-81
Active Directory, 481-488
    DNS, 487-488
    domains, 483-486
    global catalog, 482-483
    organizational units, 486-487
    schema, 482
    sites, 483
Active Server Pages, 307
ActiveX Data Object, 307
adding users, 78-79

Address Resolution Protocol, 428-429. *See also* protocols
administrative tasks, with MMC, 143-146
Advanced Peer-to-Peer Networking, 25
alternate volumes, 488-490
anonymous user access, restricting, 390-391
APPN. *See* Advanced Peer-to-Peer Networking
AppStation, 147
ARP. *See* Address Resolution Protocol
AT command, 162-164
Audit Policy editor, 81-82
audit trails, 393-394
authority hierarchy, 139
autoloaders, 116

B

backup domain controllers, 54, 61, 69
backups, 114-120, 394-395
    media choices, 115-117
    NTBackup, 118-119
    open files, 117-118
    placing the backup system, 119-120
    scheduling, 118-119
    third-party applications, 119
BDC. *See* backup domain controllers
BIND boot file, 221
boot partition, 104
boot problems, 432-438
    boot phase problems, 437
    emergency repair disk, 437-438
    Intel boot phase, 433-434
    load phase, 434-435
    load phase problems, 437
    Registry settings for boot
        information, 436
BOOTP. *See* Bootstrap Protocol
Bootstrap Protocol, 271. *See also*
    protocols
bridges, 45-46
broadcast name resolution, 245-247
broadcast storm, 17
broadcasting, 17
browser elections, 174-175
Browser Monitor, 177, 426
Browser service, 170-178
browsing
    basics, 170-171
    enhancing, 176-178
    multiple client, 171-175
    on the WAN, 175-176
browsing environments, multiple client,
    171-175
    browser elections, 174-175
    client commonalities, 172
    NT issues, 172-173
    Windows for Workgroups issues,
        174
    Windows 95 issues, 173-174

 C

C2 Configuration Manager, 395-396
cache file, 220
caching
    by DHCP clients, 270
    name servers, 238-240
    network data, 149
callback, 352
canonical name (CNAME) record,
    221-222
capacity planning, 443
CD-ROM contents, 537-547
    admin tools, 538-541
    diagnostic tools, 541-543
    IP utilities, 543-545
    miscellaneous utilities, 545-547
    RAS utilities, 545
Challenge Handshake Authentication
    Protocol, 351. *See also* protocols
changing hidden attributes of files, 60
CHAP. *See* Challenge Handshake
    Authentication Protocol
choosing a file system, 479
choosing hardware and software, 52-58
    hard drives, 57-58
    from hardware compatibility list,
        52-54
    with Microsoft Compatibility tool,
        54-57
    multiprocessor systems, 58
    RAM, 57
Client Access Licenses, 68, 168-170
    License Manager, 168-169
    replication, 169-170
client workstation connections, 165-209
    considerations, 166
    Gateway Services for Novell
        networks, 197-204
    Macintosh services, 192-197
    non-NT client connections, 181-192

NT connection services, 167-181
UNIX, 204-209
clustering, 110-114
    Active/Active model, 112
    Active/Standby model, 112
    Microsoft Cluster service, 112-113
    shared disk model, 111
    shared nothing model, 111
    third-party solutions, 113, *114*
    totally redundant model, 112
    types of, 111-112
    Wolfpack, 112-113
CNAME record, 221-222
Command Scheduler, 162-163
commands
    computer configuration
        commands, 154-156
    net account command, 152-153
    net commands, 150-160
    net computer command, 157
    net config command, 154-155
    net continue command, 156
    net file command, 158-159
    net group command, 153-154
    net localgroup command, 153-154
    net name command, 153
    net pause command, 156
    net print command, 158
    net send command, 153
    net session command, 156-157
    net share command, 157-158
    net start command, 156
    net statistics command, 155-156
    net statistics workstation
        command, 155-156
    net stop command, 156
    net time command, 156
    net use command, 159
    net user command, 151-152
    net view command, 159-160
    networking commands, 150-164
    sharing commands, 157-160
    user commands, 151-154

computer configuration commands,
    154-156
configuring DNS client, 233-235
    automatically, 234-235
    manually, 233-234
configuring DNS server, 224-229
    DNS notify, 233
    domains and zones, 224-229
    round-robin lookup, 232-233
connecting clients
    LAN Manager 2.2c, 181-184
    MS-DOS, 181-184
    OS/2, 181-184
    Windows 3.11, 184-188
    Windows 95, 188-192
copying administration client tools, 184
cost benefit, 441
cost of ownership, reducing, 146-150
Crystal Reports, 308
CSMA/CD protocol, 3, 6-9, 10. *See also*
    protocols

 D

database files, 219-222
    BIND boot file, 221
    cache file, 220
    reverse lookup file, 220
    zone file, 220
database redundancy, 120
DC. *See* domain controller
DDNS. *See* Dynamic DNS services
default users, 78
Deputies, 139, *140*
Dfs. *See* Distributed File System
DHCP. *See* Dynamic Host Configuration
    Protocol
diagnostic tools for NT, 133-134, 420-427
    built-in tools, 420-423
    Resource Kit tools, 423-428
Dial-Up Scripting Command Language,
    349
Directory Replicator service, 120-124

distance-vector routing, 36-37
Distributed File System, 488-490
DNS. *See* Domain Name System
domain controllers, 480-481, 494
    promotion, 496-500
domain models, 69-73
Domain Monitor, 73, *74*, 425
Domain Name System, 211-241, 487-488.
    See also Microsoft DNS
        caching name servers, 238
        database files, 219-222
        domains and subdomains, 217, 237
        dynamic update functions, 241
        evolution of, 240-241
        forwarders and slaves, 218-219
        Incremental Transfer Protocol, 241
        integrating into a diverse network,
            236-240
        integrating with WINS/DHCP,
            229-232
        and IPv6 (IPng), 240
        load balancing, 238
        management, 514-515
        name servers, 217-218
        queries, 218
        redundancy, 237-238
        resource records, 219-222
        RFC support, 223
        Secure DNS, 241
        setup, 495-496
        using to resolve NetBIOS names,
            248
        and WINS, 222-223
        zones, 216-217
domain organization, 481-490
domain registration, 215-216
domain structures
        centralized domain example, 491
        converting from existing, 492-493
        decentralized domain example,
            492
domains in Active Directory, 483-486
        forests, 484-486

multimaster replication, 486
trees, 483-484
trusts, 483
dual-boot installation, 479-480
dual power supplies, 97-98
duplexing, 100
Dynamic DNS services, 241, 516
Dynamic Host Configuration Protocol,
    42, 269-275, 514-516. *See also* protocols
        address allocation process, 273-275
        Bootstrap Protocol, 271
        caching clients, 270
        compatibility, 271-272
        configuring and managing,
            276-282
        installing, 276
        network components, 283-284
        overview, 270-273
        Registry settings, 282
        related RFCs, 271-272
        security issues, 282-283
        and WINS, 243-285

E

EA. *See* Enterprise Administrator
emergency repair disk, 437-438
encryption, 391
Enterprise Administrator, 139-142
enterprise organization, 491
Ethernet, 6-11
        access control, 6-9
        common Ethertypes, 8
        common SAPs, 9
        Fast Ethernet, 10-11
        physical connections, 9-10
        versions of, 6
Event Viewer, 423, *424*
export servers, 121-122
external RAID arrays, 109, *110*

F

fail-over solution, 113
FAT vs. NTFS, 61-63, 479
FDDI. *See* Fiber Distributed Data Interface
Fiber Distributed Data Interface, 13-16
    beaconing, 15
    built-in redundancy, 15-16
    differences from Token Ring, 14
    error correction, 14-15
    synchronous and asynchronous traffic, 14
File Transfer Protocol, 4. *See also* protocols
    security, 389
firewalls, 380-385
    packet filtering, 381-382
    proxy firewalls, 382
    TCP/IP ports, 383-386
    using, 383
    vendors, 385, 387
forests, 484-486
forwarders, 218-219
FrontPage Server Extensions, 308
FTP. *See* File Transfer Protocol
functionality testing, 444-445

 G

global catalog, 482-483
Gopher service, configuring, 306

 H

hard drive requirements, 57-58
hardware
    built in series: 90-92
    failure probability, 90-92
    in parallel, 92
    requirements, 57-58
Hardware Compatibility List, 52-54

Hardware Detection tool, 420-421
HCL. *See* Hardware Compatibility List
help command, 526-528
Help Desk, 128
help resources, 525-535
host adapter cards, 99
host record, 221
Hosts file, 34
HTTP. *See* HyperText Transfer Protocol
HyperText Transfer Protocol, 4. *See also* protocols

 I

IGRP/EIGRP. *See* Interior Gateway Routing Protocol
import computers, 123-124
import/export systems, setting up, 121-124
Incremental Transfer Protocol, 241. *See also* protocols
Index Server, 308
installing
    as backup domain controller, 61
    basic steps, 59-61
    Dial-Up Networking, 341
    a dual-boot system, 479-480
    FAT vs. New Technology File System (NTFS), 61-63
    licensing, 68
    Macintosh services, 192
    Microsoft DNS server, 224
    Microsoft Installer, 149
    a mirrored drive, 105
    a modem, 341-345
    overview, 58-59
    as primary domain controller, 61
    queried information, 63-64
    as standalone server, 54
    a striped disk array, 108-109
    unattended, 64-68
    Windows NT, 58-69
    Workstation vs. Server or Server/E, 61

Integrated Services Digital Network, 340
IntelliMirror, 149
Interior Gateway Routing Protocol,
40-41. *See also* distance vector routing;
protocols
International Standards Organization
(ISO), 2
Internet
avoiding bottleneck, 327
connecting to, 323-326
help, 531-532
management tools, 328
services, 287-328
throughput requirements, 326-327
Internet Connection Services for RRAS,
360
Internet domains, 212-216
second-level, 215-216
top-level, 213-215
Whois database, 216
Internet Information Server, 288-311
Active Server Pages, 307
ActiveX Data Object, 307
configuring, 299-306
configuring FTP service, 306
configuring Gopher service, 306
configuring WWW service, 301-306
Crystal Reports, 308
FrontPage Server extensions, 308
hardware requirements, 290-291
Index Server, 308
installing, 292-299
memory, 291
NetShow, 307-308
NT 4.0 Option Pack, 309-311
placement, 291-292
publishing directories, 297-298
removing services, 297
selecting ODBC drivers, 298
selecting services, 295-296
software components, 289-290
upgrading, 298-299

Internetwork Information Center, 31-33
and second-level domains, 215-216
Internetwork Packet
Exchange/Sequenced Packet
Exchange protocol, 25-26, 338, 356-357.
See also protocols
InterNIC. *See* Internetwork Information
Center
inventory, hardware and software,
127-129
inverse queries, 218
IP addresses, 30-34
IP management, 513-524
cost vs. benefit, 515-516
key features, 517-518
Meta IP, 523-524
NetID, 520-522
QIP, 518-520
staffing, 515-516
IPConfig utility, 429-430
IPSec, 397-398
IPX/SPX. *See* Internetwork Packet
Exchange/Sequenced Packet
Exchange protocol
ISDN. *See* Integrated Services Digital
Network
ISO. *See* International Standards
Organization
iterative queries, 218
ITP. *See* Incremental Transfer Protocol

L

LAN. *See* local area networks
LAN Manager 2.2c, connecting clients,
181-184
LDAP. *See* Lightweight Directory Access
Protocol
licensing, 68, 168-170
Lightweight Directory Access Protocol,
4. *See also* protocols
link-state routing, 37

LMHOSTS file, 247-248
load balancing
    alternate volumes, 488-490
    DNS traffic, 238
local area networks
    Ethernet, 6-11
    Fiber Distributed Data Interface,
      13-16
    Token Ring, 11-13
    types of, 5-17
Local Security Authority, 178
logon script variables, 85
LSA. *See* Local Security Authority

▼ M

Macintosh services, 192-197
    installing, 192
    logon, 192-196
    volumes, 196-197
mail exchange (MX) record, 221
Management Information Bases, 28-30
Marshals, 139, *140*
master domain model, 72
mean time between failure value, 90-91
Meta IP, 523-524
MIBs. *See* Management Information
  Bases
Microsoft Challenge Handshake
  Authentication Protocol, 351-352. *See*
  also protocols
Microsoft Compatibility Tool, 54-57
Microsoft DNS
    configuring the client, 233-235
    configuring the server, 224-236
    DNS Manager, 235
    installing, 224
    logging, 236
    managing, 235-236
    Nslookup, 235-236
    special configuration items,
      232-233
    statistics, 235

Microsoft Installer, 149
Microsoft Management Console,
  142-146, 235
Microsoft Network Monitor, 451-452
Microsoft Proxy Server, 311-323
    common services configuration,
      322
    installing and configuring, 314-320
    managing, 320-323
    shared services, 321-322
    SOCKS, 312-313, 322-323
    Web, 313, 323
    WinSock, 313, 323
Microsoft WINS
    configuration options, 260-261
    configuring, 258-264
    installing, 257-258
    Preferences configuration
      parameters, 264
    Registry settings, 265
    Replication Partners configuration
      parameters, 259-263
migrating from NetWare, 86-87
migrating to Windows NT 5.0, 490-502
Migration Tool for NetWare, 86-87
mirroring, 100, *102*, 104-108
    installing, 105
    NT support for, 105-108
    recovering a data disk, 106
    recovering a system disk, 107
MMC. *See* Microsoft Management
  Console
modems
    detecting, 343-344
    Dialup Properties, 344-345
    installing, 341-345
monitoring program. *See* RoboMon
MPR. *See* Multi-Protocol Router feature
MS-CHAP. *See* Microsoft Challenge
  Handshake Authentication Protocol
MS-DOS
    connecting clients, 181-184
    scripts, 160-162
    startup disk, 181-183

multihoming, 98-99

multimaster replication, 486

multiple client browsing environments, 171-175

    browser elections, 174-175

    client commonalities, 172

    NT issues, 172-173

    Windows for Workgroups issues, 174

    Windows 95 issues, 173-174

multiple master domain model, 72-73

multiple node solution, 113

Multi-Protocol Router feature, 42

multiprotocol routers, 49

MX record, 221

▼ N

name server record, 221

native mode, 13-18, 500-501, *502*

NAUs. *See* network addressable units

NDIS. *See* Network Driver Interface Specifications

net commands, 150-160

    net account command, 152-153

    net computer command, 157

    net config command, 154-155

    net continue command, 156

    net file command, 158-159

    net group command, 153-154

    net localgroup command, 153-154

    net name command, 153

    net pause command, 156

    net print command, 158

    net send command, 153

    net session command, 156-157

    net share command, 157-158

    net start command, 156

    net statistics command, 155-156

    net statistics workstation command, 155-156

    net stop command, 156

net time command, 156

net use command, 159

net user command, 151-152

net view command, 159-160

NetBEUI. *See* NetBIOS Extended User Interface

NetBIOS

    registration of names, 245-247

NetBIOS Extended User Interface, 26, 338-339, 355-356

NetBIOS over TCP/IP, 34-36, 245-246

    name mapping, 35

    NBTStat command, 35-36

    node types, 35

NetID, 520-522

NetLogon Service, 178-181

    clients, 178-179

    domain controllers, 179-181

    Registry settings, 180

NetShow, 307-308

NetWare

    enterprise considerations in integration, 204

    Gateway Services for, 199-204

    integration tools based in NT Server, 197-204

    Link Services Protocol, 25

    migrating from, 86-87

NetWatch, 426

network addressable units, 24

network analyzers, 450-454

    Microsoft Network Monitor, 451-452

Network Client Administrator, 181-184

Network Driver Interface Specifications, 5

network monitoring standards, 446

    RMON, 447-448

    RMON-2, 448-449

    RMON-3, 449-450

    SNMP and MIB, 447

network probes, 452-456

networking commands, 150-164

networks
 administration, 125-164
 hardware, 45-49
 maximum utilization, 18-20
 monitoring standards, 446
 physical characteristics, 17-18
 protocols, 23-36
 tuning, 416-418
newsgroup help, 532-534
NFS servers, 206-208
 NT network client configuration, 207
 UNIX configuration, 207-208
NLSP. *See* NetWare Link Services Protocol
Nslookup, 235-236
NT routing table, 43-45
 adding routes, 44-45
NT startup floppy disk, 107-108
NT Workstation options, 480
ntconfig.pol policy file, 76
NTFS vs. FAT, 61-63, 479
NWLink protocol, 198-199. *See also* protocols

▼ O

online help, 526-528, 530-531
Open Shortest Path First Protocol, 38-40.
 See also link-state routing; protocols
 areas, 39
 autonomous systems, 39
 support in Windows NT, 39-40
Open Systems Interconnect reference model, 2-4
 Windows NT in, 4-5
optical media
 compact disk recordable, 116
 compact disk rewritable, 117
 digital versatile disk, 117
 magneto-optical, 117
OSI. *See* Open Systems Interconnect reference model

OSPF. *See* Open Shortest Path First Protocol
OS/2, connecting clients, 181-184

▼ P

Package Command Manager, 131-132
packages
 creating, 129-130
 installing, 131-132
 sending, 130-131
packet filtering, 381-382
PAP. *See* Password Authentication Protocol
parity, 101-102, *103*
Password Authentication Protocol, 350.
 See also protocols
passwords, 392-393
PDC. *See* primary domain controllers
Performance Monitor, 404-416
 Alert view, 410-411, *412*
 capacity planning, 417-418
 Chart view, 407-410
 files, 415
 fundamentals, 404-407
 Log view, 411-412, *413*
 Registry parameters, 415-416
 Report view, 412-414
 shortcut keys, 414
 views, 405-407
phonebook entries, adding, 345-347
ping command, 430-431
Plain Old Telephone Service, 340
planning for Windows NT 5.0, 477-502
Point-to-Point Protocol, 339. *See also* protocols
Point-to-Point Tunneling Protocol, 339.
 See also protocols
pointer record, 222
POTS. *See* Plain Old Telephone Service
PPP. *See* Point-to-Point Protocol
PPTP. *See* Point-to-Point Tunneling Protocol

primary domain controllers, 54, 61, 69, 494
proactive planning, 440
protocols
ARP, 428-429
BOOTP, 271
CHAP, 351
collision-based protocols, 21-22
CSMA/CD, 3, 6-9, 10
DHCP, 42, 514-516
FTP, 4
HTTP, 4
IGRP/EIGRP, 40-41
included in TCP/IP protocol suite, 27
IPX/SPX, 25-26, 338, 356-357
ITP, 241
LDAP, 4
NetBEUI, 26
NLSP, 25
NWLink, 198-199
OSPF, 38-40
PAP, 350
PPP, 339
PPTP, 339
RIP, 25-26, 37-38
routing, 36-41
SAP, 25-26
SMT, 13-14
SMTP, 2-3, 4
SLIP, 339-340
SNA, 23-25
SNAP, 6
SNMP, 28-30
SPAP, 351
token-based protocols, 20-21
TCP, 4
TCP/IP, 26-28
UDP, 4
XNS, 25
proxy firewalls, 382

 Q

QIP, 518-520
querying the DNS host, 218
querying the SMS database, 129

 R

RAID level 5, 108-109
RAID levels, 99-104
RAM requirements, 57
RAS. *See* Remote Access Service
recovering
a data disk, 106
a failed striped drive, 109
a system disk, 107
recursive queries, 218
redundancy, 89-124
alternate volumes, 488-490
redundant databases, 120
redundant DNS, 237-238
registering a domain, 215-216
regression testing, 445
reliability testing, 444
remote access security, 395
Remote Access Service, 329-372
adding phonebook entries, 345-347
automating connection with scripts, 347-349
clients and servers, 331
configuring clients, 341-353
connection protocols, 339-340
enterprise considerations, 361-368
hardware guidelines, 365-366
installing the RAS server, 354-360
managing, 358-360
modem options, 366-368
monitoring the connection, 353
network protocols, 337-339
office to office connectivity using, 364
security settings, 349-352
setting protocols, 336

superthin client technology, 335
thin client technology, 334
transport methods, 340-341
using a private service provider, 363-364
using an ISP, 361-363
vendors, 366, 367
remote control, 333
remote network monitoring, 447-450
remote node, 332-333
remoteboot clients, 184
removing Windows NT, 69
repeaters, 45-46
Resource Kit, 534-535
resource records, 219-222, 227-229
    canonical name (CNAME record), 221-222
    host record, 221
    mail exchange (MX) record, 221
    name server record, 221
    pointer record, 222
reverse lookup file, 220
RIP. *See* Routing Information Protocol
RMON. *See* remote network monitoring
RoboMon, 135-139
routers, 48-49
Routing and Remote Access Service, 42, 331
    administration, 371-372
    advantages, 369
    features, 369
    installing, 370-371
Routing Information Protocol, 25-26, 37-38. *See also* distance-vector routing; protocols
    limitations, 37
    removing routing loops, 38
    support in NT, 38
routing protocols, 36-41. *See also* protocols
routing tables, 41-45
    NT routing table, 43-45

RRAS. *See* Routing and Remote Access Service
rules, 135, 136-138

▼ **S**

SAMBA server package, 205-206
    NT network client requirements, 205
    UNIX configuration, 205-206
SAP. *See* Service Advertising Protocol
schema, 482
SCL. *See* Dial-Up Scripting Command Language
scopes
    active leases, 281
    active options, 279-280
    creating, 278-279
    defined, 269
    superscopes, 281-282
scripting languages available for NT, 160
scripts, 160-162
    to automate RAS connection, 347-349
    MS-DOS, 160-162
    in NT 5.0, 162
security, 373-399
    encryption, 391
    expectations, 379
    firewalls, 380-385
    FTP and WWW service security, 389-390
    goals, 378-379
    IPSec, 397-398
    key questions, 375-376
    NT issues, 385-396
    policies, 377-378
    remote access, 395
    risks, 377
    too little vs. too much, 376-377
    Virtual Private Networking, 398-399

Serial Line Internet Protocol, 339-340. *See also* protocols
server commands, 156-157
Server Enterprise Edition (Server/E), 61
Server Intelligent Storage, 149-150
Server Manager, 73-75
server types, 480-481
servers, upgrading, 493-494
Service Advertising Protocol, 25-26. *See also* protocols
Setup Manager, 64-68
seven-layer model, 2-4
shares, 488-490
sharing commands, 157-160
Shiva Password Authentication Protocol, 351. *See also* protocols
Simple Mail Transfer Protocol, 2-3, 4. *See also* protocols
Simple Network Management Protocol, 28-30. *See also* protocols
    and MIB, 447
    packet types, 28
    polling intervals, 29
    proxy agents, 28-29
    traps, 134
    with Windows NT, 29-30
simulating a network, 465-475
    data reduction, 467-468
    lifecycle management, 475
    simulators, 468-475
    topology, 465-466
    traffic, 466-467
simulators, 468-475
    COMNET Predictor, 469-471, *472*
    NetMaker XA, 471-475
single domain model, 71
sites, 483
slaves, 218-219
SLIP. *See* Serial Line Internet Protocol
SMP systems, 58
SMS. *See* Systems Management Server
SMT protocol. *See* station management protocol
SMTP. *See* Simple Mail Transfer Protocol

SNA. *See* Systems Network Architecture
SNAP. *See* Subnetwork Access Protocol
Snap-Ins, 142, 146
SNMP. *See* Simple Network Management Protocol
SOCKS Proxy Server, 312-313, 322-323
source route bridging, 46-47
source route transparent bridging, 47
SPAP. *See* Shiva Password Authentication Protocol
stand-alone server, 480-481
standards organizations, 2-5
station management protocol, 13-14. *See also* protocols
Steelhead. *See* Routing and Remote Access Service
striping, 100, *101*
    with parity, 108-109
Subnetwork Access Protocol, 6. *See also* protocols
superthin client technology, 335
switches, 47-48
symmetric multiprocessors (SMP), 58
system partition, 104
System Policy Editor, 75-77
    default system policies, 76
    modifying system policies, 77
    ntconfig.pol policy file, 76
system requirements, 478-479
Systems Management Server, 126-134
    hardware/software inventory, 127-129
    Help Desk, 128
    Network Monitor, 134
    Package Command Manager, 131-132
    querying, 129
    remote diagnostic tools, 132-134
    Sites window, 127-129
    software distribution, 129-132
    Windows NT Administrative Tools, 134
    Windows NT Diagnostics tools, 133-134, 420-427

Systems Network Architecture, 23-25
  Advanced Peer-to-Peer
    Networking, 25
  routing, 24
  sessions, 24
  subarea network, 23-24

▼ T

tape libraries, 116
tape media
  Advanced Intelligent Tape, 116
  Digital Linear Tape, 115
  4MM DAT, 115
TaskStation, 147
TCP. *See* Transmission Control Protocol
TCP/IP, 26-28, 337-338, 357-358
  configuring, 30-34
  filtering, 388-389
  IPv6 (IPng), 240
  NetBIOS over, 34-36
  ports, 383-386
  troubleshooting, 428-432
TDI. *See* Transport Driver Interface
TechNet, 528-529
test lab, 456-459
  environment, 456-457
  hardware, 457-459
testing
  acceptance, 445-446
  benefits, 440-443
  functionality, 444-445
  goals, 443
  and management, 442-443
  regression, 445
  reliability, 444
  throughput, 444
  your network, 446-465
testing applications, 460-464
  analyzing results, 462-464
  network setup, 460
  running the test, 461-462

thin client technology, 166-167, 334
third-party administration tools, 134-142
  Enterprise Administrator, 139-142
  RoboMon, 135-139
throughput expectations, 17-22
  maximum utilization, 18-20
  physical characteristics, 17-18
  token-based protocols, 20-21
throughput testing, 444
Token Ring, 11-13
  beaconing, 13
  ring stations, 11-13
  types of frames, 11
tracert, 431-432
translational bridging, 46
Transmission Control Protocol, 4. *See
  also* protocols
transparent bridging, 46
Transport Driver Interface, 5
trees, 483-484
  creating an NT 5.0 domain tree,
    494-501
troubleshooting, 418-438
  attempting to fix problems, 420
  boot problems, 432-438
  defining problem, 419
  diagnostic tools for NT, 420-427
  locating problem, 419
  reviewing changes, 419-420
  scheduled jobs, 164
  TCP/IP, 428-432
trust relationships, 71-72
trusts, 483
tuning NT systems, 402-418
  networks, 416-418
  Performance Monitor, 404-416
  seven habits, 402-404
two-digit date problem. *See* Year 2000
  problem

U

UDP. *See* User Datagram Protocol
uninterruptable power supplies, 93-97
    configuring, 94-96
    testing, 96-97
UNIX client connections, 204-209
    applications servers, 208-209
    file servers, 204-208
    NFS servers, 206-208
    SAMBA server package, 205-206
    utility vendors, 209
upgrading
    servers, 493-494
    to Windows NT 5.0, 478-481
UPS. *See* uninterruptable power supplies
user and computer accounts, 75-87
user commands, 151-154
User Datagram Protocol, 4. *See also*
  protocols
user groups, 85-86
    global groups, 86
    help resources, 533
    local groups, 86
User Manager, 78-81
    for Domains, 78, 140
user profiles, 82-85
    local profiles, 83
    logon scripts, 84-85
    mandatory profiles, 83-84
    roaming profiles, 83
    settings, 82-83
    slow connections, 84
user rights and policies, 79-82
    Account Policy editor, 79-81
    Audit Policy editor, 81-82
    User Rights Policy editor, 81

 V

Virtual Private Networking, 398-399

 W

WAN browsing, 175-176
Web Proxy Server, 313, 323
Whois database, 216
Windows Internet Naming Service. *See
also* Microsoft WINS
    and DHCP, 243-285
    and DNS, 222-223
    impact on network, 266-269
    integrating with DNS, 229-232
    LAN implementation, 266, *267*
    name queries, 252-254
    node types, 251-252
    Proxy Service, 255-257
    registration, 250-251
    release, 251
    renewal, 251
    replication, 254-255
    WAN implementation, 266-269
Windows 95, connecting clients, 188-192
Windows NT
    Administrative Tools, 134
    audit trails, 393-394
    backups, 394-395
    C2 Configuration Manager,
      395-396
    client connection services, 167-181
    Diagnostic tools, 133-134, 420-427
    help resources, 525-535
    installing, 58-69
    migrating to, 490-502
    passwords, 392-393
    planning for 5.0, 477-502
    removing, 69
    requirements for Intel-based
      systems, *53*
    scripting, 162
    securing servers, 390
    security issues, 385-396
    Setup Manager, 64-68
    upgrading to 5.0, 478-481
    user groups, 533
    vulnerabilities, 391-392

Windows Scripting Host, 162
Windows startup disk, 181-183
Windows 3.11, connecting clients, 184-188
WINS. *See* Windows Internet Naming Service
WinSock Proxy Server, 313, 323
Wolfpack, 112-113
workgroup models, 69-70
WWW service
    configuring 301-306
    security, 389-390

 X

Xerox Network Systems network protocol, 25. *See also* protocols
XNS. *See* Xerox Network Systems network protocol
X.25, 340-341

 Y

Year 2000 problem, 503-512
    contingency plans, 511-512
    estimating costs to fix, 507
    planning a solution, 506-508
    testing and certification, 509-512
    what will fail, 504-506

 Z

ZAK. *See* Zero Administration Kit
ZAW. *See* Zero Administration for Windows
Zero Administration for Windows, 146-150
    in NT 5.0, 148-150
Zero Administration Kit, 147-148
    distribution modes, 147-148
    installation modes, 147
zone file, 220
zones, 216-217, 224-229